Fraud
Casebook

Fraud Casebook

Lessons from the Bad Side of Business

Edited by Joseph T. Wells

BICENTENNIAL
1807
WILEY
2007
BICENTENNIAL

John Wiley & Sons, Inc.

The case studies presented in this book are based on actual cases. Names, dates, locations, and some facts have been changed to protect the privacy of the organizations and individuals involved.

All amounts are in U.S. dollars unless otherwise specified.

Library of Congress Cataloging-in-Publication Data:

Fraud casebook : lessons from the bad side of business / Joseph T. Wells.

p. cm.

Includes index.

ISBN 978-0-470-13468-9 (pbk.)

1. Fraud–Case studies.   I. Wells, Joseph T.

HV6691.F737 2007

363.25′963–dc22

2007009247

10 9 8 7 6 5 4 3 2 1

For Barry C. Melancon:
A true giant in the accounting profession

Contents

Preface

Fraud, as you will read in the following pages, is not committed by accounting systems or computers. It is carried out by living, breathing human beings who outwardly seem no different from you and me. Occupational frauds—those offenses that occur in the workplace—are all too common; nearly every company has been a victim or will be in the future.

It would be easy to say that this phenomenon happens because of greedy, dishonest people. But greed is a natural human trait. And all of us lie. So that explanation falls short of predicting who will turn to occupational fraud. More often, as you will see, fraudsters appear to be ordinary individuals who believe that they are caught in extraordinary circumstances. They are frequently upstanding, God-fearing, patriotic citizens who despise crime as much as the rest of us. Moreover, they don't really look at themselves as criminals. But they certainly are.

I have been fascinated with the motives and morals of white-collar criminals for close to 40 years. Preventing, detecting, and investigating fraud has become my life's work. It didn't start out that way, though; I graduated with an accounting degree and became an auditor before being accepted as a special agent of the Federal Bureau of Investigation. Fraud cases, large and small, were my bread and butter. After nearly 10 years, I left to start my own consulting firm specializing in white-collar crime issues. And in the late 1980s, I helped form the Association of Certified Fraud Examiners (ACFE), the world's largest antifraud organization, where I still serve as chairman.

Along the way, I've lectured to thousands of antifraud professionals, traveled to nearly every corner of Earth, taught in the graduate school at the University of Texas at Austin, conducted independent research on the causal factors of fraud, and written extensively on the topic.

This book, my thirteenth, pulls together the experiences of fraud examiners from across the globe, each of whom has provided details about a case he or she has investigated. Although the literary styles are as unique as the people who wrote them, all the chapters drive home a number of universal themes. First, those who commit fraud usually do so without a grand plan; instead, they made bad decisions, one after the other. Second, like water, fraud follows the path of least resistance. That is, these offenses are never more complicated than they need to be in order to accomplish the perpetrator's illicit goals. So you will notice that many of these schemes are the essence of simplicity.

Third, occupational fraud follows definite patterns. We first determined that fact in 1996 with the release of the ACFE's first *Report to the Nation on Occupational Fraud and Abuse,* which consisted of an in-depth study of over 2,000 actual cases furnished to us by certified fraud examiners. The *Report* has been replicated three times since then. We've been able to classify frauds by the methods used to commit them. There are three broad categories—asset misappropriations, corruption, and fraudulent financial statements—and there are numerous subschemes.

Fraud Casebook: Lessons from the Bad Side of Business is organized around these schemes, which has subsequently been dubbed the "Fraud Tree." Part I is devoted to the most common offenses, asset misappropriations. Part II covers corruption; Part III details fraudulent financial statements, the least common but by far the most expensive occupational frauds; and Part IV focuses on a variety of other fraud schemes.

Each case involves four areas. *Why* the fraud was committed is an important human interest story. *How* the fraud was committed gives the accounting and other technical details. *Lessons learned* offers sound advice on what went wrong. And *preventing future occurrences* shows what must be done to keep the same kind of schemes from happening again. You will notice that many of these stories don't have pleasant outcomes; justice was not served and lives were changed forever. My experience in this field has taught me that when fraud occurs, there are no winners. That makes prevention the ultimate goal. And that process begins with educating ourselves.

Lessons from the Bad Side of Business can be utilized by academics wishing to expose their students to the realities of fraud. It can easily be an accompaniment to one of several fraud texts, including my own, *Principles of Fraud Examination.* But practitioners, managers, and business owners will also learn a great deal in these pages. Finally, those with a general interest in occupational fraud will discover that this book is simply a fascinating read.

Thanks go first to the ACFE members who wrote the case studies. They didn't do it for money; the profits are earmarked for the ACFE General Scholarship Fund, which provides grants to deserving college students. Good writers know that there is nothing easy about this craft, and they are therefore commended for their efforts. Authors also are aware of the critical symbiotic relationship that exists with their editing team. John Gill, Kassi Underwood, and Andi McNeal of the ACFE Research Department did an outstanding job in that regard. Finally, I appreciate the assistance of Tim Burgard of John Wiley & Sons, Inc., who wouldn't give up until I agreed to take on this project.

Fraud is a serious problem that goes much beyond monetary losses. It costs jobs, raises, corporate reputations, and individual dignity. *Fraud Casebook: Lessons from the Bad Side of Business* will shed light into the dark corners of government and commerce so that we can hopefully avert, in the future, some of the same mistakes we have made in the past.

Joseph T. Wells, CFE, CPA
Austin, Texas
June 2007

Asset Misappropriation

CHAPTER 1

High Art, Low Value: How A Connoisseur Became A Convict

ELLEN A. FISCHER

If there were a law that required people to trade their names for a single adjective, Lawrence Fairbanks would be *Cosmopolitan*. A tallish, gaunt man of 45, Lawrence held the position of Assistant Vice Chancellor of Communications—the glitziest job in the glitziest department of Aesop University. In the vast sea of academe, Lawrence's ship steered clear of the lecture halls, laboratories, and weekly beer orgies on Fraternity Row. I doubt that Lawrence ever met a professor, much less a student. Instead, he sailed the waters of media and public relations. Lawrence was in charge of making sure that the university's good side was featured in every last magazine, newspaper, and brochure that dropped off the printer.

The position of AVC-Communications fit Lawrence like a second skin. He had been recruited by Aesop from a renowned magazine empire, and it showed. Two decades in the publishing world had secured him the professional trust and personal admiration of the writers, editors, photographers, and graphic artists who produced award-winning publications on behalf of the university.

Moreover, Lawrence wore the cultured charisma of a man well studied in the arts. His knowledge and taste far surpassed the better-known works you might guess on *Jeopardy!* or in a game of Trivial Pursuit. Lawrence was captivated by the black-and-white photography of the early twentieth century. He was versed in original oil paintings and ceramic pieces by important—though not mainstream—artisans in New York, San Francisco, and London. The breadth of Lawrence's interests included antiques—all kinds of antiques, ranging from old books to the earliest cameras, apothecary items, steam trunk luggage, and toys. Lawrence also had a fondness for period furniture of the sort you might find in a museum. Art was Lawrence's life.

Lawrence's high regard among the university communications creative staff was shared by the administrative employees who reported to him. Though fluent in the language of the elite, Lawrence Fairbanks was no snob. He always greeted the accounting clerks, the administrative assistant, and the receptionist by name. At Christmas, he arranged a destination luncheon and tour of the newly opened museum—the one that had a year-long waiting list. Every employee in the department was invited.

Lawrence's glad-handing social ease endeared his university colleagues and impressed the literati and glitterati of the media and art worlds. It also won him a lovely, intelligent wife. Having waited until his late 30s to marry, Lawrence was now the father of six-year-old Ruthie and three-year-old Bobby. It was touching to see how a keen art connoisseur had reserved the outer surface of his office desk as a minigallery for the framed works of his two little crayon masters.

Lawrence's wife, Allison, worked as a midlevel corporate attorney; despite their dual income, which exceeded $250,000 a year, the family home was unpretentious. In a city that sweats opulence, the Fairbanks' home stood unremarkably among other homes of its style in a neighborhood better known for its nearness to prominent cultural venues than its prominent residents. The cozy, single-story clapboard house of pre–World War II construction had three bedrooms and a single bathroom. It was just big enough for four people who, by all appearances, followed the script of the American Dream.

But there was more to Lawrence's life than his wife, his children, and his job—and there was certainly more than met the eye to the way he approached his love of art. Normally, when one speaks of a love of art, one refers to a hobby that provides enjoyment and enrichment. Normally, one's most cherished pieces are shared with family.

Normally.

We often hear that the most public personalities can mask the most private souls. And, while the inner reflections of a private soul are normal, the secret, shame-driven need for certain objects is called "obsession." No one—not even Allison Fairbanks—knew the extent of Lawrence's love for art, nor the lengths to which he would go to acquire it, hide it, and ultimately dupe employer and supplier alike into feeding his passion.

Art nourished Lawrence's troubled heart even as it starved his soul to death.

Art was Lawrence's life.

THE FACE OF MANY

Aesop University, the largest campus in a state university system, enjoys an eminence that rivals the Ivy League. Founded in 1871, Aesop grew from a state teacher's college to an institution with a world reputation for scholarship, research, and community service.

Modestly put, the university produces and attracts the "Who's Who" of every imaginable field. Every orange and burgundy sweatshirt in the student bookstore proclaims its logo, *Omnibus Punim,* which is translated to mean "The Face of Many." Aesop's family portrait includes famous actors, Olympic athletes, a Supreme Court Justice, and several Nobel laureates. The Aesop Medical School successfully pioneers new treatments for the most hopeless conditions. Its doctors have ministered to the destitute and distinguished alike.

On any give day, Aesop's total student enrollment reaches 35,000 among its undergraduate, graduate, and professional schools. To keep this educational behemoth running, Aesop employs upwards of 25,000 staff and faculty. And though situated in the highest-rent district of one of the three largest cities in the United States, Aesop's 500-acre campus has earned the *über*-school its very own zip code. Aesop's football team, the Thundering Bison, has secured the celebrity campus a regular spot on the 11 o'clock news. More important, its $3-billion budget has won it a set of permanent box seats in the crosshairs of the state legislature.

The university's in-house business and technology experts have patiently guided this tradition-steeped grandfather of higher education toward the Information Age. With the steady, gentle prodding that got Daddy to trade his turntable for a CD player, Aesop eventually migrated from its old record-keeping system of manila folders and microfilm to the "Give-it-to-me-now!" world of computers.

By the mid-1990s, Aesop's entire purchasing and accounts payable system was computerized. Just enter a log-on ID and password, and an authorized employee is soon staring at any financial transaction processed in any of the university's departments. Push another few buttons, and you'll know which employee entered a purchase request before he or she fired it off to the campus's central Accounts Payable Department. You'll see the serial number of the university check and the day it was cut. You'll even know whether that check was sent out to the vendor through the U.S. mail or whether it was first sent back to the department that requested the payment.

Any business with as many moving parts as Aesop University must make sure that its bills are paid efficiently, but not recklessly. So along with the streamlining of the accounts payable process comes a few built-in security measures. One big safeguard is the university's purchasing policies—in particular, the policy that dictates spending limits.

Aesop's "Low-Value" Purchase Delegation Policy places a ceiling on how much any one campus department can spend with a single vendor on a given day without obtaining formal approval from the Central Purchasing department. Exceeding that limit causes the Materiel Acquisition and Disbursement (MAD) automated system to halt a department's purchase request and reroute it to campus's Central Purchasing unit.

That is, if more than $2,500 worth of business per day—plus a small additional margin for tax and delivery—is going to any one supplier, Central Purchasing will automatically gain control of the purchase. There are all kinds of good reasons, too—for example, making sure that old Aesop, a public university, is given the best deal in the marketplace and that it obeys a long list of state and federal laws.

You can almost see the buyers in Central Purchasing standing there, sneering, arms folded, tapping their feet and wondering what the accounting assistant in the Norwegian Poetry department was thinking when he ordered $2,984.32 worth of Viking translation guides from the Oslo Down company. That type of order immediately results in an e-mail from one of those sneering foot-tappers to the immediate supervisor of the accounting assistant in the Department of Norwegian Poetry.

You might question how a fiscally responsible outfit could extend so much green rope, every day, to a few hundred campus departments. Yet that is exactly the rationale behind the Low Value Purchase Authority—a mouthful of a term that simply means that a $3 billion university is placing up to $2,500-and-change worth of trust in any one department to buy whatever it needs from a single vendor on a given day.

The Low Value Order (LVO) policy allows an organizational giant like Aesop University to function more efficiently by not paralyzing Central Purchasing with routine, nonrecurring purchases. Sure, it involves a measure of risk, but the alternative is a mountain of overdue payments and a premier university with some really bad credit.

Aesop University's purchasing policies and automated safeguards served the institution well. But not for long.

DESIGNING A FRAUD

It began with a midmorning phone call from a hoity-toity furniture store—the kind that omits the word "furniture" from its name. A man identifying himself as "Squire's chief financial officer" called the Aesop University Internal Audit department and told our receptionist that he needed to speak to an auditor. He had to report a fraud.

Our receptionist directed the call, just as she did every other one that struck her as odd, to me. I am one of 25 audit professionals in the Aesop Audit department. Since Aesop is the largest of the 12 campuses in our state university system, there is more than enough work to occupy an audit staff of our size.

Ours is a department of specialty units dedicated to particular areas of the campus such as health care or, in my case, a specific discipline like forensics. Although six of us are Certified Fraud Examiners, I am the audit manager of investigations. That is, I am responsible for looking into matters of alleged financial misconduct. Or to be less euphemistic, alleged stealing.

I answered my ringing extension as I always do, with my first and last name. Satisfied that he had an auditor on the line, Mr. CFO repeated his announcement—he was calling to report a fraud. He knew it was fraud because Mr. CFO had previously been an auditor for a "Big 8" accounting firm.

Mr. CFO then informed me that he was holding a photocopy of Invoice Number 5432, bearing Squire's logo. The invoice, in the amount of $2,664, requested payment for "design and illustration services." It also made reference to one of Aesop University's fancy publications, *Bison Quarterly,* a glossy magazine with feature articles on our institution.

Mr. CFO continued. Invoice No. 5432, he said, was accompanied by a recently cut university check in the same amount, payable to Squire. Lawrence Fairbanks, the Assistant Vice Chancellor who oversaw our university's publications unit, had authorized the payment.

Fairbanks's signature was more than legible—it was artistic. Moreover, the billing and shipping addresses were in care of his university office.

"Just a minute," I said to Mr. CFO. "I can look up the invoice on our system." Using our MAD system, it took all of 90 seconds to get the electronic version of Invoice 5432 on my computer screen.

"Okay," I said. "Invoice 5432 certainly looks like a normal type of expense for the Communications Department." But, I wondered aloud to Mr. CFO, why was a furniture store calling me to discuss it?

Then the explosion:

Mr. CFO explained that the hoity-toity store personnel immediately recognized Lawrence Fairbanks as a regular customer, but they didn't know—or care—about his fancy university title.

And, while the invoice copy that accompanied the university check described "design and illustration services" for *Bison Quarterly,* Squire's own copy of that same invoice instead authorized the fabrication of a one-of-a-kind chaise lounge. Prophetically, this chair—or rather, this *chaise*—was named "Ophelia," the psychologically and physically doomed heroine in the Shakespearian tragedy *Hamlet.*

As I silently recalled a verse from our high school production, the Bard was trumped by this chilling quote from Mr. CFO:

"Lady, I don't know squat about magazines. Should I make the chair or not?"

Just the Fax

If there's one thing I know, it's that big guns make big holes, and I sensed that Mr. Lawrence Fairbanks had fired a cannon. I asked Mr. CFO to fax me everything he had that pertained to Invoice 5432. Within moments, I heard the tinkling of the fax phone in our copy room a few yards away from my office.

As I lifted the warm pages from the fax tray, I first inspected Invoice 5432, for $2,664, the version that Lawrence Fairbanks had enclosed with the university's check. It read "design and illustration services for *Bison Quarterly.*" Along came a copy of a low-value purchase order (LVO, for short) in the amount of $2,400. The $264 difference was for sales tax and delivery.

Finally, the fax printed out Squire's version of Invoice 5432. It looked similar to Aesop's copy. The layouts of the invoices were identical. The billing address, "Mr. Lawrence Fairbanks, c/o Aesop University Communications," was the same. Even the boxy, 3-D logos at the top center of the invoices matched.

But the descriptions of the purchases did not.

In the body of the Squire invoice, in place of "design and illustration services," were details for the fabrication of a one-of-a-kind "Ophelia Chaise." It gave precise instructions for the fabric and color—mauve damask, to be exact. It also contained a note that Squire was to contact Lawrence Fairbanks when the chair was ready.

While my first impulse was to carry my handful of trouble straight into the office of the audit director, Frank Adams, I slowly walked back to my own office to eat a banana and contemplate. Was this a one-time indiscretion on the part of a respected university official, or was this a slip-up in an ongoing scheme?

I clicked my mouse on the icon that led me back to MAD, and I input the department code for University Communications. The department had a $4 million annual budget. If I was going to find more examples of the "Squire type," I knew that I would have to drill carefully. I started by typing the four-digit code that the University Communications department used to identify publications expenses on the ledger.

A list of transactions cascaded down my computer screen. As I scrolled through them, I noticed that many of the amounts over the past year or two were under $2,500— many by only a dollar or two. I also noticed a number of "regular" payments in identical amounts, paid to the same vendors over the course of two to six months. The amounts were rarely under $1,000 and never more than $2,499.

I clicked open 20 payments. The online LVO and invoice details were similarly worded: "design and illustration," "stock photos," "reprints of original artwork," or "printing and layout." All made reference to an Aesop magazine, newsletter, or brochure.

Next, I examined the vendors' addresses. One was in San Francisco, another in New York, and still another in Chicago. Publishing ignoramus that I am, it made no sense that so much of the design and illustration work was done out of town. I chose one vendor named Lincoln Photography, partly because it had a San Francisco address and partly because MAD displayed six consecutively numbered invoices under the low-value threshold.

I Googled the address. Not surprisingly, what I got back was not Lincoln Photography, purveyors of stock shots, but Lincoln Galleries, exclusive dealers specializing in early twentieth-century black-and-white photographs snapped by artists who probably tortured themselves to death.

Finally, I broke the news to Frank, the audit director. He listened to my account of the phone conversation with Mr. CFO, the faxed Ophelia Chaise invoice, and the low-value payments to out-of-town art galleries. Frank uttered a one-syllable expletive, and, with that colorful pronouncement, he authorized me to proceed with a full investigation.

The central purpose was clear: to identify the bogus invoices, to quantify the total loss to Aesop, and to collect the evidence to prove it to the university police and the district attorney.

I started by isolating payments that fit a handful of criteria:

- One or more payments to a single vendor
- Under $2,500
- Consecutive or closely numbered invoices
- One-word vendor names
- Vendor address out of town, or out of the United States, or in a major city
- Vendor address in the "artisan" sections of our city

Given that University Communications was an artsy kind of business to begin with, I expected that my initial search for phony transactions would include some that were really A-OK. Yet I wanted to make certain that I wasn't dancing over any rocks that were covering up snakes.

Eventually, I identified 52 vendors and 200 LVO purchases that spanned a three-year period, and I obtained copies of the front and back of each cancelled university check.

You Can Take It to the Bank

As the paper drifted in, I started matching up the endorsements on the backs of the checks with the vendor names on the in-house versions of the invoices. Some of the mismatches were so obvious, it hurt. For example, the check that Aesop issued to "Redhill Publishing" in New York City was endorsed and deposited by "Redhill Antiquarian Books." The payee names on the checks were always close enough to the vendors' true names that they were less likely to notice the "slight" inaccuracy. In the end, vendors are far more concerned that the checks they deposit stay deposited—and you can take an Aesop University check to the bank.

Discretion was not only the better part of valor; it was the only way to keep an investigation of a high-profile character from a famous institution from being publicized prematurely. During these early stages, when we only had one invoice for a fussy purple chair, Frank decided to inform only his boss and campus in-house attorney.

My challenge was to have the vendors respond to my requests to mail and/or fax me copies of the authentic invoices without tipping our hand. Anyone who calls our main office number reaches a recording that announces, "You have reached the Aesop University Audit Department." I came up with a way to minimize the perceived stature of the department by transforming my name from Ellen the Audit Manager into Poor Ellie the Temporary Bookkeeper. Sure, Mata Hari is a more exotic nom de guerre, but Ellie was easy to remember.

I timed each call toward the end of the business day, adjusting for different time zones. That way, whoever answered the vendor's phone would know that Poor Ellie was stuck working late. I began each call by raising my speaking voice half an octave and beginning with the words "Um, hi."

The story was pretty much the same: Poor Ellie was slogging her way through thousands of university payment records. She had to make sure that Aesop's main Accounts Payable department had a copy of each and every invoice that it paid over the past three years. For some reason, the university lost a slew of invoices during that time, and Poor Ellie had to ask the vendors for copies. Poor Ellie had to get the job done—or else.

Pathetic? Sure, but it worked. In came the proof.

Fairbanks's methodology was obvious. He not only had doctored the description of the purchases, but he applied his own artistic flair—and some common desktop publishing tools—to redo the vendors' logos. In some cases, Fairbanks created a new letterhead for the vendor, eliminating telltale verbiage like "dealers in antiques since 1947" that might have alerted the support staff in University Communications and campus Accounts Payable.

Over three years running, Lawrence Fairbanks spent $475,000 of Aesop's money on lithographs, serigraphs, original oils, photographs, antique luggage, books, and cameras. Cartoons, sculptures, and ceramic pots. Strange space-age looking lamps with Swedish names. More fussy chairs. A phrenology head and three taxidermy specimens—all encased in glass; all incredibly dead.

It was time for me to interview Assistant Vice Chancellor Lawrence Fairbanks. Frank and I first met with Fairbanks's boss, Lennie Scott, to give him the background of the case and to solicit his assistance in getting Fairbanks to submit to an interview. Scott was surprised and outraged. Within 30 minutes of our meeting, he sent us a copy of the e-mail in which he instructed Lawrence Fairbanks to come to the Aesop Audit Department at 10 a.m. the following day to discuss some questionable transactions.

DECORATING THE TRAP

Before Fairbanks arrived, I did some interior decorating in our conference room. On our massive, bleached oak conference table, I arranged the files for the 52 vendors in five open cartons, so that the folder tabs with their names were visible. Along the way, we also had gotten a private investigator to take snapshots of the buildings of the 30 or so local galleries and furniture stores that Fairbanks patronized. I opened the photo album to the picture of the Squire storefront and set it at the edge of the conference table, nearest the door.

Fairbanks couldn't miss it.

Lawrence Fairbanks arrived at the Aesop Audit Department reception area at 10 a.m. sharp. Frank and I each shook Fairbanks's hand outside the closed door of the windowless conference room where I had set up shop.

Frank led the way in and sat in one of the chairs across the table from where Fairbanks and I would sit next to each other. As I had learned in several Certified Fraud Examiner training seminars, my sitting beside Fairbanks would allow me develop the rapport that would, with a measure of luck, lead to his unburdening.

Neither Frank nor I expected what Lawrence Fairbanks did next. Upon eyeing the opened photo album and the cartons arranged on the conference table, Fairbanks pivoted on his heels, marched straight out of the room, and, with increasing velocity, through the reception area and out of the suite. I heard no *ding* from the elevator—he had taken the stairs.

Early that afternoon, Frank received a call from the campus attorney whom he had notified earlier about our investigation and our pending interview of Lawrence Fairbanks. Upon leaving the Aesop Audit suite, Fairbanks did not stop until he reached the office of his attorney, Arnold Kruger.

Kruger assured the campus attorney that Lawrence Fairbanks would return to Aesop Audit the very next morning and that he would cooperate fully in an interview. But there was a catch. Apparently, the connoisseur had kept nearly everything that he had purchased and was offering to assist the university in recouping the ill-spent funds by selling off the goods. Kruger was trying to dissuade Aesop's officials from prosecuting Fairbanks in the criminal arena by allowing him to make the university "whole" again.

Then there was the sympathy factor: Kruger explained that Lawrence Fairbanks was a very troubled soul who had been under psychiatric care. He was not a thief; he was sick, and he was prepared to make it all up to the university. The campus attorney told us that he would not recommend that criminal prosecution be avoided. However, he did make an agreement with Kruger that the university would support his client's efforts to mitigate the loss.

The next morning, Lawrence Fairbanks returned to the Aesop Audit conference room. Slouching in a maroon V-neck sweater, a 1960s rock band haircut overshadowing his ashen face, the connoisseur confessed. In carefully measured sentences, Fairbanks recounted how he got away with his first purchase—a $10,000 oil painting that he split into four "low-value" orders for "design and layout" services. In the earlier days, he would take an actual invoice, cut and paste the logo into a less telltale version of the vendor's name onto another sheet of paper, and photocopy the whole thing. Then he discovered it was easier to fabricate the entire invoice using simple word processing graphics. He began to crack a faintly proud smile.

"How did the vendors react to getting checks drawn on Aesop University's bank account and not yours?" I asked.

As I had guessed, the vendors really didn't care, and Fairbanks knew they wouldn't. Aesop is a player in the art world, and Fairbanks's position in the university was prestigious. No one questioned the fact that the checks were coming from Aesop. A few must have assumed that Fairbanks was purchasing art and fancy furniture on the university's behalf.

"Who else in University Communications knew what you were doing?" I asked.

Eyes intense, Fairbanks adamantly replied, "No one!"

Fairbanks explained that, as with most top-level officials, he did not do windows. That is, he had administrative employees processing the invoices—the sanitized versions. He even knew how to skirt the "checks and balances" in his department that provided for a secondary review of each transaction by an accounting supervisor. So long as there was a budget for the "publications" purchases, the busy accounting supervisor, always immersed in details, was not going question him.

And what of Fairbanks's wife?

With downcast eyes, Fairbanks began to sob as he proclaimed how much he loved Allison and dreaded how this was going to shatter her life. She knew nothing of his purchases.

A Thieving Pack Rat

But, how did Fairbanks keep Allison from knowing? Did he bring the merchandise home?

"No." He sighed. "That is my sickness."

Fairbanks unfolded the story of a poor child peering through store windows in a depressed downtown area. It had been his goal to gain the education and social standing that would gain him the finest things that money could buy. Along the way, Fairbanks branched out from the banality of department store goods and into the esoterica of fine art and antiques.

Even more than the acceptance he enjoyed from the art world, Fairbanks was following a noble calling. He was saving old, dark photographs of people who didn't matter anymore, even though their images had become collectors' items. He was preventing old books, antiques, and the strangest objets d'art from being erased from their place of honor in the world. And he was creating new pieces—like the Ophelia Chaise—that would be the antiques of tomorrow.

They mattered; he mattered. And he kept them from harm's way in a public storage facility. Over the past three years, Fairbanks had rented three contiguous storage rooms in one of those "You-Haul-It, You-Store-It" places. Many items, he assured me, were still in their original packing.

Aesop University was not paying for the storage. I checked.

Before our interview concluded, Fairbanks had a question for me. I thought he was going to raise the usual concerns about what would happen next, whether he would go to jail, and so on.

Instead, he startled me by asking, "Tell me—is this the most sophisticated scheme you've ever seen?"

Not vindictively, but honestly, I replied, "No, Lawrence, it isn't."

As Fairbanks ambled out of the Aesop Audit suite, he looked more insulted than contrite.

The police and the district attorney pronounced the case a "slam dunk," and Fairbanks was sentenced to full restitution and a one-year house arrest.

In a sweet, three-bedroom home of prewar construction, Allison, Bobby, and Ruthie Fairbanks were awakened from the American Dream. Allison divorced Lawrence and moved out of state. At the conclusion of his house arrest, Fairbanks moved to the same city, to be near the kids. He now supports himself as a freelance magazine writer on the subject of arts and culture.

LESSONS LEARNED

Our investigation provided incontrovertible proof of Aesop's monetary loss of $475,000, not to mention a detailed confession. However, we all agreed that the process would have been a lot easier had Lawrence Fairbanks set fire to his acquisitions or dumped them in the river.

The investigation in the Audit Department was within our control, but the agreement between Arnold Kruger and the campus attorney was not. We all intuited that the sale of the Fairbanks collection would not abolish the loss or, as Fairbanks optimistically asserted, net Aesop a profit. However, the university now was obliged to take custody of, and account for, all of the merchandise that awaited us in the three storage lockers.

As auditors, Frank and I knew better than to handle it ourselves. We called in experts. On a wet, dreary November morning, clad in blue jeans and old sneakers, I joined two similarly attired curators from the Aesop University art museum. Lawrence Fairbanks met us, keys in hand.

I had come to the storage facility equipped with an Excel spreadsheet that served as an inventory of all of the items from the vendors' actual invoices, including a title, physical description, and, where applicable, the artist's or gallery's serial number.

The curators brought two cameras, kid gloves, bubble wrap, and a university truck to transport the collection to a secure room that had been reserved in the Aesop administration building. The door to the secure room had been outfitted with an emergency installation of a dual-custody lock. One curator had a key; and the offset key was given to the receptionist of the area outside of the secure room. We planned it so that both "unrelated" employees had to be present in order to admit the appraisers and, eventually, the buyers.

Again, as auditors, Frank and I would not take custody of these unwanted assets. Still, we knew that we had to play a major role in protecting Aesop from being accused of breaching the attorneys' agreement—or even compromising the criminal case—if one of the purchased items had been "lost" or damaged.

Lawrence Fairbanks raised the first of the three corrugated metal doors to reveal a fully packed locker. It looked just as he described it—most of the items were still in their original cartons, unopened.

All day long, the curators methodically opened each carton and removed the pieces. We jointly identified the pieces, and as I checked off each item, both of the curators, Lawrence Fairbanks, and I each initialed the line item on the Excel spreadsheet.

The curators placed index cards bearing the inventory number that I had assigned in front of each piece, and they simultaneously photographed the items. We wanted to make certain that, if one camera failed, there would be a second photograph.

The curators then encased each item in bubble wrap, affixed a sticker bearing the same inventory number, and loaded the pieces onto a dolly. When the dolly was full, Lawrence Fairbanks would close down and lock the metal door, and he and one of us would "escort" the dolly to the truck. The driver, an experienced employee of the Aesop Museum, would carefully load the objects into the back, as Fairbanks watched.

We would not allow Fairbanks to leave our presence while either the storage lockers or the truck were unlocked. Finally, when the process was complete, everyone, including the truck driver, signed the inventory listing, which I took back to the Aesop Audit Department. I immediately faxed the listing to all who were present at the storage facility and to Arnold Kruger and the campus attorney.

For several months beyond Lawrence Fairbanks's house arrest, University Communications served its own time with some heavy-duty bookkeeping that resulted from the attorneys' agreement. It was quite a burden as the auction houses dribbled $100,000 worth of sales proceeds, in piecemeal fashion, back to Aesop.

I didn't ask what became of one of the more curious items, "squirrels under glass," after one of the curators mentioned that it is illegal to sell taxidermy specimens in this state.

The biggest lesson in all of this—and one that served us well—was that an investigator will, at some point, lose complete ownership of the case. As auditors, we were not in the position to tell the campus attorney to back off from an agreement with the subject's lawyer—one that almost created more work than the investigation itself.

However, by adopting a flexible posture and applying our expertise in the areas of record keeping, safeguarding, and accountability, we were able to exert our own special brand of control over an unexpected complication.

RECOMMENDATIONS TO PREVENT FUTURE OCCURRENCES

Separate Accounting Duties and Implement Secondary Purchase Approvals at All Employee Levels

Assistant Vice Chancellor Fairbanks was uniquely positioned to commit major fraud through his position of authority and trust in the Aesop Communications Department. Traditional business controls, such as separation of accounting duties and secondary approvals of purchases, were limited to subordinate staff in the past. High-level officials were practically immune to scrutiny, which enabled Fairbanks to rack up an astronomical bill in fraudulent activity. It is important to separate accounting duties and have secondary approvals of purchases, regardless of an employee's rank.

Monitor for Suspicious Activity

A member of senior finance staff—not a department-level accountant or any of the subordinate departments—should be hired as an independent monitor for the entire organization. The monitor should look for signs of trouble: repeat payments to the same vendor, payments just under the low-value threshold, vendor names and addresses that seem incongruous with the online descriptions of the expenses. The monitor should report anything that appears strange or suspicious.

Redefine Job Descriptions to Maintain Integrity

Human resource experts should review and update the accounting supervisor's written job description. The supervisor should understand that she is as responsible for the integrity of the expenses she approves as she is for the bookkeeping detail.

When the accounting supervisor in Aesop University Communications accidentally took delivery of a large package from the San Francisco–based Lincoln Galleries, she immediately recognized the address from the many invoices she had approved for Lincoln Photography. The supervisor said that she had a "funny feeling" about the package. She was not afraid of angering Lawrence Fairbanks by questioning him about the delivery. To the contrary, the supervisor was more fearful that a serious inquiry might cause unnecessary harm to her boss's reputation.

The accounting supervisor lacked the healthy perspective of an overseer. She was entirely focused on making sure that the individual "publications expenses" were charged to the correct ledger codes and that they fit safely over the bottom line. A specific job description that clearly stated her duties may have prompted the accounting supervisor to inspect the package more closely and put a stop the fraud in a timely manner.

Implement Tip Line

Finally, though not the direct result of this particular case, Aesop University implemented a 24-hour whistleblower hotline that supports anonymous complaints. Had the hotline existed during his acquisition of the Fairbanks collection, Lawrence might only have squirreled away one locker's worth of stuff.

Ellen A. Fischer, CFE, CIA, is the audit manager responsible for all investigations in a large research university. During the past 20 years, she has conducted investigations of complex and high-profile fraud cases toward their successful prosecution. Ms. Fischer enjoys writing about her cases almost as much as she does investigating them.

CHAPTER 2

The Ambitious Payroll Manager

JOHN TONSICK

When Dena Brenner entered a room, people noticed. Her bright blue eyes were framed with blonde, shoulder-length tresses. She wore stylish, expensive clothes that flattered her slender figure. Never too much makeup and just the right amount of jewelry, Dena looked much younger than the 37-year-old mother of three that she was.

Only six years earlier, after finishing her associates degree, Dena went to work in the payroll department of Sure Growth Seed Company, a family-owned business based in Ohio. Three years later, Sure Growth was acquired by a much larger establishment, International Agricultural Seed, commonly known as IAS. Dena quickly attracted the attention of the new owners and was offered a position as corporate payroll manager, requiring her to relocate to the West Coast. She worked at the company's corporate headquarters, the same building occupied by top management. It didn't take long for her to become a favorite of those in the executive suite. Thoughtful, cheery, and flirtatious, Dena was responsive to every administrative whim. The company's CEO held Dena in particularly high regard. He took an active role in protecting her interests and advancing her career. If you were to ask anyone at IAS, they would tell you with certainty that she was on her way to bigger and better things.

Dena's husband, Ron, stood in contrast to his polished and professional wife. Tall and stocky, he was a quiet, plain-spoken man. He'd spent most of his adult life working low-level jobs in the dairy industry. Married for 15 years, Ron and Dena had three beautiful daughters. As is usually the case with fraud, things aren't always what they seem. As much as Dena was loved by her superiors, she was viewed with mistrust by many of her peers and subordinates. Instead of a charming problem-solver, they saw her as arrogant, cold, and condescending. Even worse, they thought, was the way she treated her husband. Unable to find work in the family's new hometown, Ron enrolled in college and became a full-time student. When he wasn't in class, he took care of the girls. He was the family cook, chauffeur, housekeeper, and, most important, errand boy. He meekly complied with Dena's every demand.

By most accounts, Dena was a taskmaster when it came to dealing with Ron. Even the slightest transgression would send her into a withering tirade. Though kinder to her daughters, she treated them the same way as her other possessions. They were cared for, but were viewed more like accessories.

There was one more thing that bothered Dena's coworkers: her lifestyle. Sure, she made a decent salary, but no one could understand how she was able to live so extravagantly. She wore beautiful clothing and jewelry. Dena and her family lived in a spacious five-bedroom house in one of the area's nicest neighborhoods. The Brenner home was richly appointed with tasteful furnishings and artwork. Dena and Ron both drove new cars, and all three girls attended private school. Even more curious were her two horses, to which she seemed more attached than to her own daughters. When anyone dared to ask how she could afford these things, Dena responded quickly with a story of inherited wealth and wise investments.

Sure Growth Seed Company began in 1865. The American Civil War had just ended, and a reunited America was headed back to work. At that time, more than half of all the country's citizens earned their living as farmers, and the company found the perfect moment to begin selling agricultural seed. As America grew and prospered, so did the new business. Becoming an industry innovator, Sure Growth provided high-quality, high-yield seeds that were resistant to drought and pests.

At the dawn of the new millennium, the U.S. agricultural business was bigger than ever; it had also changed dramatically. Family farms played a much smaller role in an industry that was now dominated by large corporations. One was International Agricultural Seed, a global company that had grown through a series of mergers. As IAS followed its plan to become a market leader, Sure Growth was added to its list of acquisitions. With thousands of employees and facilities around the world, IAS was sophisticated. It was an environment conducive to the ambitions of Dena Brenner.

A Suspicious Transfer

Klaus Dieter had been with IAS in Europe for more than a dozen years. A handsome, blond, athletic man in his mid-30s, he acted as if he were born in the executive suite. His English was nearly perfect, with only his name and the slight hint of a German accent divulging his roots. Klaus made it a point of pride to know every aspect of IAS's business, a trait that allowed him to move up the corporate ladder quickly. To most, it was a foregone conclusion that he would head the company someday.

When Klaus arrived at headquarters, Dena had been the payroll manager for nearly three years, and the IAS executive team seemed more enamored with her than ever. By this time she had placed her mark on the department's operations. With support from the CEO and other executives, she moved payroll to the director of human resources. "That's where it belongs," she said confidently. Besides, like the CEO, the human resource director was Dena's good friend and supporter. In addition to changing the reporting relationship, she had a new payroll system installed. Using the complexities of the new system as justification, she replaced all of the department's long-term employees with her own hand-picked staff.

Just as Klaus made it a point to know every aspect of IAS's business, Dena made it a point to endear herself to every executive at the company. Klaus seemed to be the lone holdout. For reasons unknown, and in spite of Dena's best efforts, she just couldn't seem to bring him under her spell. Klaus assumed his new role as treasurer with his usual enthusiasm and love for details. It was his job to make sure that IAS had sufficient financial resources to operate the business and to continue the company's growth; that meant keeping a close eye on cash flow. In only his second month as treasurer, Klaus noted something odd in the numbers. The company payroll was processed every two weeks and, with only minor fluctuations, came in at roughly $4 million. During the last payroll cycle, the number was $4.7 million. Surprised at the large increase, Klaus phoned Dena, who was away on business in Chicago.

"What happened?" he asked.

"I'm not sure," replied Dena, "but I'll find out right away." The next day, she was back in the office and $700,000 had been wired into the company's bank account. "Problem solved," explained Dena. "Just a bank error."

With a plausible explanation and the money's quick and safe return to the company account, most of Klaus's peers would have dismissed the issue and moved on to something else. No doubt Dena's quick resolution would have earned their praise. But that wasn't Klaus's style. Besides, $700,000 was a lot of money. If it was a bank error, shouldn't someone explain how it happened? Something else was bothering Klaus. Dena was always responsive to executive requests, but her abrupt return from Chicago seemed a bit over the top, even for her. Couldn't she have just made some phone calls?

Acting on his suspicion, Klaus phoned my colleague. He explained the situation and asked if it made sense.

"Where did the money come from?" we asked.

"I don't know," replied Klaus.

"Why don't you call the bank to see if you can find out?" we suggested. Within a short time, he got an answer that infuriated him: The money had been wire transferred from Dena Brenner's personal bank account.

MEMORY LOSS

Distressed and angry, Klaus did a little digging on his own. He learned that the $700,000 in question related to three payroll transfers. All three were made to Dena's bank account number but used the name of Yuet Chi, a former IAS employee who'd left the company more than two years ago. Klaus asked our firm to launch an investigation.

The next morning my colleague, Carrie Lane, was shown to the board room at IAS's corporate headquarters. At the center of the room was a massive black marble conference table surrounded by high-backed black leather chairs. The pale gray walls, expensive artwork, and thick gray carpeting seemed to soften the bright sunshine that was streaming through the windows. It was in stark contrast to the moods of those who would soon occupy it.

Dena Brenner walked nervously into the conference room—impeccably dressed, but distraught. She was followed by her boss, Dan Redfern, the Vice President of Human Resources. Carrie made some brief introductions and told Dena that she was trying to sort out what happened with regard to the bank error.

"I'm never doing anything again without getting someone's name in blood," said Dena. The simple bank error she described just the day before sounded a bit more complicated now. "From time to time, Amanda Salazar sends me e-mails requesting special payments for employees," Dena explained. Amanda was an HR manager who, like Dena, worked for Dan. "Since the e-mails came from Amanda, I never questioned them. I've processed lots of them over the years," she said.

"These payments are nearly a month old," replied Carrie. "How were you able to get the bank to reverse them?"

"It was just a matter of finding the right person," explained Dena. When Carrie asked her the name of her contact at the bank, Dena refused to provide it. "I don't think she was supposed to do what she did," she said. "I don't want to get her in trouble."

"Do you recognize the name Yuet Chi?" asked Carrie.

"No," replied Dena.

"These transfers are very large. Aren't they unusual?"

"Not really," Dena said unconvincingly. When shown the bank account number to which the transfers had been made, she claimed she didn't recognize it. Finally, Carrie showed Dena a fax from the bank indicating that the account belonged to Dena and her husband, Ron.

Dena's face turned ashen. After several minutes, she said, "I've returned. . . ." Then her voice trailed off.

"You've returned the money?" asked Carrie.

"No," said Dena. "I didn't take it." After a long pause she said, "I'm feeling uncomfortable. I don't know what will happen to me." Crying now, she asked, "Will I be prosecuted? I would talk if I had a guarantee of no prosecution."

Carrie could make no promises but encouraged her to start from the beginning. "Did you know Yuet Chi?" she asked.

"I just picked him," Dena said solemnly. "I don't remember why, maybe because he was terminated." The first theft had taken place a year earlier. She reactivated Chi's account in the payroll master, changed his bank account number to hers, and transferred $40,000. After the transfer, she changed the account number back to Chi's and deactivated his file. As Dena recounted her thefts, Carrie began to add up the numbers; they totaled $1.2 million.

"I still have it," Dena said softly. "I have all the money. Between my checking and savings accounts, a money market fund, and my children's bank accounts, I have all of the money. I can get it for you today."

"Did you take anything else?" asked Carrie.

"No," said Dena, "I swear on a stack of bibles." She then prepared and signed a written statement admitting to the thefts, agreeing to return the stolen money and to help the company document the transactions.

Dena was escorted to the door by security. A short time later, she returned to the office with a cashier's check payable to the company for $500,000. She agreed to meet with Carrie and me the next day at a fast food restaurant near the office. We both watched intently out the window, awaiting Dena's arrival. Right on time, a shiny new black SUV pulled into the lot. She stepped out of the car dressed in faded blue jeans and a sweat shirt. With no makeup and dark circles under her eyes, she looked as if she'd had a long night. Carrie introduced us.

"I know you've been through a lot in the last 24 hours," I said, "but I have to ask you some more questions. Did you take anything more than you've already told us about?" I asked.

"Absolutely not." she said.

"Now would be a good time to tell us," I said, "because we're going to keep looking." With a quizzical look, Dena asked, "How long do you think it's going to take?" Fighting the urge to smile, I said, "Probably a couple of weeks."

Dena and I met once more at the fast food restaurant. She assured me that I was wasting my time in looking further. She told me that all of the money had been taken in the same way: using the payroll system and the name of Yuet Chi. She told me that no one else at IAS was involved. "Even my husband didn't know until the day I was sent home," she said.

We made a copy of Dena's hard drive and began downloading electronic copies of IAS's payroll registers. Carrie and I interviewed Dena's coworkers and reviewed paper files. The interviews seemed to confirm Dena's assertion that she had worked alone. Our examination of documents did reveal a clue: Each payroll register was missing one page. We later learned that these showed the transfers to Dena's bank account. A search of Dena's hard drive revealed no hints, but we hit the jackpot with the electronic payroll registers. Sorting disbursements by bank account number, we uncovered more than a dozen new transfers to Dena's bank account using the names of three additional terminated employees, totaling $700,000. The next day Carrie and I sat in a quiet corner booth at a coffee shop. Across from us sat Dena and her husband, Ron, whom Carrie and I were meeting for the very first time.

"Dena, we found another $700,000," I said. A distressed Dena looked at me and said, "No. I didn't do it." She then dropped her head and stared silently into her lap.

"I knew you guys were gonna do this!" Ron shouted angrily. "You're going to blame her for stuff she didn't even do!"

I assured Ron that we had no reason to do that. For the next half hour, I repeated my allegations several times, but Dena continued to adamantly deny it. Except for these brief exchanges, there was silence between us. Finally, Ron couldn't stand it any more. "Did you take the money?" he asked his wife.

"Yeah, I took it." Dena said.

"Why didn't you say that half an hour ago?" he shot back angrily.

"I forgot," Dena whispered.

After years of passively doing Dena's bidding, Ron seemed empowered by the situation. "Could you excuse us for a moment?" he asked. "Of course," I said. Ron grabbed Dena by the arm and took her outside. Through the coffee shop window, Carrie and I could see the two of them engaged in a heated conversation. A few minutes later, Ron walked briskly back to the booth with his wife in tow.

"You know about the property in Michigan," he said. We had done a search for assets but had no reason to check in Michigan. "Of course we know about that," I said.

Well, we did now.

"It's worth about $400,000," Ron said. "We paid cash for it. You can have that, too."

THE LAW WINS

Now that the investigation was complete, IAS turned its attention to recovering its losses. Dena had already returned $1.2 million. Our discovery of the additional thefts meant that she needed to come up with another $700,000. Out of ready cash, she was no longer in the mood to cooperate. IAS filed a civil suit against her seeking recovery of the stolen funds, plus the cost of the investigation. Faced with the expense of litigation and the overwhelming evidence of her guilt, Dena settled the civil suit.

She agreed to repay her remaining debt to IAS by surrendering the property in Michigan, her home, cars, jewelry, furniture, and artwork. As she dispassionately described the assets that she would surrender, tears welled up in her eyes when she got to the horses. "Please make sure they find a good home. They're my pets," she said, sobbing. Dena showed no such emotion when offering up her children's personal belongings.

It wasn't over yet. IAS wanted more than restitution; it wanted Dena to be punished. With pressure from Klaus, the company filed criminal charges and asked me to assist. I prepared several binders of evidence gathered during the investigation and took them to Derek Thompson, head of the district attorney's White Collar Crime Unit. We spent several hours reviewing it. The binders included Dena's signed confession and a detailed description of what she had done and how she had done it. They also included original documents and computer files to support each illicit transfer to her account. "We don't usually get cases that are this well prepared," Derek said. "It could take some time, but I'm ready to get started." Paul Kole, a D.A. investigator, was assigned to work on the case.

Several months passed after our meeting. There had been no arrest and, except for a few inquiries from Paul, not much seemed to be happening. At one point, on a hot summer day with temperatures well over 100 degrees, Dena's neighbors noticed smoke coming from her chimney. Unable to imagine why anyone would light a fire on such a hot day, they summoned the fire department. They arrived to find Dena burning documents in her fireplace. After that, IAS grew increasingly concerned that Dena would escape prosecution. Those fears were soon laid to rest.

Dena and Ron were moving out of the beautiful home that was no longer theirs. Along with the house, most of their possessions had been sold, and they were returning to Ohio with the children. As they placed the last of their meager belongings in a rented trailer, Paul walked up the driveway with a warrant for Dena's arrest. "I won't put the cuffs on you in front of the children," he said, "but you'll have to come with me." Out in the street, Dena was handcuffed and placed into the back of the squad car. Leaving the children behind, Ron walked out and spoke to his wife through the open window. "I'm still going to Ohio with the kids," he said flatly. "I'm also filing for a divorce." Ron turned and walked to the driveway without looking back. Paul drove away with Dena, who was about to spend her first night in jail.

Dena was charged with multiple counts of theft, money laundering, and tax evasion. A conviction on all counts could put her in prison for decades. Derek offered her a deal. In exchange for a guilty plea, he would recommend a sentence of nine years. Dena was stunned. In nine years, her children would be grown. She never expected to see prison, much less a sentence of this length. She declined the deal and asked for a jury trial.

Derek subpoenaed Dena's bank statements and gave them to Paul, who immediately came to me. "John, I wouldn't know where to start with these things. Can you help?" I agreed. Dena had given me photocopies of some of her bank statements, but I had never seen most of them. I noticed numerous large deposits ranging from $4,000 to $50,000. I asked Paul to subpoena the supporting details from the bank. The information provided only deepened Dena's problems.

Part of her job as payroll manager was to prepare and file the company's tax returns. Over the years, she made large overpayments to various state and federal tax authorities. Once the returns were filed and paid, she applied for refunds. Those checks, made payable to IAS, came directly to Dena. She simply endorsed them "Pay to the order of Dena Brenner" and deposited them to her checking account. The misappropriated refunds totaled $350,000.

Derek added the additional thefts to Dena's previous charges, along with multiple counts of forgery and computer fraud. If convicted on all counts and given the maximum sentence for each charge, Dena could spend the rest of her life in prison.

Derek asked me to appear as a witness for the prosecution at Dena's criminal trial. By the time I testified, she had been incarcerated for nearly a year. When she entered the courtroom, I was shocked by her appearance. Dena was wearing a prison-issue navy blue jumpsuit and white tennis shoes. She was shackled at the waist and ankles, causing her to shuffle when she walked. With no makeup and long gray roots in her washed-out blond hair, there was almost no trace of the stylish young woman I first met. After hearing my testimony and reviewing the evidence gathered during our investigation, the jury found Dena guilty of all charges. She was sentenced to 15 years in state prison.

Lessons Learned

The Dena Brenner investigation was successful on many levels, but two aspects stood out. First, IAS realized immediately that it needed help. The company called an outside expert as soon as it suspected a problem and listened to our advice. Internal investigations are often undertaken by individuals who lack the necessary tools, training, and experience. Frequently they do more harm than good. Many times suspects are confronted prematurely, without adequate proof, which allows them to conceal or destroy evidence and alert co-conspirators. Critical evidence is often ignored or handled improperly, rendering it useless in a judicial setting. Because IAS called experienced investigators first, we were able to put together a clear, convincing case of what Dena did and how she did it. This was a critical factor in winning the civil action and the criminal conviction.

Second, the sequence of the investigation provided maximum benefit to the organization. By conducting a thorough inquiry, the company compiled all of the evidence and information necessary to proceed with the civil suit. This helped keep the time and expense to a minimum. Similarly, when filing criminal charges, most of the work was already done for the D.A. It wasn't necessary for the government to tie up scarce resources investigating a complex crime. This brought the case to trial more quickly. It also provided the prosecutors with a road map for presenting the criminal case in a way that easily won a conviction.

RECOMMENDATIONS TO PREVENT FUTURE OCCURRENCES

The circumstances that allowed Dena Brenner to commit fraud against her employer are all too common. We recommended a number of changes.

Supervisory Review

The payroll master file includes the employee's name, address, Social Security number, rate of pay, and bank account number—the kind of information that changes infrequently or not all. Dena was the only IAS employee with access to this file. She was authorized to make changes without anyone's approval. Not only could she alter data in existing records, she was also free to add or delete employee names. We advised management to review and approve all payroll master file changes. We recommended that changes be reviewed and approved by a supervisor to ensure that all changes have been properly authorized and are made correctly.

The payroll register shows the details for each disbursement to each employee. In an attempt to conceal her thefts, Dena removed the page showing her fraudulent disbursements immediately after the payroll was processed. It didn't matter much anyway, because no one at IAS ever saw it but Dena.

Post Payroll to General Ledger

Another control weakness that helped Dena conceal her fraud involved the payroll system itself, which had the capacity to post transactions to the general ledger electronically after each pay period. Dena feared that this might inadvertently disclose her theft, so she refused to let the posting occur automatically. "There's a bug in the system and I just don't trust it," she told management. Each pay period, Dena would prepare a "manual journal entry," allocating her fraudulent transfers to a huge number of expense accounts in various departments. By splitting them up and spreading them around, Dena made her transactions more difficult to spot by anyone who might be looking.

Frequent Reconciliation of Payroll Account

Before she began making fraudulent transfers, Dena tested the system to see if she would be caught. Rather than use the wire transfers, Dena authorized two fraudulent payroll checks that were never cashed. If someone noticed them, she could simply say that they were errors. But they weren't discovered because the payroll bank account hadn't been properly reconciled for more than two years. At the time Dena's fraud was uncovered, the payroll bank account had more than 500 outstanding checks totaling $700,000, including the two checks used by Dena to test the system. We recommended that the controller's office reconcile the account each month and that it be reviewed and approved by a supervisor.

Segregation of Duties   IAS did not have an internal audit department. However, we recommended that someone not involved in processing payroll observe the distribution of paychecks and earnings statements. This recommendation was to help ensure that no more "Yuet Chis" would show up on the list.

Long before she began using the payroll system, Dena stole from her employer by overpaying the taxes and then applying for refunds, which she kept. This was possible because Dena prepared the returns and no one checked them for accuracy. Additionally, tax refund checks were mailed directly to her. So we recommended that payroll be reviewed, approved, and mailed by someone other than the preparer. We also suggested that refund checks be sent directly to a "lockbox" at the bank.

> John Tonsick, CFE, CPA, is a forensic accountant and keynote speaker. He provides consulting services in the areas of fraud, internal controls, and expert witnessing. Mr. Tonsick is a graduate of Robert Morris University and has nearly 30 years of experience in preventing, detecting, and investigating white-collar crime.

CHAPTER 3

The Insider

CRAIG R. SINNAMON

Not long after 20-year-old Stefanne Rider was hired at Majestic Bank, she became the most popular teller in the office. Tall and slender with strawberry blond hair and hazel eyes, she had a smile that could light a small town. Stefanne was one of four children raised in blue-collar, rural Morgantown, Pennsylvania, by her mother, Cindy.

Her father, Sam, owned and operated a local furniture store—his pride and joy. When large chain stores moved into the area, his business experienced lean years, but he and Cindy always managed to make ends meet.

After Stefanne graduated from high school at age 18, she was accepted to attend Saint Joseph's University in Philadelphia. She immediately fell in love with the campus and begged her father to let her go. But how would Sam afford to send his daughter to the college of her dreams? The family qualified for some financial assistance, but not nearly enough to afford tuition, room and board, a meal plan, and books. Sam and Cindy mortgaged their modest home of 27 years, and Stefanne took out student loans to cover the remaining costs.

Stefanne reveled in college life. She studied Communications and received full honors her first two years. In September, at the start of her junior year, life was perfect. Then the unthinkable happened.

The remnants of Hurricane Ivan barreled through Morgantown and pummeled the area, dumping more than eight inches of rain in two days. A creek near Sam's store flooded. He fought tooth and nail to combat the rising water, but his efforts were futile. Within a few hours, the storm wiped out the building and all of the furniture inside. Most of all, it devastated Sam. One cost-cutting measure he had employed in order to send Stefanne to college was dropping his expensive flood insurance coverage. Now his business was destroyed, and he had to start over from scratch.

Stefanne returned home from college, placing her dreams on hold so she could contribute to the family. She took a job as a teller at Majestic Bank. The branch manager, Lena Santana, knew Stefanne well. Lena remembered giving her lollipops years ago through the drive-up window when Stefanne accompanied Sam to the bank to make the daily deposit. Stefanne already knew many of the customers in town and possessed the attributes necessary to be successful in her new position.

Majestic Bank is a large, regional bank based in Pittsburgh with approximately $110 billion in assets, over 9,500 employees, and a network of 850 community banking offices spanning from Maine to southern Virginia. It was founded over 17 years ago, starting with four branches in a small western Pennsylvania town. There exists a corporate culture of camaraderie and an entrepreneurial spirit. Employees are referred to as team members.

Majestic invests significant resources into the Loss Prevention and Security (LP&S) function. LP&S is segregated into two primary areas, Loss Prevention and Mitigation, and Fraud Investigations. Loss Prevention/Mitigation employs a large team of highly trained analysts at a central site. Their function is to maintain and review various software applications designed to detect and reduce losses associated with fraud. The Fraud Investigations team consists of a smaller group of professionals, each strategically located throughout the bank's footprint. Many are retired law enforcement detectives. Others, like me, are career bankers. I joined the team after two years in retail banking and seven years as a corporate auditor.

What Did You Do with My Money?

Carolyn Sasser, a career banker and a member of my team, was one of a couple of investigators responsible for investigating all forms of bank fraud cases originating in the greater Philadelphia area. She was in the process of reviewing what appeared to be a routine counterfeit check case on a humid summer afternoon in her tiny office in Rosemont, Pennsylvania. The victim in this case was a customer named Thomas White. He opened an account more than 10 years ago. Thomas, a retired World War II Air Force pilot, stopped by the local Majestic branch in the Chestnut Hill section of Philadelphia to withdraw $100 cash before going to the grocery store. Soon after handing his withdrawal slip to the teller, he was stunned to learn his account was overdrawn.

"How could that be?" he asked. "Didn't my Social Security deposit post to my account last Friday?"

"Yes," the teller replied politely. "But you also wrote three checks to your account last night," she continued.

"That's impossible! I need to speak to Gina immediately," he demanded.

Gina Stevens, the branch manager, had opened his account at the Chestnut Hill branch. She and Mr. White got along famously. But now he was fuming. "What is going on with this bank?" he asked Gina curtly before she could even say hello.

Gina listened intently to Mr. White's problem. To her, it sounded like a case of counterfeit checks. "We will take care of you, Mr. White," she reassured him. Gina completed the necessary paperwork and opened a new account for him. Majestic reimbursed Mr. White in full but he terminated his relationship with the bank a few days later, sighting concerns over security.

Carolyn reviewed the checks contained in his file. The check stock used by the counterfeiters really resonated with Carolyn. "Didn't I recently work on a case with similar-looking fakes?" she asked herself aloud. She then looked at the back of the check and observed a stamp from Kingdom Bank based in New Jersey. "Kingdom Bank?" she wondered. "I've been speaking with their Security Department a lot lately."

After a few minutes of reviewing Mr. White's file, Carolyn realized that this was no ordinary counterfeit check situation. Luckily, she was fanatical about organizing her files. She quickly was able to pull a few cases, and compared them to Mr. White's. All of them were relatively small (under $4,500 loss), so Carolyn had placed them on the back burner while she tended to larger issues. Each victim customer noticed the activity soon after it began. She found three other counterfeit cases with similar attributes—individual checks less than $1,500, same check stock, similar handwriting, all negotiated through Kingdom Bank in New Jersey. Carolyn called Tim Carter, the security officer at Kingdom. "Not only were all of them deposited at our bank," he informed Carolyn, "but they all went through the same ATM machine at one of our branches in Trenton! All four of our customers immediately withdrew all of the money from their accounts using the same ATM."

It was obvious that these seemingly small cases were associated with the same check fraud ring. Carolyn knew that LP&S likely had more problems. She immediately called Mary McFadden, another Majestic Bank fraud investigator in Freehold, New Jersey, to see if she had any similar issues.

Mary took copious notes as Carolyn provided details of her cases.

"Wait a second," Mary said, "What was that last account number?"

It was Mr. White's. "Carolyn," she continued, "that is a passbook savings account. I just received a small counterfeit check case involving checks that posted to a statement savings account. How is it possible that checks can post to *savings* accounts?" she asked. Mary pulled the case file.

"You know what? My victim customer's name is James White. Let me look at the back of the checks…yep, Kingdom Bank. You know what else, Carolyn?" Mary continued. "All the victim customers' names are common: Tom White, James White, Mark Williams, Tom Jones, Michael Smith. This doesn't appear to be a dumpster-diving operation. These victims were targeted systematically."

Carolyn agreed, "You're right. I smell an internal fraud. Let's get Kathy and Craig on the line."

FOLLOWING THE FOOTPRINTS

I had just returned to my office after lunch and was sifting through the mountain of paperwork on my desk when the phone rang. It was my manager, Kathy Backman, the corporate internal fraud manager at Majestic Bank. She manages a team of five analysts and three investigators trained to proactively identify and investigate various types of internal fraud, such as branch cash embezzlements, payroll fraud, and general ledger frauds. I am one of the three internal investigators reporting to Kathy.

"Craig, I need you right away," she said, on a mission.

"What's up?" I asked.

"I'll explain when you get here," she replied.

I scurried to Kathy's office, four doors down from mine. "What's going on?"

"Carolyn and Mary are on the phone with me now," she said. The women explained to me the circumstances that preceded their call.

"Well, it appears a bank employee has compromised your victims' accounts," I stated.

"Craig, research the 'Footprint Report' to determine if the same employee queried the victims' accounts before the counterfeit checks were negotiated," Kathy instructed.

The "Footprint Report" was created by Majestic's IT Department at Kathy's behest a couple of years ago after she suspected an insider was stealing customer account information. She could not prove her theory due to the bank's inability to monitor employee inquiry activity. The "Footprint Report" captures all customer profile/account queries performed by staff directly on the bank's mainframe system. A team member must use his or her unique user ID and password to directly access it. If someone queries a customer profile/account directly on the mainframe system, the "Footprint Report" will capture the activity and the associated user ID.

I reviewed the bank statements associated with the five customer accounts and started my research with two of them that contained minimal account activity. "It should be easy to isolate a common user ID with these two accounts. The customer's infrequent activity should result in fewer account queries," I concluded. I first searched "Footprint Report" for victim Tom White's account. Mr. White's deposit activity consisted only of a monthly direct deposit of his Social Security. He writes some checks to pay his monthly bills and only on occasion withdraws cash over the counter at his local branch. I noticed the first counterfeit check posted to his account on July 9, so I started with a date range search beginning June 1 to July 8. There were a couple of inquiries performed by team members. I cataloged the user IDs and query dates/times on a spreadsheet. I searched the "Footprint Report" for the next victim customer, Mark Williams, and cataloged the queries as I did with Mr. White account. "Bingo!" I said. "We have a hit!" I noticed that the same user ID performed queries on the accounts owned by White and Williams less than two weeks before the counterfeit checks posted.

I searched the system for the owner of this user ID. It was Stefanne Rider at the Morgantown branch. Why would a teller in rural Pennsylvania want details for a customer residing an hour and a half away in Philadelphia? I then reviewed Mr. White's account and noticed that Stefanne asked for his name and account number on June 30 at 12:05 p.m. on the mainframe system. I further observed that Stefanne queried Mr. White's profile and account number on the mainframe system at this time, and also several other rather common names within just a few minutes, some only seconds apart. She appeared to be haphazardly searching for customers.

In no time I was able to trace the three remaining profiles to Stefanne's user ID. Counterfeit checks began to post to each account within two weeks of her inquiries. Coincidentally, all five victims resided and performed their banking in the greater Philadelphia area or New Jersey, hours away from Stefanne's Morgantown branch. It was obvious that she was the point of compromise. I phoned Kathy right away. "I think we have our suspect," I said. We discovered that Stefanne was on vacation visiting family in Ohio for the remainder of the week and was scheduled to return the following Monday.

"Great," said Kathy, "This gives us the opportunity to investigate further and determine the scope of this case. There are probably more victims out there. We can interview Stefanne the day she returns from vacation and maintain the element of surprise so she doesn't have the opportunity to concoct a story behind her activity. However, let's disable her system access immediately, just in case. Solicit the help of the analysts to conduct comprehensive research. We need to identify as many actual and potential victims as soon as possible, so you'll need their help. Report your findings to me by the end of the week," she stated.

"So much for catching up on my paperwork," I said aloud as I journeyed to my office to set up a conference call with the analysts.

Kathy's team and I worked long hours to link Stefanne's inquiries to customer accounts victimized by counterfeit check activity. By the end of the week, we linked her to 18 victims of counterfeit check activity, with total bank losses exceeding $54,000. The fraud had begun only a couple of months before. Victims spanned from Maine to Virginia, and all had common names. Every counterfeit was negotiated at Kingdom Bank and clearly originated from the same check stock. Each one contained very similar handwriting. It was also evident that the "ring" had an insider working at Kingdom, as the identities of many confirmed Majestic victims were used to open accounts at Kingdom. Finally, we knew that many more of our customers had been compromised by Stefanne, as she performed inquiries on countless others. The analysts closely monitored these accounts while regional management and Kathy painstakingly devised the appropriate action plan, including contacting the customers, freezing their accounts, and offering free identity theft protection.

During the investigation, we determined that Stefanne maintained an employee checking account at Majestic. I reviewed her account and identified several nonpayroll cash deposits in amounts ranging from $400 to $1,000. She had deposited over $10,000 just over the past few months. I explained our findings to Kathy, who then reported the results to regional management. Next, we contacted Lena, Stefanne's manager, but did not disclose the nature of our investigation. We needed to obtain some background information prior to the interview. Lena advised us of the unfortunate circumstances that recently befell Stefanne and her family, insisting that she was a top performer, loved by her team and the Morgantown customers.

"If she did anything wrong, I'm sure she'll have a legitimate explanation," Lena insisted. "She's a sweet girl and I would stake my reputation on her."

"What makes you think she did anything wrong?" Kathy asked.

"Well, any time loss prevention calls, it usually means someone is in trouble," Lena replied.

"That's not true," Kathy said. "We simply think Stefanne may have some information to help us with a current investigation. Please ask her to report to the Administration Building first thing Monday morning to meet with Craig."

It was 9:30 a.m. and the start of what would be a productive work week. A trembling Stefanne Rider arrived at our office. When I went to introduce myself, I was startled to see that an older gentleman who identified himself as Sam Rider, her father, accompanied her. He wanted to participate in the interview with his daughter. I told him that the meeting pertained to a private bank matter, and I could not allow him to be present. Sam was clearly agitated, but he acquiesced and waited in the lobby.

As we entered our conference room, I introduced Stefanne to Tracy Blattner, an employee relations representative from Majestic, and directed her to a chair in the middle of the room. The table was previously moved to the side so there would be no obstruction between us. Tracy sat in a chair several feet behind to witness the interview. Stefanne remained visibly nervous, clutching her purse in her lap with her arms crossed, head down, and eyes tentatively peeking at me from under her strawberry blond bangs. She rocked slightly back and forth in her chair as I began asking her some basic background questions about her education, job responsibilities, and family life in an effort to develop a rapport with her. As I learned more about Stefanne, I began to sense the anxiety building in her. She appeared sheepish and spoke almost with a whisper.

Before I was able to begin asking Stefanne questions pertaining to the case, she began to sob. I placed my memo pad to the side, pulled my chair closer to her, and asked, "Is there something you want to talk about? You seem to have the weight of the world on your shoulders, and I'd like to help you in any way I can."

"I don't think there is anything you can do to help me," she responded, tears streaming down her face.

RUNNING ON EMPTY

It took the better part of an hour to settle Stefanne down so that she could speak to me coherently. She eventually confessed to selling customer identities and account numbers to a ring operating out of Philadelphia.

Stefanne had met a young man named Buck while employed as a barmaid at a pub near campus. A regular patron, he had befriended her not long after she began working there. Buck was brash and flirtatious with slicked-back dark hair and a rail-thin build. Although nobody actually knew how he made a living, he appeared to have a lot of money. He drove brand-new import cars, dressed to the nines, and tipped better than any other patron. One night he approached Stefanne after hearing from the bar owner that she was leaving school to tend to a family crisis. He also had learned she accepted a job with Majestic Bank as a full-time teller.

He approached Stefanne. "I'm sorry to hear about your family situation. It sounds pretty bad. I hear you took a job at a bank, huh?" Buck asked.

"I need to help pay the family bills, my own credit card bills, and put food on the table—at least until things get better. I'm devastated that I have to leave school, but I have no choice," Stefanne said.

Buck then made his pitch. "Listen, I think I can help your family and get you back to school in no time, but you need to do something for me," he said. "You take that job with the bank, and I'll give you $200 for every customer account you give me, along with each of their Social Security numbers, addresses, birth dates, phone numbers—any information you can access."

"But isn't that against the law? What in the world are you going to do with it?" she asked.

Buck explained that his friends needed the information to make and cash counterfeit checks, and customer identities to open bank accounts and establish credit lines.

"I don't know," Stefanne said.

Buck interrupted, "You want to help your family, right? You want to return to school, right? If you turn me down, you'll probably never come back to college. Anyway, nobody gets hurt in the end. The bank has millions of dollars and will reimburse the customers."

"But what if we get caught?" Stefanne asked.

"I'll tell you what," Buck said. "After your shift I'll take you to my friend's house and show you how it works. Deal?" he asked persuasively. Stefanne reluctantly agreed.

Her shift ended at 2:30 a.m., and she met Buck outside of her dorm. He drove her to an old, rundown row home somewhere in North Philadelphia. Buck navigated through a complex network of small side streets and dark alleys so Stefanne would not be able to determine the exact location of the property. They entered from behind the row home and proceeded down a dark stairway to the basement. There, they met a man who called himself "Taz." Taz was an older, heavyset African American man who wore a prosthetic leg.

"This is the girl who is going to join our team," Buck said, as he rushed to the basement. Frightened, Stefanne stood at the base of the stairway. Taz grinned and motioned her into the basement. As she made her way toward the men, Stefanne's eyes were drawn to what appeared to be a modern studio equipped with laptop computers, digital cameras, stacks of blank checks and credit cards, and laminating equipment. "This is where it all happens," Taz explained proudly.

The men explained that the information she agreed to provide would be used to create counterfeit checks and fake IDs. Taz provided the fakes to a group of "runners" who would open bank accounts and negotiate the counterfeit checks.

"We'll also tell the runners to apply for loans using the identities you give us," Taz continued. He had a partner who recruited homeless people. "They'll do anything to make a few bucks," he explained. "Stefanne, we'll make more money than you can imagine," Taz promised. "And your job is the easy part. It's the runners who risk getting caught."

It didn't take them long to convince Stefanne to agree to the scheme. She would have done almost anything just to get out of that row house!

Buck returned Stefanne to her dormitory. "I'll call you on your cell in a few weeks and let you know how we're going to do this," he told her.

Two months later, Stefanne was already a favorite teller at the Morgantown branch. One day during her lunch break, her cell phone rang. It was Buck.

"I got $600 and need some customers, Stefanne," he said without even introducing himself. She knew exactly what he meant. "Meet me at Burger King after the bank closes tomorrow and don't target customers that go to your branch. That would be too obvious."

Stefanne returned to her station and quickly decided it would be easiest to query common names on the bank's mainframe system.

Ultimately, Stefanne confessed to stealing the identities of over 55 Majestic depositors. She explained that she would meet Buck once per week and exchange customer screen prints for cash.

"I still can't believe I did this," she whispered to herself as she completed a written statement.

"Did you tell your dad?" I asked.

"I told him this morning after I was asked to come here," she responded. "I wouldn't have involved my dad if Buck didn't call me on my way here. He made it clear that I was not to cooperate with you. I immediately called my dad and told him everything. That's why he came with me this morning. He had no idea what I was doing. He just thought I was making extra commissions by cross-selling bank products. He pleaded with me to cooperate with you. I wasn't sure I would until you started asking me questions."

When the interview was complete and her written statement was secured, Tracy informed Stefanne that her employment with Majestic Bank was terminated. After handing me the keys to her teller cash drawer, I escorted an emotionally drained young woman from the conference room. I watched her approach her father and collapse into his arms.

Stefanne later offered a treasure trove of information to law enforcement. The intelligence she provided resulted in the arrest of several criminals and the breakup of an organized crime ring operating out of Philadelphia. She avoided jail time by cooperating with the prosecution of these criminals, but received five years probation and was ordered to pay $66,000 of restitution to Majestic Bank.

The promising future of this once-exuberant, intelligent young woman changed forever the day she decided to enter into the criminal underground world of identity theft and check fraud—a fact she will be reminded of each and every time she completes a job application.

Lessons Learned

I learned a great deal as a result of this and other identity theft cases involving Majestic Bank customers.

Information Security—Restrict and Monitor

In today's environment, it is critical for every organization to develop and implement enterprise-wide countermeasures to external and insider attacks against their information technology environment. Majestic Bank recognized the risks associated with insider attacks and the need to restrict employee access to sensitive information to only those who require it to perform their job. One countermeasure currently under management consideration is biometric technology. Rather than requiring a customer to provide an easily counterfeited driver's license and secondary form of identification, a customer can authenticate his or her identity with a mere scan of a fingertip.

It is no less critical for organizations to monitor employee access to sensitive company data. For example, Majestic Bank's "Footprint Report" was a relatively new tool that enabled us to identify the single point of compromise. Although it was instrumental in identifying the suspect after the fraud was well under way, we have further enhanced the surveillance of employee system activity. As such, Majestic Bank implemented new business intelligence software to proactively monitor employee access to sensitive company data by capturing anomalous teller inquiry activity, such as:

- Inquiries to the bank's teller processing system with no corresponding customer transactions
- Inquiries on customers residing outside of the teller's predetermined geographic region
- An unusually high volume of inquiries in comparison to historical volumes associated with a given teller
- An unusually high volume of inquiries performed by a teller on a predetermined list of common names, such as "Smith," "Jones," and so on

Employee Assistance Programs

Majestic Bank partners with an organization that offers a wide variety of programs designed to support Majestic team members with just about any life issue, such as financial crises, child care issues, and elder care. Lena Santana failed to recognize the extent of Stefanne's dire situation and direct her to the employee assistance program (EAP). Perhaps Stefanne could have received the help she needed before resorting to nefarious activity.

Customer Retention—Identity Theft Assistance Unit

LP&S and Retail Management had difficulty coordinating proper notification to the identity theft victims. The bank did not have standardized procedures, which created an atmosphere of confusion with respect to roles and responsibilities and did not allow the bank to adequately leverage its resources to respond to customer needs in a timely, organized fashion. LP&S quickly recognized the need to provide victims a single point of contact to facilitate customer retention. As such, LP&S established an Identity Theft Assistance Unit consisting of five highly trained team members charged with the responsibility to respond to the needs of identity theft victims.

LP&S Case Management

Carolyn and Mary utilized years of investigative experience and open dialogue to link multiple fraudulent events (i.e., counterfeit checks) to a single point of compromise. The importance of open communication and dialogue within an organization cannot be overstated. Oftentimes, entities unknowingly maintain a "silo" approach in their day-to-day operations. Majestic Bank's LP&S Department now nurtures a culture of open, honest dialogue among its team members.

Tip Line

Although Stefanne pilfered customer identities stealthily, many insiders fail to exercise such discretion. Majestic Bank provides all team members with an anonymous internal hotline to report unusual or suspicious activity to LP&S. However, only one LP&S team member is currently assigned the responsibility to man the hotline between 8 a.m. and 5 p.m. Because callers often are forced to leave information on a recorded message, many fail to provide sufficient, actionable information. Messages are also sometimes inaudible due to a poor phone line connection. LP&S recommended management consider outsourcing this function to a company that can deliver live, 24/7 coverage by personnel trained to extract detailed information from each caller, while ensuring 100% confidentiality.

RECOMMENDATIONS TO PREVENT FUTURE OCCURRENCES

Information Security

All companies, including financial institutions, should make it a priority to understand the current threats to their IT infrastructure and consider leveraging technology to defend against attacks from external and internal sources.

Background Checks

Organizations should utilize a comprehensive applicant screening process inclusive of criminal background and credit checks, especially for those positions requiring extensive cash handling and access to sensitive company information, such as customer profiles.

Zero Tolerance Policy

Executive management at Majestic Bank has taken a stance against fraud committed by its team members. They maintain a "Code of Conduct and Ethics" that must be signed by every newly hired team member. In addition, all team members must review the code during each annual performance review and sign a document acknowledging it, which states in plain language the fiduciary duty of everyone to refrain from transactions or behavior that seems even slightly inappropriate and report suspected fraud to appropriate personnel. The code also specifically addresses the bank's position regarding fraud, namely "zero tolerance and prosecution of the offenders." This document can serve as a deterrent and sets the appropriate tone from the top.

Customer Education

Majestic Bank uses every communication avenue at its disposal to educate customers on how to protect themselves from identity theft. The bank's Web site contains a prominently displayed section dedicated to these issues. Each branch displays signage warning customers of the threats associated with identity theft. Brochures are also on display in branches and are periodically enclosed with customer statement mailings to educate people about the risks. The call center often plays an audio message alerting customers waiting on hold to the danger and warning signs of identity theft.

The bank advertises and offers a software product that is linked to the three major credit bureaus. This provides customers with instant access to their credit files, automatically monitors changes or inquiries to credit files, and alerts customers to any unauthorized accounts opened in their name.

Employee Training

Financial institutions should conduct ongoing employee training about identity theft. At a minimum, they should develop written policies and procedures governing disclosure of customer information, and use them as a basis to train employees. Employees should be trained to recognize fraudulent attempts to obtain customer information and execute the necessary prevention techniques to protect customer information from internal and external threats, such as shredding documents containing sensitive company or customer information, avoiding unauthorized access to computers, and limiting the amount of information provided over certain communication channels like e-mail and telephone. Majestic Bank's LP&S and Legal departments provide on-site and web-based employee training covering these and many other issues associated with the security of customer information and related privacy regulations.

Craig Sinnamon, CFE, is a regional fraud investigations manager with a large financial institution. He is a graduate of Beaver College (now known as Arcadia University) and has 11 years of auditing and fraud investigations experience in the financial services industry.

CHAPTER 4

Aloha, Hawaii!

DOMINIC A. D'ORAZIO

Marin Jensen seemed to have it all. A self-proclaimed family man, he married a lovely gal named Julia and had two young children. His wife stayed home to manage the active lives of their kids, while Marin appeared to be a model employee at the American Logistics Agency. From the exterior, their lives were picture perfect.

The Jensens' home was nestled away on a quiet tree-lined cul-de-sac in one of the Northeast's more affluent communities. The two-story colonial sits on two acres of beautifully landscaped property that was purchased by the Jensens for almost $400,000. The dead-end street was ideal for the kids, since it does not have a heavy flow of traffic. A state park is located near the neighborhood, which is used for various athletic competitions and has an adjoining farm that resembles what daily lives were like before the advent of the industrial age. Because of the proximity to the state park, one can bike around the neighborhood in the late afternoon and spot deer meandering through the residents' yards.

At first glance, one might surmise that the area consists of the type of folks who spend a great portion of their professional lives climbing the corporate ladder. Indeed, this is not the type of neighborhood one would associate with a middle-management government worker. Of course, it is no crime for a middle-management employee to live in such a neighborhood. Certainly there are other ways to accumulate the type of wealth one would need to afford the property, but if the lifestyle one is living cannot be explained by the income one is earning, questions arise.

Marin's home, though modest compared to some of the more elegant houses that dot this high-income town, contained features common among families who prefer to have amenities close to them. For example, the backyard contained a playground area and an in-ground swimming pool, surrounded by flowers and bushes. These quiet and serene conditions could persuade one to meditate. Like many of their neighbors, the Jensens employed landscapers who mow and edge the lawn, trim the bushes, and maintain the yard.

Marin took pride in coaching his children's sports teams and running the usual family taxi service, transporting his kids to their respective sports and extracurricular activities. While most of today's families own minivans, the Jensens had the original family conveyance: a station wagon.

After working for American Logistics for several years, Marin rose to the position of senior logistics management specialist. He was considered likable, and several program directors wanted to use his services. During one particular year, he split his work time between his main office and two other customers. When a third customer inquired about his services, Marin's supervisor stated he had already used up his available work time for the year. The prospective third customer suggested that if Marin would agree to work for him, he would be willing to pay for the overtime. Marin agreed to put in the time, over and above his normal workweek. Once his work for the third customer was finished, Marin began to struggle financially. He had become accustomed to the extra cash. With his real estate taxes climbing, he had to come up with another way to supplement his salary.

The American Logistics Agency is a part of the federal government, located in the northeast region of the United States. As an integrated entity, it develops, fields, and sustains base command and control, intelligence, surveillance, and reconnaissance systems. American Logistics deals with research and development, management, and distribution of equipment to support soldiers who are fighting overseas. The company employs about 10,000 people worldwide and is also supported by thousands of contractors.

Although American Logistics is located on a site with other federal government entities that covers over 1,000 acres of prime real estate, it is self-sustained, complete with its own fire and police departments, post office, supermarket, gas station, church, child care center, liquor store, thrift shop, credit union, and motor pool. It also contains a range of outdoor amenities: three swimming pools, a physical fitness center, tennis courts, softball fields, a bowling center, a golf course, an athletic complex, and a picnic area.

As typical of any federal government entity, and in addition to its list of researchers, procurement officials, and logistics specialists, American Logistics also employs lawyers, internal auditors, and criminal investigators, along with a resource management office and a personnel office that ensures the agency is properly financed and staffed.

American Logistics is one of the state's largest employers and produces $3.4 billion for the state's economy.

The Copycat

As supervisor to Marin, Arthur Kiley never had any complaints. But one Monday, that changed. After Marin made photocopies of his new travel order, he mistakenly left the document in the machine. Mr. Kiley was the first to notice, and when he looked at the travel order, he observed that the signature block had been cut out of a previously signed order and taped to the new one.

"Marin, may I ask what you're doing with this signature taped to your travel order?" asked Mr. Kiley.

Marin replied that he was simply trying to make the signatures darker because when he faxed them to the ticketing office, the color was muted.

Later that day, Mr. Kiley approached Marin again to inquire about the taped travel order. Still, Marin assured him that he was "just making sure the signature was dark enough to be legible for the ticketing office." Mr. Kiley pressed on, threatening him with an audit of his past reimbursements of travel claims if he didn't come clean.

At the end of the day, Marin had not 'fessed up to any wrongdoing, so Mr. Kiley decided to do a little detective work. It didn't take long for evidence to surface. When he looked inside Marin's trashcan, he found a travel order with the signature cut out of it, copies of pay stubs, and copies of other travel orders where the initial "J" was handwritten by Marin. The "J" pertained to the first name of Mr. Kiley's boss, Mr. James Heyward, who was the authorizing official for Marin's travel orders and subsequent travel voucher claims.

Mr. Kiley contacted Samuel Mezzacante at American Logistics' legal office for guidance. Upon being informed of the possible fraud, Mr. Mezzacante first contacted the criminal investigators. Next, he called my department, the internal review evaluators, and set up a meeting to examine the evidence. Mr. Mezzacante requested our services to review Marin's travel vouchers and to determine how many vouchers were fraudulently filed.

In the meantime, Mr. Kiley had obtained several of Marin's settlement vouchers and tried to compare the dates of supposed travel to what Marin was actually doing on those dates. The settlement vouchers were subsequently turned over to us in the Internal Review Evaluator Department.

We notified the Defense Finance and Accounting Service and requested copies of all vouchers that were paid to Marin. It took several weeks to receive all of the copies. We had asked for vouchers going back five years, which meant the Finance Service had to research within their archives to find them, make copies of the documents, and mail them to us.

The next step was to contact the Bank of Commons, the contractor that managed the Government Travel Card program. All government travelers are required to use the Government Travel Card for all official travel-related expenses such as hotels, car rentals, limousines, airlines, or trains.

Since I had three staff members working on this review, I decided to divide the scope of the project into three timeframes. Each member worked on a one-and-a-half-year timeframe.

Have Committed Fraud, Will Travel

While reviewing Marin's travel vouchers and receipts, we noticed that on trips down to Springfield, Virginia, he stayed at a hotel chain that was not familiar to us. We searched the Internet to find the phone number of the hotel's corporate office. When we contacted them, they confirmed that the hotel was located in four cities in Virginia—but none in Springfield.

In an attempt to give Marin the benefit of the doubt, we contacted Joseph Somers, an evaluator from our corporate office in Virginia, and asked him to go to Springfield to the address listed on the hotel receipt and verify whether any hotel existed at that location. Perhaps Marin had accidentally listed the wrong hotel name. When Joseph tried to go to the address, he could not find it. None of the locals were aware of a hotel with a similar address either. The hotel simply did not exist.

The next day, Joseph called our office and reported his findings. Afterward, we drafted a letter and sent it certified mail to see if there was any chance that Joseph was mistaken. The letter was returned a few weeks later, stamped NSA—No Such Address. Our fears began to take shape. This scheme would require us to research the records and "leave no stone unturned," as our director, Martin Dais, instructed us. In other words, Mr. Dais told us to check every receipt and contact every vendor and to ask for legitimate receipts from the companies involved. We were also to ask the vendors if Marin had stayed in their establishments or used their car rental services as he claimed on his travel vouchers.

On some claims, Marin would use his Government Travel Card to charge for car rentals with one company, while his travel vouchers would show that he used a different one: Alamo Rent-A-Car. In all of those cases, Marin's claim for River Run Rent-A-Car was higher than his actual charge on his Government Travel Card. Also, when we looked at the River Run receipts that were attached to his vouchers, we noticed that the receipts were always in the same position on the letter-size paper, which indicated that Marin had a template in his computer's hard drive and was printing out his receipts as he needed them for "proof" of his various trips. We contacted the corporate headquarters for River Run and asked if Marin had used the agency to rent cars for his business trips. The River Run official told us that Marin was not showing up in their database as ever having rented a car. The official also faxed us an example of a valid receipt. When we compared that receipt to the ones that Marin had printed, we realized that the only difference was a five-digit code that appeared at the bottom of the valid receipt. This code identified either the person handling the transaction or a specific River Run agency office.

When we compared Marin's travel claims to his Government Travel Card charges, we noticed that he had used his Government Travel Card to charge train tickets at the station nearest to the airport. However, on Marin's travel vouchers, he would claim that he took a limousine from his residence to the airport and back. The cost was always under $75, which would have required him to submit a receipt to our finance office. So an $11 charge (cost of train ticket) became a claim for $74 (cost of limousine), a net profit of $63 for each direction for each trip that Marin claimed.

Another travel voucher showed that he had gone to a location in northeast Pennsylvania. However, his Government Travel Card transactions showed that he was gambling in an Atlantic City, casino located in southeastern New Jersey. We thought it unlikely that Marin was capable of being in two places at the same time.

As we scrutinized the travel vouchers, we realized that each year Marin's claims would grow to a larger amount. Also, when we conducted a review of Government Travel Card transactions, Marin's name came up because he was using the Government Travel Card in restaurants close to his residence. These types of transactions are classified as a misuse of the Travel Card since there was no official purpose for him to eat at the local restaurants. At the end of that particular review, the names of the misusers were turned over to their respective directors who coordinated discipline with the personnel office. When Marin was notified that he was found to have misused the Travel Card, he probably thought he got away with submitting all of the fraudulent vouchers. After receiving administrative disciplinary action, he began upping the ante by claiming parking costs of $18 per night at the hotel that did not exist in Springfield, Virginia.

We noticed a pattern developing while reviewing the travel vouchers. Marin would always leave a few days before his scheduled date of departure or would always stay a few days after his travel had ended. After piecing his travel vouchers together, we noticed that over a three-month stretch, Marin was basically on the road 100 percent of his time. For example, his travel vouchers showed him leaving on a Monday and returning on a Thursday. Then he would leave the next day (Friday) and return Tuesday. Again, he would leave the next day (Wednesday) and return Monday, and so on. I joked to my staff that he might as well not even unpack. Obviously, we questioned whether he was actually on travel status the whole time.

Another claim showed that Marin had traveled to Virginia for a meeting. We contacted the host for that meeting and were told that Marin had called ahead to say that his car broke down. The host had cancelled the meeting and scheduled it for another day. While Marin did not stay in Virginia for his entire travel time, the documentation on his voucher claimed that he stayed there for three days.

In one part of the review, we noticed Marin had scheduled a trip in February—just a few months back. He made reservations through the government ticketing office for a plane ticket that took him to Savannah, Georgia. On the day that he departed for Savannah, he went to the Delta Airlines counter and charged a round-trip flight to Savannah through his Government Travel Card. Then he went to the Continental Airlines counter and had the counter person exchange his government-issued round-trip ticket to Savannah for a one-way personal ticket returning from Los Angeles. A few weeks after returning from Savannah, he called Continental and had the company exchange the one-way trip from Los Angeles to a round-trip ticket to Hawaii for July 15. Since that date had not yet come, we knew that Marin was planning a vacation. We had to work fast.

PERMANENT VACATION

During the course of our investigation, Marin had his security clearance taken away from him, which meant that he could not work on any classified or secret work. In essence, he was relegated to administrative duties that were very minor and that did not require any type of security clearance. Soon after, Marin's computer was taken way from him so that the forensic investigators could retrieve all of his electronic mail, along with any files he may have stored in his hard drive.

Having no security clearance or a computer to do even minor tasks, Marin wrote an e-mail during the week of April 11 to Mr. Kiley, claiming that since he no longer had a way to complete his work, he felt that there was nothing to do but resign from American Logistics. His last day was April 15. We had to get all of our paperwork to the prosecuting attorney before Marin could go to Hawaii.

While checking his computer files, the forensic investigator retrieved electronic files for his fabricated hotel claims and for his car rental claims, which is what the internal evaluators had suspected all along. In addition to the files, there was e-mail correspondence between Marin and his wife, who asked him point blank when the next travel check was coming in. They needed the proceeds to pay for the current month's mortgage. The Jensens were desperate to make this scheme work.

In the early stages of our investigation and while working with the criminal investigators, Agent Stone Huntington and Agent Thomas Harter, we learned that the office of the U.S. Attorney only took cases that exceeded a certain dollar amount. Once we calculated that the scheme exceeded $100,000, Agents Huntington and Harter brought it to the attention of the U.S. Attorney's Office. After showing Giovanni Falcone, the Assistant U.S. Attorney, what we had pieced together, he had us go back to all of the voucher claims and reconstruct them to allow for valid claims to which Marin may have been entitled. It was this reconstruction that forced us to compare the travel voucher claims against his Government Travel Card charges. Unfortunately for Marin, he didn't realize that he was leaving a trail whenever he used his Government Travel Card.

Falcone told the investigation team that he needed the field work done at least 30 days before July 15 so that he could have the warrant signed and issued to Marin before he left for Hawaii.

Agents Huntington and Harter, along with a couple of local police officers, went to Marin's house around 5:00 p.m. on July 14 with a warrant for his arrest. As he was handcuffed and led out of his house, his wife came running down the stairs to ask "Marin, what about our trip to Hawaii?"

Huntington and Harter advised Marin of his Miranda rights. The two agents drove him to the county jail where he would spend the night. Along the way, the two agents asked Marin why he carried out this scheme to defraud the federal government. He replied that he worked harder than most people in the federal government but was not justly compensated for his work.

The next day Huntington and Harter escorted Marin to the federal courthouse at the state capital. At Marin's arraignment before the federal judge, his attorney asked if Marin could go to Hawaii with his family since they were scheduled to depart that day. But the judge confined Marin to the state of his residence. Meanwhile, his wife took the children and spent a week in Hawaii without him.

Marin was charged with one count of wire fraud covering over 150 fraudulent vouchers and totaling over $150,000. He was found guilty and was ordered to pay $151,460 to the federal government for fabricating expense vouchers. He was also sentenced to 20 months in federal prison and ordered to serve three years of supervised release upon the completion of the prison term. According to the transcript filed in the federal court, Marin took the money over a five-year period to pay off mounting credit card debt.

LESSONS LEARNED

After talking to various parties who were involved in ensuring that Marin traveled and performed his duties in conjunction with his travel orders, no one could unequivocally state that he or she knew exactly whether Marin had properly performed his duties. He fell through the cracks. He had everyone fooled. If he worked for Mr. Kiley, he would tell customers A and B that he was working for his immediate supervisor. Other times he would tell Mr. Kiley that he was working for customer A or B, regardless of where he was. Mr. Kiley had no control of Mr. Jensen, nor did he corroborate with customer A or B to attest that Mr. Jensen was indeed traveling for them. It was sheer luck that Mr. Kiley found the taped travel order in the copier—and sheer stupidity for Marin.

Although many "red flags" appeared during the perpetuation of this fraudulent scheme, nobody investigated them. For example, when the travel account for one customer had totally been expended, the budget analyst did not ask why all of the funds were spent. Individuals who are responsible to review and authorize the travel claims need to ensure that they review them for accuracy and legitimacy.

RECOMMENDATIONS TO PREVENT FUTURE OCCURRENCES

Implement Electronic Travel Order and Travel Voucher Claim System

Since the scheme unfolded, American Logistics has started using a new electronic travel order and travel voucher claim processing system. Controls are set to prevent the oversight of individuals who might manipulate the system, like Marin. Still, the individuals who are responsible for authorizing travel claims should review them for accuracy and legitimacy.

Require and Check for Appropriate Documentation

Travelers should submit appropriate documentation (i.e., receipts for any costs at $75 or higher) when filing their travel voucher claims. Otherwise, the voucher should be returned to the traveler until he or she can support the claim.

Use Common Sense

Ensure that the travel voucher claims, especially where the traveler has to list them, pass the commonsense test. For example, parking costs to stay at a particular hotel are usually charged to the room and appear on the final hotel bill. If the traveler claims parking fees, but they do not appear on the hotel bill, the authorizing official should investigate the claim.

Establish and/or Utilize a Cross-Communication System within the Organization

All authorizing officials should take the time to review vouchers for padded or incorrect claims. Establish a system that ensures that all departments are notified and capable of reacting when a false claim is uncovered so that proper actions can be taken to minimize damage and weed out those individuals responsible for the fraud. Directors who have oversight of employees should be included in the voucher-reviewing process, so that they can cumulatively corroborate the travel status of the employee.

Inform the Travelers of Consequences and Maintain a Watchful Presence

Travelers should be aware of the consequences of filing false claims. Communicate the penalties that can be imposed. Also, periodically conduct independent reviews so that selected travelers can be contacted directly and questioned about individual charges.

Dominic A. D'Orazio, CGFM, is a senior evaluator for a U.S. Army Internal Review Office in the northeastern United States. He has assisted the criminal investigators on numerous cases involving white-collar crime. Mr. D'Orazio is a graduate of Philadelphia University and has over 28 years of experience in auditing.

CHAPTER 5

What About Pete?

MICHAEL GOLDMAN

This is a story about failed partnerships, failed marriages, and rampant bankruptcy fraud. What once appeared to be a successful company progressed through a legitimate bankruptcy filing, followed by a postpetition looting of funds. There are related-party transactions, ghost payroll checks, benefit withholdings, quadruple-entry accounting, mortgage application fraud, wire and mail fraud, money laundering, and fraudulently filed bankruptcy operating reports. The story isn't over yet, but so far there have been more than $5 million in civil judgments issued and settlement payments made by five banks that were unwitting participants in these various schemes.

It began with Fred Morgan, the owner of Gopher Design. Fred was in his mid-40s, smooth and charismatic, and always well dressed. He was slender and a little frail looking, a bona fide lady's man, but definitely not the type who would do well in prison. People have one of two reactions after meeting Fred. The majority liked and trusted him instantly. But a small minority of us felt the urgent need to check our pockets and take a quick shower after shaking his hand.

Mrs. Morgan was not as physically attractive as her husband, but had been a winner of the gene-pool lottery in other ways. Her father had built a hugely successful business empire that created enough wealth to keep his offspring very comfortable for multiple generations. Her parents didn't seem to like her husband particularly, but they were there with open arms and an open checkbook whenever anyone in the family needed money. There was no apparent reason why Fred would ever resort to theft when he was married to such a huge source of wealth.

Fred's number-two guy, Pete Slowinski, was almost the exact opposite of Fred. While Fred could sell ice to an Eskimo, Pete seemed to rub everyone the wrong way. He was rough, tough, and gruff. Physically, he was short, squat, and very muscular. And his face was very flat, as if he had been hit with a shovel in his formative years. His blank stare of ignorance was a stark contrast to Fred's apparent total knowledge about almost anything you could think to talk about.

When anyone who knew him was asked if Fred was capable of committing fraud, they answered that he was smart enough and gutsy enough, but there was no reason for it; his wife's family was wealthy beyond belief, and Fred could dip into that trough whenever he wished. The same question about Pete elicited a unanimous answer: He didn't have the brains to defraud anybody; he just did what he was told.

The differences between the two men even extended to their choices in women. Mrs. Morgan was the definition of "shrew." Employees literally quaked in fear when she walked through the office. She was loud, obnoxious, and totally abrasive. Fred was rumored to have an Italian girlfriend in Italy, whom he visited often. Mrs. Slowinski, Pete's wife, was a quiet woman well liked by everyone in the company. Employees generally felt bad for her because Pete had a public affair with the company's shipping clerk, a very plain and quiet young woman.

Gopher Design had been a successful graphic arts company for more than a decade. Its client list included many large advertising agencies, Fortune 500 companies, local restaurants, and nonprofit agencies. Gopher's customers had a tough time in the years when businesses were hit by the dearth of advertising that followed the 9/11 attacks, weakness in the hospitality industry, and massive changes in charitable donation patterns resulting from changes in tax laws, and disasters—some natural, some not. Technology changes that impacted both the way that design work is done and the way that Gopher's customers disseminate their information created a great need for large capital spending. Despite this, Gopher had not suffered the economic hardships that many of its competitors experienced.

Fred and a partner had run Gopher together since its inception, but eventually had a falling out. The partner left the business, sued Fred in state court, and won his case. Fred continued to operate the business, but had been ordered by the court to buy out his former partner for an amount in excess of $1 million. Rather than make this payment, he placed the company into voluntary Chapter 11 bankruptcy.

Gopher's bankruptcy case appeared to progress normally, but slowly. The debtor's bank suspected check kiting at various times but was never able to prove anything more than careless cash management. Personal lawsuits against the bank president filed by Fred and by other companies that his family owned kept anyone from investigating him too thoroughly. The bankruptcy court finally confirmed a plan where Gopher would pay its secured debt in full and about 33 cents on the dollar of all its other prepetition debts. Everybody was looking forward to Gopher emerging from the bankruptcy process as a healthy, rehabilitated company.

Rather than serve as the poster child for bankruptcy success, Gopher crashed and burned immediately upon its release from court supervision. It emerged from bankruptcy with no cash and hopelessly insolvent. The U.S. Trustee immediately stepped in, put Gopher back into bankruptcy, and appointed a Chapter 7 trustee to investigate what had happened.

CALL TO DUTY

I was at the base of a mountain in central Quebec when the Chapter 7 trustee called my cell phone, introduced himself, and told me that the U.S. Trustee had recommended that he call me to help investigate Gopher. I had served as examiner in a bankruptcy case involving allegations of fraud both prior to and after the bankruptcy filing, so the U.S. Trustee was familiar with my work. He went on to explain that because there was no money at all in the bankruptcy estate, there was a good chance that I may never get paid for taking the case. I must have been drunk on the fresh mountain air, the overwhelming beauty all around me, and the joy of being with my family—I said I'd do it.

My first day back from vacation, I met Fred and an attorney from the trustee's firm outside Gopher's offices. Fred was pacing back and forth, totally distraught when we arrived—the alarm company had discontinued service, the building had been broken into, and most of the sophisticated computer equipment was missing. Fred took us inside and showed us the point of the break-in. Interestingly, the splinters still on the door all pointed to the door being kicked out from the inside. Some of the "stolen" computers were subsequently found, much later, to have been given to employees in lieu of amounts that Fred owed to them.

I asked Fred to give us a tour of the facility. We started with his office, which was totally empty except for a box of monthly operating reports that he had filed with the bankruptcy court. He explained that he was only a figurehead in the company and that Pete Slowinski ran absolutely everything. When I asked about the operating reports, he answered that he didn't understand a single thing on them, he was totally baffled by numbers and accounting, and that all he did was sign what his accountants prepared for him.

As we walked through the various cubicles, Fred became more and more distraught at each set of dangling wires where computer equipment used to be. He didn't know where any of the company's business records were or how we could get in contact with the former accounting staff, or how anything could possibly be figured out. If only he had stayed more involved, things may have worked out so much better, he whined. After all, he lost more than any creditor—his livelihood, his reputation, and all his personal net worth were gone with Gopher.

Fred's only contribution to the investigation was the ability to tell us who sat in each of the cubicles. He claimed not to know anything else about the business. File cabinets were all locked, and Fred had no idea where the keys were. Pete's office was jammed full of clutter—files and paper were everywhere. Despite the office being an incredible firetrap full of stuff, the only usable documents were a very impressive collection of carry-out menus from practically every restaurant within a five-mile radius. It was clear from the food stains on them that the menus were not there to sample different design styles.

The cubicle next to the accountant's had been vacant. There were dirty, dusty boxes jammed under the work surfaces. When I opened them, I found binders of batch reports showing inputs (billings to customers, invoices from vendors, commissions due) into the accounting system and some of the outputs (accounts payable checks paid) from the system. I was thrilled as I carried boxes out to my vehicle. This was a very messy and overwhelming way to start an investigation, but at least all those boxes gave me justification as to why an accountant might need a business truck if the IRS ever questioned my tax deductions.

A few days later, Fred attended a meeting at the U.S. Trustee's office. This was a chance for the Chapter 7 trustee to ask him questions about anything related to the case, under oath. Unfortunately, we still didn't have enough information to know what to ask. All we had to go on at this point were copies of cancelled checks provided by the bank and the monthly operating reports submitted by Fred. He wanted so very badly to help us, he said, but he just didn't know anything.

It turned out that Fred was familiar enough with the operating reports to be able to boastfully point out that he had stopped drawing a salary after the first few months of the case. He did this, he said, because the company couldn't afford him and he wanted it to succeed. Later in the questioning he admitted that the company had been paying large bills for credit cards in his name, but that was only because the company had no credit and Fred was personally paying for expenditures the company needed. Later still, he admitted that the company had made payments for personal loans taken out by him, but that was only fair since he was not otherwise being compensated for all his efforts on the company's behalf. There was already enough inconsistency here for the case to get interesting.

IT'S ALL IN THE DETAILS

Back in my office, I had to figure out what to do with three truckloads worth of boxes of batch reports. My initial hunch was that since the salesmen spoke highly of Fred, he probably hadn't cheated his salespeople out of their commissions. If I compared the sales used to calculate commissions to the sales recorded in the general ledger and in the receivables system, I was bound to find discrepancies that would prove that sales were being diverted. I gave up on this after two weeks; every single item I looked at traced through all the documents just as it should have.

I visited with the bank president who had been unlucky enough to be Gopher's lender. He was convinced that Fred had been kiting checks, and gave me more boxes containing 28 months' worth of bank statements and cancelled checks. Another week of charting and diagramming the ins and outs of the bank account showed that looking for kited checks was also was a dead-end endeavor.

One curious element did pop up from the bank account work, but I didn't know what it meant or what to do with it: Fred used many different banks for his personal accounts and for the other companies that he controlled. I noticed this when I reviewed deposits into Gopher's accounts and from the endorsements on the backs of some of the checks that Gopher had written to Fred.

Stymied, I turned to the monthly operating reports. All of the activity reported through Gopher's main bank tied out to the bank statements. All of the activity reported through Gopher's secondary bank also tied out the bank statements. But if everything was tying out, there should have been more cash. It didn't make sense. I needed to look at the detail behind the reports and accounting batches.

Crawling around under the desks at Gopher's offices again, I found more boxes of documents in the area where human resources used to work. This was the good stuff: original deposit slips, copies of the checks that customers had remitted, and original remittance advices showing what the customers had paid for.

What a difference original source documents make. I noticed that in some months, the batch reports that had original source documents attached to them did not trace through to the monthly operating reports. "How could this be?" I wondered, since I had already tied out most of the batch reports. Retracing some of my prior steps made the answer obvious: There were often two different sets of batch reports for the same transaction.

What happened was that a customer would remit payment to Gopher, the payment would be recorded in the accounting system, and the appropriate batch report would be generated. At a later time, someone would go into the system and change the batch report to be a different date, a different amount, and sometimes even a different customer. But why?

Again, the answers were in the details. Actual deposit slips found with the original batch reports showed the existence of eight additional bank accounts in four different names. None of these was authorized by the bankruptcy court and none was property of Gopher, but all had Gopher's customer's checks being deposited in them.

With documentation of Gopher's money being deposited into non-Gopher accounts, the trustee was now able to subpoena bank records for all of the accounts I had identified and for any other accounts that we knew of that were held by Fred, his wife, his children, or his companies. We now had most of the pieces of the puzzle.

Fred had been diverting customer payments to his own bank accounts and to the bank accounts of companies controlled by him. He even diverted money to a company owned by Fred's adolescent son. When Gopher needed money, Fred would return some (but not all) of what had been diverted.

For example, when BL Publications, a customer, made a $150,000 payment to Gopher, Fred had it deposited into one of his unauthorized bank accounts. He might then transfer $130,000 of this back into Gopher's bank account. A batch sheet may be prepared showing this deposit as consisting of $115,000 from BL Publications and the remaining $15,000 as having come from three other customers in payment of their invoices.

Later Fred might transfer $20,000 from one of Gopher's official bank accounts to the other. The transfer going out of one bank account would be correctly accounted for as an intercompany transfer. The deposit into the second account, however, would be accounted for as having been received from BL Publications, thereby clearing more of the amount still showing as open on their account from the original diversion of funds. The result of all this was that Gopher received $130,000 in cash, Fred received $20,000 in cash, and $150,000 of the bankruptcy estate's accounts receivable were marked as "paid."

These discoveries explained why there was money missing. They also explained why the bank president had suspected kiting: Every time a Gopher check bounced, it had been covered by a deposit from another account. Fred was covering the cash shortages he had created with some of the money he had diverted. It looked like kiting but was entirely different.

It was significant that all of the cash diversions went into accounts that only Fred had access to, because this made it clear who was committing the fraud. Many of the batch details attached to original deposits had notes on them from the accounting staff indicating where to deposit the money "per Fred" or "per FM," further sealing the case against him. Most of these were initialed by Fred himself. He could no longer claim ignorance and noninvolvement with the accounting process, as his initials were on source documents on almost a daily basis.

DIRECT DEPOSIT

Where was Pete during these daily diversions? His absence was both curious and troubling. In all the boxes and boxes of documents I reviewed, I never found a diversion of customer money to Pete. I never even found evidence that he had been there. While reviewing Fred's personal bank accounts, I found one instance where Pete wrote a personal check to Fred for $50,000. That check bounced and was never replaced. Why did Pete pay Fred $50,000? If the money really was owed, why was it never repaid after the check bounced? These questions gnawed at me.

I interviewed some of Gopher's vendors, all of whom were furious at being cheated by Fred. Some of them tipped me off about having some of their bills paid from a bank account in a state 1,600 miles away, which would have been an invaluable clue if I had not already found that that bank was being used. None of them mentioned Pete in any role other than Fred's stooge.

I also interviewed some of Gopher's former employees, all of whom were also furious at being cheated by Fred. Some provided sworn affidavits about being directed by Fred to divert Gopher's receipts to bank accounts that did not belong to the company. They provided more information on the use of the out-of-state bank account. They related rumors of Fred's exotic European girlfriend, whom I never found any actual evidence of. But again, nothing about Pete.

I had reviewed the backs of all the cancelled checks written during the bankruptcy process, and had noticed that one of the employees seemed to sign his paychecks with a number of different signatures and used six different banks. He also had twice as many paychecks as he should have had based on the company's pay cycle. My hypothesis was that Pete printed up a fake ID and cashed these extra checks, but nothing could be proven. Even so, it would be a very small fraud compared to how much money was missing, overall.

The dimwitted, clueless Pete Slowinski had managed to slide through this entire train wreck without ruffling anyone's feathers and without leaving any kind of paper trail. Almost. He didn't get away without ruffling his wife.

During an interview with the recently divorced ex-Mrs. Slowinski, she mentioned that her former husband had moved into a very expensive house with his new girlfriend. Oh yes, there was also once a strange call from a bank rejecting one of Gopher's deposits that had not been properly endorsed. That call from the bank never made sense to her, because Pete was never involved with Gopher's finances and she didn't know anyone who used that bank.

Our investigation had not turned up the existence of the new house or of that strange bank account, because they were both in Pete's girlfriend's name. When an FBI agent assigned to further the investigation reviewed the mortgage application for the house, she found the applicant's income grossly overstated compared to her payroll records at the debtor. This finding of mortgage fraud was good enough for a subpoena of the girlfriend's bank records, and that is where we found the money that Pete had diverted.

Fred's scheme had been to convert money received by the debtor into his own. But Pete was more clever. Rather than invoicing customers for work done by Gopher on the company's accounting system, Pete had just typed up invoices instructing the customers to pay directly to his own post office box. The sale never appeared in Gopher's records, and no one ever knew to look for the money.

THE OUTCOME OF THE INVESTIGATION

Two three-inch binders of evidence against Fred were presented to the judge in bankruptcy court. Fred, who began the case professing to know nothing of finance and accounting, convinced the judge that he was able to represent himself due to his background in finance and investments and his daily involvement in the debtor's affairs. He did a stellar job; by the time he was done, the judge had assessed him with over $5 million of judgments and penalties. The judge also instructed the trustee to have Fred referred back to the justice department for criminal prosecution.

The money Fred took has not all been found. Hundreds of thousands of dollars were traced to family members, and hundreds of thousands more were paid to lawyers as either fees or retainers. I am not aware of any record of large matters that these lawyers handled for Fred. Client confidentiality rules can make lawyers a good place to park money that needs to be hidden for a while.

The Morgans received an uncontested divorce and agreed to a huge child support settlement so that Fred's family would have first dibs on whatever money does turn up. However, since Fred was still living with his wife and family six months after the divorce decree, the divorce is being challenged as a sham. Our theory is that his Italian girlfriend never existed, but was instead a setup if a justification for a quick divorce was needed.

Fred filed for personal bankruptcy, but because the judgments against him are fraud-related, they are not dischargeable. The criminal case is proceeding.

Pete, however, had all his stolen money nicely tied up in one piece of real estate. In addition to the theft from the bankruptcy estate, charges are being prepared against him and his girlfriend for mortgage fraud, money laundering, mail fraud, and wire fraud.

Six different banks had accepted checks made payable to Gopher and allowed them to be deposited into accounts that did not belong to the company. None was properly endorsed. Two banks made the argument that as an officer of the company, Fred had authority to endorse Gopher's checks, but under bankruptcy procedures, he never had the authority to open undisclosed additional bank accounts. Five of these six banks have made restitution to the bankruptcy estate, and the sixth appears to be headed to litigation with the trustee.

LESSONS LEARNED

As bad guys, both Fred and Pete had their strong points and their weaknesses. Their strengths were almost enough to get them through their frauds scot-free. Ultimately, though, it was their individual weaknesses that gave them away.

Fred was an arrogant showoff who thought he was smarter than everyone else. Every alter-ego company that he made up had some permutation of his initials as its name. He concocted what he must have considered such a grand scheme that he didn't feel that he needed to destroy the evidence totally. He smoothly and continuously changed his story as more and more evidence was unpeeled. His final, passionate speech to the bankruptcy judge was that he was so smart that if he had done anything wrong, he would not have left that much evidence lying around. Nobody bought his professions of total ignorance at the beginning of the case, nor did anyone buy his pretense of being too smart to have done what he was accused of at the end of the case.

Pete was the real sleeper. Except for that one $50,000 check that raised my suspicion, he went through this case like a ghost. He didn't leave a trace. Unlike Fred, he had no need to keep trophies or score cards, so no evidence was left behind. Through most of the case I thought that $50,000 check amounted to Pete giving Fred a percentage of what Fred was allowing him to steal.

In hindsight, my guess is that Pete was trying to hide money from his wife, in anticipation of divorce. If he had just left the money as marital property and allowed his wife to keep half, I never would have thought to interview his wife, there would never have been a chance for her to mention that returned deposit from the bank and the big new house her husband was living in, and the reason to investigate Pete never would have been turned over to the FBI.

In a fraud investigation, you have to follow your hunches. If something feels wrong, it usually is—even if you can't explain why. A fraud investigator needs to be tenacious in pulling on all those little strings that seem out of place.

Fraud shows up in the flow of details. In this case the summary reports and the accounting entries supporting them were all faked. I would never have found this if I hadn't taken the investigation all the way back to source documents. If I had started with source documents and merely traced them into the accounting records, I wouldn't have found the fraud, either, as there were two sets of records: those that were entered from the source documents and those that were made up to support what Fred wanted to show on the operating report. The only way to have found this fraud was to start at one end of the reporting flow and trace all the way through to the other—in this case, from the bankruptcy operating reports all the way back to source documents.

By the time I identified and documented all of Fred's fraud, I had used up the time allotted for the investigation. Pete almost escaped. I like to think that if there had been more time, I could have started with the original source shipping documents from Federal Express and traced them through the accounting system to the bankruptcy operating reports, and that would have uncovered Pete's fraud.

Looking back at Fred and Pete, at the impressions they created and at the assumptions everybody made about them, I can't help but be reminded that fraud is deception. When fraud is suspected, nothing can be assumed or taken at face value, because the better the fraud, the easier it is to be deceived. Both people and computer-generated printouts can be very different from what they pretend to be.

RECOMMENDATIONS TO PREVENT FUTURE OCCURRENCES

The Problem of Owner-Committed Fraud

At this point in the story, I should be prescribing how to prevent this type of fraud from happening again. Unfortunately, I can't. Collusion in a company can defeat almost every control, especially when the collusion is among the most senior people.

It is likely that the type of activity described here occurred at Gopher for years. I have seen owners stealing from their own companies time and time again; it is called tax fraud, and unless a taxing authority catches on, there are usually no other victims to complain.

Typically, somebody's greed is what undoes them. Fraudsters become addicted to the free and easy money, and they take more and more until it becomes a noticeable problem. I have worked on cases of brother against brother, husband against wife, and partner against partner, and in almost every case, both sides were initially in on the fraud. The fraud becomes a problem when one partner takes more than the other partner, and the less egregious party starts a fight for his or her "fair share" of the spoils. The lawsuit that led to Gopher's bankruptcy may have been triggered because Fred was taking out more cash than his partner.

Detection

Owner-committed fraud may not be preventable, but it is detectable. This is usually done by conducting either a lifestyle audit or a detailed comparison of the business's inputs to the reported outputs. The devil is in the details—for example, a laundromat that uses too much water and electricity for the amount of quarters it says it received either has very inefficient machines or an owner walking out with very heavy pockets each night.

Study Bankruptcy Operating Reports Thoroughly

In this case, the fraud could have been detected earlier if the bankruptcy operating reports had been studied more thoroughly. There were printouts from the accounting system to back up every schedule and make them appear accurate, but the reports were not consistent from one schedule to the next. For example, the cash disbursements listed in the disbursement schedule did not equal the total disbursements shown in the bank account summary schedule. Many of the schedules were internally consistent each month but did not roll forward from month to month. These reports had a wide distribution, but it doesn't appear that they were adequately focused on by any of the parties who received them until all the money was gone.

The evidence indicates that Fred was a diligent debtor-in-possession during the initial months of Gopher's bankruptcy. Most likely Fred was establishing credibility with the various parties overseeing the case while he earned a good understanding of how the system worked. These well-behaved months were followed by what looks like two months of experimenting—minor inconsistencies and inconsequential fabrications in the accounting data were submitted with the operating reports, and nobody noticed them. This probing was followed by a couple more months of low-level cash diversions, always small enough that they could be excused away and returned if detected. They weren't.

Pay Attention to the Details

In today's environment of automation, budget cuts, not enough time, and information overload, it is more important than ever to stay focused on the details and always to tug on those little strings of inconsistency that occasionally stick out. One of the best ways to prevent large frauds is to detect them when they are still small frauds.

Michael Goldman, CFE, MBA, CPA, CVA, is principal of Michael Goldman and Associates, LLC, in Deerfield, Illinois, a practice focusing on fraud, valuation, and insolvency. He is an expert witness and has experience in cases involving fraud, solvency, fairness, commercial damages, marital dissolutions, valuation issues, professional malpractice, and bankruptcy issues.

CHAPTER 6

Check, Please

PETER PARILLO

Every weekday, millions of people wake up at the break of dawn, take a shower, get dressed, and hit the road to the office. Julie Rizzo was no different. She left her apartment at 6:15 every morning to catch the 6:20 express bus from Brooklyn to Manhattan. Upon arrival to her stop, she walked to the same coffee stand on the corner of Fifth Avenue and East 45th and ordered her usual breakfast: a large cup of coffee, light and sweet, and a plain bagel with a thin layer of cream cheese. Clutching her breakfast in a brown paper bag, she continued down the street, entered her building, and rode the elevator to the fifth floor. Like clockwork, Julie arrived at the office at 7:00 a.m. sharp. Sitting at her desk, sipping her coffee and enjoying the bagel, she began her day. She reconciled bank statements, reviewed invoices, checked inventory levels, placed orders, answered the telephone, and wrote checks—the usual.

Julie was gifted in bookkeeping and excelled in the subject in high school. In her senior year, she decided college was not for her, opting instead to work immediately after graduation. Since she lacked any real experience, Julie knew that it would be difficult to find a job, so she decided to ask her uncle Dominick if he needed any assistance with the bookkeeping for his wholesale jewelry business. Because accounting was not his area of expertise, Dominick needed an employee he could trust. The timing was perfect. Both agreed to terms, and soon after Julie graduated, she began working for her uncle as his bookkeeper, a position she held for over a decade.

If you were to meet Julie, you would not see a criminal but rather a normal everyday woman who worked hard to make ends meet. Happily married to her husband for over 15 years and with two children, she had the perfect life—or so it seemed.

Good Gold Wholesale was a small but successful wholesale jewelry business in the heart of Manhattan. Dominick imported the finest gold possible and was a supplier to some well-known retailers. The business grossed approximately $10 million a year and employed eight people full time, ten during the holidays to help with the increased volume of shipments. Of the eight full-time employees, six were family members, including Julie. The business was very well respected. It had been around for a long time and was considered to be one of the most reliable wholesalers in the jewelry district. Started in the 1960s by Dominick's father and built on the premise of honest business, it was established back when a handshake was as good as a written contract and profit, though important, was second to reputation. Dominick believed in his employees and trusted that they would perform to the best of their ability with honesty and integrity.

ONE MESS LEADS TO ANOTHER

After graduating from college, I joined a small accounting firm in Manhattan that specialized in write-up work, which offered me diversified business experience. The office was located in Midtown; the view from the twenty-second floor was breathtaking. Though small, the firm had fairly prestigious clients who enjoyed the personal attention and immediate turnaround that we provided. There were also many smaller clients, including several jewelry wholesalers.

One of my first assignments was Good Gold Wholesale. When I met Dominick for the first time, I noticed that his handshake was firm and solid. He seemed to be an honest businessman. Julie was quiet and hardly spoke unless I asked her a question. It was as if she were analyzing me and the level of skill I possessed. I could tell that she was very smart.

When I performed my duties, Julie was always there to assist me. One particular month, a conflict in my schedule occurred and I would have to do my work for Good Gold a week early. Julie was on top of things; I felt confident that the information I needed would be available. I called her office and was quickly transferred to voice mail. Her message stated that she would be out for two weeks and, if the call was urgent, to contact Dominick. When I informed my manager, he remarked that it was strange; she never took more than a day or two off at a time. I called Dominick to ask if I could come into the office and gather the information I needed.

"Her desk is a mess, but come on in," he replied.

At Good Gold, I was buzzed in through the security door, which slammed shut behind me. Dominick was waiting on the other side. When we reached Julie's desk, he turned to me and said with a smirk, "Good luck."

Dominick was right. It *was* a mess. Files and papers were strewn about with several half-empty coffee cups. One of Julie's cousins was getting married overseas, so Dominick surprised her with tickets to attend the wedding and to stay a few extra days.

Luckily, I knew exactly what information I needed and where to locate it. But as I began my search, I realized it was going to be harder than expected. I decided to organize her desk into files, which I thought Julie would appreciate. As I sifted through the information and labeled the various items using Julie's pen, I sometimes wrote names incorrectly and would use the eraser on her pen to correct my mistakes. Not thinking much of this, I completed organizing the invoices and began working on the bank statements. I opened an envelope addressed from a bank and several dozen checks fell out. Again I didn't give it a second thought. As I reviewed the cancelled checks, I noticed two payments to American Express and several other vendors that I did not recognize. As I looked more closely, I noticed in the memo section different credit card numbers, which I presumed meant that Dominick had two accounts. But when I asked him, he responded, "No, why would I want to do that? Keeping track of one card is hard enough." At that point I did not tell him what I had found, deciding it would be better to conduct more research first.

SOME SLIGHT ALTERATIONS

As I gathered information from Julie's desk and loaded my briefcase with folders, I tried to convince myself that there was a logical explanation. I was just overreacting. Julie was a wife and a mother of two children. Why would she steal from her own uncle? I glanced at the calendar. I had four days to figure it out.

When I returned to my office, I went directly to the copy room. After making copies of all of the documents I'd obtained from Julie's desk, I began analyzing the information, starting with the invoices. There were the obvious payments for gas, electric, insurance, shipping, and professional fees. In addition, there were a few miscellaneous items, such as plastic bags used for shipping and inventory. Everything appeared to be in order.

I then turned my attention to the bank statements and the cancelled checks. Over 30 had been written. There was something strange about the American Express checks, so I put them aside to analyze the remaining ones. Some of the vendors I immediately recognized—they were catalog companies that sold home accessories. I thought that perhaps Dominick ordered something. Just in case, I added this to my list of questions for him. I continued reviewing the remaining checks and noticed there were two payments each for telephone and electric expenses. Additionally, there were two different account numbers written in the memo section of the checks to the telephone company.

I put together the invoices paid for the month and pulled out the telephone records. The account matched one of the checks, and it had been paid in full. I called the customer service number and waited patiently as music played.

"Hello, my name is Tracy. May I please have your account number?"

I began to stutter and fumble for the check as she repeated, "Account number please." I read the numbers off the bottom of the check.

"Hello, Mr. Miller, how can I assist with your account today?" she asked.

I replied, "I wanted to see what address you have on file. For some reason the invoices seem to be arriving later and later every month."

"I'm looking at your account and don't see that you ever paid late," the representative said, "Could it be that you have a new mail carrier?"

"Maybe," I replied, "but I don't see the mail carrier, so I am not certain."

I began thinking of past conversations I had with Julie when we talked about us both growing up in Brooklyn. I recalled her mentioning that she lived on Benson Avenue.

I asked the representative, "You do have the correct address? Benson Avenue, right?"

The representative tapped on her keyboard before she said, "That is right, 2551 Benson Avenue." After I hung up, I knew that this was going to be a sensitive issue, and if I was to prove what Julie was doing, I had to gather as much evidence as possible.

I began listing all of the checks in Excel and documenting the check numbers, payees, amounts, information in the memo sections, and corresponding invoice numbers. I highlighted checks in question and made copies of all the checks and invoices, which I saved to my hard drive. With only four days to build my case, I had to go back to Good Gold. Placing the original documentation and the copies in my briefcase, I headed out the door. As I walked into the store, I began to think about what I was going to tell Dominick. I knew that I couldn't reveal too much before I had a strong case. Again the door slammed behind me. I knew that if I continued down this path and was wrong, there was a good chance I would be fired. When Dominick walked by, I told him I had missed some of the documents I needed when I was there earlier and asked him if he knew where Julie kept them. He replied, "You can check her desk drawers. I don't bother looking for anything there anymore. I needed a pen one time and used one of hers, but she insists on using those damn erasable ones and they always smudge. Feel free to go through her desk. If you clean it up, you will be doing her a favor."

I sat down at Julie's desk and started opening up the drawers. In the first one, I found personal items: a pair of dress shoes, hair products, and various magazines. As I took them out, I noticed that some of the names of the magazines matched the names on the checks. After I emptied the majority of the drawers, I saw several folders in the back and discovered one of the most important pieces of the puzzle: blank invoices. They represented various vendors: office supplies, repairs, cleaning, messenger services, and pest control. For the first time, the evidence started to take shape.

Unfortunately, there was only seven months of activity available. Dominick kept documentation in the office and placed all prior years in storage. I listed the vendors by group and noted the amounts paid for each. I was surprised to find that over the past seven months, Julie may have stolen $32,000. I wondered how long this had been going on. As I placed the information in my briefcase, I knew I would have to inform my manager. I told Dominick that I was heading home and asked if he would be available the next day for a meeting.

"Sure, I guess. What's up?" he inquired. I told him that I might have some questions about some transactions, but I needed to do some more research first. The next morning I caught the early train into Manhattan. The office was still empty when I arrived at six o'clock. After flipping the lights on and making a fresh pot of coffee, I printed multiple copies of the information and waited for my manager, Rob. When he arrived, I told him that we had an issue with Good Gold. He called Lori, a senior partner with experience in fraud investigations, to review the information I put together. I explained to her that after receiving the cancelled checks from the bank, Julie would erase the names and replace them with fictitious vendors. Lori recommended that the next step was to formulate a plan to interview Julie. I then suggested to Lori that since we had copies of the checks before Julie altered them, all we had to do was to allow her to make the changes and obtain the altered checks afterward. Then we would have all the necessary evidence.

"That's a great idea. We just have to make certain that Dominick is on board with it." Lori said. I called Dominick and asked him to come to our office. When he arrived, I escorted him to the conference room. After taking our seats, Lori began, "Dominick, we have discovered some suspicious activity that you should be aware of. Peter will explain to you what he has found, and if you have any questions, we will do our best to answer them."

I began explaining what I had discovered and supported my findings with copies of the documents. Dominick, shocked, asked, "What do I do now? Do I fire her?"

"No," Lori stated. "We want you to do nothing right now."

"Nothing?!" he screamed. "How do you expect me to do nothing?"

I then told Dominick we expected that when Julie returned to work on Monday, she would alter the checks and we would be able to confront her. Though reluctant, he finally agreed. The next step was for me to go back to Good Gold and put all of the information back in its original place. That was going to be easy; Julie's desk was a mess. Then we only had to wait for her return.

THE TRUTH COMES OUT

I woke up Monday morning later than I wanted to. It took a few seconds for my eyes to focus on the time. Then it hit me: 7:30! I jumped out of bed and quickly put on my suit. I was able to catch the next train for the city and make it into the office shortly before 9:00. After I grabbed a cup of coffee and settled in, I called Julie.

As the phone rang, I heard, "Good Gold, can I help you?" It was Julie. I asked her about her vacation, and we chatted a bit before I proposed coming in on Thursday and Friday. Julie hesitated but said, "Sure, that will be fine. I may have to work a little late, but I should be done by Thursday." I told her I'd see her then and felt relieved as I hung up the phone. The plan was in motion.

On Wednesday, I met with Lori and Rob. Lori was direct with her instructions. "All you have to do is go in as planned and obtain the checks and invoices. After you confirm that the checks were altered, call me and I will come to Good Gold with Rob to ask Julie some questions." That night, as I made my way home, I was thinking of what would happen to Julie. Her uncle had every right to press charges. But would he have the courage to have his niece arrested and possibly cause major turmoil in the family? It was late and I had to get some sleep. In a few hours all of my questions would be answered.

The next morning I woke up greeted by a gust of cold air. Finally I reached the building where Good Gold was located. As I rang the bell, Julie quickly let me in. "Here you go—all the information you need." She pointed to a desk that was approximately 10 feet from hers. Perfect, I thought. But how was I going to look through the information and call the office without her overhearing me? This was going to be a challenge. As I sifted through the documents, I noticed the invoices Julie created. I then looked through the cancelled checks. As expected, they were altered. I needed to call Lori, but how? A few minutes later, Julie went to the restroom. I seized the opportunity to phone Lori, but was transferred into voice mail. I left her a message. After an hour or so, I finally heard the doorbell. It was Lori and Rob. Julie, surprised to see them, asked, "How are you two doing? I guess they're bringing out the big guns for us."

Lori responded, "Hi, Julie, we're here to see Dominick to discuss tax options. He's expecting us. We know where he is, so we'll just go back there and see if he is ready."

In a few moments I heard Dominick's voice: "Julie and Peter, can you both come in here? You two should be part of this meeting." I looked at Julie and shrugged my shoulders, playing it off as if I did not know what was going on. Julie walked ahead of me as I gathered the necessary information: the original checks, altered checks, blank invoices, and false invoices she had created.

After we entered Dominick's office, I shut the door behind us and took a seat at the conference table across from Julie. Lori looked at her and said, "Julie, Peter was here last week and discovered that you have been altering checks and creating false vendors for your personal benefit."

Julie interrupted: "But I didn't do anything."

Lori cut her off. "Before you say anything that will harm you further, I suggest that you listen to Peter." I explained to Julie what I had found. I informed her that I knew about the fake vendors, the blank invoices and multiple payments. Julie glanced at the information. Then she looked around the room, as if trying to think of an explanation. Realizing that she was trying to conjure up a story that would somehow make sense, I told her, "Julie, I have copies of the checks."

She looked at me briefly and then averted her eyes. This time I was more precise. "Julie, I have copies of the checks. I know you altered them." Julie's facial expression changed. Her eyes swelled up and she began to cry, knowing that that she was caught. Then Dominick started crying. I guess it was difficult for him to accept that his own niece would steal from him. He turned to Julie and said, "I want you to tell us everything: when you first started and how you did this. Then we need to see how we will fix this mess."

Over the next few hours, Julie said that she first started stealing a few years back by paying for a personal magazine subscription. She explained, "As long as the lights were kept on and no one called for payment, Dominick assumed that all was well. I realized that it was easy to buy things for myself."

Julie created over 50 different fake vendors, ordering the forms from the printer. Since the invoices were blank, she would type them up using the typewriter by her desk. To avoid being noticed, Julie would come in early or work quickly when Dominick left the office. After she finished explaining all of the details, Dominick asked the last question, "How much did you take from me?" Julie looked down at her lap and said, "I'm not sure; about $300,000."

Over the past 10-plus years Julie was able to steal hundreds of thousand of dollars. Dominick then turned to Lori and asked what he should do. Lori discussed all of the options, one of which was to press charges. Dominick shook his head no and then said, "I have a better idea. Julie will continue to work here at half of her salary until the debt is paid off. Since you know what to look for, I would hope Julie would not go back to her bad ways. If you find that she does, I will have no choice but to have her arrested." Everyone was surprised, especially Julie. She began to cry again and hugged her uncle. As I packed up, Dominick pulled Lori and me aside and said, "You did well. From now on I want Peter to do the work, nobody else." Lori smiled and replied, "Dominick, I'll call you in the morning. We have a lot to talk about. We need to discuss computer-based general ledger programs." He rolled his eyes. "Great, more money to spend." Lori and I looked at him. Dominick said, "I know, I know, this is for the best."

LESSONS LEARNED

After this investigation, I realized that being a family member does not eliminate the temptation to steal. It does, however, provide a false sense of security to business owners who wrongfully assume that their relatives are always honest and trustworthy.

Dominick learned the hard way that he must be actively involved in all aspects of his business. Soon after the meeting with Julie, he installed a computer system and a tailored general ledger program. In addition, he revoked his niece's check-signing rights and submitted a new signature card to the bank.

RECOMMENDATIONS TO PREVENT FUTURE OCCURRENCES

Computer-Based Ledger System

Utilizing a computer-based general ledger system allows multiple preventive actions to be implemented. There are many inexpensive prepackaged general ledger programs out there for small businesses. Dominick decided to go with a tailored system, and we were able to implement these systems:

- Access controls to prevent the addition of new vendors (to deter fictitious expenses) and customers (to deter fictitious refunds). Only Dominick had the ability to add new vendors and customers.
- Edit reports to highlight any changes to vendor or customer information.
- Monthly sign-off of journal entries and check runs. Dominick became very involved with the financial side of his business, reviewing information thoroughly.
- Implementation of purchase orders and establishment of limits so excess merchandise was not purchased.
- Ratio analysis. This is an easy and cost-effective way to allow tracking trends to isolate peaks and valleys and inquire to why they occurred.
- Monthly inventory counts. Dominick insisted that a live inventory count be performed at the end of every month. In addition, on several occasions, a "surprise" inventory count was conducted.
- Computer-generated checks. After implementation of the computer system, Dominick threw out the typewriter and copier and invested in an all-in-one unit that had the ability to print checks. This allowed for additional control when using prenumbered check stock that Dominick kept locked away in his office.
- Check-signing authority. Dominick removed Julie from the signature card and is now the only person authorized to sign checks.

Peter Parillo, CFE, CPA, CBM, is an internal audit director for Vonage Holdings Corp., in Holmdel, New Jersey. Mr. Parillo graduated from the College of Staten Island and has over 10 years of experience in conducting fraud investigations. He resides in Freehold, New Jersey, with his wife, Lori, and his two children, Victoria and Peter.

CHAPTER 7

The MoJo Skim Twins

JOHN F. KRONICK

To look at them, you'd swear Maureen "Mo" Frugali and Joann "Jo" Brennan were sisters, maybe even twins. Both were in their early 50s. Each had the same flat, unkempt hairdo. They were short and pudgy, making them waddle when they walked. Their frumpy, wrinkled clothes looked more like nightgowns than dresses.

Mo and Jo were peas from the same pod. The two were raised a few miles apart in a blue-collar area of New Jersey. Their stories were remarkably similar. Life was not easy for their families, struggling to make ends meet in a rapidly expanding economy with high inflation. They pinched every penny to make sure there was enough money for rent, food, and utilities. Mo's father was a metalworker, her mother, a homemaker trying to raise four children. Jo's parents divorced when she was 14, and she lived mostly with her two sisters and her mother, a part-time middle school teacher. Her father worked as an electrician in New York City and was always away, even before the divorce. Through their teen years, Mo and Jo took on many babysitting jobs to help their parents pay bills and have a little spending money.

Neither girl enjoyed studying. In fact, both barely graduated from high school. Their people skills eventually landed them jobs at doctors' offices as receptionists and ultimately bookkeeper and administrative assistant positions, handling claim submissions. It was through their jobs that they met. Jo called Mo to request a patient's records and they struck up a conversation. One thing led to another, and the two decided to meet for lunch. They had so much in common; they wanted to trade childhood stories. Mo asked Jo over for a visit, and from that time forward, the two women were nearly inseparable. Over the next two years, Mo and Jo did just about everything together. Soon Mo married Bob, and Jo married Marvin; unfortunately neither marriage was very fulfilling.

After three years in the same position with no advancement or significant pay increases, Mo realized that work in the doctor's office was going nowhere. She dreamed of earning more money and moving up. One day she noticed a help-wanted ad for Colossal Healthcare, the biggest in the state. The company was looking for claims payment clerks, which was right up Mo's alley. She had spent the last three years coding payment forms and submitting them to Colossal for the doctor's office. She was excited to have a skill that could command a high hourly pay rate. She applied, interviewed, and was hired.

Mo got into the rhythm of the claim processing routine, learned the business cycle, and soon realized that the volume was rapidly increasing. Management promoted Mo to claims supervisor and promised her more help. No sooner had Mo settled into her new position than she asked Jo to join her at Colossal. Jo didn't have to think twice. She applied and was hired within a few days. The MoJo twins were on their way.

Mo and Jo slowly climbed the Colossal corporate ladder, occasionally taking a leave of absence to have a baby. With work and child rearing, there was little time to enjoy life. Neither woman liked parenting, as they were preoccupied with having enough money to pay their family bills. Neither husband brought home much money, and living in the New York City area was expensive. Between child care and commuting expenses, there was barely enough for a night out on the town.

Meanwhile, Mo and Jo became masters in the art of claim processing. The work continued to pile up, and additional help was always scarce. Colossal management decided it was time to rethink the staffing issue and sought to create a training group that could produce an efficient, effective claims processing team in a fraction of the time that it normally took. Their choice to head up such a training group was obvious—Mo and Jo. So began the MoJo training force.

As Mo and Jo worked with the company's real-time claims processing systems, they became experts in identifying shortcuts. They learned how to manipulate the system to eliminate bottlenecks and speed up claim payments. While in a training session one day, Mo remarked to Jo that they could probably create and pay claims without the company ever knowing about it. She explained that training claims were processed along with real ones. The checks on training claims were reversed out of the production systems to arrive at actual claim processing totals for the day.

"Whoa," Mo exclaimed. "The company wouldn't even know what the real payment amounts were, since no one ever reconciled the totals."

In her 15 years with Colossal, Mo said she'd never seen the company auditors review the claim processing details; rather, they derived the real claims totals by subtracting the training totals she provided. It sure would be nice to take home some of that money. Jo imagined what she would do with hundreds, if not thousands, of training claims dollars. "It might be fun to test the auditors to see if they can catch a bogus claim and check," Jo speculated. "It would make us look good if we could show that we know the systems so well that we can identify weaknesses," Mo added. "Maybe they'd even give us a raise if we were successful."

"Okay, let's try," Jo agreed, and at it they went.

THE BIGGER THEY ARE...

Colossal Healthcare, headquartered in New York City, was one of the nation's largest nonprofit health claims processor. In business for nearly 50 years, with offices in several other cities in the Empire State, Colossal prided itself on its size and stature in the health care industry. With its impressive, large computerized claims processing operations and state-of-the-art systems, the 1970s were good years for Colossal. The company attracted the best and brightest systems developers, accountants, auditors, and claims processors, as well as the most stalwart of customer companies, including many from the Fortune 1000.

Over several decades, health care rates had increased somewhere in the range of 800% from the 1960s. State legislators were unwilling to approve further rate hikes for Colossal until its management could prove that it was successful in scaling back its bloated costs. Colossal was ordered to change its external audit firm and institute self-review and operational practices that would identify and eliminate fraud, waste, and inefficiencies in the company. The new auditing firm produced a management report disclosing many operational deficiencies and management lapses. As a result, a major reorganization was mandated, a new chief executive and board were established, and new processes were instituted. One of those included development of auditing practices using the existing information technology audit (IT audit) group to assist the regulatory internal auditors to detect fraud. The legislature determined that Colossal should be able to uncover fraudulent claims to the tune of at least 1% or 2% of total payments, which would be within the industry levels. With claims exceeding $7 billion per year, the legislature expected that at least $70 million in fraud should be detected and recovered. As the acting director of IT audit, I knew this was going to challenge my skills to develop innovative fraud detection techniques. The staff consisted of only seven auditors; we were already stretched to the limit, and now there was the added burden of aiding the regulatory auditors in fraud detection duties.

FAKE IDs

No sooner had the fraud investigation mandate come down than I was called into a meeting with the other audit directors to discuss the extent of our involvement. Colossal's senior management was taking a radical approach by turning everything upside down to determine whether there was any underlying fraud. Such measures included group credentialing, physician certification and validation, contract review, and ultimately claim examination. This was no small effort, as there were well over 15,000 groups, 5,000 physicians, 10,000 contracts, and 14 million claims.

A special group of regulatory auditors began the process when my team was called to assist in validating physician names in the database. In addition, we were asked to initiate an automated process to uncover claims fraud. With two of my staff, I constructed a high-level plan and timeline for claim fraud discovery.

"Where do we begin?" I asked. "What would be the most obvious type of claim fraud?" We could, I surmised, divide up claims by groups, physicians, hospitals, types of claims, and the like. We decided to start simple. "Let's write a program to identify a very basic fraud search," I said. "We'll check medical claims for the masculine sex to see if any male has received a hysterectomy procedure. That would clearly be a fraud." We wrote a routine to cover all hysterectomy claims for a six-month period, sorting by sex and extracting any male claims results. BINGO! A total of five claims printed out, and one of the patients was a five-year-old boy. We had our very first potential fraud audit result. I instructed my team to research the five claims to verify that the sex was not a coding mistake. Within 30 minutes, my staff came back, laughing about what we had found. It seems payments had been issued on that young boy who had received, over the past two years, not one but two hysterectomies. Additionally, two of the claims were processed using deceased physicians to authorize them, and one was paid to a post office (PO) box address, even though Colossal's system did not allow that. This last payment stood out. How did that claim slip by and get paid? We needed to solve the mystery.

After a weeklong investigation, a top technical staff member, Jack Greer, came to discuss the PO box payment with me. He had traced the check from payout back through the origination process and had run into a problem. The claim had been authorized by a supervisor whose identification (ID) was temporary on our mainframe customer information control system (CICS). In other words, someone had set up the impermanent ID (Claire37) to authorize and pay this claim. Since the CICS was a "real-time" system with no existing audit logs, it was virtually impossible to determine exactly who had initiated it. However, one thing was clear: The ID belonged to someone in Colossal who had supervisory capabilities and privileged access to our systems. Our investigation identified several other fraudulent claims that Claire37 had authorized, and showed that they had indeed been paid. We also discovered that someone had first created a temporary ID in order to then create the Claire37 ID, both of whom were still unknown.

MUM'S THE WORD

I could see from our initial work that we would probably uncover much more fraud than we had anticipated. I instructed my staff to keep the current investigation under wraps and disclose no details to anyone without my permission. I also met with the director of regulatory audit to discuss our findings. If my initial suppositions were correct, we might have a major internal fraud ring on our hands, and I wanted everyone working together to resolve this case and preserve evidence in the event we needed to prosecute. We did not know whether the perpetrators were internal or external, hackers, or disgruntled employees.

Working round the clock, the IT audit staff gathered all CICS temporary IDs and records of claims processed by them over the past six months. We sorted by agent and further organized them by those that had authorized claims payments to PO boxes. It would take an intentional act by an employee in a supervisory capacity to manipulate the system to pay a claim to a PO box address. What we hadn't yet figured out was where the manipulation had occurred and why these claims weren't flagged for review. We narrowed the search to an inside job; we knew we had to find someone who had access to the systems, could initiate claim agent IDs, and could change authorized payment addresses.

To understand how the CICS system worked and how claims were paid, Jack, Bill Taylor, the manager of regulatory audit, and I called for a meeting with the head of the training section, Mo Frugali, who had also invited her right-hand staff person, Jo Brennan.

Mo immediately asked why we were digging into the matter. To protect our real goals, I told them that we were reviewing changes in systems as part of an audit, and we needed their help to understand the online claims processing system. My explanation didn't put either of the women at ease. The atmosphere was tense, and we noted the women provided almost monosyllabic answers.

"Can a claims agent change claims IDs?" I asked.

"No," said Mo.

"Can a claims agent change payment addresses on a claim once it is ready for payment?" I asked more forcefully.

"No," chimed Mo and Jo, almost in unison.

"Who can create processing IDs?" I asked.

"Only authorized claims agents and supervisors can access accounts in the CICS production regions, and they are set up by the security administration group in the CICS operations center," Mo informed us.

At a loss as to how we could acquire more information from them, I looked directly at Mo and then Jo, and asked, "You both have claims agent supervisor authority in the CICS training region, right?" Both of the women were startled by and unprepared for this question.

"Yes," Mo said hesitantly. Jo looked at her. "But that's the CICS test region, not the production region."

"How many trainers have CICS IDs?" I asked.

"Ten, maybe twelve," Jo replied.

"And can a trainer create temporary IDs? Or create another to process test claims?" Jack asked, following my lead.

"In the CICS test environment, yes," Mo stated.

"What about in the production region?" I inquired.

"Huh? No," Mo sheepishly responded.

"Are you called upon to resolve processing problems in the course of the day? You know, when the normal processors can't solve a problem? Don't you provide that type of production assistance?" I asked.

"Umm, well, yes," Mo replied. It was both frustrating and exciting to know that we were on the trail of uncovering this mystery, and it seemed that Mo and Jo were dragging down the investigation.

"Well," Jack began, "don't you log onto the systems with production IDs and try to fix claims that are stuck in the processing stream? Isn't that what people call you for during the day, aside from training?"

"We try to help process problem claims," Jo replied, without providing details.

"And what IDs do you use when you do that?" I asked.

"Well," Mo replied, "there are around twelve people that get called for these issues. We use our initial log-on IDs, and then CICS prompts us for our agent IDs. Then the claim is fixed and forwarded real-time for final disposition and/or payment."

We were still clueless. We were looking for a smoking gun, but so far, we hadn't even figured out how claims IDs could be created and deleted without a trace. I was sure that Mo and Jo could provide insight into that matter. I was frustrated by the fact that they were far from helpful—and even a bit of a stumbling block. Bill approached me after the meeting and asked to speak to me privately.

"Did you see the way Mo and Jo acted in the interview? Did you watch their facial expressions and eye contact during the questioning?" he asked.

"Not really. I was more interested in following the trail of the questions, and trying to figure out the logic," I replied.

"Well, I study people as part of my job, and I would stake my reputation on the fact that those two were hiding something. Their answers were not straightforward or forthcoming. They were nervous and avoided eye contact. That's a dead giveaway," Bill insisted. "I guarantee this: If they are in cahoots, they will get caught because of their greed. It's human nature to keep doing what you've been doing as long as you're not caught." The more you get away with something, the more you think you're invincible. The fact that you weren't able to catch Mo or Jo in anything just serves to embolden them to continue. Mark my words."

"Let's start with their processing IDs and check to see what claims they processed over the last six months," I said.

"I'm going to do a background check on those two. See where they live, and how they live," Bill concluded.

When Bill left, Jack was waiting to see me. I could tell he was excited—and on to something good. "I think I figured out how those claims IDs are being created and deleted without a trace. I had systems administration turn on CICS logging over the past week, and we watched claims IDs and followed any that were created in that time. We particularly focused on claims touched by the training supervisors," Jack said, almost unable to contain himself.

"Well, don't leave me hanging. What did you find out?" I asked, almost ready to choke him for the information.

"Apparently we have a number of matches on claims IDs that were created to process bogus claims and then deleted. And those were created by Mo and deleted by Jo." Jack beamed. I could hardly believe it. Mo had been with the company for some 20 years, and Jo for just a little less. They were Colossal's star trainers. How could this be happening?

"Show me what you've got," I told Jack, hoping that he could positively identify how these fraudulent claims were being processed.

"It gets interesting," said Jack. "Remember, Mo and Jo know our systems inside and out. They can do virtually anything on them. Management has trusted them to self-police their activities. So they used their imagination to play the system. Apparently, a claim agent training supervisor creates a training ID, which is modified to allow it to process CICS production transactions. Only a claims supervisor has the capability to override the training nature of those IDs, which are used to create a claim that is either a training account or a real subscriber that is pending closure for nonpayment of premium, is inactive or the subscriber status is deceased, but the account has not yet been coded. Now, it gets better." Jack chuckled.

"I worked with Bill to set up a sting operation," he continued. "We noticed that some of the payments to PO boxes were cashed by the same person even though the box numbers were different. But Bill was one step ahead of them. He put people on surveillance at the post offices with the help of the U.S. Postal Inspection Service. Sure enough, one of the perpetrators came by and picked up one of the payments and was followed to the bank. As soon as that person cashed the check, he was apprehended, with the help of the local police department. Fearing the worst, he began to spill his guts, incriminating our two star trainers."

"Now that we know how they are executing some of the fraud, can we prove it? And is the dollar amount high enough to get the local district attorney to prosecute?" I asked.

"No problem," Jack replied. "We have traced this back for the last ten years, and by our calculations, these two have stolen over $11 million."

"Yikes!" I replied, startled that it had been going on for so long. "What can we prove?"

"Well, that's the bad part. We can only prove about $285,000 in fraudulent claims over the last six months," Jack said. I told him to round up the records, put them in chronological order, and start re-creating the scenario for law enforcement. In the meantime, I called Bill, and we arranged to meet first with Mo and then with Jo. I called Mo and told her that we needed a few minutes of her time to check a claim ID, and she hesitantly agreed.

Mo maintained a poker face throughout the questioning. She offered no confession and no corroboration. Mo, Bill, and I listened to Jack recite the scheme. Bill informed Mo that her fellow cohort who had cashed the checks had been arrested earlier that day. Mo showed little emotion. "You can't prove anything," she replied.

We began to disclose the real evidence, linking her ID to several of the bogus claims, and proving by both log-in and building access records that she was indeed the real culprit. I could see the panic in her eyes, but she offered no details. Then Bill presented some more information. Apparently, Mo was living high on the hog, having just bought a new home in a wealthy suburb of New Jersey, and was putting in a $50,000 in-ground pool, all on a modest salary. New cars, extravagant vacations, and other trappings of wealth were all disclosed in the meeting; Bill had been thorough. Mo was shocked at how much information we had gathered, but still she would not confess. Finally, we told her the jig was up; unless she agreed to play ball with us, she was going to be arrested and taken to jail. Bill even reminded her that she would lose her retirement benefits if she was terminated for cause and prosecuted. Mo was unmoved. True to our word, we had already contacted the police and filed the necessary charges beforehand, and a policeman was standing outside. Since Mo would not cooperate, we brought in the officer, and she was led off the premises in handcuffs and taken to jail.

Jo was another story. Having kept the pair isolated, we brought Jo into another room where other regulatory auditors and human resource personnel interviewed her, disclosing the volumes of data documenting the fraud scheme. Jo panicked. Like Mo, she too was in danger of losing her retirement benefits and receiving a jail term if convicted. Bill came into the room and tried to coax her to reveal her fraud activities. She admitted that she had done some wrong deeds, but she would not confess to specific fraudulent transactions. Perhaps she and Mo had previously discussed the issue. Maybe they believed that even if they were caught, the sophistication of their crime would be over the heads of any jury members and they would not be convicted. In any event, Jo was arrested on site and led from the premises in handcuffs.

COLOSSAL FRAUD DESERVES A LIKE PUNISHMENT

Mo and Jo were able to post bail the very next day and were out on the street looking for their next job. Mo, pending her trial, landed work at a competitor's health care claims processing company. We could not do a thing about it since privacy and hiring laws prohibited us from giving a bad reference or disclosing pending litigation. In the end, though, prosecution was successful, and both women were convicted of the fraud, spent some time in prison, and paid restitution. While it was not the full $11 million we believe they stole, at least they were branded as felons and probably will not have the opportunity to commit this kind of scheme again. But I remind myself what Bill told me: People will keep committing crimes until they get caught. And history tells us that people repeat their past, mistakes and all. Unless companies wise up, these kinds of frauds will continue to occur, costing all of us in the end.

LESSONS LEARNED

While implementing the fraud detection program, I learned that no one was above reproach. We found that employees, doctors, hospitals, customers, subscribers, groups, and companies had all been involved in fraudulent claim activities. It's enough to make your head swim. It did, however, help us to convince management to implement sweeping changes in claims processing, monitoring, and auditing. The before-and-after picture of Colossal's stance on data integrity and security was astounding.

The MoJo scheme reminded me there can always be a bad apple in the barrel, but it's not always possible to pick it out before it affects everyone. Colossal needed more audits, controls, and other fraud countermeasures. There were no system checks to make up for the shortfall, and systems, being neutral, were at the mercy of corrupt individuals.

Was Colossal any different from other health care claims companies? No, it was just bigger. Unfortunately for management, it was a game of catch-up to try to stop the hemorrhaging of claim fraud dollars with an already overworked audit and control staff—one that was not up to the challenge technically.

As Lord Acton first uttered, "Power corrupts, and absolute power corrupts absolutely." So, too, absolute power that has no checks and balances, no controls or accountability, is certain to run amuck. Mo and Jo, as the star trainers, should not have been able to move from the training environment into production without strong audit controls and supervisory review. Colossal learned the hard way, but many other companies may still be relying on a key set of employees who have inappropriate authority and unbridled power to execute transactions. Such authority, it is assumed, is provided with complete trust that employees will do the right thing all the time. We all know that is a foolish notion. Colossal proved this point.

It took multimillion-dollar fraud schemes and state legislature mandates to force Colossal to rethink its strategy regarding audits and proactive controls. Based on our early efforts at automated fraud detection, a new breed of software was developed in the health care industry to assist companies.

Colossal hired fresh management and members of the board of directors to revamp its systems, replaced its external auditing firm, and also brought in specialized consultants to help management implement a state-of-the-art fraud management and reporting system. Significant resources were added to the audit and control functions. Colossal was forever changed.

RECOMMENDATIONS TO PREVENT FUTURE OCCURRENCES

This fraud was a wake-up call for Colossal management. What they learned and what they chose to do about it were impressive. Here are some of the ways that the company chose to remediate the fraud problem.

Fraud Awareness

Colossal changed its posture about fraud. Instead of denying it exists, management decided to identify it as an ever-present danger and implemented employee awareness and training programs to identify and report fraud.

Fraud Prevention Hotline

Colossal instituted a toll-free number to encourage customers, employees, subscribers, and anyone else who is aware of a health care fraud to call and report it. Colossal provides identity concealment to those who request it.

Audit and Control

The company updated its audit routines to include annual fraud audit detection programs from certified bodies, and requires all current and future audit personnel to complete training and execute fraud examinations. Colossal requires claim agent ID quarterly audits based on sample selection. Real-time claim agent ID creation is prohibited, and independent oversight of them is instituted.

Background Checks

Colossal requires background screenings prior to hiring employees in sensitive areas.

Segregation of Duties: Production versus Training and Development

Colossal was a textbook case where monitoring for effective segregation of duties was defective or nonexistent. Colossal implemented tough new measures to prevent training and development personnel from performing production functions. Audit routines were added to ensure compliance.

Quarterly Recertification of Key or Privileged Systems Users

Colossal also implemented quarterly reviews of key systems and requires management recertification of all system user functions and entitlements.

John F. Kronick, CPA, CISA, CISSP-ISSAP, ISSMP, CISM, CITP, PMP, is director, Information Security, at Citigroup, N.A. in New York. He has over 25 years of professional experience, 14 of which have been in information security, fraud audit and risk assurance services, health care, and consumer services sectors. He holds an MBA from the University of South Dakota and a BSBA in Accounting/ Finance from Phillips University.

CHAPTER 8

The Mole

MANUEL PEREIRA

Tom Grey had four years of banking experience when he joined our financial institution. He worked closely with our customers, handling their most confidential information. Some described him as a loner who was constantly trying to figure out a way to make big money. Others knew him as a playboy who repeatedly ended romantic relationships with coworkers in favor of newer employees.

I am no stranger to moles, those insipid insiders who have plagued the counter-espionage services of every intelligence agency known. It was a life I thought I had left behind when I turned in my FBI credentials, top secret clearance, and government-issued firearm for a more peaceful life with predictable hours at a financial institution. During my tenure with "the Bureau," I spent five years on the Foreign Counter Intelligence (FCI) squad chasing spy types from East Germany, the Soviet Union, and Czechoslovakia. But with the fall of the Berlin Wall, I, like many of the Bureau's FCI resources, was reassigned to the White Collar Crime unit, which is where I spent the final years of my career.

I manage a group of 14 fraud investigators for a midsize bank that operates solely in California. About a third of us were ex-cops. The rest of our department included a few with criminal justice degrees and others with retail loss prevention and claims processing experience.

Our work was routine for the most part; the fraud we mitigated daily was usually as obvious as the proverbial nose on one's face. Besides the ever-present counterfeiters and check washers, we chased after credit card thieves, angry ex-boyfriends with an ATM card and PIN trustingly provided in happier days, wayward children whose "spitting image of their father" included a remarkable talent for replicating dad's signature, and the occasional wallet-grabbing hooker. Together, those made up an interesting yet predictable array of cases. Losses had been quite substantial before I accepted the position, growing at a rate of about 10% annually, a trend management wanted to stop.

Employing a more cohesive investigative approach, we began to earn a reputation as a financial institution that had you arrested the moment you pulled that flimsy fake ID out of your pocket. We started making house calls, which was one thing back in my federal days but quite another with neither gun nor badge. Our persistence and in-your-face investigative styles, while perhaps unorthodox for a financial institution, rewarded us with the desired results. Life was good in the world of bank fraud and forgery—or so we thought. But on one particularly cold day in January, some events unfolded that threatened to ruin what had been a downward trend in losses.

THE DOG HAS ITS DAY

Investigators love to talk about their cases, whether boasting or complaining. It was one of the few benefits of being confined to tightly cramped spaces. While it may seem less than conducive as a productive work environment, the truth is that if investigators had their own offices, they would likely never share what was going on in their worlds. Thus, bits and pieces of information that often are linked to make investigations successful would never happen. It was one such morning that the investigators for the check and credit card fraud areas entered my office to discuss some disturbing parallels in their newest cases.

I listened to similar stories about sharp increases in fraud activity and large dollar losses committed by criminals who are "just too good." But bank fraudsters aren't the most erudite criminals in comparison to the large and complex Wall Street types we often read about over coffee. Branch personnel often called with questions about the "Capival Bank" or "Bank of Stattes" cashier's checks that were being presented for payment. The average white-collar street thug, at least in California, was a horrible speller with a less-than-admirable command of proper grammar. Oftentimes they are in such a hurry to negotiate a counterfeit check that they forget to sign the item or are oblivious that the MICR line is crooked, double printed, or misaligned.

As we discussed the team's worrisome trends and anomalies, I became particularly concerned when I learned that in three instances, imposters had visited branches posing as legitimate customers and had successfully negotiated large withdrawals of cash. The fraudsters had everything they needed to make the visit a successful one, including a driver's license and, most disturbing of all, the secret pass code we use for many of our customers to protect them from this very thing. Silly words, like the name of their dog or their favorite flower, which in my opinion is so much more effective than a mother's maiden name or a date of birth, can both be easily discovered. The odds of a fraudster pulling out a fake or stolen ID and correctly providing our teller with the name of our customer's Shar-pei, "Mr. Toodles," would be extremely slim, if not impossible. Yet here we were with thousands of dollars in losses and mysterious impersonators who knew not only the name of Mr. Toodles on the Jones account, but Rosebud, Snookie Bear, and Chrysanthemum on the Smith, Gomez, and Hawks accounts, respectively. It had been more than a few years since I had left my cold war escapades, but one thing was certain: These fraudsters weren't guessing their way to success. They had help that only an insider could offer. We had a mole, and he wasn't showing any signs of stopping.

INFORMATION HIGHWAY

In a typical month, we received four or five telephone calls from various law enforcement agencies that had discovered during a traffic stop that the speeder or expired tag holder was not only concealing the usual stolen weapon and a few grams of crack, but was also in possession of stolen financial information. People were often found to be harboring copious amounts of stolen credit reports, credit cards in various names, ATM cards with PIN numbers, and stolen checkbooks.

One such call came just days after we began suspecting that an insider was stealing information. The arresting officer in a town 100 miles away advised that he had discovered documents that we would be interested in. When I pressed him for more details, he explained that he had been searching a suspect's car and in the process had discovered what appeared to be "customer information."

"I can see your customer's name, address, account number, mother's maiden name, date of birth, license number, password, and account balances," he advised.

I was a bit stumped for a moment, naively assuming that a customer had carelessly thrown away his bank statements with pass codes written on them, so I asked him to fax the seized documents to me. As our team anxiously gathered around the machine, listening to the steady clicking of the agonizingly slow printer, our eyes grew wide. Customer account profiles printed from terminals within our company headquarters appeared: the worst possible scenario and the final confirmation of the existence of our mole.

The walls of my office began to look like a war zone as we tacked up large pieces of poster board in columns around the room. Our lists of check cashing suspects, photos of account imposters, and employee suspects were voluminous. As we proceeded, the case grew. We found numerous similarities that linked recent frauds with the existence of a mole. We listed victims under their respective fraudster and wrote loss totals beside their names. To an outsider, it probably looked like a serial killer investigation on *NYPD Blue*, but for us, it was an attempt to grasp the scope of what we were facing. We were racing against the clock and we knew from experience that it was much better to face the press with the employee fraudster in jail than empty-handed.

After the case was laid out, we began analyzing our losses using a relatively new tool that tracked teller access through computer surveillance. A few long days passed until we were able to link most of the damage to one employee who was hired the prior year. We had almost 40 victim accounts. Nearly 30 of them had been accessed by a staff member who worked in the Telephone Operations Center, answering customer inquires. While he was clearly our best target, approximately 10 of these accounts were seemingly untouched by him, leaving us with some doubt about whether we had identified the only perpetrator or if others were involved.

Before we could accuse anyone, we would need more proof. We began studying the account profiles seized in the traffic stop. The more we looked at these documents, the more confused we became. None was accessed by the primary suspect, yet all of the accounts had been victims of fraudulent activities. Most of the information contained in these seized documents was accurate when compared to the current customer database, but some of the data was pure nonsense. Customers holding an average amount of $1,200 were showing balances of $1,000,000. Some of our customers were at the right street address but in the wrong city, or their account numbers were correct while their Social Security numbers were not.

We continued to review and theorize, searching for links to our mole, until one of our team, a criminal justice graduate, asked what seemed like a meaningless question: "When can an employee manipulate an account without any repercussion?" He stood next to the war desk staring at the information with a quizzical expression on his face.

The ex-cops looked at him impatiently. "When we spend our time asking stupid questions we don't catch the bad guys," one said, turning back to the growing labyrinth on the wall.

The criminal justice graduate seemed a bit dejected so I decided to take him seriously and at least pretend to consider the question. I thought for a moment, and my mind drifted back to a very long week when I first started with the bank. I looked at him; he shook his head slowly with a devious smile that told me he too had been thinking.

"Actually, it's not a stupid question." I put my arm around the ex-copper and continued. "In teller training class you can add a million dollars to an account, change the addresses all you want, and do whatever else. In those classes, they work with real accounts. These documents, my friends, were taken from that class during somebody's first days on the job. When we see who on our list was in teller training class during the week these were printed, we have our mole."

The following morning we called Tom in for an interview. He was in the teller class from which the seized profiles were stolen and was also the employee who had accessed 30 of the 40 compromised accounts. We made our suspicions known to the feds and the U.S. Attorney's Office. None of these agencies objected to us conducting the initial interview, partly because they had nothing to lose, and they know that employees are often more likely to confess to a company investigator who can only take away their job, as compared to a federal agent who can take away their freedom.

Tom was nervous from the start. His answers were indicative of deception, and when confronted with our suspicions, his rebuttals were weak and lacking conviction. He was street savvy, though: not afraid to look me in the eyes while attempting to remain cool and unaffected. I offered him what I considered to be the best motivator for those who are wise to the game: the chance to tell authorities his story first and be the one who fingers everyone else rather than the one who ends up getting the finger. I told him that everyone knew what he did. The rest was up to him. After two hours of who, why, what, where, and when, he became agitated.

"So what do you want me to do, lie about myself? You want me to tell a lie? Fine. What do you want me to confess?"

So you did do it, I thought to myself, leaning over so that our knees were just inches apart, attempting to invade his personal space without being too obvious. "You would do that for me? You would lie about a crime you didn't commit just because I asked you to?"

He looked away for a moment before announcing, "Well, you don't believe what I have been telling you—that I didn't do it—so I may as well just confess. You ain't interested in the truth, that's for damn sure."

He looked away again and was sliding up into his chair to move farther away from my knee. I could see that he was losing his aggression and determination. It was a good time to downplay his involvement in the entire caper in an effort to make confession palatable to him.

"You know, Tom, if you were the ringleader in all of this, then I am wasting my time, but I don't think you are. I think somebody asked you to do this. You want to know why? Because the losses in this investigation have gotten pretty high—and I don't see a Lexus outside in your parking spot."

"That's for damn sure," Tom replied.

"So what I need to know is this: Did you provide account information to just one person, or were you selling this information all over town?"

There is a moment in a successful interview when the weight of the world becomes heavy and the lies have stretched to capacity. It is then that the suspect's body confesses before his mouth catches up with it. The breath he has been holding finally escapes.

Tom's shoulders dropped and he sighed. "I don't want to go to jail."

An experienced interviewer knows that the suspect has just confessed. For the most part, the fight was over. This is a time to say nothing, to allow the tears to well up.

"I don't want to go to jail," he whispered again, shaking his head. The room grew quiet and I leaned closer. I wasn't going to speak; it was his show now. I mirrored his posture and bent forward in sympathy and understanding to encourage his continued cooperation. I nodded my head compassionately.

Then someone spoke, but it wasn't Tom. Management had requested an observer in the room, and unfortunately, he didn't have the experience to know when to be quiet. He couldn't handle the uncomfortable silence and gave in to his need to say something—anything. He asked about a totally unrelated element of the crime, jerking Tom away from thoughts of jail, his child, and losing his job and reputation. Tom answered the question calmly, but when he finished, he stood up and announced, "I'm done," and walked out.

I went home disappointed and troubled, a feeling that occasionally follows an extensive interview—especially when I know the suspect's life will be forever altered. I knew that although he didn't confess, we had him, and that he was probably pacing the floor of his home at that very moment. I thought about his son. I was a single parent. It was hard at times, and I wondered if he, too, had a mountain of bills and if fraud was supposed to be his way out. From what we had learned from other staff members and his file, he wasn't a drug abuser, had never been arrested or chronically unemployed, and wasn't mad at our company and seeking revenge. We did our job well and stopped him early. We had discovered our mole, and that didn't happen often.

THE KING FALLS

The FBI agent told me that when they arrived at Tom's home a few days later, he took only a few minutes to confess. He immediately turned over the name of Raphael Kingston, a local criminal whom they believed to be the ringleader of an organization that included counterfeiters, bank employees, check cashers, imposters, and manufacturers of fraudulent documents. He had recruited Tom to get a job at the bank for the primary purpose of removing confidential information. When the police raided Kingston's home, they encountered his roommate, an enormous naked man running through the kitchen nearly scared out of his mind. He later became a key witness against Kingston, admitting that he had made all of the fake driver's licenses and counterfeit checks used in the scheme. Together they had used a network of prostitutes, welfare moms, and low-level gang members to impersonate bank customers and to cash checks from their accounts, affecting our bank and several others.

I was eventually called to testify and told my story. I explained what had happened to arouse our suspicions and how we had narrowed our search down to Tom.

On cross examination, Kingston's defense attorney asked the anticipated questions: "Do you possess any information which proves that your employee provided this information directly to my client?"

"No, I don't."

"Did you see your employee provide any stolen records to my client?"

"No, I did not."

"Have you seen my client's name on anything associated with this case that even suggests he had anything to do with this investigation?"

It's always a smart move for a defense attorney to read through the documents he receives during discovery. It is also important not to ask any questions for which you are not relatively certain of the answer. If Kingston's attorney had practiced this advice, he would not have asked that particular question.

"Yes, one of the counterfeit checks was made out to your client and he negotiated it at one of our branches."

Fraudsters can be bad spellers and sloppy printers. They are also impatient and greedy much of the time. Cashing that check wasn't a great idea, especially for someone denying participation in a bank fraud scheme.

The first trial of Kingston ended in a mistrial. As it turns out, I wasn't the only one tired and exhausted, because the judge learned that one of the jurors had fallen asleep during testimony late in the afternoon as the trial was about to end. As was his duty, the judge called in all of the jurors in and asked how many of them had nodded off at any time during the prior weeks. Three sheepishly raised their hands.

A new trial was ordered. I wasn't called to testify.

I never found out much about Kingston other than what I learned while watching him in the courtroom during my testimony. He appeared disinterested in the proceedings, dressed in his designer jeans covered with patches from various NBA teams. I learned that he had been on probation for robbery with a firearm at the time he initiated his scheme against area banks. After his second trial, he was found guilty and was sentenced to 51 months in prison. According to the sentencing report, there were over 60 victims in the case. Kingston was ordered to pay restitution of nearly $100,000. He received 29 felony convictions. Five other participants entered into plea agreements for their parts in the scheme. Tom was sentenced to six months in jail.

LESSONS LEARNED

One of my mentors was fond of saying "Confess early and often." I think in these days of identity theft, and now with the never-ending stream of compromises, there is certainly some value in adopting this creed if and when your information is compromised. Informing your customers that you have taken every imaginable step to prevent data leaks but were a victim of someone you trusted is something most people can relate to. There are numerous stories about the Social Security Administration, tax preparers, credit agencies, banks, and even hospitals dealing with employees who have stolen confidential information and have used that information for profit.

Our initial contact with account holders to inform them of the compromise was handled without excuses or any shadowing of the truth. A letter sent to them stated:

> I am sorry to inform you that your information has been compromised. We are saddened and surprised that someone we trusted has let us all down this way. What I can tell you is that this person was identified quickly and has been indicted and will be prosecuted. I am calling to apologize and to reimburse you for the funds that were removed from your account.

Most of the responses we received, even from the most initially indignant of our customers, were understanding. It wasn't that we forgot to lock the door to a branch or had been careless with a laptop. We simply had a bad apple in the bin. Some were less conciliatory and asked, "Don't you do background checks?" We explained that we do, but that this employee had no criminal record. Many people assume that employees who commit occupational fraud have long and lengthy rap sheets: perhaps petty theft, possession of a controlled substance, and a few embezzlement indictments under their belt. This is, of course, far from the truth. In reality, only 7% of bank employees who steal from their employer are ever charged with a crime. They are free to move from bank to bank, and many do just that. And while the discovery of the stolen training class documents proved that Tom had taken the job with one purpose in mind, I can't think of anything human resources, his department managers, or anyone else could have done to isolate him as a potential criminal during the hiring process. He was just another guy who walked, talked, and looked like everyone else. But then again, he was a mole, and that's what they do.

RECOMMENDATIONS TO PREVENT
FUTURE OCCURRENCES

Fraud Policies Introduced to Employees: The Perception of Detection

Creating the perception of detection is an integral part of preventing occupational fraud in today's workplace. While handing out our fraud policy, which outlines specific nontolerable acts, I inform employees that everything they do via e-mail, on any terminal, or on the telephone is subject to corporate surveillance and recording. I tell the stories of those who have gone before, their aspirations and their untimely demise. After this, we review the federal statutes for bank fraud and computer secrecy. I let them know that there are cameras that look like cameras and cameras that look like clocks and smoke detectors.

More Surveillance

One technique we use is to create a report that lists how many times each teller looks at an account without performing a transaction. We created a position for one investigator to review this report and to initiate an investigation against all of the high scorers. Curiosity that leads to violating a consumer's privacy may start with one innocent peek to see how much your boss makes, how much your next-door neighbor deposits on a monthly basis, or to check up on an old flame. Inquisitiveness is great when it comes to scientific pursuits and space exploration, but bad when it comes to banking and customer privacy.

Manuel Pereira is a former Special Agent with the Federal Bureau of Investigation, previously assigned to the White Collar Crime and Foreign Counter Intelligence squads. He has eight years experience directing the security and loss prevention efforts for a West Coast financial institution.

CHAPTER 9

Her Passion for Fashion

BETHMARA KESSLER

Bobbi Jean Donnelly was hardened by her humble beginnings in rural Mississippi. The fourth of six children in a blue-collar working-class family, she spent the early years of her life in hand-me-down clothes, living in the shadow of the siblings that came before her.

As the result of public school zoning policies, Bobbi Jean attended class with some of Mississippi's most prominent families. At a young age her self-image plummeted as she endured the ridicule and torment inflicted upon her by the girls in designer clothes who would chant, "Poor, poor Bobbi Jean, she can't get her clothing clean!" Instead of submitting to her plight, the scrappy schoolgirl confronted her oppressors, frequently landing in the midst of large playground brawls. Eventually she learned to use her charm and wit instead of her fists—she won over the critical in-crowd and gained some popularity in middle school and high school.

Determined to rise above her roots, Bobbi Jean left Mississippi after high school to chase after her dream of becoming "somebody." Not sure what she would do for living, she headed to New York City and landed a job with a temp agency. Luck was on her side; Bobbi Jean's first assignment was temping for the design house of a major fashion retailer. This eventually led to a full-time job that lasted three years. Over the next eight years she continued to hold high-profile administrative support roles for fashion executives until finally landing her most lucrative position at Mod Fashions, Inc.

When she joined Mod Fashions, Bobbi Jean was newly married and had recently moved with her husband into a very attractive home in a New Jersey suburb. The house was beautifully appointed with fine upscale furnishings. The property was sprawling, complete with a swimming pool.

For Bobbi Jean, image was everything. She worked hard to project a family portrait of affluence, lying to coworkers about her "privileged" upbringing in Mississippi. Bobbi Jean's stories were so convincing that no one questioned the extent of her designer wardrobe. She was always decked out in the latest high-end clothes and accessories from head to toe. Hermès, Prada, Gucci, Chanel, and Louis Vuitton were some of her favorite designers. Bobbi Jean sported a brand-new outfit every day and was the envy of all of her coworkers. Her shoe collection could rival anyone's, containing hundreds of pairs from designers like Jimmy Choo and Manolo Blahnik. In the end, her passion for fashion would be her downfall.

Mod Fashions, Inc. was a hip multibillion-dollar retailer based in Kansas City, Missouri. Launched in 1970 by a brother and sister team, Steven and Debra Cammamod, it rose from its humble beginnings—a small mom-and-pop store on the outskirts of a big city—to a chain of over 2,000 stores across the country that carries every trendy must-have of the season.

When Steven and Debra started the business, they surrounded themselves with a handful of trusted friends and advisors. For the first five years, Mod Fashions was run solely by the small posse they had assembled.

As the business grew, so did the need to expand the team to help manage the day-to-day requirements of the company. After eight highly profitable years, the Cammamods built a crackerjack team from the retail industry's who's who in fashion. Two years later the company went public. Over the years the business became a multidivisional giant boasting over 75,000 employees worldwide.

Ron Dawson joined the company to run its design division, the incredibly fast-paced place where fashion is created. He had a cadre of 40 designers and design contractors, supported by a team of 20 individuals with various back-office support expertise. The team was based out of New York, over 1,000 miles away from Mod Fashion's home office in Kansas City.

When Ron joined the Mod team, he quickly began the search for an administrative assistant. He knew the importance of having a great assistant—one he could trust. Ron placed an advertisement in the *New York Times* classified section and was inundated with résumés from people clamoring to join the world of fashion. As he reviewed the applicants, one stood out from the crowd. Bobbi Jean Donnelly was a seasoned professional with several years of experience supporting senior executives in the industry. Ron was so impressed by her captivating personality during the interview that he immediately extended an offer, which she quickly accepted.

The chemistry was there; Ron and Bobbi Jean hit it off right away. After working together for only a short while, their connection grew strong. Ron's trust in his new assistant was solidified. People throughout the company could not stop talking about her. "Bobbi Jean is amazing," they said. Ron didn't hesitate to take her with him to Kansas City, where she would interact with all of the senior executives' assistants and home office support personnel. From the Accounts Payable Department to the executive suite, she charmed them all.

With the accolades pouring in, Ron quickly propelled Bobbi Jean from her position as his administrative assistant to office manager. That promotion entailed a significant increase in responsibility and authority. In addition to managing Ron's needs, Bobbi Jean also supervised the remaining support personnel and prepared and oversaw the Design Department's budget, a task that Ron despised. She was more than willing to shield him from mundane financial tasks. His least favorite was the review of expense reports submitted by his staff. Ron gave Bobbi Jean the responsibility of providing the first level of review; he relied on her to make sure that the expenses were valid before he signed them. On a few occasions, when Ron was traveling out of town or swamped with work, he asked Bobbi Jean to sign the expense reports on his behalf.

DESIGN ON MORE THAN A DIME

I joined the Mod team three and a half years after Bobbi Jean was hired. As the business grew, management decided it was time to build a robust Internal Audit Department. That's where I came in. My internal audit team was conducting a routine and relatively straightforward travel and expense audit, which was not expected to reveal any major surprises.

We developed a program designed to ensure that the corporate travel and expense policy was followed by employees and to confirm that adequate internal controls in the processing and payment of expense reports were operating effectively. The team scoped a sample of individuals and transactions to test. The people selected were from those employees who submitted the highest dollar amounts over the course of the year for reimbursement. Moreover, transactions were randomly selected across the total population of expenses submitted.

The approach and criteria used to audit the transactions differed significantly from the approach used to audit the individuals. The transactions were reviewed for compliance with the policy, proper authorization and approval, and the legitimacy of the expense. That work yielded no major surprises. The more interesting results of the work were in the review of individuals. My team looked at all expense reports submitted by the selected employees over a one-year period. We were looking at the expenses based on the employee's role in the company and for any patterns of activity that seemed unusual. It didn't take long for us to identify a pattern from one area of the business—the Design Department. There were several individuals who devised very inventive ways of submitting expenses on more than one occasion for reimbursement, demonstrating that their creativity was not limited to fashion.

My lead auditor, Mike Stuart, entered my office with piles of paper spilling over his arms. He was animated as he shared the details of the expense reports he reviewed.

"You have to see this," he said. "There are at least six people that are submitting their American Express bills for reimbursement instead of the detailed receipts for individual expenses. On most of them, I can't tell if the charges are even for a legitimate business purpose; some of them definitely look odd."

As Mike took me through the documents, the bills began to show a pattern: one month of charges, plus the next month a late fee with the old and new charges combined. In essence, at least three employees were submitting the same charges twice, one of which included a seemingly fake late fee.

Mike indicated that the three people were part of the design team in New York. So I asked him to bring in all of the expense reports for the employees in that department. As Mike and I flipped through those documents, we began to uncover more red flags.

Several of the employees submitted New York City taxi receipts for reimbursement, a legitimate business expense when conducting business in different locations in Manhattan. Upon examination of the actual taxi receipts, Mike and I noticed multiple receipts that appeared to come from the same taxi on the same day.

I am a born and raised New Yorker. Hailing a taxi in New York City is quite a feat— getting the same taxi twice, let alone several times in one day, is virtually impossible. New York City taxis are regulated, and all have electronic meters that print receipts. The receipts all show the taxi medallion number, which is how we were able to identify that they came from the same taxi. Below the medallion number is the trip number. I became very suspicious when the multiple receipts had sequential trip numbers on the same day. The time stamps on the receipts had small gaps between the end time of the receipt first in sequence and the begin time of the next one. In some cases there were five or six sequential taxi receipts. Upon further inspection, the tear pattern of the bottom of the earlier receipt in the sequence was an exact match for the tear pattern at the top of the one following it.

Mike and I also found several cases of meal receipts being submitted twice. The detailed bill usually presented at the end of the meal was separated from the credit card receipt for the same meal, and each was submitted separately for reimbursement. On a few occasions the person submitting the receipt would put different tip amounts and totals on each of the documents to make the duplication less obvious.

"Who had the most expenses this year on the design team?" I asked Mike, after a quick scan of the reports.

"The office manager, Bobbi Jean Donnelly; she charged about $115,000 worth of expenses this past year," he responded.

I asked Mike how much her boss, Ron Dawson, submitted.

"About $40,000," he replied.

It seemed strange that Bobbi Jean's expenses would be so much higher than Ron's. It also disturbed me that her name came up in all of the schemes we had identified at this point.

I went to meet with our general counsel, Fred Jackson, and informed him of what we had identified in the audit. He agreed that we needed to conduct a thorough investigation of the design team's expenses. As we'd begin the broader investigation, I would make sure that we thoroughly reviewed the activities of Bobbi Jean.

THE FRAUDULENT FIVE

Mike and I sat down to develop an investigation strategy. The volume of expense reports submitted by the design team was daunting. It would be impossible to effectively review every one of them in detail. We decided first to acquire a solid understanding of the organizational structure and normal business activities of the design team. Then we would do a high-level review of the expense reports submitted by each individual. Based on that review, we would be able to identify any individuals who had expenses or patterns of activity that were inconsistent with normal business expenses. We would put those aside to conduct a deeper analysis.

Mike and I went to meet with the director who was responsible for communicating with the design team on their budget, Jack Stevens. Jack had spent quite a bit of time in New York with Ron, Bobbi Jean, and the team to learn about their functions in the business and understand in depth how they operated.

"You have to understand that what the design team does is art, not science. A lot of the expenses that you will see in their budget will look unusual." This is the first thing that Jack said to us. Formally trained as an accountant and finance person, he admitted to having a hard time wrapping his mind around the types of expenses that came through the department.

As Jack took us through the organizational structure and budget of the design team, he explained that the group's role was to create new products for the company. The team traveled extensively around the world to be influenced and inspired by fashions and lifestyle trends. On those trips, team members would immerse themselves in local culture, entertainment, and shopping experiences. People would frequently buy things on the trips to serve as reminders of inspiration when they returned to the office. They call those purchases "samples." In New York, the team would create presentation projects, often incorporating their samples, to present to various merchants around the company. Jack showed us books of photographs that captured some of the presentations—they were awe-inspiring. Out of these, new ideas would be born and new products created.

The meeting with Jack provided just the right amount of context for our investigation. Mike and I sifted through the piles of expense reports and set aside approximately six individuals whom we would review in detail, in addition to the three we were already planning to look at.

We decided that the best approach would be to use our audit software, Interactive Data Extraction & Analysis (IDEA^{TM}). The expense reports were manual, which would make that difficult. In fact, submissions from these individuals were recorded in such a sloppy fashion that it was hard to truly analyze the patterns of data effectively. In all nine cases the expenses were submitted over many months, making it difficult to piece together all of the elements of the alleged business activities. Mike and I agreed that it would be worthwhile to invest the time of some members of our team to help build a database of the expense detail to facilitate the review. That investment paid off. The data read like tea leaves, giving us insight into the potential fates of each of the individuals. In four cases, expenses appeared reasonable and appropriate. For the five remaining people, it was clear that there were some problems that would need to be rectified.

Seth Warren, George Miller, Robin Simmons, Rose Waller, and Bobbi Jean Donnelly were systematically and routinely submitting expenses multiple times for reimbursement. Mike and I nicknamed them the "Fraudulent Five." By using IDEA to identify duplicate amounts quickly, we were able to isolate the expense reports that we needed to review in tandem. For example, the data would show us the exact amount, say $123.42, processed twice, and we would look at the different expense reports that corresponded with those charges. Mike and I looked at the receipts that were submitted as support. It became easy to separate the duplicates, and in some cases, those that were submitted multiple times. Seth appeared to be quite gutsy; he actually submitted a $132.86 charge for a car service five times over the course of seven months.

Mike and I also used IDEA to analyze expenses submitted from the same vendor for similar amounts, expenses incurred in the same week based on the detailed receipt information, and multiple submissions of the same expense category for the same day. Once we identified the Fraudulent Five as individuals involved in similar schemes, we analyzed the patterns of data across them as a group and found a few instances where Seth and Robin submitted the identical expenses. When they traveled together and had a meal, one would pay with their credit card and the other would get the detailed receipt and submit it as if they paid cash for the meal. Through various schemes, the Fraudulent Five submitted approximately $75,000 in false expenses.

About $12,000 was attributable to Bobbi Jean. I still had a nagging feeling about the sheer amount of expenses she was submitting. Using IDEA, I ran further analyses on her expenses to roll them up by category. I was very surprised to see that the majority of her purchases were samples. It particularly struck me as odd because that would mean that in her capacity as office manager, Bobbi Jean also had the luxury of traveling around the world with the design team to make decisions about fashion trends. I looked at her sample purchases and was overwhelmed. At times I can be considered a "fashion emergency," so the names of some of the designer clothes, shoes, and accessories that Bobbi Jean purchased didn't register with me, but the prices did. Seven-hundred and fifty dollars for a pair of Jimmy Choo shoes, $875 for a Hermès scarf, $1,250 for a Prada wallet: all samples and all coded to various projects that the design team appeared to have done for Mod Fashions.

Using IDEA, I extracted all travel-related expenses submitted by Bobbi Jean to see if the sample purchases correlated to trips that other design team members took. I thought that this would at least validate that her role could be broader than it appeared and that I was worrying about all of these charges for no reason. I was very surprised to see that she did go on several trips with the team. Upon further review, I found a trip to London that seemed to further validate Bobbi Jean's importance on the design team. It appeared that Ron had sent her to London to meet with 12 students to recruit interns for Mod Fashions. Bobbi Jean had submitted over $6,000 for a one-week trip to do the recruiting; she had wined and dined the interns at the finest restaurants in London, including one outing that cost $1,386. Surely if all of these charges were fraudulent, Ron would have picked it up in his own budget review.

I went back to the general counsel and took him through the circumstances of each individual. We decided that it was time to sit down with Ron to share the details of the investigation when he came to Kansas City. I had never met this design prodigy, but he was definitely a legendary figure at Mod Fashions. Fred warned me about the need to be delicate: "He is creative and might be a bit sensitive."

Ron was wildly charismatic, bursting through the door of our conference room like a gust of wind. Fred introduced us, and Ron made it clear that he did not like auditors. He was very kind in ensuring that I didn't take his comment personally, but it was clear that he was not interested in becoming friends. As Fred and I took him through the schemes of the Fraudulent Five and the $75,000, it was apparent that he was disappointed and disgusted by his staff's conduct. He shared that Seth was a wheeler-dealer type so he wasn't surprised, but the rest really caught him off guard. The person that disappointed Ron the most was his trusted manager, Bobbi Jean.

"I pay her so well. Why would she steal $12,000?" he asked. "Her family is so wealthy; I can't understand why she would need the money!"

Ron was really distressed. Deep down, he knew that Steven and Debra would be displeased with him for harboring a collection of untrustworthy employees.

Next, Fred discussed a game plan. We collectively agreed that Fred and I would fly to New York to meet with each person and give them a chance to explain themselves. Bobbi Jean would be a problem, though; she was out on maternity leave, at home in the suburbs of New Jersey. Fred and I would have to organize a way to connect with her while we were there on our trip.

A (Corrupt) Design for Living

Fred and I arrived at the design office in New York bright and early on a Wednesday morning. We were clearly out of place in our corporate suits. The environment was casual, trendy, and very hip; we were not. Ron greeted us and quickly shepherded us into a small but exquisite conference room with floor-to-ceiling windows, a phenomenal view, and some of the most incredible objects d'art that I have ever seen. Ron introduced us to the human resources director, Anne Skully. We discussed our plan for interviewing Seth, George, Robin, and Rose. Anne would be present during the interviews along with Fred and me.

George and Rose were quick interviews. They both readily admitted to the complete extent of their actions, taking full accountability for what they had done. Robin was a bit ornery. She put up a strong wall of resistance, denying any impropriety until directly confronted with each and every expense report. Ultimately, she bowed her head and accepted defeat.

Seth was a completely different story. He was slick, as Ron had warned us. As we presented him with the evidence of each of his fraudulent acts, he responded with indignant outrage at "the incompetence" of his assistant. Seth poured on the charm as he explained that he was incredibly disorganized and incapable of even dreaming up the type of schemes we were accusing him of committing. He claimed that he gave his assistant wads of crumbled receipts to sort through and process.

"She is not very intelligent," he asserted. "This is all a mistake and it's her fault."

Despite Seth's best efforts to deflect responsibility, his explanations did not make sense. Fred and I questioned him in excruciating detail about his process for giving his receipts to his assistant. He could not explain how she would have duplicate receipts to process for him over the course of many months unless he repeatedly gave them to her in a piecemeal fashion. Seth, George, Robin, and Rose were terminated that day.

It was 2:30 p.m. when Ron, Anne, Fred, and I reconnected in the conference room to discuss how we were going to handle Bobbi Jean. Despite feeling betrayed, Ron insisted that we allow her to exit Mod Fashions gracefully. We decided that Fred and I would call her at home, explain what we found, and tell her that we would allow her to finish out her maternity leave and resign without returning to the office. Ron and Anne left the conference room so Fred and I could get down to business.

As we were getting ready to make the phone call, I decided to ask Ron one more question. I walked to his office where he and Anne were meeting, and interrupted the two of them.

"I hate to bother you, Ron, but I just need to ask you one thing before we call Bobbi Jean. How much do you think she submits per year in expenses through her travel and expense reports?"

"Probably about $10,000 to $12,000 per year," he answered.

My stomach sank as I continued, "So if I told you the amount was more than $100,000 a year, it would surprise you?"

It looked like someone had knocked the wind out of Ron. "That can't be! What are you talking about!?"

I explained that the biggest category of expenses was samples, and went on to enumerate the types of purchases I saw. Ron calmly looked me straight in the eye as he attempted to hide his rage and whispered, "She was not authorized to purchase samples."

Fred and I agreed that we needed to terminate Bobbi Jean immediately and then figure out the extent of her fraudulent activities and what actions to pursue. We called her and explained that we had found approximately $12,000 of expenses that she had fraudulently submitted for reimbursement. Bobbi Jean was confident yet guarded as she insisted that there must be a mistake. She went on to explain that her workload was so great that it was possible that she had accidentally submitted things for reimbursement on more than one occasion, and if so, it was in error. Fred then went on to tell her that we also believed that a large number of expenses that she submitted were not valid; they were possibly personal in nature. Bobbi Jean was cautiously dismissive as she said, "You just have no idea what I really do for the design team."

Fred explained the conditions of her termination and indicated that we would do some additional work to determine if we would take any further action. As parting words, he suggested that she seek the assistance of a lawyer regarding this situation.

Fred and I flew back to Kansas City that Wednesday evening. I spent Thursday and Friday working with my team to pull together all of Bobbi Jean's expense reports and receipts and catalog them for a detailed review with Ron that I scheduled for the following week.

On Monday morning I flew to New York with two suitcases in tow, which contained meticulously prepared binders of the reports and supporting receipts that my team had pieced together. Ron and I agreed to meet at an office that he was able to borrow, a considerable distance from the design office. He was hesitant as he eyed the suitcases, but cordially invited me into the beautiful office overlooking Central Park. He offered me a cup of coffee and we got down to business.

I pulled all of the binders out of the suitcases, organized them chronologically, and began reviewing them with Ron. For the next two days I received an accelerated education in fashion and began to bond with Ron in a way that neither of us expected. We were both infuriated by the audacity of Bobbi Jean as we separated the expenses into piles of those that appeared to be legitimate, those that were clearly fraudulent, and those that were questionable. Ron easily recognized a lot of Bobbi Jean's clothing, shoes, and accessory purchases as things that she wore to work on a regular basis.

Mod Fashion's expense reporting process requires individuals to give descriptions for the business purpose of an expense and have their boss sign off on the actual expense report. Ron was amazed by the accuracy with which his signature was replicated. Every expense report had a signature that reasonably appeared to be his own. However, we compared documents that he actually did sign with those he did not, and viewing the documents side by side clearly showed the anomalies in the forged signature. With Ron's tutelage into the world of fashion, I was able to clearly see that in many cases Bobbi Jean's receipts did not match up to her explanations. Before meeting Ron, I did not know that Jimmy Choo exclusively sold shoes, handbags, and small accessories. On several occasions Bobbi Jean submitted Jimmy Choo receipts but claimed that they were blouses and pants. Ron showed me that a close look at the receipt clearly indicated a size of 7.5, which is not a clothing size but a shoe size. A savvy fashion buff would have easily seen the pattern of deception.

Ron lost it when we came across the expenses for Bobbi Jean's trip to London to interview the design interns. He quickly pulled out his calendar and confirmed that the dates of that trip coincided with a vacation that she and her husband took to London.

A final tally of her fraud was approximately $275,000 over two and a half years. Almost 95% of the expenses that she submitted to Mod Fashions for reimbursement were false.

I called Fred to discuss our findings. We agreed that the right thing to do was to talk to the district attorney in New York and see if they would prosecute Bobbi Jean criminally for her actions. Our case was assigned to Assistant District Attorney Wendy Simmons. I met with Wendy at her office in downtown Manhattan. She was impressed with the organization and detail of the documentation that we provided for the case, and she readily agreed to prosecute Bobbi Jean.

Several weeks after meeting with Wendy, she called to tell me that she met with Bobbi Jean and her lawyer. Wendy shared that Bobbi Jean was very impressive and confident during their interview, denying all of the allegations and offering to provide witnesses who would substantiate her position of innocence. She claimed that all of her purchases were legitimate, authorized, and part of normal business practices of the design team. Wendy said that she would need to meet with these witnesses and Ron to decide if there really was a case to pursue.

Wendy met with Ron and the three witnesses Bobbi Jean produced, all ex-employees of Mod Fashions: Jackie Adams and John Bresnin, who were terminated for poor performance and had a clear ax to grind with Ron; and Holly Wilson, who left the business to start her own company. Jackie and John were cool yet adamant about the authenticity of Bobbi Jean's purchases and legitimacy of her actions. But Wendy quickly sized them up and concluded that they were disgruntled ex-employees who would not be credible witnesses for the defense.

Wendy called me to confirm that she was now confident in the case against Bobbi Jean, and would sit down with her and her lawyer to discuss the possibility of a plea agreement. At first, Bobbi Jean was adamant about her innocence and refused to consider any plea agreement. Ron and I testified before a grand jury that subsequently handed down an indictment against Bobbi Jean. Eventually she decided to avoid a messy court battle and accepted a plea that came with a jail sentence of 6 to 12 months.

Several months later I testified in unemployment court to justify our termination of Seth Warren for cause. The judge was very patient with Seth, allowing him to explain the "mistake." Before he denied Seth any unemployment benefits, the judge said, "Sir, you must expect that the whole lot of us are 'not very intelligent,' as you claim your 'poor hardworking assistant' to be, if you expect us to believe that you did not intentionally and systematically time the submission of your expense receipts with the explicit purpose of defrauding the company for your personal benefit." Visibly deflated, Seth did not seem to be so slick after all.

I went to Bobbi Jean's sentencing hearing and watched as she stood apprehensively; her body language did not exude her usual confidence. The understated and unfashionable outfit she wore was ironic considering that her passion for fashion was the cause of her downfall. Bobbi Jean was ushered away in handcuffs with her head down, never turning back even to say good-bye to her husband. As she left the room, I thought about the baby she left at home. I wondered if she regretted her actions—or just getting caught.

LESSONS LEARNED

When this was all over, I worked with the management team to recap the breakdowns and lessons learned that enabled Bobbi Jean and the rest of the Fraudulent Five to commit their acts. We all agreed that there were many important lessons to take away from this.

Ron placed too much trust in Bobbi Jean, giving her authority that went virtually unchecked. Checks and balances must be in place and operating effectively. Leaders should not delegate their fiduciary responsibilities. Once Ron allowed Bobbi Jean to sign expense reports and manage the design department's budget, he did not engage in the level of review that would have alerted him to the fraudulent activities.

By signing the expense reports for the design team on Ron's behalf and managing the budget, Bobbi Jean could pad certain budget categories in the planning process by submitting details described only as "other" or "miscellaneous." She could also monitor and control the budget lines that everyone's expenses hit to prevent variances that Ron might want to review in more detail. Therefore, when she would submit her fraudulent expenses, she would code them to budget line items that were running under budget. Ron didn't suspect a thing.

There also needs to be a clear definition of roles and responsibilities between the staff who sign expense reports and those who process them. At Mod Fashions there was confusion as to what exactly the manager's signature on an expense report meant. For us, it was not clear whether it indicated that the manager was authorizing the expenses as reasonable or that the manager reviewed the report and supporting detail and was attesting to the validity of the expense. Management thought it was the former, and the travel and expense processors thought it was the latter. The result was that neither could thoroughly monitor expenses that employees were submitting across the company.

On a personal note, Ron and I became good friends and colleagues. Despite his early resistance, the journey we took together through this set of unfortunate circumstances bonded us. As an added benefit, my taste in fashion has definitely improved as a result of our friendship.

RECOMMENDATIONS TO PREVENT FUTURE OCCURRENCES

Use Clear Supporting Documentation for Travel and Expense Reports

We modified our travel and expense policy to be black and white in respect to appropriate supporting documentation for expenses. We now require original documentation and prohibit things like credit card statements and photocopies. This prevents employees from submitting duplicate expenses for reimbursement.

Use Corporate Credit Cards for Business Expenses

We now require all employees to use their corporate credit card for business expenses. This has significantly reduced the amount of expenses for which people claim to have paid cash and reduces the ability to split the credit card receipt from the detailed receipt and submit both for reimbursement.

Train Travel and Expense Processors

We have trained our travel and expense (T&E) processors in the basics of identifying the red flags of fraud. Using the actual receipts submitted by the Fraudulent Five with some additional educational materials, I put together a training class for the processors to demonstrate what fraud looks like and to increase their awareness of various schemes.

Update Technology

Both the internal audit team and the T&E team have considerably expanded use of the audit software, IDEA, to proactively look for warning patterns of fraud in the T&E data.

The T&E has also developed auditing protocols that allow it to be most efficient in auditing T&E data. Team members separate big spenders from the rest of the population. Much as Mike and I did during our initial internal audit, they look at those big spenders in detail for patterns that appear odd on a quarterly basis. In addition, they randomly select expense reports to review against a set of audit criteria on a weekly basis.

Bethmara Kessler, CFE, CISA, leads enterprise business risk management for a Fortune 500 company. Her 25-career has spanned various audit and risk management roles involving fraud investigation and ethics compliance in the retail, entertainment, consumer products, and public accounting industries. Ms. Kessler received her BBA in Accounting from Baruch College.

CHAPTER 10

An Unaffordable Complex

JEFFREY D. BARSKY

At an early age, Christine Cross immigrated to America with her parents. The first in her family to go to college, she worked hard to achieve a degree in accounting and was proud of her accomplishment when she became a CPA.

After graduating, Christine married and she and her husband, Jimmy, found jobs with Affordable Housing, Inc. (AHI), a charity that developed, owned, and managed a large number of housing projects for low-income families and the elderly. After several years of working together, Jimmy developed some health issues and resigned.

Christine was originally hired as an internal auditor and, within two years of employment, she was promoted to the director of fiscal services. She possessed a dominant personality and demanded respect from everyone. AHI employees who reported to Christine knew not to question her authority. She had terminated more than one person for disagreeing with her.

Yet despite her quick rise, she would complain of feeling underappreciated. She did not think that management recognized her professionalism—according to her, they didn't acknowledge or even realize how hard she worked for the company. She claimed to have back problems due to her stressful job. Because of this, she needed to take work home. This conveniently also explained why she was absent from the office on many occasions.

Although Christine was the predominant breadwinner, the family lived an extravagant lifestyle. It included, among other things, expensive cars, pricy real estate investments, and exotic travel. Christine's Harley-Davidson motorcycle was modified at a custom shop, costing tens of thousands of dollars. Jimmy owned two motorcycles that were worth a combined $30,000. They shared four relatively new vehicles and a custom-built trailer used to transport their motorcycles long distances.

The couple traveled to warm locations to escape the winters in Cold Creek, North Dakota, and often discussed their luxurious foreign travels with AHI employees. Christine and Jimmy publicly reminisced about traveling to Florida, where they stayed at a pricy condominium.

The couple also was proud of the fact that they sent their children to the best private schools and expensive colleges. It was well known by AHI employees that Christine and Jimmy spared no expense for the education of their kids.

Everyone wondered how the Cross family could afford this lavish lifestyle on one salary. However, no one wanted to risk his or her job by confronting Christine.

NOT SO AFFORDABLE, AFTER ALL

Affordable Housing, Inc., was a large not-for-profit charity located in Cold Creek, North Dakota, that provided services to economically disadvantaged residents of the community. One of their divisions developed, owned, and managed approximately 20 affordable housing apartment projects that provided low-cost housing to qualified low-income families and elderly tenants. Tenants' total household income levels may not exceed certain amounts to be eligible to live in the apartments. The projects charged tenants a rent equal to a certain percentage of their income. The balance of the rent was paid by the Cold Creek Housing Authority, which received some of its funds from the federal government. The subsidies received from the Cold Creek Housing Authority allowed the apartment projects to meet their operating needs without charging tenants a higher rent.

The record keeping for subsidized housing was complicated. An owner was required to maintain more records for this type of housing than in a typical apartment complex. Evidence of tenants' income levels had to be proved on a regular basis. This step, which is required by the regulatory agreement with the housing authority, was to ensure that the tenants are qualified based on their total household income. The owner needed to also prepare monthly reports, which provided the housing authority with support for the rent charged to each tenant so that the housing authority knew how much to pay the owner.

Christine hired people with limited accounting experience, and, as a result, the accounting staff was far from effective. Furthermore, AHI management focused on its goals of providing services to the citizens of the community, not the strength of the accounting department and its related internal controls. An inexperienced accounting staff and complex reporting requirements resulted in records that were behind and often insufficient. For example, bank reconciliations often were not completed on a monthly basis.

While AHI had reasonable polices and procedures, they were not always followed and therefore were not effective. The combination of Christine's forceful personality and the lack of experience in the accounting department made it possible for Christine to get away with breaking the rules. In violation of company policy, Christine instructed the employee who received the mail to give the unopened bank statements directly to her. This allowed her to destroy or alter checks before other individuals ever saw them. According to company policy, disbursements required approval by someone other than the person who requested the payment. In many cases, Christine made the check request and then approved the invoice for payment anyway. She was then able to obtain payments for companies that were controlled by her or her husband. But as it turned out, these "companies" were nothing more than bank accounts that were controlled by them and used to deposit AHI checks.

WHEN IT RAINS, IT POURS

Most of AHI's apartment projects operated at a small cash surplus. However, one project, Raintree Apartments, was an exception. Raintree had received favorable rent increases from the housing authority over the years, generating a cash surplus of approximately $4 million. Raintree also had nagging water penetration problems, so management decided to commence a renovation project to correct them. This included replacement of windows and casements and a redesign of the roof line to eliminate the leaks. Alison Kramer, the AHI internal architect, along with outside consultants, prepared a construction budget of $2 million, well within the project's cash surplus. As required by the housing authority, management sought and received approval to commence the renovation project.

One fall day, Alison received two calls—one from the general contractor and another from the inspecting architect—both of whom complained about not having their draw request paid. When Alison contacted Christine about the situation, she was told that Raintree Apartment's funds were invested in the stock market, and they had suffered a significant decline. Christine asked Alison to slow down the renovation project so that the funds would have ample time to recover in value before they were needed to pay bills. She also demanded that Alison obtain her approval before committing to any additional work in excess of $100,000. Unbeknownst to Alison at the time, the statement regarding the decline in value of the stock market made no sense because an investment of surplus funds in this manner was in violation of the regulatory agreement between the housing authority and AHI. It turned out that the funds were not invested in the market, anyway.

Alison requested and received copies of the paid bill file on the renovation project from another AHI employee. Upon reviewing the paid bills and draw requests, she noticed certain payments totaling over $700,000 that she had not approved. This aroused her suspicions. One of the bills she had not approved was listed as being paid to the architect. Mysteriously, it contained two different type fonts. Once Alison called the architect's office, she determined that this payment had not been received. She also contacted the general contractor and located certain bills listed to him that he had not received.

Bothered by her discovery, Alison disclosed the findings to her supervisor. Management was concerned, among other things, with two issues: Since government funds appeared to be involved, there could be legal consequences to the organization. Also, if the public became aware of the fact that AHI had been defrauded by an employee, there could be a negative impact on AHI's ability to raise contributions.

Management contacted their law firm for advice, which suggested that a complete investigation be conducted and appropriate steps taken to resolve the matter. The law firm recommended me to AHI, and after an initial meeting, I was engaged to conduct an investigation.

RAIN(TREE) CHECK

I began the investigation by conducting an interview with Alison Kramer and obtaining several important documents: a copy of the list she prepared of questionable checks written from a checking account of Raintree Apartments; copies of the approved construction contract, along with the typical documents evidencing payment to the contractor such as draw requests and change orders; and a copy of the approved architect agreement. Alison also provided me with a copy of a fax from Christine's home, which was a Housing Authority "approved" construction contract in the amount of $2.1 million. This approval was $200,000 higher than the actual construction contract with the general contractor, Williams Construction Company, Inc. I then obtained copies of invoices and draw requests in support of actual payments to Williams and the architect, Martin Stewart, from the Accounting Department. I reviewed all of these documents with Alison for unusual items.

One significant example of an unusual item was an invoice in support of a payment to J&C Design in the amount of $275,000. This invoice was a draw request allegedly for the general contractor, Williams, which indicated payments should be made to the "architect," J&C Design, for payment to Williams. Over the years, I have reviewed a substantial number of invoices and documents related to construction and never saw an example where the architect receives payment and then pays the general contractor for the construction work.

There were several other unusual things about this draw request. First, it stated that the contract amount was $2.35 million, or $450,000 higher than the actual contract amount of $1.9 million. Interestingly, the contract amount listed did not even agree with the approved Housing Authority contract amount of $2.1 million. Second, the draw requested indicated that the contract price was increased by "approved" change orders in the amount of $250,000. It is very unusual for approved change orders to be in round numbers. According to the actual change orders on file, the contract amount was actually decreased by approximately $82,000. Therefore, the change orders were overstated by $332,000, and the adjusted contract price (original contract price plus change orders) was overstated by $782,000.

To continue the investigation, I obtained copies of the bank statements for the Raintree Apartments checking account from which the renovation project were paid. I quickly determined that the account had been opened for a period of three years. I also deduced that, on average, only two to three checks were written per month. Accordingly, I decided to review all checks written on the account.

During my review, I noticed that many of the checks appeared altered or were missing altogether. I requested and obtained an authorization letter from the client, giving the bank permission to provide me with copies of all cancelled checks.

Also, consistent with my usual practice, I asked Alison for additional names of AHI employees whom she thought would be helpful to interview. She suggested Bill Miller in accounting. Christine had hired Bill 10 years earlier on a part-time basis while he attended a local university. Upon graduation, he began working for AHI full time, where he progressed from an assistant bookkeeper to senior accounting supervisor. In recent years, Bill was responsible for preparing accounting analyses and schedules that were provided to the outside auditors of the various AHI entities. While preparing these schedules and analyses, Bill noticed certain checks payable to vendors that he did not recognize—namely, Jimmy's Metal Works and J&C Design. He provided me with a list of seven payments made to these vendors in the approximate amount of $62,000. He had been afraid to bring these items to AHI Management or to the outside auditors for fear that he would be fired if management ignored the issue or if he was wrong.

Bill also told me that he noticed that one of the outside auditors, Michael Woods, appeared nervous when dealing with transactions involving Raintree Apartments. This only occurred on the Raintree audit. Bill was not the only one to notice the odd behavior. During some water cooler conversations, employees learned that Michael was having an affair with an AHI employee, which Christine also knew about. The employees surmised that Christine used this as leverage to force Michael to ignore suspicious items. It is possible that he knew something was not right, but failed to look into it for fear of having his affair exposed.

At this point, I received the requested checks from the bank and decided to review them as the next step in the investigation. I compared them to the ones in AHI's files. I also now had an original check as it had cleared the bank from the batch of checks that had been missing. My review revealed that many of the checks had been altered. For example, one supplied by the bank was written to Jimmy's Metal Works in the amount of $195,000. The payee was altered to "Williams Construction Company, Inc." on the copy of the check in AHI's files. Inspection of the back of this check as it originally cleared the bank revealed that it was endorsed "For deposit only, Jimmy's Metal Works" with a bank account number. On the back of this check in AHI's files, the endorsement was altered to read "For deposit only, Williams Construction Company, Inc." with a bank account number. From this I surmised that the check was written to Jimmy's Metal Works and deposited into a bank account in its name. Later the check was altered to read "payable to Williams Construction Company, Inc.," an approved AHI vendor.

In addition, I noticed that all but two of the checks missing from AHI records were written to Jimmy's Metal Works, J&C Design, Jimmy Cross, or Christine Cross. Most— but not all—of the checks found in the AHI files that were written to the Crosses or to one of their controlled entities were altered in a similar manner to the check in the amount of $195,000 to Williams. A review of public records revealed that Jimmy's Metal Works and J&C Design were not registered or licensed companies. It was not difficult to surmise that J&C stood for Jimmy and Christine.

The invoices supporting these payments were generally draw requests to Williams Construction Company, Inc. or invoices to Jimmy's Metal Works and J&C Design. As mentioned, the draw requests had inflated amounts well in excess of the actual contract amount. The invoices to Jimmy's Metal Works and J&C Design were without any address or phone number and were described as "services rendered." Many of the invoices and check requests were not in the file.

Later in the investigation, I was able to subpoena the checking account statements for Jimmy's Metal Works, J&C Design, and Jimmy and Christine Cross. In summary, I determined that of the total of $2.6 million disbursed from this account from its inception,

$1.55 million was disbursed to Jimmy and Christine Cross or companies under their control.

Bill suggested I interview Carl Perry in accounting, another AHI employee. Carl described certain aspects of the accounting system and how bills were approved and paid. Carl told me that Christine had a "system" requiring that if the bank questioned any Raintree checks made payable to Jimmy's Metal Works or J&C Design, he was to confirm that they should be honored. In addition to providing me with notes he had maintained, Carl told me about conversations that occurred with four other AHI employees about suspicious vendors being paid that seemed to be linked to Christine and Jimmy. According to Carl, several employees were aware of something but afraid to come forward.

Next, he described some of the Crosses' purchases. According to Carl, the couple would show him pictures of some of their prized possessions, including the cars, the motorcycles, their expensive condo in Florida, and furnishings for their new house.

Based on the interviews conducted and documents examined, I became aware of some payments from other AHI checking accounts to one of the entities in the Cross empire. As a result, I obtained bank statements, cancelled checks, and cash disbursement journals for as many years back as possible for review. I then noted any check made payable to Jimmy Cross, Christine Cross, J&C Design, and Jimmy's Metal Works. Also, I took a sample of checks payable to other vendors and reviewed the supporting documents to determine if any of these checks appeared linked to the Crosses. In summary, I located $2.48 million in checks payable to the Crosses or one of their controlled entities.

A Place for Everyone and Everything in Its Place

Upon completing an initial review of documents and conducting several interviews, I met with outside legal counsel to consider the appropriate steps to recover funds from the Crosses. Counsel decided that sufficient information existed to file a civil lawsuit. Once the suit was filed, I requested that outside legal counsel subpoena the bank records of Jimmy's Metal Works, J&C Design, and the Crosses. Access to these bank records provided me with a history of deposits into their bank accounts. I was able to determine the source of most of these deposits. The sources included transfers from other Cross-controlled accounts, payroll from AHI, and deposits of fraudulent checks from AHI. This helped minimize the risk that I had missed major defalcations during my review of AHI records.

Near the conclusion of my engagement, I prepared a written report that was forwarded to AHI's insurance company. I cooperated with their investigator by responding to questions and providing him with documents as requested. The insurance company made a payment up to the limits of the policy, but it was less than the amount of the total loss suffered by AHI.

During the investigation, I was consulted by AHI management and outside legal counsel about potential negligence by the outside audit firm. Instead of filing a lawsuit against the auditors, I suggested that AHI have a meeting with the audit firm and discuss a potential settlement. Ultimately, a settlement was reached between them, which provided a payment to AHI without the need to file and litigate a lawsuit, saving professional fees.

I also cooperated with local authorities who had commenced a criminal investigation, which resulted in indictments of both Jimmy and Christine Cross. The authorities were very helpful to AHI. They gave the Crosses a large incentive—a plea bargain carrying a modest sentence—for turning over the majority of the assets purchased with AHI funds. In the end, Jimmy and Christine agreed, which minimized legal and other professional fees, while still allowing recovery. Christine received a sentence of 1 to 3 months and Jimmy was sentenced to 6 to 12 months.

AHI sold the real estate and other assets it received from the Crosses. From these sales, insurance proceeds, and the proceeds from the settlement with the auditors, AHI collected almost all of its loss of $2.48 million. Because AHI was able to satisfy the housing authority that all funds were returned, no action was taken against it. Fortunately, the case did not appear to have any negative impact on the organization's ability to raise contributions from the public.

Lessons Learned

In concept, the fraud uncovered was quite simple. Phony invoices and other supporting documents were created to support fraudulent payments to nonexistent vendors. As a result, the investigation was simple, as well. All that was required was for me to follow certain basic fraud investigation techniques, such as interviewing witnesses and examining and maintaining the chain of custody of documents. However, certain aspects of the investigation were difficult and time consuming. It took a long time to retrieve copies of checks from the bank. Also, because AHI wrote so many checks, reviewing even a sample of disbursements from the other AHI accounts was time consuming.

From the beginning, there were many signs of potential fraud occurring. Christine and Jimmy's extravagant lifestyle was a clue. How could a family afford this lifestyle on one salary? Also, Christine chose inexperienced employees to work in the Accounting Department because they were less likely to discover the fraud. Due to her controlling nature, they would be also less likely to expose the scheme if they became aware of it. Allowing Christine so much control over a poorly functioning Accounting Department should have been avoided.

Another red flag was poor record keeping. The records were constantly behind. One way to cover up a fraud is to create phony documents while altering other documents. It takes a lot of time to create phony invoices and draw requests. When an employee uses his or her time in this manner, the result is that other duties are not performed, and the books and records are delinquent and often incomplete. It is harder to spot fraudulent transactions in incomplete records. In addition, Christine took documents out of the office to her home. Perhaps this was because the task of creating phony documents and altering others was a risky endeavor at the office.

RECOMMENDATIONS TO PREVENT FUTURE OCCURRENCES

Segregation of Duties

AHI should have enforced its policy of having someone other than the employee who wrote checks reconcile the bank statements. The individual who prepared the bank reconciliation should receive the bank statements unopened from the mail clerk. One classic internal control policy is segregation of duties. There are several examples where this control could have prevented the losses incurred by AHI. The bank statements should not have been transmitted from the mail clerk to Christine. She should not have been allowed to reconcile the Raintree bank account used to pay for the major renovation project because she was also the person writing checks from this account. This reconciliation should have been performed by another AHI employee who received the bank statements directly from the mail clerk. In addition, Christine should not have been able to approve invoices when she wrote the checks and check requests. Having so much control over these transactions permitted her to create and approve phony invoices, cut the checks to pay them, and destroy or alter documents to cover up the fraud.

Monitor Budgets

It is important to develop a system to monitor the cost of major renovation or construction projects. This system should include an approved renovation or construction budget with monthly comparisons of budget to cost incurred and estimated costs to complete. The system should also consider written confirmation of contract terms with major contractors hired by AHI.

Implement Fraud Hotline

AHI should encourage employees to come forward if they suspect fraud. A good way to promote this is to implement a fraud hotline. Employees and customers are more likely to report occurrences of fraud if the tip line is anonymous.

Hire Experienced Accountants

It would be beneficial for AHI to hire individuals with sufficient experience in accounting and internal controls. The company should also hire an internal auditor who can monitor the progress of AHI's changes to and compliance with internal controls.

Confine Records to Office

A policy should be established and enforced that prohibits employees from removing records from the office. Taking important records home allows employees the opportunity to alter or embellish documents, resulting in fraud.

Jeffrey D. Barsky, CPA, has a forensic accounting practice in the Washington, D.C., area. He provides fraud examinations, performs tracing of funds, prepares and rebuts damage analysis, and consults with attorneys in civil and criminal litigation. Mr. Barsky is a graduate of the American University and has more than 20 years of experience in forensic accounting services.

CHAPTER 11

A Taxing Problem

ANDREW H. KAUTZ

A ngela Bauer was the youngest of six children and the only girl. She wasn't particularly attractive, but she made up for that with a pleasant nature, and people warmed to her quickly. She was also a social person, quick to join others for coffee or a drink after work, and was well liked by her coworkers. Unfortunately, her social skills did not carry over into her academic life. She didn't graduate from high school, but she eventually obtained a GED. In later years, she managed to finish a few bookkeeping and business courses at a local community college, but she never completed the degree requirements.

Despite her limited education, Angela managed to gain an understanding of how businesses operate, and she built a career working for small construction companies. She was known as someone who was always willing to help, charming enough to convince most people that she was a capable and loyal employee.

Angela met her husband, Don, when they were both would-be students at the community college. Don may not have known it at the time, but he was a perfect match for Angela. His easygoing, almost naive, approach to life fit well with her take-charge nature. As Don would later remark, "Angela would give me my allowance, and that's what I could spend myself. She handled everything else." Don worked as a telephone adjuster for a small insurance company. It was not a glamorous job, nor very challenging, but it suited him. By the time they were in their early 40s, Angela and Don had two children and had settled into a comfortable existence. Like most middle-class parents, they were determined to give their children a better life. The drive to provide for her children was very strong in Angela, and anyone that knew her could see that her kids truly were the center of her world.

Angela worked for Agassiz, a midsize construction company, for over 10 years, starting as a clerk and working her way up to the accounts payable area. Her duties included issuing checks to vendors, but she had no check signing authority. She later left Agassiz to take a better-paying job a year before the fraud was discovered.

Agassiz is a closely held collection of companies involved in road and commercial building construction. It is highly respected in the industry and known for its quality work. The owners have always believed that their success is directly attributable to the hard work and dedication of their more than 200 employees. The family-owned nature of the business permeates the work environment and has created a high degree of trust and reliance on individuals. While employees are expected to give 100% to the company, they are rewarded when those efforts succeed.

Agassiz's operations had expanded over the years, but its internal controls had not grown with the organization. This was especially true in the accounting area, where employees had sole control over many functions, often with little oversight and a great deal of responsibility.

OFF THE RECORD

My first contact at Agassiz was with the senior administrator, Diane Stapleton. She had been with the company for over 20 years. My call to Agassiz was prompted by a notice I had received regarding a potential employee dishonesty claim. Diane was upset by the fact that someone may have stolen from the company, while, at the same time, she had trouble believing it was true. As in many cases of employee fraud, the scheme was discovered completely by accident. A government auditor had been winding up a review of Agassiz's books when she questioned an amount recorded as a sales tax payment. The government had no record of having received the amount, yet the company's books showed that it had been paid. Diane's first inkling of a problem came when she couldn't find the check or any documentation to support the payment. She knew that the records were up to date, and since the missing check had been issued over a year earlier, there was no reason for it not to be on file. Diane told the auditor she would do some more digging and get back to her with more information. What Diane didn't know was that she was on the brink of uncovering a fraud that would occupy her time for the next several months and shake her trust in coworkers for many more.

When she could not find the check, Diane telephoned Angela at her new job. Even though Angela had left Agassiz almost a year earlier, Diane often called her with questions because it saved her some time—and she welcomed the opportunity to talk with her old friend. They had worked together for 10 years and she had relied heavily on Angela, especially in regard to accounts payable. After a few minutes of catching up, Diane asked about the payment the auditor was questioning. Not surprisingly, Angela wasn't much help, and she told Diane that she couldn't recall anything about it. What was surprising was the fact that Angela abruptly cut off the conversation, saying that she was very busy.

Diane was frustrated. Not only had she spent most of the day with the government auditor, she now had to spend more time tracking down a missing check. Then it hit her: She could call the bank and have it send over a copy. It would be faster than trying to locate it by herself.

When she picked up the fax from the bank the next day, any frustration she still felt was quickly replaced by confusion. There on the payee line, where she expected to see "Ministry of Finance," was the name "HWC Bank." There was a credit card number written on the memo line, but she knew the company's credit card number by heart, and this was not it. The writing was clearly Angela's, but whom did the credit card belong to? Diane had a thought. She pulled one of Angela's old expense claims and checked the number of the credit card that Angela had used to pay for a course she had attended. It was the same as the one on the check she was holding. Why would the numbers be the same? What was going on?

Then it finally sank in. The missing check, the lack of backup documentation, the incorrect payee, Angela's abrupt manner: Angela had stolen the money. That appeared to be the only explanation. But it wasn't an explanation at all. They had worked together for years; Angela wouldn't have done that. Diane needed to talk to someone about this, so she headed straight to Bill's office.

Bill Morgan was one of the two owners of Agassiz. When Bill heard Diane's story, he didn't know what to say. He treated his employees like family, and he couldn't even fathom that one would steal from him. He took another look at the check and compared it to the credit card number on the expense report; there was no mistaking what he was seeing. He looked up from his desk and said to Diane, "See what you can find out without raising any flags."

Digging Up the Dirt

Diane was not quite sure what to do next. She reasoned that since the check had been disguised as a tax payment, she would check the records for other similar items. While she had hoped that she wouldn't find anything else, Diane had a sick feeling that there would be more. It didn't take long for her fears to be realized, as she quickly determined that another "tax payment" was missing from the files. When she reported this to Bill, they both knew what had to come next. Bill looked at her and said, "Let's go back as far as we can and look at all the companies Angela was involved with."

Diane rolled up her sleeves and got to work. She pulled all the bank statements for the three companies for which Angela had been responsible and reviewed them for missing checks. This was no minor feat as many of the records were in a large trailer that was used for storing old files. Investigating a former coworker—a friend—was unpleasant enough, and the visits to the trailer just made it worse. As Diane worked her way through the pile of statements, she discovered several checks with white-out in the payee area. The payee name written on top matched what the records showed, but there was obviously something else underneath.

Each time Diane determined that a check was missing or found one with White-Out, she made a copy of the bank statement and requested the check from the bank. It wasn't long before one of the checks that the bank faxed back showed "Angela Bauer" as the payee. Any lingering doubts that Diane had were completely wiped out when she saw that name. After looking through several boxes of bank statements, cleared checks, and accounting records, Diane noticed that in one month there were two disbursements payable to the HWC Bank for Bill's company credit card. When she turned the checks over and examined the reverse side, she noticed that one had a teller stamp while the other did not. She knew that the credit card payment was always made in person by Angela or someone else from the office, so there should be a manual teller stamp on any legitimate payment.

Determined to get to the bottom of this, Diane pulled out the credit card statements and found the one for the corresponding month. She examined it several times, to be sure, but there was only one payment credited. Now she had more to look for. She went back to the beginning of the pile of bank statements and looked for double payments to the HWC Bank credit card. Each time she found a double payment, and there were several, she checked the HWC Bank credit card statement to verify that the check without a manual teller stamp did not appear as a credit to the account. The bank would not, or could not, give her any information on the accounts.

After 18 days of paper cuts and dusty file boxes, Diane had reached the end of her investigation and her rope. She had determined that Angela's scheme spanned almost six years. It involved 54 checks ranging in amount from $1,181.54 to $25,080.00 for a total of nearly $462,000. Of those 54 checks, 34 had altered payees and 20 were payable to the HWC Bank, which had not been credited to any Agassiz bank account or credit card.

As she looked at the white-out on the checks, Diane realized how obvious it looked after the fact. The correction fluid left noticeable evidence of an alteration but it had never been questioned by the bank. Then again, since Angela had been responsible for reconciling the bank statements, no one at Agassiz had questioned it, either. All in all, it was a devastating revelation for Diane. At the end of her story, she told me, "Each time I found a missing or altered check or duplicate credit card payment, I just couldn't believe it! I kept asking myself, Why? I was angry and felt totally betrayed. This was one coworker that I considered a friend."

The next day, I sat down to my first meeting with Agassiz at their main office. The grim faces around the boardroom table belonged to Diane, Bill, and their in-house legal counsel, Norman Mayer. None of them had been in this type of a situation before, including Norman, who had experience in the criminal justice system. I explained the process for making a claim under their fidelity bond. When broken down into the various parts, bond claims are not overly complicated, but to someone unfamiliar with the process, it can seem like an endless paper chase.

After I finished my presentation, Diane summarized her findings. I was quite impressed. For someone with no investigative experience, she had done an excellent job at "digging up the dirt." She had copies of all the checks that were found in the files and that had cleared the bank. The only thing that was missing was the other side of the equation. Where had the money gone? That was going to be my job. In any employee theft claim, I try early to determine where the money went and whether I can recover any of it. In this case I was optimistic, yet still skeptical, when Diane told me that Angela was living in a very large house on the outskirts of the city. I had been down this road before only to find that the large house had an equally large first, and in some cases second, mortgage. By the time most employee frauds are discovered, the money is usually long gone—frittered away on a gambling or drug addiction or spent on extravagances that have little resale value.

Later that evening I took a drive past the Bauer home. I was stunned to see where they were living. The house itself was not that large, only 2,400 square feet, but the four-car garage, curved driveway, and two-acre lot made it look like a small country mansion. Even with the partially finished landscaping, the property had to be worth at least $300,000. A passerby would certainly think that the Bauers were quite a successful family. With a combined take home income of about $4,000 a month, the only way they could afford to live in that house while raising two kids and driving expensive vehicles was through Angela's "extra income."

From the information Diane had given me, I knew that the late-model Oldsmobile parked in the driveway was Angela's. I wondered whether she was enjoying the early summer evening, oblivious to the investigation that was headed her way, or whether she was sitting in her house fretting over the call she had from Diane about "that check." Diane sent me the information she had compiled, which clearly showed that the funds had been misappropriated. Angela was the payee on many of the checks, but I still didn't know where the money had gone. To get this information, I retained legal counsel to obtain an order requiring HWC Bank to disclose the details of the accounts into which the checks had been deposited. The court granted the order, which required HWC to identify the account holders and produce statements and related information.

The initial package of documents from the bank provided me with just the information I needed. While I had assumed that Angela was an account holder, it turned out that there was another, her husband, Don Bauer. He was named along with Angela on two bank accounts and was the sole signer on a credit card that had been credited with the proceeds of several of the checks. This immediately made me wonder whether Don was involved in the scheme, either actively or passively, or if there was some other explanation. Either way it raised the possibility of recovering from Don, given that he had apparently benefited from Angela's fraud. This would become very important as it would mean that I would be able to recover assets owned either solely or jointly by Don, including his vehicle and his share of the family home.

Over the next couple of months, information from the HWC Bank slowly trickled in. As each package of statements arrived, I entered all the transactions from the bank and credit card accounts into a spreadsheet that allowed me to look at their financial activity over a six-year period. My primary goal was to confirm that each check was credited to an account held by Don and/or Angela. Secondary goals were to determine how the funds were used, locate any assets that may have been purchased, and determine whether there were accounts at other financial institutions. An unexpected result of my analysis was the discovery of two large deposits to one of the Bauer accounts. When Diane checked Agassiz files, she confirmed that these funds were also misappropriated, bringing the number of disbursements to 56 and totaling more than $485,000.

It was now 80 days since Diane had discovered the first check, and it was time to bring things out in the open. Legal counsel was putting the final touches on a statement of claim against Don and Angela, along with applications for orders to seize Don's truck, garnish bank accounts in their names, and place a notice of pending litigation on their house.

As support for what I was alleging against the Bauers, I had prepared a spreadsheet that showed $485,952 had been misappropriated from three of the Agassiz companies over a period of six years. My analysis showed that $118,822 of this amount had been credited to Don's HWC Bank credit card and $268,685 had been deposited into accounts held jointly by Angela and Don. Based on the limited financial information I had, I was also able to show that on an average monthly basis, the Bauers were spending almost twice their estimated $4,000 monthly take-home pay. Over six years, the couple had spent between $200,000 and $400,000 more than they had earned. The variance was due to the fact that I still did not have all the credit card and statements that the Bauers held, including the bank account where Don's paychecks were deposited. However, I did have evidence that Don's truck payments and the house mortgage payment came out of HWC Bank where some of the checks had been deposited. This was important information, as it would provide support for our applications to seize or tie up the Bauers' assets. The information was obviously compelling, as the court granted the orders. While this was a victory, it was far from the end of the road.

One hundred four days after discovery of the scheme, Don and Angela were served with our statement of claim and the related orders. Don was served at work, which had to be embarrassing, but the seizure of his luxury pickup truck must have been like a kick in the stomach. The next day I received a call from the Bauers' legal counsel who wanted to talk settlement. Don claimed that he knew nothing about Angela's actions, but he was prepared to turn over his share of the joint assets in exchange for the return of his truck. Angela was claiming that the bulk of the money was spent on gambling. She was also prepared to forfeit their assets. In exchange, they both wanted a complete release. It was difficult to determine whether this was a good deal because I did not have a complete picture of everything that had taken place, nor did I know what their assets were worth. To me it sounded like they were trying to throw out a quick offer and then run for the hills. I was not prepared to play by their rules, so I instructed counsel to continue the action against the Bauers.

BETWEEN A ROCK AND A HARD PLACE

Angela did not defend the action or file any affidavits in response. She essentially gave up. This was pretty much as I had predicted; after all, she really had no defense. She had been caught red-handed. Until this point I only had a portion of the Bauers' financial records. This meant that the picture was not complete, and I couldn't show the full extent of Don's benefit from Angela's scheme. If Don was going to defend himself, he was going to have to disclose all of his financial records, which I could use to strengthen the case against him. If not, I would get a default judgment. It was a classic Catch-22. Don was legally entitled to half of the family assets. A successful defense for him would mean that he would walk away with money that I was hoping to get back. He continued to deny any involvement in Angela's scheme, and elected to defend the action. I had no evidence to show that he was actively involved or knew anything about her scheme, yet he had benefited from it. As a result, it was not going to be easy to obtain a judgment against him. I would need to show that he had actual or constructive knowledge that Angela had improperly taken money from Agassiz and that he received those funds.

In order to avoid the time and expense of a full trial, I opted to try for a summary judgment. As part of the legal process, Don was required to provide an affidavit, his financial records, and submit to an examination under oath. For Don, having to turn over the additional financial records simply made a bad situation worse. With the additional information he provided, I was able to show that over the period of the scheme, the Bauers had spent in excess of $900,000 in cash yet had brought home only $330,000. This left an unexplained shortfall of approximately $570,000.

While every fraud has its own unique set of facts, they all have one thing in common: victims. This case had more than usual. Not only had Agassiz been victimized by Angela, but her family had been, as well. Their children were in for a very rough and undeserved ride in the months to come. Whether Don was also a victim is a matter of opinion. On the one hand, there was nothing to show that he knew what she was doing. But he had lived in the house and driven the truck that had been paid for, at least in part, by the fruits of Angela's fraudulent labor. Regardless of how you look at it, there is no doubt that it was a sorry situation. Don was clearly a broken man. Not only had he been blind to what was going on, but he had been blindsided. In his words, "I'm just telling you that from the time that Angela and I got married to the time I found out about this, nothing ever changed. Nothing drastic enough to catch my attention."

Four hundred sixty-eight days after Diane's original discovery, the attorneys presented their case to the judge. My analysis clearly showed that the Bauers had been spending like there was no tomorrow. During the period of the fraud, they withdrew over $120,000 in cash from their accounts, wrote checks totaling more than $150,000, and made over $250,000 in payments to their credit cards. While I did not know who the Bauers had written all the checks to, the credit card purchases clearly included trips, furniture, expensive clothing, appliances, and electronics. It was obvious to me that that the funds had been used to benefit the Bauer family and increase their assets. I only hoped that the court would see it the same way.

While it took over six months to render a decision, the court granted judgment against Angela for the full amount of the fraud. The decision against Don was not what I hoped, but it was pretty much what I had expected. The court ruled that there was ample uncontested evidence to show that this was not a case where Angela has squandered the money on a gambling or drug addiction, but instead had used it for the betterment of the family, including Don. Given that, the court found him liable for 50% of the funds that had been credited to his accounts, which totaled approximately $193,000.

With the judgment, there was really nothing left for Don and Angela to do but turn over the proceeds from the sale of their assets. I understand that they are no longer living together. Don has apparently left the province, while Angela has remained where she was, but without the "country mansion."

LESSONS LEARNED

This case provided an interesting lesson in recovering losses from an alleged nonparty to a fraud. I have recovered funds from financial institutions on several occasions and even had spouses not involved in the fraud agree to turn over certain low-value assets. The issues are complex and the burden of proof required is understandably high, so there is a lot of work required, and this option is not appropriate for every case. To get the biggest bang for your "legal buck," it is important to retain counsel familiar with this type of litigation. Most important, never forget that litigation is expensive and the justice system moves forward on its own schedule, not yours.

Recommendations to Prevent Future Occurrences

Segregation of Duties

From a strictly "mechanical" point of view, the main reason that Angela was able to continue her scheme for such a long time was the lack of segregation of duties. Angela was responsible for issuing the checks and reconciling the bank account. This left her with the ability to walk through Agassiz's records and erase her footprints afterward. Had the bank reconciliation been the responsibility of another employee, the fraud would have been uncovered shortly after it started.

Update Controls as Company Grows

It would have been beneficial for Agassiz to have reassessed its controls on an annual basis. While the company had expanded over the years, its controls had not. This is a very common occurrence, particularly in closely held companies.

It is important to realize that controls will not stop an employee from stealing. The best they can do is to minimize the opportunities and maximize the chance that a fraud scheme will be discovered early.

It would be easy to end the discussion by saying that Agassiz should have had tighter controls or paid more attention to the finances, or that the auditors should have done a better job, but I think it is more complicated than that. I believe that the real issue involves the trust that Agassiz placed in Angela. They believed that she would do her job to the best of her ability and took for granted that she would not do anything to harm the company. Unfortunately, they were wrong.

Trust your employees, but spend that trust wisely.

Andrew H. Kautz, CFE, is a senior corporate risk adjuster with The Guarantee Company of North America, Toronto, Ontario. Mr. Kautz has over 25 years of experience investigating fraud and pursuing recovery. He has also designed fraud-related policies and procedures and is a frequent speaker to groups interested in fraud prevention, detection, and investigation.

CHAPTER 12

Phantom Links In The Supply Chain

CHRISTOPHER J. KELLY

By all appearances, Tom Kellogg was a rising star in the field of supply chain management. His duties included coordinating the flow of raw materials and components to ensure that finished products are completed cost-effectively and on time, while also minimizing the inventory. Tom had recently held this position at a manufacturer of computer peripherals, providing him with seemingly good experience. He claimed to have received an undergraduate degree from a West Coast university and completed some graduate work in accounting toward an MBA. A large and imposing man, he towered well over six feet tall and had the physique of an NFL lineman. His hair and his bushy mustache were always carefully groomed and his nails were neatly manicured. Armani suits and colorful ties contrasted with his starched white silk shirts and well-polished shoes. He drove a Cadillac, one of several luxury cars that graced his suburban home's driveway. He was a dedicated family man who reveled in the position as coach of his son's Little League team. His employment history was less than ideal, with his two previous positions lasting for less than one year each. However, Tom's impressive credentials, his dapper image, and his ambition were features that most employers found attractive when International Electronic Assemblers Inc., known as IEA, hired him.

IEA is an automobile, aviation, and computer components subcontractor headquartered in a suburb of Dallas, Texas. Wholly owned by a regional private equity fund, IEA emerged from Chapter 11 bankruptcy protection after the disastrous acquisition of a printed circuit board manufacturer. Unlike many companies reorganized in bankruptcy, IEA's management remained intact. The chief executive officer (CEO) also functioned as the primary salesman and marketer. Other longtime members of the management team anchored production, engineering, and finance.

IEA based its business model on the labor-intensive manufacture of products such as automobile and airplane wire harness assemblies and industrial lighting products for various industrial uses. Its primary customers were government entities, both foreign and domestic, and a substantial base of relatively small businesses. The company struggled with the development of profitable customer relationships after its reorganization and emergence from bankruptcy. The lack of profitability forced budget and salary reductions that were painful for employees and management alike.

Liquidity for IEA was provided by a $6 million asset-based loan from American Bank of Dallas. The loan was collateralized by inventory and customer accounts receivable less than 90 days old. The amount outstanding under the line of credit usually came perilously close to the maximum allowed by the loan agreement. The CEO, Matt Kramer, was on the brink of signing a major new customer contract that he was convinced would be the breakthrough required to obtain more favorable financing and produce long-term profitability for the company. Matt needed short-term forbearance from the bank, which was currently concerned about the breach of loan covenants based on financial statement ratios. He also needed some patience from the owners, who thought they might never see a return on an investment that had already been reduced in bankruptcy court.

HELD ACCOUNTABLE

In April of that year, a Dallas bank was alerted by its security software regarding a possible check-kiting scheme. Sirens sounded as the result of a large number of checks deposited and paid of similar amounts—approximately $18,000 to $25,000—processed through these suspicious accounts. The bank demanded that all of the accounts, which had a variety of names, be closed immediately. Although IEA was the payer or payee on these checks, the company was not notified. Shortly thereafter, the owner of the closed accounts reopened them at different banks in the same area. Unbeknownst to the account owner, the Federal Reserve Bank of Dallas identified the newly opened accounts as money laundering suspects. Though they were at different banks under different corporate names, they all used the same taxpayer identification number. Further investigation by the Federal Reserve Bank disclosed that all of the items being deposited into the accounts were drawn on IEA. This discovery prompted a warning call to American Bank, the payee bank on IEA's checks.

The American Bank security officer noted with concern that IEA was not only their checking account customer, but also had a multimillion-dollar loan. He immediately conferred with the company's loan officer and launched an investigation including a field audit of the accounts receivable pledged by IEA as collateral. The report identified a total of $4 million of accounts receivable under the suspicious customer names, out of a total of less than $8 million on IEA's books. The other accounts having the same tax identification number were recognized as suppliers to IEA. As a result of cooperation among the banks, American Bank determined that Tom Kellogg's wife was the owner of the suspicious accounts. She had used her maiden name to open them, and Tom himself was listed as an additional signer. The bank requested a meeting with IEA's management to inform them of its findings—a meeting to which an unsuspecting Tom was invited.

Tom, upon being confronted with American Bank's investigative report, admitted both the supplier and customer accounts were under his direct or indirect control. However, he maintained that the "suspicious" suppliers were real companies that sold genuine components to IEA. Even if these claims proved to be true, this was a blatant violation of the company's conflict-of-interest policy. The company terminated Tom but inexplicably did not require him to vacate his office and turn over his computer for more than a week.

Tom's admitted involvement with these customers and suppliers dealt an additional blow to American Bank's already-diminished confidence in IEA. The bank was concerned about the lack of profitability, inadequate liquidity, and anemic sales growth at IEA even before it had been notified by the Federal Reserve Bank of suspected irregularities. The possibility that a significant portion of the accounts receivable might not be collectible became a source of grave concern. Following the meeting with the company, American Bank adjusted IEA's borrowing base calculation to exclude the $4 million of accounts receivable attributable to the Tom Kellogg–related customers. As a result IEA was thrown into default of its loan covenants. The bank then made demand for repayment of its loans, offset the remaining balance in the company's checking account, and began returning checks drawn on the account. Not honoring checks payable to the company's suppliers would trigger an immediate crisis of confidence among IEA's suppliers and customers, casting doubt on the ability of the company to continue operations and meet payroll. The downward spiral of IEA appeared fatal.

However, later on the same day as the meeting with the bank, Matt proudly announced that a major new customer had committed to orders that would increase IEA's sales and profitability by about 50% over the next two years. This new customer, a division of a respected public company, initiated several large purchase orders, clearly indicating a valuable relationship that would change IEA's future prospects. Based on this new development, which American Bank verified directly with the customer, a decision was made to forebear on the loan repayment demand and to resume payment of checks. The bank decided that it was worth a small additional risk to wait until the smoke cleared and see if the company could be turned around and the loan repaid. The alternative—to liquidate the remaining receivables and inventory—would result in a large monetary loss to the bank and elimination of IEA's jobs when the doors were closed. The private equity fund that owned the company agreed to make a substantial injection of capital to restore the liquidity necessary to meet operating requirements. The capital would enable the company to hire and train the additional employees necessary to handle the new customer orders. IEA was stabilized and the bleeding stopped, but the questions regarding Tom's actions were unanswered.

Fraud Dismissed

I had not heard from Patterson Hewett, managing director of a Dallas-based private equity fund, for several years until his phone call. I previously assisted IEA, one of his portfolio companies, with its restructuring while it was in Chapter 11 bankruptcy. During that project I became familiar with IEA's business and established a good rapport with the CEO, Matt. While Matt initially had been supportive of my suggested changes to the IEA management structure, I heard from others that it was "business as usual." Finding out that IEA might once again be in financial trouble was not a surprise.

As he recounted the matter concerning Tom, Patterson was obviously distressed. "I'm under a lot of pressure on this one," he said. "Both American Bank and my investors are all over me, and they expect a complete investigation." He was eager for me to start on the project as he remembered that I was a Certified Fraud Examiner and familiar with IEA.

Since my prior engagement had been financial rather than operational, my direct contacts at the company had been limited to Matt and to James Porter, the chief financial officer. During the bankruptcy restructuring I recommended that James be assigned to a less demanding position. Matt, however, felt that James should be given a chance to redeem himself as CFO. James continued in this function until being reassigned to an operational area within the company pending the outcome of my investigation. Patterson brought in a certified public accountant (CPA) who worked on other projects for their firm to replace James. This change provided American Bank with assurance that funds were released only for legitimate supply and operating expenses.

On Friday afternoon I met with IEA's senior management team to go over the investigation process. Ken Daley, outside counsel for the company, attended as well. Ken had a background in prosecuting white-collar fraud from a stint with the U.S. Attorney's Office. I presented an overview of the investigation plan along with a list of the specific documents and reports needed to start. I would later schedule interviews with select employees and managers. The IEA management team assured me that I had their full cooperation, and expressed certainty that Tom had acted alone. Ken and I agreed to stay in touch as my investigation progressed.

The following Monday morning I arrived at the IEA facility to find the requested documents stacked on a conference room table. There were purchase orders and invoices for the suspicious suppliers and customers for the past four years. The documents also included IEA's monthly accounts receivable and accounts payable. Custom reports showed the detail of each invoice sorted by account and date, and this information was also provided in electronic form for my further analysis. I had a great deal of information but not much time, since Tom had agreed to be deposed by Ken the following week.

I began by reviewing the suspicious customer accounts. There were six different ones, and all of the purchase orders were identical except for the customer name and logo. The same products were being ordered over and over again. Repetitive orders are not unusual; however, each of these resulted in IEA invoices between $18,000 and $24,000. The interim CFO confirmed that the cut for review was $25,000, putting these invoices just under the radar of IEA's auditors.

I also requested suspicious customers' credit files. I found that each had been set up within days of the others, and all had local addresses that were fictitious—either vacant lots or residences where the occupant had never heard of the company. The "salesman" assigned to all of them was Tom, even though his job did not include sales. The contact phone number for each belonged to his wife. All of these customers had been approved for credit sales by James, the CFO.

I then tracked the path of the "products" through the IEA plant. Each was shown on the work-in-process reports as being assembled; however, none of them could be found in the finished goods inventory. The shipping dock was my next stop. Since all of the invoices indicated the products were sold for "customer pickup," they should have been recorded in the shipping log. There was no record of the products being picked up. Because these phantom customers had been making real payments for nonexistent products, I next wanted to confirm that IEA had received them. I matched copies of the customer checks to the invoices and found that payment was received just before each invoice reached 90 days. Past that time, the delinquent invoices would have been put on the collection list and eliminated from American Bank's allowed borrowing base. After confirming that Tom's phantom customers had purchased phantom products with real money, I was ready to investigate the suspicious suppliers.

I had determined that payments made by IEA to the six suspicious suppliers accounted for a substantial percentage of the company's cost of goods sold. Each of these purchase orders showed Tom as both the buyer and the approver of the order. He also initiated the check request and authorized the issuance of checks on the same day that the purchase order was received. I confirmed with accounts payable that Tom personally picked up these checks to pay the suppliers. Tom's paper companies were folding.

The difference between payments made to the phantom suppliers by IEA and cash received from the phantom customers was $1.5 million. This was the amount of cash stolen from the company. There was also the matter of nearly $4 million of bogus accounts receivable that IEA had to remove from its books. Tom's complex fraud scheme had apparently been a full-time job.

Ken and I met to prepare for Tom's deposition. I designed questions that Ken could use to walk Tom step-by-step through my findings. Tom arrived for his deposition impeccably dressed and accompanied by his wife and attorney. After he was sworn in and answered background questions, Ken proceeded with a line of questioning that destroyed any illusion that these companies were "real." Rather than deny the scheme, Tom admitted that he had initially lied. "Yes, I created these phony suppliers and customers," he said. "But it was with the express knowledge and consent of the company." When asked to identify specific individuals he said, "Matt Kramer and the IEA management team." Ken then asked Tom, "Can you explain why management encouraged you to steal from the company?"

Tom's response was disturbingly plausible: "IEA needed the additional accounts receivable as collateral for the American Bank loan that was keeping them afloat until they could land a large and profitable customer account." He added, "They were willing to let me take a commission in order to create the phony collateral."

Had Tom really been following orders, or was he just using the facts as a justification for his actions? After the deposition, Ken reminded me that Tom had admitted fraud, even if other members of management were involved. The new issue was whether Matt and the management team had been complicit. American Bank had continued to loan operating funds to IEA based on those fraudulent accounts receivable, and the company would probably have collapsed if it had not landed the large new account that dramatically improved its fortunes.

At his deposition, Tom produced his personal tax returns and the most recent bank statements for the customer accounts. The tax returns showed a half million dollars of "commission income," none of which was supported by W2 or 1099 forms, in addition to his base salary from IEA. The only evidence that Tom offered to support his claims of management complicity was his own testimony. Matt and the other managers adamantly denied Tom's allegations.

After Tom's deposition, I interviewed IEA's accounts receivable and accounts payable clerks, both of whom reported to the former CFO, James. They thought that there was "something fishy" about these particular suppliers and customers, but neither clerk felt that he could afford to question Tom. The fact that James signed checks payable to the suppliers and accepted payments from the customers seemed to make it legitimate. Although I was eager to interview IEA's senior management team individually, Patterson, who represented the private equity fund, asked me to discontinue the investigation. Patterson also rejected Ken's suggestion that IEA management submit to lie detector tests. The investigation was over.

A LONG RUN FOR A SHORT SLIDE

I submitted my written report to Patterson several days later. I did not have an opportunity to review the suppliers and customers' bank accounts because the private equity fund was unwilling to absorb the additional cost. Patterson told me that he and his partners had decided to build on the new customer opportunity at IEA and try to make the company profitable and valuable. A search of Tom's assets indicated that prospects for any form of monetary recovery were minimal.

With the additional capital injection into the company, American Bank had confidence that its loan would be repaid. The private equity fund hired a new chief operating officer for IEA so Matt could focus his efforts on developing additional new customer relationships. An experienced CFO replaced James, who continued as an employee of the company in an operations area. American Bank did not suffer any loss from the fraud, so the owners were unwilling to file charges that might implicate IEA's management and imperil their investment. Tom filed personal bankruptcy and moved to Chicago, where he reportedly landed a job as supply chain manager for a computer peripherals company.

I was frustrated because the investigation was incomplete. Tom had confessed to fraud, but the authorities would not proceed without a complaint. The owners and the bank were determined to focus on the future rather than the past. Had Tom acted alone in creating and executing this complicated scheme? Had he planned, if discovered, to implicate management and cause a standoff? Had management been complicit in order to buy time for the company to become profitable? Or had Tom planned to drive IEA into bankruptcy in the hope that his phantom customers would get lost in Chapter 7 liquidation?

The unfinished investigation left me with many more unanswered questions:

- Why didn't the field auditors from American Bank discover the phantom customers? Nearly 60% of the accounts receivable of the company, which served as primary collateral for the bank's multimillion-dollar loan, were fraudulent. When confirming the validity of accounts receivable at IEA, it appeared that the bank's field auditors contacted Tom's wife for customer verification of amounts owed.

- Was it possible for a fraud of this magnitude to succeed without detection by other members of IEA's management team? Matt was not only the CEO but the primary salesperson. Tom had no responsibility for customer relationships, yet his phantom customers accounted for a significant percentage of IEA's total sales. Hindsight is a great benefit, but it is hard to believe that management was totally unaware of the fraud.

- Why didn't the outside auditors notice the growth in accounts receivable while sales were flat and cash was decreasing? The changes in the balance sheet and cash flows over the four-year period of the fraud should have clearly indicated that something was wrong. By keeping each transaction below the $25,000 review threshold, Tom avoided auditor scrutiny of his phantom suppliers and customers.

- Was James merely incompetent, or was he an active co-conspirator with Tom? James permitted Tom to pick up large checks to pay his suppliers immediately rather than using the mail. He also allowed Tom to submit large payments for his customers—just in time to avoid collection efforts for being 90 days delinquent. James appeared to be more ineffective than dishonest.

- Was Matt directing his CFO to allow Tom to generate the accounts receivable that would enable the company's continued borrowing from American Bank? The bank made demand on its loan as soon as it determined that elimination of the phantom accounts receivable from the borrowing base left it undersecured. If not for the major new customer and a large injection of capital, IEA would not have survived.

- Why did Tom complicate his fraud scheme by setting up phantom customers, when he could have simply stolen the funds paid to his phantom suppliers? The suppliers took cash out of the company, while the customers brought some of that back and provided receivables as collateral for the bank's loan. Either IEA management encouraged the scheme to supply collateral for the loan (possibly being unaware of Tom's massive theft), or maybe Tom thought he had a better chance of avoiding prosecution if he could implicate IEA's management.

The bottom line is this: Tom stole $1.5 million from IEA over a four-year period. He provided sworn testimony and submitted personal tax returns claiming $500,000 of the missing $1.5 million as "commissions." Unless the owners sued Tom, the case was closed.

LESSONS LEARNED

The red flags surrounding Tom and his activities should have been obvious, yet he continued his fraud over a period of four years. How was it possible that IEA's management, owners, auditors, and bankers did not detect any of these warning signs? There were many reasons why this fraud succeeded.

First of all, IEA hired Tom to fill a critical and sensitive management function without performing a background investigation. The company should have questioned his short tenure with previous employers. Later it was confirmed that his academic credentials were false or enhanced.

Second, IEA did not have a formal procedure for approving suppliers and customers. The only outside verification was a phone call to the number included with other new account information provided by Tom. The person who answered the phone and provided the confirmation was his wife.

James Porter attained his position as CFO because of his long-term "loyalty to the company" rather than his experience or competence.His entire career was with IEA. His narrow scope of work and lack of professional training failed to provide the preparation necessary to function as an effective CFO. James wanted to please Matt, his CEO, and avoid any friction with other members of the management team. He allowed Tom to set up the phantom suppliers and customers without formal approval, and permitted payments on nonstandard terms.

Finally, IEA's corporate culture discouraged employees from reporting situations that were overtly suspicious. The accounts payable clerk allowed Tom to pick up payments from IEA to the phantom suppliers on the same day that he submitted purchase orders. In addition, the accounts receivable clerk permitted him to deliver payments to IEA from the phantom customers immediately prior to going 90 days past due. Although both of these clerks knew that the transactions were irregular, neither of them reported these concerns.

RECOMMENDATIONS TO PREVENT FUTURE OCCURRENCES

As a result of the investigation, I made these recommendations to the client:

Background Checks

Careful screening of prospective employees, especially those who will have access to key accounting and process systems, is critical. Background checks should always include employment and education verification, with zero tolerance for résumé enhancements or omissions. Prospective suppliers and customers must be evaluated as carefully as new employees. The verification process should confirm their good standing, trade references, corporate identity, and creditworthiness.

Encourage Tips

The company should contract with a third–party corporate compliance agent. Employees should be encouraged to report fraudulent activities or suspicious behavior via a confidential hotline.

Tone at the Top

Management must set standards of performance, honesty, and integrity that apply to all employees. The corporate culture within any organization follows the tone at the top. In an open culture, managers do not intimidate employees into making exceptions to approved operating procedures.

The absence of these controls and disciplines at IEA brought the company dangerously close to the brink of destruction by a fraudster. Although Tom was caught and admitted his scam, he was not prosecuted. It is likely that he is continuing his fraudster career with his new employer in Chicago.

Christopher J. Kelly, CFE, is a director at the Dallas, Texas, office of LECG, LLC, a global expert services firm that provides independent expert testimony, original authoritative studies, and strategic consulting services. Mr. Kelly received his BBA and MBA from Creighton University and has been involved in litigation consulting and fraud investigations for over 16 years.

CHAPTER 13

The Trusting Business Owner

DAVID H. GLUSMAN

In his stylish office, the impeccably dressed chief executive officer (CEO) of American Men's Clothing (AMC) placed the telephone receiver into its cradle and paused for a moment. Joseph Jones's muscles tensed. His mind raced as he considered the demands the person on the other end of the line had just imposed upon him. Then he stood up from his desk, walked into the controller's office, and invited him on an errand to the North Region Bank. At the bank, Joseph requested a $500,000 wire transfer to an attorney in Pennsylvania. The bank officer knew the company's owner well and was aware that the CEO was still relatively new to the company, but he also knew that the owner trusted Joseph completely. They had discussed business with the bank together, and the CEO was permitted to sign all checks and bank documents on his own.

Joseph had indicated to the banking officer at North Region Bank that the wire transfer was necessitated by some quick-moving business transactions. Joseph told the bank officer that the wire transfer was to go to the offices of an attorney in Pennsylvania who was acting as an escrow agent on the pending purchase of a substantial quantity of fabric for the fall line of suits. The owner was out of the country and the documentation for the wire transfer was in order, so the banker executed the transfer.

What wasn't known to the banker or to the owner of AMC at that time was that Joseph had previously pleaded *nolo contendre* to a charge of defrauding his former client. Joseph was a certified public accountant (CPA) who had used his position of trust to defraud clients out of hundreds of thousands of dollars. As part of his plea, he was making restitution payments from his salary. He had told the AMC Human Resources Department that his payments to a Pennsylvania court were part of a child support issue from his earlier marriage. In fact, as would later be revealed, Joseph was not being honest with his probation officer. When he was hired by AMC, he provided the probation officer with a copy of his pay stub, and his restitution was based on that information. Also, when the arrangements were made with the probation officer, Joseph was living in a rented home. He subsequently received a substantial raise, which, as part of his initial negotiations, provided for a very low starting salary and an increase 60 days later to a salary comparable to his experience level and the position's responsibilities. Joseph never showed the probation officer an updated pay stub. This allowed him to arrange for low payments for restitution while enjoying an increasingly lavish lifestyle and a newly purchased multimillion-dollar home. The call he had received was from the probation officer who had just found out about Joseph's real earnings, as well as the value of his home. She made a demand that he could not meet on his own. Joseph would have to make alternative arrangements.

American Men's Clothing was founded in 1946 by cousins Albert, Marvin, and Charlie Schwartz, who were tailors. Years later, Marvin died and his portion of the company had been purchased from his estate. Charlie died shortly after Joseph was hired to run the company and keep it alive after all of the cousins had passed away. Charlie had been impressed when he met Joseph and recommended that Albert hire him to work for AMC.

AMC was a high-quality manufacturer of men's suits, some women's business outfits, and men's separates. It was one of the few remaining such manufacturers that had all of the manufacturing facilities in the United States. At the time of the defalcation, AMC employed over 150 staff in the manufacturing plant and the outlet.

The company had grown over the years, but still operated much like it had when the three cousins had started out. Many of the employees had been with AMC for much of its history, and the accounting controls had not changed much over the years. One of the owners had always signed the checks, so Albert thought that employee theft could not occur. There was simply too much checkbook surveillance. In addition, as occurs in many small family businesses, the owners used the company coffers for personal expenses, including gifts for their wives, nonbusiness travel, and related items. The accounting department did not question expenditures for the top brass.

WHERE THERE'S A WILL, THERE'S A WAY

The following week, when Albert returned from his business trip abroad, the banker called and advised him that the company had nearly exhausted its line of credit and was desperately close to a cash shortage. He wanted to know if Albert was in a position to put up additional collateral to extend the corporate line of credit. This confused Albert, as he was sure there was at least an additional $500,000 available in the line of credit. After reviewing company financial records with the controller, Albert was advised of the transfer that Joseph had authorized during his absence. He was flabbergasted. Albert knew there was no reason for a wire transfer to an attorney in Pennsylvania. His pulse quickened as he thought about the current condition of his company. He placed a call to his longtime trusted attorney, Bruce Roth.

I was just finishing my morning cup of coffee at my desk on the 24th floor of 1601 Market Street when I received a call from one of my partners. I was the director of Litigation Support Services at the firm.

"Come down to my office. I have an attorney named Bruce Roth on the phone, and he needs us to do some checking for him right away. He thinks his client, a menswear clothing store owner, may have been ripped off by an employee." A short telephone conversation with legal counsel revealed the essence of the concerns and helped me set the initial course of action.

I started organizing the forensic accounting engagement at AMC just a few hours later. It was the beginning of Memorial Day weekend, and my initial thoughts were to safeguard the assets of the company, making sure the financial records could be secured, and schedule the staff to leave for the job site on Monday morning. I arranged for a private guard service to be put in place right away. I was advised that the primary suspect in the misappropriation was away for the holiday weekend and wasn't expected to return to the company headquarters until Wednesday morning.

The initial concerns that related to the shortage in the line of credit expanded within a very short period of time. Even before I started investigating the details of the defalcation, I initiated an investigation into the background of Joseph, CEO and suspect. Together with the attorney, we determined that he had a criminal record. Then something eerie happened. Without being alerted to the possible fraud, a former employee faxed the owner of AMC a photocopy of a newspaper article that had appeared in a Pennsylvania paper explaining Joseph's previous *nolo contendre* plea.

When Albert, who at that point was the sole owner and chairman of the board of AMC, asked the controller whether he knew anything about a $500,000 wire transfer, he acknowledged that he had accompanied Joseph to the bank the previous week. When Albert asked the controller why he had done that, he replied, "Mr. Schwartz, you told me to trust him; you told me that he had your full faith and trust and that I was to follow his orders explicitly. I have done that since the day you hired him."

During the holiday weekend, additional calls with legal counsel led us to also understand the degree to which Joseph had ingratiated himself with the chairman of AMC. Albert had rewritten his will less than a year earlier and had made Joseph a 10% owner of the company upon his death. We worked with Albert's lawyer over the weekend to add a codicil to the will, eliminating Joseph from any eventual inheritance.

THE BIG IDEA™

Our preliminary discussions and review of documents revealed Joseph's history of deception and a long list of misappropriated funds that severely undermined the company's financial stability. We determined that the purpose of the attempted wire transfer was to make restitution for the prior defalcation that Joseph had committed at his previous company. This was not known by AMC or Albert, despite the routine background check conducted by AMC attorneys. In addition, numerous payments were made to a female friend of Joseph, authorized by the CEO as casual labor, when in fact no work had been performed. There were payments to contractors for maintenance and improvements made to Joseph's new home, which was determined to be worth $1.8 million based on an appraisal. The original purchase price was $300,000 and the house had been extensively renovated and expanded in the meantime. Joseph routinely submitted exorbitant expense account statements without supporting receipts. He gave himself unauthorized salary increases, in addition to several salary advances that were provided to him under rushed circumstances. Joseph initiated payments to the controller and other employees to obtain their participation in the deception. AMC's telephone expenses included seven cell phones, including Joseph's own, his girlfriends' (2), his ex-wife's, and his three children's, totaling over $600 per month for almost three years.

In just over 30 months, Joseph had misappropriated over $1.4 million from the company he was entrusted to lead. By utilizing a variety of techniques over the Memorial Day weekend, I was able to determine most of the issues that had been revealed in the preliminary discussions in significant detail.

With IDEA™ software, I performed an analysis of the accounts payable and cash disbursement records for the entire time frame of Joseph's employment at AMC. IDEA allowed me to perform an analysis of several million transactions without spending significant staff time. By utilizing IDEA, we were able to perform cross-reference checks between vendor names, vendor addresses, telephone numbers, and, in the case of payroll records, Social Security numbers.

The use of the IDEA software allowed for a complete computer-based analysis of the various transactions that were initially uncovered. My interview with the controller, as well as an interview with the director of human resources and the head of the accounts payable department, allowed for a fairly rapid understanding of the various methods that were used and the places that would most likely reveal the depth and scope of the employee defalcation orchestrated by Joseph.

Buried among the repairs and maintenance expenses for the company's two physical locations were payments for expenditures ranging from routine weekly lawn service to the installation of a state-of-the-art bathroom/spa facility in Joseph's home. Additional expenditures included fencing, a security system (both the installation as well as the monthly monitoring expenses), and a telephone system.

"Casual labor"—a category that is utilized for hiring temporary workers for moving large quantities of finished goods—was used for part of the fraud. The documentation that had been provided to the accounts payable department included photocopies of money orders. The money orders had been purchased by Joseph in denominations ranging from $25 to $100. He made photocopies of the money orders (often 5 to 10 at a time) and submitted them for reimbursement of his payment for "casual labor." In fact, when the banks were questioned with regard to the ultimate disposition of the money orders, it was determined that Joseph had purchased them, made the photocopies, and deposited each of the money orders back in his own bank account, generally within a 24- to 48-hour period. "Casual labor," which previously ran between $3,000 and $5,000 per year, was now costing between $20,000 and $25,000 under Joseph's method of reimbursement. The accounts payable department and the controller had previously handled expense accounts for the owners without documentation. So the accounting department thought nothing of routine reimbursements on expense accounts without any documentation. Even on the face of the expense reports, most of the expenditures were clearly without business purpose. Joseph's expense reports often had headings as obfuscating as "dinner," without any indication of where, why, or who might have accompanied him.

GREASING THE WHEELS

Upon questioning the controller, the accounts payable director, and the human resource director, I also determined that each of them was provided with relatively small perks after Joseph joined AMC. Individually, none of these perks was extraordinary or exorbitant, but they helped Joseph smooth the way for each of these individuals to inadvertently assist him in more significant frauds. The controller had a minor emergency in his family; his daughter had run over some nails in the road and needed four tires, but did he not have a credit card to pay for it. With Joseph's approval, he used the company credit card to arrange for the replacement of his daughter's tires. When the bill came in, the controller attempted to repay the company for the borrowed money, but Joseph waved him away, saying "Don't worry, you worked a lot that month; it's on the house." Although the man indicated that he felt slightly uncomfortable with the company taking responsibility for his personal expenses, he accepted Joseph's generosity.

The accounts payable supervisor was provided with a vacation package on AMC's tab when, instead of paying for four or five hours of overtime during a particularly difficult period, Joseph suggested that the supervisor and his wife "go somewhere warm." Then he scheduled a flight and a weeklong vacation in the Caribbean, all expenses included. The human resources director was also given an extra week of vacation time at one point. When she indicated that she wasn't going to make any plans because her budget was tight, Joseph again offered to pay for the airfare and accommodations at the same Caribbean resort he had previously used for the accounts payable manager.

The documentation of each of these items was completed by obtaining photocopies of the underlying checks and/or other records, and preparing them for submission to the insurance company. Fortunately, AMC had fidelity bond insurance during Joseph's entire tenure.

During the second week of my investigation at AMC, I received a telephone call from legal counsel for the company indicating that I was going to be visited at company headquarters by an FBI agent. The bank officer, upon learning that the transfer that he had authorized was, in fact, fraudulent, had notified his manager. Because a federal bank institution was involved, the bank's legal counsel decided it was appropriate to notify the federal regulatory authorities, who would then notify the FBI. During the ensuing meeting, the FBI agent asked for photocopies of all of the documentation that I had put together.

When the research on the first charges concluded, I learned that the original crime was a theft from a client, as well. Joseph held a CPA certificate and had a part-time practice. He cheated a client out of over $650,000 by using the client's bank account information to transfer funds to an account he had set up to support a girlfriend.

Subsequently, the federal government indicted Joseph. About two years later, he pled guilty and received a five-year minimum sentence for a single count of federal wire fraud.

A LAST-DITCH EFFORT

While the fraud in this case far exceeds the average amount across all businesses, the losses were not unusual for a family-owned business. In addition, the types of fraudulent transactions and the factors that allowed them to occur at AMC are very common.

In terms of the resolution of the fraudulent action at AMC, I conducted a detailed analysis of all of the company's payroll and financial transactions over the course of Joseph's tenure. A variety of computerized transaction analysis methods were used to identify possible fraudulent activities. I then sought supporting documentation for possible illegal transactions. All of these data were then assembled into a claim that was filed with the company's fidelity bond carrier. The claim totaled $1.6 million. Initially the bonding company rejected the claim under the theory that the company's oversight of its financial transactions was so inadequate that the transactions were not fraudulent. We worked with the company's legal counsel and together were able to establish that fraud indeed existed and that it was properly defined under the employee fidelity bond that was in place. That resulted in a $1.4 million insurance payment (the policy limits). As these proceedings were occurring, we worked with AMC to establish proper financial control procedures and management reporting procedures, which have continued to work effectively at the company.

The original background check was performed by AMC's law firm, but the company never clarified exactly how it had missed Joseph's previous criminal activities. When I uncovered the criminal history, my investigator suspected that timing was the issue. The investigation into Joseph's background had been performed so soon after his plea agreement that the system might not have recorded the event at the time of the initial inquiry by the law firm.

To make the case even more tragic, two weeks after the fraud was uncovered, Albert had had a fatal heart attack on the shop floor. Fortunately, Albert's attorney had written that codicil to the will during that fateful Memorial Day weekend, eliminating Joseph's bequest.

LESSONS LEARNED

Pressure to commit fraud can come from personal financial problems, personal vices such as gambling or excessive debt, and unrealistic deadlines or performance goals. In the AMC case, Joseph was under extreme financial pressure; he owned a very expensive house with a mortgage that he could not afford on his salary. He lived a very lavish lifestyle characterized by the newest and most expensive possessions, including the newest girlfriends. Joseph was also hiding his previous fraud case and was worried about this information being uncovered. All of these pressures led him to commit fraud.

Family-owned businesses are especially susceptible to employee fraud because they may not have the staff or organizational structure to implement adequate financial controls efficiently. A variety of other situations may explain the absence of proper financial controls at AMC. For example, as the company grew and evolved, the informal financial procedures of its early days were never updated.

At AMC, several factors created an open opportunity for fraud. The financial controls in the company never changed, even though it had grown to $35 million in annual sales. The company employed only a controller and an accounting manager. It did not employ a chief financial officer with the proper perspective and skills to lead financial operations. The past "minor" indiscretions by the owners in making personal payments from the company coffers allowed the controller and the accounts payable staff to view "personal" expenditures by the upper echelon of management to be acceptable. The company's founder and owner was in his 70s and was not as active in day-to-day management as he had once been. As the CEO, Joseph could authorize large expenditures and could sign checks without a second signature. He was able to gain the support of the controller and accounting staff through subtle coercion and financial rewards and reimbursements.

The company had fallen on hard times as competition from overseas manufacturing increased. Joseph was hired to rejuvenate the business and restore it to its previous position. He was able to achieve some initial success, which resulted in the owners giving him unusual latitude in financial matters. In addition, he was able to charm the owners and establish a close personal relationship with Albert. The situation of the trusted employee is one of the most common elements in employee fraud. With blind trust, employees are more likely to commit fraudulent transactions.

RECOMMENDATIONS TO PREVENT FUTURE OCCURRENCES

Segregation of Duties

Proper segregation of duties is important so that there are built-in checks and balances whereby a single employee is not able to complete a financial transaction on his or her own. For example, in the area of cash receipts, one employee should gather all of the funds received and prepare a bank deposit. A second employee should verify the amount of that deposit and actually make the deposit. One employee should approve expenditures, and a second employee should make the actual payment (write the check). A third employee should sign the check, reviewing all of the underlying paperwork and documentation.

Check for Supporting Documentation

All financial transactions should have proper supporting documentation. Expense account reimbursements must be supported by receipts, paychecks must be supported by proper time recordings, and accounts payable items must be supported by detailed invoices.

Limit Authorized Size of Transactions

Strict limits on the authorized size of each transaction before a review or countersignature is required. For example, there should be a specific dollar limit on the checks that can be signed by one individual. All checks greater than this amount must have two signatures.

Proper Reporting

With today's computerized accounting systems, it is easy to create management reports that highlight the financial transactions that are susceptible to fraud and of interest to the company's owners. The purpose of these reports is to allow owners the ability to review important financial transactions to ensure that they are in line with established policies and limits. In small family-owned businesses, where efficiency is especially important, this reporting process can focus only on the exceptions—those transactions that exceed the dollar amount or other parameters that management wants to review.

Periodic Audits

The third component of fraud prevention is periodic audits of transactions and procedures that are subject to fraud. Family-owned businesses usually do not have an audit staff that is separate from the accounting and financial management staff. Therefore, it may be difficult for the company's staff to conduct an objective and independent internal audit. This task may be handled by the company's accounting firm as part of its annual engagement. Separate reports on possible duplicate payments and review of the payees' addresses can also be helpful in preventing fraud.

Communication

Another component of prevention is communication. Owners and senior management should clearly express their concern for employee honesty. Management should set high standards for honesty and communicate the expectation that employees comply with them. This will go a long way in deterring fraud and will indicate support for any employees who may be aware of fraudulent activities.

Background Checks

Conduct thorough background checks on all employee candidates. The law firm did not conduct a thorough enough background check on Joseph before he was hired at AMC. It is important to keep in mind that fraudsters often go to great lengths to protect themselves, even fabricating previous employment history and education. To flush them out, it can be important to arrange for a second search of public records by a competent and ethical investigator more than 30 days after the initial search. Review all application information with candidates, ask detailed questions to reveal gaps in employment history and education, and explore red flags.

Conduct complete reference checks—including criminal, education, employment, residence, credit, Social Security, driving record, and professional affiliation and license. Ask schools—not the applicant—to send transcripts, and make sure they agree in all material aspects with the representation of the applicant. Administering psychological and behavioral testing for management positions should also be considered.

David H. Glusman, CPA, CFS, is the director of forensic accounting and litigation support services at Margolis & Company, P.C., of Bala Cynwyd, Pennsylvania. His firm provides forensic accounting and business valuation services. Mr. Glusman is also the lead author of *Fiduciary Duties and Liabilities: Tax and Accountant's Guide* **(CCH, 2007).**

CHAPTER 14

The $13 Million Man

JOHN FRANCOLLA

When Jerry Terranova, a 20-year-old from Chicago, moved to New Port Ritchie, Florida, a suburb of Tampa, a family member who was employed by American Insurance Company suggested that he apply for a position there. Shortly thereafter, Jerry was hired as a data entry clerk in the Corporate Controllers Department of the insurance company. A minimal background check was completed since this was a low-entry position. From the beginning, Jerry was well liked by his associates and his management team. After one year, his supervisor rated him above average and quickly provided him with many new challenges and additional responsibilities. Jerry gave everyone the impression that he had plenty of money. His hobbies, like refurbishing antique automobiles, were expensive. Jerry constantly offered advice on how to make fast cash. His favorite pastime was betting on sporting events, especially football games, with a local bookie.

The American Insurance Company (AIC) was established in 1867 and is considered one of the strongest financial institutions in the world. The headquarters is located in New York City and has representation in 20 countries around the world. AIC sells life and health insurance, pensions, annuities, 401KS, and auto and home insurance. AIC employs millions of people in sales and back-office operations in 30 dispersed locations. The administrative office in Tampa handles the accounting function for the company.

ON THE RADAR

I was in my office in New York City as part of a Special Investigation Unit when I received a telephone call from Dan Murray, a collection manager of a federal credit union in Sonoma, Arizona.

"How can I help you?" I asked.

"Well," he began, "my president has released a memorandum to all employees that any deposit of $20,000 or more should be reviewed and possibly investigated. On the date of the memorandum, I observed that a $6,490,357.69 check made payable to a Magnolia HealthCare LLC and issued by AIC was deposited into the company's account. I tried to contact AIC to verify this check. I noticed that it was being sent to a nearby residential address in a low-income area of Sonoma, AZ. When I visited the address, I saw that it was a run-down single-family home. Finally, I spoke to someone in the Tampa, Florida, office whom I asked to verify whether or not the $6,490,357.69 check was bona fide. An unknown female indicated that she had reviewed the electronic check register and it appears to have been approved and issued properly."

Dan, who previously worked for an investigative unit at another company, found this to be suspicious and asked her to contact the authorizer of the check and get back to him. When nobody returned his call, he reached out to my company's Special Investigation Unit.

"Would you fax me a photocopy of the check?" I asked.

Once I received the copy I would complete a preliminary investigation. Dan placed a voluntary freeze on the account until I verified the check and we agreed to complete a joint investigation.

Next I contacted the officer in charge of the Tampa office and asked if he could have one of his directors provide me with copies of the paperwork authorizing this check. Taylor Dooley, the vice president, said he would obtain the information and deal directly with me. He mentioned that he believed that one of his employees did contact the authorizer of the Magnolia HealthCare check: a woman by the name of Mary Barillo. When questioned, she stated that she did not authorize the issuance of the check.

The next day, Taylor contacted me and advised that several people from his organization had investigated this case by interviewing coworkers and documenting their responses. The employees determined that on the same day, another sizable check for the amount of $6,225,165.06 was issued to Real Estate Investments Professionals LLC on North 73rd Avenue in Sonoma, Arizona.

I suggested that Taylor instruct his employees to stop contacting anyone within or outside the company and that I would lead the investigation from here on out. Last, I recommended that whoever was involved should document their efforts. As part of my investigation, I would speak with each of the members.

I contacted Tom MacDonald, director of accounting in Tampa, to determine what was completed by his unit. Tom told me that Jerry Terranova, one of his employees, had allegedly received a telephone call from our Bridgewater, New Jersey, office, and that an unknown caller wanted two checks issued as soon as possible: one for Magnolia HealthCare LLC and the other to Real Estate Investors Professionals LLC. Jerry provided the caller with a voucher number for the two checks. Jerry told Tom that he did not recall whether the caller was a female or a male. After receiving the fax, he prepared the entries necessary to issue the checks. Jerry then went to his associate, Rhonda Madison, whose job was to approve the entries prior to having the checks issued. She verified the authorizing signature on the two accounting forms by comparing it with a signature on an electronic file. The signatures appeared identical to that of Mary Barillo, the approver. The two checks totaling $12,715,522.75 were then issued electronically and mailed to the designated addresses. When Rhonda was interviewed, she acknowledged making sure that Mary was within her approval limit of $50 million for requesting checks to be issued by the company to a provider.

I called Dan, who answered his telephone on the first ring.

"Hello, John. Do we have a check fraud?"

"We sure do," I replied, "and American Insurance Company will always be grateful to you."

I told Dan that on the same day, a second check was issued improperly to Real Estate Investors Professionals, in the amount of $6,225,165.06. Dan reviewed his online credit union system.

"I don't see a check for that amount and that date," he said.

He agreed to send a message to other banks and credit unions to see if anyone local had deposited the Real Estate Investors Professionals LLC check.

I told him two stop payments had been placed today on our administrative electronic check payment file, just in case the checks resurfaced at another financial institution. This internal action would minimize the potential loss for AIC.

Next, I told Dan that the U.S. Postal Inspection Service was aware of this situation and that they had suggested that I work jointly with them. Dan was willing to help and promised to send me copies of the documentation used to open the Magnolia HealthCare LLC account on East Scenic Avenue in Sonoma, Arizona. He said that the ownership of this account changed from Frank Tilos to Jorge Castera two days after the issued date of the check. Furthermore, the prior address on the credit union records was the same as the address shown on the Real Estate Investors Professionals LLC check: North 73rd Avenue in Sonoma, Arizona.

I told Dan that James Turner, a U.S. Postal Inspector, was assigned to this case and we were planning to visit the Tampa office next week to interview Jerry Terranova regarding his involvement in this case. Then we would interview Frank Tilos and Jorge Castera, his account holders.

THAT GUILTY LOOK

The day of the interview, we reserved a small conference room. James Turner, my partner in the investigation, felt that I should begin by myself and invite him into the interview after a few moments. I contacted Jerry's supervisor, Tom MacDonald, and asked if he would accompany us in the conference room. He entered the room and introduced me to Jerry. When I initially made eye contact with the suspect, I noticed that around his neck, he wore a gold chain that had to be worth more than $1,000. Jerry's attire was flashy, overall. He reminded me of John Travolta from *Saturday Night Fever*.

"Jerry," I began, "you are being interviewed because you were the one who apparently received a telephone call from someone claiming to be from the Bridgewater, New Jersey, facility. Can you tell us exactly what transpired with the issuance of the two checks to Magnolia HealthCare LLC and Real Estate Investors Professionals LLC?"

Jerry said that he received a telephone call from an unknown person which he believed then to possibly have been a man; earlier he had told Tom that he could not remember the gender. This individual said that he needed to have two checks issued as soon as possible.

Jerry began the story: "I furnished the caller with voucher numbers that needed to be entered on the accounting form. Then I received a fax from Bridgewater, New Jersey, and the accounting forms listing the two checks that needed to be issued and mailed to the Arizona addresses. As usual, I prepared the jackets for the two check requests and gave them to Rhonda Madison for approval. She verified the signature on the accounting form and that the two checks were within her approval limit. Next, the checks were sent to the addresses on record."

We asked Jerry who entered the voucher numbers on the accounting forms and who sent the fax addressed "Attn: Jerry." In all instances, he stated that it had to be the person whom he believed to be an unknown male from the Bridgewater facility.

I told Jerry that I had reviewed the telephone records from Bridgewater and another local installation in New Jersey and no one had contacted him requesting the issuance of the two checks. He insisted that someone did telephone him that day, but changed his story to claim that possibly the call could have been made from another facility. I reminded him that the emergency contact at the Tampa office was Rhonda Madison, not him. Next, I pulled out his employment application and the fax from Bridgewater, along with other accounting forms, and arranged them on the desk before Jerry.

"Do you see the similarities in handwriting on your application and the rest of the forms I have here?" I asked.

Jerry agreed that his writing compared favorably to that of the alleged unknown person's handwriting, but he would not admit to completing these forms.

I asked him why on the Bridgewater, New Jersey, fax sheet, his fax number appeared rather than the sender's fax number. Jerry could not offer a reasonable explanation.

"Jerry, I want to point out that the area code of the number listed on the fax memorandum and the area code on your employment application are identical," I said, hoping to break him.

"I did not write the fax document received from Bridgewater, New Jersey!" he swore.

I asked Jerry to review an old original accounting form that was completed by Mary Barillo a couple of weeks prior to the two checks being generated. He agreed that the approver signature on the original form and the two recent accounting forms were identical and that someone could have superimposed her signature on the recent accounting forms. He also agreed that the accounting form shown to him had to be the one that was used to superimpose her signature. Jerry suggested that the unknown person in the Bridgewater, New Jersey, office probably created the duplicates prior to sending them to him.

I informed Jerry that Bridgewater personnel did not have any original forms since the accounting forms are FedExed directly to Tampa. We concluded that the improper forms had to be created in Tampa, Florida, prior to faxing the information to him.

I offered a possible scenario, suggesting that by using the original accounting form, an individual could have scanned the document, creating a new file on a computer. The writings on the new document located on a computer could be modified by name or amount of check, producing an accounting form with the approver's signature.

HE'S GOTTA GO

At this time, he showed concern and asked me if we could take a bathroom break. As Jerry and I left the conference room together, he asked me what was going to happen to him regarding his employment or with law enforcement. I advised him that it was a very serious situation and that the person who was instrumental in issuing these checks could face criminal charges. Then we entered the men's room and he went into a private stall. He was there for a long time without speaking.

When he finally emerged from the stall, he said, "Why don't you hire a forensic handwriting expert to find out if I did actually write those documents to generate the two checks?"

"Why don't we just return to the conference room?" I replied.

It was now time to update James, my partner in the investigation, so that he could enter the interview and begin the second phase of our plan. James decided that he would play the "bad guy" and wanted to take a couple of minutes to interview Jerry.

James explained to Jerry that he was working with me on an investigation for the Sonoma, Arizona, grand jury under an assistant U.S. attorney.

"Jerry, you are a target of the investigation because you are the one who improperly requested that the two checks be issued and mailed to the Arizona addresses. The Assistant U.S. Attorney believes that the investigation will point to potential federal criminal violations of mail and wire fraud. This is very serious," he continued.

James then presented Jerry with a subpoena to testify before the grand jury in Sonoma, Arizona. The subpoena also requested that he provide sufficient quantity of fingerprints, palm prints, and handwriting samples for expert comparison. James advised the suspect to engage the services of a criminal attorney.

At this point, Jerry was unsettled once again. He did not provide any additional information, so I advised him that I was in touch with our Legal Department and that, effective immediately, he would be placed on administrative leave of absence until a decision was made by senior management. Finally, I asked for his badge and escorted him out of the building.

I returned to the conference room, where James and I discussed the case. We agreed that Jerry Terranova was the one who had the two checks issued and mailed to the Arizona addresses. But the question remained: Why would Jerry be part of a scheme to issue two checks totaling approximately $13 million? I suggested that gambling was probably part of the problem. James felt that it had to be more than just gambling. Maybe Jerry felt that if he was already breaking the law, then why not write the check for more than the amount he owed to a bookie? That way, he would make a profit from the deal.

James and I decided that we needed to review telephone records for a couple of months originating from or received by Jerry Terranova's Tampa office. Also, we needed to identify all the players in this check fraud scenario. We would have to travel to Sonoma, Arizona, to interview Frank Tilos and Jorge Castera, the account holders.

The following week, James and I decided that we would go unannounced to interview Frank Tilos. Through reviews of external databases, we were able to determine that Frank Tilos had many companies, one being Dynamic Realty, located on North 59th Avenue in Sonoma, Arizona.

When we approached Dynamic Realty, the plan was that as the business investigator, I would enter first, followed by James. In this manner, if anything went wrong, my savior, the U.S. Postal Inspector, would have enough time to react. The room was reasonably large with many desks and people working. I approached the receptionist's area close to the door and asked the woman behind the desk if I could speak with Frank Tilos. She pointed to an elderly man, short in stature, in his 60s.

The receptionist asked us to follow her to where her boss was sitting. I introduced myself. Then James told Frank that he was a U.S. Postal Inspector. I mentioned that American Insurance Company was investigating the issuance of two checks: one to a Magnolia HealthCare LLC and the other to Real Estate Investors Professionals LLC. I asked Frank if he could shed some light on why these checks were issued.

Frank Tilos explained that he created Magnolia HealthCare LLC with a former partner a couple of years ago. He subsequently bought his partner's share and became the sole owner. Later he transferred the ownership to Jorge Castera. Magnolia HealthCare LLC was an adult care home with no clients. This company operated out of a single-family home on East Scenic Avenue. Frank mentioned that Jorge Castera lived at that address and was responsible for managing the property.

He confirmed that the $6,490,357.69 American Insurance check payable to Magnolia HealthCare LLC was mailed to East Scenic Avenue. Frank said he had received a telephone call from Jorge Castera who had said, "I'm rich!" and explained that he had received the check. Jorge thought that the check was "play money" and jokingly referred to it as "money from heaven."

Frank continued, "I instructed Jorge to deposit the check into the Magnolia HealthCare credit union account. I never expected that it would clear the credit union. I also remember telling Jorge that it was possibly a gift or a settlement from a prior adult care home client that had resided at the Scenic Avenue address. When the credit union rejected the check, I told Jorge it could have been due to the recent change of ownership from between us," he explained.

Then we asked Frank about a company called Real Estate Investors Professionals LLC. He stated that he created this company to serve as a "shell company" to purchase real estate. Once again, Frank changed the ownership over to Jorge. He said that the North 73rd Avenue, Sonoma, Arizona, was his home address.

"Do you remember receiving a check payable to Real Estate Investors Professionals totaling $6,225,165.06 at your home address?" James pressed on.

"No," Frank contended, "I never received this check."

"Are you aware of any scheme to obtain fraudulent checks, Frank?" asked James.

"No."

REACH OUT AND TOUCH SOMEONE

As part of the investigation in Arizona, James was able to obtain telephone records from Frank's residence through a subpoena. Utilizing an external database, we identified additional individuals who could have been involved in the scheme. At this point in the interview, James began throwing these names at Frank. This proved to Frank that we knew a lot about the fraud.

"Vincent Tusso, David Romito, Hilario Romito, and Larry Romito? Do any of these names ring a bell?" James asked.

"No," Frank replied.

"Do you know a Vincent Tusso, Cappios Café, Barter Brokers, or Child's Play Computer?" James listed.

"No."

Finally James told Frank that at the time the two fraudulent checks were issued from AIC, there were numerous telephone calls back and forth from his two residential telephone lines to these entities and individuals.

"I don't know these people, nor did I make any of these telephone calls!" Frank exclaimed.

We asked him if Jorge Castera was in the office or if he would be expected later.

"He's over there."

Once again, the two of us walked to Jorge's work station, introduced ourselves, and began the interview. Jorge confirmed that his address was 1517 East Scenic Avenue. He also confirmed that he managed Magnolia HealthCare LLC and admitted to receiving the $6,490,357.69 check payable to Magnolia HealthCare. Jorge mentioned that he contacted Frank Tilos, who suggested that possibly an insurance company issued the check on behalf of an elderly client.

After Jorge consulted with Frank, he deposited the check into his account at the credit union. Later, when Frank contacted the credit union to determine if the check had cleared, he was told that the check was cancelled. Next, he confirmed that he was the current owner of Real Estate Investors Professionals LLC. When asked if he received a $6,225,165.06 check from American Insurance Company, Jorge denied ever having received it.

We concluded the interview by asking him if he knew a David Romito, Larry Romito, Hilario Romito, John Terranova, or Vincent Tusso. Jorge swore that none of the names sounded familiar. James mentioned that Larry and David Romito had contacted Frank Tilos's residential telephone number on regular bases.

"I told you. I do not know any of those people," Jorge replied.

"Well, then," James said, "I advise you to hire a criminal attorney, since this case is currently with the Sonoma, Arizona, grand jury."

In following the remaining leads from the telephone records, the investigation returned to New Port Ritchie, Florida. We had to determine who else was involved in this fraud scheme. We needed to identify and interview Larry Romito, who had made several phone calls to Frank Tilos. Through an external database we were able to find that Larry Romito lived in New Port Ritchie. At times, there had been telephone calls from Barter Brokers to Arizona. The owner of Barter Brokers was a Vincent Tusso, who also lived in New Port Ritchie.

James and I drove to the address where Larry Romito supposedly lived. I knocked. A woman opened the door and introduced herself as Ella Romito, who was apparently divorced from Larry. I asked if Mr. Romito was at home and Ella began to cry. After some questioning, she explained that yesterday morning a couple of men came to her home and took her former husband away. We found that Larry's real name was Hilario. When we mentioned the name Café Caprios, she said that her son, Michael Kennedy, was the owner and that the café was no longer in operation. She provided us with her son's address.

As we left the house, James contacted the local U.S. Postal Inspection Service to find out if Larry had a criminal record or was currently incarcerated. On the way to Michael Kennedy's home, James received a call confirming that Larry was in jail and had been arrested recently. He apparently had a revolver with no serial number in his possession. The individual James was speaking with stated that Larry—or Hilario Romito—had been arrested several times for bookmaking, robberies, and other crimes.

We contacted Michael Kennedy, a nurse in his early 30s, and the owner of the defunct Café Caprios. When asked of his relationship to Larry Romito, he stated that he was his stepfather. Michael told us that, for approximately six months, Larry took over running the café while he was recovering from a motorcycle accident.

James once again mentioned some of the names of the people in Arizona, but Michael did not know them. We also cited the many telephone calls that were made from Café Caprios to Arizona. Michael concluded that his stepfather must have made the calls, since he was at home during that time. When James asked about Vincent Tusso, Michael said he knew him and his two sons.

"Vincent Tusso Sr. owns a pawnshop and a computer company in New Port Ritchie," Michael said. "My stepdad and Mr. Tusso are close friends. Larry used to work for him at the pawnshop."

The next day, James and I drove to Barters Brokers, a pawnshop in New Port Ritchie. When I opened the door, I saw an elderly man sitting behind the desk.

"Are you Vincent Tusso?" I asked.

"Who would like to know?" replied the man.

"An investigator from American Insurance Company," I responded.

"Can I see some identification?" Vincent asked.

I reached into my pocket. "Here's my business card. The other gentleman is James Turner, U.S. Postal Inspector."

We asked him if he knew Larry Romito.

"Sure, I'm friendly with the Romito family. I've known them for 13 years. Romito was arrested last week by a federal agency for an illegal firearms sale. I'm trying to raise money for his bail."

"Do you know anything else about the Romito family?" I asked.

"Larry hangs out in Café Caprios in New Port Ritchie. My son, Vincent Jr., and his friend Jerry Terranova—"

"Jerry Terranova? What can you tell us about this man?" I asked.

"Well, he spent a lot of time with my son. Vincent Jr. helped the boy fix his computer when it crashed."

James and I concluded that Vincent's son must have shown Jerry how to scan a document to produce two accounting forms with Mary Barillo's signature.

It's Child's Play

Next, we told Vincent that a number of telephone calls between suspects in an investigation had been made to and from both Barter Brokers and Child's Play Computer, both of which he owned. Calls were also made to Romito's mother and brother in California. Vince admitted to speaking to David Romito on the telephone but claimed he never met him. We asked for directions to Child's Play Computer Store.

"It's next door," he said.

"A pawnshop and a computer store side by side. Very unusual," I whispered to my cohort.

Since my investigation was in conjunction with U.S. Postal Authorities, and under direction of the Sonoma, Arizona, grand jury, the Assistant U.S. Attorney handling the case was contacted by Frank Tilos's attorney. He said that his client would testify in substance to lessen his future sentence. He indicated that Frank had received a telephone call from Larry Romito, the nephew of his ex-wife. Larry was trying to obtain guidance on how to establish a new or use an existing corporation. Frank advised that he had two dormant corporations, one called Magnolia HealthCare LLC and the other, Real Estate Investors Professionals LLC. After hearing about the two corporations, Larry decided to visit Frank in Sonoma.

At Frank Tilos's home, Larry Romito told him that he had "legitimate claim checks" coming from an AIC. Larry wanted to invest some of the funds in real estate and to withdraw some of the money. He claimed to have done this before, using a coffee shop in the name of his son (Café Caprios) and a computer company in Florida. The checks were tax free since they were personal injury claims. He also mentioned that he had a relationship with an insider at the American Insurance Company who could issue the checks.

They decided to use the two corporations owned by Frank Tilos. Frank suggested that he would transfer the corporations to Jorge Castera so that he, Frank, would appear to be uninvolved. On one occasion, Larry had Frank fax the exact name of the corporation to an individual at American Insurance Company to issue the check in question. A subsequent check payable to Magnolia HealthCare LLC was received. Frank and Jorge were dumbfounded at the face amount. They discussed this matter with Larry Romito, who advised them to deposit this check. A few days later, they were advised that the check did not clear. They contacted Larry; he told them that there was some problem with the check and that they would receive smaller-denomination checks in the near future.

Jorge and Frank copped a plea to furnish documentation against Jerry Terranova and Larry Romito. Two years later, the Sonoma, Arizona, grand jury indicted Jerry, a former American Insurance Company employee, and Larry Romito on three counts: two on mail fraud and one on conspiracy under U.S. Mail Fraud Statute.

James's assumption had been correct. Jerry admitted that because of his gambling habits, he needed to issue a couple of checks to Larry Romito, his bookie. Initially, the amounts were supposed to be a lot less. However, he felt confident that no one would be able to implicate him in this fraud and decided to make the checks greater in anticipation that a portion of the checks would come back to him. Due to the watchful eye of the credit union, AIC, and the U.S. Postal Service, Jerry was convicted and sentenced. The $13 million man received five years probation and 200 hours of community service. Larry Romito received additional probation time, to be completed after serving his previous sentence.

There was no monetary loss to American Insurance Company, which stood to lose $12,715,522.75. The credit union emerged unscathed, as well.

LESSONS LEARNED

This investigation took several years from start to finish and revealed the importance of involving law enforcement agencies as soon as possible. Through combined efforts, we were able to identify at least four individuals in the fraud and identify another $6,225,165.06 that would have been a loss for AIC.

The investigation revealed four internal control weaknesses, which related to the inappropriate approval limits across lines of business and the check approval process:

1. Approval limits were excessive for employees in the company.

2. The approval system for issuance of emergency checks was not subject to proper internal controls.

3. Fraud awareness throughout the company was necessary. Employees should know whom to contact when a fraud may exist.

4. We should have requested assistance from law enforcement agencies early in the investigation.

RECOMMENDATIONS TO PREVENT FUTURE OCCURRENCES

Although fraud is impossible to eliminate completely in a company, there are many ways to reduce it.

Approval Limits for Checks

Internal auditors should be assigned an audit across all lines of business to establish approval limits by level. Even at the senior vice president level, additional checks and balances should be established. The emergency approval system should be strengthened by involving a quality control group, as well as supervisory involvement. One should not be able to authorize the issuance of over $1,000 without multiple approvals and verification with the source.

Fraud Awareness

Fraud awareness should be a key component throughout the company to assure that the right people are notified when a fraud may occur. American Insurance Company has established, on a yearly basis, a weeklong fraud awareness training. The clear message given to all employees is this: "Undetected fraud directly impacts a company's bottom line."

Fraud Hotlines

Ongoing advertisement of a company fraud hotline that provides an efficient notification process is vital. This hotline should be manned by experienced investigators.

Update Technology

Updated technology helps investigators identify fraud quickly. Information system security personnel work hand in hand with the Special Investigation Unit to establish controls and monitoring tools to minimize fraud with and through the computer.

John Francolla, CFE, FLMI, retired from MetLife after 41 years of service. During his career he conducted thousands of investigations on internal and external fraud. He also trained employees in fraud awareness. Mr. Francolla is a graduate of Capital University and has over four decades of experience in detecting, preventing, and assisting in prosecuting white-collar crime.

CHAPTER 15

They Didn't Know Jack

JANET McHARD

The management of Garden Grove was pleased with their technology manager, Jack Gallegos. By all appearances, he was keeping both the Internet and storefront services of the business supplied with computer hardware and software. But Jack was good at hiding things. It turns out that Garden Grove didn't know Jack.

Jack was 23 years old when he responded to Garden Grove's ad seeking an information technology (IT) manager. On his résumé, he listed a bachelor's degree in business with an emphasis in management of information systems. The résumé also sported logos indicating he was certified in both Microsoft and Cisco computer systems and networks. For so young a professional, he appeared to have had a remarkable education and career.

Jack loved muscle cars. He even owned a restored classic Mustang with a shiny black coat and purple flames whipping down the sides. This was not a vehicle to commute in; this was to show off, to take to car shows, and to brag about. Jack even posted a picture of it on his Web site.

When he applied to Garden Grove, he stapled his résumé to his application rather than providing the information requested. He did not furnish contact numbers for his previous employers, his supervisors' names, or the reasons for leaving. But Jack did sign the application, giving Garden Grove explicit permission to check references. The company did not, which turned out to be a costly mistake.

Garden Grove was the professional passion of Mike King, who had earned a degree in horticulture and was fond of creating new plants. He had spent his entire life in the desert. Having seen many droughts, he developed a knack for making water-hungry plants tolerant to dry weather. He founded Garden Grove so he would have a market for these plants. Mike's particular skill was in maintaining the lush beauty of plants while reducing water usage. Located in the desert Southwest, Mike had found himself a niche that everyone in the community could use. He found it easy to market in communities that were subject to mandatory water rationing. With Mike's products, customers could relandscape with bright, colorful, and lush plants.

Mike and his wife, Sandy, shared the management responsibilities, and under their direction, the company had grown from one small storefront to a robust retail business with several locations and thriving Internet sales. Their inventory was grown onsite at Garden Grove's main location, which also included a retail store.

I didn't know any of this the bright, sunny day I received a call from Garden Grove's general counsel, Lyle Washington. He asked me drive out to Garden Grove and meet with him, Mike King, and their new IT manager, Cathy Delamar.

I worked for a public accounting firm in the desert Southwest. My practice was exclusively litigation support, primarily involving fraud examination and prevention. Over the years, I was used to hearing from potential clients shocked to discover that a trusted employee may have stolen from them. Garden Grove was in exactly that state when their attorney called asking for my help.

When I arrived, I noticed that the gardens were vibrant with flowering plants. The cherry sage and the vitex both were gathering bees by the dozens. I found my way across the lot to the metal building bearing a small "Office" sign.

I was surprised to find that there was no secretary. I wandered down the hall that bisected the building and was looking for anyone who could direct me to my meeting. I stuck my head in a couple of open office doors, only to find warrens of cubicles, some of which were occupied, but no one turned around to greet me. It seemed that the office was truly an employee-only area and that it didn't get many visitors.

Finally, a casually dressed woman in her early 30s saw me from the corner of her eye. She held the phone away from her ear and mouthed to ask if I was the fraud examiner. When she hung up, she introduced herself as Cathy Delamar. Then she gathered some papers and showed me to our meeting.

Cathy introduced me to Mike King, a fit man in his 40s with close-cropped hair. His demeanor was direct and businesslike. His pride for creating new plants was obvious as he told me the history of Garden Grove. Lyle Washington was fit, too, with hair as silver as Mike's was black. Lyle and Mike were both in khakis, with Mike's shirt bearing the Garden Grove logo. We sat down in an airy conference room. Mike, Cathy, and Lyle told me about Jack Gallegos, their former technology manager.

MAY I QUOTE YOU ON THAT?

Jack had recently left his job, saying that he needed to care for a sick relative and would not be back. Jack's resignation phone call coincided with the deadline Mike had given him to provide copies of the Microsoft and Cisco system and networking certificates Jack claimed on his résumé. A short time later, Garden Grove hired Cathy as Jack's replacement. She got to work doing the equipment inventory that Mike had been requesting from Jack for months but had never received.

Cathy's project turned out to be more difficult than expected. At first, she thought the easiest way to proceed was to take the list prepared by the Accounting Department and then find the equipment. It wasn't that easy. When Cathy found many items missing, she decided to examine the purchases to get a better description; then she could just match them up. But when she pulled the invoices, she knew something was wrong and immediately informed Mike. He told me that Garden Grove had recently experienced a period of significant growth. In fact, Jack was the company's first IT manager. Previously they had outsourced the function, but with continuing expansion, they felt they needed someone dedicated to their IT system. Mike and Sandy had just opened a third retail store and the hits to their Web site increased. They were hoping to find some technology solutions for their inventory and Internet sales challenges. When they interviewed Jack, he seemed to have the expertise they needed.

Not long after he started working for Garden Grove, there had been a fire in one of the portable buildings of the office complex, which appeared to have been caused by an electrical problem and was completely accidental. But it had set Garden Grove back technologically because several computers and the backup system were in the building. For the first few months of his tenure, Jack's primary duty was to repair, replace, and reconstruct the infrastructure. Mike had seen and approved higher-than-normal purchases coming from his technology manager and thought the increased spending was as a result of the fire.

I spent some time with Mike, Cathy, and their attorney learning about their company and industry. Sometimes a case is made on the details particular to a specific business. We talked about the mail and Internet ordering systems they used. I inquired about the location of Jack's workspace and found that Cathy now occupied his cubicle. I made a mental note about the isolation of the employees I had seen during my search for the meeting, realizing anyone could easily conceal his or her activities due to the physical layout of Garden Grove's office space.

Next Cathy outlined her discoveries during the equipment inventory she performed. She saw the first red flag when she started looking for a particular server. She knew Garden Grove didn't have any of them from the manufacturer listed, so she started digging deeper and found more missing equipment. Mike and Cathy realized that the server and the other items that she couldn't find had been purchased from Wired World—Jack's previous employer. Mike asked Cathy to pull all the invoices from this business and determine if those items were on site.

Cathy gave me copies of the paperwork and explained why they didn't seem right. She noted that since computer equipment, particularly hardware, had serial numbers, suppliers almost always list those numbers on their invoices. The ones from Wired World had no serial numbers. Then I pointed out that there was another problem: These documents were merely quotes and did not show that the products had actually been purchased. Nevertheless, Garden Grove's accounting department had paid Wired World, and Mike had signed his approval on all of the large invoices.

Cathy and Mike had made another interesting discovery. The quotes listed the salesperson as "Mary" and gave her phone number. Mike handed me a "Personnel Information Sheet" that Jack had filled out when he was hired. The sheet listed his emergency contact as Mary Montgomery at the same phone number. The salesperson at Wired World and Jack's personal emergency contact were one and the same. With this combination of facts, I knew I had grounds to launch an investigation.

WIRED UP

After leaving the meeting, I began my investigation in earnest. I turned to my computer and started by researching the players in this case. I first ran a public records check on Jack Gallegos. I didn't find any criminal actions filed against him, but I did find a civil action against someone with the same name and date of birth. It was a few years old, and the cause was unpaid debt.

Next I focused on Wired World. I discovered that the company did not have a listing in the online phone book; clearly it was not a retail company depending on walk-in traffic. I then searched the secretary of state's corporation listings to see what was on public record. Wired World had been incorporated five years ago and was active but not in good standing. This usually meant that it had not kept up with its annual filings or was delinquent in taxes or fees.

Finally I found that the principal address of the corporation was different from the street address printed on the quotes. The one registered with the secretary of state appeared to be in a residential area. The quotes showed an address on Camino Norte while the state records showed an address on Oakland Drive. The corporate inquiry record listed two officers, Mary Kane and Arthur Holmes. Mary was also the sole director listed.

Mary was a director of Wired World; "Mary" was the salesperson on the quotes; and Mary Montgomery was the name of Jack's emergency contact. Even though the last names didn't match, I decided to look further to see if these "Marys" were, in fact, the same person. I searched the records of the local tax assessor's office, which showed that Arthur Holmes was the owner of the Oakland Drive property, a residential address. The owner of the Camino Norte property listed on the quotes was Mary Kane.

Now I needed to determine why Mary had so many last names and what her relationship was to Jack. Searching the state court records, I found a divorce proceeding with Mary Montgomery Holmes as the petitioner and Arthur Holmes as the respondent. When I got a copy of the final decree, I found that Montgomery was her maiden name, restored as part of the divorce proceedings. I also found that she got possession of "the business Wired World, Inc., including all assets and liabilities," and the real property located on Camino Norte. Arthur Holmes got possession of the Oakland Drive home.

I performed some broad Internet searches hoping to hit on the relationship between Jack and Mary. That's when I found out about Jack's love of classic cars. I also discovered that Mary was a former Miss Kansas, having won that crown in the late 1970s. Up to that point in the investigation, I had hypothesized that Jack and Mary were romantically involved. Now, knowing Mary's approximate age, I adjusted my hypothesis to a possible mother-son relationship (which we found out later was the case).

Some things I *didn't* find in my research were also fascinating; Jack seemed to have fallen off the earth. His old phone number was no longer connected. He had no new listings. I could find no references to him following his departure from Garden Grove. It had been three months since Jack resigned, and in that time he seemed to have disappeared from public view. The police were going to have to locate this suspect if they wanted to talk to him. As a private consultant, I didn't have the legal muscle to require him to show up to any interviews, and I didn't have legal access to the law enforcement databases that might have given me a clue to his whereabouts.

A few days later Garden Grove gave me a copy of all of the documents they had concerning Jack and the equipment purchases, including the inventory Cathy had prepared and the equipment they had apparently paid for but could not locate. She also provided copies of the supporting documents from the Accounting Department, which were primarily the quotes from Wired World, and the cancelled checks used to pay them.

As I analyzed the information, I realized that the invoice number was constructed in this format: yymmddxx. Thus, a quote dated June 5, 2007, would be numbered 07060502. I was unable to determine the meaning of the last two digits. Nine of the quotes showed purchase order numbers that were exactly the same as the invoice. Since purchase order numbers are assigned by the purchasing company, and invoice numbers are assigned by the selling company, it is unlikely for them to match. I also found two quotes that carried identical invoice numbers, even though they were issued two weeks apart.

The cancelled checks revealed their own host of clues. Twelve of them issued to Wired World were endorsed by hand with "Wired World" and a signature written in the endorsement area. Comparison of this signature to that of Mary Montgomery on the divorce documents showed enough similarity to make me believe that professional handwriting analysis might prove fruitful if the case required it.

I also found one check written to Wired World that was endorsed by Jack Gallegos. Three without signature endorsements showed only checking account numbers; the writing of those numbers appeared consistent with Jack's handwriting on his application and personnel information sheet, particularly since he had a specific way of writing a "5" that made it look more like an "S."

After comparing the supporting documentation to the missing equipment listing, Cathy and I identified three overlapping classes of problem transactions. The classes concerned equipment:

1. Purchased from Wired World that could not be located on the premises
2. Bought from Wired World at a price far greater than normal market price
3. Not produced by the manufacturer listed in the description

All of the problem transactions fell into the first category, and about half of them also fell into the second or third. The final analysis determined that just over $26,000 of equipment had been purchased from Wired World that could not be located.

JUST THE FACTS, MA'AM

Mike and Lyle wanted to file criminal charges against Jack. Having completed my preliminary analysis, it was now time to contact law enforcement to see how much of my help they needed. I called the best white-collar investigator at the local police department, Detective Jerry Martinez, and I walked him through the investigation to date. We discussed my findings, my interviews of the employees at Garden Grove, and my analysis and research. He was intrigued by the relationship between Jack Gallegos and Mary Montgomery.

One of the county prosecutors Detective Martinez worked with regularly was a white-collar crime specialist. We both knew this increased our chances of getting an indictment on the charges. Finally, he told me what the county prosecutor would need to take the case to grand jury for indictment. There were two things in particular: (1) a concise set of documents with a summary cover letter and (2) an interview of the suspect by law enforcement. The first item would be easy because I had already assembled most of that information. Since I was unable to locate Jack, the police would have to handle the other.

I went back to my office and began preparing a report for Detective Martinez. My first step was to go back through the information I had collected with an eye toward what would be necessary to prove the legal elements of embezzlement:

- Converting to the person's own use
- Anything of value
- With which the person has been entrusted
- With fraudulent intent to deprive the owner thereof

My letter concentrated on the facts of the case, leading off with contact data for Garden Grove and the last known address for the suspect, Jack. I then laid out what I had gathered, including the information about Wired World and Mary Montgomery. For each piece of information, I attached the documents that supported that fact. I included all of the quotes/invoices from Wired World paid by Garden Grove and copies of the cancelled checks, front and back.

I put the letter and all the exhibits, tabbed to match the references, into a three-ring binder and sent it off to Detective Martinez. Garden Grove also got a copy; they would use this to file a claim on their employee dishonesty insurance policy.

After receiving my notebook, Detective Martinez called to tell me that he was going to present the case to the prosecutor and that he would contact me if they needed any further help. He said that with the information I had collected, he was certain that they could get an indictment.

Two months later, I received a grand jury subpoena. I had been notified about testifying for the Garden Grove case. The subpoena was for an appearance *tomorrow*. First, I called my client to let them know I'd been summoned. It was a surprise to them; they didn't know the case had progressed that far. They asked me to inform them of any updates after my appearance.

Next I called Detective Martinez. He said the prosecutor would have him provide all the basic information of the case. My job would be to be available to the grand jury in case the jurors had specific questions. The detective expected the whole appearance to be shorter than 30 minutes for both of us.

So, the next morning, I donned my best suit and reported to the courthouse. I ran into Detective Martinez in the hall outside the grand jury room, and he and I traded stories until the time came for us to testify. He told me that he keeps my report on his desk and shows it to victims as a guide for what a good case file should look like. I was gratified by the compliment.

Just then, the door opened and Detective Martinez was called in to give his testimony using my file copy of the report and documents. He was in front of the jury about 20 minutes, as I paced the hallway outside the jury room. As Detective Martinez came out, I was asked to go in.

The grand jury convened in a large sunlit room around a conference table big enough to seat the 20 or so members of the jury comfortably. The clerk directed me to a seat at one end of the long table. The jury foreperson was a middle-age man with dark, curly hair. I made eye contact and answered his concerns about the inventory methodology.

The rest of the jurors had clearly been working together for a while. I answered their questions, most of which concerned computer jargon in the inventory listing. Inside of 10 minutes I was back out in the hallway, waiting with Detective Martinez to see if the jury would return an indictment against Jack Gallegos for embezzlement. They did.

Unfortunately, although we had an indictment, we had no Jack Gallegos. It took more than a month for him to be found and arraigned, and another six months before an attorney entered an appearance on Gallegos's behalf. The case is still pending.

LESSONS LEARNED

This case drove home the point that personnel files often contain crucial information that can make or break a case. It is surprising that many times this file is overlooked. I've often used the direct deposit information provided by the employee to show that company funds were diverted into personal accounts. This case showed me that emergency contact and previous employer information is just as important as banking data.

RECOMMENDATIONS TO PREVENT FUTURE OCCURRENCES

Background Checks

A criminal background check would not have helped in this case; Jack had not been indicted or convicted of any crime. However, calling previous employers might have provided Garden Grove with some clues about the kind of employee Jack would be. An interview with his prior employer, Wired World, might have provided the interviewer with information to make a decision either not to hire Jack or to at least analyze purchases from his former employer more closely.

Garden Grove did not require copies of professional licensing certifications. Although Mike had asked for these all along, he did not give any deadlines and let Jack work without providing them. When Mike insisted on these certifications—prompted after Jack had supposedly gone to a continuing education conference but couldn't produce anything to prove attendance—Jack quit. If Garden Grove had been more persistent up front about getting copies, Jack might have gone elsewhere to find a job.

Now Garden Grove requires all applicants to provide employment dates and supervisor contact information for all prior employers. Attaching a résumé to the application is acceptable only if the applicant also provides all the information requested.

Review Payment Documentation

No one at Garden Grove looked closely at the documents supporting payments to Wired World. No one noticed that these were quotes, not invoices. No one was aware that Jack was buying most of the IT supplies from one small vendor. There was no policy requiring multiple quotes or price shopping for purchases.

These days, Mike reviews invoices carefully. He looks for more than just his employees' initials and request for payment. Now he makes sure invoices appear genuine. Mike asks more questions of his employees about the purchases they make. He also checks to make sure the vendors are reputable and legitimate.

Fraud Education and Reporting

Garden Grove has consciously created a safety net to help protect against fraud. They now educate their staff about how fraud can occur in the workplace and how to report any actions that might seem unethical. They have set up an internal communication policy so that people who have concerns can call Mike and Lyle directly. In doing this, Garden Grove has added all their employees to their antifraud system, and everyone knows that fraud is something that Mike will be looking for.

With the changes to its hiring policies and communication methods, Garden Grove knows all of its workers. Had all these systems been in place when they hired him, they might even have known Jack.

Janet M. McHard, CFE, MBA, CPA, CFD, is a senior manager in the Litigation and Valuation Services Department of Meyners & Company, LLC, in Albuquerque, New Mexico. She leads the firm's fraud investigation and prevention team, working with privately held companies, nonprofit organizations, and governmental entities. Ms. McHard is also a popular speaker on fraud-related topics.

The Skim Sisters

ADAM K. BOWEN

From an early age, Ellen Lowry and Josephine Rodriguez were inseparable. Like sisters, these two childhood friends grew up just three doors from one another in the suburbs of Atlanta, Georgia. Both were from middle-class families. Ellen's father was a small business owner, her mother a teacher. Josephine's mother passed away when she was very young. Her father spent most of his time working, often picking up graveyard shifts to make ends meet. As a result, Josephine spent many nights at the Lowry dinner table, even joining the Lowry family vacations on occasion.

When the time came, Ellen went off to college and Josephine entered the workforce. Despite their differing paths in life, they remained close. The two spoke often, double-dated, and even promised each other that their own children would grow up together, just as they had. After graduation, Ellen married her college sweetheart. Josephine was, of course, the maid of honor.

After Ellen settled down, the bond between her and Josephine strengthened. A few years later, when Josephine married, Ellen arranged for the reception to be held at the hotel where she managed front desk operations. Josephine felt indebted to her friend for arranging such a beautiful location for her wedding reception, complete with catering from the hotel restaurant. Ellen had been so supportive throughout Josephine's life; she wished she could repay the favors.

Shortly after getting married, Josephine became pregnant. With a new family on the horizon, she scoured her local community for a better-paying job—one with the health benefits every future mother needs. She wasn't surprised when Ellen stepped up to the plate and offered her a position as a housekeeper in the Atlanta hotel where she worked. The job didn't pay much above minimum wage but offered advancement opportunities and great benefits, including health insurance. Ellen also promised her that she would have a job to return to after the baby was born. Josephine was grateful; Ellen had always been more like a sister than a friend.

Several months after starting to work with Ellen, Josephine gave birth. To show appreciation to her friend for years of kindness, she and her husband named their baby girl Ellen. Six weeks later, Josephine returned to work to find that her previous supervisor, the director of housekeeping, had quit. Ellen was on the search for a new housekeeping director—one she could count on. She offered Josephine the job, which paid significantly more than her current wage.

Josephine was again extremely appreciative but hesitant to accept a job with so much responsibility, especially with her new family. Nonetheless, Ellen convinced her to take the position.

"I'll be here to support you," Ellen promised. "Just like always."

Even Josephine was shocked by her friend's generosity with this gesture.

"Why would she entrust me with such a huge responsibility after only a few months of being on the job?" she wondered. But Josephine was eager to help Ellen in return for her generosity in the past. She would do anything she could to repay her. After all, that's what sisters are for.

ALL THAT GLITTERS IS NOT GOLD

The Excelsior Inn, located in Atlanta, Georgia, is your typical antebellum southern hotel. It had existed in one form or another since 1859. The clientele were upper-middle-class travelers coming to and from Atlanta on vacation. The Excelsior frequently had business clients, as well. A modest sales and marketing department had opened in recent years to attract convention groups and wedding receptions. The new additions to the hotel were such a hit with the wedding crowd that hotel management decided to construct a new 15,000-square-foot convention and reception center in 1989 to host large events.

In 1994, the Excelsior went through a massive renovation and reorganization. The inn was acquired by Premier Properties Limited, a hotel management company headquartered in Charleston, South Carolina. Construction crews spent months restoring the inn's vaulted ceilings, floor-to-ceiling windows, restaurant, and 215 guest rooms. When construction and restoration was complete, the hotel had regained its illustrious splendor. Entering the hotel lobby, guests encountered large, round mahogany columns that rose elegantly from the travertine floor 15 feet to support the ornate gold-leaf ceilings. Crown molding, expensive wallpapers, and designer carpets were installed throughout.

Guest rooms at the Excelsior were wonderfully appointed. Most featured luxurious bedding and expensive Egyptian cotton linens. High-end bath soaps, shampoos, and lotions were provided free of charge. Business centers with computers and fax machines were installed throughout the property so business clients could work during their stay. The hotel restaurant provided a free sit-down breakfast to each guest and offered a sumptuous menu for both lunch and dinner.

Premier Properties also brought an experienced hotel management and housekeeping team on board to take the new Excelsior to the peak of success. I was hired as hotel general manager in 1994 and oversaw the hiring of the remainder of the staff and subsequently the hotel's renovation. To manage front desk operations, I hired a young and fresh hospitality management graduate from the area, Ellen Lowry. The hotel soon became quite popular among travelers to Atlanta. The Excelsior was even featured in a 15-page spread in the travel magazine *Tourism Today* in the summer of 1995, just in time for the Summer Olympics held in Atlanta the next year.

By 1999, the Excelsior was posting record profits. Occupancy rates before renovation had approximated 53% per year. After the renovation and reorganization, the Excelsior had reached an astonishing 92% occupancy rate. At an average rate of $225 per night, the hotel was earning well over $16 million in revenues annually. Premier Properties was happy, I was happy, and our guests were happy.

I left the day-to-day operations of the hotel to my staff. I had the utmost trust and confidence in my team that everything would be handled while I attended primarily to sales and marketing for large groups. Premier Properties set an occupancy goal of 95% for the Excelsior by 2001. I was determined to hit the target. With such a great property and wonderful team on my side, I was sure it could be done.

CLEANING UP MONEY

As the Excelsior's general manager, I had total responsibility for all hotel operations. Although the Excelsior was a well-oiled machine by the fall of 1999, I routinely spent one to two days a week in the office handling the usual guest complaints, staffing issues, and vendor calls. The remainder of my time was spent on marketing, sales, and the future growth of the Excelsior. Despite my erratic schedule, I always phoned my department heads each morning I was away for a status update. One Thursday morning in October of 1999, I phoned the Excelsior's front desk from my cell phone while I was traveling to a marketing opportunity.

My call was answered by one of my best desk agents, Edgar Riley, a young man who worked the morning shift so he could attend night classes at the local university. When I asked for Ellen Lowry, still the front desk operations manager, Edgar informed me she was out sick. Concerned about Ellen, I went on to inquire about the hotel's status. Edgar informed me that a gentleman had been calling the front desk all morning demanding to speak to Ellen. He had been screaming something about his refund and insisting on a call back from management. When Edgar had tried to access his records on the hotel computer, they were nowhere to be found. According to hotel records, the gentleman had never been an Excelsior guest.

I decided to return the call. Obviously the man had an issue that needed to be resolved, and I had always striven to make guest satisfaction my highest priority. I took the gentleman's name and number down and hung up with Edgar. I pulled over to a local gas station to refuel. Atlanta was very cold that October; it felt as if the frost would never melt from my windshield. I could still see my breath as I exhaled inside the car. The gas station attendant ran out and began to fill up my car. I picked up the phone and dialed the gentleman.

A sharp but soft-spoken voice answered and I identified myself as the Excelsior Inn's general manager. "My front desk agent informs me that you had an issue with your recent stay at our inn," I said. "Can you tell me about your experience?"

"Well," the man began, "I checked in your hotel with that front desk manager, Ellen, paid her $760 cash for three nights, and didn't see a housekeeper for two days! It was like I wasn't even there!"

Disturbed that one of the Excelsior's guests would go without housekeeping service for over half of his stay, I inquired further. "Sir, did you inform the front desk of this issue?" I asked. "You bet I did," he exclaimed. "Every day! But they kept saying they didn't show me in the computer and would have the manager call me back."

"Did she?" I wondered.

"Yeah, finally. Then the housekeeping manager, Josephine, showed up and cleaned my room. I was promised some sort of refund that I haven't received. I think I deserve at least partial compensation," he said. I hung up, promising to get to the bottom of the situation and resolve his issues.

While the gas station attendant finished filling up my car, I made another call: this time, to cancel my marketing appointment. Several things about my discussion with the mystery guest just didn't make sense. Why wasn't he documented as a guest in the hotel computer? Why wasn't his room cleaned until the third day of his stay? And why did the housekeeping manager clean his room herself? The housekeeping manager rarely cleaned rooms unless the department was extremely shorthanded, which hadn't been the case at the Excelsior since I took over.

I drove back across town to the hotel. When I arrived, I went straight to my office and began accessing the hotel's accounting records. Indeed, records failed to show the gentleman as having been a guest of the Excelsior. Furthermore, the cash accounting system showed no cash transactions taking place on the day in question. I was perplexed. Could this guy be crazy?

I almost abandoned the issue altogether until I decided to look at the housekeeping records for the room. I accessed the hotel's housekeeping system and discovered that 198 sets of linens and bath towels had been washed and signed out of the laundry for housekeeping's daily rotation, 13 by Josephine herself. But hotel accounting showed only 185 suites had guests on the same day. Where could the additional linens have gone? Either laundry had made a mistake, or there were additional guests who had not been accounted for. Either way, I was determined to get to the bottom of it.

Not Quite a Full House

I have never been a person to start in the past and work my way forward. I knew that the best place to begin to understand this situation was to see if it was currently taking place. The quickest way to determine if the Excelsior had unregistered guests was to pull a list of vacant rooms per the hotel accounting records and personally inspect each room. From my tiny office on the Excelsior's second floor, I accessed the hotel's active inventory. From my terminal, I generated a report that listed each unoccupied unit.

Out of the 215 guest rooms at the Excelsior, 179 were listed as occupied that Thursday. Another 5 rooms had been taken out of service by the inn's maintenance staff, which was routine for carpet cleaning, painting, and other repairs, leaving 31 guest rooms vacant. I journeyed down the hallway from my office to the stairwell and then around a corner on the ground floor to the first room on my list: 106. I inserted my master key and opened the door. The room was vacant. The bed was made. The carpet still had vacuum marks from the last housekeeping service.

I moved on to the next room: 110. Same process, same result. I continued to inspect all of the remaining vacant rooms with no sign of occupation. I wasn't surprised; my team was top notch. Perhaps they had just made a mistake in the linen count that day. I was sure now that the guest who had complained was just wrong. Maybe he had called the wrong hotel, or perhaps he was trying to swindle the Excelsior. People tried that all the time, calling up with crackpot complaints demanding a refund or cash payment.

"Yes, that's it," I thought. "This guy is lying and he's trying to defraud the hotel." I couldn't believe I had been duped by this person! How could I have cancelled such an important marketing appointment to participate in some wild goose chase after a guest that had never even stepped foot in the Excelsior? "Oh well," I thought. I suppose it was better to be safe than sorry.

"Maybe I can reschedule my marketing meeting for this afternoon," I pondered, returning to my office. Rounding the corner from the second-floor elevator bay, I spotted Josephine Rodriguez, the director of housekeeping. She reached down to the bottom of her service cart to retrieve a set of bed linens. Her vacuum cleaner was sitting off to the side. The vacuum's cord was lying in a bundled mess on the floor, as if it had just been used. I noticed the room number next to the open door: 218.

I thought quickly. I just knew I had seen 218 somewhere recently. "On a report maybe?" I wondered. I passed by Josephine and we exchanged the usual pleasantries. I inquired as to why she was cleaning rooms that day.

"Are you shorthanded?" I asked. "Oh, yes sir, several girls have been out sick recently and I'm picking up the slack," she replied.

"Great work, Josephine! You're a great team player." I remarked. She was visibly nervous. I dismissed her behavior as simply a result of her demanding workload and I continued on to my office.

The bright, warm sun began peeking through my window, which overlooked the hotel's courtyard, gardens, and pool. These were the days I really enjoyed making sales calls, when the sky was clear and the sun was shining. I couldn't wait to reschedule my meeting and get out of the office, forgetting all this worry about someone stealing from the Excelsior. I sat down at my desk and reached for my Rolodex. The business card I needed was neatly tucked away there.

As I pulled the business card out with my right hand, I reached my left hand over to begin dialing the telephone. Just as I placed the phone receiver to my ear, I glanced down at my desktop. Directly in front of me was a maintenance request. In order to take a room out of active inventory, a maintenance request must be completed and submitted to the front desk for processing. The request form required several things, namely a valid reason and two signatures from management.

This particular maintenance request was signed by Ellen Lowry and Josephine Rodriguez. The reason for taking the room out of service was "routine deep cleaning." This was a common reason, actually. Deep cleaning usually included a carpet and bedding shampoo, fresh paint, and a service of the room's air conditioner. Premier Properties required each room to undergo a deep cleaning annually. Because the Excelsior's inventory included over 200 rooms, several rooms were out of service at any one time for deep cleaning.

Routine deep cleanings were always performed by an outside contractor hired by Premier Properties. None of the Excelsior's staff was allowed to participate in the deep cleaning of any room. This was a way for the parent company to have an independent annual inspection of each unit to ensure the hotel was being properly maintained. The unusual thing about this particular maintenance request was that it was for room 218. And I had just seen Josephine Rodriguez, an Excelsior employee, working in 218.

The pieces were coming together. I stood up from my desk, walked toward my office door, and exited into the second-floor hallway. I stared down toward the end of the corridor, where I had seen Rodriguez cleaning room 218 just 10 minutes earlier. My heart was racing; I suddenly realized I had walked right by and didn't even notice what was happening. "How many times have I walked by and not noticed?" I wondered. Josephine was gone now. I walked down the hallway, toward 218. I approached the door and inserted my key.

A red light flashed, a sign my key wasn't going to open the door. Only two things could prevent my key from working: Either it had been deactivated by the front desk, or someone in the room had locked the door from the inside. My key had worked just 10 minutes earlier when I was inspecting rooms, leaving the obvious choice for why it suddenly stopped working. Someone was on the other side of the door, occupying room 218.

I knocked. No response. I knocked again, this time harder, louder and faster. Someone shouted from behind the door. "Hold on a moment, I will be right there," a female voice called out. I waited.

"Who is that?" I thought to myself. I heard the door latch swing back, the handle turn. The door opened in front of me. A tall young woman in her early 30s stood before me. I looked around her; a laptop sat on the bed and papers were strewn about the table and floor. The smell of fresh deodorizer emanated from the room.

"Excuse my interruption, ma'am," I said politely. "I am the hotel's general manager, and I'd like to personally inquire about how your stay has been so far."

"Oh, just wonderful," she exclaimed. "I have just been so pleased with the accommodations. I will definitely visit again when I return to Atlanta." I began to inquire about the specifics of the young woman's trip. She had checked into the Excelsior without a reservation on Monday evening, was staying for four nights, and had paid cash at check-in. Ellen Lowry had assisted her in the check-in process. Josephine Rodriguez had cleaned her room every day since she checked in.

I thanked the woman for her comments, apologized for interrupting her, and went on my way. I paid a visit to each of the four other rooms listed as out of service in the hotel accounting system. Each room was occupied by a guest or guests. In each case, I introduced myself as the hotel manager, gathered information about their stay, and thanked them for their patronage. I didn't want to let on that my visit was any more than a courtesy call.

My conversations with these guests were similar. Every guest had checked in over the past week with Ellen Lowry and had paid cash at check-in. They were each paying an average of $115 per night, about $100 less per night than the Excelsior's standard rates. Not only was the hotel being cheated on the revenue from the skimmed cash, but these guests were getting great deals. I hypothesized that the discounted price contributed to the slim likelihood for complaints for subpar service in the way of housekeeping and other typical guest amenities.

I now had enough information to report my concerns to Premier Properties and await further guidance on the investigation. Within days, an internal audit team and fraud investigator from the company's home office reported to the Excelsior. Ironically, Ellen escorted them to my office. Her look when I welcomed them said it all: time to face the music.

Facing the Music

Once the initial meeting with Premier's auditors was complete, the team set out to comb through the hotel's accounting and housekeeping records. The goal of their analysis was to uncover how the fraud had been perpetrated and approximately how much had been compromised. Another goal was to estimate how deep inside the organization the fraud extended. How much was lost? How many people were involved? Who was involved? These were all questions the investigation attempted to uncover.

After the auditors' first day at the Excelsior, Ellen and Josephine were aware their scheme had been discovered. Nonetheless, the investigation continued as every hotel employee was interviewed by investigators. Because evidence pointed to Ellen as the lead fraudster in the scheme, Josephine was interviewed first. Shortly after the discussion began, she broke down in tears and divulged the details of the plot.

Ellen had pressured her into going along with the scam. Josephine claimed to have been compensated an extra $100 a week in cash by Ellen to continue cleaning the unregistered rooms. Ellen used Josephine's personal feelings of indebtedness for her wedding and job promotion to pressure her into assisting with the fraud. Josephine wanted to give her daughter the home she herself had always dreamed of as a child. She didn't want to spend her nights away at work to provide for her family, as her father had done.

With Josephine's signed confession in hand and a mountain of evidence to support it, Ellen Lowry was called in for her interview. The interviewer from Premier confronted her with tough questions about the out-of-service rooms and unregistered guests.

"I don't know anything about this!" she exclaimed.

When the interviewer provided a copy of Josephine's signed confession, Ellen claimed she had been working undercover for the hotel, gathering evidence to support terminating Josephine for stealing. Of course, the evidence showed otherwise. Ellen ultimately admitted to the fraud and signed a confession of her own.

"I feel as if the world has been lifted off my shoulders," she said with a sigh.

Ellen Lowry provided investigators with a detailed journal she had maintained that accounted for almost every dollar of skimmed funds. She had perpetrated the fraud for over a year, beginning shortly before the Excelsior's previous house-keeping director had been fired. According to her confession, the prior director had refused to go along with the scheme, which led Ellen to find an excuse to terminate her. When Ellen Lowry hired Josephine as director, all the pieces of her plot came together.

For 14 months, Ellen had defrauded the Excelsior out of approximately $95,000 in revenue. To entice guests to pay cash for their stay, instead of the more popular credit card used by frequent travelers, she offered them a special discount. The substantial discount, almost 50% in most cases, resulted in more guests paying cash than would have usually, giving her even more opportunities to skim.

When the corporate office or I analyzed key front desk ratios as part of our internal controls, we noticed that the level of actual cash inflow at the front desk remained steady. Because sales for the Excelsior were rising so rapidly during that time, Ellen was able to combine her discount scheme with increasing business to defraud the hotel without raising suspicions. Since her theft was small at first, usually only one to two guests a week, she was able to fly under the radar.

In the end, Ellen just got greedy. When her fraud was uncovered, she was up to over 10 guests a week. This number of rooms exceeded Josephine's capacity to clean and service on her own. Ellen's greed did her accomplice in. When Josephine was unable to keep up with all the unregistered rooms, guests started complaining. And they were complaining to more people than just the Skim Sisters.

Both women were terminated from their positions at the Excelsior and the fraud was turned over to legal counsel and ultimately the authorities. Before trial, Josephine cut a deal with the district attorney. In exchange for no jail time, she testified against Ellen at her trial. Josephine served three years of probation and repaid over $10,000 in restitution to Premier Properties. Ellen was convicted and spent five years in state prison. She was also ordered to pay over $100,000 in fines and restitution.

LESSONS LEARNED

I learned a great deal about methods to prevent and/or detect fraudulent activities throughout the investigation. Most important, I now have a better understanding of the importance of employee background checks. During her trial, it was uncovered that Ellen had been terminated from a prior position with another hotel due to suspicions of fraud.

This was a very important fact; if I had known about it, I would not have hired her as the Excelsior front desk manager.

I also realized that a significant number of frauds take place in environments where strong fiduciary relationships exist. As the Excelsior's general manager, I was preoccupied with sales and marketing calls. Even though I spent two days a week in the office, I left the lion's share of responsibilities for the hotel's operation on Ellen's shoulders. She was able to use, or misuse, my trust to perpetrate her fraud. The one or two days per week I spent in the office weren't enough to address all the issues of a large hotel. Ellen knew that and used it to her advantage.

Properly implemented segregated duties are vital to prevent frauds of this kind from occurring. Because Ellen was managing the front desk, she had the responsibility of filling in when a clerk called in. This often left her working two shifts a day, five or more days a week. With that kind of exposure to incoming guests, she had ample opportunity to perpetrate and cover up her crime. Because only one clerk worked the front desk at a given time, Ellen had no other hotel employees to contend with.

Mandatory vacations and time off are essential to ensuring that fraud is detected early. Ellen's scam was uncovered when she was home sick, a rare occurrence given her dedication to working uncovered shifts. If she had been required to take vacation, or had rotating days off each week, it would have been easier to detect her fraud. Employees should be required to take suitable time off.

After I contacted the corporate office to report my suspicions, I was advised to discuss my discoveries with no one. I later understood why this was important. Fraud investigators spent significant time in the Excelsior case to determine how and where Ellen was placing the skimmed cash. An analysis of bank records showed that she had set up a separate checking account at her bank where she was depositing the cash proceeds from her fraud. She was then transferring the cash to several investment and personal loan accounts she had opened.

If Ellen had been tipped off earlier in the investigation, she could have potentially moved the cash, making it difficult for investigators to track down. Luckily, she had spent only approximately half of her take. Premier was able to recover the remaining amount, in addition to Lowry's restitution.

I also learned the importance of establishing a concern hotline for guests and employees. Unregistered guests who had complaints about their stay and service were reporting their concerns to the Excelsior's front desk — in essence, to Ellen. If an outside line, a third-party concerns system, had been established, then perhaps the fraud could have been detected sooner.

RECOMMENDATIONS TO PREVENT FUTURE OCCURRENCES

Based on the lessons we learned from Ellen and Josephine, the Excelsior changed its policies and procedures to include the measures that follow.

Background Checks

The Excelsior now conducts background screenings prior to hiring employees in sensitive positions. Even though the cost of these screenings can be prohibitive for some organizations, the potential savings in fraud and other losses is often more than enough to compensate.

Segregation of Duties

Effectively segregating certain duties among personnel is vital. Now at the Excelsior, two clerks always occupy the front desk. The desk clerks work on a rotating schedule, so the same two rarely work together twice in any seven-day period. When a guest checks in and pays cash with one desk clerk, the other desk clerk must verify the cash amount received, as well. When each shift ends, both front desk clerks independently count the cash proceeds from their shift and deposit them in the hotel's safe together.

Additionally, management at the Excelsior is now prohibited from working more than one shift per week in a fill-in capacity. Any shift left open by a sick or vacationing employee must be offered to another existing front desk clerk before being taken on by management. In the event that a manager does have to fill in for a desk clerk, the general manager verifies all cash activity the following business day.

Surveillance

Premier Properties also invested in a small, in-house surveillance system for the Excelsior's front desk area. This type of system is a must-have at many hotels to ensure any instances of robbery are caught on tape. Furthermore, the surveillance system, which was relatively inexpensive, monitors each guest as they check in. The videotapes provide an independent resource for management to verify certain transactions, should the need arise.

Mandatory Vacation

It is essential that employees be required to take frequent time off and use their vacation time. The Excelsior now requires employees to take time off. A cross-training program has also begun where, for two weeks prior to taking vacation, an employee will train another hotel employee in his or her job responsibilities. Not only does this practice better prepare existing employees to take on other roles at the hotel, it also puts a fresh set of eyes on each position, which contributes to fraud prevention and detection.

Hotlines

Every company should have a hotline number for employees or customers to report concerns. Since the Excelsior's fraud, Premier Properties has contracted with an outside agency to provide employee and guest concern hotline services. All reports of fraud are forwarded to the corporate office, not the individual property, to ensure each report is appropriately investigated.

Other Measures

Premier Properties still requires the Excelsior to take each room out of service once during a 12-month period for deep cleaning. Now, however, the corporate office reviews the Excelsior's inventory records via a remote Internet connection and selects the rooms that will be taken out of service and when. This level of independence regarding out of service rooms has helped to prevent a recurrence of the Skim Sisters' fraud.

Hotels and other lodging establishments face unique risks regarding vacant inventory. Astute fraudsters realize that with hotels, there is no missing merchandise to count when theft has occurred. Therefore, it is incredibly easy to fill a vacant room, pocket the proceeds, and clean the room without being detected. Now at the Excelsior, a manager independent of the front desk must personally inspect every room that is out of service for maintenance reasons. Additionally, a random sample of vacant rooms must also be inspected weekly.

The best recommendation for managers to prevent fraud in the future is to always be visible, attentive, and involved. Businesses that have managers who espouse ethical behaviors throughout the organization will have less occurrences of fraud than organizations that do not have these individuals. Potential fraudsters are less inclined to act on fraud opportunities in organizations where management emphasizes and enforces ethical behavior standards both internally and externally.

Adam K. Bowen, CFE, CPA, M.Acc, is an accountant with Georgia Power Company, a subsidiary of Southern Company. Based in Atlanta, Southern Company is one of the largest generators of electricity in the nation. Mr. Bowen is a graduate of the University of West Florida.

CHAPTER 17

No Such Thing as a Free Lunch

SUZANNE COGGINS

Patti Clinton was a struggling 23-year-old mother with a 5-year-old son. She rarely referred to his father, and it was common knowledge that she couldn't count on child support. Little was known about her family background, but she was an intelligent young woman just trying to make a decent living.

Patti applied for a position as a front desk assistant at the Family Wellness Practice Center. Though she had no experience in medical offices, she was willing to learn. Her pleasant smile and demeanor led the office manager, Lucy Green, to believe that Patti would be a wonderful match for the practice.

During the interview, Patti admitted that her work history was spotty, but attributed it to constant chaos in her relationship with her son's father. She declared that she was now focused and ready to start a career in medical office assisting.

When the Family Wellness Practice Center opened, Dr. Richard Steever had a vision to provide top-notch medical care. After finding an easily accessible first-floor office suite in an ideal location, he proudly had his name painted on the double doors.

With everything in place, Dr. Steever's practice began. Soon after, his appointment book filled up. He and his staff were overwhelmed. Not anticipating such rapid growth, Lucy scrambled to hire additional help. Before long, the office staff had grown from two to six. Scheduling patients and exams and calling in prescriptions became paramount. Patient satisfaction was high.

THE LUNCHTIME BANDIT

In Dr. Steever's office, there was a rule: The rookie employee covered the workplace while the rest of the personnel went to lunch. Day in and day out, Patti was left alone, manning the front desk while everyone but the doctor ate out.

It wasn't long before she started showing suspicious behavior. First, Lucy noticed that Patti's wardrobe was undergoing a transformation.

"Sandra, have you noticed that Patti seems to be wearing a lot of new clothes these days?" she asked the insurance clerk. "How can she afford them? I don't even have the money to dress like that, and I'm married—with a second income!"

"I've noticed the new clothes," Sandra answered after a long pause, "and she has also been buying her son some expensive toys during her lunch breaks."

Sandra leaned over her turkey sandwich and whispered, "Do you think she could be stealing money from the office?"

Both women made a decision to keep their eyes and ears open. They would not say anything to the doctor because at this point, it was merely speculation.

Lucy and Sandra didn't have to wait long. As luck would have it, later that week a patient came in with a statement that she had received from Dr. Steever's office. Mrs. Dawson was quite upset about her bill. Included in the amount due was a $50 copayment.

"I don't owe this," she explained to Lucy. "I paid $50 cash to the girl at the front desk." Then she produced the receipt. Mrs. Dawson claimed that at the time she paid the copayment, the girl at the front desk took the money but did not voluntarily give her a receipt. "I practically had to beg for it," she said. Lucy apologized profusely, made a copy of the cash receipt, and assured the patient that she would not be billed for the $50 copayment again.

When the office closed for the day, Lucy went to the cash receipt book to try to find the carbon copy of the receipt issued. The book was a generic fill-in-the-blank type. In the upper right-hand corner there was a blank place for the person filling out the receipt to hand-write a number. The space was always left blank. Numbering receipts was not a procedure that was followed. So, she went to the date indicated and tried to find the carbon copy. But she couldn't find one. Looking carefully to see if any pages had been ripped out, she noted that none were missing. Could someone have a duplicate receipt book? It seemed possible since it was available at any office supply store.

Next, Lucy accessed the insurance file. She pulled Mrs. Dawson's chart to see if there was any indication of a $50 cash payment or to see if there were any errors. To her surprise, she discovered that the paperwork for billing the insurance company was not in the file. Then she pulled the master list and searched for Mrs. Dawson's name. She scanned the list three times but was unable to find any documentation stating that the insurance company had been billed for this visit.

The next morning, Lucy called a private meeting with Sandra. She inquired about a backlog of unbilled insurance issues. Sandra assured her that all the paperwork had been submitted. Since completing a daily cash log was not part of the office procedure, they could not check if a cash entry had been made. They did, however, go to the patient sign-in list for that date. A cursory check of two patients that had been seen before and after Mrs. Dawson revealed that there was no insurance activity and no paperwork for those patients, either. Before they went any further, Lucy and Sandra decided that it was time to call in the doctor. Neither one of them wanted to approach Dr. Steever with this discovery. He was a kind and generous man, a physician they admired and respected. Most of all, they knew he completely trusted his staff. He would be devastated. Dr. Steever was committed to his staff, having said on many occasions, "My success will be reflected in your paychecks." Lucy and Sandra contemplated how this situation would reflect on them since it was their responsibility to see that all office and insurance functions were accurate.

After hours, the women approached Dr. Steever to explain what they had found. He was shocked. "How could this be happening?" he asked.

Everyone was silent. Finally the doctor said, "This is out of my league. I'll call the police for advice. I don't want to accuse her if she's innocent."

TRAIL OF TEARS

Soon after, I received a call from Detective Duane Lunsford. He was one of three local police officers who had accepted our invitation to attend an all-day fraud seminar with our Certified Fraud Examiners. As president of our local chapter, I decided that one of our goals for the year was to involve local law enforcement officers in our training. We knew that every policeman or woman knew exactly how to handcuff and arrest someone. But fraud investigation education was minimal. Detective Lunsford asked if I could come by to review the case with him.

He informed me that Dr. Steever had met with the chief of police that morning and the matter had been turned over to him. Detective Lunsford was tall, and wore a starched white shirt with a blue pin-striped tie. The only indication that he was a police officer was the shiny police badge clipped to his belt. The following day we visited Dr. Steever's office. Initially we met with Lucy. Clearly, she felt some responsibility for the circumstances. During the interview, she repeatedly said, "I guess I should have checked her references more carefully."

I requested that she take us through a typical day at the office. We started with the morning appointments. When patients come in, they are given a copy of the sign-in sheet. The requested information consisted of a date, name, the time of sign-in, and the insurance company. There was a column beside that was to be filled in with a checkmark when the patient was called back to the examination room.

"Almost all patients are seen by scheduled appointment. It is rare that we would have any drop-ins," Lucy explained.

Next, I wanted to start an information trail for all patients from the time they made an appointment until their visits were paid. I asked her if the schedule was listed in a computerized module or in a book. No, she said, they were in an appointment book, written by hand in pencil.

I asked if the appointments were transferred to a daily master sheet, which could help me determine the payment method for each visit. Lucy said that the only sheet with names was generated by the appointment clerk who calls the day before to remind patients of their appointment.

Detective Lunsford had already told me about their method of collecting cash. I reviewed that procedure with Lucy, who confirmed that when cash was taken, it was placed in a cardboard box under the reception counter. There was no cash log at all. I then asked how often the cash was counted and a deposit made.

"Whenever," she replied. Lucy said that sometimes they were so busy that there was no time at the end of the day. In that case, they deferred the task until someone had the time. A review of deposit slips showed intervals of up to five days between deposits.

Intrigued by the cavalier attitude toward cash collection, I asked if there was ever reconciliation between the cash receipt book and the amount of money in the brown cardboard box. Lucy said that they had always just counted up what was there and entered it as "cash" on the deposit slip. No effort had been made to show a correlation between the cash receipt book and the money collected.

"Some people never ask for a cash receipt," she explained. "However," she added, "payment information is also contained on the three-part insurance form. The last, or yellow sheet, is the patient copy. The office copy also shows if a patient paid with cash." But I discovered that there was no tracking of cash payments from those forms, either.

A quick review of the cash receipt book revealed a generic, unnumbered, two-part book. Over half of the copies were barely legible and the space for the signature of the person authorizing the transaction was blank. Lucy explained that the top copy was always stamped with the doctor's name. Thus, it was impossible to tell who had issued the receipt.

She sensed my surprise after she described how the funds were handled. Lucy proceeded to explain that the cardboard box was almost like a petty cash fund to them. Even the doctor had taken money out of the box to pay for pizza and drinks for an impromptu office party.

Next, we interviewed Sandra. She explained the check-in procedure, which was pretty straightforward. At the time the patient registered and presented insurance information, a three-part insurance form was completed then placed in the person's file. It was then handed to the front desk clerk, who passed it to the nurse. After the appointment, the nurse handed the entire file back to the front desk clerk, who totaled the charges for the visit and handled copayments, ranging from $15 to $75. If the patients had not met their insurance deductible, the full amount was due, which varied from $150 to $500. Occasionally there was a cash-paying uninsured patient. But these were rare occasions.

The files were then filed in a portable plastic container, which Sandra picked up daily to perform her entries into the insurance billing system. I asked her if she ever ran a checklist against billable visits and the sign-in sheet for the day. She looked at me over the top of her glasses and sighed. "No," she said, "we really never felt the need to do that."

Lucy then helped us by reconstructing the schedule of the office personnel. She showed us the calendar for everyone involved in front desk activities. After carefully reviewing the schedule, Detective Lunsford and I determined that Patti was responsible for front desk collections approximately one and a half to two hours per business day. Because she covered lunch, she was unsupervised during this time. Furthermore, our suspect shared the same lunch block as the doctor. Hence, patients were not seen when Patti was on break. Lucy also indicated that our suspect readily volunteered to cover the front desk if someone needed to leave for an appointment.

Feeling confident now that Patti had been given the opportunity and means to steal cash from the office, we conducted a thorough paper audit of daily patient sign-in sheets against insurance billings. Each business day for the past six months was pulled and a chart was established, matching patient sign-in sheets with insurance claims.

After this task was completed, a clear picture developed. Each week, several patients who had signed in did not appear on the insurance billing. When we discovered a case like this, the person's file was pulled to make sure that unbilled insurance papers hadn't been accidentally left there. When we were satisfied that none of this documentation existed, we contacted the patients to verify that they were in Dr. Steever's office on the day indicated on the sign-in sheet. We were able to confirm with several people that they were, in fact, in the office for treatment. Thankfully, most of them agreed to provide us the patient copy of their insurance form.

We guessed that Patti had destroyed the insurance paper and returned the patient folder to the filing area. She had unlimited access to the records room. Although there was a procedure for signing patient charts in and out, certain aspects of it had not been followed. It was impossible to determine who pulled the chart and for what purpose.

The investigation revealed that every patient who had been seen by the doctor, but did not have corresponding insurance paperwork, had appointments when Patti was covering the front desk alone. All insurance billing omissions occurred between the hours of 11 a.m. and 1 p.m.

The doctor used a payroll billing service, so there was excellent documentation of days and hours worked. Time sheets were filled out and signed by each employee. The office manager had kept meticulous time and attendance records. Next, we created a spreadsheet of Patti's daily schedule. A second spreadsheet was made to show the days and times of the appointments that had insurance billing omissions. We then reproduced the second one on a transparent overlay. When we placed the transparency over Patti's schedule, it matched perfectly. Compiling this information had been a lot of work, but the two spreadsheets spoke volumes. There was no doubt that we had the right suspect.

Detective Lunsford wanted to take one more step. He reconstructed everyone's schedule on a spreadsheet. By doing this he wanted to show that the other employees were not at the front desk when these patients were seen.

ALL'S WELL THAT ENDS WELL

We reviewed our findings with Dr. Steever and Lucy. Detective Lunsford informed them that he felt he had enough evidence to charge the perpetrator for embezzlement. The following day, when Patti reported for work, Detective Lunsford was waiting for her. He took her into a private room and explained that there was money missing from the office and that they would like to talk with her at headquarters. She agreed and they left in the cruiser for the police department.

Detective Lunsford had previously agreed that actions in the doctor's office would be low key. His approach with Patti would be "firm but supportive." He wanted to gain her trust and be able to question her without evoking an emotional component. Hence, there were no handcuffs and no dramatic arrest scene.

Once they arrived at the police department, Detective Lunsford took Patti into his pink flamingo interrogation room. While I was not present, I could visualize the entire scenario—the slender young woman sitting across from this imposing figure in a room designed specifically to wear a suspect down. Detective Lunsford spared me no details later as he explained the interrogation. Patti denied any involvement. Then he left her in the room for 20 minutes, allowing her some time to think. When he returned, the detective brought the spreadsheets we had constructed.

"When I told her that we had documentation that the missing cash occurred while she was alone at the front desk, she started to cry," he explained. Patti then told the detective her version of what happened. When she first started at Dr. Steever's office, everyone was nice and helpful. A month into her job, coworkers began leaving her alone at the front desk while they all went to lunch. Patti said she had never stolen anything before, but one day she needed $20 for her son's preschool field trip. After she took the cash, she realized that she would have to destroy the insurance paperwork.

Patti explained that she did not take money for a few weeks after that. Then she gradually began taking more cash copayments. To conceal the evidence, she folded the insurance paperwork and put it in her purse, destroying it when she got home. After patients began requesting receipts for cash, she went out and bought a duplicate receipt book.

The embezzlement slowly escalated. Patti said she realized that no one missed the money and no questions were asked, so she continued to dip into the cash box. The day Mrs. Dawson came in with the bill for the copayment, she remembered that she forgot to destroy the woman's insurance paperwork. After she explained everything, the confession was written and signed. The following week, Detective Lunsford called me. The day after signing the confession, Patti had hired an attorney and was claiming that the confession was forced. She alleged that the detective had terrified and intimidated her into signing it.

For the next couple of months, I did not hear from Detective Lunsford. When I called to inquire about the status of the case, he chuckled.

"Well, I had to jump through some hoops, but we re-arrested her, and guess where she was?"

"Where?" I asked.

"In another doctor's office!" he exclaimed. "This time we marched in with a warrant for her arrest, handcuffed her, and brought her right to jail."

Because this was a first offense, Patti was given suspended jail time, community service, fined, and ordered to make restitution. Her family stepped in and repaid the embezzled money. Dr. Steever was able to recover about 75% of his unfiled insurance claims by submitting them to some insurance companies with a letter of explanation. The amount taken was estimated at $2,500 to $3,000. The unbilled insurance claims totaled $15,000.

LESSONS LEARNED

Assisting in this case showed me how important it is for law enforcement to have the knowledge and the skills to investigate financial crimes. Even prosecutors say that as attorneys, they know the law, but do not have enough expertise in fraud to prosecute the increasing volume of cases.

The doctor was completely committed to providing the best possible medical care. In fact, he was so focused on that aspect that he neglected to address critical areas in his practice that involved money—the very thing that would permit him to continue to offer the best service. Regardless of your career path or business, it is important to know the risk of fraud and ways to prevent it.

When establishing setup costs for his practice, Dr. Steever had splurged on medical equipment, office furniture, and a state-of-the-art patient filing system. But when it came to the financial aspect, he relied on a bare-bones setup of records and documentation, along with a family member who helped with the accounting procedures. This was a system that had no methods to prevent embezzlement of cash.

RECOMMENDATIONS TO PREVENT FUTURE OCCURRENCES

Establish a Clear Procedure for Collecting and Storing Cash

A cash log with the amount, time, date, and name of the client should be established and maintained. All cash should be kept in a locked box. There should be no reason whatsoever that cash should be removed until it needs to be counted and reconciled. Cash should be reconciled on a daily basis. In case a discrepancy is discovered, it is much easier to review one day rather than reconstruct a long period of time. If employees are aware of this practice, it can also serve as a deterrent. Furthermore, large amounts of cash should not be kept in the office.

Record All Petty Cash Withdrawals

A petty cash box needs to be established with a designated amount of money for expenditures like office parties. A valid receipt should be deposited into the petty cash box for every purchase. That reconciliation should be done at least on a weekly basis. It should be the objective of the office to purchase as much as possible by company check, purchase orders, or authorized credit.

Extensive Cash Receipt Documentation

I recommend preprinted, numbered cash receipts with the name of the firm, address, and phone number. A review of the carbon copies should be conducted routinely.

A procedure should be established for voiding receipts that include approval from a supervisor.

Start-Up Businesses Should Monitor Accounting Closely

For any start-up businesses, it is critical to give careful attention to all aspects of accounting. While I realize that leather furniture and ambient lighting all make for a comfy waiting room, I would rather know that my money and my assets were protected by solid accounting procedures and fraud deterrents. Relying on family or friends to help set up office accounting procedures can be a mistake. When it comes to the books and the money, seek qualified and experienced professionals.

In addition, plan for growth. As in Dr. Steever's case, the rapid increase in patients was surprising for both him and his staff, and he was not well positioned for expansion. Chaotic cash-handling led to destruction of insurance billing documents. The loss was not just the cash copayment. The entire documentation of the office visit was destroyed. Equip small businesses with up-to-date software programs to prepare for growth.

Suzanne Coggins, CFE, is the owner of Lindsey Consulting in Fort Mill, South Carolina. She provides proactive fraud consultation to small start-up companies. Ms. Coggins holds an associate's degree in industrial health and safety and a BS from Liberty University. She has 30 years of experience in worker's compensation fraud and fraud education, prevention, and detection.

CHAPTER 18

The Dirty Custodian

PAUL J. HARVEY

On the outside, Art Dixson appeared to be a simple, hardworking, middle-age man. He was never noted for flashy clothes or fancy cars. For many years, his home was a modest rental apartment unit. He was single and not socially active.

To the few who knew him well, Art was a fan of horse racing. To them, he boasted of winning substantial wagers at a local track. Art was also proud of his history as a state-licensed boxing promoter. His fighter was an impressive 21–4–2 with 19 knockouts. And, known also only to a few people, at one time Art had been a reserve deputy sheriff who completed a very tough training academy in Los Angeles.

Art was one of those guys who seemed to be working all the time. While employed full time as a custodial supervisor in the Unified School District, he also maintained a position with a very large hospital as a contract custodial supervisor. Given his two jobs, his management of a successful boxer and his frugal lifestyle, Art was not a person who would be a likely suspect for large-scale theft of public funds.

Unfortunately, what people didn't know about Art was that at the time he was employed by the Unified School District, he was already a felon. In the early 1980s he was convicted of burglary and grand theft after stealing property from his employer, where he had worked as a custodial manager.

The Unified School District consisted of nearly 20 campuses and several noneducational facilities. It had an enrollment of over 18,000 students and employed hundreds of teachers, administrators, and clerical and facilities persons.

The district was well known throughout the state as a poor minority school system—it was actually bordering on insolvency—and it had become a near-academic failure, as well. After receiving a $27 million modernization grant from the state, things were looking up. Unfortunately, trouble was coming. While it was promising to see 16 of the school sites renovated, the survival of the district was doubtful. The County Office of Education had hired a fiscal advisor, Greg Richards, to oversee and control the finances and deal with a fiery, no-nonsense superintendent. There was little peace in this organization, which served a community of over 110,000 residents. Nepotism, favoritism, and outright indifference to fiscal problems were sending this organization into a downward spiral.

One October day I received a call from my chief, asking me to report to the city manager's office with him and my captain. I had been a police officer for more than 22 years and a fraud investigator for over 16. I had just received my CFE accreditation six months earlier. The district was not a new target for my investigations; I had been there many times before.

The meeting was intriguing. The city manager, police chief, and my captain were there as well as Richards and the new superintendent. The discussion focused on an impending fiscal crisis that could have criminal ramifications and then a plea for the police department to provide assistance. Richards—a retired longtime school administrator and one of the most brilliant men I've worked with—told us what he had found. In the grant to modernize the campuses, almost all of the work was to be done by outside contractors through a project manager. Yet there were substantial budget provisions for services, particularly for the substitute custodial account. According to the district's organizational chart, there were between 35 and 40 regular custodians and no more than 3 substitutes. While the regulars provided typical janitorial services, the others filled in for ill or injured regulars. They also provided general clean-up assistance where the school sites were being renovated.

The budget for the past school year provided $160,000 to cover the substitute custodians. Richards said it was peculiar that this account was so heavily funded. At an approximate gross payroll cost of $9.25 per hour, the three substitutes would cost about $70,000 per year if they worked the maximum 208-hour months. But during his review, Richards said that expenses for substitute custodians for the first quarter had already reached $320,000. At this rate, the yearly cost would be more than $1.2 million, a figure four times greater than allocated in the budget.

In an attempt to verify this anomaly, Richards contacted Art's supervisor, who confirmed that Art had actually hired seven, rather than three, substitute custodians. Later in the day, Richards spoke with Art, who said he had to hire extra substitutes to cover the workload created by the modernization project. Richards found these explanations to be feeble at best. Art bragged about winning a sizable amount of money at the horse track and commented that his business venture involving the promotion of professional boxers was really taking off. Richards told me that he thought it odd that Art would mention these things unless he was trying to lay a foundation for an explanation of recent wealth. Shortly after this conversation, Richards learned that Art had purchased a new luxury automobile, which we later found cost $40,000. It was even more interesting to note that there was no lien holder listed, which was a sure indication that it was purchased for cash.

The fiscal advisor looked at the payroll records and discovered there were neither 3 nor 7 substitute custodians, but actually as many as 77! Investigating further, he found that each had been paid a staggering amount of money. The most glaring detail was that many of them were paid for more than 40 hours per week, yet not a single one was paid overtime. Although they worked far in excess of regular hours, they were consistently and without exception paid at straight time. None was receiving any form of fringe benefits.

Richards then examined many of the personnel applications on file for the substitute custodians and saw that every one had been given preliminary approval by Art. Only a handful had undergone the normal and required process of school board approval. It seemed that whoever Art approved was hired.

Finally, Mr. Richards contacted two very trusted employees in the payroll department. It was then that he learned that on paydays, the district office was so overrun that they decided to hand out the checks to supervisors for distribution to their employees. They remembered that every month for about a year, Art picked up a large stack of checks by 9 a. m. on paydays. The payroll department was most appreciative. Of course, so was Art.

Richards turned to me and said that he had gone as far as he could without tipping anyone off, but thought that what he had seen so far constituted a strong suspicion that a fraudulent payroll scheme might be in progress. I had to concur, and based on the preliminary information, it was reasonable to conduct an investigation.

A GHOSTLY PAYROLL

Fortunately, I got the green light to proceed. Unfortunately, everyone wanted it done yesterday. There were myriad issues to deal with, not the least of which were legal considerations. Some wanted me to apply the idiot test, which says that given the circumstances, any imbecile could see that a crime had occurred—now go and arrest him! While there are many different legal theories that might fit the circumstances, they require the requisite intent. Many also require proof of the suspect's knowledge. Each statute involves elements that have to be proven individually. It was obvious that hundreds of thousands of dollars had been wrongly expended, but this alone does not establish that a crime occurred. There may be serious breaches of a fiduciary duty, carelessness, sloppy accounting, and reckless oversight, but under California statutes, such things amount to civil wrongs, not crimes. It was my job to establish that a criminal offense occurred and that the standard of proof was beyond a reasonable doubt.

I used a timeline to understand the patterns of the system and the actions of the suspects. During the prior six months, the payroll was always closed by the twenty-fifth of the month. By the tenth of the following month, always on a nonholiday Friday, the checks were distributed. At this point in my investigation, November 25 had passed, and the next distribution was to be December 8. This left me two weeks to find and examine evidence and implement a plan.

The first step involved collecting every evidentiary document available. In my experience, these things have a habit of growing feet and walking away if not seized very early in an investigation. Over the next several days, I had personnel files and time sheets removed from the district office, sometimes after midnight. The superintendent helped in accessing the prior-month payroll warrants from the County Office of Education.

Next, I put all of the information in a simple spreadsheet that included name, address, telephone, Social Security number, date of birth, and emergency contact name(s). With this, I could access motor vehicle, arrest, victim, and witness records from police files.

These revealed aliases, addresses, Social Security numbers, and dates of birth that in several instances differed from the employment records. Some of the suspects had felony convictions that should have disqualified them from employment with the district. It was obvious that required background checks were not run on these individuals.

The spreadsheet showed commonalities. Several of the suspects had the same address. Two of them were issued traffic citations at different times for an identical vehicle. One was reported as deceased a year before he applied for the job—yet payroll warrants were issued to him under two aliases for several months. Another phantom employee and his wife were identified as receiving money each month in their real names, as well as in aliases.

I cataloged the payroll warrants from the prior month by name, check number, location cashed, and endorsement information. I found the markings on a cashed check very helpful in establishing how, when, where, and by whom it was negotiated. The data showed that many of the suspects cashed their payroll warrants at the same time at the same establishments. Most of these businesses take photographs of their customers and checks, which is priceless evidence. The vast majority of the warrants were negotiated for cash; only a few were deposited into bank accounts. This is consistent with phantom payroll.

The employees had not been approved by the school board as required. None of the files contained I-9 forms and only a few had W-4 forms. Art Dixon had signed the applications, and each bore his initials. When compared to legitimate personnel files, they were very obviously fakes.

I next entered the prior six-month payroll records and time sheets in another spreadsheet. When I sorted them by the number of hours worked in a given month, I found the most significant patterns. With the exception of just a few names (later determined to be genuine employees), each and every suspect was paid for more than 40 hours a week. All were in whole numbers (no partial hours), and the gross amounts were the same in each month. As Richards had already found, none of these individuals was paid at the overtime rate even though they supposedly worked more than 40 hours each week. Art Dixson approved every time sheet, as evidenced by his signature on each.

Finally, I needed to corroborate my findings. With dozens of possible perpetrators, there just had to be one who would be willing to cooperate without jeopardizing the investigation. I decided to interview a young woman named Lynn Powers who had received just a few payroll warrants and had no criminal history. My partner and I arrived at her house early one evening. As she opened the door, I could see small children playing in the living room. I gave her the usual cop greeting: "Hi, Lynn. We're police officers. Can we talk to you for a moment?" She said, "I know what this is about. Come on in." Art Dixson's life was about to change.

Lynn said she had expected us to come one day and ask her about her "work" at the school district. She told us a man who owned a hair salon had enlisted her to fill out a phony employment application. She knew him only as Mr. T. Thereafter, she had to fill out a time sheet and turn it in before the end of the month. Around the tenth of the next month, she was given a check, which she cashed and kept about $200. The remaining money (usually more than $1,000) went to Mr. T. Based on her information, I was able to identify him and determine that he was receiving checks in two different names, as was one of his employees at the hair salon. Lynn furnished information about several others in the neighborhood who were also participating in the scheme; these names matched ones I already had. She confirmed that none of these people, including her, ever worked for the district.

It was time to prepare the case. Art was clearly the major figure in the scheme to introduce phantom employees into the district's payroll. Mr. T was also a player in this scheme, so he was also named.

Our arrest-planning meeting included a captain, a sergeant, and our narcotics surveillance team whose specialty was undercover work. We excluded all other backup personnel from this meeting because fewer people involved lessened the risk that the operation would be compromised before being executed. I obtained a search warrant for Art's home and automobiles as well as Mr. T's business and cars.

On December 8, the surveillance team watched Art as he left his apartment at 5:30 a.m., followed him to several school sites, and tailed him as he picked up the checks and drove outside the city, where he met with three women and handed out the payroll warrant envelopes to them. At this point he was detained. I arrived just in time to watch.

The women, mother and daughters, admitted they had no right to these checks and confirmed they never worked for the district. They gave the same statements as Lynn Powers, except they received their checks directly from Art, and had done so for many months. For each one, they were paid $200 and gave the balance directly back to Art in cash—about $1,000 per check.

We searched Art's car and found the remaining December payroll warrants on the front seat. They had been carefully sorted with true employees in one small stack and phantom employees in another, much larger stack. We also found handwritten "Pay-Owe" sheets from prior months listing the phantom employees, which clearly showed Art's primitive tracking of who received a check and when the person paid him his cut.

Before the day was out, we searched Art's other cars and home and Mr. T's business and seized over $60,000 in illicit payroll warrants. I spent an hour and a half interviewing Art. He admitted to receiving around $150,000 from the scheme and claimed that "Mr. T" had gotten about $250,000. Most important to the investigation was Art's admission to being the main perpetrator behind the entire fraud. We arrested Mr. T.

THE CLEANUP

I spent the next seven months hunting down more than 70 phantom employees and interviewing them before the case could be filed. Surprisingly, most were fairly cooperative. They all offered the same story—that they were acquainted with Art or Mr. T and were solicited to participate in the fraud at a very difficult time in their lives. Many believed that they were selected because they were on relief.

The district brought a civil action against Art. Judgments totaling $150,000 were obtained. Art's bank accounts and luxury car were levied by the civil court.

The case was presented to the district attorney's office for consideration of a criminal complaint. This is where the real work began. We were gifted with a very talented and energetic prosecutor. Together, we sorted and marked the huge volume of documents. For compliance with discovery, we duplicated dozens of taped interviews that had been transcribed. The case was meticulously prepared.

Toward the end of the trial, the prosecutor showed the video of Art's confession. The defense lawyer objected, arguing, unsuccessfully, that Art was coerced into being interviewed without an attorney. This is where video evidence was crucial. When Art took the stand, he turned out to be our best witness! When confronted with inconsistencies between his taped statement and testimony, he said he had not lied but offered "nontruths" when interviewed after his arrest. The jury took just over an hour to convict him on all counts.

Art was sentenced to five years in state prison, followed by a three-year parole period.

Several others, including Mr. T, were separately prosecuted for their parts in this scheme and other crimes that were discovered during the investigation.

LESSONS LEARNED

Every case should be carefully critiqued at its conclusion. All aspects, from inception to conclusion, need to be reviewed. There are always things that we can learn to do differently and more efficiently next time.

Urgency and Secrecy

In this case, both urgency and secrecy were required. That severely limited the time before making an arrest and the number of personnel needed to get to that point. Each time a payday came and went, so did over $60,000. The best time to intervene in this case was on a payday, when the suspects could be caught in the act. In smaller municipalities or corporations where word travels quickly, it doesn't take much for someone to catch on. So, the longer it takes to make an arrest, the more likely it becomes that the secrecy will be breached. The fewer people "in the know," the better.

The Effect of Publicity

In a criminal case arising from a public entity, we learned that some consideration should be made about how the publicity is handled. After the arrest, the district seemed to come apart at the seams. Everyone demanded to know what happened and why. Many different political machines went into motion. Elected officials were incensed that they weren't briefed prior to the arrests. Publicity also affected the process to fire Art. There actually were some in management of the district who believed that Art should not have been fired until convicted, but rather put on paid administrative leave. More important, I knew that other crimes were being committed within the district. The last thing that I wanted was for any potential whistle-blowers to fear that their tips might not be dealt with professionally. Also, I found that having the search warrant affidavits sealed during the critical investigative stages was helpful in not adding fuel to the fire. Release of such information often compromises the investigation and parallel investigations that may arise.

Interviewing a Perpetrator

There is nothing more important to an interview than planning. After all, Art confessed, and the confession was admitted into evidence. I had formulated the questions and prepared for his responses. I was thankful we had videotaped the interview. It played very well to the jury and really sank Art's claim of being under duress to give a statement without an attorney being present. When interviewing Art, I learned how important it was to control the questioning, allowing him time to fully answer my questions, especially when he was not being truthful. Nothing derails a perpetrator in court faster than his or her own lies, especially when viewed by a jury on a large-screen television display.

Evidence Handling

In a case like this, where there are literally thousands of pieces of evidence, there must be a system for cataloging, copying, and securing it. One of the best systems today is digital storage, although it was not available during this investigation. Digital audio and video recordings, photographs, and document scans can be priceless in large cases. When working on any investigation, use what has been referred to as the vertical system as opposed to horizontal filing. The vertical system involves the orderly sorting and keeping of documents in clearly marked folders, stored vertically in boxes. The horizontal system involves sloppily laying all documents horizontally in a box (or boxes) until needed.

When preparing for discovery or any other copy processes, first create a folder as a "master copy file" of all documents that will be needed. Carefully produce clear photocopies of every piece of evidence. Reduce the size of legal documents to fit onto letter-size paper. Later, when a copy job is required, this master can be used to produce as many sets as needed, all of which will be of the best quality possible. I could have saved many hours of tedious sorting of evidence by doing this during the district's investigation.

And remember those simple spreadsheets? They are wonderful until your computer locks up and your last several hours of work are lost. That happened twice in this case. I found that setting frequent backups and backing up every computer session virtually eliminated data loss caused by crashes and freezes.

RECOMMENDATIONS TO PREVENT FUTURE OCCURRENCES

It must sound like a broken record to anyone who investigates financial crimes: "There were no controls in place ... someone circumvented the controls ... we're too short-handed to have duties segregated ... we don't usually run background checks." So we must continue to preach the same message.

After Art Dixson was arrested, the superintendent issued an executive order to all employees. It was posted on the entrances to the district office and at all school sites. Anyone with any information regarding fraud committed against the district was to report it immediately—and we were the only two persons to whom fraud tips were to be made. Failure of any employee to adhere to this order would result in his or her dismissal.

While this method may seem unusual, it worked. Over the next three years, more than a dozen workers were arrested and convicted of various fraud offenses. Many of the leads came from anonymous tipsters employed by the district.

This case resulted in major personnel, payroll, and accounting office policy change recommendations:

- All prospective employees are fingerprinted and checked for criminal convictions prior to being submitted to the board of education for approval.
- No prospective employee is permitted to commence work until approved by the board and entered into the personnel and payroll systems.
- No employee is entered into the payroll system without a supervisor's written approval. Those approved for inclusion must first have complete personnel packages (I-9, W-4, employment application, criminal history check, and board approval).
- All payroll warrants are distributed at the district office or at the various school sites by the principal or his or her designee.
- Budgets for most noncertificated positions are reviewed every month.

Paul J. Harvey, CFE, is a retired detective sergeant with over 28 years of experience in criminal and civil fraud investigations. Mr. Harvey is the owner of Victory Investigations in Redding, California, providing consulting and investigative services for victims of fraud-related crimes.

CHAPTER 19

The Video Game

CARLOS L. HOLT

J oe Detmer and his family had come to know and love their community. The military base was the center of life. Despite being classified as "remote and isolated," this large installation was located in a town with a population of 40,000. The base itself was home to almost 10,000 military personnel and approximately the same number of dependent family members. Many of the town residents were employed there. Life in the town had benefits, including clean air, low crime, and an unusually inexpensive cost of living. Housing was particularly affordable. With so many residents connected to the base, the entire community was completely supportive of military operations. Patriotism was high. The annual Fourth of July event included one of the largest fireworks shows around, as well as bands, food, and military displays. The commanding general was more recognizable than the town mayor.

Joe, a married military retiree, had been the manager of the video rental store for five years. His paycheck, on top of his military retirement funds, provided a nice living in this rural setting. He was selected as manager because he seemed stable, committed, and responsive to direction from Samuel, the services manager.

SUPPORTING THE TROOPS

There is a kinder and gentler aspect of the U.S. military, known as Morale, Welfare, and Recreation (MWR). This service includes family counseling, organized sports leagues, financial planning, child care centers, a golf course, a bowling center, and numerous business operations. The business operations branch includes six convenience stores, four restaurants, a high-volume gas station, car repair and rental, two barber shops, a beauty salon, vending machine operations, movie rentals, and a large retail store called the PX or Post-Exchange. Together, these generate over $48 million in annual revenue. Profits are funneled directly back into the community for ventures such as gymnasiums, child and youth programs, and family events.

The video store was a cross between a concessionaire vendor and a direct sales operation. The contractor acquired and provided the movies and equipment, and MWR employees ran the store. A percentage of sales was sent directly to the contractor, and the remainder was retained by MWR. The contractor happened to be a disabled individual who rarely visited the operation and lived across the country. He sent the movies by mail and spoke with personnel on a regular basis. He also provided the software and stand-alone computer system used in the video store. He had personally written the software and tailored it to the video rental operation. Monthly reports were generated and sent to him by mail. Older movies were sold at the store and the proceeds split 50/50 between him and MWR.

Daphney Ingersol, the new MWR director, was quickly coming into her own and feeling very comfortable instituting change in order to effectively serve the wide customer base and carry out the wishes of the commanding general. By all accounts, MWR was doing an excellent job in many areas and was receiving many accolades. Daphney, however, was pushing ahead, never content with the status quo.

Her staff was strong. Ruth Bard, the business operations head and a recently retired military officer, was extremely committed to supporting military members and their families. If a product or service was needed or desired, she would see that it was provided by the most convenient method at the lowest price. In some cases, she knowingly lost money in order to provide necessary products for low-ranking military families. Milk, diapers, formula, and children's needs were marked up a maximum of 5% over cost. Dry cleaning and tailoring services were priced only to break even. Near–first-run movies were free at the base theater. Car washes were only 50 cents.

Another valuable member of Ruth's team was Samuel Washington, the services manager. His responsibilities included the dry cleaning/tailoring facility, barber and beauty shops, movie rentals, vending operations, phone centers, the car wash, all concessionaire vendors, and several other small-service businesses. Samuel worked endless hours, sometimes seven days a week. He never turned anyone down who asked for his help. As a result, his plate was about as full as it could be. He was in his late 50s and had worked for MWR for over 10 years. He expected to stay in the area indefinitely and had no plans to retire. Samuel was frequently on the defense about the video rental store. Ruth had never been happy with its bottom line and always believed it was run inefficiently. She questioned Samuel many times, but he always provided some reason as to why sales were lower or costs were higher than expected. Samuel often related Joe's recent excuses, which seemed to placate Ruth only temporarily.

Meanwhile, I had been assigned duties as a contracting officer with MWR and was still an active-duty military officer. In my previous assignment, I served as the accounting officer and had just obtained my Certified Internal Auditor (CIA) designation. Daphney tasked me with taking over the Management, Analysis, and Control (MAC) office. At the time, I was collecting information and preparing to write a new internal control instruction. Daphney had asked me to create a proactive approach that identified and assessed risk areas. She wanted scheduled and unscheduled reviews of each activity to be conducted by the MAC office, with an emphasis on efficiency, effectiveness, and fraud detection. My two-member staff and I had scarcely begun our assignment when Samuel, the services manager, piqued my interest.

"Officer Holt, I have some information that might concern you," Samuel called out. "One of the video store employees came over a short while ago and mentioned a strange occurrence with one of the customers."

THE BUCK STOPS HERE

A private by the name of Marvin Buck had stopped by the video rental store to pay for a past-due rental. His name was on the list that MWR sent to the first sergeant of each command once a month, which was composed of the names of all service members who had bad checks, overdue movie rentals, overdue library fees, or any other debt owed to MWR. When Private Buck was contacted by his first sergeant about his movie rental fees, he promptly went into the video rental store and paid what he owed. Since he was due to transfer in a few weeks, he decided to close his account. Later Private Buck discovered he had lost his receipt and went back to the store. Wendy Parnell, the clerk on duty, printed a copy of his account, which showed he had received a large refund as his last transaction. She was unable to explain the transaction since the video store did not offer refunds. Any customer desiring a refund was to be sent to Samuel. Refunds were rare, usually necessary only when someone paid the cost for a lost movie, then located the original one.

Since Joe was off for the day, Wendy took the matter to Samuel, who then brought the matter to my attention. I first asked him if Wendy was a reliable source. He advised me that she seemed to be an honest college student with a good reputation. Next I spoke on the phone with Wendy and asked her to bring me copies of the mysterious transaction, reminding her keep everything strictly confidential. I called together my MAC crew. We discussed the possibilities and ultimately decided to interview Wendy to determine if she had any additional information. We would begin reviewing the MWR daily activity reports (DAR) and accompanying paperwork from the store. In particular, we would keep an eye out for anything that might be related to refunds.

Later that day, Wendy showed me a printout of the customer account in question. As had been related, there was a refund listed as the final transaction on Private Buck's account in the amount of $131.69. This seemed like an odd total, but I kept an open mind. It could have been some sort of legitimate attempt to balance an account, even out inventory, or some other nonstandard but innocent action. The refund was entered at closing on a night that two part-time employees were working. I asked Wendy to search through a few days' final transactions to see if any more were present. The next time I saw her, she brought me printouts of several more refunds, which resembled the first one. All of them had similar surrounding circumstances. Each was the final transaction of the night, and each ranged from $20 to $200. Looking over the work schedules and time cards revealed that no single person was present on all of the nights the refunds were issued. From this, my staff and I reasoned that either multiple employees or Joe himself had to be involved. We decided that we could no longer continue the investigation in secret. We would need to interview all of the employees, look at all of the books and records over the last year, and take a full account of funds, sales, and inventory. It was our conclusion that Joe could not be present in the video store during this investigation. If he was involved, he would be in a position to destroy information and influence the staff during interviews.

BEATING THE SYSTEM

In my update to Daphney, I told her that I was asking Ruth to place Joe on paid administrative leave until the investigation was complete. Needless to say, neither Daphney nor Ruth was happy to learn of the possibility of theft. Daphney wanted to root out the problems quickly. I was very impressed when just a week later she informed the commanding general of the possible fraud. This worked to motivate our small MAC team to unveil the truth as quickly as we could. In the past, when leaders react to bad news by trying to minimize the problem, investigations were delayed.

While waiting for the finalization of Joe's administrative leave, we learned that the contractor had provided new hardware and software almost two years ago but had never been installed. The system kept only the last three transactions of any customer account, along with the current balance and a listing of all movies in the customer's possession. In order to view any of a particular customer's transactions, other than the last three, one would have to sequentially scroll through each day's business looking for ones belonging to that account.

Meanwhile, my MAC staff found some surprising results from the review of the DARs and computer printouts. Refunds were not broken out separately on the computer printout. Looking at any particular day, it was impossible to determine if any refunds had been issued. The system-generated reports had been designed by the contractor. Apparently, he had not solicited input from a CFE when he designed them, and they were insufficient for recognizing strange transactions. The accounting technician who handled video store paperwork said that she had thought it very odd; since she joined MWR a few months ago, the store had balanced "to the penny" every single day. She knew that five or six employees worked out of the one cash drawer seven days a week and could not understand how they could be so precise. Not one of the 40-plus activities within MWR—not even the library—came close to such a record.

We decided that Samuel and I would present to Joe the administrative leave order early on Thursday before the store opened. We included a computer specialist on our team. At 8:30 a.m. we entered the store and informed Joe of the bad news. Samuel asked him for his keys and if he had anything else on his person that belonged to the store. He answered, "No, not a thing." Joe seemed very surprised as the events unfolded, although he didn't ask any questions or attempt to protest our actions. This was something I thought particularly telling. I noticed Joe's hands tremble quite a bit as he handed his keys to Samuel. We had planned not to question Joe until after we had obtained some of the facts about what was going on. We recognized that the store manager might never return, as nothing prevented him from turning in his resignation at any time.

Joe was long gone by the time his closest ally and self-titled assistant manager, Sally, arrived. By all accounts, Sally and Joe seemed to be an odd pair, but each fiercely protected the other. As we expected, she immediately began a series of seemingly unending questions about what was going on and why Joe wasn't at the store. "This is all unnecessary. Everything was going just fine around here," she exclaimed repeatedly. Even after being assured that this was just a routine audit, Sally continued to be confrontational. Surprisingly, she did manage to finish out her shift that day. The following day, she arrived for work five minutes late and said she had forgotten something in her car. She came back in after a few minutes and stated that she was quitting. Sally left the building and never returned. She even waited several weeks before contacting MWR about her final paycheck.

HONESTY NOT THE POLICY

The MAC staff quickly found that there were no procedures and policies to deter or prevent fraud that were specific to the video store. New employees learned what old employees taught them, which were verbally related by Joe and sometimes posted on the wall. The unwritten procedure for closing the store was simple. First, they were to lock the doors at 10:00 p.m. and finalize any customer purchases. Then the computer system printout was to be obtained and the cash counted. The MWR daily activity report was completed the next morning by either Joe or Sally, who then filled out the deposit slip and walked the deposit bag to the finance center.

Store policy allowed any employee to open a new customer account, but only Joe was allowed to close them. He kept a list of accounts that had no activity for six months or more so that he could close them out "when he had time." Wendy stated that on occasion, Joe asked her to review the several thousand accounts at random, looking for ones with no recent activity, then to make him a list of those account numbers. He kept the list underneath the cash register. On the morning of the "takeover," as we had begun calling it, I located the one-page list of account numbers. About half of the names and numbers had been crossed off, as if they had already been closed. I decided to pull up a few of those accounts to see what might be revealed. We found that each account number had already been issued to a new customer. Most interesting was that the initial transaction for each new customer was a large refund. A close analysis revealed that all of the refunds had actually been issued on the day before the customer opened the account, yet it was still displayed on the customer's statement. I had already tasked our computer rep with installing the new software and hardware and moving all of the account data over.

As we began plugging refund transaction times and amounts into a spreadsheet alongside employee work schedules, it became apparent that only one person had any correlation to the refunds: Joe. As we had already seen, the refunds were the final transactions of the night, all recorded within several minutes of 10:00 p.m. Joe was present on each day following this activity. Not one refund had been issued when he didn't work the following day. The transactions were inputted using various cashier IDs.

Our hypothesis took shape. Joe was somehow entering refunds on the previous night's sales, and only on accounts he was about to close. He knew closing the account caused the account number to be reassigned. Because the system only showed the last three transactions for each account, the false refund would likely be more than three deep in a very short time. Thus, the customer would probably never see it. Joe would have to print a new system report each morning before filling out the DAR. He would then destroy the original system report and remove the "refund" cash from the safe, leaving enough money for the deposit and the change fund. On his last day, Joe had not yet opened the safe. Since we did find a $200 refund on the previous night's sales, we concluded that he had the original system report on his person, as we didn't find it in the trash or anywhere in the store. Of course when we counted the cash, we found the extra $200.

After reviewing each and every entry, we plugged all refunds into our spreadsheet. It became clear that the scheme had been occurring for some time and steps had apparently been taken to cover it. First, only transactions going back eight and a half months were present, and one of those months contained no information. It appeared that Joe was erasing data as far back as he could in order to hide the fraud. It was January at the time, and the figures only went back through May. The entire month of July was also missing. We began guessing that Joe either erased the wrong month accidentally or eliminated July's entries in particular due to the large amount of activity. The total of the seven and a half months of data showed $13,264 in refunds had been entered. They were all found to be among the last transactions of the day. In 225 business days, 140 of them showed refunds. There was every reason to believe the missing months contained similar activity.

Analysis of some of the particular transactions revealed the following interesting data.

Date	Transaction Sequence #	Time	Transaction
03 Nov	165 of 166	10:05 p.m.	$1.90 rental fee
	166 of 166	10:01 p.m.	$102.20 refund
05 Nov	93 of 94	9:53 p.m.	$5.30 rental fee
	94 of 94	10:00 a.m.	$100.00 refund
15 Dec	216 of 218	10:09 p.m.	$1.90 rental fee
	217 of 218	10:01 p.m.	$50.00 refund
	218 of 218	10:02 p.m.	$3.24 refund

These transactions reveal that the time is out of sequence with the transaction number. It appeared that whoever was entering the transactions had gotten lazy and careless. Instead of ensuring the refunds were always entered at a time *after* the last legitimate transaction, the fraudster was carelessly using 10:00 p.m. and 10:01 p.m., believing that since the store closed at 10:00 p.m., there would be no further entries. (The store did not usually have late business.) Even more careless was the November 5 transaction, when 10:00 a.m. was used instead of 10:00 p.m.

We still didn't know how the times were being manipulated. One good aspect of the computer program was the transaction sequence numbers, which could not be overridden. Without them, it could have been made to appear as if the transactions took place in the middle of the day's sales, instead of always at the end. Another striking realization was that if the fraudster was resetting the time to make it appear that the entries were at night, it wasn't someone working that night. Night-shift employees would not need to reset the time. They would have been free to enter transactions immediately after closing. Thus the time/sequence errors provided valuable information. One final telling observation was of a small $3.24 refund. The perpetrator had felt it necessary to go back and balance the books after entering a fraudulent "overpayment" for $50.00. Although perpetrators sometimes use odd amounts so that the false transactions won't stick out, it appeared that the fraudster was doing this so that the cash would balance "to the penny," as the accounting clerk had already told us it had. Who, other than the manager, would be interested in ensuring that the books balanced? We theorized Joe was incorrectly assuming that having the cash balance perfectly would prevent scrutiny.

THE MISSING MOVIES

One by one, we interviewed each of the other six employees. Among the information we obtained was that in years past, it was necessary to back up the computer each night at closing. The accumulated monthly data were then sent to the contractor. Almost three years earlier, Joe announced he would begin doing all of the backups himself. He eventually announced that they were no longer required. Another item of interest was the night Sally asked a fellow employee for a ride home. When the coworker dropped her off, she asked Sally if she could go inside and use the telephone. While making a call, she noticed what appeared to be about 30 videos, very similar to what the store rented, still in the boxes on Sally's living room floor. Not wanting to sound accusing, the coworker never asked about it. But most surprising of all was the fact that most employees stated that despite the afternoon or the nightly cash count sometimes coming up short, Joe always claimed to find it later. One employee was very concerned when she was short $130 for the evening— only about five days before our "takeover." In an attempt to protect herself, she took the extra step of printing two system reports from the computer, taking the extra copy home for safekeeping. The next day when she phoned Joe, he told her not to worry, that all was fine, and the shortage had been found. Fortunately, she still had the extra report, which she gave to me. After looking at the document for only a few seconds, I knew Joe was our guy.

The computer specialist had implemented the new software with all of the account data within two days. This system was much faster and contained many new features, including the ability to view all of the transactions related to each account, not just the last three. By experimentation, we learned that in order to enter information at a time other than the current one, the computer clock could be reset, and the system could completely shut down and be restarted. Then the computer time was reset to the actual time and the system again shut down and restarted. It was not possible to override the transaction sequence number. Our computer specialist was unable to retrieve the apparently deleted account data from July and all months prior to May.

Conversations with the contractor were quite revealing. He stated that for some time, he had been unable to obtain any backup data from Joe. He needed the data not only to verify sales and the percentage he was due, but also to know which movies were renting well and which ones weren't. He was operating almost blindly since the only information he obtained was from the infrequent verbal conversations with Joe and his monthly check from the Finance Department. He believed Joe had been avoiding most of his calls. As far back as three or four years ago, the computer disks were sent less and less frequently and finally not at all. He continued to send new movies each week, sometimes several copies of each, hoping this is what the military members wanted to rent. Joe had not provided him with an inventory in a long time. He was disturbed by Joe's failure to install the new computer system. The contractor said that Joe initially seemed pleased to receive the new system, but then began offering excuses not to use it. He was confused by Joe's initial expertise with computers and software then later his apparent lack of abilities. He suspected Detmer played dumb when it suited him. The contractor agreed to send us a new list of the movies he had furnished during the last year. We soon received the list and compared it to the on-hand inventory. This revealed yet another problem that I already suspected. Many of the new movies were not in the store. In fact, the computer data showed they had never been rented. The final tally revealed at least 300 different movies, and several copies of each, that were not present and had apparently been stolen. Since several copies of each had been provided, we calculated that over 1,500 tapes could actually be missing. All of the employees believed that Sally was the sole person responsible for putting new movies into service. This, coupled with the sighting of movies on her living room floor, indicated she had something to hide. We tried several times to reach her by calling and knocking on her door but were unsuccessful.

A Mostly Happy Ending

After reaching our conclusions about the thefts and putting together the report and supporting evidence, I reviewed the information with Daphney. She contacted the criminal investigation agency and updated the commanding general. The criminal investigator needed little time to understand the matter. By that point, we had enough evidence to call Joe in for an interview, during which we would seek his admission. He appeared pale and scared when he showed up at the investigator's office. During the initial information verification with the investigator, Joe surprisingly admitted to taking small sums of money from the store. He said he had taken $5 to $20 on only a few occasions, amounting to no more than $100 during his employment, but he adamantly denied anything else. His denials became less and less credible as I showed him how his work schedule coincided perfectly with the false refunds.

Next, we displayed the out-of-sequence transactions. This really seemed to shock him; I believe he never knew he had made these slip-ups. We also showed him the sworn statements from all of the employees, reading selected sections from several. Joe winced at some of the information, as if he were being shot with a pellet rifle. As the interview proceeded, he became quiet. Last, I decided to reveal the two different system reports, from the same night's business. One had sales of $130 more than the other one. The lesser one, which Detmer had turned into the finance office, had his signature on it and the deposit slip, and the DAR showed that the cash had balanced to the penny. When I pressed play on the VCR that I already had cued up, I showed Joe the security video of the employees leaving the store that night around 10:30. I fast-forwarded all the way until Joe arrived early the next morning. I was able to show him that no one else had entered the store during the entire period between when the employees left and when he could be seen arriving. No one else had yet entered when he could be seen leaving with the DAR, his doctored computer printout, and the deposit in his hand.

I told Joe the local DA would likely find it *impossible* that anyone else had entered the $130 refund transaction and printed a new computer report after the employees left that night. I pointed at the stack of about 30 tapes and asked if he would like to view each one of them. At this point, he began to discuss his options. He finally decided to submit his resignation and sign a statement admitting to stealing $13,264. We explained that making an admission, and possibly being issued a summons for a court date, was preferable to having law enforcement come into his home unannounced and arrest him. He claimed to have "no knowledge" of why the computer files were erased and said that he didn't make any false refunds in those months anyway. Although neither of us believed him, we decided to take the admission statement he was offering to sign. We could always take any additional information to the DA's office after a forensic computer examination was completed. Joe steadfastly denied knowing anything about the missing movies.

Two of the criminal investigators tried numerous times to have Sally come in for an interview, but each time she flatly refused—slamming down the phone or shutting the door in their face. The only information we ever obtained was an old flyer found posted in her trailer park offering movies for sale. Although there was no name on the flyer, the phone number was traced to Sally's old cell phone, which had since been disconnected. With nowhere to go, we dropped further attempts to tie Sally into the missing movies, later estimated to be worth over $40,000.

Joe quickly obtained a lawyer and recanted some of what he earlier admitted and attempted to minimize the rest. The forensic computer examination turned up no usable information except that special software had apparently been used to delete the files. The DA called me to testify to the methods, extent, and amounts of the fraud, and Joe decided to plead guilty. He received six months in the county jail, restitution of $13,264, court fees, and a fine. The military staff judge advocate also sent Detmer a letter advising of him that except to receive medical care, he was no longer allowed on the military base. In our remote area, this was a harsh penalty.

LESSONS LEARNED

The most striking and basic element of this case was the absence of proper internal controls. Processes were not reviewed or documented in the first place. The contractor-designed software and system reports were woefully deficient. No one had reviewed either for weaknesses prior to placing them into use. Once Joe discovered a flaw in the software and the report, he exploited it to the maximum extent. He knew that neither Samuel nor the distant and disabled contractor was likely to uncover his scheme. Samuel's busy schedule did not allow him enough time to monitor the video store. No audits or inspections had taken place to discover the scheme. Thus, Joe continued unabated for a long time. He successfully erased all but the last few months' computer files so that evidence of thefts only amounted to $13,264, even though he likely misappropriated upward of $60,000. Joe admitted to taking his wife on twice-monthly gambling trips to his favorite casino, where he was well known. Like many embezzlers, he fit the classic "Fraud Triangle" developed by Dr. Donald Cressey: unshareable need, perceived opportunity, and rationalization. Joe's unshareable need was his gambling habit; his perceived opportunity was the software weakness and the lack of adequate oversight. During his initial confession, he related that he had worked many extra hours that he never turned in, thus rationalizing his actions.

RECOMMENDATIONS TO PREVENT FUTURE OCCURRENCES

Updated Technology

The software that Joe used was out of date. Because it was not advanced, he could easily reset the time on the computer, making his refunds appear to have been made at the end of a business day. Furthermore, the reports failed to show refunds. This program was insufficient. Software that is used to account for assets should undergo complete review, including risk management and certification by qualified individuals.

Segregation of Duties

Staff should be cross-trained in order to alternate duties. This would eliminate cases like this one, where Joe Detmer was solely responsible for system reports and closing accounts. He and Sally, his likely cohort, completed the daily activity reports, filled out the deposit slips, and took the bag of money to the finance office. No one watched to ensure that they were being honest. Samuel could not adequately supervise the many businesses that he oversaw. All activities should receive proper oversight. In addition, all major processes should be documented and reviewed. Standardized processes would have provided a basis for review by others.

Surprise Audits

Even though the movies belonged to the contractor, they were under custody of MWR. An inventory would have uncovered the many missing movies. An audit would have uncovered numerous weaknesses and indicators of possible fraud.

Also, sales receipt deposits should be made out and the amounts of those deposits called in nightly if the deposit itself cannot be made. This would have required a noticeable effort to change the deposit amount after the previous days' sales were altered. Finally, accounting personnel should be trained to report out-of-the-ordinary occurrences. Had the accounting technician reported the unbelievable cash over/short history to the MAC office, a review could have taken place.

Carlos L. Holt, CFE, CIA, CGAP, is an auditor and investigator for the United States federal government in Charleston, South Carolina. He also teaches accounting and finance courses at Park University. Mr. Holt earned his graduate degree at Central Michigan University and has over 10 years of experience in fraud-related cases.

CHAPTER 20

Bet Your Life on It

HOWARD B. GROBSTEIN AND JOSHUA R. TEEPLE

At only five feet tall, Tasanee Pho had a slight presence wherever she went. Her brown hair was cropped in a bob around a dark-complected face. She bore a distinctive mole on her right cheek. Tasanee's customary anonymity stopped at the doors of the community casino in New Jersey, where she was pleasantly greeted by many dealers and other casino employees who recognized her as a valuable and long-standing patron. Over the years, she racked up over $1 million in activity on her preferred player's card. Though this seems to be a lot of money for someone with a modest background and less than $80,000 of annual household income, it's easy to do when the stake money is not your own.

Tasanee was a simple person; her home life as a little girl in Thailand was basic. Because of the lifestyle she had grown up with, she did not dress expensively, drove a basic four-door import sedan, and appeared unpretentious to most everyone she met. Her only real extravagance in life was her insatiable desire for gambling, which ultimately led to her downfall.

She and her husband were married 30 years ago, when she was only 20. After immigrating to the United States, they built a loving home for their family and made the most of what they had. Tasanee was a resident alien and green card holder.

Her family plodded along as solid middle-class citizens. They were by no means wealthy, but they did more than just eke out a living. Tasanee had some failed sideline businesses in the health care industry, but aside from her gambling habit, no other significant financial obligations weighed her down.

Tasanee worked with the Big Apple Special Events Foundation for nearly a decade. Until her criminal habits were uncovered, her reputation among coworkers was untarnished. Her peers not only held her professional abilities in high regard, but found her a pleasant and caring person to be around. Over the years, Tasanee changed positions within the Accounting Department, eventually serving as the accounts receivable clerk. Her duties in that capacity included, among others, receiving all incoming checks and cash from all departments and the mail room; making up the deposit slips for those funds, and physically depositing the funds in the foundation's bank account. Unfortunately, Tasanee was also tasked with receiving the bank statements and preparing the reconciliations for that very same account.

The accounting department in which Tasanee worked was on the foundation's top floor. She shared offices with other accounting personnel including her immediate officemate and friend, Gloria Richardson, who was the foundation's accounts payable clerk. Upon entering their shared office, one could not help noticing the stark difference between Tasanee's and Gloria's work spaces. While Gloria's desk was the definition of efficient order and cleanliness, Tasanee's cubicle appeared to have been struck by an indoor hurricane. Stacks of papers piled up on her desk in utter disarray, following some arcane filing system known only to Tasanee. Her filing cabinets and drawers overflowed with half-completed files, wrinkled invoices, and a seemingly endless supply of personal memorabilia including photographs, correspondence, bank statements, deposit slips, and documents related to other business endeavors in which she was engaged.

Perhaps no one else in the foundation was as surprised by Tasanee's arrest as Gloria, who said, "She is such a sweet person. Always happy to lend a hand or offer a kind word when I was feeling a little down. I cannot believe that she has done something like this." Interviews of more foundation personnel revealed that others shared Gloria's incredulity. Tasanee, it seems, was a well liked and respected long-term employee.

A BIG APPLE IN THE BIG APPLE

The Big Apple Special Events Foundation resides in the heart of Manhattan's art and culture district. Its primary purpose is to serve as a host venue for musical acts, theater performances, and special exhibitions. The foundation houses modern theatrical equipment with superb acoustics on its main stage. For exhibitors and performance groups, the foundation provides ancillary services, such as box office operations, beverage sales, maintenance, and security. The foundation enjoys an impeccable reputation among its patrons and greater New York in general. Organized as a not-for-profit organization, the foundation's superior standing attracts some of the largest performance groups in the country, in addition to special exhibitors. It is not unusual for it to run critically acclaimed musicals and top-billing dramatic performances.

The foundation operates with an annual budget of $60 million. Over the past several years, it expanded its facilities by adding an $80 million state-of-the-art exhibition hall. Due to the normal bureaucracy accompanying such a large capital project, the accounting department processed a large amount of financial activity. The stress of the additional activity and the abnormally high volume of financial transactions on the department made it easier for Tasanee to cover her tracks.

The foundation maintains a staff of nearly 150 full-time employees and a board comprised of 20 influential socialites. Employees enjoy the culture they work in, although the deadlines and the constant turnover of performers and exhibitors can become stressful. Its staff and board members consistently strive to be consummate professionals. The foundation's success rate in fulfilling its commitment as a superior special events facility has been nothing short of phenomenal. Unlike its contemporaries, its philanthropy elevates it above the for-profit enterprises, allowing it to be more discriminating in the events it hosts.

The foundation operates with four significant revenue streams. The first results from donations elicited from the business and private community. These funds typically arrive in check form. The second source is incoming checks derived from the use of the events facilities by outside parties. Often the foundation runs special programs on behalf of outside parties in conjunction with use of those facilities. The third revenue stream comes in from performance and exhibition ticket sales. These sales are made through the box office, in person, on the phone, or through Ticketmaster. Although most ticket sales are rung up in credit card or check form, some currency is also taken in. The fourth revenue stream results from the cash-only bars run at the performances and exhibitions themselves. The revenues from the bars can be significant, depending on the particular event and day of the week, sometimes approaching $20,000 for a busy weekend. To a lesser extent, the foundation also earns commissions on concession sales made by event coordinators themselves.

For the last five years, all of this money passed through Tasanee's hands.

BLACK TUESDAY

Colin Reznik arrived at work on a brisk Tuesday morning in October, expecting an average day. He liked his job and had showed superior ability as the foundation's chief financial officer for the last two years, serving as the controller for several years before that position. Although his external accountants were in the offices for the annual financial statement audit, he felt that his department was in order and that the engagement had been going quite smoothly. The accounting firm's partner in charge of the foundation's audit, Bob Ross, had nurtured the relationship for over 10 years. Although the foundation was a relatively small client for a national accounting firm, the prestige associated with servicing the account made it worthwhile. The audit team thought they had the engagement dialed in and knew exactly what to look for. As it turns out, this seemingly typical Tuesday was to be full of unpleasant surprises.

The foundation's controller, Herbert Kolowitz, served as the primary liaison between the accounting department and the auditors. He would often pass on standard document requests to his subordinates, Tasanee and Gloria. As she had for the prior four financial statement audits, that Tuesday morning Tasanee handed the audit team's accountant in charge, Suzanne Ortega, the bank reconciliation file, replete with the year's bank statements.

Suzanne took Tasanee's file to the boardroom where they were sequestered and asked a staff person to review the year-end bank reconciliation and trace the book and bank balances to their respective supporting documentation. While looking at the bank statement, one of the staff accountants signaled for Suzanne's attention. "Will you take a look at this? It might be my imagination, but something looks funny on this bank statement."

Intrigued, Suzanne leaned over the accountant's shoulder to scrutinize the document. After several moments of study, she responded in kind. "I think I see what you are talking about." She placed her finger on the section of the statement where the beginning balance, less payments, plus deposits equals the ending balance. "It looks like the ending balance is crooked or something, and it feels like it has an edge. Almost like it was taped there."

She held the statement closer to the light. The staff accountant nodded in agreement and said, "That number is definitely taped on there."

Suzanne absorbed the significance of this discovery and started to have an awful feeling in her stomach. Going off a hunch, she instructed the staff accountant to review the balances on the other bank statements in the file to see if any of those numbers matched the modified year-end balance. As the staff accountant began that process, Suzanne did what was natural for any auditor to do upon encountering some impropriety in their engagement. She called the partner in charge.

As Suzanne was explaining the situation to Bob on the phone, the staff accountant hastily interrupted the call. Within minutes, he had found the same balance to the penny on a bank statement from three months prior. Now, Suzanne thought, we really have a problem.

Bob arrived at the foundation shortly after lunch. After reviewing the documentation himself and knowing that Tasanee was responsible for preparing the bank reconciliations, he decided to call her in for an interview to get to the bottom of the story.

After inviting her to sit down at the conference table, Bob began his questioning: "We noticed something a little weird with this bank statement. It looks like this balance from three months ago is cut and pasted onto the new one. Any idea why that would be?" His query was met with silence from the other side of the table, so he pressed his point. "Tasanee, I really need to understand what is going on here before we speak with Colin and Herbert. I want you to help me understand why a bank statement would be modified in such a way. Do you know why this would happen?"

"No," Tasanee replied.

Sensing that he would get nothing further from Tasanee, Bob decided to have her return to her office and move up the food chain to Herbert.

As soon as he posed the same questions to Herbert, Bob could tell that he was absolutely in the dark. Herbert appeared stunned that something like this could happen when he reviews and signs off on Tasanee's bank reconciliations. Bob knew it was time to present the situation to Colin.

As Colin entered the conference room, the tension was palpable. Bob immediately showed the suspect bank statement to Colin, explaining the situation as best he could. There was no soft way to break the news. Bob read the crushing effect of the discovery on Colin's face. Colin turned to leave the room and said, "I have to talk to Tasanee."

Back in his own office with Herbert, Colin called in Tasanee. She stood in front of him while he asked, "Why is this number taped on this bank statement?" Tasanee's head slumped onto her chest as she started crying. She did not need to say a word; Colin knew right then that she had robbed the foundation. "How bad is it?" he asked.

Tasanee wiped her eyes on the back of her sleeve, took a deep breath, and in a barely audible whisper, she gave Colin the tragic news: "Over one and a half million."

Fifteen minutes later, Colin had recovered from the shock enough to proceed with the next step in damage control. He first called the president of the foundation and the chairman of the board. Telling them about the fraud was one of the most difficult things he had ever done. Next, he called the foundation's attorney to give him the story. The attorney advised that Colin should contact the police and file a report with them. The New York Police Department (NYPD) arrived, took several statements from foundation employees, and arrested Tasanee, hauling her away in handcuffs. The foundation was rocked to its core.

CALLING IN THE CAVALRY

Two days after the arrest we arrived at the offices of Gary West, the foundation's outside counsel, for an interview to determine whether we were the right forensic accountants to investigate Tasanee's actions. In addition to the three of us, Colin and the foundation's president were also in attendance. Gary West is a stone-faced all-business litigator who had no compunctions with raking us over the coals about our professional qualifications and relevant experience. After an hour of Gary's inquiries, he came to realize that we were the perfect forensic accountants to investigate this type of fraud.

We were hired to identify how Tasanee perpetrated the fraud and quantify the amount of the loss so that the foundation could file a claim with its insurance carrier. The insurance company required that the foundation provide evidence supporting the nature of the loss and quantify the loss up to the insurance policy limits. In addition, the insurance company required that such information be provided within 90 days of reporting the loss. This deadline was moot, however, because the foundation's charter required audited financial statements in half that time. When the audit team discovered the impropriety, it put further work on the audit on hold, pending the results of a forensic investigation into the fraudulent activities. Thus, in actuality we had only five weeks to complete our investigation; thereafter the foundation's auditors would complete the audit.

Given the tight timeline, we started our work the very next day. Our initial on-site visit to the foundation began with an interview of Colin. He expressed utter shock and dismay over the events that had transpired over the preceding days. Colin felt as if he had failed in his duties to the foundation and its board of directors since this horrible crime had taken place under his watch. He also experienced a sense of betrayal of the trust he had placed in a long-term employee.

Colin provided us with background information regarding the foundation. He explained how Tasanee worked with others, named those foundation employees she interfaced with on a regular basis, and described certain aspects of her personality and her general daily routine. Colin explained how he, as chief financial officer, worked with Tasanee. He detailed the nature of her interactions with Herbert, as her immediate supervisor and the foundation's controller. Essentially, Colin was responsible for overseeing all of the strategic and financial functions of the foundation. He was also responsible for the financial aspects of building the multimillion-dollar exhibition hall. Colin relied heavily on Herbert for monitoring the more detailed accounting and general ledger functions. The two met formally once a week to review financial activities, but interacted daily to discuss current and ongoing issues related to the accounting function of the foundation.

The interview with Colin was very insightful. He painted a picture of how the foundation was supposed to operate under normal conditions. We next turned our attention to Herbert, a stressed-out man with thinning silver hair that always seemed out of place. His responsibilities were crucial to the foundation's operation. He managed the general ledger and oversaw the accounts receivable and accounts payable functions. Herbert was also the primary reviewer of the foundation's bank reconciliations. Immediately after beginning our interview of Herbert, we became concerned about his apparent lack of control over those critical functions. We learned that Herbert was several months behind in his detailed review of the general ledger. He also acknowledged that he performed only a superficial review of the monthly bank reconciliations. When we relayed this information to Colin, he was very disappointed to learn that his controller was not performing the functions he expected of him.

The most informative part of Herbert's interview occurred when he described the individual responsibilities of the personnel he supervised in the accounting department. He explained that all funds received by the foundation, whether donations, bar receipts, ticket sales, event programs, or concessions, ultimately passed through Tasanee's hands. On an almost daily basis, Tasanee walked down the block to the bank's branch office and personally made the foundation's deposits. Her visits were so frequent that she was on a first-name basis with many of the branch's employees. The foundation's deposit slips were stored in the drawers of Tasanee's desks, where she was in sole control of them.

We absorbed Herbert's words as he described the extent of the responsibilities placed in Tasanee's hands, but were amazed when he casually indicated that in addition to the myriad of duties she performed as the accounts receivable clerk, she was also solely responsible for preparing the foundation's monthly bank reconciliation. We came to understand that Tasanee exercised complete control of the cash function within the foundation—from the time the cash came in the door, to delivery at the local bank branch, and finally to the reconciliation of the monthly bank statements. Herbert's Adam's apple became stuck at the top of his throat as if it had knotted up as he described the extent of power the slight woman wielded within the foundation.

Later that day, we met with Gloria Richardson, the accounts payable clerk, and Mario Hernandez, the foundation's bar manager. These were two people who interacted with Tasanee on a regular basis, and it was important to determine their professional and personal involvement with her. We tend to approach our investigations assuming that all parties are guilty of some participation in the crime. In essence, we play an elimination game, narrowing down all suspects and methods to perpetrate the crime. During our interviews of Colin, Herbert, Gloria, and Mario, we were able to eliminate them as accomplices with a high degree of certainty. Of course, we would not be completely comfortable with that assessment until we had documented exactly how Tasanee perpetrated the crime.

After completing the initial round of interviews, we thoroughly examined Tasanee's work space. The desk in her cubicle was in utter disarray. The NYPD had been the first responders to the crime scene and had rifled through the drawers. At the investigating officer's direction, many documents had been removed as evidence for the criminal investigation. Colin and Herbert directed us to a drawer in Tasanee's desk that was stuffed with bank documentation including bank statements, cancelled checks, deposit slips, and bank reconciliations. There was no discernible method to the filing, so we began sorting through the information and organizing it based on type of document and relevant dates. Because we still did not understand how Tasanee committed the fraud, we methodically examined the bank statements and deposit slips in search of unusual transactions or other evidence. We also examined cancelled checks to see if there were payments made to related or unusual parties. We knew that the auditors had been provided with a bank statement that appeared to be altered, and we were looking for this kind of documentation as a lead. Our search did not take long to bear fruit.

We came across multiple copies of bank statements for the same account and month; however, the various statements reflected different ending balances. The statements looked legitimate; they contained the bank's emblem in color and had some bank information printed on the reverse side. We then found multiple bank reconciliations corresponding to the different versions of the bank statement. Various aspects of the bank reconciliations agreed with the various bank statements. Looking at the documentation, we were unable to distinguish the legitimate statements from the altered ones. We knew that obtaining original copies of the foundation's bank statements directly from the bank would be critical to our investigation, since we needed access to a reliable set of records.

The next morning, Colin arranged a meeting at the foundation's local bank branch down the block. Not surprisingly, the bank was very familiar with the foundation's account. This was due not only to the large balances maintained by the foundation (even larger in recent times as a result of the massive expansion taking place), but also because the foundation was an icon that garnered well-deserved respect in the community. It was an honor for the bank to be chosen by the foundation. We met with Henry Jones, the bank's vice president. He was extremely accommodating and expressed willingness to assist the foundation in any way he could. We advised Henry that we needed a clean set of all bank statements including copies of all deposit slips, cancelled checks, and other enclosures for a three-year period. In the interest of time and because we did not know when the fraud began, we asked that the bank provide the most recent documentation first and work backward in time. We also requested that the documentation be delivered directly to our team in order to maintain its integrity. This was crucial as we had not completely eliminated the possibility of collusion among any of the remaining foundation employees.

We had asked Colin to arrange another meeting for that day—this time with the original discoverers of the fraud. We traveled to the offices of the foundation's external auditors and sat across the shiny granite conference table from Bob and Suzanne as they detailed the initial discovery of the crime and the implications of that discovery on the foundation's audit. Although the crime would be memorialized in the foundation's financial statements and a loss from the defalcation recorded therein, the auditors would need to gain a certain comfort level that the fraud was isolated to Tasanee. Bob and Suzanne were unable to enlighten us as to how the crime was perpetrated.

After concluding our meeting with the auditors, Colin took us on the subway to One Police Plaza for a meeting with the detectives working on the case. This encounter turned out to be extremely productive for the detectives and us. We provided the NYPD with the multiple iterations of various bank statements and bank reconciliations we had identified as suspicious. They, in turn, allowed us to view the actual altered bank statements with taped numbers that had been confiscated at the foundation when they arrested Tasanee, in addition to ancillary documents that would be used in the criminal case against her. While the police had what they felt was sufficient documentation—including Tasanee's confession—to warrant an indictment, they still had not figured out exactly how she committed the fraud. Nor had we, for that matter.

After two intensive days of developing background and acquiring information, it was time to figure out how the fraud was committed and how we were going to quantify it. We knew that Tasanee was altering bank statements and manipulating false bank reconciliations to cover her tracks, but how was she actually stealing the money? In her confession, she indicated that she had manipulated the timing of checks that came in the door. What did this mean? We were not going to get any information from her. As a foreign national, she was deemed a flight risk and was incarcerated in a jail cell. Colin had some intriguing thoughts on the matter that pushed us in the right direction. He had figured that Tasanee had somehow concealed the cash defalcation by utilizing checks made payable to the foundation for various purposes, such as donations and event programs. How could she have accomplished this concealment? Wouldn't the donations be understated if this were the case? Wouldn't there be other red flags popping up in the review of the foundation's financial activity? The answer was simple. Because Tasanee had full control of many of the related accounting functions, compounded with a lack of oversight from Herbert, she manipulated the financial reporting to very effectively cover her illicit activities.

We undertook an even more thorough review of the bank documentation in Tasanee's work area. While examining the records, we identified a key piece of evidence that allowed us to better understand the fraud and how it was being reported on the books and records of the foundation. We began comparing foundation deposit slips to each other. Some of the deposit slips attached to the monthly bank statements did not have the mechanical stamp customarily imprinted by the bank teller when the deposit is made. Duplicate deposit slips for the same days were found under stacks of papers on Tasanee's desk. These deposit slips showed more checks and less cash being deposited. They also differed in another key way: They had stamps indicating that these were the deposits that had actually been made with the bank. We had found the smoking gun.

After that point, the investigation really started to come together. Tasanee controlled all of the funds that came through the foundation. Donations were routed to her in the envelopes in which they arrived. No one logged these donations or matched them to pledges prior to Tasanee taking control of these checks. Tasanee also received checks for event programs. Bar receipts from the previous evening's performance—all cash—were accounted for by the bar manager and then forwarded to Tasanee for deposit in the bank. The same process applied to concession sales. Tasanee completed the deposit slips, walked the funds to the bank, received and opened the monthly bank statements, and prepared the reconciliations on them.

The seasoned accounts receivable clerk stashed checks that came in for donations and special events. As cash became available from bar and concession sales, she exchanged cash meant for deposit for checks in equal amounts so that the total deposits for bar and concession sales reconciled to bar and concession sales reports. At the end of the month, Tasanee altered the bank reconciliations using "plug figures" to show an ending cash balance that agreed to bank statements that she had altered through a detailed process in which she cut and pasted ending balances from prior statements to more recent statements and reproduced using a color copier to complete the illusion. This process was necessary because Tasanee actually recorded the correct balances and transactions in the general ledger, thereby overriding any red flags that might be raised in a review of the general ledger and its subsidiary reports. Over a five-year period, the variance between actual cash in the bank and the amount recorded in the general ledger had grown to over $1.5 million. She accounted for this in "plug figures"— a fictional mix of outstanding checks and deposits in transit that Herbert did not catch on to. The breadth of her thievery was more easily concealed because of the large deposits being made for the funding of the construction project and the additional strain on the accounting department that capital project caused.

Armed with the knowledge of how the fraud was perpetrated, it was time to develop a methodology to quantify and report it. The other piece of the documentation was compiled from all of the foundation's deposit slip carbon copies attached to the daily deposit detail—often there was more than one deposit for a single day. Although we looked at every deposit slip carbon copy for the previous three years, we paid particular attention to those that did not have the mechanical bank stamp on them. We immediately identified those as suspect or false deposit slips, as Tasanee had destroyed many of the actual carbon copies of the deposit slips presented to the bank. Our approach was to record the amount of cash and checks recorded on the deposit slip carbon copies maintained within the foundation to the corresponding deposit slips obtained from the bank and tally up the difference between cash deposited per the carbon copy of the deposit slip and the cash deposited per the bank documentation. The excess of cash recorded on the false deposit slip carbon copies over the amount actually deposited to the bank equaled the amount of the defalcation.

In order to record these variances methodically and keep track of the massive amount of information we were processing in a very limited amount of time, we designed a custom database application using Microsoft Access. We utilized the interface form in this application to record all of the pertinent information from the foundation and bank documentation. By applying a high-tech approach to a relatively low-tech document review, our team was able to record the requisite information in a very efficient manner all the while minimizing the risk of data entry errors through the use of double-entry and hash total reconciliations. The investigation was further enhanced by making the interface screens in the database application intuitive, thereby easing the laborious data entry process.

All told, we examined 1,539 deposit slips covering a three-year period in a matter of three weeks. The amount of the allowable insurance claim was $1 million. We identified and documented a cumulative variance closer to $1.05 million, so there was a little wiggle room within the insurance claim. Having reached this amount, our goal was accomplished.

GAMBLING ON PRISON

From the foundation's perspective, we helped make the best of an extremely unpleasant situation. Not only was the foundation remunerated for a substantial portion of the theft, but Tasanee was also successfully prosecuted for her crime.

We produced a comprehensive report for the foundation that detailed how the crime was committed. We documented over $1 million of theft and secured the foundation's insurance claim. The findings that resulted from our investigation enhanced law enforcement's understanding of the crime and enabled the foundation to put measures in place to protect against future occurrences of such crimes.

The foundation's board members were aware of the difficulties associated with filing criminal charges in a white-collar fraud scheme. Would the district attorney make an indictment? Was there enough evidence for a conviction? Would the punishment fit the crime? Despite these uncertainties, the foundation proceeded with the criminal action to demonstrate that this type of behavior would not be tolerated.

Tasanee pled guilty to nearly 30 felony counts, including grand theft, embezzlement, and computer fraud. She was sentenced to 10 years in prison and immediate deportation to Thailand upon her release. She is also compelled to return the stolen funds to the foundation plus 10% interest. It is highly unlikely these monies will ever be recovered as they appear to have all been squandered on her gambling habit.

Tasanee's criminal actions affected a great many people. Not only did she destroy her future and split up her immediate family, but her crime also brought to light Herbert's weaknesses as a controller, which resulted in his termination.

LESSONS LEARNED

While this investigation presented several unique challenges, we saw it as a tremendous opportunity for us to hone our interviewing and organizational skills. During the initial phases of the engagement, we spent several entire days interviewing foundation personnel at all levels and in all areas in addition to bankers, accountants, and law enforcement. Dealing with the latter was particularly exciting as the investigation detectives made us feel that our contributions were of particular value to the criminal matter. We have gained a true appreciation for face-to-face interviewing techniques and the information that can be elicited through proper application of those techniques.

The second most important aspect of this investigation relates to organization and document management. By obtaining third-party documentation from the bank, we had a master set of indisputable records. When we combined the bank documentation with the boxes and boxes of paper held at the foundation, we had a bona fide library of records to sort through. We verified and streamlined our work by developing a custom Microsoft Access database application to review and record the contents of the documents. We methodically maintained originals in a massive set of binders that referred back to a master inventory. A reference was placed on each database record so that the paper document could be located in the binders in no time. This referencing was of particular use during the insurance company's examination of our report and findings.

One other lesson that stands out for us is the importance of recognizing luck in an investigation. If we had not determined the significance of the missing bank stamps on the deposit slips—the smoking gun—our investigation would not have come together as quickly as it did, nor would we have been able to quantify the theft as efficiently. We believe that the outcome at the end of the day would have been the same, but we do value having this bit of serendipity occur at the beginning of the investigation.

RECOMMENDATIONS TO PREVENT FUTURE OCCURRENCES

Our report on the investigation of Tasanee's fraud did not necessarily outline remedial steps for the foundation. Rather, it highlighted certain weaknesses within the accounting function. As a result of recognizing those weaknesses, Colin implemented several accounting controls to help protect against future instances of fraud.

Segregate and Rotate Duties

The foundation now segregates duties for the cash function. A different employee performs each of these functions: receiving and opening the bank statement, preparing the bank reconciliation, receiving incoming checks, preparing deposit slips, and physically making deposits. It is also important for duties of key accounting personnel to be rotated so that no employee exercises all power in any single area.

Review Bank Reconciliations

Now there is a higher-level review of the bank reconciliations at the foundation. In particular, there is greater scrutiny of the deposits in transit and outstanding checks.

Mandatory Vacations

The foundation also implemented mandatory vacation time. This allows the company to discover possible fraud while the employee is away.

Use Protective Services to Transport Cash

Perhaps the most effective new control in place is the most simple. The foundation now utilizes an armored transport service to deliver its incoming cash to the bank's drop box.

Howard B. Grobstein, CFE, CPA, is a partner in the Litigation & Insolvency Department of Grobstein, Horwath & Company LLP. He provides litigation consulting, expert witness testimony, fraud examinations, and forensic accounting services. Mr. Grobstein is a graduate of California State University, Northridge, and has 15 years of experience in handling fraud and litigation matters.

Joshua R. Teeple, CFE, CPA, is a partner in the Litigation & Insolvency Department of Grobstein, Horwath & Company LLP. He provides litigation consulting, data extraction and manipulation, fraud examinations, and forensic accounting services. Mr. Teeple is a graduate of University of Colorado and has nine years of experience in fraud and litigation matters.

CHAPTER 21

When Petty Cash Isn't Petty

KAREN FREY

An upstanding member of the community, Jeri Hansen was active in her church and the school's PTA, and served as a troop leader while her daughter was a Girl Scout. Married to her high school sweetheart for 14 years and now a mother of three, she was one of the most trusted employees at Foster Foods. Short and attractive, Jeri dressed well without being ostentatious and lived in a frame house—nice but not extravagant—on a country road. Although she drove a new vehicle, it was leased, not purchased. Little about her lifestyle suggested that she was supplementing the family income at her employer's expense.

Jeri had worked for Foster Foods in various positions for more than 15 years and had been in charge of petty cash accounting and reconciliation for the last 10. She also served as the accounts payable clerk. Her reputation was company-wide: If you want something reimbursed through petty cash, be sure that your documentation is both complete and accurate, or it won't get past Jeri.

Foster's finance and accounting staff was small, so Jeri knew a great deal about how the company worked, including the types of information the different officers wanted, expected, and relied on. She also knew how the independent auditors worked and the types of documents and summaries they normally requested. Occasionally Jeri appeared to resent her clerical status, believing that she knew more and could perform as well as some of the employees with better job titles and salaries. However, she was still diligent about making certain that her bosses and the auditors received everything that they needed to facilitate their work. "It would be a lot easier if I just get that *for* you" was her standard offer.

Founded in 1953 by brothers Arthur and Louis, Foster Foods began humbly in an old hog barn on the family farm, where they turned out a processed jam from excess fruit. Andrew Foster (son of Louis) recalls his father describing some of the early days. "It took a long time to learn the best way to make it—our pigs were the happiest ones around, because every time we goofed up they ate the mistakes." But learn they did, and despite some misadventures when fruitstuff ended up covering everyone and everything in sight, they developed a product that sold as fast as they could make it.

In 1975 Andrew assumed leadership as president and changed the strategy to an emphasis on research and development of specialty dried fruit products. By 1986 the changeover was complete, and the Fosters enlarged their product line and facilities in order to satisfy the rapidly growing demand. Today the company continues to develop new and innovative technologies. Utilizing its core competencies in research, development, and process engineering, Foster Foods currently manufactures more than 200 products in two facilities located in a mid-Atlantic state as well as several facilities in the Fiji Islands, and exports to more than 80 countries around the world.

The transformation took its toll, however. In the late 1990s Foster Foods was working to recover from a difficult period. Having filed for protection under Chapter 11 of the bankruptcy code, the company found that many of its suppliers and former creditors would no longer accept its checks—they demanded cash. Many businesses maintain a petty cash fund in order to pay small expenses, such as postage due, delivery fees, and other small cash purchases. At Foster Foods, though, long-haul company truck drivers also used petty cash to pay for highway and bridge tolls, minor repairs, and fuel at gas stations that would not accept their company's fuel charge cards. In addition, some deliveries to headquarters were on a cash-on-delivery (COD) basis.

For each petty cash disbursement, the custodian—Jeri—completed a petty cash voucher indicating the date and amount of the disbursement and to whom it was made. The person requesting the funds signed the document to acknowledge receiving the cash.

Because drivers received cash *before* each trip, they did not know exactly how much they needed; the amount they received in advance varied depending on the length of their trips. Upon returning, the drivers gave Jeri the receipts for cash they had spent, together with any remaining money. For example, if the driver started out with $250 and spent $160 for fuel and $19 for tolls, he would give her his two receipts totaling $179 plus his $71 remaining cash. Jeri would take the original petty cash voucher, cross off the $250 written there, and write in $179. She would complete the voucher by indicating the total of the expenses that were for fuel ($160) and tolls ($19), and attach the receipts to support the costs. Both the voucher (with its receipts attached) and the $71 went into the petty cash box.

After a number of trips, when the box filled up with vouchers and ran low, it was time to reimburse petty cash. As part of that process, Jeri completed a reimbursement envelope. On its face, she summarized the petty cash vouchers inside with their dates, to whom each item was paid, and an accounting distribution of the expenses. After entering all of them, Jeri added the columns, with the sum of the "Total" column indicating the amount of reimbursement needed. She placed the vouchers with their receipts inside the envelope and submitted it to the controller to request replenishment of petty cash. An internal control measure directed the controller to review the contents of the envelope before approving the replenishment. Then the treasurer would write a check to cash and give it to Jeri, who took it to the local bank.

TAKING A VACATION DAY

He wasn't looking when he found it. As the new chief financial officer of Foster Foods, Dan Jenkins had many more important things to worry about than something as insignificant as petty cash. Besides, Jeri clearly had things under control. On several occasions she had brought to his attention anomalies that a less astute person might have missed. No . . . petty cash could wait.

But one day Dan had a question and Jeri had the day off. In looking for the answer to his inquiry, Dan noticed a substantial petty cash disbursement to an equipment supplier—normally one paid by check. He remembers it well. "That transaction just didn't pass the 'smell test,' so I called the controller and said, 'We have a problem.'" By the end of the day, the two of them had found several occasions when invoices were indeed paid by check and the very same were "paid" again through petty cash. Dan Jenkins and Roger Stevens (the controller) began telephoning suppliers. "I have a question about this invoice—do you have any indication that we paid twice?" Their efforts failed to turn up a single supplier that had received duplicate payments. It was time to determine the nature and size of the problem.

Foster Foods asked its CPA firm to examine the petty cash records. The young accountant assigned to the case spent several weeks going through their records for the previous five years. He was able to identify more than 200 discrepancies totaling about $60,000—enough that Jenkins decided to call in the police and file criminal charges. The accountant had found three types of discrepancies:

- Duplicate payments where invoices were paid once by check and "paid" a second time through petty cash.

- Incorrect totals reported, where the total was greater than the attached receipts. Using the earlier example, the receipts for $179 may have been attached to a petty cash voucher that incorrectly read $279 or $379 or more.

- Incorrect transfers of information, where the amount written was greater than what was inside the envelope. Returning to the original example, the reimbursement envelope might contain a petty cash voucher correctly completed for $179 with the two valid receipts totaling $179 attached, but the summary line on the reimbursement envelope would indicate a total of $279.

Of all the discrepancies identified, the third type was certainly the easiest to detect. Because Jeri freely admitted that most of the petty cash vouchers and all of the envelopes bore her handwriting, it also provided the best evidence of intent to defraud the company. "I must have copied it wrong" would not serve as an excuse for the number and amounts of these issues. Things already seemed bad enough from Foster's point of view, but they were going to get worse. . . .

A LACK OF SUPPORT

Lindsay Dumont, the assistant district attorney assigned to investigate and prosecute the case, described herself as "not a numbers person." Since she was not satisfied with her understanding received from the initial Certified Public Accountant report, Lindsay first asked for only one thing: a more specific, down-to-earth explanation of the findings that would help her to present the case in court. In her words, "All I need is an 'accounting information and evidence for dummies' course." So we sat down together at the police station to work with the sealed carton of evidence.

From the very first envelope, it was apparent that the young and rather inexperienced CPA had missed a lot. We soon realized that what he had identified were only the most obvious discrepancies described earlier—just the tip of the iceberg. "I don't think we can just let these other things pass," Lindsay decided. "Can you check everything one more time?" The second review was eye-opening; I found not only additional occurrences of the types of irregularities just described, but several more methods that Jeri used to divert cash from the company's coffers to her own pockets. If she had more ingenious tricks, I missed them. Most were fairly obvious if someone took the time to look. Here are some of the other things she did:

- *Submitted receipts to petty cash more than one time.* When a driver paid cash for fuel and asked for a receipt, once in a while he received two copies. Jeri started submitting both of them for "reimbursement," attached to two different petty cash vouchers. Of course, one represented a proper accounting of the amount spent on behalf of Foster Foods for fuel, but Jeri used the second copy to divert cash for her own use. In more daring instances, two vouchers with identical receipts were in the very same petty cash envelope. Other times, some of them were dated weeks apart. In fact, that is what tipped me off. It made no sense at all to think that a driver would wait a couple of weeks to submit a receipt for reimbursement.

- *Used photocopies as support for additional payouts from petty cash.* Some tolls and other receipts were photocopied and cut to size, and the copies were submitted as support for payments a second or even a third time. When you find several toll documents that are stamped with the same date, the same collection window, and the same time that is recorded *to the nearest second*, you can be quite certain that you have fakes. The Massachusetts Turnpike was particularly prone to this type of problem because the records were printed in black ink on white paper stock—precisely what you would normally get from a photocopier. Receipts from other states would have been more difficult to replicate, and certainly not merely by photocopying them. The Pennsylvania Turnpike, for example, issued receipts on a stiff, manila-colored ticket with a green stripe; others used a shiny silver paper, colored punch cards, or multicolored inks.

- *Altered receipts.* Altered receipts can be tough to identify and even tougher to prove, but it can become quite obvious when it is combined with submitting both copies on two different vouchers, one of the schemes described previously. In one case, the first fuel receipt that came through was reimbursed for $60; the second copy, with the same service station location, date, invoice number, number of gallons, and price per gallon had a one ("1") inked in ahead of the total, so that the new total read $160.

  In another example, a UPS receipt for a COD package had "$1379.70" written in the "amount" box. The ink of the first digit was not quite the same color or thickness as the rest, and it was squeezed in against the left side of the box. Most people who run out of room when writing crowd the *right* side of the available space; think of any particularly large check that you wrote out by hand.

Unfortunately, although it appeared that $1,000 was diverted for Hansen's own use by entering a one ("1") at the front of the receipt, the evidence was not sufficient to prove it. UPS keeps its copy of such records for only one year. In addition, because *only* the UPS receipt supported the petty cash voucher, I was unable to determine either the supplier or the correct amount.

- *Petty cash vouchers had no supporting receipts at all.* By itself, this may not seem important. You might be able to imagine some circumstances that would result in a petty cash disbursement without a receipt. However, it becomes important if we examine the pattern. Arranging the items by date of occurrence revealed that, in the first three years, the only discrepancies involved the drivers' records. That is, petty cash vouchers were for $100 or $200 or so more than the attached documents. Not until August of the third year was there a single example of a petty cash payment without a receipt. Yet by May, two years later, this had occurred on 44 separate occasions, almost impossible from a simple error.

  Looking for patterns that evolve over time also provided additional evidence of some of the techniques described earlier. For example, Jeri did not use petty cash to "pay" for an item that had already been paid by check until the fourth year. Once she came up with that method, however, she used it on at least 25 more occasions between February and May of the following year.

- *Petty cash vouchers were made out for amounts where the "supporting" invoice specifically stated that no payment was due.* Toward the end of the time in question, Jeri became more and more inventive in finding ways to take Foster Foods' cash for herself. In one case, the company had a credit memo as a result of returning goods to a supplier; Jeri attached that to a petty cash voucher and removed money in the amount of the credit. In another case, the supplier had been paid in advance and the invoice was clearly marked as such, but Jeri used it to divert the funds anyway.

- *Both original and corrected invoices for an item were submitted for reimbursement.* In a variation of submitting both copies of a two-part receipt, two vouchers were made out to pay the same company for the same item, but for two different amounts. The second supporting invoice was clearly marked "revised," but Jeri removed petty cash, once to pay the correct invoice, and once for herself.

By the time we identified all of these incidents, we had established that approximately $100,000 had been diverted, quite a sum for a petty cash account. At this point, Foster Foods decided not to pursue the investigation any further, reasoning that there was already enough evidence for the district attorney to secure a conviction. Regardless of what the total was, the company was unlikely to recover much of anything from Jeri. Perhaps they did not want to know the full extent of the damage.

CAN WE RENEGOTIATE?

Lindsay Dumont was pleased with the additional information uncovered in the second investigation, and the district attorney's office went to court with more than 200 counts against Jeri Hansen, including (1) theft by unlawful taking, (2) theft by failure to make required disposition of funds received, and (3) multiple counts of tampering with records or identification with intent to deceive—a separate count for each of the falsified petty cash envelopes and/or vouchers.

Although Andrew Foster wanted to see Jeri "hung out to dry in the town square," that did not happen. Protesting to the very end "I didn't do it," Jeri was led in tears into the courtroom. However, the hearing proceeded and she admitted many incriminating things, including that the handwriting on all of the petty cash envelopes and vouchers was hers; that she was aware that amounts on credit memos indicated what the company should be receiving, not paying; and that she knew that certain vendors were to be paid through regular accounts payable procedures rather than through petty cash. Jeri and her attorney worked out a deal in which she was sentenced to 24 months of probation and ordered to make restitution—though in an amount substantially less than what she was found to have taken. She managed to repay nearly $18,000 right away, partly by cashing in her retirement fund. Unfortunately, she quickly defaulted on the schedule of payments set forth in the judge's order, and she was soon back in court.

"I know I haven't complied with the order, but I just can't come up with the money to make the payments," Jeri insisted. Despite this claim, she proposed (and the court agreed to) a suspension of the probation provisions in order to allow her to get caught up on the payments. The judge also gave her a new, more lenient, schedule. As you might expect, within just a few months she was back in court—and she never made a single payment. This time probation was revoked, and she was sentenced to serve the remainder of her 24-month sentence in the county jail.

LESSONS LEARNED

Several internal control weaknesses contributed to the loss of so much money. Most likely Jeri did not analyze them and plot to take advantage, but over time she noticed the controls were becoming automatic or skipped entirely. The first discrepancy involved a difference of just $20. But after five weeks passed and it remained undiscovered, she may have decided to test the system with the second $20 "error," her first true attempt to defraud the company.

That one went undiscovered as well, and Jeri Hansen had found a new source of income. As the months and years went by, like a boulder rolling downhill, the discrepancies started coming faster—first only once, then twice, until toward the end she was stealing as many as 10 times a month. As the frequency increased, so did the amounts—first $100 at a time, then $200, then $300. They also started becoming more imaginative and diverse. When Hansen, in the last year or so of the fraud, began "paying" vendors a "second time" through petty cash, the amounts grew into the upper hundreds and then thousands per incident. The largest was a single withdrawal of $3,030.

Jeri had too much control and not enough supervision. She was the petty cash custodian and also served as the accounts payable (AP) clerk in later years. An AP clerk examines invoices and compares them to purchase orders, receiving reports, and other documents. Upon finding proper authorization and support, the AP clerk forwards the documents to a different person, who writes the checks for payment. As both the AP clerk and the petty cash custodian, Jeri had full access to the information she needed to submit to petty cash items paid through regular channels. But how did she know she wouldn't get caught?

This is where a lack of internal controls enters the picture. The company's written procedures required Jeri to submit petty cash reimbursement requests to the controller for review and approval. However, no controller ever checked the receipts against the envelope summary. The reviews were nonexistent; approvals were automatic. Hansen had worked for Foster Foods for a long time. She was a valued and trusted employee, one who took few vacations and fewer sick days; one who was such a stickler for details—to the penny—that her reputation was company-wide. More than one controller apparently believed he had no reason to check the contents of the envelopes against the summary. After all, petty cash represented such a, well, "petty" amount, and Jeri had the situation well in hand. More important things demanded their time.

You might wonder, "Wouldn't the outside auditors have caught this?" And indeed, many of the things described here would be quite obvious to anyone who looked. However, the auditors considered petty cash to be so small as to be immaterial; that is, whether it was absolutely correct or whether it contained some degree of misstatement would have no effect on the judgment of financial statement users. For that reason, the outside auditors ignored petty cash.

RECOMMENDATIONS TO PREVENT FUTURE OCCURRENCES

One thing necessary to prevent future occurrences is to eliminate opportunities. Even in this age of technology, where computers have opened a whole new world of opportunity for fraud, the age-old themes still apply, such as segregation of duties and supervision. Based on the lessons learned, Foster Foods instituted a number of changes to its policies and procedures.

Segregation of Duties

One of the most basic yet often overlooked areas of fraud prevention is segregating duties so that any one person's ability to both perpetrate and conceal irregularities is very small. In response to the findings, Foster Foods has separated the duties formerly handled by Jeri Hansen so that petty cash and accounts payable are no longer handled by the same person. Further, the procedures have been changed so that one person prepares the vouchers and makes the disbursements, and a different person reviews the transactions, reconciles the cash, and prepares the summary when it is time to request reimbursements.

Supervision and Controls

Jeri never could have begun her five-year journey into fraud had the various controllers at Foster Foods followed their own written procedures. With adequate supervision and review, the first $20 error would have been found quickly; Jeri would have been reprimanded and probably would have apologized profusely while making a solemn vow to herself not to let that happen again. Written procedures or controls are of little good to a company if they are ignored. Foster Foods now requires that the controller initial the summary envelopes to accept responsibility for their contents.

Another opportunity for fraud detection could have been realized with analytical work regarding the truck fleet's fuel efficiency. Regular analysis of trucks' mileage versus gas consumption—something you would think would have the ongoing attention of management—would have signaled a problem to the controller quite early. Almost from the first incident, he would have noticed that one of the company's trucks was extremely inefficient in its fuel consumption compared to the rest, indicating either a problem with the truck or with purchases. Fuel analysis is now done regularly.

Mandatory Time Off

Combined with the lack of segregation of duties, refusal to take time off from the job is a red flag signaling possible fraud and cover-up. Foster Foods now requires that everyone in the accounting section be cross-trained and that each employee take a minimum of one week of vacation per year.

Be Aware

Because cash is the most liquid asset and can be transferred easily, the risk of theft is great. In addition to instituting effective control procedures, management needs to be aware of what employees are doing. Unfortunately, it is all too common that the most tireless and trusted worker, who never takes a day off, is the very one defrauding the company.

Karen Frey, Ph.D., CPA, is an associate professor at Gettysburg College. After more than a decade of practical experience in accounting and auditing, she earned a Ph.D. from the University of Maryland. Her research interests include managerial and forensic accounting, and she continues to consult on fraud cases.

CHAPTER 22

Where Did My Money Go?

ROBERT BARR

Cheryl Swanson was a typical suburbanite from Galveston, Texas. A high school graduate, she had worked as the office manager for Dr. Roberta Martin for over 12 years. Her husband, Paul, was a physical education teacher and coach for the parochial high school. She had two teenage kids—one son and one daughter, a junior and a sophomore in high school. Cheryl and Paul each had a salary of $45,000 per year.

Dr. Martin's husband and son had both died several years earlier, and she had no other living relatives. Due to the long relationship Cheryl had with the doctor, she was named the sole heir in the doctor's will.

Family was very important to Cheryl. Any time she was not at work, she was doing something with them. Her son and daughter were very committed to school and community activities, and Cheryl and Paul attended events to support their children. Though they were often short of cash, Cheryl liked to spend on her kids whenever she could. Cheryl and Paul were always saving to take nice vacations. They traveled all over the United States, often driving rather than flying to save money.

Dr. Roberta Martin was a well-known psychiatrist in the Houston area. In addition to her M.D. in psychiatry, she had also gone back to school and earned a Ph.D. in psychology. A Phi Beta Kappa, she was a very intelligent woman who thoroughly enjoyed her psychiatric practice. Dr. Martin had just turned 60.

She had a large practice, with a staff of 18 to 20 psychotherapists who specialized in drug rehabilitation. Dr. Martin had monthly accounts receivables of about $600,000, with the vast majority being billed to insurance companies.

For many years, the doctor had managed the business side of her practice with help from Cheryl. She had been rather meticulous in the management, reviewing the cash receipts and reconciling the amounts received to the number and types of patients seen that day. Although the checks were prepared and signed by Cheryl, Dr. Martin also cosigned every check, as she required two signatures. The doctor opened the bank statements each month before giving them to Cheryl. Once Cheryl had reconciled all three bank accounts, Dr. Martin reviewed and approved them. Dr. Martin also opened and reviewed the monthly account statements for her three investment brokerage accounts and one IRA account. Afterward, she gave the statements to Cheryl to file.

Dr. Martin did a reasonably good job of maintaining supervisory control over all of the business activities in her practice.

Like many physicians, however, the doctor wanted to practice medicine, not manage a business. In March, a well-known psychiatric hospital company approached Dr. Martin with the idea of helping manage her practice so that she could spend more time with patients. The doctor was intrigued and asked what the management company would do for her. Dr. Martin had a list of required activities, and the management company was willing to take on all of those requirements. As part of the agreement, the office staff and psychotherapists would become employees of the management company and would be eligible for improved benefits that the doctor could not offer. In addition, the management company would:

- Supervise the office manager and staff to ensure accurate accounting for the doctor's practice business activities
- Have management personnel onsite at the doctor's office at least one half-day for three days each week
- Maintain files on insurance claims
- Oversee the bill payment function and cosign all of the checks prepared by the office manager
- Monitor all bank deposits and reconcile them
- Review and approve the bank account reconciliations prepared by Cheryl each month for all three accounts
- Review the doctor's monthly brokerage statements for any unusual activity

For these services, the management company would be paid $7,500 per month.

The agreement was signed in late March, and the management company took over supervision of the practice as of April 1. The first week, they were in the office every day. The doctor was elated with the company's attentiveness and was thrilled to spend less time with the business side of the practice.

In the second week, once the procedures and accounting records had been established, Bonnie, the management company representative, was in the office for three half-days to supervise the business and cosign the checks. Since Bonnie was only in the office for a few hours, Dr. Martin often did not even see her but assumed that matters were being handled as agreed.

But after three weeks, Bonnie quit and was not replaced. As a result, no one from the management company ever set foot in the doctor's office again. With Dr. Martin no longer reviewing the details of the practice, and with no supervision from the management company, Cheryl had all of the opportunity she needed to get cash for her family. She started paying personal bills and sending the checks out with only one signature, and she quickly learned that the bank did not verify that there were two signatures on the checks. For several months, Cheryl continued to keep the accounting records set up by the management company. She also reviewed the brokerage account statements and learned how much money the doctor actually had.

In early August, Cheryl, Paul, and the kids went on a two-week vacation. As was generally the case, Cheryl spent lavishly on the holiday and had charged a large amount on their credit cards. With school about to start, both kids needed new uniforms. But there was a problem: Cheryl had charged the credit cards to their limits, and she had neither the cash nor the credit to buy the clothes needed for the kids. So Cheryl simply wrote a check on the doctor's practice account to "cash" for $2,500. The tellers at the bank knew Cheryl and did not verify the signature, as was required by bank policy for checks over $500. The tellers gave her the cash, and Cheryl realized that it would be no problem for her to supplement her income.

Once Cheryl discovered how easy it was to steal from the doctor, she decided to try taking some money from the brokerage accounts. In her first attempt, she used the doctor's signature stamp to prepare the request for withdrawal, but the brokerage firm would not allow a facsimile signature. So she forged the doctor's name, withdrew funds, and put them in Dr. Martin's practice account. From there, she could write checks and take money as she pleased.

The IRA that Was MIA

By November the following year, Cheryl had withdrawn all of the funds from the doctor's regular brokerage accounts along with $251,000 from Dr. Martin's individual retirement account (IRA). In early December, the broker called to ask about the large withdrawal from the IRA account. He asked to speak to the doctor, but Cheryl told him that the physician was too busy with patients to talk and had decided to make some other investments. The broker again insisted that he speak to Dr. Martin, but Cheryl claimed the doctor knew about the withdrawals and was not interested in speaking to him.

Luckily for Dr. Martin, the broker persisted and called her home to inquire about the withdrawals from the IRA account and what Cheryl had told him. The doctor indicated that if she was going to make other investments, she would have used her other brokerage account, not the IRA. The broker then told Dr. Martin that the other brokerage account with his security firm had already been emptied to a zero balance. Dr. Martin was furious and asked why she had not been notified of such transactions.

Even though it was already 10 p.m., Dr. Martin immediately called her attorney. They discussed the situation and decided that Cheryl may have made the withdrawals. The attorney called me at 2 a.m. and asked me to meet him at Dr. Martin's office at 6 a.m. He told me what they thought might have happened and that he wanted me to help investigate the matter. I am a practicing Certified Public Accountant with over 20 years of experience in auditing, fraud examination, and litigation consulting. I had previously worked for the attorney in other litigation cases as an expert witness.

On my suggestion, we called a 24-hour locksmith and had the locks to the offices changed before Cheryl could arrive. The attorney also arranged for an off-duty police officer to be in the reception room to keep Cheryl from getting into the offices. We checked the doctor's mailbox in the office building and found the bank statements that had been delivered after Cheryl had picked up the mail the day before. I opened them and started looking at the cancelled checks, noticing numerous payments to members of the office staff, including a large number to Becky Bolton, one of the psychotherapists. Becky was always one of the first people to arrive in the morning, so when she got there, the attorney and I asked her about the checks. She claimed that Cheryl would make the checks payable to one of the office staff and ask them to go to the bank to cash the check for the doctor, who needed some cash. These checks were not for small amounts—they ranged from $2,500 to $9,000. Cheryl was always careful to keep the amount under the $10,000 limit so that the cash transactions were not reported to the IRS.

We asked Dr. Martin, and she indicated that she used her debit card to get cash and that she had never asked Cheryl to obtain money for her. When Cheryl arrived for work, the attorney told her that she had been terminated and that she would not be allowed to enter the offices. Cheryl said that she had some personal items and that she needed to retrieve them. The attorney told her to make a list and that we would make sure that they were delivered to her that day, but that she would not be allowed to enter the offices. Cheryl tried her key, but found that the locks had been changed. She even attempted to climb into the office through the reception window, only to be pulled out by the policeman who was there. After being carried out of the window three times by the officer, and warned that she would be arrested if she persisted, Cheryl finally left Dr. Martin's office.

Dr. Martin and her attorney asked me to assist them in finding out how much money had been stolen, how it had been stolen, and how many people in the office were involved in the scheme. They also asked me to determine whether there was any possibility of recovery of funds from the management company, the bank, or the brokerage firms.

That first day in Dr. Martin's office, I found that there were virtually no business and accounting records. The only check stubs were those written in the last two days—everything else was gone. We did have the November bank statements and cancelled checks, but that was it. There were no details of amounts that had been billed to the insurance companies or the patients directly. We also found that there were no copies of the brokerage statements any time after July of the previous year. By then I recognized that I had a big job ahead of me.

CASHING OUT

Since we had only the November bank statement and cancelled checks available, I began looking at these items. The doctor's attorneys filed a lawsuit against Cheryl, the bank, the management company, and all three of the security brokerage companies, and of course, we requested copies of all documents in connection with each of the defendants.

I began analyzing the November bank statements. Since there were a number of unauthorized checks that were payable to four of the doctor's employees, we decided to question each of them.

The first interview was with Gene Henley, who indicated to us that Cheryl had asked him to go to the bank and cash a check for the doctor. Cheryl told him that the doctor needed some currency and was too busy to go to the bank. She made the check payable to Gene for $4,000 and instructed him to see one of three particular bank tellers, as they knew the doctor well and would take care of the transaction more quickly than anyone else. Gene did as he was told, saying that he had done this at Cheryl's request seven or eight times with amounts ranging from $4,000 to $9,000. He also said that almost everyone in the office had cashed checks like this at one time or another.

The next interview was with Laurie Dillon, a psychotherapist who had been with the doctor for about five months. I asked Laurie about two checks for $2,500 and $6,000. Additionally, Laurie said that Cheryl had asked her to go to the bank three other times in November, but Laurie did not feel comfortable with this process and had declined. Cheryl had told her that if she did not go, she would tell the doctor and have her fired. Laurie held her ground and refused to go to the bank because she did not like to carry that amount of currency with her and she did not believe Cheryl when she said the money was for the doctor. Laurie told me that she knew that the doctor did not carry cash—she always used her credit cards.

The interview with Becky Bolton, another of Dr. Martin's psychotherapists, was very interesting. Becky felt a lot of pressure as a psychotherapist and had requested one hour off each morning and each afternoon so that she could "recharge" and be ready for the next patient. Cheryl often asked if Becky would go to the bank for the doctor during the breaks, which Becky was willing to do.

I asked Becky if she was aware of how many checks she had taken to the bank in November. She said that it would be at least 12 because Cheryl asked her to go about three times each week. Becky said that the checks were often in the $3,000 to $9,000 range but that she really never paid much attention to the amounts since it was not her money. When told that she had gone to the bank 14 times in November, Becky was not at all surprised. However, she was somewhat taken aback that these checks totaled $66,000.

Becky told me that Cheryl had started asking her to negotiate checks a little over a year earlier and that originally they were made payable to "cash." However, one of the bank tellers told her that the bank's policies were changing and that the checks would need to be made payable to an individual. When Becky informed Cheryl of this, she began making the checks payable to the person that she had go to the bank each time.

Becky also told me a bit about Cheryl—that she was very dedicated to her two teenage children and that they liked to take nice vacations. She indicated that last July Cheryl's family, along with some friends, had spent two weeks at the nicest hotel suite in Aruba. I asked if she thought that Cheryl and her husband could afford a trip like that. Becky said that she thought that Dr. Martin might have helped them.

Once the bank finally provided all of the microfilm copies of the doctor's finances, the detail work began. We had three years' worth of transactions, which included about 400 checks and 35 deposits per month, many with 20 to 30 documents attached—nearly 40,000 pages of microfilm. The quality of the copies was poor at best, and some were completely illegible.

I started preparing a database listing the check date, check number, payee, amount, and, if the check was cashed at the bank, the number of the teller. Once the information was completed, I went over the payments with Dr. Martin to determine whether they were valid expenses for the practice, or if they needed further investigation. She stated that she never sent anyone to the bank to get cash for her; for security reasons, she did not like to carry currency.

In going through the finances, the doctor identified a number of payments that she said were not for her medical practice and that were unauthorized. The first of these were several checks to a travel agency that Dr. Martin had not used since her last vacation three years earlier, when she went on a Mediterranean cruise. The travel agency provided copies of all of the invoices, tickets, hotel reservations, and other expenses. The records showed that Cheryl had charged her family's entire trip to Aruba to the doctor's travel agency account, including the four families that joined them. They flew first class and stayed in a suite at the finest hotel on the beach, all courtesy of the doctor. The total cost was in excess of $143,000.

I was able to interview one of the families that went with Cheryl to Aruba, who claimed Cheryl told them that she had won over $500,000 at a slot machine in Las Vegas and that she had wanted to share the proceeds with her friends. But Cheryl was able to contact the other two families and tell them not to talk to us about the trip.

The doctor also pointed out questionable payments to clothing stores, consultants, construction companies, and certain of her employees. The investigation into these expenses showed that most were fraudulent. The clothing store payments were for purchases of clothing by Cheryl. The nearly $100,000 to the consultants and the construction companies were mostly for remodeling of Cheryl's home.

The database also indicated several deposits that had unusual items, including large checks from insurance companies that were only partially deposited into the doctor's bank account. The remaining balances were taken in cash, money orders, and cashier's checks. We found one check from an insurance company paying the doctor about $85,000. Cheryl had stamped the back of the check with the doctor's signature and deposited approximately $22,000 into the doctor's bank accounts. She took the rest in several ways. First, Cheryl had obtained $21,500 in money orders. Four of them were payable to Ford Motor Credit for $413.50 each. The cancelled money orders matched Cheryl's vehicle loan account number, the monthly payment on her vehicle. All of the other money orders were also used for Cheryl's personal expenses, including $6,000 for the catering, bartender, servers, and maids for her family's Christmas party.

Cheryl had also obtained $33,000 in cashiers' checks from the proceeds of the insurance money. Two of the cashiers' checks (one for $1,000 and one for $5,000) were paid to employees of the doctor for alleged Christmas bonuses. There were also two cashiers' checks payable to American Express, one for $4,000 and one for $10,000. The account numbers revealed that the $4,000 cashiers' check was credited to Dr. Martin's American Express account but the $10,000 check was credited to Cheryl's American Express account. Moreover, there were two cashiers' checks payable to Dr. Martin, one for $8,000 and one for $5,000. The $8,000 check was negotiated using the doctor's signature stamp and was presented at the bank for cash. The doctor says that she never saw any of this money. The $5,000 check was actually deposited into the doctor's personal bank account. Dr. Martin told me that she had never authorized any payments like these.

I also tested the deposits made after Cheryl had been terminated as compared to the ones that had been made when she handled the office duties. Shortly after the management company had taken over, no currency was deposited into the bank for insurance copayments. Before the management company was hired, $400 to $700 per week was being credited to the doctor's bank accounts. After Cheryl was terminated, there was again $400 to $700 in currency being deposited into Dr. Martin's accounts. Although I could not prove the exact amount taken, I estimated that Cheryl likely took about $2,000 per month in currency for copayments over a period of about 15 months, or an additional $30,000 in theft proceeds.

An Unhappy Ending

This investigation took several months to complete. Although Dr. Martin had sued Cheryl, the bank, the management company, and the security brokerage firms, she also made it clear to her attorney that she wanted Cheryl to go to jail.

The bank had requested an analysis of the transactions in the 60 days before the discovery of the fraud. The liability of the bank, by federal law and by contract with the depositors, is limited to 60 days. In this case, that amounted to about $115,000. However, 95% of the checks in this branch were cashed by 3 of 29 tellers. Although we never said the word "collusion," the facts spoke for themselves.

To start the pursuit of criminal prosecution, Dr. Martin's lawyer called the district attorney's office and scheduled a meeting to go over all of the evidence that we had compiled. At the end of the three days, the investigators said that this case would be a "slam dunk" because of the degree of documentation that I had provided and that it would be easy to get an indictment for a number of charges. I left the DA's offices believing that charges would soon be forthcoming against Cheryl.

However, this was not the case at all. The district attorney's office sat on this material for well over two and a half years before taking any of it to a grand jury. Calls to the DA's office did not help move the case along. But after almost three years, the grand jury indicted Cheryl Swanson on 34 counts. Cheryl was an insulin-dependent diabetic. The evening of the charges, she told all of her family good night and took an extreme dose of insulin just as she went to bed. Her husband said he knew she was dead when he tried to wake her up the next morning. Paramedics were called, but it was clear that Cheryl had passed away at least six hours previously.

After being terminated by Dr. Martin, Cheryl had gone to work in the office of the parochial high school in her community—the same one where her husband worked as a physical education teacher. Almost immediately after her death, news of the indictment was released, and the school began looking into their records, and found that in the almost three years that she had worked there, Cheryl had been able to steal almost $400,000.

Subsequent to Cheryl's demise, settlement negotiations took place with the remaining defendants in the civil litigation. The bank did not want to go to trial because the tellers had not followed written instructions that required all checks presented for cash to be traced to the signature card. Since the litigation was filed before limits on punitive damages in Texas, the institution was sufficiently frightened of what a jury might do and so it settled for an amount in excess of $750,000.

Next was the deposition of the chief financial officer of the management company who negotiated the agreement for the doctor's practice. Counsel started by asking whether the company had done the things that it had agreed to do.

Did it cosign all of the checks? Not after the first three weeks. Did it go to the doctor's office and supervise the office administration? Not after the first three weeks. Did it review the bank account reconciliations? No. Did it review the insurance billings? No. Did it review the reconciliation of insurance billings to insurance receipts? No. Did it review the reconciliation of patients seen to insurance billings, patient billings, and cash receipts? No. Did it review the doctor's security brokerage statements to ensure proper accounting? No. Did it ensure the maintenance of insurance billing files? No. Did it collect the fee of $7,500 per month for providing these services? Yes, absolutely.

When counsel had finished these few questions, he said, "I have no further questions." The entire deposition lasted less than 30 minutes. Less than a week later, the management company settled with a payment of $1 million to the doctor.

It took several more years before the three security brokerage firms settled with the doctor. After all of the expenses and legal fees, the doctor ended up with about $1.1 million of the $1.5 million that had been taken by Cheryl.

LESSONS LEARNED

Dr. Martin found another management company to help her. At my recommendation, she obtained references from several other doctors who were using the management company to determine that they were legitimate and effective.

Dr. Martin negotiated several items to include in the new management contract. First, she demanded that the bank account reconciliations be prepared and approved no later than the fifteenth day of each month. Second, the management company would prepare and give to the doctor an analysis of insurance billings and collections no later than the tenth day of each month. Third, the company would prepare two accounts receivable listings—one for patients and one for insurance companies—and give them to the doctor no later than the tenth day of each month.

At my recommendation, the doctor began having the bank account statements mailed to her home rather than to the office. Dr. Martin now opens the bank statement, reviews the statement, and reviews the cancelled checks (and later the images of the cancelled checks) to ensure that all were paid to authorized vendors and are for reasonable amounts.

She then takes the statement to the management company so that it can prepare the bank account reconciliations. We initiated this compensating control due to the small size of the administrative staff and the inability to segregate functions as would be done in a larger company.

Additionally, Dr. Martin reviews receivables each month and compares collections to the amounts deposited into the practice bank accounts. She also monitors the receivables with the insurance companies to ensure positive cash flow for her practice.

RECOMMENDATIONS TO PREVENT FUTURE OCCURRENCES

Background Checks

Dr. Martin says that she wishes that the parochial school had called her for a reference about Cheryl, as she would have told them exactly what had happened and that Cheryl could not be trusted. The doctor now checks references on all new employees. She obtains a release from the prospective employee to allow previous employers to release information without liability. The doctor asks to speak with the person's direct supervisor for the previous three places of employment and makes specific inquiries about the integrity of the candidate. Dr. Martin says that this has caused her not to hire two persons for employment. In both cases, there were problems with the person's integrity; in one case, the person had given a written statement admitting to theft from the company. Dr. Martin believes that getting these references has helped her to stop additional fraud losses at her practice and that similar procedures would help other companies to stop fraud losses.

Supervisory Review

At my recommendation, Dr. Martin now receives the bank statements for her accounts at her home address rather than the office. She reviews them and the images of the cancelled checks to ensure that the transactions are authorized.

Robert Barr, Jr., CFE, CPA, is a manager with Harper & Pearson Company, P.C. in Houston, Texas. His firm provides public accounting, fraud examination, consulting, and expert witness services. Mr. Barr is a University of Houston graduate with over 25 years of experience in detecting and preventing white-collar crime. He teaches a graduate-level fraud examination course at UH.

CHAPTER 23

Three Strikes and You're Out!

MARY BEST

Dan Knorr was liked by everyone he worked with in the Lawrencetown Parks and Recreation Department. Stocky, with an easy smile and an outgoing personality, he seemed much younger than his 45 years. Dan and his wife, Margie, often had parties at their large, pleasant house where coworkers and guests were treated to plenty of food and drinks. The Knorrs also liked to travel to popular places including Las Vegas, Florida, and the Dominican Republic at least a couple of times a year.

At work, Dan was a conscientious if somewhat unremarkable employee, having slowly worked his way up the ranks in the City's Parks and Recreation Department. After an amalgamation of the city with several adjoining municipalities five years after his hire, Dan's responsibilities increased along with the population base using the recreation programs. Eventually his dedication and long service earned him the position of assistant department manager, where he performed administrative tasks, such as budgeting and approving invoices. When the department manager moved to another position, Dan replaced her as acting manager of Parks and Recreation. He was an easygoing boss and not too demanding of his staff.

The city and each of its surrounding regional municipalities had many organizations devoted to programs such as baseball, football, soccer. The Parks and Recreation employees were especially prized for their knowledge. As a result, Dan Knorr was invited to become a board member for a number of groups and generously consented to the volunteer time required. He became the treasurer for one of these nonprofits, the Regional Recreation Association, an umbrella organization for activities around the area. Generous and well liked, Dan Knorr was considered a solid member of the community. The municipality of Lawrencetown was incorporated in the mid-1700s. Although it is situated on a natural harbor, its remote location, northern exposure, and cold Atlantic winter winds have kept the population growth at a standstill compared to the big coastal cities farther south. While it enjoys a seasonal population boost in the summer months, Lawrencetown is a small city by most standards, with a permanent population of only around 60,000.

Lawrencetown's staff consisted of about 50 employees prior to the amalgamation. Afterward, most of the staff in the consolidated municipalities were given jobs in the new structure, and the number of employees doubled overnight. They work in all the usual departments, including police, fire protection, public works, planning and development, water and sewer, and parks and recreation. There is no internal audit function.

Parks and Recreation is busy since Lawrencetown is a very sports-minded community. Fall fitness classes are well attended and winter sports are keenly competitive. Even spring and summer teams, recreation programs, and water sports are very popular with students out of school with parents looking to keep their children busy.

Internal controls are made difficult by the perpetual registrations for programs—small dollar amounts, many different volunteer organizations to deal with, and lots of cash. The Parks and Recreation Department is also responsible for operating certain athletic facilities, including several arenas and pools, soccer and baseball fields, and other venues. In addition the department operates a subsidy program for various community youth sports organizations. To help them with their operating costs, Lawrencetown contributes a set amount each year for every child registered. For instance, a youth soccer association might get $50 per child; if 200 children are participating, the group would receive a total annual subsidy of $10,000.

Characterized by a busy environment, low staff turnover, lots of cash transactions, and a focus on the delivery of successful recreation programs, the Parks and Recreation Department did not consider financial controls its top priority.

A DOUBLE HEADER

In late March, an innocent inquiry by the chairman of the Parks and Recreation Committee one Monday morning started the ball rolling. The chairman asked Wendell Short, an employee working in the Parks and Recreation Department, how much the city had paid to the East Town Minor Hockey Association for the current and previous year. This group was in his municipal electoral district, and the chairman was anxious to know the level of support prior to his appearance at a major hockey tournament. Normally the chairman would have asked Dan Knorr, the acting manager. However, Dan was out of town. As a result, Wendell took the call. Wendell could only find the current year's East Town file. He asked the city's Finance Department for the information it had. The Finance Department produced the requested listing of payments made to this organization for both years. But when he received the list, Wendell was puzzled. Right at the top, it showed two large payments in the current year: one in January for $25,650 and one in March for $25,000. Why two? Wendell recognized the March figure since he had requested that amount only a couple of weeks earlier. But what was the January payment? Wendell concluded that it must have been an accidental double payment.

Since he figured he'd have to get the earlier payment back from the association, Wendell decided to phone East Town's treasurer, Charlie Howard. But when he called, Charlie said he didn't remember receiving any January payment at all; in fact, he had been very late in requesting the organization's annual subsidy. After checking, he phoned Wendell back to confirm that the only money the East Town Minor Hockey Association had received since early the previous year was in March for $25,000. This information substantially complicated matters. Wendell knew he still had to get back to the chairman, and to do this, he had to clear up the matter of the January payment for $25,650. His next move was back to the city's Finance Department. He told the manager, Will LeMain, what he was looking for and got help from the staff to retrieve source documents for the two payments. The check requisition forms requesting the payments were pulled, along with the cleared checks. Wendell brought along the current year's subsidy file, and he and Will began studying the paperwork.

First, they verified the March payment. The subsidy file from East Town contained an itemized listing of 500 children registered for hockey in the fall of the previous year. Along with this was a memo from Charlie Howard requesting the annual payment of $50 per child, or $25,000 total. The check requisition for payment by the city was prepared by Wendell, properly approved by Dan Knorr, the department manager, and paid by the Finance Department. The March payment was good. Wendell and Will then turned their attention to the January payment. The check requisition for this payment showed 513 children at $50 per child, or $25,650. However, there was no supporting information at all. The requisition was both prepared and approved by Dan Knorr. Both checks were made out in the name of East Town Minor Hockey Association, and the same address was printed on the face of the checks. However, the reverse of the checks were not the same. The March cancelled check showed a stamp by Scotiabank. The January cancelled check showed a Firstbank stamp but a different bank account number.

Next, disbursements to a completely separate regional organization, the Halton County Baseball Association, were examined. Wendell Short had been suspicious of a payment to them the year before, since the city generally funded only municipal organizations. But he was new in his position then, and Dan Knorr reassured him that the payment was okay. Recalling this incident, Wendell now wondered whether looking at these transactions might help shed some light on the East Town Minor Hockey payments. Although the checks were made out to two completely separate organizations, they had been deposited to the exact same bank account!

Obviously, something was wrong. A telephone call to Charlie Howard, East Town's treasurer, confirmed that their organization's bank was Scotiabank, not Firstbank, and Charlie reiterated that East Town had not received any payments from the city in January. The president of Halton County Baseball Association confirmed that the organization's bank was not Firstbank. In fact, the president told Wendell that the baseball association did not receive any funding from the city at all.

Check requisitions to the Halton County Baseball Association were also initiated and approved by Dan Knorr. No supporting documents were found. So far the investigation had taken about three days. At this point, Wendell and Will believed there was something wrong, that city funds were being somehow diverted, and that Dan Knorr was the only common thread that tied the transactions together.

As manager of finance, Will LeMain decided to present the information to the city's chief administrative officer, who quickly informed other key people: the mayor, the chairman of finance, the chief of police, the director of human resources, and the city attorney. They decided to move quickly. Upon his return to the office the next day, Dan Knorr was confronted. When he offered no explanation, he was suspended from his position and escorted off the premises.

Since there was no internal staff to do a thorough investigation, the city looked to a professional accounting firm for help. Having recently assisted with several cases related to fraud, I got the assignment. My instructions from the city were to review the information that had been gathered on the suspected fraud and, if their suspicions proved true, to delve further to determine the time frame and methods used by Dan Knorr to divert funds and to quantify the amounts involved. All of these events, from the initial question by the chairman of the Parks and Recreation committee to hiring an investigator, took less than a week.

A HOME RUN

After briefing me on the background, the chief administrative officer asked me how I planned to go about investigating the situation. "Oh, by the way," he said, "there's a city council meeting two weeks from yesterday, and we're hoping you'll attend it to explain things." I thought to myself, "If Dan Knorr were actually responsible for the fake requisitions, he'd had 13 years of employment to perfect his technique. And they want me to find out all about it in 13 days!" I laid out my planned approach for the investigation. "I think I'd like to start the process on two fronts," I explained. "First, we need to look at all payments from the Parks and Recreation Department to recreation or sports organizations. Starting with the current year and working back, we'll identify any suspicious transactions. Second, I want to get into Dan Knorr's office as soon as possible to see whether there's any useful evidence there." I met with Charlie McAskill, the big, burly chief of police for Lawrencetown, to get into Dan Knorr's office. McAskill had locked the office soon after Knorr had been suspended. Now we were going to see what we could find.

My first impression was that the workspace was messy. It was also big, with a large desk, a credenza on one side, and a floor-to-ceiling bookcase. Papers and files were everywhere. Stacked loosely around the perimeter of the desk were several uneven piles, one leaning against the computer monitor for support. Boxes of papers were stowed under the desk and beside the credenza.

"Whew!" Chief McAskill said. "You've got your work cut out for you."

We needed to catalog what was there, and we had to make sure we could identify where it came from.

"Do you need a helper from the Police Department?" the chief asked. I quickly said yes. I felt it was a good idea to have two people there at all times in case any questions arose later about chain of custody.

Once my helper arrived, I started by tagging all the boxes, shelves, and piles, working from the door around the office and back again in a systematic fashion. I began to hit pay dirt at the desk. In the drawers and in boxes underneath were bank statements and deposit slips from a Firstbank account called "Regional Recreation Association." A quick comparison showed that the account number was the one identified by Wendell Short and Will LeMain on the back of the suspicious checks to East Town Minor Hockey Association and Halton County Baseball Association. I also found some credit card statements in Dan Knorr's name, from several different credit card companies. A few personal joint bank statements and personal bills were also there. On the top of the desk were several old subsidy files from a previous year.

Meanwhile, upstairs in Finance, the tedious work of going through the general ledger accounts and pulling supporting documents was proceeding. Slowly emerging from the mass of transactions was a list of checks and payments that looked suspicious. Lack of support, authorizations by Dan Knorr for his own requisitions, and Firstbank endorsements isolated these payments from many legitimate ones.

Now that I had plenty of information to work with, I needed to figure out what was going on. As a starting point, I used the check dated in January of the current year for $25,650 to East Town Minor Hockey Association. At Dan Knorr's desk, I found a "Quick Deposit" slip to the Regional Recreation Association bank account, listing the check from the city along with a small cash amount. Since I happened to be a Firstbank customer myself, I recognized the "Quick Deposit" slip as the kind you just fill in and drop in a slot for the tellers to process later. I traced the resulting amount to the January Firstbank account statement for Regional Recreation Association found in Dan Knorr's office. It exactly matched a deposit on January 22.

I thought, "How was a check made payable to East Town Minor Hockey Association able to get deposited into an account called Regional Recreation Association?" A quick flip-over of the cleared check showed the endorsement signature of "Charlie Howard." Later I would confirm with him that this was a forgery. So now I knew for certain that the city's check had been deposited in Regional Recreation Association's bank account on January 22. The next item was a check for $8,595 coming out of the account on January 23; the payment was made to Capital Credit Card Services. Recalling that I had cataloged several Capital Credit Card bills in the personal information found at Dan Knorr's desk, I pulled out the statement showing a payment on January 28 for $8,595. The credit card was in the name of Dan Knorr and was sent to his business address. The incriminating trail was now complete. Starting with a city check, the money had gone through an intermediate bank account and right to Dan Knorr's personal credit card.

As I investigated further, the details that follow began to emerge.

Eleven years prior, Dan Knorr became treasurer of Regional Recreation Association, an organization formed to promote and assist in offering all types of recreational activities in the Lawrencetown area. Three years later, this association merged with another recreational organization, keeping the same name but obtaining a broader countywide mandate and a larger budget funded by several levels of government. Dan was treasurer of both the old and the new organization, remaining in this position for five years.

A Firstbank account was opened in Dan's first year on the job for the association. He and two other directors were signing officers, with two signatures required on checks. The bank account address was the association's post office box number. When the new treasurer of Regional Recreation finally took over for Dan, she opened a new account for the organization at a different bank in a more convenient location. The new treasurer assumed the Firstbank account was closed. However, it wasn't. Dan left Regional Recreation Association's Firstbank account opened, merely changing the address to that of the city's Recreation Department. That way, the monthly bank statements were delivered directly to Dan at work. He used the Firstbank account as a conduit to cash improperly obtained checks and withdraw the funds for his personal use. I found that four years after the new treasurer took over, Dan Knorr began diverting money from the city through phony check requisitions for various sports associations into Regional Recreation Association's Firstbank account. These amounts started reasonably small, with check amounts between $900 and $2,500. However, they grew quickly to include individual checks as high as $9,500, $15,000, and the one that was ultimately found for $25,650 in January. In total, Dan extracted approximately $500,000 in a little over six years. No wonder he was able to afford expensive trips and lavish parties!

In order to get the checks issued from the city, Dan had to prepare a check requisition. He cleverly used legitimate organizations as payees and reasonable explanations for the requests. As a result, authorizations by the Recreation Department manager were primarily a check to see if the budget for that particular type of activity was exceeded. Dan prepared a great many valid requisitions that looked no different from the fictitious ones. Supporting documents weren't typically attached to the check requisitions, since it was assumed that the details of individual registrants were kept in files to be easily viewed at any time.

When Dan became acting manager of Parks and Recreation, he was able to approve his own check requisitions, along with those of others. This made the process of obtaining checks even easier, although budget constraints still remained as a ceiling on what was ultimately available. However, I later discovered that the dollar amounts of the fraudulent checks did not push the related accounts over budget because Dan was falsely inflating them. This was very ingenious on his part since he knew that budgets are watched very strictly in any municipality. For instance, if the proper amount of subsidy for a certain association was based on registrations of approximately 350 participants and the budget was inflated to provide for 500 participants, the excess would leave a slack amount available for Dan to divert without raising any red flags. Additionally, the amalgamation of the city and the municipalities afforded an opportunity to increase the recreation program budget areas substantially, as the numbers from the combined entities were not initially known.

Checks for a variety of recreational organizations were commonly addressed to the Parks and Recreation Department at the City of Lawrencetown. Since many of these volunteer organizations had no permanent addresses and the treasurers were constantly changing, it was not unusual to have the city address listed and the checks picked up. However, this practice allowed Dan to be able to intercept a check without it being mailed to the organization, something that may have exposed the scheme earlier.

Accordingly, the sports organizations to which extra checks were payable did not know about them since they were receiving their correct subsidies through regular channels. Similarly, the Regional Recreation Association did not know about the unusual activities in its unknown bank account. And finally the victim, the City of Lawrencetown, did not realize anything was amiss, since the checks were cleverly concealed amid other similar payments and the amounts did not exceed the previously inflated budget levels. It was almost a bulletproof plan, and I understood why the scheme had gone undetected for so many years.

Since the Regional Recreation Association sounded like an umbrella organization for several different sports groups, the bank never questioned any of the deposits. But just to make sure, Dan always used the drop box to avoiding any face-to-face questions from tellers. Payments were all done by check. Remembering that the account required two signatures, I noted that Dan Knorr was always one of the signers. I asked the other two signing officers to confirm their signatures on several checks made out to Dan Knorr's credit cards or personal bills. They were forgeries.

Although the full investigation took the better part of a month to complete, I had enough details to attend the closed session of City Council as promised. I presented the East Town Minor Hockey example. Seeing the incriminating trail with their own eyes saved a lot of explanations. However, there was still plenty of heated discussion and lots of questions. Dan Knorr had no doubt been clever, but the councilors agreed that troubling issues remained about the city's internal controls.

THE FINAL INNING

Based on the outcome of the investigation, Dan Knorr was charged by the police with theft and forgery. Not surprisingly, his temporary job suspension became permanent. Out of work and facing financial ruin and public humiliation, he was beginning to reap the ugly consequences of his illicit activity. Dan pleaded guilty to both charges. Prior to sentencing, his lawyer prepared a written request to the court for leniency. Everyone connected with the case was keenly interested to find out what Dan Knorr had to say about his actions. He began by corroborating the evidence outlined in my written report. This included key points on inflating city budgets in advance, obtaining checks through false check requisitions, and using Regional Recreation Association's bank account as a conduit. The submission got more interesting after that, since it dealt with Dan's motivation for the crime. It noted that he fully expected to get caught in "year one," although it never stated exactly what year that was. He claimed that he fully intended on repaying the amounts he had "borrowed," but this became increasingly unrealistic and eventually impossible as the amounts grew larger. One could argue that the underlying reasons for Dan's behavior lay in a deep desire to please everyone around him: his family, friends, and coworkers. This caused him to do such things as always pick up the tab for meals, drinks, and entertainment and to make substantial donations to a variety of good causes. These expenses were well beyond his means, but the stolen money offered him the way to pay for them. Coupled with this were two common vices: drinking and gambling. Dan played the lottery on an ever-increasing basis with the hope that he would win big and be able to repay the amounts he had stolen. That never happened. As a result, drinking became a problem.

The submission commented on the acute suffering Dan was currently undergoing as a result of his actions. Loss of prestige in the community was cited along with financial ruin and the prospect of extremely limited future job prospects. Also it was noted that Dan had received many letters of support from stalwart members of the community. The submission concluded that since Dan was no danger to the public, had always been a hard worker, and was extremely remorseful, he was a prime candidate for conditional sentencing.

However, the submission did not generate much sympathy for him. While showing the human face of the crime, it also confirmed that Dan fully understood what he was doing. Areas such as budget manipulation and the intricate mechanics of exploiting operating procedures at the city and the bank indicated a level of sophistication that went far beyond spur-of-the-moment actions. Also, while Dan accepted responsibility for what he had done, it didn't appear that he accepted much blame for his actions. Instead he hinted that the situation resulted from the city's poor controls and the bank's lax procedures in not requiring financial statements or confirmation of signing officers. Finally, although the submission outlined the generous things Dan did with the city's money, conspicuously absent was any mention of his purchases for personal gratification such as expensive trips to popular vacation destinations.

The sentence was delivered in the historic downtown courthouse, jammed with curious onlookers and people more directly affected by Dan's activities. Although the judge toyed with the benefits of house arrest in the sentencing preamble, causing representatives of the City of Lawrencetown in attendance to hold their collective breaths, in the end that was not adequate punishment for such premeditated activity. Dan was sentenced to two years in prison. He served about half of the time in a maximum-security federal penitentiary, hopefully a grim deterrent to others who might contemplate similar activities. Since his release, Dan Knorr has led a quiet life out of the public eye. He keeps busy with jobs as a manual laborer and over the course of time has dropped out of sight almost completely.

LESSONS LEARNED

Everyone connected with this case learned something. The City of Lawrencetown learned that gaps in internal controls are an open invitation to fraud. Accordingly, it moved swiftly to plug the leaks highlighted by the investigation. Managers were strictly reminded to review supporting documents carefully before approving check requisitions, and they were no longer allowed to approve their own disbursements. Mailing procedures for suppliers' checks were revamped to minimize any possibilities for interception. Pickup of checks was discouraged. The sports subsidy program was reviewed carefully to determine the correct amounts, and the budgets were reduced correspondingly.

In addition, the investigation had uncovered a couple of interesting side issues. The city had encountered considerable difficulty in finding documents from earlier years, and data kept in a software program no longer in use was unreadable. This prompted city leaders to look at better methods for cataloging paper-based financial information and to discuss with their computer consultants ways to access older electronic records.

Personally, I learned a number of things. I gained insight into some different methods used to conceal fraudulent activities, adding this information to my toolkit for future reference. Also, I learned a lot about how to deal with large groups of very different stakeholders. For example, the issues that were important to elected members on City Council, who had to deal with the public, were entirely different from those of the Parks and Recreation Department, whose members were primarily interested in whether the investigation would affect their sports subsidy program.

I was intrigued that the fraud had gone on for such a long time without being detected. I saw that the reasons for this lay in Dan's ability to seize opportunities to improve his plan each year to reduce the possibilities for detection. Inflating the budgets was a brilliant stroke. Also, upon finding that a department manager could approve his own check requisitions, Dan quickly shifted to this approach, which eliminated any concerns around getting fake disbursements approved. Ultimately, though, Dan made a key mistake in handing control of the sports subsidy program to another employee, which led to exposure of the plan.

Two final lessons were learned about public perception and punishment. The letters of support for Dan Knorr made me wonder whether people didn't care or just didn't understand how fraud ultimately affects everyone. However, perhaps these people were simply too close to Dan to see the bigger picture. I also observed that while the justice system may sometimes seem to be too lenient on white-collar crime, it isn't always that way. In this particular case, the courts cracked down hard. Dan Knorr learned the tough way that timeworn old cliché: "Crime Doesn't Pay."

RECOMMENDATIONS TO PREVENT FUTURE OCCURRENCES

Segregation of Duties

For small entities that have volunteers for treasurers, like Regional Recreation Association, a regular changeover of signing officers is important to keep a situation like this one from going on a long time. It can be hard to find a competent treasurer, and as a result organizations tend to hang on to the good ones as long as they can. But a change brings in new thoughts and ideas as well as fresh eyes to review financial controls.

Communication with Banks

Authorized signatories for a nonprofit organization should make sure to confirm with the bank that the previous signing officers have been replaced. Any time an organization changes banks, a letter from the prior financial institution should be obtained confirming that the earlier account has been closed and all funds have been transferred to a new account. Directors should be trained not only to find out what the organization does but what controls are in place. Finally, although a financial audit is not a panacea to uncover fraud, it would have been a deterrent in this case since covering up the amounts running through the bank account would have required extra effort.

Strict Enforcement of Organization Rules

For regular businesses and larger organizations like municipalities, fraudulent activity can result when existing rules are bent without anyone realizing it. In the City of Lawrencetown, check requisitions were required to be approved, but somewhere along the way it became acceptable to allow the managers to approve their own requisitions. A good dose of common sense would tell you that this sounds like a dangerous practice, which it turned out to be. Accordingly, approvals need to be done by someone other than the person purchasing or receiving the items.

Required Documentation for Payments

As a final recommendation, payments should provide proof that the goods or services were necessary to the organization and therefore were properly authorized in the first place (purchase orders), that they were actually received and used by the organization (receiving reports), and that there are valid requests to pay (suppliers' invoices). Matching of these documents and adequate segregation of duties in these key areas helps to make internal controls work to prevent fraud.

Mary Best, CFE, CA, is a partner with Arsenault Best Cameron Ellis, a public accounting firm operating in Canada's Atlantic region as part of the AC Group of Independent Accounting Firms. Ms. Best has been in public accounting for over 30 years, including 14 years as a partner with an international chartered accounting firm.

24

Country Club Fraud—What a Steal!

JOHN BOEKWEG

Melody Gunther was an unmarried 23-year-old woman who believed that life had treated her unfairly. She was not born into a wealthy family. In fact, her parents divorced when she was a teenager, and her mother and siblings struggled financially as a result. Although the neighborhood Melody grew up in was not in the most affluent part of town, she had friends and acquaintances from school who came from wealthy families. Seeing the lifestyles and opportunities enjoyed by her peers caused her to want more in life than she could afford.

After graduating from high school, Melody worked a series of part-time jobs while still living at home with her mother. She was never paid enough to support her spending habits, so she was constantly looking for job opportunities with a higher hourly wage. Eventually she found work as a teller in a local bank.

While employed at the bank, Melody fell deeper and deeper into debt. She had purchased a new car, was racking up credit card charges, and having trouble making the minimum monthly payments. In order to avoid bankruptcy, she stole some money from the till to cover some of her debt payments with the intention of paying it back as soon as she received her next paycheck. The theft was discovered immediately, and she was terminated.

After her termination, Melody quickly found employment at a local country club as a receptionist. Her position made her the first person members contacted when they entered the clubhouse. She charmed everyone with her smile and flirted with the older, wealthy men. When given the opportunity, she complained to them about her troubles to garner sympathy. Occasionally a member would even give her money to lend support.

Melody's coworkers were becoming frustrated with her laziness. She was constantly filing her nails and doing her makeup. She arrived late, left early, and took long lunch breaks. The club's board of directors had recently terminated the club manager and was in the process of hiring a new one. In the meantime, nobody was managing Melody or the office staff.

WELCOME TO THE CLUB

The club features an 18-hole, par 72 golf course located on 7,000 square yards of real estate in Sanpete County, Utah. Additional amenities include a clubhouse, a swimming pool, and a pro shop. The club's revenues consist of monthly dues and assessments from its 300 members, green fees, and restaurant and bar revenues. The year our firm was hired to conduct the audit, the club had gross revenues of $1.8 million and total assets of $3.7 million.

The club's management team consisted of Jake Trembell, the general manager, who was responsible for accounting and administrative operations; Barney Lewis, the head chef, who handled the club's restaurant and bar operations; Lee Johnson, the golf pro, in charge of the golf course; and Ed Manning, the chief engineer, who was responsible for maintenance of the facilities and grounds. Each of these individuals managed a certain number of employees and reported directly to the board of directors.

Shortly after Jake hired Melody as the receptionist, he was terminated. The board of directors decided to combine the duties of the general manager with those of the head chef, making Barney the one responsible for the office staff. Since Barney was more concerned with the restaurant than the accounting or administrative operations, the office staff was often unsupervised—and accounting controls were largely ignored.

Barney relied on Colleen Peterson, the club's part-time accountant, to oversee the accounting functions. She worked five four-hour shifts each week. Colleen used the other two office staff, Ruth Johnson, a part-time accounting technician, and Melody, the receptionist, to perform various accounting duties to assist her in the maintenance of the general ledger and member billing systems and to generate financial reports for the monthly board meetings. Ruth and Melody did not report to Colleen.

The executive committee of the board of directors assumed responsibility for monitoring the club's finances and engaging an auditor to conduct the annual audit. The committee would also meet monthly to review the financial reports prepared by Colleen and her staff. Financial results were discussed and material budget variances and individually significant transactions were reviewed. The committee was made up of three or four board members with experience in finance or accounting who interacted regularly with Barney and Colleen during the course of the month.

As one might expect, the club's culture was fairly laid back, and there were no formal internal control policies and procedures. To make matters worse, a lot of cash circulated throughout the club because that was the members' preferred method of payment for restaurant and bar tabs. There were four different petty cash boxes. Each had up to $5,000 at any given time and was managed by four different people. All of the office staff had access to the key to the safe where the petty cash was stored at the end of the day. Petty cash was reconciled four to five times a year, and those reconciliations were performed by the same people who handled the petty cash boxes.

The receptionist was typically responsible for receiving payments from members at the front desk, opening the mail, preparing the deposit for the bank, posting member payments to the member billing and accounting system, and taking the deposit to the bank. While bank reconciliations were performed monthly, they were not reviewed by the general manager or an officer independent of the accounting process.

Member accounts were not reconciled on a regular basis, and there were "ZZ" accounts set up to record transactions arising from non–member-sponsored events, which included significant alcohol purchases and food consumption. These "ZZ" accounts were monitored only by the head chef.

The club functioned with Barney at the helm for about six months until Doug Anderson, a new board member, was appointed to be the chair of the executive committee. Doug was a Certified Public Accountant with 32 years of auditing experience with one of the Big Six accounting firms. It didn't take him long to notice some major problems with the way the club was being run.

The first change Doug made was to hire a general manager with a finance background. The new general manager, Ed Wilkins, was given the charge to exert more control and oversight over the club's accounting processes and procedures. This was a daunting task for Ed since the office staff was not accustomed to following formal rules. He quickly realized that Melody was lazy and a potential liability to the club, so he terminated her employment about two weeks prior to the annual audit.

The second change Doug made was to fire the club's current auditor, who had never provided the board of directors a management letter that would have revealed material weaknesses in internal control. In fact, the auditor never reviewed internal controls as part of his engagement. Our audit firm was retained to conduct the financial statement audit for the year-end. I was the lead auditor on the engagement.

My first task was to gain an understanding of the club's internal control policies and procedures and significant accounting processes. In order to do so, I had to meet with Ed and Colleen and interview them about their responsibilities and the duties of those in control of accounting, asset custody, and authorization. At the time, Ed had been employed by the club for only about a week, and wasn't much help. But Colleen revealed several issues that were of great concern; lack of segregation of duties within the accounting department was foremost among them.

I asked Colleen if the club had experienced any fraud as a result of poor segregation of duties. She replied that there hadn't been any to her knowledge, but that that would be difficult to judge since there had been no one overseeing any of the accounting functions, and she only worked in the evenings and early mornings, when there is little going on in the clubhouse.

Nothing Petty about It

A few weeks after my interviews and internal control walk throughs, but prior to Melody's termination, we received a tip from Colleen that some petty cash was missing from the safe. She had noticed the discrepancy that day when she was reconciling one of the petty cash boxes, as required by one of the new accounting policies Ed had established. She was not sure who had stolen it, or if it had, for certain, been stolen, but the amount missing totaled approximately $2,200, and she felt that she should inform the auditors. Little did she know that this would only be the tip of the iceberg.

After receiving Colleen's phone call, I called a meeting with the audit team to discuss the tip and to assess the scope of the potential fraud. The audit team consisted of me, the audit manager, a senior auditor, a new staff auditor, and the managing partner.

In the meeting we discussed the phone call and the impact it would have on our assessment of fraud risk. Although we were all feeling somewhat uncomfortable about this new engagement, we did not consider it necessary to withdraw since the club appeared to have accounting records sufficient to conduct the audit. However, we decided to modify our standard audit approach to address the fraud risk factors identified in our meeting. The modified approach would incorporate all of our traditional procedures, but would focus more attention on areas with substantial inherent risk. Therefore, we discussed the process of each significant transaction class and the key employees involved. Our discussion led us to conclude that, among other things, our procedures would need to include an examination of all:

- Petty cash disbursements and replenishments and related reconciliations. Specifically, we wanted to learn whether the use of all petty cash was authorized, accounted for, and supported by adequate documentation and reconciliation. We further wanted to determine whether replenishments to the petty cash accounts were properly approved and recorded to the petty cash subsidiary ledgers.

- Bank reconciliations, paying particular attention to deposits, wire transfers, and general ledger adjustments to cash. We wanted to learn whether deposits were complete and valid, and whether they cleared the bank in a timely manner. We also needed to determine whether nonroutine wire transfers were authorized and appropriate. General ledger adjustments would be tested for adequate supporting documentation.

- Member accounts. We wanted to determine whether member accounts were being reconciled and payments were being properly applied.

- Check disbursements from the operating account to ensure that vendors were approved and valid, payments were authorized and supported by adequate supporting documentation, and cancelled checks contained the proper signors, payees, and endorsements.

Fieldwork was scheduled to last one week. On the first day, I gave Diane, the senior auditor, the assignment of examining bank reconciliations and testing petty cash while Tanya, a staff auditor, and I began reconciling and testing member accounts. Within an hour of commencing her examination, Diane noticed a strange trend occurring within the operating account.

"Why would a deposit totaling $27,845 that was prepared November 30 fail to clear the bank until January 2? And why would a deposit totaling $28,779 made December 31 fail to clear the bank before February 17?" she asked.

I agreed that it appeared suspicious and requested to see the support for the November deposit. As I reviewed the support, I noticed that it contained copies of checks made by members to pay their monthly assessment bill with payment dates ranging from November to December. I also noticed that there were no cash payments included in the deposit. As I reviewed the deposit, I wondered why a deposit dated November 30 would have member payment checks dated in December. This appeared very unusual, so I addressed the issue with Colleen.

BETTER SAFE THAN SORRY

Colleen was perplexed by the problem and didn't have an answer. After researching the issue for a few hours, she returned with Ed.

"There appears to be a discrepancy in cash, but we don't know why," he said. "Several of the members' accounts within the member billing system reflect balances that do not agree to the statements mailed to them. Since the statements were generated from the member billing system, the statements' balances should reflect the balances in the system."

I asked who was responsible for controlling and mailing the member statements. Ed confirmed that it was Melody. She was also responsible for posting member payments to the billing system and preparing the daily deposit. It turned out that nobody independent of the billing function was reviewing the bills prior to mailing them.

Colleen compiled all of the member statements for one year that had been mailed to members, and prepared a schedule, by member, summarizing the invoice balances compared to the billing system balances at the end of each month. The differences between the invoices and the billing system were summarized and totaled approximately $50,000. It was noted that the invoices that differed from their related billing system balances had been obviously altered. Some of the fonts shown on the statements reflected what appeared to be those from by a typewriter.

After the differences had been quantified, the questionable payments on each account were traced through to the cash receipts subsidiary ledger within the accounting system and then to the bank deposit slip. All of the payments that cleared the bank were checks. There were no cash deposits. Since many members paid their account balances with cash, it appeared that someone had been stealing the cash. All the evidence appeared to suggest that one of the office staff—probably Melody—was the perpetrator.

I was unable to interview Melody since she was no longer with the organization and was unwilling to cooperate with the investigation. So I interviewed Ruth Johnson, the part-time office staff member who was usually present during the hours Melody worked. I asked Ruth to describe her duties.

"I am primarily responsible for helping Colleen pay the bills and post the vendor payments within the accounts payable module of the accounting system. On occasion, I assist her by preparing the monthly financial report to the board," she replied.

Next I asked, "Do you have or have you had any responsibilities for opening the mail, collecting and processing cash or check receipts, making deposits, or posting transactions to the member billing system?"

"All of those duties used to be performed by Melody, but Ed is considering cross-training me to perform the member billing function."

"Did you observe anything unusual about Melody or how she performed her duties?" I continued.

"Melody seemed to devote a lot of attention to the member billing statements each month. She would print them from the system, then manually type corrections to the ones that she claimed were generated by the system but that could not be changed within the system. I don't know what those changes were. I suspect they were probably mailing address changes or member status changes. It's not unusual for member data to change when members move or upgrade their memberships, and our system is old and doesn't handle that process very well."

"Did you ever observe Melody steal cash or assets, or has anyone ever communicated to you their suspicion that Melody might be stealing cash or assets?" I asked.

"No," she replied, "but I do recall hearing that someone saw her in the office after she was terminated, getting into the safe. When she was asked what she was doing, she replied that she forgot to reconcile petty cash and to make the last deposit. I guess the person who saw her didn't realize that she had been terminated."

It began coming together for me. "How was she able to get into the clubhouse and the office without a key? Did she still have her keys?"

"Yes. When she was terminated, management obviously overlooked that one small detail," Ruth said sarcastically.

LAPPING UP THE CASH

After my interview with Ruth, and based on all of the other evidence observed, it appeared that Melody had engaged in a lapping scheme, which involves stealing money from one member's account and covering the shortage by applying a later payment by a different member. I met with Ed and Colleen, who were performing their own investigation in conjunction with ours, and communicated the results of my interview with Ruth. Ed mentioned that Ruth's testimony was consistent with that of other employees who had observed Melody's behavior in the final weeks leading up to her termination. He agreed that all of the evidence pointed to Melody. Colleen said that she had suspected her early on, even prior to her termination, when the $2,200 in petty cash came up missing. When Colleen confronted Melody about the missing cash, she denied any involvement and said that she would never have taken the money and suggested that the bar manager or restaurant manager were the ones who may have stolen it. Even though there was no conclusive evidence at that time, Melody was suspected because of rumors circulating about her termination from the bank and the events surrounding it. When I asked why she was hired and retained despite the rumors, Colleen said that Melody had been given a raise by the prior club manager and it was difficult for current management to justify termination for cause right after giving a raise.

After completing our preliminary investigation and compiling, analyzing, and evaluating the information available, we determined that Melody had perpetuated a lapping scheme for nearly eight months. Since she was responsible for opening the mail, collecting payments at the front counter from members, preparing the daily deposit, and managing the member billing system, she had access to and control of nearly the entire phase of the cash receipts transaction process. This enabled her to steal cash and cover it up easily. Her scheme would work, however, only if she retained exclusive control of the process. When she was terminated, her fraud was quickly detected.

Melody would keep the cash she collected from payments and replace it with checks subsequently received. She would hold the bank deposit open until she could replace the stolen money with later checks. This resulted in a lead time of one to two months from the date the deposit was initially prepared to the date it was actually made. Although the cash that was stolen was not applied to the member accounts within the system, Melody would manually alter the member statements that were generated from the system to reflect payments on the affected members' accounts so that they were not aware that their account balances were misstated. Since the member accounts were not reconciled independently, the overstated member accounts were not detected.

After the audit was completed, it was determined that member accounts were short $52,800. In addition, the $2,200 of missing petty cash could not be located. We concluded that Melody stole that money the night she returned to the clubhouse after her termination, before she surrendered her keys. This resulted in a total theft loss of $55,000.

After Melody's termination, but before the fraud was uncovered, members began receiving statements reflecting higher account receivable balances than expected. At that time, things went from bad to worse. Ed began dealing with numerous complaints from members demanding an explanation. In order to address concerns proactively and to show that he was on top of the matter, Ed unwisely sent a letter to all the members without first consulting the board on the matter, which stated:

ALERT A message from your new Club Manager. Please check your statements carefully!

Over the last two weeks we have discovered numerous errors, discrepancies, and posting irregularities with regards to member accounts that have occurred over the last couple of months. Many of you have already called to ask what is happening with your account. One of our goals is to provide you with ongoing current and accurate information on your account. To this end, I am asking that each of you review your last month's statement very carefully and inform me of any inaccuracies in statement balances, monthly charges, or payments that may not have shown up on your account. Any questions or comments will be reviewed in an expeditious manner.

This letter was mailed before the investigation was effectively under way, and the ensuing controversy posed a major challenge to the board in resolving the matter in a timely and efficient manner. Alarmed members suspected that millions of dollars had been stolen by the board and club management. Lawsuits were being threatened, and several board members resigned before the investigation was completed and a final loss had been determined.

The good news was that the club had insurance that covered $50,000 of the loss. Melody paid the remaining $5,000 in a plea deal that allowed her to walk away without the club pressing charges.

LESSONS LEARNED

The most significant lesson learned from this case was how important it is for an organization to have a strong control environment and a board of directors and management group that proactively and effectively communicates and enforces internal control policies and procedures. Melody would not have had the opportunity to commit fraud had management and the board been more attuned to the risks inherent in the organization and the access employees had to cash and other assets. Moreover, it was okay for employees to arrive late to work and leave early, or to have free meals from the restaurant or bar. The restaurant manager hosted parties at the clubhouse for his friends, and they would consume an inordinate amount of alcohol without paying for it. There was no accountability to anyone, because nobody knew who was really in charge.

Another lesson I learned was the importance of professional skepticism when conducting an audit. I have since approached every audit that I perform with the presumption that someone in the organization is committing fraud and it's my job to find it. This attitude has dramatically altered my audit approach from one of a cookie-cutter, routine nature to one where procedures are crafted that directly address certain fraud risks assessed at the beginning of an audit. More specifically, my audits are focused more on testing internal controls, conducting interviews, and performing analytical procedures in order to identify potential fraud risks.

Finally, I learned the importance of communication. There are good times and bad times to communicate fraud to the stakeholders. Had Ed waited to inform all of the members of the problem until the scope of the fraud had been determined, the results of the investigation would have been less alarming. Furthermore, when the appropriate time to inform the membership was determined, it should have been done under the direction of the board and by the board, not the new club manager. This did not bode well for Ed in the long run. Although he was competent, eventually he was terminated because he was a poor communicator.

RECOMMENDATIONS TO PREVENT FUTURE OCCURRENCES

Segregation of Duties

Melody was responsible for receiving payments from members, opening the mail, preparing and making the daily deposit, and posting the receipts to member accounts.

These duties should be segregated in order to prevent someone from having access to both physical assets and the related accounting records, or to all phases of a transaction. An administrative assistant should continue to open the mail and prepare each deposit, but a prelist should be prepared that summarizes the cash and checks received. The prelist should be forwarded to another office staff member or the bookkeeper to post receipts to member accounts, and the deposit should be forwarded to the club manager for review. The club manager and one other person should take the deposit to the bank each day. Alternatively, the bank could arrange to pick up the deposit at the clubhouse. This would ensure a timely deposit and eliminate the need for two employees to accompany the deposit to the bank.

The club manager should receive all bank statements and cancelled checks unopened. The club manager should review them prior to delivering them to the accounting clerk for reconciliation. The club manager should also review the bank reconciliation after it is prepared.

Office staff should be cross-trained and share certain aspects of each others' duties. For example, some months Colleen could assume the cash receipts and deposit preparation duties, while Ruth posts those cash receipts to the member accounts. Cross-training may be accomplished for other accounting functions, as well. This would result in better controls over the various accounting functions and would allow employees to assume the responsibilities of coworkers in an emergency.

The club manager should periodically perform independent checks on the work completed by office staff involved in all accounting functions. A thorough screening process should be followed when hiring individuals who will have access to assets susceptible to misappropriation. Had the club performed a background check on Melody, the fraud may have been prevented.

Timeliness of Deposits

Although the board of directors passed a resolution requiring a daily bank deposit for all amounts over $500, this policy was never followed, as we observed. This was evidenced when we noticed that two deposits, one approximately $27,000 and the other approximately $28,800, did not clear the bank in a timely manner. Had these deposits been made in a timely manner, Melody's ability to divert funds would have been greatly reduced. Deposits should be made every day. In rare circumstances when a deposit must wait until the following day, it should be secured in a safe with access limited to only a few key employees.

Cash Receipts

Although the club had a receipting function in place when cash was received from a member, it wasn't being used effectively or consistently. The club should reevaluate its policy on how members make payments on their accounts. Two options that may improve controls over the cash receipts process follow.

1.   The club manager, or another individual independent of the cash handling and recording functions, should match the cash received to the prenumbered cash receipt when reviewing the deposit.

2.   Have a "no-cash" policy. Accept only checks and credit/debit card payments.

If the club elects to continue receiving cash and checks at the front desk, a member should be required to place the payment in a drop box at instead of giving it directly to the office staff. Access to the drop box should be limited to a few select individuals who are always accompanied by another individual when retrieving cash and checks for deposit.

Petty Cash Procedures

The club's petty cash was reconciled only four to five times a year and was located in a safe in the office that could be accessed by any of the office staff. Due to the significant balances in the petty cash accounts, two people should be present at all times whenever a disbursement from petty cash is made. All disbursements should be approved by an authorized and designated petty cash custodian and supported by a prenumbered petty cash voucher, together with a supporting invoice or receipt. Reconciliation should occur regularly, and the club manager should review and approve the reconciliation.

Centralization of Authority

According to the club's bylaws, the officers of the organization consists of four managers: a club manager, a chef/food services manager, a golf course superintendent, and a golf professional. These managers are responsible for their own departments and report directly to the board of directors. The problem with this organization structure is that there may be confusion about who is really accountable for particular areas within the club and to whom employees are responsible. The result, as evidenced by the lax control environment, was that some areas did not receive adequate attention. Centralization of authority can prevent such misunderstandings and increase administrative efficiency and control.

The club should hire a full-time general manager. This individual should be ultimately responsible for all departments and should chair a management committee comprised of him- or herself and four department managers: an office manger, a chef/food service manager, a golf course superintendent, and a golf professional. The office manager should take charge and ensure that the office and accounting staff are adhering to established accounting policies and procedures. The committee should meet weekly to coordinate activities and responsibilities and to resolve issues relating to the general operations of the club. The general manager should report to the board of directors regularly to receive instruction and ensure that resolutions are carried out.

John Boekweg, CPA, is an audit manager at HEB Certified Public Accountants in Salt Lake City, Utah. His firm provides forensic accounting, auditing, litigation support, and expert witness services. Mr. Boekweg obtained an undergraduate degree in accounting and information systems from Brigham Young University and an MBA from Utah State University. He has over 12 years of experience in auditing and forensic accounting.

CHAPTER 25

Where in the World is Dina Sanchez?

BRIANA J. PACIOREK

aria Vasquez was a large, middle-age woman with short blond, layered hair. Her attire was never flashy or inappropriate. Rimless glasses and minimal makeup were all that accessorized her face. Her smile was pleasant and friendly. She looked like your everyday mom—someone who would go out of her way to help you.

Growing up in Argentina, Maria worked hard in high school and earned a business degree from the university. After marrying Pedro, her longtime love, she worked at various jobs, but her husband was the breadwinner. For a while, Pedro ran his own delivery business and Maria balanced the books.

With hopes of a prosperous life, Maria and Pedro moved to the United States. They did not have children, so they brought Maria's mother with them. The three lived together in a modest three-bedroom house in North Miami, surrounded by palm trees and situated on the Intracoastal Waterway. It was a dream come true for all of them.

Pedro was a self-employed painter who worked less than 30 hours a week. Maria found a job doing accounting for a small company but left after she had problems getting along with her boss. At that point, she contacted JobMart, a staffing agency, and was soon placed at Safe Protect, a subsidiary of a huge conglomerate known as Martz.

Safe Protect manufactured and sold safes to residential and commercial customers. A temporary employee, Maria worked in the tax department helping others perform various administrative tasks. Just one month after I was hired to work in the corporate internal audit department for Martz, Maria was given the responsibility of preparing sales tax returns for various states.

Safe Protect is a world leader in the security products industry. Headquartered in Miami, the company has been in existence for more than 150 years and has had numerous acquisitions along the way. Since the early 1900s, the company's way of ridding itself of competitors has been to buy them out. Starting out with just three employees and revenues under $50,000, today the company employs 45,000 workers and has gross revenues exceeding $4 billion.

As you can imagine, Safe Protect went through many changes as it developed and grew to its current size. In the beginning, the company catered only to small general stores and the wealthy elite. Today's customers also include large corporations, hotels, governmental agencies, banks, museums, and casinos.

Safe Protect is the largest subsidiary of Martz. For this reason, I spent a significant amount of time performing audits and reviews at the company headquarters during my first year in internal audit. Other than a few minor issues here and there, the audits of Safe Protect went smoothly. Overall, the company seemed to be operating efficiently. Employees appeared happy and business was booming. In the process, I was fortunate to become very familiar with the organization and build strong relationships with senior management. One fall, I transferred into the newly developed forensic audit group and found myself traveling to many of Martz's other subsidiaries.

NOT A GENUINE ENDORSEMENT

Thanksgiving had just passed and I returned to the office after a visit with my family. It was historically a quiet time of the year for my department, as everyone was preoccupied with holiday spirit and many employees were taking much-needed vacations before the end of the year. I was sitting in my windowless office catching up on e-mail when my phone rang. It was Peter Nellis, Safe Protect controller, with a request to meet and discuss an urgent matter. I grabbed a pen and a notepad and quickly made my way to his office on the fourth floor. I sat on the other side of Peter's desk, joined by Margaret Lewis, director of the tax department. They believed they may have uncovered a fraud in the company.

Margaret had been out of the office on business the day before. Sometime that afternoon, she received a call from Bridget Kingston, senior legal counsel at the company, who told her of events that transpired during her absence. Earlier that morning, Sarah Jasper, tax associate, was engaged in a phone conversation with Bill Trent, a representative from the State of Kansas Department of Revenue. Bill claimed he did not receive the June sales tax return and payment from Safe Protect. Surprised to hear this, Sarah offered to look into the issue and give Bill a call back. After phoning the accounts payable shared service center in Chicago, Sarah learned that there had been a check dated in July for $78,965 (for June's payment) made payable to the Kansas Department of Revenue that cleared the bank. Sarah received an image of the cleared check and forwarded it to Bill. Upon Sarah's follow-up discussion, he said the endorsement was not genuine. He faxed Sarah a copy of a check with the proper endorsement stamp on the back as a comparison. Neither the account numbers in the endorsements nor the name on the account matched. The Kansas Department of Revenue endorsement stamp read "Deposit only KS Dept. of Revenue." However, the endorsement stamp on the suspicious check read "Kansas DOR." Because Margaret was away on business, Sarah reported the suspicious activity to Bridget in the company's legal department. Bridget immediately attempted to reach Margaret on her cell phone to explain what had happened. In the meantime, Bridget informed Peter about the matter. Following company policy, Peter turned the matter over to forensic audit for investigation. Maria was the only individual responsible for the Kansas account; her duties which encompassed preparing sales tax returns, requesting payment, and physically handling the checks before mailing. Strangely enough, Maria had recently left the company—her last day was on September 9, and it was now November.

WHAT'S MY NAME, AGAIN?

Before I could dig deep into the investigation, I needed to learn more about Maria. I received only limited details on Maria's background from Margaret, so I decided to interview her former coworkers, Sarah Jasper and Paula Martinez. But before I talked to them, I requested bank records for all checks that cleared the bank since Maria's employment. I knew it would take a few days to get this evidence, and I didn't want to lose any time waiting for it. Sarah, who handled the initial discovery with the State of Kansas, worked closely with Maria in the sales tax department. Paula, currently with the licensing compliance department at Safe Protect, used to work closely with Maria. They knew her for approximately two years and three and a half years, respectively. While Paula had a closer personal relationship with her, both socialized with Maria on several occasions outside of the workplace.

Sarah and Paula each described instances where they found that Maria was using a different name. Sarah recalled receiving an e-mail from someone named "Dina Sanchez" from an address she did not recognize. Sarah said she could tell the communication was from Maria because it read "Louisiana" in the subject line, and it was responding to a question she had asked Maria concerning the Louisiana tax return. Sarah replied, but never received a response from Maria. The e-mail was received between September 13 and 17, about a week following Maria's last day of employment at Safe Protect. Paula described an instance where she heard Maria's mother call her "Dina" during a time in July when Maria and her mother visited Paula at her home. Upon inquiry as to why she was called "Dina," Maria claimed that "Dina" was her middle name.

On another occasion, Paula also recalled receiving an e-mail from a "Dina Sanchez." When asked if the e-mail was from her, Maria claimed she was using a friend's account. Once Paula stopped by Maria's home in North Miami to see why she was not returning any phone calls or e-mails. At the door, Paula was greeted by a couple who recently moved into the house. She asked if they knew where Maria was. The couple replied they did not know where the previous owner was and that her name was "Dina," not "Maria." The couple showed Paula a stack of Dina's mail that they didn't know what to do with because they did not have her forwarding address.

Paula informed me of an incident that occurred approximately three years earlier, when Maria had "run into some trouble with the law." She recalled that Maria's husband asked her if he could borrow $25,000 to help get his wife "out of trouble." During my interview with Sarah, I learned that money was to bail Maria out of jail. Sarah didn't know why Maria was there, but believed that it was linked to one of Maria's previous jobs.

I learned many additional interesting tidbits about Maria during the investigation:

- Sarah claimed she heard from Paula that Maria bought a Social Security card or was using a fake Social Security card after arriving in the United States.

- Paula claimed Maria wore a Rolex watch and drove a Mercedes and that her husband drove a Lincoln Navigator. They were supposedly building a new house in Boynton Beach, Florida.

- Both Paula and Sarah said Maria never liked to talk about herself.

- Maria had been to Paula's home on several occasions, but Paula was never invited over for Maria to return the favor.

- Maria had been offered a full-time position by Safe Protect on more than one occasion, but always turned it down.

- Paula recalled that Maria wanted to become a regular full-time employee of the company but did not want to have a background check performed on her.

- Maria supposedly had friends or some sort of connection to someone in Port St. Lucie, Florida.

Could Maria really be Dina Sanchez? My next step was to examine the checks I requested from the accounts payable department. But before I performed this review I did two things. First, I asked a colleague in the security department to perform a background check on "Maria Vasquez" and "Dina Sanchez." Second, I decided to do some quick investigating into the bank where the suspicious check was deposited. When I could not reach the manager, I decided to call the bank's fraud department. Although the representative could not divulge information about the owner of the "Kansas DOR" account, he was able to provide yes or no answers. As a result of my questions, he confirmed the names "Kansas DOR" and "Dina Sanchez," and he said that the account was still open.

Feeling that I had made progress and that we had the right suspect, I performed a full examination of the cleared checks I had received. Out of 60 checks made payable to Kansas DOR and requested by Maria during her employment at the company, 25 had been intercepted. I was able to determine this by comparing the endorsement information on the back of the checks to the actual endorsement stamp used by the Kansas Department of Revenue. The total was just under $430,000. Now the investigation was getting interesting.

After uncovering this information, an injunction and writ of attachment freezing Maria's bank accounts were immediately filed. Thereafter, I had a phone discussion with Lucy Santos, an in-house counsel for the bank, who confirmed Maria had two personal accounts in the name of Dina Sanchez and one as "Kansas DOR." According to Ms. Santos, Maria opened the business account in February of the previous year under "Kansas DOR," filed by her as an "assumed name certificate" with the Florida Secretary of State. Ms. Santos confirmed that the bank had frozen all of Maria's accounts and ordered all bank statements and records relating to them. The balance in the Kansas DOR account was -$5.90, and the balances in the two personal ones were -$7.02 and $187.52. In addition, Ms. Santos provided a number of deposits made into the Kansas DOR account. Every amount was matched to Safe Protect checks that were known to be intercepted. It turned out that Maria had sent a request to the accounts payable department to change a vendor name in the vendor master file. The change request was to abbreviate the vendor name "State of Kansas, Director of Taxation, Department of Revenue" to "Kansas DOR," and was sent from Maria's Safe Protect e-mail account. Included were requests to change "State of Nebraska Department of Revenue" to "Nebraska DOR" and to change "State of Vermont Department of Taxes" to "Vermont Department of Taxes."

I obtained a copy of the e-mail and change request by Maria from the accounts payable department. There was clearly no supervisory approval. The hardcopy form did, however, contain initials and a date by the individual who processed the change in the vendor master file. According to the accounts payable supervisor, there was no process in place to ensure all changes made to master files were approved before *or after* being entered into the system.

Not long after uncovering all of this, I caught up with my colleague who performed a background investigation of "Maria Vasquez" and "Dina Sanchez." As it turned out, our suspect's real name was Dina Sanchez, and she was using the identity of Maria Vasquez, a woman who was more than 10 years older. It was revealed that Dina used Maria's information in order to obtain a Florida driver's license under the name of Maria Vasquez at her residence in Port Saint Lucie, Florida. Dina then used Maria's Social Security number and falsified Florida driver's license to apply for work with the JobMart temporary staffing agency. It was later revealed by a Miami detective that Dina Sanchez had a criminal record and had been arrested and jailed at her first place of employment after she arrived in the United States.

JobMart provided copies of the last two paychecks sent to Dina (under the name of Maria Vasquez) to her home address in North Miami. The earlier check was endorsed using the same signature of "M. Vasquez" that she used on all of her documents while working at Safe Protect. The second check appeared to have been endorsed by someone else (a "Maria Vasquez" signature that did not match the other check), and was paid after we found out Dina had already left the United States. JobMart personnel records under the name Maria Vasquez (Dina) revealed that she had listed her home address as 19 W. Esimo Avenue, Port Saint Lucie, Florida, the home of the real Maria. Research of the property revealed that the home was purchased in January of the previous year by Andreas Marco Dion and Maria Estrellita Vasquez de Dion for $85,000. There was no mortgage or other lien on this property.

The real Maria claimed to have known Dina as her accountant. Maria said that Dina stole her identity, although she had not filed a police report. We had reason to believe these women may have conspired to commit this fraud because we found a photograph of Dina, her husband, her mother, and Maria together in the Port Saint Lucie home, suggesting they were friends. Maria refused to cooperate with the investigation and declined, through her attorney, to be contacted.

The Well-Traveled Fraudster

Ultimately, I was able to determine what Dina had done based on a review of tax return documentation and discussions with Margaret. She had manipulated system reports, tax returns, and controls in order to intercept checks and conceal the fraud. Dina was responsible for running the monthly sales tax reports from the Safe Protect system; she was the only individual who knew how to perform this task. Most of the check interceptions were accomplished as a result of modifying total sales reported and then creating falsified returns.

For example, the April tax returns submitted for review in May showed sales tax due of $58,300 and use tax due of $2,000, totaling $60,300. However, the check requests made by Dina were for $35,700 and $24,600 (summing to the correct total due of $60,300). It is unknown why the approver of these check requests did not question why the amounts were broken out the way they were. The individual was no longer with the company at the time of the investigation.

Dina then prepared a second set of returns or, more precisely, a second sales tax return, as she rarely tampered with the use tax return. The numbers for this falsified sales tax return were derived by falsifying the system report to illustrate a lower amount of sales, which would ultimately calculate a lower amount of taxes due. Keeping with the April tax return example, the sales in the system report were lowered in order to calculate only $33,700 of sales taxes due and $2,000 of use tax due. The difference in total taxes due between the original system report and the falsified system report equals $24,600, the amount of   the second check requested by Dina.

After she received the two checks requested from accounts payable, Dina attached the falsified system report with lower reported sales to the falsified sales tax return and the actual use tax return, included the check for $35,700, and mailed it to the State of Kansas. She then intercepted the check for $24,600.

In February, Dina did not mail the January tax returns and checks to the State of Kansas. She simply intercepted the checks. Subsequently, in March, she requested an additional check, under the guise of an unclaimed property filing, and used this to pay for the January and February returns together.

For the March returns, Dina presented the same sales tax return as backup to both the tax director and the tax manager, on separate occasions, and each person authorized a check request for the return. She mailed the first check with the return and intercepted the second check.

Another manipulation involved the April and May returns of the following year. The tax director reviewed the April sales tax return, which showed tax due of $82,200, and the use tax return, showing tax due of $1,005. He signed both of the returns and the check requests, ensuring that the individual checks requested matched each return. Dina did not mail either of the April returns or the checks to the State of Kansas. Instead, she intercepted both of them.

The following month, Dina prepared the May returns and submitted them to the tax director for approval. The returns signed by him showed sales tax due of $57,100 and use tax due of $1,300. Again, the tax director ensured that the individual check requests matched each of the returns. Dina also failed to mail the May returns to the Kansas Department of Revenue.

Instead, she created falsified sales tax returns for April and May in the amounts of $28,495 and $26,300. These, along with the original April and May use tax returns and the May check of $57,100, were submitted to the Kansas Department of Revenue. Both of the falsified sales tax returns contained a forged/photocopied representation of the tax director's signature.

The most unbelievable aspect of this part of the story is that we were able to understand all of these methods Dina employed to cover the fraud because she was kind enough to leave the original and falsified system reports and tax returns in Safe Protect's files.

There was just one unanswered question: Where was Dina Sanchez now? We found information suggesting that Dina and her family were now in Barcelona, Spain. With the perpetrator living outside of the United States, an arrest would certainly be more difficult.

Regardless, I completed a report containing the details of the investigation, the facts uncovered, and the evidence gathered. I also put together a timeline of the events that occurred during the fraud. I shared my report with local Miami police and the Secret Service, walking them through information. Robert Murphy, a Miami detective, was so impressed that he offered me a job with his department! We hope that Dina will one day be caught and punished.

LESSONS LEARNED

The most obvious internal control breakdown that enabled Dina to launch her scheme was in the maintenance and control of the vendor master file. The company did not have a process in place to approve changes being made to the file. I wondered why the accounts payable clerk never questioned Dina's change requests.

When I found out that Dina was able to manipulate numbers in the system's sales tax reports, I couldn't believe there wasn't a control in place to prohibit modification. Luckily, after talking with someone in the information technology department, I learned they had the capability of implementing this type of control.

Through her scheming and manipulation of tax returns, Dina had been late in mailing payments to the State of Kansas on at least two occasions. Because of the lack of a centralized process for the receipt and tracking of the tax department mail, she was able to get her hands on the late-payment notices before anyone ever knew they existed. Out of the kindness of her heart, and to keep her scheme going without raising suspicion, she paid these late payment fees out of her own pocket. Of course, it was with the money she had embezzled from the company.

I found some holes in the company's control over making payments to state tax departments. While check requests (for payment to a vendor) appeared to be properly approved, there was no process to review payments in the aggregate on a weekly or monthly basis. For example, the tax director would approve Dina's check request on one day. A few days later he approved a second check request in the same amount for the same tax return. Had someone been responsible for a week or month's worth of check requests or payments, he or she could have caught the duplicates. Further, there was no system in place to ensure that all checks were accounted for and mailed to the appropriate vendor. Throughout the investigation, I remember feeling bothered by the fact that Dina was a temporary employee at the time she defrauded the company. I naturally assumed temps would have little access to the company's assets. But I uncovered these facts:

- Signed contracts were not in place with JobMart, the temporary staffing firm providing services to the company.
- There was no policy requiring JobMart to conduct and furnish background checks.
- Temporary employees had physical access to cash and checks.
- There was no policy regarding the length of time a person could work as a temporary employee.
- There were not adequate limitations on a temporary employee's access to the company's systems.

RECOMMENDATIONS TO PREVENT FUTURE OCCURRENCES

Vendor Master File

All change requests to the vendor master file should be documented and approved by a supervisor prior to entry into records.

Safe Protect System

A system control was put in place. In addition, those that are exported into another program should not be able to be manipulated.

Payment Process—Tax Department

A complete listing of approved check requests and disbursements should be reviewed on a weekly and monthly basis by the tax director, who looks for unusual items, duplications, and split payments. In order to ensure the safeguarding of company funds, state tax departments are now paid via wire. For any state unable to accept wire payment, the supporting tax returns should be sent to the accounts payable shared service center, where they are matched to the checks and mailed directly to the appropriate state.

Mail Receipt and Tracking

The tax department assistant is now responsible for opening all of the mail, inputting the receipt of any notices received from state tax departments, and ensuring distribution to the appropriate individuals. The tax director monitors the list of notices received from state tax departments to ensure timely resolution and reconciliation of the items.

Briana J. Paciorek, CFE, is a manager in the Fraud & Forensic Services practice at Solomon Edwards Group, LLC, in Philadelphia, Pennsylvania. Her group specializes in providing fraud investigation, detection, and prevention services to clients. Ms. Paciorek is a graduate of Babson College and has seven years of experience in external, internal, and forensic audits.

CHAPTER 26

School of Fraud

NESSAN RONAN

Roger Kaunda lived life in the fast lane. Tall and imposing, he had a well-deserved reputation for being a ladies' man. Roger was about 35 years old when I met him. He had a degree in public administration and worked as an administrative officer for the specialized accountancy college in the South African country of Lesotho. Before working there, he was a teller with one of the country's major banks.

Roger was well liked as the administrative officer. The staff especially appreciated his willingness to recommend that the college repaint their houses. There was no doubt that he had great interpersonal skills. Roger knew the best person to contact when there was a problem or a difficult job to be completed. He had an excellent relationship with the director of the college, who relied heavily on him to keep the wheels moving.

Roger was married with two young children. His wife, Gladys, was a secretary in the same bank where Roger once worked. Rumor had it that she was not very happy in the marriage. Whenever Gladys would complain about the excessive time he spent away from home, he would retort, "I gave you two babies, what more do you want?"

Some of his colleagues often remarked that Roger seemed to neglect his wife and children. He was fond of taking weekend trips with one of his many girlfriends. He was known to take plane trips to South Africa to visit one mistress in particular.

Roger was a great believer in the powers of the witch doctor. His friends thought that he was able to engage in risky behavior due to his belief in traditional medicine. His remedy was to get medicine from the witch doctor if he had a work or domestic problem. He believed that all he had to do in order to harm someone he didn't like was to buy the appropriate medicine. Roger would laugh heartily when boasting about the latest concoction that he had acquired. He told everyone that he had the most powerful witch doctor in the mountains.

I never saw Roger in a bad mood. He seemed to go through life with childlike optimism. He was always on the move, trying to solve some problem or sort out some human relations issues. One day I remarked to a colleague, "I hope you realize the great job Roger is doing for all of us." My colleague readily agreed with my assessment of Roger.

The College of Accountancy was established in 1980 with financial assistance from the World Bank. Its specific purpose was to train professional accountants for both the public and private sectors. Most of central and southern Africa at that time was emerging from colonialism and was making serious strides in developing its professional cadre.

The college also received significant technical assistance from the United Nations Development Programme (UNDP), the International Labour Organization (ILO), and the governments of Britain and the United States. As a result, the national government was very eager for the college to be a success. The technical help meant that international staff could be recruited to work alongside their national counterparts, who came from the United States, England, Scotland, Australia, and Ireland.

The college had two campuses at that time, one in the political capital and the other in the commercial capital. It had about 2,000 students enrolled in accountancy, banking, and financial management classes. Most were graduate students studying commerce and economics. Because the country was ruled under British power until 1964, all of the courses offered at the college focused on internationalization. These students were trained for British professional accountancy qualifications; specifically, they were prepared to become involved in the Chartered Association of Certified Accountants and the Chartered Institute of Management Accountants. The banking courses were offered by the Chartered Institute of Bankers in the United Kingdom. The financial management course was also UK-based.

When I arrived at the college as ILO Chief Technical Adviser in Accountancy, the institution was beginning a second phase of technical assistance. The first phase had by all accounts been a complete failure. During a period of 10 years, not one professional accountant had been produced. The image was so bad that the firms in the country had decided to establish their own college of accountancy. Both international and bilateral donors were extremely concerned with the clear lack of progress. It's fair to say that they agreed to a second phase of assistance only very reluctantly.

Many explanations were offered for the lack of academic success, ranging from poor students to lecturers not committed to their work. There was also a strong suspicion that the director of the college lacked leadership and strategic skills. In reality, all of these reasons were true. The tragedy was that the lack of success was hampering the economic development of the country, the poorest in Africa. There was only one qualified accountant in the entire government. Among the chartered accountancy firms, all the partners were expatriates. In the private sector, there were about 20 qualified accountants. It was urgent to increase the supply of accountants in a nation that screamed for development and the alleviation of poverty. This was the only public sector college of accountancy in the country, which meant that both the national government and the international donors were anxious for the college to start producing qualified professional accountants.

THE LETTER

About six months after arriving at the college from Ireland, I was required to take over the directorship of the college. About a month into the new post, I was faced with the biggest challenge of my career. I remember the day well. It was a Tuesday, one of those beautiful African mornings with blessed sunshine and only a hint of breeze. I looked out my office window and stood for a minute admiring the jacaranda trees waving gently in the wind.

After taking in the inspirational sight of the trees in full bloom, my secretary, Leomile, brought me the morning mail. One of the letters was unusually addressed to "The ELO man." I laughed, realizing that they meant "The ILO man." I can resist everything except curiosity, so I decided to open the letter immediately. It consisted of one page torn out of a child's notebook. I must have read it 20 times. It completely bewildered me. Here I was in the middle of a foreign country with very little knowledge of anything African, and I was confronted with what seemed like a very sensitive issue. The letter, written in pencil, stated:

> Mr. ELO man, be warned. Your administrative officer is robbing the college. You don't know him but be warned. He will come to a bad end. He is involved in a lot of things. Don't ignore this.

The letter was not signed. I wondered if the sender was playing a practical joke on me. What credence should I give to an anonymous letter?

As I was pondering my next move, I remembered my experience in Ireland when I worked as an accountant. I had discovered two frauds as the result of tip-offs. With this in mind, I could not ignore the letter, but at the same time, I wondered how the authorities would react to my suspicions. After all, I was a Caucasian expatriate in a country that had only recently won its independence from white rule. If this had happened in Ireland, I would have no problem deciding what to do. However, I realized that if I did nothing (and that would have been easy), it might come back to haunt me later. I looked back out onto the peaceful jacaranda trees and thought long and hard about my decision for the rest of the day.

CHECK-HAPPY

I decided that before taking any action that I would consult my friend, Marty, who had been working in the country for about two years. He had a strong appreciation of the culture and knew the local language. As soon as we met that day, Marty could see that I was very agitated about something. After I briefly described the situation to him, he scratched his head and warned me to be very careful. His main piece of advice was that I should work through the "national" employees.

I wanted to proceed carefully because I was suspicious of Happy Banda, the college's accountant, and felt that he might be working in collusion with the administrative assistant, Roger, in a possible fraud. Happy was a small, middle-age man with a goatee. He was single and had a reputation for carrying a good supply of condoms in his briefcase, often boasting about his conquests. He had been with the college for about five years and had a relaxed style of management.

The college had recently hired an assistant accountant due to the increase in the workload. David Mtonga was in his mid-20s, married with a young daughter. He had recently completed his technician accountant qualification. He was a quiet, introverted person with a serious outlook on life.

I decided that I would engage the assistance of David to carry out a preliminary forensic audit. I called David to my office and explained my concerns to him. I arranged to meet him at his house, and I put him on notice that the information was most confidential. If the two officers got any hint that we were investigating fraud, they would likely destroy the evidence.

David lived in a township within the suburbs of the college. I greeted him and his wife and then fully briefed him about my suspicions. We worked out a strategy to carry out a preliminary forensic audit. We would conduct the investigation after hours in order to avoid controversy. We agreed not to waste any time and to start the investigation the following evening.

We spent every evening for two weeks sifting through the latest purchase orders and invoices. The evidence was shocking. In our view, fraud was clearly visible from the financial records. We compiled a preliminary report, and I then called the permanent secretary in the Ministry of Education and explained that we had established what appeared to be a prima facie case of fraudulent activity at the college.

I recommended that he request two internal auditors from the office of the auditor general to assist us. Internal auditors in the office of the auditor general have extensive powers. They may go into premises and demand access to documents and compel testimony from people. They also have the powers of arrest. The permanent secretary took my advice. I decided to wait for the internal auditors and not to pursue the investigation on my own. About a month later, they arrived at the college.

The two auditors investigated the purchase of supplies, the rendering of services, and the operation of the transport system. The rendering of services appeared a prime candidate for fraud. The auditors discovered that Roger would issue a purchase order to a painting contractor who was hired to paint a staff member's house. The college would be invoiced with the cost and Roger would approve it for payment. Happy would write a check for the invoice and pass it to the principal for signing. Then the check would be taken to Roger, who would take it to the painting contractor. The problem was that Roger, Happy, and the painting contractor had conspired to defraud the college. In fact, no houses were painted and all the payments were fraudulent. The three conspirators shared the proceeds of their scam, which the auditors estimated to be about $50,000.

The next area of investigation was in the purchase of supplies. Some invoices were selected for scrutiny; there was no record of supplies having been received for many of them. The auditors visited the suppliers and found that a considerable number of the invoices were false. Although it wasn't clear if the suppliers were involved in defrauding the college, certainly the invoices didn't represent supplies.

We estimated that these fraudulent invoices amounted to about $40,000. Moreover, we determined that the accountant was in the practice of forging the college principal's signature. The second signature on the check belonged to an academic, who was apparently in the habit of relying on the principal's signature and didn't bother to check the supporting documentation.

The third and final area of the investigation dealt with the operation of the transport system. The college had about 10 motor vehicles, and the purchase of fuel was a major activity. Again, the auditors found massive fraud. The administrative officer would approve invoices and receive checks for gasoline that was never purchased. Since Roger controlled the transport system, no checks and balances were in operation. This fraud cost the college about $30,000. In total, the two officers defrauded the college of about $120,000.

TRIPLE THREAT

One of the auditors entered my office at noon one day. He told me that he had obtained all of the fraud-related evidence and was going to challenge the two suspects. He casually remarked that the accountant, in addition to forging the principal's signature on the illegitimate checks, had also tried to forge *my* signature. It was one surprise after another. Just two days prior, I had been threatened by Roger. He said that he was going to complain about me to the president of the country and ask that I be deported. I informed the auditors of this threat and they went to the secretary, who briefed the president on the matter. Roger also said that he was going to poison me. So the auditors warned me not to go to the canteen during the investigation.

One day things came to a climax. I had a visit from one of the auditors, who told me that Roger had threatened my sons. I reported this incident to the police, and they quickly drove up to the college to escort Roger and Happy to the police station in handcuffs. There they were interrogated and charged with fraud.

Although I was relieved that the two officers had been removed from the college, I still had many reservations. Would the evidence be sufficient in a court of law? Would the evidence be "lost," and would these two men be found not guilty? Worst of all, the college might reemploy the men. As the alleged frauds had taken place over a period of six years and the college had the same public auditors during the entire period, I decided to visit the senior partner in the audit firm.

Before my visit, I made sure not to state my reason for making the appointment. I was shown into the plush boardroom of the firm and invited to pour myself a soft drink. Very soon the senior partner arrived and greeted me warmly. I told him briefly what we had discovered regarding the fraud at the college. The partner nodded and said, "Yes, I am very sure there is fraud going on there." This came as a surprise to me. If he believed that fraud was going on, why had the auditors not taken any specific steps to report it when carrying out the audits?

I decided to also visit the chairman of the college's finance committee. He was the chief accountant of a large multinational company. Unlike the audit partner, he didn't suspect that fraud was taking place. He agreed that we should allow the law to take its course. But he suggested that we should request that the public auditors to provide us with a report on their observations on the fraud. In particular, we wanted to know why the public auditors had not discovered these frauds during the course of their audits over a period of six years.

WHEN THE END DOESN'T JUSTIFY THE MEANS

Finally, Roger and Happy were officially suspended from their posts at the college. The government auditors filed a detailed 100-page report on what they had discovered. I sent a copy to the Ministry of Education and convened a meeting of the College Board.

Our lawyers were briefed on the matter and given a copy of the auditors' report. I also filed a report outlining the circumstances that led us to suspect fraud in the first place. Roger and Happy were brought before a magistrate's court. They pleaded not guilty to all counts of fraud and theft and were released on bail on their own sureties.

In the meantime, the public auditors responded to our request for an explanation of why they had not discovered the fraud. The auditors stated that their procedures were designed, among other things, to uncover fraud if it exists. But they pointed out that the discovery of fraud is not one of their functions. This is the responsibility of management. They also emphasized that considering the annual expenditure of the college over six years, the amount of loss due to the fraud was not material. While the auditors may have been technically correct, some of us in management felt that they were not giving sufficient weight to the $120,000 that had been stolen as well as severe disruption to the functioning of the college. There was also the issue that the discovery of the fraud caused trauma to staff members and led to a lower morale. All in all, we weren't impressed with the manner in which the auditors dealt with the fraud and, in particular, their attempt to hide behind the technicality of "materiality."

The college requested that the government auditors establish if there was collusion between the suppliers and the suspended officers. We also asked them to investigate whether the principal of the college, who was on study leave during this time, was in any way implicated in the fraud. In the case of the suppliers, the auditors were unable to establish a link which would stand up in court. But there was a strong suspicion that they must have had some involvement. Otherwise, it is difficult to see how the officers could have obtained the false invoices.

In the case of the principal, the auditors were satisfied that he was not involved in the fraud. But they did remark that he was certainly negligent for not ensuring that proper accounting controls were in place. It seems that he failed to exercise proper supervision over the work of the accountant and the administrative officer, both of whom reported directly to him.

When the officers' case came before the courts, Happy was found to have fled the country and was working as a salesman in a neighboring country. Roger turned up for his court hearing, but when the case was tried, we found that most of the evidence was missing. Due to the fact that he was the nephew of the minister of education, his case was dismissed. Happy was subsequently shot dead in the neighboring country by bandits who robbed him for the large sum of money he boasted about carrying.

Some time later I saw Roger crossing the road in the town where the college was located. He was shabbily dressed and noticeably thinner. His suave appearance and confident smile had disappeared. His wife had left him, and he was unable to get another job. In some ways I couldn't help feeling sorry for him. I wondered if he would have taken the path to fraud if he had a chance to do it all over again.

LESSONS LEARNED

The first lesson I learned was that investigating fraud in a Third World country is very different from carrying out such an investigation in a developed nation. It seemed to me that there was a greater tolerance of fraud and corruption in Africa. Even the public auditors seemed to accept that fraud was taking place in the college. I was surprised by the fact that Roger wanted to poison me. He didn't seem to realize that the investigation would go on irrespective of whether I was there or not. I learned that it is crucial to have a sufficient knowledge of the country or region's culture where one is conducting an investigation, to ensure that all precautions are taken to safeguard oneself and one's family.

It's important that a thorough investigation be carried out before any administrative action is taken. Looking back, I can see that if I had suspended the two officers before we found the evidence, they might have launched a legal action for unfair dismissal. This would have distracted us from our task of collecting evidence.

Carrying out a lifestyle analysis on one of the officers assisted in pointing us in the right direction. I have come to believe that fraud is committed by two groups of people: those in need and those with greed. Roger combined both motives to sustain his extramarital affairs.

I think it is fair to observe that an organization shouldn't rely on its public auditors alone to discover fraud. The public auditors in this case have firmly rejected any attempts to hold them responsible for discovering the fraud. It is management's responsibility, they claim, to ensure that controls are in place to prevent and detect fraud.

An investigator may do a tremendous job in uncovering fraud and may compile a solid file of evidence, but it's worthless if the legal system doesn't support the process. It's not sufficient that fraud examiners do their work properly; they must also able to rely on a legal system that is efficient, transparent, and not corrupted by either political or financial influence.

The two fraudsters grew confident over the six years they had been perpetrating their financial crimes. It helped them that the same principal was employed during the entire time. They had studied his methods and knew how to outfox him. They also knew how to forge his signature. They came to recognize that the internal controls he exercised were designed to send a warning to employees, but they were not strong enough to prevent them from committing fraud.

Roger, who was clearly the leader in the fraudulent activities, worked himself into a corner with his extramarital affairs, which required more and more funds to sustain. Clearly he was living beyond his means, and he exploited the weak financial controls of the college to fund a style of living that he had become accustomed to. It's likely that he would have continued stealing from the college if he had not been discovered. There was a pattern to his frauds. He became more daring in his actions and steadily increased the amount of money he was stealing. Clearly the more frauds he was getting away with, the more confident he became and the more risks he took.

It became clear during the investigation that some of the staff members at the college knew about the fraudulent activities that were going on, but they decided to stay silent. It's difficult to fault them, given the hostile environment that existed for whistle-blowers.

RECOMMENDATIONS TO PREVENT FUTURE OCCURRENCES

Implement Strict Internal Controls

A strict system of internal controls is of paramount importance to prevent fraud in any organization. There should be clear division of labor in order to prevent one person from doing a number of different jobs, especially where it involves disbursement of funds. An important dimension of the system should be the rotation of staff, if feasible.

Mandatory Vacations and Time Off

Both the administrative officer and the accountant in this case had been at their respective posts for a considerable period of time without taking any mandatory vacations. In order to ensure that an organization can test the effectiveness of its internal control system, employees should be required to take mandatory vacations and time off. During the periods when the staff is away, take the opportunity to test the system of internal control and review a sample to make sure that everything is in order. Senior management should take an interest in the operations of the internal control system. They should arrange for random checks to be carried out on the accounting records. In this case the most senior manager, the principal, didn't provide proper oversight of the work of his immediate staff. This resulted in an exploitation of the obvious weaknesses in the system.

Conduct Lifestyle Analyses

I would recommend that internal auditors and senior management conduct lifestyle analysis to identify possible fraudulent activities. Also, it is clear that some staff know when fraud is taking place, even though they have no involvement in it. Staff should be encouraged to report their well-grounded suspicions to management. At the same time, management should ensure that whistle-blowers are protected from adverse consequences when they do report their suspicions.

Set an Ethical Tone at the Top

A code of ethics that is concise and coherent should be disseminated to all staff members to minimize the incidence of fraud. Top management should make it known that the prevention of fraud is everyone's business. Good governance principles need to be announced, and employees should be made aware that their organization is serious about fraud prevention. Top management should lead by example and observe the highest ethical and managerial standards. The board of the organization needs to put governance on the agenda and make it clear that observing good financial governance is a cornerstone of the management of the organization. There must be zero tolerance for fraud and corruption and no ambiguity about the issue.

Nessan Ronan is a professor of accountancy at the National University of Lesotho. He has extensive experience in accountancy theory and has worked for over 40 years for organizations in Europe and Africa. In teaching, research, and consultancy, Mr. Ronan specializes in forensic accounting and corporate governance.

CHAPTER 27

Price Check on Register One

DWIGHT TAYLOR

C lifton and Holly Harmon had been married for 14 years. They grew up in a small town and knew each other for most of their lives. Like many people, they struggled to raise their three children and meet the monthly bills with their paychecks from the local chicken packing plant. There wasn't much work around Cherokee, Iowa, and what there was didn't pay well.

They decided to pack up the family and move about three hours south to Des Moines for higher-paying jobs and an opportunity to improve their lives. They found an apartment in Grimes, a small town about 10 miles outside of town. After they enrolled the kids in school, Clifton landed a job in a food processing plant. The pay was better than he had been making in Cherokee, but it still fell short of what was necessary to support the family.

Holly had held many different positions over the years, but she lacked specialized skills. She didn't want to go back to work but knew that it would take two paychecks to pay the rent. After working in the packing plant in Cherokee, Holly swore that she would never go back into a factory. She was thrilled when she was hired as a cashier at a large national superstore.

Cathy Lester, one of Holly's best friends, had moved to Des Moines about a year earlier and had encouraged Holly to do the same. Cathy was a single mother of two who, like Holly, had grown up in Cherokee. She married young and had her first child soon after. The second came along a year later—about the same time her husband decided he didn't want to be married. Cathy worked as an office assistant, and although she was still struggling to make ends meet, she was better off than if she had stayed in Cherokee.

Shelly North was Holly's sister. She was divorced with three kids, and also struggled to pay her bills. But unlike her sister, Shelly was satisfied with living in a small town. She had other family members around, and it was a safe place for the kids. Shelly rented a modest house in Cherokee and was doing fine until health problems forced her to quit her job. Child support payments from her ex-husband were not always on time, and sometimes didn't come at all, so she relied on government assistance.

Amelia Leach was born in California, but her family moved to Cherokee when she was a child. Even though she grew up in Iowa, she always wanted to see the world. So it was not surprising to anyone when just after high school she left Cherokee to seek her fortune. Amelia was a bright, attractive young woman. She had a magnetic personality and the potential to be successful in life. But a combination of growing up too fast, associating with the wrong people, and taking shortcuts led her to trouble. She was first arrested in Colorado for forgery at age 20. That was followed by three more arrests within a year. Over the next two decades, Amelia would find herself in and out of jail, in and out of marriage, and finally back to Iowa.

But she was always on the lookout for the easiest way to make a buck. The fact that she always got caught didn't stop her from believing that her next scam would be the one to put her over the top.

CAUGHT ON CAMERA

Thanksgiving had just come and gone, and I was gearing up for what I expected to be an active holiday season. I am a 20-year veteran in law enforcement and had been doing fraud and forgery investigation for the past 4 years. Since I am the only fraud detective in my department, my desk is constantly overloaded with paperwork. I usually have between 20 and 30 active cases, and sometimes as many as 50. With Christmas approaching and the stores filled with shoppers, there was more opportunity and motivation for fraud to occur.

I am also a questioned-document examiner. When I received a call from Chris Lawrence, the loss prevention supervisor at a large national chain store, I was about one month into my studies to receive a Certified Fraud Examiner (CFE) certification. Chris told me that he suspected an employee had been involved in stealing merchandise.

This was not the first time that I had been contacted by the store. In the past, there had been numerous forged checks or stolen credit cards and the occasional employee caught taking a few bucks out of the till. The place was equipped with a state-of-the-art surveillance system, so if Chris had any of the larceny on camera, I was confident that I would have no problem identifying the culprit.

When I arrived at the store, I met Chris Lawrence in the security area. In the office are dozens of monitors where Chris and his staff are able to watch each cash register, aisle, entrance and exit door, as well as the parking lot. All of the equipment is digital, and each color monitor has high-definition resolution. The cameras can zoom in close enough to see pictures on the driver's licenses that are presented to the checkout clerks. Video was kept for at least 90 days and could be accessed with the touch of a button.

Chris told me that he had footage of one of their employees scanning numerous items through the cash register checkout with false UPC labels, stickers with bar codes for pricing. He then showed me surveillance tape of a checkout lane during a recent two-week period. On this tape were 22 suspicious transactions that Chris had documented involving Holly Harmon operating the cash register when three other females and a male subject brought items to her. One can clearly identify the items being scanned in the video, but when the cash register transaction log is reviewed, different items show up—items that ring up at a much lower cost. For example, Holly is shown scanning a clock radio, but the transaction log indicated that it was a bar of soap. It was clear that the items being scanned had UPC labels on them that were not ringing up at the proper amount. Chris also showed me several other times when Holly would scan at the regular cost, but then turn around and void out that item from the cash register. Every time, she would leave the item in the cart and allow the individual to leave with it.

As I watched the video, it was apparent that there was one particular woman who was very active in this scheme. She was shown numerous times going through the checkout lane, and Chris had shots of her leaving the store with many items. It was clear from the footage that Holly and this other woman were very comfortable with each other. They worked with the ease and speed of two people who knew exactly what they were doing. This was obvious because as Holly was ringing merchandise out, the other woman would be placing those items in bags and putting them in her cart. Once the transaction was complete, this woman would take the receipt from Holly and quickly leave.

There were also two other unidentified women and a man who were seen performing the same transactions with Holly. Chris was able to provide me with a shot of the front license plate of the vehicle driven by the male suspect—as I said, these cameras were good.

I asked Chris how he found out about Holly's actions. He said that she had been scheduled to work but failed to come in without telling her supervisor. It is store policy for the security department to perform a review of recent activity when an employee just doesn't show up. As his staff began examining the transaction logs of Holly's register, they noticed many items being scanned at the same price. That's when they searched the videotape and started to suspect that false UPC labels were being used. Chris then had his staff look at all of Holly's activity since she began working for the store. They discovered that within just a few days of being trained and put on a cash register, she began stealing.

I went back to my station and ran a check of the plate of the vehicle. It was registered to Clifton Harmon, Holly's husband. I ran a driver's license photo of Clifton Harmon and identified him as the male subject on the videotape.

I contacted Chris and asked him to compile an itemized list of all of the fraudulent transactions and a dollar amount of the merchandise, which I would need for charging purposes. However, I knew after watching the video that we would not be able to recover everything because not all of the items could be identified from the tape. Some were placed in other containers and just removed from the store. Several times the suspects were seen loading suitcases or large plastic containers onto the checkout register's conveyor belt. If those items were empty, the suspects could have moved them with little effort, but on the tape, it was clear that they were expending an enormous amount of energy to lift them onto the belt.

The Bill Comes Due

As Chris put together the video and compiled a list of transactions, I began an investigation of Holly and her husband. A criminal history check showed that they had both been arrested for forgery, and Clifton had a previous theft charge. Now I needed to learn the identities of the other three women. Since no one at the store could tell me, there was only one choice—to contact Holly.

The Harmons' rented apartment was located about five miles from the store. Since I didn't know who might be at the residence, I took Detective Dan Stein with me. The complex where they lived consisted of several two-story buildings. Holly and Clifton lived on the ground floor, at the end of one of the buildings. I had to knock several times before Holly answered the door. When she did, I identified Dan and myself as a police officers and asked if we could step inside and speak with her. Holly escorted us in to her living room. The apartment was small and dimly lit. In the corner was a Christmas tree with gift-wrapped presents around the base, stacked two and three high.

As I began the interview, I asked Holly if she had worked for the store. She said that she had but that she had recently quit. When I asked why, she said that the hours she was working did not fit with her family life. I then let her know that I was investigating a report from her former employer about merchandise that had been sold at below-retail prices. It was obvious that this made Holly nervous. She shifted in her chair and would not maintain eye contact with me. I continued by telling her that I had videotape of her operating the cash register when these particular sales were made. I immediately saw a dramatic change in her physical appearance. Her eyes became dilated, her jaw muscles tightened, and she had trouble swallowing.

I then took out still pictures I had made from the video and laid them on the coffee table in front of her. As she looked at them, I could not help but wonder about the thoughts running through her head. I then pointed to the first picture, which showed the woman who had been the most active in this scheme. I asked Holly who that person was. She answered in a soft voice, and without making eye contact: "I don't know." Each time I showed one of the other women and asked her who they were, she repeated the same answer. It was not until I pointed to the male subject that she finally looked up at me and said, "That's my husband."

I told Holly that I suspected that she knew who the other three women were and that I also felt that she was involved in the theft of this merchandise. I advised her that she was not under arrest, she did not have to answer any of my questions, and she could consult an attorney if she wished. She no longer wanted to speak to me and asked me to leave her apartment.

As soon as Dan and I left, I contacted two other detectives from my department, and asked them to meet with me. When Tim Pettit and George Griffith arrived, I advised them of the situation involving the Harmons and told them that I was going back to the station to get a search warrant for their apartment to look for stolen merchandise. I asked them to watch the apartment and make sure that the Harmons didn't try to remove anything.

Just as I arrived back at the police station, I received a call from Detective Pettit. He said Holly had just taken some of the gift-wrapped presents from her place to the apartment next door. It certainly appeared that she was attempting to hide evidence.

Because of the exigent circumstances, and not knowing who lived in the apartment where Holly was taking the items, I told Pettit to secure her apartment until I could get the search warrant approved.

As I continued to work on the warrant, I received another call from Pettit. He advised me that he was inside the Harmons' apartment and that both Holly and Clifton were now more cooperative. They told him they would be willing to come to the station to speak with me. I advised Pettit that I was going to continue writing the search warrant, but to go ahead and bring them in. It was not long before Holly and Clifton arrived. While Clifton waited at the front desk, I took Holly to the interview room to begin questioning her and set up the video camera to record the session. I advised her of her rights and asked if she would be willing to speak with me. I then gave her the Miranda waiver form to sign. Her attitude was similar to what she exhibited in the apartment. She would not make eye contact with me, and in a very low-toned voice she said that before talking with me, she wanted to speak with an attorney. Why she didn't say that before I brought her into the interview room is unknown. It could be that once she sat down in the interview room, the reality of her situation sank in. But for whatever reason, once she told me she wanted a lawyer, the interview was over. I took her back to the lobby of the police station.

I then asked Clifton to come with me. I made sure not to allow any time for the two of them to speak to one another as they passed in the hall. When we got into the interview room and sat down, the only things on the table in front of him were the Miranda rights form and the stack of still shots I had from the video. I made sure that the picture on top of the stack was the one I had of him coming out of the store with some of the merchandise, and I also made sure it was in a position where he could easily see it.

Just as I did with Holly, I read Clifton his Miranda rights and asked if he understood them, and if he was willing to speak to me. Clifton hesitated to answer at first. He asked me what his wife had said. I told Clifton that Holly said she wanted to speak with an attorney before talking with me. I explained that he and Holly had every right to have an attorney present, but that did not change what had happened at the store. Regardless of whether they spoke to me, I was going to locate that merchandise.

"Clifton, it is time that you step up and take responsibility for your part in the theft, if for no other reason than to show that you have some remorse for what happened, and because it's the right thing to do," I said. I made it clear to him that the whole scheme would eventually be uncovered and that the more he cooperated, the faster things would go, and the sooner he would be able to start to put this behind him.

This was a critical juncture in the interview. If Clifton did not sign the waiver and agree to talk to me, it would be much harder to identify the other suspects. That additional time would give each of the other participants the opportunity to dispose of the evidence and make prosecution more difficult. At that point I just laid my pen on the waiver form and slid it over in front of Clifton. Without staring too hard at him, but still watching his reactions, I just sat there without saying anything else; I let him think about what I just said. This is sometimes the hardest part for young officers to do in order to get a confession. They are so anxious for a response that they don't allow suspects to ponder what they've been asked to do. Rookies often only let a few seconds of silence pass before they jump back in with more coaxing or more rehashing of information. Once you have laid out the foundation to suspects and you've asked them a question, *let them make the next move*. In this case, I could tell from Clifton's body language that he knew I had enough information to involve him in the scheme, and I just felt that he wanted to clear the air, so I let him sit and stare at the pen until finally he picked it up and signed the form. As soon as he did, his whole demeanor changed. It was as if someone took a weight off his shoulders. I actually saw a smile come across his face, and I knew that he would give me what I needed.

I started by confronting Clifton with the information I had received from the store. I showed him all of the still shots from the video and the cash register printouts of the transactions. I told him I knew that UPC labels had been changed in order to ring up the merchandise below its actual price. I gave him enough facts so that he understood that I knew everything about what had happened and how the scheme worked. Now Clifton had no reason to hold anything back. All I had to do was show him the pictures from the video, and one by one, he identified the three females seen on the tape.

The first person that Clifton identified was Amelia Leach, who was a friend of his wife's. He said that Holly and Amelia came to know each other when they worked at the food plant in Cherokee. They talked on the phone a lot after Holly started working for the store. Amelia had also come to Des Moines several times to visit them. He said he felt that she was the one who concocted the scheme and that she talked Holly into participating.

Clifton also identified the other two women as Shelly North, Holly's sister, and Cathy Lester, one of Holly's closest friends. He told me that Shelly lived in Cherokee and Cathy lived in Grimes. As far as he knew, neither Shelly nor Cathy had ever been in trouble with the law. He also explained his participation in the scheme. On two separate occasions, he went to the store and had items that had false UPC labels taped to them placed into his shopping cart. He said that both times, Amelia had gone to the store with him. He had watched as she took UPC labels from her pocket (which she had previously taken from other items) and put those labels on the things that he wanted. He then took the merchandise to the checkout counter, had them scanned by Holly, and left the store with the merchandise. Clifton claimed that before going to the store for the first time, Holly compiled a list of things for him to get. He put most of the blame on Amelia as the instigator of this scheme. I asked Clifton if he knew where the merchandise was. He told me that some of it was at his house and the rest was at the homes of the other participants. He said that he would go back with officers and retrieve all of the items that were in those two apartments.

After obtaining a written statement from Clifton, I contacted the county attorney, who authorized charges against Holly for theft. As Clifton went back to his apartment with the officers to retrieve the merchandise, I booked Holly and had her transported to the county jail. As it turned out, more than $4,200 in merchandise was found in the Harmon's apartment. But that was only a part of what was taken. I still needed his help in order to recover the other stolen goods.

WRAPPING UP SOME GIFTS

Clifton wanted to cooperate. I had to take advantage of that and not allow too much time to pass before the other perpetrators could be contacted. I asked Clifton if he would be willing to call Cathy and try to convince her to admit to her part in the theft and turn over any of the merchandise she had. He said that he would do whatever I needed in order to get this cleared up.

After stationing officers outside her house, I had Clifton phone Cathy. He told her that the store had found out about the theft, and the police had video of her in the store. He let her know that Holly had been arrested and that all of the items they had in their apartment had been recovered; it would be in her best interest to cooperate.

Cathy consented to a search of her house, and all of the items she received in the scheme were recovered. Since she had children at home, Cathy was allowed to turn herself in the next day and was also charged with theft.

I knew that Amelia would be the most difficult of the entire group to get to cooperate, but since Clifton was still willing to help, and the approach we took with Cathy worked, we decided to try it again. Early the next morning, Detective Griffith and I drove three hours to Cherokee. After contacting the local police and getting one of their officers to accompany us, we drove to Amelia's house and waited outside until Clifton called her. She was not as receptive as Cathy. Once Clifton explained the situation to her and told her Holly had been arrested, she hung up on him.

After Clifton told me that Amelia was not going to cooperate, I decided to go ahead and make contact with her. I was a little surprised when after only a few knocks on the door, Amelia answered. She was much friendlier than I thought she would be, and she invited us into her house. Once inside, she said that she knew why we were there and that she wanted to assist us. I have to tell you this startled me for a second. I explained that I had a warrant for her arrest and advised her of her rights. She immediately waived them and agreed to tell me what happened. She tried to put most of the blame for the planning of the scheme on Holly, but she admitted that she was a major player in putting false UPC labels on merchandise. Soon we were going through her house and piling all kinds of things on the floor in her front room. By the time we were finished, there were so many items that we had to rent a trailer to haul everything back. It turned out that Amelia had more than $5,000 in merchandise.

We followed the same plan with Holly's sister, Shelly. Clifton called her as we waited down the street. Shelly cooperated—she was crying when she opened the door. After being advised of her rights, she told us of her involvement in the theft. She then went around the house and brought everything she had stolen to us. The total of her theft was $1,500.

After all of the items were collected, we recovered more than $12,000 in merchandise and made five arrests. Clifton, Shelly, and Cathy were placed on probation and ordered to pay restitution for their parts in the scheme. Holly and Amelia were not so lucky. Since it was obvious that they were the main planners of theft, they each received 10-year prison sentences in addition to orders of restitution.

LESSONS LEARNED

We were lucky to recover the majority of the goods. The store had an excellent surveillance system. Without the videotaped evidence, it is extremely unlikely that things would have progressed as quickly and smoothly. It allowed us to identify the perpetrators, figure out the scheme, and identify most of the stolen merchandise.

It is good that the store has policies in place to check on employees who abruptly quit, but I wonder if they would have detected this scheme if Holly had not been so fast to leave. What if she would have stopped switching UPC labels for a time and then submitted a two-week notice? Would the store have been as diligent in going back over her cash register transactions? When I posed that question to Chris, he said he's not sure if they would have caught it. After all, it was a very busy time of year.

I also learned that effective interview techniques can break a case wide open. Although Holly refused to talk, my interview with Clifton turned the case. I laid out the evidence so that he knew I was aware of the scheme and his participation. I then waited for him to make the next move. He knew he was caught and that his best option was cooperation. Without his help, it would have taken much longer to track down the other suspects, and I have no doubt that we would have had a much more limited recovery of the merchandise.

RECOMMENDATIONS TO PREVENT FUTURE OCCURRENCES

Background Checks

Holly had a previous criminal record. If the store had conducted a background check, it is unlikely it would have given her a position as a cashier.

Improved Monitoring

The store is in the process of redesigning its software to flag for unusual activity, such as numerous voided items from a single register. Also, the store will be more proactive in randomly reviewing register transactions logs and comparing them to the videotapes. Of course, no store can review every sale, but it can randomly select several transactions per day or per week to examine more thoroughly.

Increased Perception of Detection

The store should let its employees, particularly the cashiers, know that it is monitoring for unusual activity and that it selects transactions randomly for further scrutiny.

These measures will help, but I bet I'll be back at the store again. There will always be people like Holly and Amelia who are on the lookout for that next scam to make a few quick bucks.

Dwight Taylor, CFE, DRE, is a detective who has been in law enforcement for two decades, a fraud and forgery investigator for five years, and a questioned document examiner for four. He is president of the DART Group, a firm that develops drug testing policies and training to aid companies in identifying fraudulent activity and drug use in the workplace.

28

The Sky Is the Limit

BRIAN E. BROWNING

D r. Reginald Lear began his administrative career in higher education as the president of a small northern college. After eight years, he moved to Kentucky to take another job as a university president. There he was hailed for his vision and strong leadership. He increased the endowment from $183 million to more than $400 million. Following an extensive search, Dr. Lear was selected as the next president of Hardwell University. The school offered him a compensation package that ranked highly for college presidents, exceeding $700,000.

"We've got to commit ourselves to giving the state the very best university it can afford. That's the philosophy that I'll bring to this challenging position," he said upon his appointment. Unfortunately, Dr. Lear's idea of affording the very best was not what anyone had in mind.

OLD SCHOOL

Hardwell University is a well-established college with over two centuries of history. It began as a small school, but eventually became one of the few land-grant universities in the country. There are currently 9,000 faculty and staff and an annual enrollment reaching approximately 42,000 students. Several campuses comprise the academic system, with an annual operating budget of $1 billion; less than 40% is funded from state appropriations.

This institution prides itself on its efforts to become a top research facility. However, the school was struggling with a decline in state funding and increases in annual operating costs, which meant significant tuition hikes and cuts in departmental budgets, staffing, and salary.

My office was located off-campus in the bottom level of a converted department store. Windowless and with poor artificial lighting, the moisture content was so high we had to use two dehumidifiers daily. It was the perfect place for a team of 13 internal auditors.

I was employed by Hardwell's flagship campus and, as a senior investigative auditor, handled most fraud-related issues. The majority of the cases we received were the typical small-dollar shortages and thefts committed by employees with access to petty cash accounts or those who received money in their departments from students or staff. This investigation was different.

IN PLANE VIEW

The fraud was not discovered by an anonymous phone call, nor was it the result of a routine audit. The controversy began when a local news outlet questioned Dr. Lear's desire to purchase a new university airplane to replace the aging twin-turbo propeller plane that had been used for 20 years. The local media expressed concern about such an extravagant investment during a time of budget cuts, layoffs, and double-digit tuition increases. So they filed an open records request for copies of flight logs to determine if the president could justify spending an estimated $4 million on a jet plane.

The media discovered that the aircraft was used extensively; however, they decided to further scrutinize the actual destinations and purposes of the flights, starting at the time that Dr. Lear was appointed at Hardwell. He was then questioned about several of the trips, particularly flights to Alabama, where it was rumored that he had a personal relationship with the president of a college there. When the local media outlet asked Dr. Lear about the purpose of a few of these trips, he replied he had attended meetings to search for a new athletic director. Of course, they sought to confirm his statement and discovered that few such meetings took place. In fact, Dr. Lear and the president of the Alabama college had attended a black-tie event at the same time as one of his supposed scheduled events.

This led the media to examine other activities. They found that he had used a company credit card for questionable expenditures, including a $6,000 overseas flight. Evidence also suggested that he awarded a $300,000 no-bid contract to a former business associate. It didn't take long for the governor and chairman of the board of trustees to appoint a special committee to investigate these allegations. Finally, the chairman requested that the university's internal audit department conduct a thorough review of all financial matters related to Dr. Lear.

A LIFESTYLE FIT FOR A PRESIDENT

I was determined, yet apprehensive, about preparing for what I knew would be a series of interviews with Dr. Lear. Undoubtedly there would be pressure from state and university officials, as well as the public, to get to the bottom of these allegations as quickly as possible. Although there were only 14 months of information to review, it included all types of expenditures as well as several contracts initiated and approved by Dr. Lear. Mark Beasley, director of internal audit, determined that the best approach was to utilize the full resources of our office by assigning different areas of the investigation to all 13 auditors.

My role was to review and question Dr. Lear and other employees. Shortly after we began, Dr. Lear announced he would reimburse the university several thousand dollars for numerous private and commercial flights, regardless of the fact that some trips involved business. He felt this would clear the air and reduce further questioning. My investigative skills immediately told me this was a red flag. If I was in his position, and someone had questioned me about improper flights, I certainly would not pay *extra* for legitimate business-related trips. Therefore, the logical place to begin the investigation was to review all flight logs for the university plane.

Our office requested a copy of Dr. Lear's calendar, which listed all of his appointments, and compared them with the flight logs. In the associate director's dimly lit office, we analyzed pages and pages of information and determined that Hardwell had incurred nearly $24,000 for air travel considered personal (or of incidental benefit to the school). Some of the trips that Dr. Lear took included attending athletic events with the president of the Alabama school, visits to Kentucky related to his divorce, and certain occasions when the university plane flew empty to pick him up and return home. This was only the tip of the iceberg; we kept digging.

When he had begun his short tenure, the university had agreed to provide Dr. Lear a travel credit card, which is made available to all employees. Charges for travel are made to the card, statements are then sent to the employee for payment, and the employee submits appropriate documentation for reimbursement. However, an exception was made for Dr. Lear. The school paid for his monthly statements in lieu of reimbursements—another red flag. One of the senior auditors reviewed the charges and identified several purchases, including clothing, flowers, restaurant charges, and a trip to Greece, totaling over $7,200 in personal expenses.

As the auditors continued to investigate, we felt it was time to begin questioning Dr. Lear. The next day I drove to the state capital with three state auditors. I was surprised to find that the university president had an office suite in a rather lavish downtown building near the state capitol, away from the campus. We were led into a conference room with a large round table. Shortly thereafter, we were greeted by Dr. Lear. After brief introductions we commenced questioning.

"Can you explain the nature of these purchases on your travel card?" I asked, pointing out some seemingly personal items on our review.

He replied that the clothing was an emergency purchase and the flowers were charged by mistake.

"That seems to be a reasonable excuse, but it's still personal," I remarked. Next I showed him the airfare to Greece. "Now, can you explain this $6,000 airline ticket?"

"I attended a board meeting at New York College in Athens, and they were supposed to reimburse the university," he replied.

They did, in fact, reimburse Hardwell after I contacted them several months later.

There were other charges, such as concierge-level hotel rooms and entertainment expenses on the travel card. One receipt for a hotel in Denver, Colorado, reflected a charge of $1,165 for one night. Dr. Lear claimed that $900 of this amount was associated with a meal at the hotel's restaurant, but no receipt or further explanation was provided.

The president's staff said they had a difficult time obtaining receipts for charges to the travel card. When asked about his lack of documentation, he stated, "I attempted to turn in all the receipts I had, but do admit I probably could have done a better job." Although not necessarily fraudulent, this was clearly a violation of university policies. There was still plenty of explaining for Dr. Lear to do.

When he was hired, his contract allowed for reasonable moving expenses from his former residence. The key word here is *reasonable*. The cost of his move was, in fact, a whopping $14,000. A couple of weeks into the investigation, I called the representative for the moving company used to transport Dr. Lear's belongings. He informed me that at the end of the move, Dr. Lear had instructed his movers to add 20% gratuity to the bill for a job well done, which they refused to do.

The next day I met with Dr. Lear and asked him if he recalled making the gratuity offer.

"No, absolutely not," he replied. "However, I did feel they deserved a tip and recall asking my chief of staff about the policy regarding gratuities."

"Well," I began, "I've already questioned your chief of staff and she does not recall any conversation with you or the moving company in regards to gratuities. Therefore, if you deny offering the gratuity, but recall asking your chief of staff who knows nothing about it, then why would the moving company report it? Do you think you could be confused?"

Dr. Lear paused for a moment, then glanced away and replied, "I don't know . . . I just don't know." I could hardly restrain myself from calling him out on what was obviously another dishonest answer. As the investigation progressed, we started to realize the effect our findings would have on the institution and on Dr. Lear's presidency. There were numerous front-page headlines and state legislative inquiries as to the status of our inquiry.

One of the many fringe benefits Dr. Lear received as the president of Hardwell University was the use of a large residence owned by the school. During his brief tenure, Dr. Lear was allowed to make reasonable modifications to the home. Prior to his appointment, it had undergone a $787,000 renovation. Dr. Lear requested an additional $400,000 in improvements. As our internal audit team began to review some of these expenses, we were astonished by the president's lavish spending habits. This was an individual who just weeks earlier had explained to students that a 15% tuition increase was necessary to fund rising operational costs. He bought two entertainment systems totaling over $14,000, a $7,000 Persian rug, two armoires, a $5,000 stainless steel gas grill, and a $1,200 invisible dog fence. Some of these items were in direct violation of purchasing guidelines. I met Mike Lawler, the executive director of Facilities Services, at the residence to look at these items.

As I entered the foyer, I said, "Okay, where's that famous Persian rug?"

"You're standing on it," he replied.

"This thing cost $7,000? You have got to be kidding me."

In my view, it was the ugliest rug I had ever laid eyes on. I finished inspecting the remaining items with Mike and then asked Dr. Lear for a justification of the purchases. In short, he claimed to believe them to be reasonable and thought they would add value to the residence in the future.

One of the most surprising expenses was the amount spent on telecommunications—$64,000 for residential installments. The telephone system alone was valued at $30,000. It consisted of five lines and a cordless speaker phone in nearly every main room. Also, Dr. Lear requested a $20,000 telephone to be installed on the university plane. When asked, he stated he wasn't aware of the cost. This seemed strange, as the bill was sent to his office account.

No Parting Gift

The investigation seemed to end as quickly as it had begun. Normally, a fraud of this magnitude, with one or two investigators working on it, would have taken quite a while to put together. However, with the full resources of our office, we wrapped up everything in about a month. Once we issued our report, the media and state legislators were demanding answers: How could this have happened? Why were policies circumvented?

As the investigation progressed, Dr. Lear refused demands to resign. However, before the final report was released to the public—and after immense pressure and a meeting with the governor and the vice chair of the board—he relinquished his presidency.

The agreement included a $400,000 severance package, which the state felt was the best course of action to avoid a lengthy legal quarrel. As part of the settlement, Dr. Lear confirmed there were no other issues, which, if discovered, could void the deal.

Although the audit report had been released, the outcome of the investigation was still being processed as the university sought answers. Several senior administrators were requested to appear before a state legislative committee less than two weeks after Dr. Lear's resignation. They all said that they should have done more to curtail Dr. Lear's spending and that, ultimately, they were responsible. A summary of our findings included:

- Dr. Lear's travel was rarely handled in accordance with university procedures. Questionable travel expenses exceeded $23,000.

- Dr. Lear's credit card was used to purchase nearly $1,200 in personal items, approximately $3,000 in excess lodging rates, and over $800 in entertainment and meal overpayments.

- Dr. Lear requested nearly $500,000 worth of renovations done at the president's residence, which included a $7,000 Persian rug and a $5,000 gas grill.

- The university spent over $64,000 on telecommunications items for Dr. Lear, including a $20,000 phone installed on the plane.

- Two no-bid contracts with friends of Dr. Lear were determined to have been unfair and consisted of favorable treatment.

- Nearly $165,000 was spent on entertainment-related expenses for a single football season, and holiday receptions exceeded $73,000.

As the state legislators continued to grill administrators, and with the announcement of the president's resignation, preparations were under way to collect and ship Dr. Lear's belongings from his office. Another auditor and I oversaw the process to ensure that no university property was inadvertently packed with his personal items.

Upon arrival, I entered the president's extravagant office. I sat down at his desk. My colleague and I began sifting through the desk drawers, removing any university records. We never expected to discover anything surprising; however, we did find something eye-opening. I pulled out a hardcopy of Dr. Lear's calendar, which listed all of his appointments dating back several months. At first glance it appeared to be a copy of what was already provided to us. But as we scanned through the pages, we noticed some trips to the same destination in Alabama that were not on the copy we'd seen. I immediately contacted the audit director and explained what we had found. He instructed me to return to the office as soon as possible.

As one might imagine, this was damaging information for Dr. Lear. He had lied to us during the investigation by providing an alternate calendar. After further questioning of his staff, it was determined he had instructed Jan Blackledge, his administrative assistant, to remove certain personal appointments from the calendar. This action raised another issue—Dr. Lear had altered a public document.

"He just highlighted the personal appointments he did not want to be shown on the calendar. I never gave it a second thought," explained Jan.

The governor and legislators were infuriated once they were informed of the alterations. Without hesitation, the governor said he considered Dr. Lear's severance package null and void. However, the state's attorney general reviewed the matter and determined there was insufficient information to file criminal charges against Dr. Lear.

Lessons Learned

This case opened my eyes to the fact that anyone, regardless of his or her position, is capable of committing fraud. The president of a public university is no different. During the investigation we discovered that Dr. Lear had instructed his staff to run all information by him instead of the board of trustees. This was an obvious red flag. It provided him with relative assurance that he could authorize or make decisions regardless of the expense, including requesting exceptions to policies and spending as if the sky was the limit.

Caps on travel expenses are intended for all employees—even senior administrators. A travel card that the university paid for allowed Dr. Lear to charge personal items. Also, the opportunity existed to engage in wasteful spending, such as concierge-level hotel rooms and extravagant meals. The travel coordinator said Dr. Lear had a standing request for the best hotel rooms since he was the college president.

Budgets should be established to limit entertainment expenditures. Dr. Lear spent tens of thousands of dollars during a single football season; alcohol purchases totaled $13,000. A few holiday receptions during the month of December alone cost over $81,000. If budgets and proper controls had been in place, excessive spending would have been prevented.

The most fundamental breakdowns were the critical internal control deficiencies in nearly every financial aspect of the president's office. The primary reason these acts occurred was the disregard of and exceptions to existing policies just to please Dr. Lear. Of the few times someone did question an expense, his response was "This is how things were handled at my previous institution." The only way internal controls succeed is if they apply to everyone—even a university president.

Most of all, I learned the importance of having a hotline and ensuring people are aware of it. At the time of the investigation, the state had a tip line that allowed employees to report allegations anonymously; however, it was not widely publicized. In addition, most employees I interviewed expressed concern over losing their jobs if they were to report suspicious spending.

RECOMMENDATIONS TO PREVENT FUTURE OCCURRENCES

University Policies for Senior-Level Positions

Four policies were revised to prevent the president and other senior-level administrators from making exceptions without approval by the Finance Committee of the board.

1. Presidents should be reimbursed for expenses in the same manner as all other university employees, which should specifically prohibit direct payment of travel cards. Lodging should be paid only at the allowable rate, and the purpose of each flight taken on the university airplane should be documented in the flight log.

2. A formal housing policy governing the president's residence should be adopted to address all expenses and major renovations. It should receive the appropriate approval from the State Building Commission. Additional projects and furnishings should be thoroughly documented and authorization obtained in writing.

3. Every organization has a responsibility to be good stewards of the taxpayer's assets. Budgets are essential. The university now requires documentation for all entertainment and special events initiated by the president's office.

4. All no-bid contracts for consulting services should include a noncompetitive purchase agreement, and any potential client that is an acquaintance of a university employee should be removed from further consideration to eliminate the possibility of favoritism. In addition, steps should be taken to ensure contracts have completed the entire approval process before the contract period begins. This includes a review by the purchasing department.

Administrative Changes

One of the main reasons Dr. Lear was able to commit many fraudulent acts was the lack of appropriate oversight. The position of chief financial officer (CFO) was created to monitor all financial aspects of the university. Although the CFO reports directly to the president, he is required to provide the board regular updates on spending by the president's office.

Additionally, an Audit Committee was created within the board, and the executive director of Internal Audit answers directly to the committee. Prior to this investigation, the executive director reported only to the president. Monthly and quarterly reports are issued to the committee along with face-to-face meetings. Also, annual audits are performed on the president's office, chancellors, and vice presidents to ensure compliance.

Whistle-Blower Protection and Hotlines

Some form of a state statute was already in place prior to the investigation of Dr. Lear, but now more emphasis is placed on protecting an individual's confidentiality. In addition, the university was required to create and widely disseminate brochures and posters informing employees and students about ways they can report suspected fraud or wasteful spending, including the use of the state audit hotline.

Proactive Approach

The internal audit department has begun conducting risk assessments of the university prior to routine audits. Part of this function includes a fraud audit. For example, once an auditor takes a sample of invoices to review for standard requirements (vendor name, date, total, quantity, etc.), he or she must physically verify the address of a few by driving by the business to ensure its legitimacy. Other examples may include verifying all employees listed in a department are actually there. These steps may seem trivial, but could uncover a fraudulent scheme.

Furthermore, fraud prevention and awareness courses are now offered to employees through the university's human resources department. These presentations provide an understanding of how fraud occurs, potential red flags, and ways to prevent fraudulent activities in higher education.

Brian E. Browning, CFE, MS, is the business manager for the Division of Finance and Administration at a public university. Mr. Browning, a graduate of the University of Tennessee, served as a senior investigative auditor prior to his current position and has over 10 years of fraud prevention, investigative, and law enforcement experience.

CHAPTER 29

Supplemental Income

JAMES E. WHITAKER

Mike Riddle was a loner, but not a recluse by any standard. Married and in his early 30s, he had a young daughter who was the apple of his eye. On Mike's desk sat a picture of the two most important women in his life: his wife, Sally, and his little girl. Although Sally's family didn't approve of her marriage, he didn't really care. She was not demanding, but she did expect to live in a nice house, drive decent cars, and measure up to the neighbors' lifestyle. Mike always assured her that they shared common goals and that he would work as hard as it took to realize them. While they would never get rich from his income as an insurance adjuster, he promised her they could and would be financially comfortable. The company had a great profit-sharing plan, and he assured Sally that he would invest their money wisely. She trusted him completely and let him handle all of the financial planning. Sally didn't agree with her family's assertions that Mike would never have any real success. Considering that his company was well established and that they obviously thought highly of her husband (according to him), they were surely destined for a comfortable middle-income lifestyle.

Mike was a claims adjuster. He worked in a small office that included him, the manager, and the office secretary. Although he specialized in property claims, he was required to work many other different types as well. He thought bodily injury, auto damage, and similar claims were boring, and it irked him that the company didn't appreciate his skills as a property adjuster and that his manager never sang his praises.

Mike thought his boss, Daryl Stepp, was a nice-enough guy but a bit of a pushover. Daryl never expected a lot and rarely, if ever, questioned Mike. He was content just to assign him files and to work the other ones himself. Besides, everyone knew that the philosophy of Protection Mutual was to let the employees do their work without too much hindrance.

Although Mike had several years of adjusting experience, he was viewed as an average performer. He was fairly dependable as an employee—usually punctual, finished his assignments, but never asked for additional duties or responsibilities. Though soft spoken and courteous, Mike did not interact well with his fellow workers.

The insurance carrier, Protection Mutual, had an impeccable reputation among its agents and insureds. The company was founded in the mid-1800s and was one of the oldest in the Midwest. Its business plan was straightforward: Sell its products through reliable and honest agents; reward them for loyalty and productivity; treat the employees well and make them a part of the company; make sure the insured was provided insurance at a competitive rate; and—most important—pay the claims owed.

When Mike Riddle came to Protection Mutual, the company had barely changed in 150 years. Technology had advanced, but the operating philosophy remained the same. Upper management believed that if the staff was treated fairly and shared in the profits, they would remain loyal. The very thought of an employee stealing from the company was unheard of.

Protection Mutual had grown quickly in the past decade and was confronted with new and increasing security and internal issues. The company's structure included a separate corporate security department and a Special Investigation Unit (SIU) for claims issues. Most internal investigations were conducted by human resource personnel in conjunction with the Security Department, which consisted mainly of auditors. There were several reasons for this structure, but it was predicated mainly on the mandates of the "old school" executives. They never wanted the SIU to be viewed as "the bad guys." To them, it was more important to have a good working relationship so that claims adjusters would work *with* SIU to identify and resolve potential frauds.

Of course, there were several deficiencies with this process, the most notable being the lack of expertise in the Human Resource Department to adequately conduct internal investigations. They had no training in this area and had little, if any, knowledge of the criminal justice system. Their main goal was to remove miscreants from the position as expeditiously as possible, which usually resulted in a settlement with the perpetrator. In this manner, the "problem" was resolved with no embarrassment or liability. This philosophy was not lost on Mike Riddle. Even if he was caught, and he thought this highly unlikely, he would just be forced to leave.

I was familiar with many of the eccentricities of the company's operations. After all, I had begun my career as an SIU investigator and had worked my way up to manager of that unit. Later I relocated to the home office and eventually became an executive in charge of other claims units, but retained direct responsibility for the SIU.

SMELLING SMOKE

One afternoon I got a call from the SIU manager, who reported to me directly. Bob Temple was a retired police lieutenant. He was smart, articulate, well educated, and a good investigator. Bob asked if I had a few minutes to speak with him. As usual, he got right to the point. "I think we may have a problem with an employee in one of our out-of-state service offices," he said.

Preliminary reports indicated that Mike Riddle may have been authorizing drafts to himself on the claims files he was working on. The secretary in the office wasn't sure what was actually going on, but something "sure seemed fishy," according to her. The checks written are referred to as "drafts," so we were looking at a situation where an employee was possibly authorizing checks to himself disguised as payments on claims.

I chose to take the lead when I found out that a new twist had been introduced: Mike Riddle had just voluntarily terminated his employment with Protection Mutual. HR would no longer be involved in the investigation, and corporate security was not adequately equipped to deal with the situation. Bob and I would be conducting the initial investigation so SIU would be directly involved. I first advised him to contact Mary Stewart, the claims secretary in Mike's old office. Mary was a long-term employee of Protection Mutual. She was detail-oriented and a hard worker. Everyone knew that she was the glue that held the office together. Because there were only three people in the office, Mary had to take on the entire clerical function. This included answering phones, setting up claims, and handling all correspondence. She was efficient and took pride in her work.

As directed, Bob contacted Mary, who told him that it appeared as if Mike had been authorizing supplemental drafts (checks) for some property claims. Over the years, both Bob and I had spent some time in her office investigating cases. Mary told us she had received a call from an insured about a draft he received. The customer had some interior smoke damage to his house as a result of a kitchen fire. He had used the restoration cleanup service that Mike, his assigned claims adjuster, had recommended. As far as the insured was concerned, the company did a great job.

The insured was questioning why, several months later, he received a draft in the amount of $965.32 for supplemental work. He indicated that Mike had already had him sign off on the claim, and as far as he was concerned, it was over and done with. He made it clear to Mary he wasn't complaining, he just didn't know what to do with this check. It was made payable to him and the restoration company. He had asked, "Do I cash it, sign it over to the other company, send it back, or what?"

Mary was very concerned. She knew something was wrong, so she immediately notified Daryl, who told her to contact SIU. The draft was made out to the insured and to "Restora*tive* Professionals, Inc." This name was very similar to Restora*tion* Professionals, Inc., a service that Protection Mutual frequently recommended to insureds as a preferred contractor. It was also the company that had done the cleanup on this particular claim. We had worked with this contractor for many years and knew the people there to be honest and dependable.

CURIOSITY KILLS THE CAT

First, we called Restoration Professionals to verify what services were performed. They confirmed that they did the initial work and closed the claim to the satisfaction of both the insured and the adjuster, Mike Riddle. They received a draft coendorsed by the insured and closed the file. There was no danger of Mike accidentally stumbling on us investigating his files since he no longer had access to the office, so we set about collecting and analyzing the information. I advised Bob to make a computer vendor run on any files that involved Restoration Professionals in the past three years, including the ones that Mike had either assisted with or handled directly.

We matched the employer identification number (EIN) for Restoration Professionals with all the files that Mike had dealt with. I obtained copies of the front and back of all drafts that had been approved by him for that EIN. Some of the checks were payable to "Restoration Professionals" and others to "Restora*tive* Professionals." We found two separate and distinct banks and deposit numbers found in these groups. The bank and deposit account numbers on all of those files matched perfectly with one of the accounts we found on the drafts made payable to "Restor*ation* Professionals." The other numbers only showed up on files handled by Mike with drafts made payable to "Restora*tive* Professionals," and they also all had another common trait: All were supplemental drafts issued at his request. On them, where the name closely resembled the legitimate vendor, the correct EIN actually was present, which allowed the drafts to go through the system undetected, even though the name was not exactly correct.

We verified with Restoration Professionals that the bank name and deposit account number belonged to them. As their EIN showed up on the supplemental drafts, we asked about each draft in question, and they verified they had not performed the work as Mike had indicated. As Bob and I discussed where to go from here, our biggest concern was that Mike was no longer required to assist in our investigation, as he was no longer an employee. We could turn it over the local law enforcement agency, but past experience told us that with their limited resources, it might be a long time before anything happened.

Bob didn't think there was a snowball's chance on a Florida beach in August that Mike would agree to speak with us. After all, why should he? I felt differently. Having had contact with Mike over the previous years, his smugness and aloofness always caught my attention. I thought that if I contacted him and told him we needed to speak with him regarding some investigative issues, he would be curious. I was banking on the fact that he would think he could outsmart us and find out what we did—and didn't—know. Of course if I guessed wrong and he refused, we would then have no alternative than to contact the law enforcement authorities and hope for the best.

I packed my bag, and Bob and I flew out to the local service office. When I met with the staff, I reiterated the fact I wanted no one to discuss this investigation—even with other company personnel. Claims people, even after switching jobs, often still communicate with each other.

While we were driving, I called Mike from my cell. No one answered, so I left a message. I made it intentionally vague and just told him to contact me. I said I was leaving the day after tomorrow and if I didn't hear from him by then, I'd have to explore other options. The web had been spun; we now just had to see if the fly would be caught.

Later that evening, my cell phone rang. It was Mike. We exchanged pleasantries and then he asked, "What exactly do you want to talk to me about?"

"It's concerning some possible irregularities found while reviewing some of your files," I responded.

"What irregularities?" he inquired. I had to be ambiguous but give him enough to rouse his curiosity.

"You know I won't talk specifics on the phone," I replied. "I've known you long enough to believe that we should discuss this face to face. You were too valuable of an employee to deserve less." Silence ensued. After a few more moments, he said, "When do you want to meet?" I suggested the next evening at 7:00 at the office. He said he wasn't sure he could make it and that he had to call me back. I knew my response was critical to his decision, so I said, "Mike, I'm leaving the day after tomorrow whether I meet with you or not. If I don't, I'll have to let someone outside the company handle this. That isn't my first choice."

He pondered this for a few seconds and said, "I'll call you back; we have a bad connection." He then hung up. Bob was convinced we wouldn't hear from him again, except maybe to say that we would need to speak with his lawyer. I was still betting on the fact that he understood the threat of us going to law enforcement, and he was deciding at that point whether to call a lawyer or to talk with us. The phone rang later. He would meet us at 7:00 p.m. the next day.

When Mike showed up, he had clearly considered that he may be arrested, so he was scoping out the office. Bob and I had strategically placed all the documentation on the table in huge binders so that Mike would see that we were prepared. Some of it was filler, but he didn't know that. It was certainly an intimidating mound.

I knew that the first three minutes of the interview were critical. We purposely allowed Mike to begin the conversation. Finally he said, "What's this all about?"

"It's about the bogus supplemental drafts you issued to yourself through your own account," I replied. I let that sink in for a few moments. He didn't deny it, but didn't say anything affirmative either.

"Mike, here's the deal," I said. "I wanted to hear your side of it before presenting it to senior management to decide the next course of action."

After pondering that for a few moments, he wanted to know what could possibly happen. I told him the options were to let him reimburse the company and possibly face a civil action or a criminal complaint. He asked why we didn't contact the police already. I told him it wouldn't have been fair to do so without learning his side of the story. I knew the issue of criminal prosecution was foremost on his mind, so I downplayed that aspect as much as I could. I told him all the possibilities and advised him that the extent of cooperation from him would certainly be considered. At that point, he said he would fully cooperate.

So Mike laid out the events of his fraud. He would fabricate a reason for additional work on a particular file and then add it to the claim. After waiting for a while—the amount of time he guessed it would take to complete the kind of job that he recorded—he'd make an invoice to reflect the job was finished. Having worked with Restoration Professionals for many years, he knew what their invoices looked like. Mike simply copied one and used it as a blank. As the adjuster, he was able to approve the invoice. Sometimes he would enter a note stating that he had personally inspected the work and had found it satisfactory.

He would then issue the draft to his bogus company, which almost duplicated the name of the legitimate one. As the EIN was correct, the secretary just issued the check. It would be made payable to the insured and the contractor, with both signatures being required. Mike already had the signature of the insured; he simply duplicated it as best he could on the bogus supplement. He would then endorse it as a company representative with a FOR DEPOSIT ONLY stamp and place it in his account. He was relying on the fact that since he was using the real EIN of the company and a similar name, it would take a very long time to uncover the fraud.

Since the secretary prepared the drafts and mailed them out, it seemed reasonable that they would end up directly at the insured's residence. Mike had this covered also. Being a small office, all three employees helped each other out. Mike, appearing to be a team player, often offered to drop the mail off at the post office. Of course, he would remove the envelope with the bogus supplemental draft. Unfortunately for him, he failed to catch the one that started the investigation.

We had drafts totaling a little over $50,000. That is all Mike would admit to, although we knew there was probably more. He gave us written permission to run a credit check and agreed to provide his bank statements and account information. When he was preparing to leave, he asked what was going to happen. I reiterated that once the investigation was completed, I'd let him know the disposition. As we were wrapping up the interview, he inquired as to how the fiscal year was going for the company. I told him we were having a good one. He then asked a question so unbelievable that Bob and I just looked at each other in amazement. "After all this is finally over, do you think I'll be able to get profit sharing again this year?"

"No," I replied.

Surprise Visit

Mike was feeling pretty good about the situation when he left and probably thought he would only be facing restitution—on his terms. But things didn't work out that way. As required by law, the incident was reported to the state Department of Insurance (DOI) as well as to the local authorities. The DOI was interested in the case. Insurance fraud is taken very seriously by most DOIs.

Mike Riddle liked being a claims adjuster, especially with the extra benefit package that he had set up for himself. He was later hired at a different carrier with basically the same duties. When asked on the application whether he had ever been convicted of a crime of theft or any insurance-related offense, he stated no. Technically, that was true—he had not even been arrested yet, let alone convicted. As several weeks went by, it appeared that he had dodged a bullet. Mike had voluntarily terminated his employment with Protection Mutual and had a clean record. On paper, he looked like the ideal candidate for a new claims adjuster. But imagine his surprise when at 1:15 p.m. on a weekday he was approached by DOI agents and the local sheriff's deputy and hauled out of the workplace in handcuffs.

Mike was arrested and spent several days in jail until his wife posted his bail. Confronted with the overwhelming evidence against him, he pleaded guilty to embezzlement and insurance fraud. Mike received time served as the actual jail sentence, was placed on five years of supervised probation, and was ordered to pay restitution in the amount of $50,000 to Protection Mutual in monthly installments. His license to act as an insurance adjuster was permanently revoked.

Mike Riddle was forced to obtain a second mortgage on his home in order to pay the attorney fees and restitution that was ordered by the court. Although he avoided a jail sentence, he no longer had a job with a steady source of income. His home was mortgaged to the hilt. Perhaps of most dire consequence was the felony record that would follow Mike for the rest of his life.

LESSONS LEARNED

The person who first discovered this theft was a coworker of the offender. Often colleagues are reluctant to squeal on their associates because they don't think that's part of their job, or they are concerned about how the company will react if they are mistaken. In this case, when Mary came forward, the fraud was uncovered and eventually resolved. Protection Mutual made sure she was honored for her honesty.

Another lesson learned centered on the risk of attempting to evoke a response from the offender in order to obtain an interview. Although it worked in this particular case, I caution other investigators in making that assumption. I carefully weigh the prospect that he or she would be alerted to the suspicion and would scramble to hide or destroy evidence. Investigators should remember that it is usually preferable to have all the evidence you can obtain before actually conducting the interview. The lesson is simple: Go with your gut, but don't rely on it. Most cases are solved by using a tried-and-true systematic approach that goes where the evidence leads you.

RECOMMENDATIONS TO PREVENT FUTURE OCCURRENCES

Implement Controls

As we began to work with the internal audit department to ascertain what controls were in place, we were struck by the fact that there were few, if any. From an SIU perspective, we naturally assumed there were sophisticated controls and that Mike just managed to slip through the cracks. Although we were somewhat dismayed that this was not the case, we also recognized this was an opportunity to become more involved with internal audit to help implement proper controls.

Software

We made recommendations to the internal audit team to implement software that would scan vendors and look for any anomalies involving EINs, supplemental payments, misspellings of the vendor's or insured's name(s), and anomalies directly tied to any specific company employee or agent. Irregularities should be investigated promptly.

Follow-Up with Clients and Vendors

The company needs to have supplemental work for any property claim authorized by an office supervisor. This is an effective deterrent. The supervisor should also randomly call both the insured and the contract vendor as a follow-up. This way, if an insured has had all of his or her work completed, the supervisor can get feedback on the handling of the claim, and the insured views the call as an act of goodwill. If the insured expresses surprise at a supplemental work order, the supervisor knows to investigate further. Calling the vendor to make sure the work was completed serves as a form of quality control. The supervisor should ask the vendor if he or she was paid on time and to evaluate the vendor's overall experience in dealing with the adjuster. Again, if the contractor expresses concern or surprise at the prospect of performing supplemental work, further investigation is required.

Employee Tip Line

I also suggest forming an employee tip line. Protection Mutual had one for reporting suspected external fraud but had no mechanism for reporting internal suspicions. One of the concerns that employees often have is that they are afraid their voice will be recognized. Our experience shows that workers won't come forward to leave a voice message either. Therefore, we had to convince the company that the tip line had to be truly anonymous in order to be effective. The most effective way to ensure anonymity is to use a third-party hotline service, such as EthicsLine.

Besides serving as an effective crime deterrent, the tip line offers a potentially persuasive defense against legal liability. By its use, the company can demonstrate its resolve to detect and prevent fraud and misconduct. It shows the employees that the business cares about and honors those who are honest and hardworking. Conversely, it demonstrates that illegal, unethical, or potentially dangerous behavior will not be tolerated.

Formal Fraud Detection and Deterrent Training

It is helpful for companies to institute a formal training program for supervisors, managers, and executives. This program needs to address internal fraud and how to detect and deter it. Companies should not stop trusting their employees, but rather institute controls to catch those who violate that faith. The best deterrent to this type of activity is an employee workforce that is both vigilant and ethical.

James E. Whitaker, CFE, is the executive director of the International Association of Arson Investigators. Mr. Whitaker is a retired police detective lieutenant and insurance executive with over with 36 years of fraud-fighting experience. He holds a bachelor's degree in criminal justice and a master's in business management.

CHAPTER 30

An Innocent Perpetrator

HOWARD C. SPARKS

As usual, Christi Wenzel arrived at the office early—ahead of the other accounting and finance staff. As the chief financial officer, she liked the quiet time that the morning afforded and the fact that it projected an image of dedication to the other employees. Her day was usually an endless series of interruptions once the office filled with her coworkers. She sat at her desk sipping her first cup of coffee, sorting through messages from the previous afternoon and reviewing exception reports generated late the day before, after all the transactions had been posted.

Christi enjoyed being the controller of Northern Electric Cooperative, one of the largest businesses in the community. She had joined the company soon after earning her certified public accountant (CPA) license and had been assigned to the audit department as a new staff member right out of college. In her third year, she worked her way up to lead the audit team.

Now, just 12 years later, she contemplated her plans to retire. She and her husband had decided that they would both leave their management positions with Northern Electric in 18 months in order to travel.

A message from a customer pulled her out of a daydream. Brooks Inc., a large construction firm, was inquiring about a discrepancy in a recent bill for renting one of Northern Electric's cranes. She recalled a similar situation several months ago. In that case, she had requested an investigation and Brooks had produced a copy of a cancelled check that had been deposited into Northern Electric's bank account. Based on that evidence, Christi had approved a special adjustment to the balance.

Meanwhile, Susanne Simpson drove into the parking lot. As she passed the Employee of the Month's space adjacent to her office building, she wondered if she'd ever have that privilege again. She pulled into an empty spot in the second row. Susanne was proud of her advancement at Northern Electric. Her employment had begun over 15 years ago, when she was hired as a temporary records clerk. Although she lacked any formal training, through hard work and dedication she had earned the respect of her coworkers and supervisors. Extensive on-the-job experience provided her with intricate knowledge of Northern Electric's accounting system, which had been the basis for her current position as accounting specialist. She enjoyed her work, largely because it offered more independence and diversity than the other clerical jobs she had performed there. Suzanne was often called on to help train new hires or to fill in when a department was shorthanded. She didn't mind these additional demands. In fact, they gave her a sense of security and importance.

Northern Electric Cooperative was founded almost 60 years ago when the town of Annelein, Massachusetts, was a booming mining community. It was formed when a large mining business offered its power-generating facilities for sale. Several local residents saw the potential for economic development that the availability of stable electrical power provided. They applied and were granted a loan from the Rural Electrification Administration. The group formed a co-op and acquired the mining company's central power plant and the surrounding land.

Over the years, Northern Electric prospered and grew along with the town. Operating as a co-op means that customers are also member-owners of the business. Annual elections are held to select directors, and members receive capital credits representing the profits earned by Northern Electric. These credits are redeemed periodically when funds are available. The board provides oversight of the chief executive officer who, in turn, appoints department executives and evaluates them. Today, the business maintains several power-generation facilities and a distribution network that extends over 100 miles, serving outlying communities and industrial operations. Northern Electric's most recent annual report indicated that it had nearly 40,000 members and revenues exceeding $100 million.

Both residential and commercial customers are billed monthly for electrical services. While most payments are received through the mail, customers can make pay over the phone or in person at the business's customer service center. Because of Northern Electric's sporadic growth, its administration and finance offices were somewhat scattered around several buildings at the main physical plant. The Finance Department, including the cash control office, is located separately from the payroll, accounts payable, and customer service centers. The customer service center has representatives and several cashiers. Clients arrive at the center and enter a queue for assistance. A representative determines the customer's needs, prepares and executes the appropriate forms, and finally sends them to a cashier if payment is required.

Daily cash collections are compared to the register totals for each cashier station and then sent over to the Cash Control Department, where they are stored in a vault overnight. Payments received by mail are sorted by the mail room and forwarded to the Cash Control Department. The customer's remittance form is sent to the Customer Service Department for recording against their accounts. The cash control office combines these mail receipts with payments made in person and prepares a bank deposit the following morning. After the deposit is prepared, it is placed in a locked deposit bag for pickup by an armored car sometime in the afternoon. Each cashier prepares a daily report comparing collections to the register totals for each respective payment category. These, along with a copy of the deposit receipt, are forwarded to accounting for recording in the cash receipts journal.

To increase Northern Electric's profit margins, management had pursued nonoperating-type transactions that included land and equipment rentals, sales of unneeded supplies and equipment, and other services. As Northern Electric's accounting specialist, Susanne had sole responsibility of recording and processing payments for these nonroutine transactions. The accounting department would receive a copy of any executed contracts between Northern Electric and customers. A debit to other receivables and a credit to miscellaneous margins would be created when appropriate. Statements and invoices would be prepared monthly by accounting and mailed to the customer. Susanne's responsibilities primarily involved examining details of any payments received by the mail room or customer service and determining the application of the payment to Northern Electric's receivables accounts. She would then prepare and transmit a journal voucher to the accounting department for posting to the appropriate accounts.

Making a Statement

Christi reread the message about the billing discrepancy as she dialed Brooks, Inc.'s phone number.

"Hello, may I speak to Bert in accounting?" she asked.

During the course of their conversation, she learned that once again, their most recent payment had not been reflected on their statement from Northern Electric. They even had a copy of the cancelled check to prove that they had paid their balance. Christi wondered how lightning could strike twice in just a couple of months—and to the same account. She decided to investigate the matter further this time. She requested that Bert fax her a copy of the cancelled check. Later in the afternoon, Christi visited cash control and had one of the clerks pull the deposit records for several days around the stamp date on the cancelled check. After hours of digging through papers, she could not locate any record of the customer's payment on any date surrounding the cancelled date stamped on it by the bank. She returned to her office to review her notes on this bill. Upon opening the file, she noticed right away that both missing payments involved a special receivables account handled by Susanne.

Christi decided it was time to delve deeper into this mystery. She requested to have Northern Electric's cash receipts and deposit records pulled for three days preceding the cancellation date on Brooks's check. Later, after the finance staff had left and the office was quiet, Christi sat down and began examining records. She had planned to trace Brooks's check backward from the deposit to determine what had happened. To her dismay, Northern Electric's cash receipts records were a mess. Not only was she unable to determine what day the check had been received, but because the individual cashier cash receipts records were missing, she couldn't even support the daily bank deposits.

The next morning, Christi talked to Northern Electric's chief executive officer (CEO), Tom Bartlett. She related the details of Brooks's payments not being properly credited and told him that she had not been able to trace the payments back from the bank deposit into Northern Electric's records. Christi agreed with Tom's recommendation that outside assistance would be prudent. He left it up to her to arrange for a preliminary investigation.

JUMPING TO CONCLUSIONS

Upon returning to her office, Christi located Heidi Roth's phone number. She was an old college classmate of Christi's who had recently opened her own firm in partnership with another local CPA. They had been good friends in college and had studied together for the CPA exam. Christi called Heidi and told her that she had discovered some discrepancies regarding a customer's payment and that management would like to hire an external investigator. She also related that her staff was too shorthanded to accomplish the task promptly.

Heidi was very interested. Most of their firm's services involved tax and bookkeeping services, and they had just entered the slow time of year. It would be a great opportunity when both partners would have significant free time available. Heidi told Christi that she could drop by later to review the details of the engagement.

When they met, Christi told Heidi the exact nature of the discrepancies occurring with Brooks's payments and the difficulties she had run into while attempting to analyze Northern Electric's cash receipts records. It was decided that Heidi would request bank copies of all the deposit items in order to determine exactly which one had included Brooks's check. Next, she would trace the deposit back to Northern Electric. Christi called Northeastern Bank. The manager said that it would take at least a week or two to have the files restored and copies generated.

Back at her office, Heidi discussed the engagement with her partner, Sue Hollingsworth. They both agreed that this would be a challenging assignment since neither of them had any prior experience with a company the size of Northern Electric. During the next week, while they awaited the bank copies, they would gain familiarity with internal controls involving the company's cash receipts.

Just over a week later, a bank courier delivered several large boxes to their office. Heidi and Sue started examining the copies to find Brooks's payment. They found that it was deposited the day before the cancellation date on the copy of the check. They then noted the deposit batch and worked backward into Northern Electric's records to trace the amount into the cash receipts. This analysis was very troubling because while most deposits shown generally agreed with Northern Electric's account, there were important differences. For example, the bank deposit containing Brooks's check did not exactly match Northern Electric's deposit total for the same day. Further, the check was not included in Northern Electric's deposit records, consistent with Christi's finding. There were, however, almost a dozen smaller checks listed by Northern Electric that were not in the bank's records. It suddenly occurred to Sue that the sum of the small checks was almost the same amount as the Brooks's check. Heidi found that although deposits were occasionally off by a few cents or dollars, the difference had not been followed up by Northern Electric's Finance Department.

Heidi arranged a meeting with Tom and Christi to discuss what she had found. Tom expressed concern over the apparent discrepancies. Christi understood. It appeared that Northern Electric's cash receipts procedures were weak and unreliable, possibly allowing someone to embezzle funds. If news of this leaked to the local paper, it would generate considerable negative publicity. Tom decided that Heidi and Sue should expand the investigation to determine whether funds were missing and, if so, to ascertain the amounts. Heidi mentioned that at some point they would probably need to interview some of the staff, but that they would use discretion.

After the meeting, Heidi proposed a time frame for continuing their investigation.

"It isn't feasible to reconstruct all of the deposits. Thousands of checks are processed through Northern Electric everyday," said Heidi.

"I know," replied Christi, "but what do you propose?"

Heidi thought for a moment before saying "We'll start by examining all of the days around Brooks's payments."

She was curious when the checks that were in Northern Electric's records were actually deposited, but kept her thoughts to herself. Heidi knew they had their work cut out for them.

About five weeks later, Heidi and Sue saw a pattern emerging in the discrepancies. The checks listed in Northern Electric's account, but missing from the reconstructed bank deposit, eventually appeared in following weeks. They surmised that someone was substituting the initial larger payment for smaller ones that nearly exactly totaled the larger check. Then the perpetrator substituted the smaller checks over the next week or two. But why? And why didn't someone performing the bank reconciliation ever investigate the differences in Northern Electric's deposits? They had tried to trace the deposits back to the cashiers but faced either incomplete or illegible daily records.

Armed with this information, Heidi and Sue started interviewing Northern Electric personnel. During these initial interviews they learned that Susanne regularly accessed the locked deposit bag in the cash control office. When a staff member had questioned her, Susanne replied, "I am looking for a check to be sure that it was properly recorded."

Heidi was surprised at this revelation. Giving employees such easy access to deposit bags was not her idea of sound internal controls. She also learned that Susanne regularly used Northern Electric's policy allowing employees to cash personal checks up to $500, and over this amount with a supervisor's approval. One cashier noted that Susanne would cash at least one check every day, and occasionally, they exceeded the $500 limit.

Heidi felt it was time to confront Susanne about the discrepancies involving transactions under her responsibility. However, Suzanne and another finance clerk refused to be interviewed. Apparently they'd received word of the missing funds and the investigation. When asked to be interviewed, Susanne said to Heidi, "This is just witch hunt."

Based on her refusal to cooperate, Susanne was terminated that afternoon. She sat in her office for a long time staring at the pictures on her walls. She finally finished packing her personal things at 5:30. On her way out she gave Christi her keys and said, "I have always given my best to this organization and would never steal a thing."

GUILTY UNTIL PROVEN INNOCENT

Heidi and Sue focused on the payments under Susanne's responsibility. They developed a theory that Susanne would receive a large balance from a customer for a nonutility payment. She would then visit the cash control office during lunch hours so that she could sort through the locked deposit bag uninterrupted. She would swap the larger check for smaller checks of approximately equal amount. She had worked at Northern Electric long enough to know the schedules and routines of most of the staff and the armored car pickup schedules. Since the deposits were equal, or nearly so, her switches could go undetected. Susanne could then negotiate personal checks for identical amounts with Northern Electric's cashiers. The next day she would return to cash control and replace her personal checks with the Northern Electric's stolen checks.

Northern Electric's attorney, Jerry Evans, arranged a meeting with the local police and district attorney to see if they would launch a criminal investigation. The district attorney felt the evidence was good and obtained search warrants for Suzanne Simpson's house and bank accounts, which was executed the next day. All of Simpson's records were seized. No funds were recovered from their home, but some of Northern Electric's records were found. When asked why she had taken the documents to her house, Susanne replied that she often brought work home when she got behind.

I received a call from Jack White, the local attorney who was representing Susanne and her husband, Ray. He briefly outlined the case against Susanne and said that she felt that she was being framed by someone, maybe Northern Electric's chief financial officer. He asked if I had time to review the investigation. I told Jack it sounded interesting and to send me a copies of what he had received so far.

In reviewing Heidi and Sue's report, I was struck by several holes in their investigation: an exact figure of the missing funds wasn't reported, and they had performed only a partial analysis of the couple's personal bank account, focusing on checks and deposits to Northern Electric. They had failed to locate any of the misappropriated funds, and nothing observed during the search of the Simpsons' home indicated that they were living lavishly. Plus, the plausibility of the scheme did not seem reasonable. For one, converting large individual checks into cash by substituting personal checks would have required Susanne to cash at least three or more personal checks for $500 each every day for 7 to 20 consecutive days. This would have been very obvious to everyone and should have attracted considerable attention right away—not a year or more later.

Following my review of Heidi and Sue's report, I decided it was important to investigate further. Specifically, I would need to complete an indirect reconstruction of the couple's income based on *all* of their bank accounts. During an interview for the local newspaper, Jerry Evans alleged that the couple had laundered the stolen funds through Ray's painting business, despite the fact that Heidi and Sue's investigation did not include a review of Ray's business account. This analysis would be difficult since all of the defendant's records were seized by the police during the search. I contacted both of the couple's banks and requested copies of bank records for the three years surrounding Heidi and Sue's analysis.

I examined all of the couple's deposits and couldn't find any funds that were unaccounted for. Virtually every deposit was either a paycheck or bona fide business payment. Based on my reconstruction of their income, the couple lived very modestly. In fact, they were just getting by. I decided it was important to eliminate suspicion that Ray's business had laundered stolen funds. I examined vendor statements and made inquiries about whether Ray ever made large cash payments in lieu of writing checks. I learned that Ray had always paid his bills by check, never cash.

I called Jack to relay my preliminary findings. "Hi, Jack, I have some news regarding the Simpson case. From my analysis, I don't reach the same conclusion as Heidi and Sue. In addition, I think that you've got a good shot at getting their testimony and report excluded with a *Daubert* challenge, which ensures that the case is proved by scientific method, not just speculation. The judge has to verify that all evidence is reliable and relevant."

Jack's tone indicated his surprise. "Really? What basis would I have for this challenge?"

"Well," I began, "Heidi and Sue's report comes up short on just about every major requirement. They lack any fraud expertise, and neither partner has had professional experience with a company even a fraction the size of Northern Electric. Didn't you find it strange that Northern Electric would hand off this kind of an investigation to a small local CPA firm without any previous work in fraud? In addition, their investigation was grossly incomplete, and their conclusions are not supported by the evidence. Northern Electric's internal controls and records appear too weak to even provide a reasonable basis to believe that funds are missing, let alone conclusively link Susanne Simpson to an embezzlement scheme. No monies have been recovered, nor have the Simpsons lived beyond the income I imputed." The news excited Jack and he asked me to compile my findings as soon as possible.

Before I could complete my report, I learned that Susanne had been diagnosed with cancer in the advanced stage. She died before the *Daubert* motion could be heard. Ray was devastated by the loss of his wife. Based on my analysis, Jerry Evans offered to release Ray from the lawsuit and allow him to keep his house in exchange for a default judgment against Susanne's estate. Northern Electric needed to pursue a judgment in order to collect a damages claim against their surety bond. On the advice of Jack White, the Simpsons' attorney, with their finances exhausted and a pile of medical bills confronting him, Ray reluctantly accepted the terms of the settlement. Christi retired early, as she and her husband had planned. They sent a postcard from Brazil some time later.

LESSONS LEARNED

It is still a mystery why an organization the size of Northern Power chose to hire grossly inexperienced investigators. To ensure a competent, reliable investigation, the company should have hired someone with requisite qualifications and experience—at the very least, someone who had experience with entities and accounting systems of this scale.

Mishandling of interviews and other evidence may permanently impair the quality of the examination.

An important lesson to be learned is the need to remain objective in all phases of a fraud investigation. Despite the best work by a competent fraud examiner, there just may not be enough evidence to identify the perpetrator. Oftentimes an organization's internal controls are simply too deficient or incomplete, which is what allowed this fraud to occur in the first place. Investigators have a professional responsibility to limit their inferences and opinions to just those that can be supported by the facts. It is incumbent on the investigator to resist pressures to point a finger at someone in order to justify the fees paid. Conclusions are appropriate only when the examiner is confident that the investigation has applied the correct methodology and sufficient evidence has been collected to support it. Investigations lacking in some respect should be presented as a summary of the facts without an opinion. Then the investigator may, if necessary, testify as a fact witness as opposed to an expert.

Reaching incorrect or unsupported conclusions can impact on the admissibility of the investigator's testimony. Failing a *Daubert* challenge can have a devastating impact on the investigator's future career as well. Further, a botched investigation may also have the unintended result of allowing the perpetrator(s) to go free.

Another important lesson that can be learned from this case is the need to carefully control information about the nature of the investigation. Through office gossip channels, most employees learned quickly about a possible fraud at Northern Electric. This information undermines the reliability of evidence collected through interviews. Careful consideration should be given to the sequencing and selection of personnel to be interviewed. Interviewing skills are the key to collection of reliable statements that would withstand rigorous cross examination at trial.

RECOMMENDATIONS TO PREVENT FUTURE OCCURRENCES

Bank Reconciliations

Bank reconciliations need to be performed in a timely manner, and discrepancies must be investigated fully. In this case, small differences in deposit amounts between the bank records and Northern Electric's records were ignored on a regular basis, which may have caused the company to lose a great deal of money.

Audit Trails

Audit trails need to exist and records retained to ensure that transactions have been recorded accurately. It should have been possible to trace deposit amounts from the bank statement to specific sources (e.g., cashier batches or mail remittances) on a daily basis at Northern Electric.

Segregation of Duties

Segregation of duties is necessary, especially in larger organizations. These segregations should be enforced through communication in procedures manuals, periodic training, and audit compliance testing.

Monitor Nonroutine Transactions

Nonroutine transactions often have a higher risk due to their smaller volumes. They generally do not receive sufficient controls and audits. To counter this increased risk, specific controls need to be developed. Periodic audits should be conducted, either by internal or by external auditors, to ensure that transactions are properly authorized and recorded. All receivables should be subject to periodic review for valuation. Direct confirmation is advisable for larger balances.

Prohibit Employees from Cashing Personal Checks at Work

Allowing employees to cash personal checks should not be permitted. This may provide an important employee benefit in some situations, but the risks should be carefully considered. If check cashing must be allowed, reasonable limits should be established.

Howard C. Sparks, Ph.D., CPA, is an associate professor of accounting and information systems at the School of Management, the University of Alaska, Fairbanks. He is also a senior associate with Northern Economic Research Associates. Dr. Sparks has over 20 years of professional experience. He holds a master's and doctorate in accounting from the University of Iowa.

CHAPTER 31

Dr. Amy

STEPHEN A. PEDNEAULT

Dr. Amy Daniels, known and referred to by her coworkers and patients as Dr. Amy, was the pride of her family. At age 33, her size and youthful appearance allowed her to pass for a college student. Amy was just four years out of dentistry school and already seeing her own patients. One of three dental providers at a small practice, Dr. Amy worked closely with Dr. Michael Grady, the owner, who offered her the rare opportunity of employment with little experience. Her family was so appreciative that at Amy's wedding, her father personally thanked Dr. Grady for taking his daughter into his practice. The entire office attended the ceremony, like one big family.

Arriving early most mornings to get a jump on her day before her first patient arrived, Dr. Amy was a hard worker. She was almost always the last to leave, finishing charts and preparing for the next day's appointments. She turned the lights off at night and back on again in the morning.

Dr. Amy was also more fortunate than her peers when it came to her compensation. Making close to six figures, her salary formula was easy and straightforward. Dr. Amy and Dr. Gerard Barrett, Dr. Grady's other employee dentist, each received a biweekly paycheck based on patient billings. Each received one-third of their total charges submitted for dental services performed during the previous two-week period. Much of Dr. Amy's salary went toward repaying her student loans.

The practice was opened almost 30 years ago by Dr. Grady and his wife, Judy. She maintained all the accounting and payroll records at their house to ensure employees had no access to these important documents. Located centrally in the city, the office was convenient for patients to walk or take the bus to their visits.

Dr. Grady's reputation among his patients and employees was that of a compassionate person who truly cared about people. He frequently went to lunch or socialized with his staff, and took interest when anyone was having personal issues. Dr. Grady often performed much-needed dental work on patients who had no means of paying. Embarrassed to take any handouts, many would offer to pay him whatever they could afford in small installments over time. Amazingly, nearly every patient paid his or her entire balance.

Not surprisingly, once word was out about Dr. Grady's practice, adding new patients was never a problem. The practice grew to three dentists, two dental assistants, two hygienists, an office manager, and part-time clerical staff. Many of them remained loyal, long-term employees who had been with Dr. Grady for 10 or more years.

Dr. Grady and his family lived modestly. Having raised two children through college, he and his wife worked tirelessly in the practice by day and kept the books and records by night. Although a very talented and experienced dentist, Dr. Grady never looked to make a million dollars. He had reached a point in his career where his focus shifted toward grooming younger dentists to possibly buy in to his practice.

Dr. Grady's plan was to discuss partnership opportunities with Amy as she continued to build her patient base. But Dr. Grady also knew not everything was stable within his office; Dr. Amy couldn't work amicably with her assistant, a long-term employee, and reassignments were necessary to accommodate her. Also, there were rumors and internal fights occurring between the hygienists and Dr. Amy, affecting both their professional and their personal relationships.

BITE MARKS

It was a Friday morning and I was catching up on things from earlier in the week. Both of my forensic associates were present. Kevin worked with me in my office, and Scott was finishing a project at his cubicle. Dan, one of the firm's founding partners, walked into my office and asked me if I would be around for the morning. He said that Dr. Grady was coming in at nine o'clock to discuss a potential problem. Dan wanted me to sit in during the meeting. He knew I had worked with Dr. Grady on past projects, having installed his accounting package and trained his wife on how to use the system.

At nine o'clock, Kevin and I walked down to the conference room where we met Dan and Dr. Grady. On the table was a large box filled with documents.

"How can we help you?" Dan asked.

Dr. Grady said he found a situation with his billing system and needed our help. Two weeks ago he overheard the receptionist discussing an account issue with a patient on the phone. The patient said she was in the office last week and had $450 worth of work performed. She made a partial payment of $200 toward her charges, and when she left she was provided a "walkout statement" reflecting an unpaid balance of $250. She then received in the mail a statement reflecting a bill of $450. She couldn't understand why her balance had changed. The office staff was unable to provide an explanation. They researched her history within the billing system, and the balance on her account reflected $250 due.

Dr. Grady asked the receptionist to have the patient come in with her paperwork. Within a half hour the patient showed up with her receipt and statement. Everyone was puzzled as to how this could have happened. Determined to solve this mystery, Dr. Grady ran some reports and called the SoftDent billing software support center. When the support center had him check his configurations, he was surprised to learn of features within his system that were disabled or never properly initiated. He was guided through different menus and screens and ultimately ran a "Transactional Audit Trail" report on the patient's account.

The report reflected the initial charges assessed as well as her partial payment. The next set of transactions was alarming. The charges were changed after the payment was applied, then on a later date changed back again. Dr. Grady showed the report to his staff, especially to those whose user names were associated with the changed transactions. That's when he first learned his employees were in the habit of logging onto computers and never logging off. It was common for one person to log into one computer, and everyone else would simply use the computer under that person's name throughout the day. He also learned that every user had the ability to change and delete transactions within SoftDent.

Dr. Grady went back to his office and revoked the rights of all the users. He then reset all their passwords, requiring his employees to set up new ones upon entering SoftDent, and returned to the front desk, where he called his staff together. He informed them they only had posting ability and that they needed to log out from SoftDent when they left their computer. He also told them there would be no more sharing of usernames and passwords.

Dr. Grady decided to see if there were similar transactions with other patients, and there were. He decided to run a complete report of the entire practice, every patient and every procedure, since the implementation of SoftDent 18 months earlier. He scanned the pages to find similar entries and highlighted them.

Now, in our office, Dr. Grady opened the box and removed the first 200 pages to show us examples of the transactions. There were over 1,500 printed pages in his box. He showed us where original charges were posted on page 25, then farther down the charges were changed on page 68, only to be restored to their original entry on page 193.

Open Wide

Based on experience, we knew something fishy had to be behind all the changed entries; we just didn't quite know what. Dr. Grady said he was unaware of any way to provide us the report electronically, so into our cars we went. Kevin and I followed the dentist back to his office, where he guided us to his computer, then shut the doors. His staff stared as we walked through, wondering who we were and what was happening. Dr. Grady had told no one of the internal investigation he was conducting.

It took me just a few minutes to have the same report up on the screen. I smiled and looked back at Kevin when I saw the option to allow the report to be saved to a file rather than printed on paper. We now had the complete 1,500-page printed report in one computer file, which Kevin and I took back to our office. Using the patient identification number and date of service, we identified a total of 4,327 transactions that had been altered. We also learned the changed fields involved the dentist number for the dentist who provided the service for each patient. There was a clear pattern of which numbers were changed and then changed back.

Weekends always seemed to get in the way of solving a mystery, except in this case, Dr. Grady was waiting for the results of our initial analysis and instructed me to call him any time, day or night. He said he wasn't sleeping anyway. The whole mess was driving him crazy. I called him at home and shared with him what we found. I asked him what the dentist numbers represented and for a list of all them assigned in his billing system. He provided me both. I then asked him if he had an attorney he used for legal work. He said he didn't have one and asked me if I could recommend someone familiar with these types of issues. I knew exactly who was best suited for this case, but I wouldn't be able to reach her until Monday. I provided Dr. Grady her name, and asked that he not talk to anyone about this matter until we spoke with counsel after the weekend.

In the meantime, I brought the file home on my laptop and performed every procedure I knew on it: sort, extract, stratify, extract again, and so forth. By Monday morning I had the advantage over Kevin in that I knew who belonged to each dentist number, and I summarized who benefited from the changes. In almost every one of these transactions, an alteration was made from the original dentist number to a second, then subsequently the original number was restored. I needed the answer to one more question to better understand why the changes were made: How were the dentists and hygienists compensated by Dr. Grady?

Monday morning, I called attorney Lisa Woods, and she conferenced in Dr. Grady. I shared with her an abbreviated version of the case history and the transactions I had summarized. An experienced litigator in employment-related matters, Lisa was already asking the doctor how the members of his practice were compensated. Dr. Grady explained that his administrative staff was paid a straight salary. For the dentists, however, Dr. Grady told us each provider was compensated on a two-week cycle based on the procedures each dentist performed during that time frame. He said he typically ran the productivity report from SoftDent on Saturday mornings that showed the procedures for each dentist for the previous two weeks. Now we had a motive. If procedures performed by one dentist were changed to a different dentist, the "changed to" dentist would benefit by having more procedures than actually performed. The larger total would lead to a larger one-third share, and thus more compensation. While not the only explanation possible, it seemed to make sense to us that the changes posted to patient transactions were part of a scheme to obtain more pay than someone would have otherwise received.

The focus of our conversation switched to Dr. Grady's dentists. Three worked at the practice during the last three years. Dr. John Stabler had worked for Dr. Grady for about four years, and left the practice 12 months previously. The changes to patient transactions continued to occur after he left and appeared in the audit report right up through the previous week. That seemed to rule him out, as he didn't seem to benefit from the changes posted for the last year. In the SoftDent system, Stabler was referred to as Doctor #3.

Then there was Dr. Gerard Barrett. Barrett worked part time and was with the practice for only a short period after Dr. Stabler left. Barrett, Doctor #4, also didn't seem to benefit from recent changes to the billings. That left only Dr. Amy, who had been with the practice the entire time. Dr. Amy was Doctor #2, and Dr. Grady was #1. I looked at the transactions extracted, and in almost every case, procedures were changed from Doctor #1 to Doctor #2, only to be changed back later to Doctor #1. I had also assigned the day of the week to each questionable transaction. While the first changes occurred throughout the weekdays, the second change almost always occurred on a Tuesday. I told Dr. Grady and Lisa Woods that I wanted to interview each of the employees, including Dr. Amy, as soon as possible. Dr. Grady confirmed that all the employees were present, except for his part-time receptionist, who wouldn't be in until after lunch.

I arrived at the practice just after 10:00 a.m. The staff members stared at me and whispered to each other as I headed to Dr. Grady's office. Dr. Grady greeted me and closed his door behind me. He said he told his staff I was coming this morning to meet with each of them. He also told them he had hired me to evaluate the practice and his internal controls and to provide him feedback and recommendations. Dr. Grady said he arranged for me to use a private office in his colleague's practice one floor below for privacy purposes.

The dentist introduced me to his staff, and I left with his office manager, Susan, to go downstairs. I explained to her that I was evaluating the practice and needed to understand each employee's role and responsibilities. I also talked with her about computer usage, including her user ID and password. Susan provided much information about the operations and her different coworkers. She gave me a list of all the users on the SoftDent system, along with the names of the employees associated with each user ID. I asked her about Dr. Amy, and learned that she spent significant time at the computer in the back and in Dr. Grady's office. She said Dr. Amy always had computer printouts and schedules in her medical coat pockets and would check on and off the computer frequently between patients. Then I brought Susan back upstairs and met with the next employee.

Interview after interview, I learned of the person's length of employment, different responsibilities, computer activity, and more facts about each coworker. I asked everyone about Dr. Amy. I listened to troubling statements about her attitude, length of time at the computers, and conflicts with fellow workers. I learned that Dr. Amy was nearly always the first person to arrive each morning and pretty much always the last person to leave each day, typically staying much later than everyone else. That was true even when she didn't have any late-afternoon patients. I also learned that Dr. Amy was privileged to park in the adjacent parking garage. I asked how she gained entry to the garage, and was told she was issued an access card that she used at the gated entrance and exit.

This information was extremely helpful. I knew right then that there must be a system tracking the garage access. If I could compare this information with the computerized transactions and payroll records, I could determine whether she was in the office at the times the changes were posted to the system. My second-to-last interview was with Dr. Amy. She was petite and looked much too young to be a dentist. I introduced myself and we went downstairs to the private office. I broke the ice by telling her of my recent debacles with my own dentist whom I recently fired after extracting a second tooth. I had learned it would cost me about $10,000 for implants to correct the problem. She seemed sympathetic and amazed that it could have happened. I believe we had established a good rapport.

I started by providing her my background as an accountant who works with medical clients to improve the practice's operations and efficiencies. I began to ask her about her background and her experiences at Dr. Grady's practice. She seemed to enjoy working there. I had her describe her responsibilities and a typical day in her working life. Then I turned to the computer system, and asked her what doctor number she was assigned in SoftDent. She said she was Doctor #2, and asked why I needed to know that. I told her that I would be looking at prior activity to gain a sense of the charges and collections and would be focusing on the practice as a whole as well as the performance of each individual dentist. She seemed fine with my response. I asked her what involvement she had with the SoftDent system, and she claimed she never posted transactions to the system. She told me that if I were to look I would never see her user ID. She said she was computer illiterate and intimidated by computers and that she had no posting responsibilities. She told me that with the number of patients she saw, she only had time to check her schedule between patients and that all the posting was done by the office staff. Dr. Amy said she hand-wrote out the charts and brought them to the front desk for posting and billing. It was clear she wasn't going to discuss anything specific regarding transactions, and since she was being less than truthful, I would save the real questions for a later date. With that I thanked her for her time and brought her upstairs. I asked her if we could meet again.

"Anytime," she replied.

During my seventh and last interview, I learned Dr. Amy was overheard at times telling patients not to worry about their balance due, that she could take care of it for them. She told one patient, "I'll take care of your deductible for you by adding an extra filling or two, if that's okay." She told others not to be alarmed if they saw extra procedures on any statements from their insurance company, that it was customary to add procedures in order to have the insurance cover their portion. I also learned Dr. Amy was slow in turning in her patient files to the front desk for charge entry and billing, oftentimes with missing information.

These new developments troubled me. If any of these allegations were true, each added new dimensions to the already expanding case against Dr. Amy. Procedures never performed could lead to criminal and civil claims by the insurance companies against Dr. Amy and, more important, Dr. Grady. As I walked back to his office, the staff was paired up in different areas, whispering and watching me. I met with him and provided a summary of the interviews. He was not pleased with this new information. He had already looked at a few of Dr. Amy's patient files and compared what was in their written charts. Today's information confirmed his worst thoughts: insurance fraud. We called the attorney and updated her on the situation.

Kevin and I spent the next two days obtaining background information on Dr. Amy to identify where she had worked, lived, banked, and owned property. We knew a civil case was coming to recover some of the proceeds, and time was of the essence. As she probably knew from the interview, the jig was up. It was Thursday and I had just gotten into the office. Dr. Grady called and said that Dr. Amy hadn't been at work for the past two days. He arrived in his office this morning and found an envelope on top of his desk. It was a letter from Dr. Amy, presumably left sometime during the night. There was an office key in the envelope as well.

Dr. Amy's letter said that Dr. Grady had harassed her and made her feel uncomfortable about her trying to have a baby. She indicated she saw in the media that he was advertising for a new dentist and that if he wanted her to leave, all he had to do was ask. The letter continued by making claims about the hostile workplace environment and that she had decided to resign, effective immediately. He was devastated by these unsubstantiated allegations attacking him personally. We called the attorney to update her on the letter and to tell her to expect a "smokescreen" from Dr. Amy to cloud the issue that she stole funds. Fortunately Lisa Woods specialized in labor law and knew exactly what to do in anticipation of any claims or suits.

Kevin and I continued to search in light of the information learned from the staff. We sorted by date, time, patient name, and user ID. We found there were no transactions within the database posted by Dr. Amy, but 48 patients had been deleted from the SoftDent system under her user name. Dr. Grady identified many of them as either her family or friends. Without a reliable backup prior to the changes, we were unable to locate more details. After talking with the office manager, Susan, I learned the garage access card number assigned to Dr. Amy. We met with a garage attendant who showed us the system, including tracking each cardholder's activity. We had the attendant print out the complete history of Dr. Amy's card number. The report showed us dates, times, travel direction (in or out), and the gate location. Back in the office Kevin was able to import the file and compare dates and times with the SoftDent transactions.

On Friday morning I decided to interview the staff again to learn more about Dr. Amy. Using Dr. Grady's office this time, I met with each of the five people working that day. When I asked each employee directly about Dr. Amy's habits and computer use, I learned she often was at the computer when she was not seeing patients. I was told that she knew how to post the change transactions because she watched other users do it all the time, and one employee told me she offered to teach Dr. Amy how to do it so she could post them herself. Dr. Amy responded that she didn't want to know how to do it and that she was too computer illiterate.

Another staff member told me Dr. Amy never worked on Mondays and worked only every other Saturday. She said Dr. Amy constantly watched the screens while coworkers posted legitimate transactions or changes and was "damn quick on the keystrokes." She stated Dr. Amy was, in fact, very good and confident on the computer. I showed her some of the changed transactions and asked how long it would take someone to post them. She said it would take under 10 seconds.

Comparing garage entry and exit times with the other employees' time clock activity and to transaction times within SoftDent, Kevin and I identified a clear pattern. In most cases the changes were posted immediately after Dr. Amy entered the garage but before the first employee arrived, or immediately before Dr. Amy exited the garage after the last employee had punched out for the day. Some others were posted while the staff was at lunch, potentially leaving Dr. Amy in the space alone. Another coincidence was that there were no changed transactions posted on Mondays. It became clear that while any one of Dr. Grady's employees could have perpetrated the changes to his SoftDent system, only one person financially benefited from the changes: Dr. Amy.

PAYING THE BILL

The next logical step was to reinterview our suspect. I left message after message, and finally Dr. Amy called me back.

"What's this all about anyway?" she asked.

I told her we were looking to understand how patient charges and billing occurred and thought she could shed light on process.

"Do I have to meet with you?"

I responded that she didn't have to do anything, but that I thought a meeting would be helpful to understanding how things worked. Dr. Amy agreed to come to my office on Thursday at 11:00. I had serious doubts about whether she would actually show up. So I was pleased when I saw her pull into our parking lot. But my pleasure was only fleeting when just moments later Dr. Amy backed out of the parking lot and drove off. Still wanting to resolve the case for Dr. Grady, I brought Bonnie from my office for a ride to Dr. Amy's house. I thought if I was going to confront Dr. Amy at her home, it would be a great idea to have a second person, a female witness, accompany me. We knocked on her door, and after what seemed like forever, Dr. Amy opened the door and asked, "Can I help you?" I asked her if she remembered me, and she said no. I told her I had sat and talked with her not a week or so ago at Dr. Grady's office. That is when she reached out and opened her right hand, offering the name and phone number of her attorney. She said if I had any questions, then that's who I should contact.

Before leaving, I asked, "Do you want to know what this is all about?"

"I would *love* to know what this is about," she replied.

As I started to tell her about the charges, she abruptly stopped me, raised her voice and said that it sounded like I was accusing her of something and that I should get off her property. She closed the door, and we went back to my car. Mission accomplished. We now knew she had an attorney and how to contact him.

Five attorneys later, we had our first meeting with her latest legal representative. He listened to Lisa Woods and me tell the story, and when we finished, his opinion was that this case sounded complicated. That's when I showed him our analysis of the transactions, along with statements from coworkers and some of the other evidence collected. Even after all of our efforts, it took the involvement of detectives from the local police department and the real threat of prison to get Dr. Amy and her attorney to come to terms with what she had done. In the end, Dr. Amy refinanced her home and wrote a check to Dr. Grady for $80,000, which covered all the "proven" thefts and his out-of-pocket costs for the investigation. The true amount of damage Dr. Amy caused may never be known, but we estimated it in the $150,000 range. Her restitution also kept her from being arrested, and she has never acknowledged any wrongdoing or even apologized to Dr. Grady.

LESSONS LEARNED

In most small businesses, and especially within physician and dental practices, it is easy to focus on generating revenue or providing medical care and leave the financial aspects to "trusted" employees. Even when an owner or provider starts out heavily involved in managing the day-to-day finances, over time there is a real risk of complacency. Dr. Grady was doing many of the right things by writing all the checks, having his wife prepare the payroll off-site, and reconciling the daily deposits. What he didn't contemplate was his staff sharing passwords, leaving themselves logged in to the systems, and delegating their responsibilities by teaching coworkers how to post transactions. Dr. Grady also let his guard down when his SoftDent system was installed and configured, in that he didn't thoroughly review the levels of access assigned to each user of his system. He also never knew of the audit features, and therefore none were ever activated. Last, Dr. Grady "trusted" his dental staff. He worked hard to create a family like atmosphere. Although much of Dr. Amy's "unusual" behavior was occurring right before his eyes, he never thought for a moment that she or anyone else within his practice would be stealing from him.

Unfortunately, the worst news for Dr. Grady was yet to come. Although we had identified the changes posted to transactions and the extra billings submitted to insurance companies for procedures Dr. Amy never performed, it wasn't until Dr. Grady started seeing her former patients that he discovered she had performed poor dental procedures. Further, she also billed for work she didn't do but should have. Dr. Grady spent much of the next few months providing free dental care either to correct what had been done or to complete procedures that had already been billed and paid. Dr. Grady photographed the teeth of every patient he corrected, both before and after, and built a case for the state dental society and the insurance companies.

In the end, nothing happened to Dr. Amy or her dental license. Dr. Grady settled with the insurance companies that, amazingly, allowed Dr. Amy to continue billing as a participating provider under her new practice.

RECOMMENDATIONS TO PREVENT FUTURE OCCURRENCES

Could Dr. Grady's situation have been prevented? Maybe. Should he have detected the problem much earlier? If Dr. Grady had known about the disputes between his staff and Dr. Amy, he may have become suspicious. Also, if he had compared what he was paying her to the actual number of patients she was seeing, he would have noticed that she was being paid more than she should have been. In his defense, the staff had begun to realize what Dr. Amy was doing and started their own mini-investigation before the case came to light. Had they shared with Dr. Grady this information, her fraud might have ended sooner.

To help prevent these types of schemes, employers should take these seven steps:

Step 1.   Know your employees (and their habits).

Step 2.   Listen to your employees. (They tried to tell Dr. Grady that something was wrong.)

Step 3.   Ensure audit features are turned on and review them.

Step 4.   Perform spot checks comparing information for consistency.

Step 5.   Review system user rights and access, and monitor them.

Step 6.   Document personnel and computer policies, and enforce them.

Step 7.   Trust, but verify.

Fraud can't be eliminated, but attention and vigilance will help prevent many schemes and catch others before the losses mount.

Stephen A. Pedneault, CFE, CPA, is the founder of Forensic Accounting Services, LLC, Glastonbury, Connecticut. His firm specializes in fraud examination, fraud prevention, and litigation services. Mr. Pedneault is a graduate of Eastern Connecticut State University and has 20 years experience in detecting and preventing white-collar crime.

CHAPTER 32

Patriotic Game

JAMES LEE

M r. Jani Chin was one of the first to join the Red Sun Corporation in Shenzhen, China. With only 50 employees, the company's staff was like a family and everyone felt a personal connection to the chief executive officer (CEO). Chin prided himself on being quick to respond to the CEO's demand to go overseas to explore new markets.

Chin joined the company soon after he graduated from a local college with a degree in electrical engineering. He grew up in a rural area of Hubei. As a son of a peasant family, he was proud of having had an opportunity to study in a university. However, after graduation, he found it difficult to find work. He had been assigned a job in a state-owned enterprise (SOE) as an electrical engineer. Salaries at SOEs are generally so low that recent college graduates could expect to make only $30 a month. Chin heard that higher wages were available in the southern part of China, particularly Shenzhen, where Premier Deng Xiao Ping had just paid a visit to encourage more investments in this special economic zone. After several interviews with foreign joint ventures, Chin was dismayed when he was turned down. His last interview was with Red Sun, a small manufacturer of telecommunications equipment for companies in Hong Kong. Chin accepted Red Sun's offer and threw away his train ticket back to Hubei.

During the first 10 years he watched Red Sun transform from a small manufacturer to a $5 billion multinational corporation. He shared in the business's success and was promoted from an engineer to a senior sales manager for two provinces in China. Then the CEO announced that since China's telecommunications market was becoming saturated, the company would start exploring new areas. He asked for managers to go overseas. To encourage volunteers, Red Sun agreed to pay senior employees a stipend of $20,000 for each year they served in a foreign country. Chin quickly volunteered and was assigned to set up an office in Quito, Ecuador.

After three years, Chin had succeeded in building a profitable operation with annual revenues of $10 million. When he received orders to move back to China, he didn't want to leave because he thought that he could increase sales even more if he were successful in winning several contracts for which he had recently submitted bids. He wrote to the CEO, arguing that given the success of the operation, he intended to stay and continue to make a contribution in Ecuador. The CEO demanded that Chin follow orders and return immediately; the plans had already been made, and his successor would be arriving in Quito shortly. Chin was surprised by the hasty arrangement. He contemplated his past years of service and did not understand why he was being sent back to China. Except for a minor conflict with a senior sales manager and some arguments with the accountants at headquarters, his record with the company was good.

When he arrived back in China, Chin was assigned to look after two provinces. They were slightly larger areas than he had been in charge of in South America. Red Sun's overseas strategy proved to be very profitable. However, success came with some costs. It was reported that a CEO of a subsidiary company in Colombia had embezzled more than a million dollars. He was arrested in China after being asked to return to attend a meeting in Shenzhen. Additionally, two financial controllers submitted their resignations about having conflicts with local management regarding internal control issues. One controller hinted to the human resources department and group financial department during an exit interview that there were other suspected fraud cases in some of the South American offices. In response, Red Sun's CEO, Mr. Sue, asked the audit director to look into these alleged frauds and to strengthen the internal controls.

A Long Trip

It is a long flight from China to Quito, Ecuador. Although I was exhausted, I found myself unable to get any sleep on the plane. As I closed my eyes, I began thinking about the events that led to this flight. A few weeks ago, the CEO's secretary called me and said, "Mr. Sue wants you to meet him in his office right away." To my surprise, Mr. Zhang, the human resources director, and Ms. Jing, the chief financial officer (CFO), were both in the CEO's office.

"Take a seat," said Mr. Sue. "When will you set off your next overseas audit?"

"Next month, according to our plan," I replied.

Ms. Jing added, "And if I recall correctly, your next overseas audit will be in Latin America."

"Yes, we'll be visiting the regional headquarters in Brazil and one sales office in Lima," I responded.

"Good. I want your team to go to Ecuador as well," Mr. Sue said. He paused and stared at me with his sharp eyes, as if searching for my response. Indeed, this was a strange expression that I had never seen. He continued, "As you know, Ms. Sheila Zhang, the regional compliance officer, completed her work a couple of months ago and submitted her report to Ms. Jing. She noted some problems in the expense accounts, particularly in Ecuador. Afterward, Mr. Chin wrote a letter to Ms. Jing charging that Ms. Zhang was biased against him because of her close relationship with David Yi, who had been Chin's previous assistant manager before Chin transferred him to Brazil. Rumor has it that the transfer was due to the fact that they were constantly arguing with one another. Chin strongly objected to the report, saying that Shelia had misinterpreted the financial data."

Ms. Jing explained further, "A few months ago, the financial controller in Ecuador, Edmund Yee, also submitted his resignation. One week later, Chin made a complaint that Yee had not sought his approval for some funds transferred to the regional headquarters. In fact, Yee is the second financial controller to submit his resignation in the past two years in Quito. From what we've learned, Chin was apparently infamous for disregarding internal controls and fighting with the controllers in Latin America."

"In his exit interview," Mr. Zhang said, "Yee defended the transfers and said they were made under urgent circumstances and according to policy, but for some reason, Chin did not want them made. Yee also hinted that he believed something disturbing was occurring in Ecuador, but he refused to give any details about it."

Mr. Sue concluded, "Obviously, we need to look into this. I want you to fly to Ecuador and conduct an independent evaluation of the whole matter. If something is wrong, we need to know. However, I want this kept strictly confidential."

I returned to my office with a copy of Sheila Zhang's compliance report and began to review it. She had made note of three points with regard to expenses:

1. Surprisingly, Mr. Chin incurred very few expenses.

2. However, sales managers had incurred exorbitant amounts of expenses, all of which were approved by Mr. Chin.

3. The business purpose of some of the gifts and entertainment expenses was in question.

The report did provide some figures and account details, but nothing further. Nor did the report mention whether she had conducted any interviews to gather more information about the reasons for the expenses.

My reminiscing of the past few days' events was cut short as the airline captain announced our descent into Quito. I looked out the window and saw the runway emerge in the middle of the high mountains. Although I had just finished a 28-hour flight, I knew the toughest journey lay ahead.

THE BEST CHINESE RESTAURANTS IN TOWN

Despite having had 15 hours of sleep, I felt dizzy when I arrived at work at 9:00 the next morning. There were two facilities in Ecuador—the headquarters in Quito and a sales office in Guayaquil. Quito had about 50 employees, including seven in the Finance and Accounting Department.

My first task was to meet with Tracy Wu, the new financial controller. She knew I had been asked to look into the problem areas identified in the compliance report. As we sat down, she told me her story. "You know, I arrived here only a month ago. Things were a bit of a mess, but I think we've finally gotten most of the important things straightened out. It helps that we have a new person in charge of Ecuador. I'm sure you might have heard something about Chin. Amazingly, he always found some excuse or reason not to comply with the procedures. Edmund Yee and our financial team in the regional headquarters often argued with him."

I asked her to elaborate. Tracy continued, "Well, for the last month, I have been busy clearing the expense reports. I did note that some of them lacked documentation. Edmund told me previously that he had challenged Chin on some of the items. But Chin just yelled at him and said that the business implications and strategy were so complicated and profound that an ordinary accountant could not be expected to understand."

We both agreed that the expense accounts needed a very thorough review, and she helped me get access to the files and documents I needed. Over the next four days, I downloaded all financial data from their computer system to my notebook computer. Using audit software, I analyzed the office's expenses. I started by analyzing the last 16 months, which was how long Edmund Yee had been the controller at this office. The top five categories of expenses during that time follow.

Entertainment	14%
Travel	19%
Salaries	18%
Telecommunication expenses	7%
Rental expenses	16%

Compared to the total, the entertainment expenses were very large, broken down as follows:

Entertainment of customers (including meals and travel)	21%
Gifts to customers	27%
Sponsorship of events for promotional purposes	28%
Exhibition expenses	24%

I selected 10 of the most material from each account, along with 10 unusual items from them, and passed them on to my team member, Peter Wang, to check the respective vouchers and supporting documentation. Meanwhile, I immersed myself in other analyses and found that nearly 70% of all of the expenses were claimed by just two individuals: Francisco Lui, a sales and marketing manager, and James Guo, a senior sales and marketing manager.

As Shelia Zhang noted in her compliance report, Chin did not claim a lot of entertainment costs. In fact, he only claimed 1% of the total expenses, an abnormally low amount compared to the company's other regional managers. I talked to Tracy Wu again to find out more about Francisco Lui and James Guo. Francisco was the protégé of Chin because he was the only Chinese employee who could speak fluent Spanish. Chin was dependent on Francisco's translation skills when dealing with important customers. He had studied foreign languages in college, majoring in Spanish and English. Indeed, Red Sun recruited him directly from the university campus five years ago. In addition, Francisco was a gambler. The local casino was a regular rendezvous for him. James was a capable and experienced salesman with an impressive track record. Before joining Red Sun, he had worked in the telecommunication industry for more than 10 years. Rumor had it that he had had a bitter argument with Chin six months ago.

I asked Tracy about the fact that Chin himself had very few expenses. She said that was odd because he had a reputation for being a big spender. She had heard that Chin was so lavish that he frequently flew with his team to Guayaquil, a popular vacation spot, on a Friday for a two-hour meeting, and then they would remain the weekend before flying back to Quito on Monday. Chin's wife supposedly accompanied him on many of these trips to do some shopping.

Based on this information, I selected some more travel and meal expenses to review. I asked Peter to test these against the supporting documentation. In the individual expenses analysis, I focused my attention on Francisco Liu, James Guo, and Chin. We closely examined the major items, such as gifts, entertainment, and meals, particularly Francisco's expenses. Frankly, Chin's expenses were not material when compared to the total, but I definitely planned to see whether his wife's travel was paid for by the company per Tracy's tip. As to the gifts claimed by James and Francisco, all were approved by Chin. However, there were no details about their purposes. The only description was "promotion of business and relationships with customers." However, they were not in breach of the authorization policy, which stated that all gifts over $10,000 should be approved by the regional director and CFO. Most of the ones given by Francisco were electronic products, clothing, and some luxury items with values ranging from $1,000 to $9,000. James's gifts were mostly in relation to the exhibitions and conferences. Again, no details were present except for the invoices showing where they were purchased.

The next day, Peter popped in my office and told me that he had completed his review of the expense vouchers and supporting documentation. "Everything they claimed seems consistent with the group's policy and procedures. All have been approved by Chin. It's really difficult for us to challenge his decision," he said.

"So did you see anything strange or unusual?" I asked. Peter replied, "Not really. However, it seems they liked to go to two local Chinese restaurants for business dinners. These must be really expensive places; some meals were over $6,000."

"How many people were at those meals?" I queried. "Seven or ten," he responded. "It seems they ordered a lot of expensive wines. My guess is they probably just took some of the bottles home with them."

I browsed through the vouchers attentively. The meal expenses were mostly from two restaurants. I couldn't help but notice that the customer receipt numbers were surprisingly close. For example, a dinner on Monday would be 4210, but then the number for a meal on Friday would be 4212. Also, I noted that some of the receipts contained the details of the order, but others only contained the word "dinner" or "banquet" with a strange writing that I did not recognize. I turned to Peter and said, "Could you do me a favor and scrutinize all these vouchers and compile a schedule showing the receipt number, date, amount, and whether we have any detail about what was ordered?"

I then reviewed the other information Peter had gathered. I immediately spotted two words, "Galapagos Island," in the travel expense list. Peter wrote that it was approved by Chin, and the business purpose listed was to build a relationship with the CEO of a local mobile phone operator and his senior management team. The amount of $12,000 was claimed by James. I dug out the respective voucher, which was attached to an invoice. The invoice was in Spanish and from a local travel agent. No details were given except for a brief sentence in Spanish and the total amount. I looked the sentence up in my Spanish dictionary. It translated to "luxury package tour for seven foreigners, including child." It seemed odd that all of the management for a local phone company would be referred to as "foreigners" and that they had brought along a child for this so-called business promotion tour. I wondered if I could get more details. Browsing through the travel expenses of Francisco and James again, I found two more items relating to the Galapagos Island—one for $6,000 claimed by James and the other for $8,000 claimed by Francisco.

I asked Myriam Ramirez, one of the accountants in the Quito office, if there were any foreigners who operated mobile phone businesses in this area. She said there weren't any that she was aware of. I also asked her about the Galapagos Island trips. I told her that I had noticed certain submissions for travel expenses that only had the invoices from the travel agents attached. "Do we normally request the travel agents to give us details on the invoices they send?" I inquired.

Myriam replied, "Yes, usually the travel agents mail the invoices, including the itinerary and copies of air tickets. You said you've noticed some without details given. Can I have a look at these?"

After a brief review, she said "Oh! These are expense vouchers submitted by the managers for their cash advances. Under our normal procedures, when the receptionist receives the request, she looks at them and passes it on to the responsible staff to confirm the services received. The claimants later forward all the paperwork detailing what they spent and returning the remaining cash, if any. So I'm surprised to see that the invoices are not attached."

"Is it possible to find out where the details are? If not, can we get them from the travel agents?" I asked. Myriam agreed to see if she could locate any more documentation in our files. The next morning as I walked in, Peter came running up to me and said, "You'd better have a look at these." In his hand were three invoices from a Chinese restaurant, for approximately $15,000. Two had only the word "dinner," but the other did have at least a partial description. As I looked through the documents, I noticed Peter grinning at me. I was about to ask him what I was looking for, but then I caught sight of the three invoice numbers. "My goodness! All of the invoice numbers are the same," I exclaimed. Peter laughed and said, "You see it now." As I examined the schedule of restaurant invoices that Peter had created, he told me that he had contacted the restaurant and confirmed that it had not prepared these. It certainly seemed as if Francisco had been using fake invoices to claim expenses.

Later that day, Myriam called and said she'd received the records from both travel agents. Chin had traveled with his wife, son, Francisco, and two other Chinese men. Eventually we identified them as some sales people in the regional headquarters. The travelers on the second trip were Chin, his wife, and three other senior management personnel from other regional offices. The third trip was taken by Chin, his secretary, and his administrative assistant. However, all these were claimed by Francisco or James. Company procedures did not allow anyone to claim expenses on behalf of others.

We were just about to finish the whole operational review as well as the financial audit. Chin was in violation of company policy for asking his subordinates to claim expenses on his behalf. Additionally, it appeared that the purposes of at least some of these trips were questionable and that the company paid for Chin's family's vacation.

Francisco had defrauded the company by using fake invoices. He and James had claimed doubtful items as gifts and other entertainment expenses. The total amount for these questionable transactions was over $90,000.

A Second Chance

I called Ms. Jing, the CFO, to inform her of what I had found so far. She said, "I think you have solid evidence. Have you interviewed them?"

"Not yet," I replied, "I intend to interview Francisco and James first. As you know, Chin is in China. So I'll interview him later."

"Ask them to explain these transactions. At the same time, convey the message to them that the whole case can be handled leniently if they disclose and explain the facts fully to us. Please keep me informed of their responses. Also, we will use your recommendations to strengthen the internal controls in order to avoid such schemes from happening again," she said.

Peter and I decided to interview Francisco first. He looked worried when he came into the room. I began by asking him about the travel expenses he had submitted. He stared at me coldly. "I think it was explained on the voucher."

"I just am trying to understand the exact details and the people involved. For example, what about this trip?" I asked, showing him the expense report for one of the Galapagos Island trips.

"Well, that was for the senior management of the local telecom company," Francisco said, slightly nonplussed.

"What does this word mean?" I asked, pointing to the word "foreigners" in Spanish.

Francisco hesitated and just said, "It refers to the people that went on the trip. Even if I told you their names, you wouldn't know who they were."

"No worries," I said. "Just give me the names of these 'foreigners' as indicated on the invoice." Francisco was desperate and so anxious to defend himself that he just stared at me. There was a long silence. I did not speak. We all stared at Francisco.

"I can't remember their names," he said feebly, then stopped. Peter broke the silence nicely and said gently, "Look, Francisco, we all know who they are. Just tell the truth."

Francisco distanced himself and said, "The voucher was passed on by Chin. How could I say no to my boss?"

I replied, "Oh! I see. What about this? I showed him another travel expense voucher. His only reply was "It was the same."

I made a signal to Peter. He said, "What about these three invoices? Francisco..."

I said calmly, "You are such a capable sales manager that Red Sun would like to give you a second chance. I think you have heard the speech by our CEO, Mr. Sue, that he hates those employees who do not admit their mistakes. Ms. Jing told me before my audit that if we found anything wrong, the most important thing was to find out the control weaknesses and prevent them from recurring. Lenient treatment will be given to anyone who is truthful and honest."

Francisco stared at the floor. Finally he raised his head and said, "I'll tell you everything I know." He went on to admit that he had submitted fake invoices and falsified the expense reports.

At the end of the interview, he croaked in a weak voice, "What about my career? They won't send me back to China, will they? I just followed my boss's instructions." Peter and I averted his eyes. We did not like being present at the end of a colleague's career.

"That decision will rest with management" was all I could reply.

Next, we interviewed James. We repeated the same technique. In fact, I was leery of him, as he looked calmer and more experienced than Francisco. When presented with the evidence, however, he admitted the falsification. He claimed that Chin made him do it and that the two of them had several bitter quarrels over the matter. He agreed to cooperate and stressed the fact that he had been forced to do this by Chin. At this point, the only person left to interview was Chin. I had gathered all of the information I needed in Ecuador, and this time, I was looking forward to the long plane ride back to China.

It was good to be home. As soon as I was back in the office, I called Chin to set up an interview. He did not seem surprised to be receiving my call. When he walked in the room, I did not know what to expect. I wondered if he would be combative and argumentative, or just keep silent and deny everything. Somewhat surprisingly, Chin was extremely cooperative and admitted to the fraud. He assured us he would be fully responsible for what he had done. He conceded he did pass the vouchers and invoices on to James and Francisco to claim the false expenses. His candid demeanor and admission certainly made my job easier; however, I wondered if his cooperation was the result of a tip-off from Francisco. Regardless, with the interviews completed, I finished my investigation report and sent it to Mr. Sue.

The next day, I received a copy of a short memorandum written by Mr. Sue to the senior vice president of Global Overseas Sales and the human resource director. Attached to the memorandum was the executive summary of my report. The memo outlined how Mr. Sue had decided to handle the case:

1. The perpetrators would be required to reimburse the company for twice the amount of money taken. If they were unable to pay immediately, they could choose that these sums to be deducted from their bonuses and share options.

2. These individuals would receive no promotions or salary increases for two years.

3. Chin would be demoted from his senior management grade, and his salary would be adjusted accordingly.

4. If any of them committed a future act of fraud, they would be fired immediately and would not receive their retirement funds, share options, or outstanding bonuses. Red Sun further reserved the right to report the case to the police.

Later, Ms. Jing phoned me to explain the rationale behind the decision. Basically, Red Sun did not have a policy of firing its employees for any wrongdoing. Mr. Sue wished to present an image of treasuring the efforts and accomplishments of every staff member in the company. However, he would not let fraud go unpunished. Instead of firing them, he gave them a chance to correct their mistakes.

LESSONS LEARNED

The whole event was written about in the company's monthly management newsletter, including what steps would be taken to prevent future occurrences. While this presumably served as a lesson, it also stressed to employees that the company was taking a more active role in fraud prevention and detection.

An internal control presentation on the red flags of fraud was prepared and distributed to all financial departments, along with the mandate to implement antifraud programs in their business units. Additionally, we were asked to conduct various workshops for senior management to help them strengthen internal controls and enhance their fraud awareness.

Two months later, my proposal for setting up an antifraud team in our internal audit department was approved. It seemed that Red Sun had learned the lesson that frauds should be prevented proactively.

The company also learned that it must be more diligent about supervising its operations around the globe. It instituted a system of strict oversight for all of its local offices. It also changed the reporting lines for its financial personnel. Previously, the chief accountant at the local level reported to the local manager. Now he or she reports directly to the regional chief financial officer. Red Sun also established a policy whereby local and regional managers are graded annually on their internal control programs and fraud prevention measures as part of their annual performance review.

RECOMMENDATIONS TO PREVENT
FUTURE OCCURRENCES

After these events, Red Sun agreed that the growth of the company must be handled in a more balanced way; that is, it would still be committed to increasing sales and efficiency, but not by sacrificing internal controls. We offered a number of specific recommendations, which the company agreed to adopt. The most important ones included these five:

1. The gift policy would be completely revised and include the following:
   a. All gifts over $1,000 must be approved by both the local chief executive and the chief financial officer. Those decisions were subject to review by the regional chief executive and regional financial director.
   b. Segregation of duties should be implemented regarding gift approval, purchases, and delivery.
   c. If possible, all gifts should bear the company's logo.

2. Entertainment expenses must not exceed preset spending limits. These schedules detail the maximum amounts allowed for different entertainment events. For example, dinner cannot exceed $30 per person unless prior approval is obtained. All staff members would be trained each year to ensure they understand this policy.

3. All employees will receive a new code of conduct that emphasizes their responsibility for fraud prevention. Training and related workshops on the new code will also be provided.

4. Employees who claim expenses for their supervisors will be subject to discipline. Previously, only the supervisor could be disciplined.

5. An extensive fraud reporting program will be implemented to encourage employees and vendors to reveal fraud or other questionable acts without fear of retribution.

James Lee, CFE, CIA, ACA, is a chartered accountant in Alcatel-Lucent's internal audit department. Previously he was a deputy internal audit director of a multinational telecommunication company. Mr. Lee holds an MBA from Melbourne University as well as master of law (commercial). He has over 20 years of experience in financial, auditing, and managing information systems.

CHAPTER 33

Would You Like the Special Poutine, If You Know What I Mean?

RICHARD ELLIOTT

Canadian Multi–Cinemas Inc. (CMC) opened their latest movie house in Toronto, Ontario, in May. Upon opening, Century 16 Cinemas became the hundredth theater owned and operated by CMC, one of the largest film exhibitors in Canada. This marked the completion of an aggressive expansion plan, adding 30 state-of-the-art theaters to the chain in just over five years. They all had multiple cinemas, stadium-style seating, large screens, birthday party rooms, games arcades, and a variety of food items at the main concession stand, as well as specialty food outlet areas.

With this challenging expansion, the company's resources were spread thin, both operationally and administratively. Support staff at the head office, including senior corporate officers, looked forward to the end of the growth phase of the company so they could concentrate on the day-to-day operations of the organization and build stronger theater management teams and theater operational systems.

May was the start of the busy season—*Spider-Man* and the latest *Star Wars* movie were hyped as the blockbusters of the summer. Not unlike any other theater complex, Century 16 Cinemas relied heavily on young, part-time help to staff the box office and the concession areas. For most part-time theater employees, it was their first job, and for many, a summer job only. Once school started in the fall, business dropped, and the theater did not need the level of staff necessary for summer operation until the next blockbuster season: Christmas.

The theater had a great opening and a great summer season. In November, in anticipation of the coming Christmas holidays and the accompanying release of holiday blockbusters, the management team at Century 16 Cinemas recruited 20 new part-time employees. One of the new employees was 16-year-old Jeremy Hamel. Jeremy was trained along with the other new recruits, and he learned quickly. He soon became a versatile em-ployee who could work all food service positions at the main concession and at the specialty food service areas located in the theater lobby. Jeremy learned how to operate the point-of-sale devices and how to make, prepare, and serve all drink and food items available at the theater, including popcorn, fries, pretzels, pizza, hamburgers, and specialty coffees.

Because of Jeremy's versatility, when the Christmas rush ended, theater management decided to keep him on as a part-time employee. Management had to reduce his hours, but once business picked up during the coming busy summer season, Jeremy would be working close to full time. That suited him. He could first concentrate on school while making a bit of pocket money, and then have a fun summer job with more hours, more money, and free movies.

Jeremy turned 17 in January. One day in early spring, he came to work very excited. All he could talk about was a used car that he had just purchased: a seven-year-old Honda Civic. The car was in poor shape, but throughout the coming weeks Jeremy had decided that he was going to fix it up and turn it into his "dream car." What Jeremy failed to realize was the cost involved in such a project, not to mention the day-to-day prices of insurance and fuel.

Jeremy desperately wanted to have the car fully reconditioned for the summer, but even with his job at Century 16 Cinemas, he could not find enough cash to achieve his goal. It seemed that everything he needed to do to his car cost more than he first estimated. Regardless, the transformation of the Honda became his obsession, and he decided he would do whatever it took to make this vehicle into something special.

POUTINE WITH YOUR FRIES?

One Friday evening Jeremy was assigned to the fry outlet, as he often was. Some of his friends came by and started joking with him about "hooking them up" with some poutine (fries, with cheese and gravy). Jeremy knew about the company's strict zero tolerance policy regarding employee theft; in fact, he had signed a theater fraud and theft policy document when he was hired. Jeremy also knew that there were cameras aimed at the various serving stations about the theater. But his friends were relentless, and Jeremy gave in to the pressure. He prepared the poutine and handed the order out to his friends.

Later that night, on the way home, Jeremy realized that he had taken a huge risk, but he had heard that other food service attendants were giving out food for free, so he felt that his actions were justified. "Who cares?" he thought. "It's just a few fries. They owe it to me anyway, given the amount of work I do and the low pay that I get."

That weekend the muffler on Jeremy's car went. He still hadn't done any of the bodywork or painting, he needed four new tires, and it was already the middle of May. He only had a few weeks left before summer. And there was this girl he met in December who was coming to work at Century 16 Cinemas for the busy summer season. He needed to make his car "road-worthy," and he needed to do it fast.

Jeremy came up with a plan. Instead of just giving product out to his friends, he would use his friends to help him steal money. On camera, it would look like a legitimate transaction. Jeremy would give his friends free fries. His friends would give Jeremy money as if pretending to pay, but Jeremy would give them back their money, plus more. Later his friends would give Jeremy the extra money that he had handed them during the so-called sales.

The plan worked. In less than one week, and over three shifts, Jeremy was able to steal $150 from the fry outlet. But he was running out of friends—or at least friends who could be trusted to help him steal in return for free product. Realizing the potential of this scam, the amount of money at stake, and his "deadline" rapidly approaching, Jeremy began to steal money from sales other than the "fake" sales he was doing with the help of his friends.

When Jeremy wanted to steal, he used his body to block his actions from the camera. He usually crumpled up bills with his right hand and put his right hand inside his apron. He then walked away from his serving station to the food preparation area so that he could pocket the money off camera. Sometimes he slipped bills into the waste basket and later pocketed the money when he made the trip to the trash compactor with the garbage. One Friday night, Jeremy stole $80, and one busy Saturday night, over $200. At this rate, he would easily have enough money to finish the repairs and beautification of his car.

NOT A PRETTY PICTURE

Alison Collins was puzzled and concerned. Just transferred to the position of general manager for Century 16 Cinemas, Toronto, she could not gain control of her cash over/shorts, which recently were becoming more "short" than "over." In addition, the operator report showing summary data of sales and tender type (cash, credit, debit, coupon, gift certificate) by food service attendant (operator) was so convoluted that she could not make sense of what was going on in the theater at the operator/treasurer level. Nothing was coherent, and Alison felt she was rapidly losing control over the handling and balancing of cash at Century 16 Cinemas. Was theft occurring in her building, or was she looking at the results of sloppy cash accounting procedures? Perhaps her food service attendants were just not capable of returning the proper change.

In an effort to grasp the situation, Alison viewed the report to see if, for every operator who was short cash and noncash tender at the end of the shift, there was a corresponding operator who was over by the same amount. For most days there were not enough overages to cover off the shortages, and although it was clear that the treasurers were not doing their job of properly attributing their cash pickups to the correct operator, it was not clear if the overall shortages were due to theft.

Alison also printed some concession audit trail reports that showed all entries made on the point-of-sale devices by operator and by time. She looked at the reports for unusual voids. There were some suspicious voids, but when she checked these against the CCTV images, nothing jumped out as fraudulent. The voids seem to occur when the operator made a legitimate mistake or the customer changed his or her mind. It appeared to Alison that, if there was theft, those guilty were not leaving evidence of the theft on the audit trail reports by entering phony voids on their tills to cancel legitimate sales they made. Operators can void product prior to the completion of a sale. This allows for the correction of errors or changing an order if the customer changes his or her mind during the sale. Once the sale is totaled, it cannot be voided. If a customer changes his or her mind once the sale is totaled, a refund must be processed, and only managers can process refunds.

Alison persistently pored over the operator reports. For one day, she noticed what she thought was an unusually high cash shortage at the fry outlet. She investigated further by reviewing the CCTV images for the shift in question. Alison did not see any theft or product giveaways, but she did notice that the food service attendant on duty at the fry outlet was acting suspiciously. To Alison, it appeared that the attendant was hiding some of his actions by blocking the CCTV camera with his body. The attendant on duty was Jeremy Hamel.

GUILTY MOVES

Alison scheduled Jeremy to work at the fry outlet for his next shift, and she had her most trusted treasurer do the cash pickups and deposits for the outlet for the young man's entire shift. In addition, Alison watched Jeremy's behavior live on the computer CCTV monitor. Again, his body language was suspicious, and, at the end of his shift, his cash was significantly short when compared to his recorded sales. Alison contacted the Loss Prevention Department at CMC head office.

Alison spoke with the director of Loss Prevention, Paul Drake, about her suspicions. Paul was confused. "Let me get this straight," he said. "You mean you suspect that an operator is stealing because he is coming up short cash at the end of the night, and there is no indication on the audit trail report that he is manipulating sales through voiding?"

"Yes," Alison replied.

Paul continued, "So you think he is taking money and making no attempt to hide his theft—not even trying to balance by not entering the sales he steals money from, or by entering and then voiding the sales he steals money from?"

"That's correct," Alison replied.

Paul thought that this was odd. Usually food service attendants who are stealing cash try to balance their recorded sales to the cash in their drawer, to avoid any suspicion. They do this by first entering the sale, then voiding it, or they simply do not enter the sale at all. By voiding or not entering the sales from which they steal money, their cash will always balance to their recorded sales and they can hide their theft. Although the cash drawer will not open if the product is voided, the food service attendant can get around this by entering a low-dollar item as the sale. This will open the cash drawer and allow the attendant to give change to the customer. If the customer pays with exact change, the attendant does not have to open the cash drawer at all, since change is not required—for exact change sales, the attendant does not have to void anything on the point-of-sale device to try to balance.

When cash is just outright short due to theft, it is most often a treasurer or manager who is taking the money. Treasurers and managers do periodic cash and noncash tender pickups from the tills. They flag these pickups by operator and device, make up deposits, and enter the pickups and deposits into the sales reporting and cash accounting systems accordingly.

"What about your inventory of fry containers?" Paul asked.

"They balance," Alison replied.

Alison understood that most retail businesses have three measures of sales: (1) recorded sales, that is, sales entered on the point-of-sale device by the operator; (2) physical cash and noncash tender received from customers for sales; and (3) sales based on the difference between opening and closing inventories, in this case determined by counting the supply of containers used for fries before and after a sales period. Alison had no discrepancies in the difference between her opening and closing counts of fry containers when compared to the number recorded by the operator as sold; both of these measures of sales balanced to each other. The discrepancy was between the two measures of sales and the cash and noncash tender for these measures of sales. Alison had more recorded sales than cash and noncash tender, and she had more sales based on inventory changes than she had cash and noncash tender.

Alison insisted that the evidence pointed toward Jeremy. She described Jeremy's body language; how he sometimes apparently used his body to block the camera. Paul agreed with Alison's suspicions, and they decided to install a covert camera at the fry outlet to augment the camera coverage of the suspected area of criminal activity.

Paul contacted Daryl Anderson at SecurTech Video Solutions, a Toronto CCTV company. He explained the area that needed coverage and suggested that Daryl install a pinhole camera in the acoustic ceiling tiles above the point of sale. Daryl had done previous work for CMC and knew the basic requirements, but Paul reminded Daryl that the camera should cover the customer being served, the counter, the point-of-sale device, the product going out to the customer, the cash drawer, and the server. Also, Paul told Daryl that if he had to locate the camera either to the left or right side of the server, he should locate it to the server's right. One morning in June, Daryl met Alison at the theater and, under Alison's supervision, installed a covert camera and VCR to videotape activities at the french fry outlet. Daryl was able to install the VCR in a locked cupboard in Alison's office, which allowed her to change tapes in private and have the VCR secured in a locked cupboard and office that no one else could access.

The theater's existing overt CCTV system was a multiplexed digital system, consisting of 2 Digital Video Recorders (DVRs) with 16 cameras per DVR, for a total of 32 cameras. The images were captured on the DVRs, but the frame rate capabilities of the system were not high enough to provide the detail needed for this investigation. Besides, the suspect was hiding his activities from the overt camera, making the covert camera necessary to determine exactly what was happening at this point of sale.

To ensure the continuity of evidence and the chain of custody, Paul instructed Alison on how to label and change the videotapes and where and how to send the tapes to Loss Prevention for analysis. Alison had to label each videotape with the date and time that she inserted the tape into the machine and the date and time that she removed it. Beside each entry on the videotape label, he instructed her to sign her name to identify her as the person changing and labeling the videotapes. Paul also instructed Alison to remove the record tab of each videotape as she removed it from the VCR.

Alison followed Paul's instructions. When she removed each videotape, she sealed it in a package and sent it by courier to the Loss Prevention department at CMC's head office.

The manager of the department, Sara Williams, analyzed the videotapes. For each of Jeremy's shifts on camera, Sara used the theater's audit trail report and matched what was recorded as sold on the report with the videotape images. Sara's analysis of the images revealed that Jeremy Hamel entered everything that he prepared and served to customers as sold on the point-of-sale device. However, the images showed that Jeremy was repeatedly stealing money from the cash drawer at the fry outlet. Sometimes he would discreetly take the money from the cash drawer or from the counter, walk away from his serving station, and pocket the money. Other times he would take the money from the cash drawer and give it to his friends, faking a sale: Jeremy would give his friends the product, his friends would pay, he would enter the sale, and then give them back their money, plus $40 or $60 more. Sara noticed on the videotape that every time Jeremy's friends approached him for the fake sales, they would "high-five" or tap knuckles with Jeremy before and/or after the fraudulent sale. Sara documented her findings for June 20, 21, and 27. The total amount stolen was $510 over the three days that Sara examined. Paul Drake verified Sara's findings and, on June 30, Paul contacted the police.

CAUGHT ON TAPE

On July 4, Sara, Paul, and Alison met with Constable Daigle and Constable McLellan of Toronto Police Services, 52 Division, to present their case, which included full documentation of the investigation: table of contents and contact sheet; Jeremy's loss summary amounts; audit trail reports; video analysis report; operator shift report; record of employment and swiped hours; statements from Alison, Sara, and Paul; and the invoice from the CCTV installer. Sara kept all original documents and prepared the evidence file in triplicate: one copy for the police, one copy for the crown, and one copy for Jeremy's legal counsel. Sara also included copies of the videotape of Jeremy's shifts in triplicate.

At the meeting with Constables Daigle and McLellan, Sara showed the videotape of the cash thefts to the officers. The officers agreed that there were sufficient grounds to arrest Jeremy, and both commented on the quality of the evidence and the documentation:

"Sara, the work you have done and the documentation you have prepared for this case would put many police officers to shame," Constable McLellan remarked.

"Well done," Constable Daigle added.

On the evening of July 4, Constables Daigle and McLellan approached Jeremy while he was working at the fry outlet, arrested him, and charged him with theft under $5,000.

Jeremy was devastated. He didn't want his parents to find out, but he was a young offender, under the age of 18. The police had to release Jeremy to the custody of his parents with a promise to appear in court on a set date. Jeremy's parents assured Alison that Jeremy would pay back every cent that he stole. Alison banned Jeremy and his friends from all CMC theaters for a period of three years.

During the investigation, Alison found out that other operators were stealing money. Jeremy indicated that he knew other operators were giving away product. When arrested by the police, Jeremy revealed that he used at least one employee to pass money to, and this was discovered by Sara on the videotape. After Jeremy's arrest, the employee was questioned by Alison, and admitted that he received money from Jeremy and that they split the cash. The employee returned the money and was dismissed by Alison. A third employee was also named by Jeremy. This employee was alleged to be stealing money at the pizza outlet. She was questioned by Alison, admitted to giving pizza out to friends, and was dismissed with cause for giving out free product.

LESSONS LEARNED

After Jeremy's arrest, the Audit and Loss Prevention Department for CMC scheduled a meeting with the management team at Century 16 Cinemas to discuss how this theft occurred and what could be done to prevent it in the future. During the meeting, the group discussed the case from all angles—from Jeremy's perspective and from the theater's perspective—to determine the root cause for the theft and to determine what corrective measures could be taken to prevent or deter employee concession theft. A description of the points of discussion follows.

Jeremy was driven by the desire to create an image for himself within a deadline. He wanted to be the cool guy with the cool wheels to impress a girl, and he had only a few weeks to create this image. This desire was much stronger than the fear of cameras, or not balancing his cash to his sales, or getting caught. In addition, when Jeremy gave the poutine to his friends, he created justification for this first act of dishonesty. Jeremy applied the same justification logic to his more serious crime of stealing cash.

During the meeting, the group agreed that the act of giving out free product is usually one short step away from stealing money and often the two go hand in hand. In Jeremy's mind, he was stealing from a company that would not miss the money. He believed that he worked hard and was underpaid, so he deserved what he stole, and he rationalized that other food service attendants were doing the same or similar things, so there was no reason why he shouldn't partake in the theft.

The theater had several preventive measures in place to detect or deter theft:

- Cameras
- Audit trail reports
- Surprise cash audits, where an operator is cashed out and balanced to recorded sales in the middle of his or her shift
- Cash balancing procedures, including log-ins and log-outs by employee, and cash pickups by treasurers or managers by till
- Cash drawers that will not open unless the total sale key is pressed
- Till product display windows for customers to follow their transactions
- Company policies regarding the consequences for employee theft
- Management/supervisory floor presence

- Performance dialogue with employees (communicating balancing performance as part of the training and ongoing process)

But there were also factors that contributed to theft:

- No consequences for operators short cash, due to poor implementation of cash balancing procedures
- Peer pressure: operators' friends demanding free product
- Cameras that didn't cover every angle of the serving area
- Limitations of the existing digital video recorders
- Difficulty in attributing sales and cash for sales to the individual who transacted the sales
- Sloppy money handling by treasurers, resulting in errors that hide theft indicators
- Lack of management focus on operator balancing performance

During the meeting, Paul and Sara discussed with the management team the importance of proper cash balancing. Paul explained, "In a perfect world of exact balancing, cash handling, transactional processing, and hardware/software operation, a cash shortage would indicate that there was theft and show you who was responsible. In the real world, what you are trying to do is eliminate as many other reasons for shortages and overages as you can so these cash variances will be indicators that theft is a strong possibility and must be investigated. That is why the cash balancing system must be kept as 'clean' as possible.

"Just because an operator is short cash, you can't assume theft. If an operator innocently gives back the wrong change, he or she will be short (or over). If an operator accidentally enters more product than he or she sells, he or she will be short. A treasurer doing the cash pickups and deposits may improperly count money or assign cash to the wrong person. This could cause cash shortages.

"If an operator balances his or her cash to recorded sales, you can't assume that there is no theft. 'Off the till' transactions allow operators to balance their cash to recorded sales and still steal money.

"If there is theft due to cash shortages, don't assume that cash shortages always indicate treasurer or manager theft, and not operator theft.

"If there is theft indicated by shortages, you can't assume that the operator assigned to the till that is short is the guilty operator. Maybe this operator was relieved and the relief operator was not set up with a separate till and float, and stole cash from the till. Maybe a dishonest treasurer or manager took money from a cash pickup at the operator's till. Even the employee setting up the floats at the beginning of the day could skim money.

"Don't assume that an overage means 'everything is okay.' 'We're over' probably is just someone forgetting to enter sales, or not giving back enough change. An overage could mean that the operator responsible made numerous off-the-till transactions, but only took some of the money from these transactions, either to avoid suspicion by being over, or because the operator couldn't properly keep track of the amount he or she could steal to balance.

"Don't take a shortage and apply it to an overage, assuming that the treasurers made an error. The shortage could be the result of one operator theft, and the overage could be the result of another operator theft."

The group agreed that Alison completed all of the necessary steps to try to come up with a suspect, and her investigation produced results. She examined the operator reports. She looked at audit trail reports and video images. She was somewhat lucky in that Jeremy was not trying to cover up his theft by balancing his reported sales to his cash. Eventually his shortages would stand out, but someone had to be looking and questioning these shortages, as Alison eventually did. She also knew the limitations of the overt CCTV system; if theft was occurring, the perpetrator would try to conceal his or her actions from the camera. Therefore, the theft of cash would not jump right out of the video. Alison knew to look for odd body language; the suspect was likely not going to steal money right in front of the camera.

The treasurers' sloppy work and lack of attention to detail cost Alison huge amounts of time during her investigation. The treasurers assigned cash to the wrong operators. They also failed to keep track of pickups and attempted to fix everything up in the office to make it appear that they were doing their job. The treasurers were partly responsible for these thefts going undetected.

RECOMMENDATIONS TO PREVENT FUTURE OCCURRENCES

Monitor Financial Transactions Closely; Do Not Ignore Mistakes

To improve the cash accounting system, Alison realized that she must enforce the requirement that anyone who transacts sales is accountable for the cash attributed to the sales that he or she processes. All agreed that floats must be set up for each operator that transacts sales and that treasurers must properly attribute cash pickups to the operator responsible for the sales that resulted in the cash picked up. When this is achieved, the operator report becomes a meaningful document that can be used more effectively as an investigative tool. Alison commented that she would have to make sure that her treasurers or managers do not merely "move things around" after the fact to make the report look the way it is supposed to. The operator report should reflect exactly what happened by operator.

Hold Employees Accountable for Financial Transaction Mistakes

Going forward, Alison agreed to set up a routine to investigate the cause of operator shortages and overages on the operator report. As part of the routine, if the shortages or overages are the result of error, management must find out who is responsible and make them accountable. If an operator is the cause of the shortages or overages, management must make that operator accountable. If the operator continues to be out of balance, management must retrain, reassign, or dismiss if necessary.

Analyze Audit Trail Reports

Alison also agreed to set up a routine to analyze the audit trail reports for unusual transactions, especially voids, and to investigate these transactions with the corresponding video images. This routine includes documenting findings, and if there is sufficient evidence of theft, dismissing the perpetrator, and/or contacting the police.

Surprise Cash Audits

Alison stressed the importance of surprise cash audits on tills. Sara and Paul agreed, and indicated that operators who are stealing and aware that their tills can be audited at any time are under pressure to keep their tills balanced. This means they have to pocket money as they steal it—they don't want to be caught with an overage in their cash drawer. And the more times an operator pockets money, the more likely he or she will be caught.

Surveillance with Many Vantage Points

Management pointed out the importance of watching operators as they process sales, preferably from a vantage point where the operators are not aware that they are being watched. Paul commented that management should look for red flags and make a note of anything they see that appears unusual. Later management can check the audit trail report and video images to confirm what they have seen. There are several things that management might see that they should investigate further. For example:

- Unnecessary or suspicious handling of money
- Items, even coins or bills, placed in a certain way that operators are using as counters to keep track of amounts they are about to steal from the cash drawer
- Operators transacting sales with customers who appear to be friends
- Operators serving other staff
- Handshaking, "high-fives," laughing, or any other familiar gestures that occur between operators and customers before or after a sale
- Operators with till display windows fully or partially obstructed
- An operator serving customers at a serving area other than at that operator's assigned till

Other Measures

When the meeting concluded, the management team thanked the Audit and Loss Prevention Department for their support. Paul summed up the overall recommendations requiring implementation to deter the specific type of theft perpetrated by Jeremy Hamel.

"To instill in operators responsibility for the money that they are entrusted with, and to ensure that operators take true ownership of the responsibility for balancing their cash, and for transacting sales correctly, managers and treasurers will:

- Assign every operator his or her own float;
- Confirm all floats in the presence of the operator given the float;
- Count all cash pickups in front of the operator at the time of pickup; and
- Fill out a sign-off agreement with the operator as to the amount picked up.

"These procedures provide accountability at the operator level for balancing recorded sales with the cash for these sales, and hold operators responsible for shortages and overages."

THE OUTCOME OF THE INVESTIGATION

After this investigation, Alison had a huge challenge in trying to improve the performance of her treasurers. Unfortunately, she had to dismiss most of them over the next few months because they could not or would not carry out the responsibilities of their job. Alison implemented new training procedures for her treasurers, but she still finds it difficult to fill this position with competent staff.

A few months after Audit and Loss Prevention personnel met with the theater management team, Jeremy's court date came up, and he pled guilty. He had no previous record or occurrences, so the judge gave him a conditional discharge, consisting of one year's probation, during which he had to perform 200 hours of community service, maintain an 11 o'clock curfew, stay in school, keep the peace, and be on good behavior. The judge took into account during sentencing that he had paid back the money he took from Century 16 Cinemas.

Jeremy was able to do so by selling his car.

Richard Elliott, CFE, is director, loss prevention, for a chain of movie theaters and entertainment complexes in Canada. He is a graduate of York University and has worked in the movie and entertainment business for over 30 years, primarily in the prevention, detection, and investigation of employee theft and fraud.

CHAPTER 34

Three-Ring Circus: An Exposé of a Corporate Commission Embezzlement

DAVID A. SCHNEIDER

Although fraudsters Alex Bedford, Van Nguyen, and Parviz Shah may have collectively acquired five college degrees at the baccalaureate level or higher, these 20-somethings were not clever enough to elude the experienced Special Investigative Unit (SIU) at Centerstone Health Systems, a leading health care insurer in the United States. This trio, in varying roles, was involved in a scheme to embezzle funds from the company. While both Alex and Van were Centerstone Health employees, Parviz's involvement was different because he acted as an external co-conspirator. All three were close friends and they enjoyed playing basketball, experiencing the nightlife, and discussing their aspirations of owning big homes and expensive cars in a ritzy suburb just north of Los Angeles.

Alex, the ringleader, took pleasure in flaunting his muscular build and natural intelligence. He had a jovial personality and was admired by many of his peers. Yet he did not hesitate to let others know that he was the one in charge. He was the father of a young daughter. Even though he was no longer with his child's mother, the two proud parents jointly paid for her private school. Alex was an eight-year Centerstone Health employee who earned his bachelor's degree in business administration during the day while working the swing shift at night. Soon after completing his degree, he began working toward an MBA with a concentration in finance at a pricy private university. Alex was in the same department all eight years of his employment with Centerstone Health, and he reached the distinction of unit lead, responsible for customer service, processing member enrollments, and various supervisory functions. Alex was known to be very technically savvy, and he knew all the ins and outs of his business unit's operations. He began to get bored with his job so he decided to obtain his Life & Health sales license in hopes of transferring to Centerstone Health's in-house sales department. Once he became licensed, he applied for the job. However, Alex was unsuccessful in securing a position so he remained in his existing role.

In appearance and demeanor, Van was Alex's polar opposite. Van was of very slight stature, and he was more of a follower than a leader. Nevertheless, he had no intellectual shortcomings. He received his undergraduate degree in history from one of the top universities in the University of California system and considered going to law school. Van was from a very close-knit family. Growing up, he saw how hard his immigrant parents worked to make a living in the United States. His father, who unquestionably was his hero, was a manufacturing manager always worried about the possibility of losing his job. Van's parents knew how important owning real estate was, and, over the years, they were able to acquire three single-family homes, one of which Van was renting.

Parviz was quite arrogant. He was athletically built, sported hoop earrings in both ears, had bleached blond hair, and wore expensive clothes and a heavy dose of cologne. He also was from an immigrant family, but unlike Van, whom he had met and befriended in high school, his family lived a much more lavish lifestyle. His mother was an extremely successful real estate agent and his father was an engineer who owned several small businesses in town. In his high school days, Parviz learned quite a bit about computer programming. Instead of attending college immediately after graduation, he began to work for his father as a software engineer. During this time, he also started his own Internet-based car poster business. He was known to be an avid fan of the science fiction trilogy *The Matrix*, starring Keanu Reeves and Laurence Fishburne. He even had a black Infinity G35 coupe with the personalized license plate "MATRIX." Parviz decided to attend college about two years after graduating high school. He attended one of the nation's most elite technical universities and graduated with double majors in economics and computer science. At the time of the investigation, Parviz was finishing his master's degree in mathematics at the same university.

Centerstone Health is a commercial health benefits company. It offers medical insurance to large and small employers, individuals and families. It has over 40,000 employees and major operations in many states. The company's products are marketed by a network of independent insurance agents and an in-house sales team. When an individual seeks medical insurance, he or she can apply for coverage in one of three general ways: by contacting an independent licensed agent, by calling the company's internal sales department, or by completing an application online or submitting a paper-based enrollment application.

The SIU is led by a former federal prosecutor. Each of the company's four geographic regions is managed by a director of investigations, two of whom are retired from the Federal Bureau of Investigations (FBI). At the time of his retirement, my manager, Jim Greer, was the supervising agent in charge of one of the local FBI offices. Each director of investigations has one investigative analyst and several investigators. I am the investigative analyst for the western region and have been employed by Centerstone Health for nearly 10 years, of which the last 3 have been in the SIU. One of my primary roles is leading large-scale data-mining studies and performing statistical analyses on medical claim payments, but I am always excited when I'm assigned the occasional investigation. The SIU is responsible for all internal and external white-collar crimes perpetrated against Centerstone Health. This largely includes physician and hospital fraud, but also consists of broker, vendor, and employee frauds.

SECRET AGENT

On an unusually crisp September morning, I received a call from a manager, Gracie Leonard, within one of my organization's membership departments. She stated that her business unit had recently received information from several upset insurance agents and one new policy holder complaining that the agent of record on file with the company was someone they had never heard of. The agents were angered because they wanted their commissions. The new policy holder, Mr. Donald Strickland, was concerned because he felt someone had inappropriately obtained his personal information. Gracie knew something was not right. She told me the common denominator was an agent named Parviz Shah. Parviz's name appeared as the agent on these particular enrollment applications, and he had skyrocketing commissions in the five months since becoming appointed to sell insurance with Centerstone Health.

Mr. Strickland had sent a long letter to Gracie detailing how he signed up for his insurance with a close family friend who had been his agent for a long time. Parviz Shah, Mr. Strickland proclaimed, was someone he had never heard of, and he demanded to know how that person was listed as the agent of record on the enrollment application. Mr. Strickland provided a copy of the documents he completed with his agent when he applied for his insurance policy. Just as he stated, the agent whose signature was on his version of the application was not Parviz's. Mr. Strickland, along with his agent, took it upon himself to phone Parviz to confront him about the matter. As a result Parviz sent Centerstone Health a letter releasing himself as the broker of record on Mr. Strickland's insurance policy. According to Mr. Strickland, Parviz claimed that there must have been some sort of mix-up and agreed to give the commissions to the original agent. Nobody was told how this so-called mix-up occurred, but Mr. Strickland was more or less satisfied when the matter was resolved. In insurance sales, it is almost unheard of for an agent to surrender his or her commissions. That struck Gracie as rather odd because commissions are the lifeblood of all insurance salespeople. She advised me that the management team had spent two weeks examining the situation. She had no idea how Parviz, a nonemployee independent sales agent, would be able to obtain copies of enrollment applications. Although foul play was suspected, the management team had no success in determining how, if, and by whom a fraud was perpetrated. Gracie needed my help and she needed it quickly.

MAIL ROOM MYSTERY

I suspected that this was an inside job. The timing was ideal because I was training the newest addition to the SIU. It was Gary Pultzer's second week with the company, and, as it turned out, this was the perfect case to acquaint him with occupational fraud. I told Gary that my immediate impression was that Parviz must have had an accomplice who worked for Centerstone Health. How else would he be able to become the official agent of record on these insurance policies, especially when the policy holders had never heard of him?

Online, Gary and I and looked up Parviz's licensing information with the California Department of Insurance. He was a newly licensed Life & Health agent. The Department of Insurance database also showed that Parviz was authorized to transact on behalf of BN&S Insurance Agency, LLC. I then had Gary go to the California Business Portal webpage to do a search on BN&S. His research showed that Parviz was the company's registered agent and both a post office box and a physical address were listed on the documentation. I then ran a business search on the physical location. The address was residential and occupied by Alex Bedford.

Who was Alex Bedford? Was he our culprit? A search of Centerstone Health's employee directory revealed that Alex was not only an employee, but that he also worked in the Membership Department within the same business unit as Gracie, the manager who had called me earlier that morning. The California Department of Insurance Web site also showed that Alex, like Parviz, was a licensed Life & Health agent. Further, Alex had been appointed to sell insurance with two of Centerstone Health's competitors. Because of the obvious conflict, that fact alone could be grounds for termination. I wondered if he had disclosed this information on his annual employee conflict-of-interest form. I then theorized that BN&S stood for the initials of Alex Bedford, Parviz Shah, and an unknown third party whose last name began with the letter "N." At this point, Gary and I high-fived and began to document the information we had gathered so far.

We were off to a fast start in cracking the case. Although we felt confident that Alex and Parviz were in cahoots to embezzle commission payments from Centerstone Health, we needed to complete the puzzle. What that meant was establishing their precise modus operandi. I called Gracie back and scheduled a time to meet with her the following day. She and Alex worked in a Centerstone Health building 20 miles northwest of my office. Gracie was not Alex's boss, but she was able to provide a detailed description of the business unit's operations and Alex's job responsibilities. She explained that her department used an imaging system to scan and process enrollment applications. That meant that when an individual or family applied for insurance, their paper-based enrollment application was scanned into a software program; this made all internal operations paperless. Once the enrollment application was scanned, it was electronically forwarded to a queue to be reviewed for completeness. If the enrollment application was missing information, such as a signature or a question that was left unanswered, it was electronically sent to a holding queue until the missing or incomplete information was obtained. Enrollment applications that were not missing information were placed in a production queue to be processed.

Now that I was knowledgeable of the unit's operations, it became apparent to me that Alex must have been intercepting enrollment applications before they were imaged. That way he would be able to affix Parviz's name and license number on them and place the applications back into the mail. Like all others working in his business unit, Alex was not authorized to possess paper-based enrollment applications. Only mail room employees were allowed to handle the paper versions that were received in the mail every morning and then processed into the imaging system. The papers were scanned daily up until 3:30 p.m. when the mail room shift ended. Those not scanned then were handled the following morning. Gary and I learned that the door was always left unlocked after the mail room employees left for the day. We already knew that Alex worked the swing shift. His regular hours were between 4:00 p.m. and 12:30 a.m. I surmised that Alex was sneaking into the basement where the mail room was located and then either inserting Parviz's agent information on the paper enrollment applications or taking the applications home with him and doing the same.

Prior to leaving Alex's work site, I called Centerstone Health's Human resources (HR) Department. I sought to obtain copies of his employment record, including his yearly performance evaluations and conflict-of-interest disclosures. Human resources told me they could have the information ready for me to pick up in two hours. Gary and I decided to eat sushi for lunch at a nearby Japanese restaurant before heading to the HR office, which was located in a different Centerstone Health office seven miles north of Alex's building. Upon arrival, we perused the documents. Alex, for the most part, received glowing yearly reviews and above-average salary increases. However, his evaluations contained some noteworthy entries. For example, his supervisor mentioned that he was a "whiz kid"; he learned and mastered new responsibilities so quickly that he became bored shortly thereafter. He also had to be warned about his excessive chatting with friends in other departments on several occasions. Overall, the content of Alex's evaluations would lead most people to believe he was nothing less than a stellar employee. More important, the review of Alex's conflict-of-interest form showed that he did not disclose that he received his Life & Health insurance agent's license just over a year earlier and that he was authorized to do business with two of Centerstone Health's competitors. I was almost certain that Alex's omission of this fact would be all Centerstone Health needed to terminate his employment, but I considered this a side note for the time being because I needed to complete the investigation at hand.

Gary and I left the HR office and traveled several more miles to Alex's residence, which also was BN&S Insurance Agency's business address, to take pictures. It is standard practice to document an investigation as thoroughly as possible. Therefore, when pictures are included in the final investigative report, it helps to give credence to the amount of detail and effort undertaken in putting the case together. Afterward, Gary and I decided to call it a day and we hopped on the highway for a long drive back to our office. As I dropped him off at his car, he expressed how eager he was to get started tomorrow to continue the investigation. I felt the same way, but also was personally thrilled to be a part of the rookie's excitement.

The next day came and I spent a good portion of the morning on the telephone with the Centerstone Health Information Technology (IT) department. After several hours, I was granted access to the systems Alex used, including his e-mail account. I pored through the contents in hopes of finding incriminating evidence. One such communication stuck out, which was sent to Alex by another worker asking why some of the employees in his unit had been electronically forwarding applications from the production queue back to the holding queue when, in fact, they were not missing any information. Alex received and viewed the e-mail two days earlier, but he had not yet responded. I decided to take a look at the imaging system for myself. As I was logging in, I noted that the password given to me by IT was the same as my normal network logon ID and there was no way to change it. I gave IT another call and was informed that all imaging system users' passwords were set to match their network IDs. That meant that any employee could log on to the imaging system as another employee. Therefore, the system's audit log would not accurately reflect who was handling the application. In my mind, this was a serious internal control issue.

I ran a search for all applications that were transferred from the production queue back to the holding queue. There was one thing in common: The majority were those in which the insurance applicant did not use an agent. These are called nonbrokered applications. For Centerstone Health, this is highly valued business because the company does not have to pay a commission. Further, of the thousands of insurance applicants applying for individual or family coverage every month, about 15% or so do not use an agent. I was on to something! If Alex was smart, and we knew he was, he would affix Parviz's name and license number to only those applications. Otherwise, the true agents would complain when their commissions were not received. Why then did Parviz's name appear on Mr. Strickland's insurance policy? To help me determine why, I called the Centerstone Health sales manager and obtained Parviz's complete book of business (an agent's list of his or her clientele information, such as each subscriber's name, policy ID number, commissions paid, etc.). Parviz had only been licensed to sell insurance for Centerstone Health for five months, but he had an astounding 250 policies from which he was receiving commissions. The total amount paid to Parviz in these five months was $13,072. Over the course of the next day and a half, Gary and I called a sample of 50 of Parviz's "clients." Each and every one of them indicated that they had never heard of Parviz and that they applied for their health insurance policies without an agent. My best guess to why Alex affixed Parviz's name and license number on Mr. Strickland's insurance application was that he made a mistake—a costly one. Up to this point I believed that Alex was sneaking into the mail room to obtain physical copies of nonbrokered enrollment applications to add Parviz's name before they were scanned. Now I had to consider the additional possibility that he too was logging on to the imaging system with other users' IDs. I figured that it would be easier for Alex to search for them there, as opposed to the mail room, because these applications were rather rare. How then would Alex insert Parviz's name and license number on those that had already been scanned? I later learned that, within the imaging system, Alex had found a way to cancel the original application. He then had a copy rescanned, but with Parviz's name and license number inserted. Alex had enough know-how to circumvent this vulnerability. It was now time to take the investigation to the next level.

CASE DISMISSED

To conclude our work, I sought to interview Alex's former manager, Paula Lee, who had recently started a new position within a different division of the company. Next we'd interview Alex. Before that could be done, I needed to obtain the blessing from HR, Legal, and Ethics & Compliance. I arranged a conference call between these parties. The HR manager, Neil Honna, said that he was apprehensive about Paula's integrity as a result of previous, unrelated dealings with her. Neil was concerned with the possibility that she would relay information back to Alex before he was interviewed. So I suggested that we arrange simultaneous questioning of both of them at their two respective work sites. The plan was for me and Randy, a colleague SIU investigator, to interview Paula while Jim and Gary interviewed Alex. The attorney from the Legal Department felt comfortable with this arrangement. However, he recommended that Neil also should be present during Alex's interview. Finally, the ethics & compliance department wanted to be notified immediately about the outcomes, and I agreed to keep them posted.

Randy and I met with Paula at precisely 4:00 p.m. It was a surprise interview. Much to my astonishment, she was entirely cooperative and extremely helpful. She told us that Alex was a "big part of the team" and that he was used as a "floater" to cover other job functions when the unit was understaffed. He was described as extraordinarily knowledgeable of all of the business unit's processes and procedures. When Paula was apprised of the allegations against Alex, she stated that if any of her former employees were intercepting enrollment applications, she would suspect him. He exuded such an aura of confidence that she would not be surprised if he thought he could get away with it. She explained that he had been involved in the initial testing and subsequent implementation of the imaging system just several years earlier. In fact, she described Alex as the "king of the imaging system."

I then asked Paula if she knew if our suspect had any friends in the company whose last name began with the letter "N." Without hesitation, Paula named Van Nguyen. She explained that Van began working for Centerstone Health in the Membership Department three years earlier. He then received his Life & Health agent's license and transferred to Centerstone Health's in-house sales department in July of the following year. Paula recounted that both Van and Alex applied for sales positions, but only Van received the transfer. He terminated his employment with Centerstone Health in April of the next year to care for his father, who had suffered a heart attack. Van's departure from Centerstone Health came among a great deal of speculation from fellow sales employees concerning his incredible sales performance. Paula explained that Van was rumored to have been receiving "inappropriate sales referrals" from friends in his former department. This was one of those "aha!" moments; one additional and previously unknown piece of the puzzle was about to be put into place. During the time Van worked as an in-house sales agent, Alex was intercepting nonbrokered enrollment applications and sending them to Van—much like what was taking place at present between Alex and Parviz. I began to draw a mental timeline and noted that Parviz's first commission check was paid the month after Van terminated his employment. Paula told us that to her knowledge the rumors surrounding Van were never established to be true. Last, but certainly not least, Paula revealed that just three weeks earlier, Van was rehired by the original membership department where he worked prior to his transfer to in-house sales. This was the same department that Alex worked in. Randy and I wrapped up the interview and rushed to Alex's work site to share what we learned with Jim and Gary.

When we arrived 15 minutes later, Alex was still being interviewed. I took out my cell phone and sent Jim a text message indicating that I had important information about the previously unknown third player whose last name began with an "N." A few minutes later, Jim emerged from the interview room, and I briefed him on everything Randy and I learned from the interview with Paula. The information came at the right time because Jim stated that Alex was being a "punk" and that, so far, he had not admitted to any wrongdoing or even knowledge of who Parviz was. Jim, with his 30 years of FBI experience, then went back into the interview room. A few minutes later, Neil scurried out. He told me that when Jim mentioned Van, Alex said that he quit working for Centerstone Health five months prior. He omitted the fact that Van had just been rehired three weeks earlier and that they were both working in the same unit. I followed Neil while he looked up Van's employee file and confirmed that he was recently rehired. Neil then went to Van's cubicle and asked him to come to Neil's office and wait.

In the meantime, Neil headed back to the unit where Alex and Van worked and gathered their personal belongings. He returned to the interview room with Alex's briefcase and asked him if it contained any Centerstone Health documents. Alex confirmed that it did contain enrollment applications and premium checks from applicants, but said that he was allowed to take work home with him. This, however, was not the case. He should not have had possession of any of these documents. When Neil confiscated the papers, Alex stated that he might need an attorney. Neil told Alex that he was free to leave at any time, but advised him that as a Centerstone Health employee, it would be a good idea to finish the interview. That is when Alex admitted he knew Parviz and that he was introduced to him by Van. For the rest of the interview, Alex remained mostly tight-lipped, but he did state—still not admitting any wrongdoing—that he was a "venture capitalist" and that he gave Parviz $3,000 to start BN&S Insurance Agency. Neil immediately placed Alex on administrative leave, and he was escorted from the building by Centerstone Health security personnel.

Jim, Neil, and I then interviewed Van. The look on his face was of utter fright. He knew the real reason he was being questioned. After Jim and I introduced ourselves as SIU fraud investigators, Van asked if he could use the rest room, and Neil was kind enough to escort him there. When they returned, Jim and I cut to the chase. Ultimately, while Van admitted that he had been friends with Parviz since high school, he refused to admit to any past or current misconduct in relation to embezzlement of commission payments. Neil placed Van on administrative leave pending further investigation.

I was not surprised to learn that Alex and Van resigned the following day, prior to what would have been their official dismissal. I worked with the sales manager to develop a letter notifying Parviz of his termination as a Centerstone Health sales agent. In the letter, we also demanded the repayment of all commissions to date. In the meantime, Gary scheduled a meeting with the California Department of Insurance to report the trio and pursue revocation of their licensure. When they decided to dismiss the case as "too difficult to prove," Jim contacted the local district attorney's office, which also declined the case because it had bigger fish to fry. Last, I entered a summary of the case into an online intelligence-sharing system developed by LexisNexis in partnership with the National Health Care Anti-Fraud Association (NHCAA). This electronic database allows corporate members of the NHCAA, such as Centerstone Health, as well as a variety of law enforcement agencies, to search for fraud schemes, trends, and perpetrators.

LESSONS LEARNED

When I logged in to my computer the following Monday morning, I came across something quite ironic. Just days before Alex resigned, the general manager of his business unit awarded him with the prestigious honor of employee of the quarter. His picture was posted on the Centerstone Health intranet homepage, and there was an article about how crucial he was to the company's success. For this honor, Alex was given a $1,000 bonus. Gary and I joked that we needed to create an SIU Wall of Shame in our office and post Alex's picture, along with photos of Van, Parviz, and fraudsters from previous investigations. We were shocked that Alex was so highly regarded among his peers and management. It must have been even more shocking to the general manager who, after he learned of the embezzlement, had to send notification letters to the 250 individuals and families whose personal information was compromised in the process.

In yet another ironic event, I received a call from the Membership Department director the month following Alex's resignation and learned that he had been hired by one of Centerstone Health's competitors. SIU investigators regularly share information with those at competing companies. I advised one of my investigative contacts at Alex's new company to read my entry in the online intelligence-sharing system. Alex had been hired as a manager for another company and was earning a significantly higher salary than he had been at Centerstone Health. In addition, Alex had hired his friend and fellow fraudster, Van. My investigative contact opened a case on Alex and Van, but she ultimately was unable to have them terminated because they were not dishonest on their job applications. Alex and Van were smart enough to terminate their employment with Centerstone Health before they were officially fired. That way, when asked by a potential new employer whether they had ever been fired, they could honestly answer no.

The most important lesson I learned is that I have little control over the decisions as far as prosecution is concerned. My investigation may have been professionally executed, but there is no guarantee law enforcement will be interested in taking the case. It was not easy to swallow the fact that Alex had moved on to greener pastures with a new company. It also was upsetting that Parviz never responded to our demand letter for repayment of the $13,072. However, I have a personal sense of satisfaction that I was able to stop this commission embezzlement relatively early. If it were not for Mr. Strickland, an astute new policy holder, the fraud could have continued for a very long time. This fact demonstrates the importance of the consumer in detecting fraud. Using a statistical technique called simple linear regression, I projected that Parviz would have received $204,342 over the next 12 months had the scheme gone on.

RECOMMENDATIONS TO PREVENT FUTURE OCCURRENCES

Physical Safeguards

The fact that the mail room was left unlocked after business hours was a major concern. This policy needed to be changed. Enrollment applications contain Protected Health Information (PHI) under the Health Insurance Portability and Accountability Act (HIPAA). Specific HIPAA provisions require health care insurers to control physical access of PHI against inappropriate acquisition.

Technical Safeguards

There was a serious internal control issue with the imaging system used by Alex's department. The password was set to be the same as the user ID, so any employee had the ability to log on to the imaging system of another. If anyone did this, the system's audit log would not accurately reflect who was processing enrollment applications. The obvious recommendation is to require legitimate passwords.

Processing of Nonbrokered Applications

Nonbrokered enrollment applications are good business for Centerstone Health because no commissions are paid. I recommended that nonbrokered applications be assigned a dummy broker number, such as 99999, before the application is scanned into the imaging system. That way, it will be clear that the insurance applicant did not use an agent.

Segregation of Duties

Alex was a jack of all trades. He was cross-trained in every facet of his department's operations, and this enabled him to perpetrate this scheme. For example, the reason he knew the imaging system's vulnerabilities was because he was the membership department liaison with IT. As the unit lead, Alex also was the person to contact whenever there was an operations problem that needed to be resolved. His responsibilities were simply too vast.

David A. Schneider, CFE, is an investigative analyst in the SIU of a leading health care insurer. He is responsible for fraud detection and investigation through data mining and statistical analysis. Mr. Schneider has uncovered massive fraud schemes, including those perpetrated by organized crime rings. He enjoys spending time with his beautiful wife and newborn daughter.

CHAPTER 35

One Bad Turn Deserves Another

FORREST BOWMAN JR. AND CHARLES F. G. KUYK III

Robert Anthony Walker was striking in appearance and demeanor. At six feet seven inches tall, he was athletic, highly intelligent, and possessed a charming personality. He attended a small liberal arts college in mid-America on a basketball scholarship and graduated with honors. The most significant facet of his personality was not so readily apparent, nor did he specifically disclose it: He was a sociopath.

As an undergraduate, he served a paid internship as an aide to a member of the state legislature. Robert went on to attend the state law school, from which he graduated in the top third of his class. He and his wife, a CPA with a major accounting firm, had one child. They had just moved from a neighboring state when he applied for a position as the chief benefits officer of the Public Employees Pension Fund. On his résumé, he stated that that he was previously employed as counsel and manager of the Corporate Benefits Department of a highly regarded medical devices manufacturer.

The Public Employees Pension Fund was created by the legislature to administer investments and pay benefits to employees of the state and its political subdivisions after specified years of service. The fund is managed by a five-member board of trustees appointed to staggered terms by the governor. The statute sets the qualifications of the five members, no more than three of whom may be of the same political party. The board, with the approval of the governor, appoints an executive director, who is in charge of the day-to-day administration. The board and the executive director also administer several other retirement and death benefits for public employees. The primary fund consists of contributions from governmental employers, as well as an annuity savings account paid for by member contributions.

When Robert applied for employment as the chief benefits officer, the fund had 150,000 active accounts, over 50,000 benefit recipients, and managed assets in excess of $9 billion. As is often the case with quasi-governmental agencies with tight operating budgets, the fund had a long history of significant understaffing and underfunding. It had just recently added an internal audit function, staffed with one employee. To keep operations running and to minimize expenses, the fund made extensive use of temporary employees for whom no background checks were required. The fund's business processes had been repeatedly criticized in audits by reputable public accounting firms and by the state audit agency.

GOVERNOR, WE HAVE A PROBLEM

The hometown newspaper in the capital city ran an article in which it listed the names, positions, and annual salaries of a number of state employees, including the recently hired Robert Walker. The next day the statehouse reporter received an anonymous call suggesting she explore the records of the federal court in a large city in an adjoining state. After following that lead, the reporter called the governor's press liaison to ask if he was aware that Robert had been convicted of federal bank fraud involving the use of stolen identification. That same evening, I (one of the coauthors of this study) received a call from counsel at the governor's office asking if he could come in the next morning to discuss an urgent matter. As an attorney with more than 40 years of criminal defense and civil litigation experience, I knew it was serious.

The governor ordered an investigation to explore how the fund went about hiring Robert. He also asked that it include the organization and supervision of an investigative audit to determine what vulnerabilities existed at the fund and to what extent any members' identities had been exploited. Within hours of the disclosure of Robert's record, a criminal investigation was opened by the U.S. Attorney. The agencies involved included the United States Secret Service, the Special Investigations Division of the State Police, and the Criminal Investigation Division of the Internal Revenue Service, all working as a team. I also retained the services of a seasoned forensic accounting practice of a large firm. This engagement was led by the other coauthor of this study, a forensic accountant (with certified fraud examiner and certified public accountant credentials) with extensive investigative experience.

In the meantime, the initial investigation into the circumstances of hiring Robert commenced. The new position of chief benefits officer was created as part of a broader plan to bring in new management to improve the operations of the fund. This was to respond to numerous complaints about the timeliness of processing applications and paying benefits.

Robert was one of 36 applicants for the position. His initial application was by e-mail, with his résumé attached. He stated that he had managed a department in his previous job and was responsible for benefit administration for 4,000 employees worldwide. Robert also claimed that he was a key member of a team that handled the "$100 million plus retirement portfolio" of the company.

At some point before his final interview, he submitted copies of his merit wage review forms spanning over two years, the most recent of which was just over six months old. It contained glowing appraisals of his performance. He sent a letter describing his work with his employer's profit-sharing plan, family health plan trust, and the group task force. In addition, Robert listed four top executives of his employer. His boss knew he intended to leave, his reason being concern about his status in a then-anticipated sale of the company.

After the final interview, the executive director of the fund told a staff attorney to contact Robert's references. A list of inquiries were prepared, which the attorney used in telephone interviews with the three of the executives he was able to contact. One question was "If Mr. Walker leaves your organization and later would like to come back, would you employ him if you had an opening?" The first interviewee answered, "Yes." The other two said that there was a policy against rehiring. The final question was "Is there anything else you think we should know before we make our hiring decisions?" All three replied negatively to this question. Because of the positive responses, the executive director decided no further reference contacts were necessary.

Very early in the investigation, we contacted the attorney for Robert's previous employer, Megan Greeley. She disclosed that he had been terminated for misconduct several months previously. He had, at company expense, obtained business cards identifying himself as corporate counsel. Although he was a law school graduate, he had never been admitted to practice in any jurisdiction.

Megan also revealed that Robert had not told anyone of another prior criminal conviction at the time of his application. After he was hired, the record came to light. The company contacted his probation officer, who advised them that Robert had paid court-ordered restitution and was discharged from probation supervision, so they had forgiven him.

Megan said that Robert had told his references they would be called in connection to his application to the fund and that he had disclosed his prior criminal convictions.

As a part of the required background investigation, Robert was required to sign a waiver authorizing any person or entity having information about him concerning the following subjects, to release such information to the state police:

1. Any history of criminal law violations or arrests
2. Driving record
3. State tax matters
4. Credit history
5. Professional license and disciplinary matters

The form requires disclosure of the applicant's date of birth and Social Security number.

Six years earlier, Walker had been convicted of using the date of birth and Social Security number of a man who was about his age, who lived in the same state, and whose name was Anthony R. Walker, to obtain credit fraudulently. That was the same date of birth and Social Security number he used on the state police waiver form in conjunction with his application to gain employment with the fund.

The form was sent to the police, who processed it. The responses raised two questions. There was no record of him having paid state taxes or of his admission to practice law. When asked about this, Robert said that he paid taxes in the adjoining state, where he had gone to college and law school and had maintained his residence. The governor's administrative assistant concluded that since he would not be practicing law in the new job, the fact was irrelevant. However, since the state police report noted an address in the adjoining state from a credit report, she sent a request to check the first four items on the form. Of course, since the date of birth and Social Security number were not his own, the state police report was positive.

He soon thereafter was offered the position of chief benefits officer of the fund. After being hired, he simply used his true date of birth and Social Security number when he filled out his payroll forms.

In the course of our investigation, we learned that Walker had been fired from his legislative internship years before for fraudulently claiming time worked. He had also been accused of stealing a credit card from a fraternity brother while in college. The reason he was not admitted to the practice of law was due to the fact that he could not pass the character and fitness screening. This information came to light fortuitously from a person who was visiting from Robert's hometown, knew his background, saw the newspaper story, and contacted the investigators.

FRINGE BENEFITS

At the time we learned of Robert's history, he had been the chief benefits officer for the fund for 10 months, during which time he enjoyed unrestricted access to the entire database of members and had the ability to determine the amount and recipient of benefits.

Our investigation sought to answer two fundamental questions:

1. What could Walker do to steal assets or information?
2. What evidence could be found to determine whether he had availed himself of these opportunities?

In pursuing these inquiries, we wished to determine if he had established a method that would permit him to misdirect benefits in the future, perhaps remotely.

Our concerns about these matters were heightened when, two months into our investigation, the U.S. Attorney with whom we were working obtained a multicount indictment against Robert based on his fraud in obtaining employment with the fund, his misconduct while on pretrial release, and allegations that he had embezzled more than $500,000 from the medical devices manufacturer whose executives' recommendations had been instrumental in his employment.

We received a request to meet with law enforcement officers to discuss how best to proceed and to what extent we could properly share information. By this time we had learned that Kay Monroe, the internal auditor, and Donna Douglas, the chief information officer, on learning of Robert's suspension and potential termination, on their own initiative took quick action to prevent any further harm, including these steps:

Step 1.   They prevented Robert from logging on to the fund's network (and thus its benefits information system) either from the office or remotely. This disabled his network and e-mail accounts.

Step 2.   They deactivated his building pass to prevent further access after hours to the fund's buildings.

Step 3.   They changed the locks on his office doors and secured his computers and the contents of his desk.

Step 4. They reviewed activity for bank accounts and authorized signers to ensure that he had not accessed fund accounts.

Step 5. They notified appropriate information technology personnel within the fund and state administrator of his termination to ensure no access would be granted.

Step 6. They stopped his network logons and e-mail communications.

Step 7. They secured his computers and the computers of other fund employees with whom he had recently collaborated.

Step 8. They intercepted his telephone voice mails and changed the password to prevent further access.

Step 9. They backed up his home directory on the network where he stored electronic files, including e-mails.

Step 10. They promptly responded to law enforcement officials' requests for information.

Kay promptly began reviewing the electronic paper trail for evidence of significant activities. It did not take her long to discover that Robert had developed inappropriate relationships with at least two female employees, one of which breached an important internal control—ensuring the separation of duties in authorizing and executing transactions.

After those preliminary steps, we began the formal and structured phase of the forensic investigation. We identified these possible fraud schemes during team brainstorming sessions:

- Creating fictitious vendors and/or paying fictitious vendor invoices from the fund's operating account
- Falsifying personal expense reports or causing fictitious payments to be made
- Rerouting member retirement contributions to a personal bank account or address
- Rerouting member pension or annuity balances to a personal account or address or those held by accomplices, particularly in instances of suspended or dormant accounts
- Creating fictitious employees (members of the fund) at participating government agencies to accumulate and receive pension benefits
- Accessing confidential member information for purposes of identity theft for personal gain or to sell to others
- Rerouting payments of deceased members
- Colluding with other fund employees to circumvent controls in order to perpetrate any of these schemes

Through examination of purchasing procedures, we determined that the risk of fictitious vendor payments and falsifying expense reports was low. We also found that

Robert did not have control over incoming money, so the possibility of misappropriation was negligible.

Just as quickly, we learned that the risk of Robert accessing confidential member information for identity theft was very high. Law enforcement officers executing a search warrant of his home discovered a compact disk (CD) with spreadsheets of deceased fund members as well as CDs containing lists of members' names. While Robert often worked from home, he had no reason to have the data on a CD, since it could have been recorded elsewhere. The fund did not make CD burners available to employees, so Robert had probably improperly used a personal CD burner to save the data. Still, there were several other ways he could have exported the information without detection (e.g., by using a third-party e-mail account from a work computer to send an e-mail containing attached files or by saving member databases to a flash drive), so the use of the CD merely raised the concern that this might have been a way to readily market vast quantities of sensitive member data.

We determined that creating ghost employees at participating government agencies would have required collusion with specific staff members at one or more of those agencies. This would also involve funding the accounts and posting the contribution, which was beyond his authority. This and rerouting member pension benefits were determined to be low-level risks.

Initially, we concluded that the possibility of Robert having rerouted member annuities was low, but later we learned that an accounting anomaly had created a population of accounts that were vulnerable. There were also several dormant and suspended accounts in danger, such as those related to deceased members.

An important aspect of the investigation was the study of the fund's member database system, the State Retirement Benefits System (SRBS). This investigation was performed to gain an understanding of the nature and extent of information processed and maintained by the fund regarding retirement and annuity savings accounts. It would explain how fraudulent transactions might have been carried out and by whom. We found that while all of the Teacher's Retirement Benefit Fund (TRBF) membership data were *viewable* by authorized users at the fund, the ability to change or update data was restricted through user access codes to only authorized employees.

The position of chief benefits officer was, of course, of particular interest to the investigation. This role included the span of control that Robert exercised and the access rights to information he was granted. We reviewed organization charts and, through numerous interviews, gained insight into his job responsibilities and department interfaces. By virtue of his senior position and duties, he required complete entry to SRBS and the database of membership information. This unlimited access to sensitive data posed the greatest risk of financial loss and of harm to individual member's identities.

From our interviews with fund staff, it was apparent that they viewed Robert's performance during his nine-month tenure to be satisfactory, if not outstanding. We asked ourselves whether this was the reflection of the turnabout of a past felon, or simply good cover for fraud?

To determine if Robert had misappropriated assets or compromised the identity of members, we conducted four avenues of investigation. We:

1. Reviewed internal controls surrounding the payment of benefits to members to ascertain how money or personal identities might have been stolen

2. Created bit-level images of the hard drives from Robert's computer and those of other senior fund officials to identify irregular contents or transmissions of information

3. Ran queries against the fund's SRBS to identify misappropriations

4. Investigated anomalies from the above searches, including detailed examinations of transactions and affected member accounts

Among the many queries we conducted were these examples, most of which focused on the time period during which Robert was employed at the fund:

*   Member accounts on the CD discovered at Robert's home

*   All accounts with the same bank routing/direct deposit account number for members with different last names

*   Accounts with the same mailing addresses for members with different last names

*   Accounts with changed names or addresses

*   Recently deceased members based on third-party death audits

*   Multiple changes in direct deposit routing

*   Accounts with returned checks

*   A search for all accounts that Robert had personally modified or updated

*   Accounts in certain age ranges

*   A cross-comparison of the results from the above query of similar addresses against the data set of deceased members

Because of the broad access to membership information inherent in Robert's position as chief benefits officer, and because of the ease with which such data could be accessed without leaving a trail, we were unable to confirm conclusively if he had misappropriated member information.

However, another scheme came to light that led to our discovery of a fraud carried out by temporary fund employees. These people were ultimately convicted on various counts, including bank fraud, misusing the Social Security number of another person, and engaging in prohibited financial transactions. No background checks had been run on any of the perpetrators.

One of these temporary employees, Sharon Smith, working in the Benefits Department during Robert's tenure, was apprehended while applying for a credit card at a department store using a false identity. She had used the Social Security number, employer, and date of birth of another employee. While responding to the call, the local police discovered a number of 1099s associated with fund members and other paperwork on her person. While executing a search warrant at her home, they later found more documents. Sharon was stealing identities for purposes of gaining credit and embezzling money from fund members.

Using a number of the queries run previously for investigating Robert, we explored the methods and extent of fraud committed by Sharon. She had apparently been processing change-of-address notices for six members to redirect benefit checks to her own address or to those of relatives and friends. She was charged with three felonies—forgery, identity deception fraud, and attempted theft—and ultimately entered a guilty plea for one count of bank fraud and 13 counts of misusing Social Security numbers. She was sentenced to 50 months' incarceration to be followed by four years of supervised release.

But it didn't stop there. While reviewing fund records to assist in the prosecution of Sharon, we discovered a fraud scheme perpetrated by yet another temporary employee, Jerry Wilson, working with external accomplices to embezzle money from deceased members.

Among the discrepancies we found that led to Jerry's scam were missing entries in various logs for data entry into SRBS to support the issuance of checks to members' beneficiaries. Members' death certificates disclosed inconsistencies with the last names of the payees. Finally, we noted a pattern of addresses clustered in one area in the city. Payments made to these accounts were all fraudulently processed by Jerry for his accomplices. There were seven checks issued, totaling in excess of $200,000.

The discovery of the last scheme delayed completion of the investigation into Robert Walker. At first, we could not determine if the most recent embezzler (Jerry) was aided by any other fund employees, but he was assisted by several people who were not.

In order to preserve the confidentiality of this phase, several interviews essential to Robert's investigation were deferred. At least one of the outside conspirators had a criminal record suggesting a potential for violence. When the investigation reached the stage that it could be submitted for prosecution, early-morning raids were conducted simultaneously at five different locations by a large contingent of law enforcement officers from several state and federal agencies. Until immediately prior to the raids, not even the fund management was apprised.

A BENEFICIAL OUTCOME

A judgment was entered against Robert by the end of the year, wherein he pleaded guilty to 23 of the 24 counts, some founded on his theft from his former employer and the deposit in banks of the stolen money, one due to his fraudulent use of a Social Security number to gain employment with the fund, and another based on a scheme he executed while in pretrial detention in which he claimed a need to visit a physician, when he was actually meeting a lover. Robert was imprisoned for 120 months, required to undergo an alcohol treatment program, subjected to supervised release of five years following prison, and ordered to pay restitution of over $1.3 million.

Sharon Smith entered a guilty plea for one count of bank fraud and 13 counts of misusing social security numbers of members and others. She was sentenced 50 months' incarceration to be followed by four years of supervised release.

As for Jerry Wilson, he pleaded guilty to eight counts of bank fraud and engaging in prohibited financial transactions and was to be imprisoned for 57 months. In addition, he was subject to supervised release for five years and was held responsible for nearly $550,000 in restitution. Jerry's six accomplices pled guilty to various counts of bank fraud and misuse of another person's Social Security number with varying amounts of prison time and restitution.

LESSONS LEARNED

Many lessons were learned from the investigation, by both management and the investigative team.

- A victim organization should act swiftly but carefully when first learning of a potential organized fraud. This will help to ensure that damage is limited and evidence is preserved. If appropriate, report the matter to law enforcement.

- Whenever possible, collaborate with a variety of disciplines, including law enforcement, legal, internal audit, forensic accounting, and information technology staff so as to capitalize on the unique and complementary skills that each professional brings to the case. This also serves to keep all team members apprised of status and direction so as to avoid duplicative efforts and misdirection.

- Conduct brainstorming sessions early in the investigation to identify possible fraud schemes. These should focus on weak links in the internal controls. Since resources to investigate possible frauds will almost always be limited, rank the suspected fraud schemes based on magnitude of potential loss and ease of execution. Document findings carefully to avoid redundant performance of analyses.

- Employ modern computer forensic tools (such as bit-level hard drive imaging systems) to acquire data in a forensically sound manner and to identify possible channels used to misappropriate and remove sensitive data.

- Use existing information technology and internal auditing staff to the greatest extent possible because their in-depth knowledge of systems and internal control procedures (or lack thereof) will prove most useful during the investigation.

RECOMMENDATIONS TO PREVENT FUTURE OCCURRENCES

A number of these lessons were transformed into alterations of the fund's policies, procedures, and personnel. Among the changes we recommended to prevent future occurrences were these:

- Severely restrict reliance on temporary employees, and when they are used, require the same background checks obtained for full-time employees.

- Increase staffing levels to eliminate or minimize the incidence of multiple roles played by individual employees that impaired internal controls.

- Tighten computer security by restricting access to certain applications, functions, and databases. Though it still relies on Social Security numbers for member information, the fund now cloaks a member's number in screen displays and reports. Password protection procedures have been strengthened and access to network drives has been restricted.

- Perform extensive analysis of financial reporting procedures and reconstruction of accounting data to identify and correct anomalies that permitted the embezzlements.

- Enhance the internal control department.

- Conduct an independent computer security review.

- Institute a routine review of all employment records to confirm use of a consistent Social Security number for each person throughout the organization.

Finally, among the important by-products of the incident was enabling legislation by the General Assembly to satisfy a federal prerequisite for a request that the Department of Justice permit state agencies' access to the FBI's National Crime Information Center (NCIC) for employment background checks.

Forrest Bowman Jr. is an attorney in a private practice in Indiana. He has 44 years of experience in fraud investigations, both as a defense attorney and as counsel for business and governmental fraud victims.

Charles F.G. Kuyk III, CFE, CPA/ABV, CVA, is an executive with Crowe Chizek and Company, LLC, and member of the firm's forensic services practice based in Chicago. He has degrees from the USAF Academy, the University of Wyoming, and DePaul University, and teaches Introduction to Commercial Fraud and Prevention and a CFE exam prep course at Northwestern University's School of Continuing Education.

CHAPTER 36

Dialing For Dollars

IAN HENDERSON

D mitri Drobyshev was a work-hard, play-hard sort of guy. He didn't spend much time with his wife, Maria, in their run-down apartment in Moscow. In college, he had been successful, earning straight As in computer science. After graduation, Dmitri was hired in the information technology (IT) Department of Vozrozhdenie Bank. The work was routine and he was often bored. On many occasions, when he told Maria he was working, he was actually lounging in seedy bars, drinking with promiscuous women. This lifestyle made him an easy target for organized crime gangs.

Global Exports LLC specialized in selling western-branded goods. The company was thriving in the former Soviet Union and Eastern Europe, and had a large number of contacts who couldn't get enough of the latest fashion trends. Treasury operations were an important aspect of the day-to-day function of the business. There were about 20 locations operating in major towns throughout the region and 30 worldwide. All of these branches used the same IT systems for accounting and treasury.

A SUSPICIOUS TRANSFER

It began with a phone call early Tuesday morning after a long holiday weekend. Universal Bank, Global Exports' primary financial institution, was querying a number of electronic funds transfers (EFTs) that had been made just before midnight the previous Friday. The bank had put several transfers on hold because the overdraft limit on the trading account had been exceeded. Transfers for over $5 million had been initiated, but only $900,000 had actually been paid. This was the balance of the account at the time the request was made.

Josef Kovacs, the assistant manager of treasury operations for Global Export's Moscow office, couldn't figure it out. He had left at 3 p.m. the previous Friday and, as far as he knew, no overnight transfers were scheduled. He made a few calls and checked the transaction log. The last one was just after 5:30 p.m.; there was no record of these late-night transactions. Only the treasury computer was able to dial in to the bank's data center and initiate these EFT transfers, so he thought it must have been a simple mistake by the bank. His boss was on vacation, so he set up a conference call with a manager in London. He also patched in IT security and the local security chief. The consensus was that it was an error; it had to be. They were using a proprietary security system developed and installed by the bank. It used strong encryption and a third-party certification authority. According to their records, none of the key codes had been used, and the log showed that there hadn't even been any administrative traffic, let alone any EFT instructions transmitted.

A follow-up call established that the transfers had all been sent to a recently opened account at Baluchi Bank in Moscow, and the authentication IDs were those of two employees who had left over three months ago. This had the hallmarks of a fraud. Josef make some calls.

Gregor Titov, the local security chief, was a former KGB officer who had contacts with the police and other law enforcement agencies in Moscow. Within 30 minutes he was with the manager of the branch of Baluchi Bank that had received the fund transfers. The manager agreed to place an immediate freeze on the account.

Josef made the initial call to Global Exports Headquarters in Cincinnati, Ohio. The nine-hour time difference didn't help to move things along quickly. It was going to be a long day. Eventually, he managed reach Joe Wallburg, the Global treasury head, while he was still at home. Joe immediately recognized the risk to their other branches since the treasury system was not secure. He agreed to dispatch an IT security specialist and a senior fraud investigator to Moscow.

THE IMAGE BECOMES CLEARER

The security specialist and the investigator had to stop in London for a few hours en route to Moscow, and I was invited to meet them. My firm specializes in the analysis of digital evidence, and in order to reduce the friction between the Universal Bank and its customer, Joe Wallburg asked if I would examine the electronic evidence and prepare a report with the relevant facts. I arranged for the hard drive from the treasury computer to be sent to me in London.

Joe explained that the immediate objective was to establish if the fraud was caused by a flaw in the treasury system itself and whether continuing to use the same system in other branches was a significant security risk.

Next I was to recover as much of the external data concerning the unauthorized EFT transactions as possible. These included telephone and security access logs from the office building where the treasury operations were located. One of the most useful logs recorded the history of all EFT data connections between the bank and its customer, based on user IDs. It didn't show the details, just the fact that a connection had occurred. This was analyzed and the relevant transactions plotted as a time-series chart.

The normal authorized EFT instructions fell within a narrow time period between about 8:00 a.m. and 5:30 p.m. on workdays, while the fraud had been performed outside of these hours. The building access logs showed that no one was inside at the time the funds were transferred. Also, the data indicated that no calls had been made to the bank data center from company telephones outside of regular office hours. We were dealing with some form of remote access, which explained why there were no records of the transactions. It seemed that the fraudster had cloned the EFT computer and set up an exact copy away from the office. It was possible that this had been an inside job since no one else had direct access to the necessary codes and security software.

Unfortunately, the bank's telephone system did not record the subscriber ID of incoming calls, and no call-back security system was in operation. The transfer instructions could have been made from anywhere in the world. A more detailed analysis of the communication logs showed that after-hours calls had taken place every Friday night for many months. Now I had a time period to examine. This fraud wasn't just a one-off attempt; it had been going on for months.

Around this time the treasury manager, who had been away, returned from holiday. As a precautionary measure, he was interviewed by the head office team. After convincing them that he was not a suspect, he provided an important clue that would eventually lead to the arrest of one of the fraudsters. For some time, the Treasury Department had received IT support from a locally recruited subcontractor, Dmitri Drobyshev. They had been impressed with his diligence and his willingness to work late. He had recently facilitated the move of the EFT computer to a new location. In order to do this, he had been provided with some test key codes in order to ensure the system was working properly. That he had all of the necessary tools to commit the fraud aroused suspicions, so Dmitri was subjected to a probing interview. He appeared to have a watertight alibi, but the security team was still convinced that he had something to do with the transfer. He certainly had a motive, an opportunity, and the required technical skills. Plus, his employment exactly matched the time period covered by the suspicious activity in the communication logs. It was decided to monitor his activities.

In the meantime, the hard drive from the treasury computer had arrived in London. I began my examination. It was important to ensure that any evidence found on the hard drive would be admissible in subsequent legal proceedings, civil or criminal. I followed the procedures set out in the "Association of Chief Police Officers Good Practice Guide for Computer Based Evidence," which indicates that no action should be taken that will change the data on a computer or other media that will be used in evidence; that we must ensure a detailed audit trail of all actions be recorded; and that these principles and any relevant laws are complied with at all times. I took a forensic image of the hard drive using special software and carried out a detailed examination of that information.

This procedure ensured that integrity of the evidence was preserved while allowing all of the data to be inspected, including passwords saved in temporary files or in unallocated areas of the hard drive. This enabled me to determine how the EFT program operated and revealed the ease with which the fraudsters were able to set up an exact copy of the EFT computer outside of the office.

Before long we were under pressure to reactivate the computer system. Since it was increasingly looking as if this were an inside job, all other branches were authorized to start using the EFT system again. But this time we had an updated set of security procedures.

My analysis was generating some interesting information. The software had been installed by Universal Bank nine months earlier, and a copy of the files and instructions had been left on the computer. Also, on at least five occasions, backup software had been used to take a copy of the entire EFT directory, including user IDs and encryption keys. The dates and times of this activity again coincided with times that Dmitri had access.

I could see from a number of spreadsheets that the computer was not being used just for EFT transactions. Despite not being connected to the local network, it was often used for word processing tasks with documents being transferred to disks. A number of documents had been left on the computer by the external auditors. Some of these were routine debtor verification letters, but one confidential document—not password protected—contained details of all of the company's bank accounts, including balances of authorizing signatories together with the varying levels of authority. This could have facilitated the fraud as it provided vital information not held on the EFT system. It was clear that the department policy, stating that this machine was to be used only for EFT transfers, had been breached many times.

A keyword search across the entire hard drive found that a "Bad Password" error message had been generated on over 5,000 occasions in the previous six months. Examination of one of the internal error logs showed that the time between password attempts was so short—just a few hundredths of a second—this could be explained only by some form of automated password hacking application. Once again, the time and dates of this activity were linked to Dmitri's work schedule.

My tentative conclusions at this stage were that although some attempts had been made to overcome the security of the EFT system on the computer located in treasury operations, this hard drive probably had been copied and the unauthorized access had been made outside of the company's premises. It seemed that Dmitri had facilitated this fraud even though he probably was not operating the computer when it was carried out. I wondered if he was linked to an organized crime gang in some way.

Meanwhile, the security team in Moscow examined videotapes and checked phone records, but this did not generate any new clues. Dmitri had been placed under 24-hour watch and his employment record was examined in detail. The surveillance showed that he was drinking heavily. Most of his time away from work was spent in a run-down bar with a number of girls who were happy to let him pay for drinks and possibly other favors. He seemed to have large amounts of cash readily available.

His previous employer at Vozrozhdenie Bank spoke very highly of him and said he was surprised when Dmitri said he was leaving to work for Global Exports. At Vozrozhdenie, he had been scheduled to receive a substantial year-end bonus, so something about his job change seemed strange. His pay as a contractor at Global Exports was about the same as what he received from his previous firm, so his resignation didn't make sense.

A background check on Dmitri did not find any secret bank accounts, and there was no sign of extravagant spending other than his activities at the local bar.

Gregor decided to revisit the Baluchi Bank to see if it had any more information. The manager there realized that he had failed to make proper inquiries about the person who had opened the bank account that received the EFT transfer. This was against policy, and he cooperated with Gregor's request for further information. Unfortunately, the documentation used to open the account was false and belonged to someone who had died the previous year. It had been opened with a zero balance two months before the fraud, and no other transactions had occurred. The only contact details were a pay-as-you-go mobile phone, which was disconnected. The bank manager provided Gregor with copies of the documents.

An Arrest Is Made

At this stage, it seemed that further progress could be made only by law enforcement authorities. Gregor persuaded the local economic crime police to take on the case. Most of the hard work had already been done.

The Moscow police arrested Dmitri. A search of his flat failed to find much in the way of incriminating evidence. They did recover a mobile phone—and many of the calls could be linked to the mobile number given by the mystery account holder at Baluchi Bank. Finally, Dmitri confessed to being involved with the fraud.

He said he was approached by a criminal gang who had discovered that he was cheating on his wife. They told him that they would reveal his indiscretions unless he did as they said. Although he did receive a few small payments, his main role was to facilitate the fraud and to act on the instructions of the gang, which had specifically targeted Global Exports LLC. When Dmitri was first approached, he was working in the IT Department of Vozrozhdenie Bank. They forced him to apply for a temporary job with Global Exports in order to carry out the scam.

Dmitri did not provide a usable description of any of the gang members. It was clear that he was terrified of them. But his explanation of the fraud matched the electronic evidence. He was charged with a number of criminal offenses. Dmitri admitted taking copies of the EFT program and passing it on to the gang, together with the test keys that he had been entrusted with.

Although the gang members were never found, all of the funds were recovered and the method of attack was identified. The computer used to dial into the Universal Bank to commit the fraud was never discovered. Dmitri was sentenced to three years in prison.

Lessons Learned

Global Exports learned many lessons as the result of this fraud. The company now ensures that all contract staff members are properly vetted and supervised. The actions of contractors are to be monitored closely to ensure that security breaches do not occur. Segregating duties is also important. No one employee should have all of the access necessary to commit a fraud. Activities and other logs must be constantly monitored. Additionally, there is now a contingency plan in place to freeze and protect relevant evidence in case of a future problem. Had these procedures been in operation, either the fraud would have been prevented or the attempts to compromise security would have been detected at a much earlier stage.

RECOMMENDATIONS TO PREVENT FUTURE OCCURRENCES

Based on the lessons learned during this investigation, Global Exports completely overhauled its security operations and incident response procedures. It also provided training for staff in the treasury, audit, and security functions.

In addition, these procedures have been implemented:

- Treasury operations worldwide are now subject to unannounced spot checks to ensure compliance with security protocols.
- Token-based two-factor authentication is now used.
- Contracts have been arranged with local security, legal, and forensic services so that a rapid response will occur to any future incident.
- A central log-vault has been set up in Cincinnati so that key system logs can be managed centrally and protected from compromise.
- Written guidance concerning use of company computers has been issued to all contractors and third parties, including auditors.
- A "clear desk policy" has been introduced in sensitive areas.

Ian Henderson, CISA, FCA, is the chief executive officer of Advanced Forensics, London, United Kingdom. He specializes in providing forensic support to companies dealing with fraud investigations. Prior to this he was head of investigations at the UK's leading financial services regulator. Mr. Henderson has over 20 years of experience in investigating complex fraud cases.

CHAPTER 37

Wake-Up Call

MICHAEL SPEIGHT

teve Tranton was a contractor in the Communication Network call center. He knew the systems inside out and the differences between prepay and postpay customers. He knew their entitlements under contract in terms of replacement equipment, financial credits, and compensation. And he didn't care about the Communication Network's policies because he was aware of the significant gap in what he was procedurally permitted to do and what he could get away with.

Steve and his like-minded colleagues quickly turned this loophole into a business, costing the company around $1.7 million over a five-month period. Our problem was the extent and depth of dishonesty in the workforce with many employees earning between $10,000 and possibly up to $20,000 dollars for dabbling in fraud—ultimately escaping with only a slap on the wrist. The most serious punishment was termination, but in most cases, no action was taken at all.

I work for the Communication Network, a wireless mobile phone provider with corporate offices, switching centers, retail stores, thousands of base stations nationwide, and over 10,000 direct employees and 8 million customers. We offer the cheapest mobile phone service available.

The industry is fiercely competitive. We deal with a complex billing environment, with multiple call plans that calculate roll-over minutes, free minutes, and half-price minutes. We take hundreds of thousands of over-the-phone credit card payments; we take cash, checks and direct debits; we offer credits, refunds, and adjustments to account balances as retention tools, ever fearful of losing customers to the opposition. And we run large (often outsourced) call centers where empowerment underpins customer care, and fraud opportunities thrive and evolve. Employee turnover is a real problem.

All these factors combine to make my job challenging. As a specialist in communications fraud control, I consistently have to balance identifying and reducing the impact of subscriber fraud, organized international call-selling, premium rate service fraud, call-back operations, voice-over Internet frauds, and a host of other technical issues too long to list— and all while not upsetting sales by standing on the intake pipe for new customers and the potential for revenue.

PAYING FOR SERVICE

Mobile telephone companies have postpay customers and prepay customers. Postpay customers are those who subscribe to the network, use the service, and receive a bill for their calls: They pay "postevent." Prepay customers are those who buy an off-the-shelf product from a nonspecialist communications outlet and purchase minutes through a voucher or by making an over-the-phone credit card recharge payment; they must pay before they can make calls.

Postpay customers are credit-checked and then provisioned into the billing system with a limit, based on their credit history, and only then are they regarded as customers. Prepay customers, however, may be anonymous. They require little servicing and are therefore cheaper to maintain, which makes them attractive from a business perspective. However, we also need postpay clients because they spend more money and generate more revenue. Prepay customers are regarded as "money in the bank," but Steve and a few people like him knew a way of ensuring that money didn't always reach the tills.

While statutes in many countries require that even prepay customers fill in a name and address form, this is largely window dressing. Nothing adverse happens to a customer who signs up as Mickey Mouse of 2 Upper Tree, Someplace Else, 12345. The details may be loaded into the billing system, but we already have the cash. What could go wrong?

Postpay customers are often with the company for the long haul. We want to give them excellent service and support. Should their account be incorrect, we bend over backward to correct it. If their phone is faulty, we'll give them a replacement or at least offer a credit. Prepay customers, however, are entitled to none of the above.

Steve's fraud was discovered by chance, but the proof was obtained through a detailed examination the system that records customer beefs, including the type of complaint and the mode of resolution.

Bear in mind that when the idea of prepaid phones was launched, it was seen as a way of controlling the increasing levels of uncollected revenue (or bad debt). Much of this was caused by subscription fraud, where a person signs up for a service using a false or stolen identity and has no intention of paying. So students, migrant workers, and low-income families—those who had difficulty obtaining an acceptable credit score—were the specific targets for such prepay services.

Unlike the marketers, accountants, business analysts, and chief financial officers, those of us in the industry who understood fraud figured this panacea for reducing bad debt was likely to be a Trojan horse. While these folks were patting themselves on the back over an inspired piece of product development, fraud managers were busy working out the loopholes and weaknesses.

Unfortunately, people like Steve were a step ahead of the game. Prepaid phones were an overnight success. Millions of people utilized the service, and by the time we had told the industry of the risks and translated them into controls, the first signs of scams were surfacing. The collective problem faced by fraud managers worldwide was convincing senior management teams of the potential for financial damage through prepay services and the speed at which it could spread.

A CALL FOR COMPLAINT

We had millions of anonymous customers making incredibly high volumes of low-level financial transactions. And we didn't seem to care about their ability to pay with real money because we apparently had it up front—credit card fraud notwithstanding, but that's an entirely different story. Daily revenue from prepay services was measured in telephone number–size figures. Sales were continuing to display strong growth with no sign of abatement. Employees were increasingly encouraged to use their imagination to retain any customer who was considering leaving our service to join the competition.

Then, one day in February, a customer complained that the minutes he had paid for with cash were not applied to his account. Although initially skeptical, the customer service adviser complied with the caller's demand to speak to a manager. His call was escalated to Susan, one of 50 team leaders. She listened to the caller's story and was confused by his complaint, but promised to investigate and get back to him before the end of the day. She applied an immediate $20 credit to his account so that he could go about his day making calls as necessary. Susan brought the case straight to my desk.

In the telephone world, there are few hard and fast rules about what appears to be a fraud and what doesn't because there are so many variants. Any communications network adding upward of 500 customers a day will undoubtedly have a fair share of fraudulent applications. But that's not the end of the story. There are many other frauds in the customer domain, such as surfing frauds, dial-through frauds, hacking, interconnect frauds, credit card frauds, equipment frauds, call-back frauds, Voice-over-IP (VoIP) frauds—I could go on. The real trick is identifying subscribers before they acquire the service. Unfortunately, many applications get through and end up being chased by the Collections Department. We are not good at separating fraud from debt because it looks the same. Usually after 90 days such customers are transferred to the bad debt category. This is true today, even though there are probably in excess of 30 indicators for subscription fraud.

The case Susan brought to me was an anonymous prepay account, so there were no subscriber details held on record. The only fraud indicators involved payment type and method, phone usage, the equipment, and the sales outlet that sold the prepay package. Susan also had a home telephone number on which she could contact the customer once we had completed our research. This in itself is rare; fraudsters tend not to provide them, and if they do, the numbers turn out to be incorrect.

During our fraud awareness presentations, Susan had come to understand the crucial number three. One fraud indicator alone is insufficient cause for concern. Two gives rise to suspicion; three signifies a strong likelihood that fraud has occurred. Susan had identified these indicators:

1. The complaint was about a payment.

2. The customer was adamant that he had paid $50 cash to a person for his calls, "just like everyone else does"—which points to occupational fraud.

3. We had no field agents taking money from customers in exchange for prepay minutes.

Postpay customers with any grievance have the right and are encouraged to complain— that way, we can demonstrate our outstanding customer service. Typical grievances were:

•   I didn't make some of the calls that have appeared on my bill.

•   I'm not paying for all these premium rate calls to sex lines because I wouldn't make calls to such numbers . . ."*but madam, do you have a teenager in your house?*"

•   Your coverage in my area is terrible.

•   My calls keep dropping out.

•   I've not received important voice mails and I'm losing business; I want compensation.

•   The phone itself isn't up to par; you're selling faulty products.

Customer service agents (CSAs) were usually authorized to deliver small-value benefits to such claimants once a script had been completed—a script that was designed to verify the caller as genuine and to weed out all but the cleverest deceivers. Typically, CSAs could issue a $20 credit for a range of complaints; over that amount would require a team leader's approval. This would have been an effective audit control, unless the team leader was involved in the scam.

Steve discovered that he had the same ability to issue credits and refunds on prepay accounts he had on postpaid accounts. And more important, nobody seemed to notice. Working through customer complaints meant delving into CSA practice, and Susan was invaluable in explaining what was acceptable and what wasn't. The customer's complaint ran something like this:

"I was in the bar as I usually am on Thursday nights, and paid $50 in cash to one of your salespeople, and I haven't received my usual $100 call credit."

The glaring problem was that we didn't have any facility where you could pay $50 to get $100 in value. Nor did any official sales staff take cash from customers. Legitimate methods of recharging a prepay account include:

•   Buying a voucher from a phone store

•   Purchasing a voucher from a retail outlet, supermarket, gas station, or corner store

•   Calling customer services and making a credit card payment

•   Using a registered online mechanism such as a bank account to transfer money electronically

Susan called the customer, and he agreed to come in and explain. The two of us interviewed him, and he painted a picture involving a public place where every night you could approach a man—allegedly one of the Communication Network sales representatives. If you gave him $50 cash and your mobile telephone number, the next day you would receive double the value you had paid him in call credits. This customer had been using the service for several weeks. The bar was busy every night he was there. Susan and I realized that if many people were using this service, then the potential for loss would be significant. On top of that, the customer said that he didn't always hand his cash to the same salesperson.

I had previously used the service of commercial mystery shoppers. So that night, our mystery shopper went to the bar. The next day, he reported that indeed he had received double the value of calls he had paid for. On a walk-through of our offices, our mystery shopper independently identified the CSA whom he had paid. He also pointed out several other CSAs on the same team whom he had seen with the salesperson, apparently colluding to recruit new customers in the bar.

At once, we formed an ad hoc investigation team made up of my senior investigator, Susan, some of her trusted peers, some network engineers, and information technology (IT) managers. We told them the scenario at hand. This provided further insight into the potential extent of the fraud, which helped drive home the urgency for those managers who had critical roles to play—ones who could supply reports or analyze data to detect unusual patterns that might imply fraud or out-of-the ordinary transactions.

With call center resource levels running at over 2,500 CSAs and 250 teams across four sites nationwide, you can bet there were plenty of refunds, adjustments, and credits being issued to angry or unhappy customers—it's a virtually constant state of operation. Our task now was to delve into the billing system using the account of the customer who started the investigation—and Steve's login identity as our jumping-off point.

The problems identified just kept growing. We had to quickly convene in mini-workshops to ensure we kept track of our findings. We first looked at prepay customers with credits of $100. Steve's list was growing, but, alarmingly, so were those of another dozen CSAs and one or two team leaders. Reviewing similarities between the perpetrator logon activities highlighted unusually high volumes of lower-value transactions, primarily $40 credits. It appears the $20 bill was the preferred currency for customers purchasing call credits in a bar at night. One link led to another, but the clincher was the one that led to a note that read "customer having major problem with his phone and has sent it back to us. Issued $200 credit and customer will buy friend's phone." The CSA responsible was particularly stupid for writing such an elaborate and unbelievable note on a prepay account—especially when phones are never part of the service deal. He was also the catalyst for report scripting. We identified thousands of larger-value credits issued for handset-related issues on prepay accounts. Our analysis confirmed these facts:

- Fraud was taking place internally in the prepay environment involving cash for credit.
- Over 100 employees had been discovered through their user IDs as having offered false credits of $50 or over. (We didn't look at the sub-$50 transactions because there were too many.)

- Between five and ten perpetrators were employed in finance (credit and debt management) rather than customer services.

- There appeared to be two distinct groups of fraudsters: The first were what we considered would be normally honest CSAs offering a single low value to a friend or family member. The second group appeared organized, operating illegitimate businesses.

- The fraud was not restricted to any one call center.

- Ex-employee user IDs and log-in passwords were being used to perpetrate and conceal fraud.

- Most fraudsters tried to cover their tracks by incorporating a written explanation on the account, such as: *Customer has bought a voucher that did not work—credited value of voucher $50.*

- The business was losing the full value of the fraud perpetrated; that is, the cash paid to the fraudsters was not being passed on to the business, plus the entire credited value was being used but not paid for. For example, the fraudster would collect $50, but we lost $100 worth of calls.

- The fraud loss was estimated at over $1 million and had been running for at least months.

- Around 20 of the worst, regular and repeat offenders were still working for the business, some on a part-time basis.

- Between 80 and 100 occasional offenders (granting illegal credits of $50 to $100) were still working for the company.

Caught in the Act

After considering the type of fraud and the widespread nature of the abuse, we concluded that preventive action was vital. A management decision was made to implement shock tactics. We already knew the serious perpetrators, about 20 of them. At each site we posted signs on the doors that read "FRAUD INVESTIGATION." At every call center the suspect CSAs were invited in for interview. Those who admitted their activities were fired immediately, provided they revealed all they knew about the fraud. Most signed an agreement to reimburse the business for the losses incurred. It was rather unorthodox, certainly unsubtle, but it worked. All interviewees elected for this form of punitive action rather than being handed over to the police. We debated at length the benefits and downsides of prosecuting the individuals, but concluded that we couldn't pick and choose who warranted this form of action. It was all or nothing. Some were visibly devastated by their actions and the outcome. Others were idiots caught up in the activity, and it was clear that a criminal prosecution would have had a catastrophic impact on their lives and that of their families—this way they got a second chance. And the sheer number of dabblers was a daunting prospect for a telecommunications company. Hundreds of other people had credited relatives' accounts for $10—and we hadn't even looked at those. Our aim was simple and clear: prevent further cash-for-credit activity.

While the interviews were taking place, I arranged for broadcast e-mails to be sent to all 10,000 staff informing them of the nature of the scam and what we had done to identify the fraudsters and to detect further incidents using IT reports and analysis.

GOOD RESULT

Fraudulent activity of this nature ceased within 24 hours. By that point, we had implemented monitoring mechanisms. Occasional outbreaks emerged as some employees tested the water to see if we were watching—and we were. Some were new hot shots in the call center who thought they'd identified the perfect loophole and were obviously not listening at the company induction courses. They were all hauled in for interview and became casualties of our one-strike-and-you're-out policy. Dishonesty was ruthlessly discouraged. And each time a scam was discovered, a follow-up broadcast e-mail kept people informed.

LESSONS LEARNED

From this single event we were able to draw up considerable ways to improve operational activity.

- There were insufficient operational controls within the customer care and billing system.
- There was no audit program to review user activities.
- Management was blind to the concept of risk in the area of customer care.
- There was no formalized management accountability for actions of CSAs.
- The IT Department was underresourced to cope with the volume of user log-in maintenance (especially IDs to be reset or cancelled).
- Greater and more formalized fraud prevention training was required. It turned out that some CSAs were aware of the scam but didn't want to get involved, even to report their suspicions.
- Tapping into the honest employees was easier than anticipated and should have been done sooner. It was clear from workshops and e-mails that dishonesty among teams had a devastating impact.
- Fraud risk management reporting was highlighted as something that had, until this point, been repeatedly bumped down the IT Department's priority list.
- The fraud team (comprising 10 people) was underresourced and focused solely on customers and network usage. We needed to look within and monitor activities such as customer services, collections, credit management, and debt recovery—those that interacted directly with customers.

- The Human Resources Department realized that there was a risk that dishonest people would slip through their net. Robust processes were developed to manage staff in departments with high levels of employee attrition and turnover (such as the call centers).

- Trust and empowerment are fine, providing employees can be monitored.

RECOMMENDATIONS TO PREVENT FUTURE OCCURRENCES

From a fraud team perspective we knew risks existed, but didn't have the resources to take action. The recommendations included:

- Providing detailed knowledge of fraud risk to the areas of the business that had the ability to prevent and detect it

- Greater scope and support for the fraud team

- Implementing formal automated audit processes to examine complex transactions, including the ability to examine hundreds of thousands of text-based notes on customer accounts

- Ensuring senior management becomes accountable for fraud losses in their areas

- Supplementing the IT Department with a dedicated security resource to better manage user IDs and access to systems

- Increasing resources within the fraud team to allow for awareness training and the ability to interact with other departments (with the aim of gaining knowledge of risk)

- Ensuring the human resources department improved its processes to better manage staff in departments with high levels of employee turnover (such as the call centers)

- Reviewing the levels of empowerment for staff with customer interaction and putting controls in place to periodically monitor CSA activity

Michael Speight has 10 years of experience in Military Intelligence and 13 years in commercial security. He has held appointments such as deputy chairman of the GSMA Fraud Forum, director of CIFAS (UK), and is currently the sole accredited fraud trainer for ATFRA. An independent consultant, he works in the financial services and investments sector of the telecommunications, health care, logistics, and transport industries.

CHAPTER 38

The Dental Queen

KENNETH J. WILSON

Lisa Thurston was an attractive woman who lived with her husband, Mark, and their two teenage sons in a modest rental house in Salem, Oregon. Their boys were active in baseball and basketball. The Thurstons were very generous, often making monetary contributions to youth programs and purchasing uniforms and sporting equipment for their children's teams. The family was highly regarded in the community by parents and kids involved in sports.

Lisa and Mark were known to be extraordinarily charitable. They paid for the airfare of a young girl from China who was being adopted by a local family. Lisa funded cosmetic surgery for a friend. When dining out, the Thurstons always picked up the tab—even if it was several hundred dollars. Lisa's parents were invited on every family vacation—all expenses paid. It was not uncommon for a trip to cost over $20,000. But the Thurstons made a point to use their credit cards in every conceivable circumstance.

The one thing Lisa loved more than spending money on others was spending it on herself. She owned a BMW with a personalized license plate that read "ENVYUS." Lisa cared a great deal about her personal appearance. She had breast enhancement surgery, purchased designer clothing, and wore expensive jewelry.

But Lisa worked only three days a week for the Franklin/Johnson Dental Clinic. She received a monthly salary of just $2,200, in addition to full benefits. After being with the business for four years, she was awarded the responsibility of paying the clinic's bills. Lisa was protective of her job and never allowed anyone to open the mail or get involved with the payments. On two separate occasions, the clinic thought it was having cash-flow problems and asked Lisa to explain it. She claimed that the issue was simply the out-of-date computer software system. During a subsequent audit, the clinic's accountant noticed the expenses for supplies had increased substantially over prior years, and costs were considerably higher than those in the typical dental clinic. The accountant wrote a report identifying the areas of concern about the business's expenditures and delivered the report to Lisa, who assured the accountant that she had everything under control. She promised to tell the dentists about the report. Instead, Lisa took it home and never shared the contents with anyone.

Despite the cash-flow problems, Lisa was well liked and trusted by the owners and other employees of the clinic. In fact, she and her husband were personal friends with the dentists. Lisa frequently asked if anyone wanted her to pick something up for them when she went out for lunch. Most of the time, her coworkers would reimburse her with cash. She often made purchases on behalf of the clinic using her personal credit card, even though she had authority to use the clinic's credit cards. The business would reimburse her by check upon presentation of a receipt.

Neither Lisa nor Mark had any formal education beyond high school. Mark had worked as a fireman and emergency medical technician (EMT) for 11 years until he was terminated for dishonest behavior. He received a lump-sum payment from his retirement fund from the city that amounted to approximately $165,000. Following his termination from the fire department, Mark started his own business, Immediate Response Services, an EMT company that provided first-aid training.

Mark's venture got off to a slow start. For the first three years, he averaged less than $16,000 annually. Most of his business came from other dental clinics in the community, perhaps because he had provided first-aid training to the Franklin/Johnson Dental Clinics' employees first. Since both of the dentists were so well known, it was easy to use them as a reference with other offices. The typical class would last two hours and would consist of six to ten employees. Mark charged $40 per person for the first-aid training. He never promoted his business aggressively. Most of the time, he was too busy with youth sports, golfing, or traveling.

When anyone asked the Thurstons how they could afford to be so generous or travel so often, they had many excuses: Mark's business was successful; Mark worked a lot of overtime; Lisa worked a lot of overtime; or they had made good investments with Mark's retirement money from the fire department.

The Franklin/Johnson Dental Clinic was family owned and had been around for many years. The owners were well known and respected in the community and in the dental profession. Both partners were active, participating in many civic organizations. The clinic employed 15 part-time and full-time staff. Apart from being family run, the dentists prided themselves with being family oriented. Most of their patients had been coming to them for many years, and all of their employees had worked there for a long time.

WALK THE (CREDIT) LINE

One summer, the owners of the Franklin/Johnson Dental Clinic happened to review their business credit card statements online. They had repeatedly asked Lisa to bring the information from home so they could be examine them, but she always had excuses. Finally, Dr. Franklin and Dr. Johnson realized they could access the data themselves over the Internet. Upon examination, they noticed that all of their credit cards and the lines of credit were at their maximum. When they confronted Lisa, she admitted she had been stealing money over the past five years and was using the business credit cards and lines of credit to pay vendors and keep the checking account balanced. All in all, she said she had stolen

$800,000, which she promised to repay if the clinic did not go to the police. Lisa signed over to the dentists two Jet-Skis, a water ski boat with trailer, a Suburban SUV, the BMW, a Rolex watch, and diamond jewelry as a good faith gesture of repaying the money she had stolen. The clinic declined to accept the BMW because she still owed more money on the auto loan than the vehicle was worth. She also provided some business records she had been keeping at her house. Lisa apologized profusely and assured them she would pay them back for everything. But after a preliminary audit was conducted by the clinic, the dentists discovered that the amount of the theft was going to be much higher than $800,000.

Dr. Franklin and Dr. Johnson realized they should contact the police department. Lisa was promptly terminated. One of the dentists accompanied her to her residence to take possession of all business records belonging to the clinic. This gave the police sufficient information to start a criminal investigation and to obtain search warrants and subpoenas for other documents belonging to the Thurstons.

SINKING OUR TEETH IN

The Salem Police Department assigned the investigation to Detective Peter Lawrence. He had been employed by the department for six years. Though young, he already had a wealth of experience investigating major crimes. It was the largest fraud the Salem Police Department had ever dealt with. The first thing Detective Lawrence did was to examine the records provided to him by the clinic. Dr. Franklin and Dr. Johnson had a verbal confession from Lisa Thurston, stating that she had embezzled $800,000 over five years. She told them she had committed the fraud by forging one dentist's signature to the checks that she used to pay her personal credit card charges. She said she had her reasons.

The clinic once had a golfing retreat for employees and spouses, and Mark wanted to participate. When he realized he didn't have any vacation time left with the fire department, he called his supervisor claiming his son was in a serious accident and he was at the hospital. When the truth came out, Mark's supervisor confronted him. Mark continued to lie about his whereabouts until he was fired. Lisa rationalized that the clinic was partly responsible for her husband's termination, perhaps because the dentists refused to lie for him. She believed that stealing the money made up for his lost salary.

"It was easy to justify committing the thefts because Mark had been fired from the fire department when he attended a clinic retreat," she had said.

Detective Lawrence now needed to collect the evidence. He started by obtaining a search warrant for the Thurstons' residence. What he found in the home was proof of an extravagant lifestyle. The garage was so filled with personal items that there was no room to park a car. Every room was full of new clothes, electronics, sports equipment, and collectibles. Financial documents were found throughout the house, showing the expenditure of substantial sums of money to support their lifestyle. Each item was photographed and collected as evidence. Detective Lawrence knew that when the investigation was over, what he found would be provided to the prosecutor, who in turn would be required to furnish to a defense attorney.

Information gathered from the search warrant provided the basis to obtain subpoenas for the records from three credit card companies that included four separate accounts. Once Detective Lawrence received the information, he discovered the accounts were not in the name of Lisa or Mark, as he expected, but in the name of Lisa's mother, Lynn Sanders. Lisa and Mark were shown as authorized signers. The mailing address for each of the statements was listed as the Thurstons' home address, not her parents'. Of the four credit cards, only one was in Mark's name. The other three had four authorized users for each, including Mark, Lisa, and both of her parents, Lynn and Lonnie Sanders. Each application used the personal and financial information of Lynn and Lonnie since they both were employed and owned their own home. Lisa and Mark, on the other hand, had very poor credit history with multiple collections and late payments. They also did not own their residence. The card applications were signed in the name of Lynn Sanders, although it appeared to Detective Lawrence the handwriting was likely that of Lisa Thurston.

On the day of the search warrant, Lisa was arrested and booked at the county jail to await a bail hearing. A prominent sign by the phones in the jail stated "All phone calls may be recorded." Detective Lawrence knew that Lisa's calls to her family members might provide leads about where some of the stolen money was located, as well as other incriminating information. When he reviewed the recording, he found that most of the calls were to her husband and her parents. Lisa told Mark whom to contact to raise her bail money, though it took three weeks to post. She also instructed him to hide evidence and assets from the police, and that her parents would need to refinance their house to raise money for her criminal defense. According to the recorded conversation, her strategy was to drag out the criminal prosecution for as long as she could before entering a guilty plea. Finally, she laughed, joking that the "boys will get a kick out of their mommy serving time."

Due to the apparent involvement of Lisa's parents, who frequently accompanied the Thurstons on expensive vacations and used credit cards for which they never made payments, Detective Lawrence also served a search warrant on the Sanders' home. He said it appeared that they had been expecting him—obviously a large document destruction party had taken place. The shredding machine was still set up and very full, and the fireplace had recently been used to burn a lot of documents. Still, the search warrant produced some items of interest.

Once Detective Lawrence felt he had sufficient information assembled, he filed a case report with the county prosecutor, John Williams. John was a seasoned prosecutor specifically assigned to the prosecutor's white-collar crime unit. He knew it would be necessary to hire an outside expert to assemble the financial information and to "follow the money."

I received a phone call from John, with whom I had previously worked in the prosecutor's office on a large drug and money-laundering case.

"How would you like to work on the largest embezzlement case ever to come through Marion County?" he asked. The more John talked, the more intrigued I became.

I agreed to a meeting the next day and left his office with three large boxes full of documents.

As a certified fraud examiner, my task was to assemble the evidence into notebooks, establish how much money was stolen and how it was spent, and, last, determine if there was any "cash hoard" from which the clinic might make some recovery. I laid out my plan to John and told him that the first thing I would do was to place a unique identification number on each document, called a Bates stamp. I typically use clear labels with sequential numbers printed on them so as to not obscure any information. I worked with all of the Thurstons' personal and business bank statements and copies of deposits and checks, the monthly statements for the various credit cards, copies of all the forged checks, and the items seized during the search warrants from the Thurstons' and Sanders's residences. In addition, the clinic provided copies of the business records Lisa had altered to conceal her embezzlement for over six years. In total, I examined over 3,800 pages. I then set out to enter all of it into an Excel spreadsheet. The spreadsheet was set up to capture as much information as possible. From it I would be able to answer the important questions John had identified.

Fighting Tooth and Nail

Two weeks after Lisa was arrested, the police took custody of her husband, Mark. He was charged with conspiracy to commit theft and money laundering. Lisa's parents were never arrested. My analysis provided the prosecutor with all of the answers he was looking for. I determined that the Thurstons and the Sanders had spent over $2.1 million over a six-and-a-half-year period. Of this amount, $1.9 million was from embezzled funds from the Franklin/Johnson Dental Clinic. There were at least 332 forged checks. Although the investigation was only able to go back six and a half years due to the absence of necessary bank records, the thefts appeared to have started prior to that time.

Apart from general living expenses and for Mark's business, the Thurstons took lavish trips to Hawaii, Canada, Florida, California, and Utah with their children and Lisa's parents. They swam with dolphins, skied, played golf, and flew first class. They spent over $32,784 on Starbucks coffee, $43,239 for jewelry, $185,218 for hotels, another $74,563 for travel-related expenses, $106,659 for sporting goods and events, $26,316 on pet food and veterinarians, and $82,429 for cash advances. Over $344,182 was charged on the credit cards as purchases made for Mark's business. It was very difficult to imagine what these charges could have been, since he instructed first-aid classes, and the highest year of legitimate income Mark ever had was $16,474.

These charges were done with the cards in Lisa's and her parents' names. An analysis of Mark's business account showed he laundered between $20,308 and $118,210 of embezzled money through his company account each year. In addition, the couple also spent over $868,352 from their personal checking account. Much of this money came from transfers from Mark's business account and the cash advances from the credit cards. Some of it also came from wages, retirement funds, and other sources.

After I completed my analysis and provided Prosecutor John Williams with my report, he amended the criminal complaint against Lisa and Mark and added a long list of additional charges. To date, Lisa and Mark have been successful in receiving one continuance after another for the start of their criminal trial, just as Lisa told Mark she planned to do in her jailhouse phone conversation.

Although the Thurstons continued to deny that Mark had any knowledge of the embezzled money, it simply is not reasonable to believe he could have helped spend all of the money without having some idea of where it came from. In addition, without his business, it would have been more difficult to launder much of the money.

From the original $1.9 million of embezzled funds, the only items the victims recovered were the few assets the Thurstons' turned over to them the day Lisa confessed and was fired. There was no investment property, no hidden bank accounts, and no cash in a safe deposit box or shoebox under the bed. The money was gone—all gone.

LESSONS LEARNED

The owners of the Franklin/Johnson Dental Clinic first reacted by blaming themselves for trusting Lisa and for not having any controls in place to identify and prevent fraud. They told me that employees had long suspected that Lisa might be embezzling money to support her lavish lifestyle. But any time someone suggested that possibility, Dr. Franklin and Dr. Johnson refused to believe that Lisa would be dishonest. After all, she was "part of the family." Now the owners have taken over control of the bank records. They take turns reconciling the statements. They have made an arrangement with their bank to receive copies of the cancelled checks, along with the monthly statements, mailed directly to their homes.

One of the problems I encountered as a certified fraud examiner was not being able to retrieve all of the necessary financial records from the banks due to the length of time that had passed; banks typically do not maintain microfilm copies beyond six or seven years. I also had to depend on the documents retrieved by the police detective during his initial investigation. Once the criminal case was filed with the prosecutor, the detective thought his job was done and went on to other cases. After I was hired, I asked the detective to obtain additional documents from the bank. Had the request been made a year earlier, the odds of having those records available would have increased substantially.

After the initial investigation, it seemed clear that Lisa intended to plead guilty. Because of that, some of the investigative effort lagged at the beginning of the case, which left more work to be done after Lisa and Mark decided to push for a trial. When cases extend over several years, time is crucial if all of the financial records are to be recovered.

The Bates numbering of all the documents was critical in our ability to easily retrieve them. The Excel spreadsheet enabled us to analyze all of the financial information. If the prosecutor needed to know how much money was spent on a specific vacation, we could tell him.

RECOMMENDATIONS TO PREVENT FUTURE OCCURRENCES

Investigate Red Flags

"Red flags" of fraud in this case were ignored. The Dental Clinic was aware that Lisa and Mark were taking extravagant vacations because Lisa shared the photographs and bragged about her trips. They also knew there were cash flow problems, yet believed Lisa when she blamed it on the computer system or other employees. Even when some of her coworkers voiced their concerns about Lisa, the owners denied it and did not look into the possibility that she was stealing from them. Businesses need to pay attention to these indicators and conduct an investigation, regardless of their close personal relationships to the employee.

Segregate Duties to Ensure Checks, Bills, and Vendors Are Legitimate

Lisa had sole responsibility for accounts payable and bank reconciliation. These duties must be separated, and owners must be closely involved in reviewing bank statements and cancelled checks. Businesses need to know their vendors. If an unknown name appears on a check or invoice, it must be investigated for legitimacy. It is equally important, when reviewing cancelled checks, to look at the back of a check. How was it endorsed? Was it cashed or deposited? Was it deposited or stamped for deposit into the account of the payee? If a second endorsement appears, to whom does it belong? Some banks will charge an extra fee to return copies of cancelled checks with the bank statement. If the bank does not offer this service, consider finding one that does. Alternatively, use a check system that retains a copy of the original check. Examine the invoices from vendors. Do they look professional? Compare the address on the invoice against those of employees. Look for the same address showing up on invoices from different vendors. Pay special attention to post office box or private mail box addresses. A "Google" or reverse directory search on the Internet will often identify whether the address is associated with a business or individual.

Kenneth J. Wilson, CFE, is the owner of Wilson Investigative Services in Olympia, Washington. His firm provides fraud examination, private investigation, consulting, and expert witness services. Mr. Wilson is a graduate of the University of Puget Sound and has more than 33 years of experience in detecting and preventing white-collar crime.

CHAPTER 39

Shirley A. Little Wouldn't Hurt!

A.T. `CHIEF" SCHWYZER

How could it have happened? That's what the Department of Energy asked itself when a valued employee of a major contractor committed fraud. All the right controls were in place to prevent administrative system abuse. There was a strong belief that no employee would jeopardize his job, especially because everyone was required to obtain a security clearance. Management, particularly at the senior level, believed that the contractor's corporate values started with trust.

Ironically, the environment was set to prevent exactly what happened. One gap in operations allowed the fraudster to take advantage of the system. The decision to give all first-line management under a second-level manager concurrent signature authority opened a crack in the administrative system. The idea was to trust employees to do the right thing in order to reduce supervision in the modern world of administrative technology, thereby allowing more time for first-line management to focus on organizational tasks. This seemly minor relief of first-line management's time became a high-speed freeway for the perpetrator to commit fraud.

Shirley A. Little's management called her a model employee. She appeared to be the consummate professional: intelligent, productive, well dressed, and personable. She was granted a security clearance well within the normal time frame. Married with two kids, she lived in an upscale neighborhood and was involved in the community.

Shirley's career was extremely successful during her first 15 years. She entered the company as a secretary. Her evaluations showed the highest level of performance. Soon she progressed to the administrative assistant field and moved up the ranks quickly. During that time, she finished her business administration degree in the evenings. When she was promoted again, it was to the professional administrative staff level. As an administrative staff member, she became a highly trusted recruiter in the personnel group. She was given responsibility as the recruiting coordinator for a number of universities and professional institutions, initially in the Southwest, then expanding to schools all across the United States. Her duties grew beyond recruiting as her skills strengthened. Many special projects were directed her way, including coordinating relatively large career fairs. She was often called on to coordinate functions for management at all levels of the company. Everyone was surprised at how much Shirley was asked to do and how much she was able to handle. Managers in the Personnel Department were especially amazed.

Besides her formal duties, Shirley was known for her willingness to help others, whether it was extra typing, buying supplies on the way to work, or filling in at a moment's notice. Often Shirley would bring treats for the employees of her section, and she was the first to remember birthdays, usually planning an office party. She was the one who organized wedding and baby showers. Overall, she felt it was her duty to make everyone feel important.

This particular characteristic may have led her to commit fraud. Perhaps she felt unappreciated and unimportant. And Shirley desperately wanted to feel important. As she progressed up the corporate ladder from secretary to senior administrative staff, the accolades were neither as frequent nor as elaborate. What once resulted in praise had become expected. Shirley had to compensate for this lack of recognition.

The company she worked for was a large contractor to the U.S. Department of Energy (DOE). It was responsible for various DOE programs across a wide spectrum. The majority of the employees had technical backgrounds, and administrative policies and procedures were tailored to these employees. A major goal was to eliminate as many bureaucratic barriers as possible without compromising the company. To that end, several policies were introduced that were smart business practices but, when combined, provided opportunities for wrongdoing.

Three policies played the major roles in this fraud: concurrent signature authority, expense voucher receipts, and security clearances.

Concurrent signature authority had been granted to all first-line management in the 1960s. Senior management wanted first-line management to be actively involved in the technologies of the group they managed. That resulted in the expectation that first-line management would spend less than half of their time in administrative functions. To ease the administrative burden, especially when first-line management had to travel, employees could have their expense vouchers and other documents signed by a manager in a sister organization.

In the early 1990s, a rising star in administration became the manager of the corporate travel group. He had a reputation for providing upper management with simple solutions to administrative barriers. His solution to the large volume of paperwork associated with filing expense vouchers was to let the line groups maintain the original expense vouchers with all the receipts attached. Staff-level employees were given the opportunity to approve their own travel before a trip with the understanding that it would be approved by the management. The expense vouchers would then be signed and submitted electronically. What was once the duty of the line group's secretary became the responsibility of the traveler. This resulted in first-line management rarely physically verifying the receipts associated with an expense voucher. The employee was trusted to do the right thing.

DOE security clearances were required for all employees, regardless of the type of work being performed. Hazel O'Leary, secretary of the Department of Energy, instituted a lower security clearance level for DOE contractor employees who performed only unclassified duties. For all employees, there was a reinvestigation every five years. These clearances gave management confidence that the company's employees could be trusted to follow the rules of the administrative policies and procedures.

Over the Budget, Under the Radar

At the time of the discovery of the fraud, I was the manager of a special examination unit in the audit department. As is the case in many large companies, the audit department usually received a number of calls requesting special projects. We had set up a group to handle these calls. This group also worked closely with our corporate attorneys and the DOE Inspector General.

Ted Gould was the senior recruiter in the personnel group and was responsible for managing the travel budget. We had worked on a number of projects together and developed a good relationship. I often used his expertise in personnel when we had delicate needs in that area. During the discovery, we were working on a couple of projects together, so a call from him was routine. What he asked was not unusual, but his tone was extremely somber.

Ted and I met within an hour of the call. He had grown even more doleful. He brought a number of regular financial reports for us to review. His concern was that his budget was being significantly overspent, and management was considering disciplinary action against him. He requested that I determine if the charges to his budget were appropriate, who had charged them, and how could he get back on budget. I accepted the assignment as a special project, and we began our process of examining the records. I told Ted that I would take the lead and John Clay, the senior auditor, would assist me.

I asked John to obtain a complete run of all the charges to Ted's budget account for the current year to date and the past three years. He also agreed to set up an examination plan for the project, which would be expanded several times as we delved deeper into our study. First and foremost, we needed to determine if the detail charges to Ted's budget account showed any red flags.

By the next morning, John was back in my office with a simplified examination plan and the detail reports. The strategy was to review all the charges for the last three years plus the year to date, making sure that all payments were appropriate. We would go further only if we found anomalies. If this were the case, we would go both to Ted and his supervisor before we initiated a complete investigation.

John had downloaded the detail reports to a Microsoft Excel template we used for analysis. The data included labor, purchases, travel, supplies, and other charges. The labor and purchases were tracked to the employees and purchases orders. We found nothing suspicious in that field. Travel and supplies were all normal except for one inconsistency: Shirley A. Little was by far the most frequent traveler and bought the most supplies. She traveled over twice as often as the other recruiters, and she had vouchered almost three times as much as the others. We did not look at the other charges at this time. This discovery was reason enough to initiate a full examination.

John and I asked for a meeting with Ted and his manager, Andrea Wollerau. Andrea was a newly promoted supervisor and was very eager to meet with us. We asked them to come to our offices so as not to alarm anyone or raise unneeded fears in their group. We met that afternoon.

The four of us convened in a small conference room in the audit department. John and I went over our initial analysis. Ted and Andrea had quite different takes on what we said. Andrea immediately began to defend Shirley by stating how hard she worked and how much of a contribution she made. Andrea ended with the now-famous words: "Shirley A. Little wouldn't hurt the company." Ted kept a low profile during the meeting until the end, when he finally stated that we found exactly what he had feared all along. Shirley A. Little was abusing the system and her privilege of authorizing her own travel. At the end of the meeting, we decided to move forward with a complete examination of Shirley's activities, including her purchases, labor, travel, supplies, and other charges. I would contact our attorneys for their input. And I agreed to brief Andrea's boss, Roger Blake.

The attorneys contacted the DOE Inspector General's office. They did not want to lead the examination, thereby eliminating the privileges, but they did want to be kept informed.

The meeting with Roger was very similar to the one with Ted and Andrea. Roger was initially shocked that there might be anything wrong with Shirley's activities. He had relied on her often for his special project needs, and she always exceeded his expectations. He agreed that it was a bit unusual for one recruiter to travel as much as Shirley and thought a full examination would be useful in order to obtain an explanation. But he ended his defense of Shirley with the same familiar words: "Shirley A. Little wouldn't hurt the company."

At the end of the week, John and I met to formalize our plan. As we chatted about our process, I could tell that he had similar thoughts about the situation: Nobody really believed that Shirley had done anything wrong except for Ted and the two of us. It was going to be an uphill struggle to convince management of her guilt if we found wrongdoing. Our plan had to be complete, the examination flawless, and the reporting extraordinarily convincing.

CONFESSIONS OF A FRAUDSTER

John and I met the following Monday afternoon in our little conference room. We blocked out the whole afternoon to draft our examination plan. First, we identified all of the documents we wanted to inspect and where they were located. These materials included time records, purchases requests, travel vouchers and receipts, supply vouchers, and the source documents of the other charges. It was important to analyze the activities of all the recruiters. We suspected that we would have to interview at least five of them, plus Shirley. Our plan was to formally interview Ted, Andrea, the previous manager, Roger, and the group's secretary, Ginger Parker, whom we expected had the travel vouchers and associated receipts. We planned on calling the placement offices at several of the schools where Shirley coordinated recruiting activities.

John and I could see where the system was weak and how someone might circumvent it. But it was hard for us to be specific beyond Ted's inadequately supported conviction that Shirley was abusing the system in authorizing more travel that was necessary. When we briefed our boss, Walter Holland, he thought that we were out on a limb. He agreed that we might have a red flag, but he was concerned that we would be accused of conducting a witch hunt. His sentiment matched ours: The plan had to be complete, the examination flawless, and the reporting extraordinarily convincing. At that point, both John and I were not convinced that even our management was going to be supportive.

I had a gut feeling that we should start with an analysis of travel. We again went to Microsoft Excel to observe Shirley's travel vouchers. We looked at dates, time of travel, location of travel, and voucher amounts. It jumped off the page: She had 54 vouchers to El Paso, Texas, and St. George, Utah, in a three-year period. The amounts were virtually the same total cost for each of the locations. We dug deeper to find that the amounts for rental cars, hotels, meals, and other expenses were identical. The only differences were the dates and the signatures of approval. Was it a red flag or a coincidence?

When we compared her labor charges to the travel dates, they did not correlate. She would charge her labor to working in our Albuquerque home base while she was on travel. One manager would approve her labor charges while another manager would approve her travel voucher.

As the red flag grew larger, we came to a decision. John believed that we should continue with a focus on Shirley's travel. But I wanted to expand our examination to all of her activities. We compromised by finishing her travel first, then looking at her other charges. We did not get very far before there was a surprise in the investigation.

Wednesday morning I received a call from Andrea. She had set up a meeting with the two of us, along with Shirley. Somehow Shirley had come to suspect that her activities were being examined. Perhaps Andrea's own investigation tipped her off.

At 1:00 that afternoon, the three of us met in Andrea's office. I had barely sat down when Shirley began sobbing uncontrollably. After being consoled by Andrea, Shirley took out her checkbook and wrote a check for approximately $12,000. She handed the check to me, stating that it was an effort to repay the company for the false travel vouchers she had submitted over the last three plus years. I thanked her for her offer but requested that she hold the check until we determined the exact amount. Andrea was so awestruck that she was silent for the rest of the meeting.

And then Shirley began to talk. She rambled over a number of topics, often stopping to sob. She wanted us to know that she was not a thief and begged us not to think poorly of her, reminding us that she was otherwise a model employee. Shirley promised to repay all that she took and ended with her own spin of those famous words: "I thought surely a little wouldn't hurt the company." It was plain to me throughout her confession that she had no idea how much she had spent. She signed a short confession written in her own handwriting, stating that she had submitted and been reimbursed for false travel vouchers. This was all that she admitted to, but I had feeling that there was more we needed to discover.

The personnel group added another challenge to our examination: Shirley was terminated immediately after our three-hour meeting. Now we had to deal with a terminated employee who was probably going to hire a lawyer. She did not want to tell her family, so she kept up a charade of working for almost another week. Her front was uncovered when her husband asked her why she did not receive a check. During that week, we focused only on her activities and charging record, and she was very cooperative.

By the end of the day I had added three more auditors to our team of two. Each was directed to analyze the detail of an area of Shirley's activities. John and I continued with the travel analysis. The other three examined labor charges, purchases and supplies, and other charges. We also obtained a complete copy of her personnel file. When we finished our review, we put all the spreadsheets on the wall and compared everything we could. We needed to interview Shirley again because there were some things we just could not understand.

When we asked her to come in again, she agreed. I took the tack that we were trying to make sure that she was given credit for the correct vouchers she had submitted. We asked to see her receipts for the trips she felt were legitimate, and she brought them in. She obviously felt that we were on her side and trying to mitigate what she had done. To her credit, she was very honest regarding her fraudulent activities during her two interviews. But as we peeled back the onion, her story became more pathetic and less believable.

THE DAMAGE

The goal of the examination was to analyze Shirley's activities to determine how much she had fraudulently received. The final total included time card fraud, purchase fraud, travel voucher fraud, supply fraud, and fraud in the other charges. While we were able to find appropriate charges in each area, the total of fraudulent activities was far greater than the $12,000 she tried to convince us. We grouped her activities into these categories: fraudulent trips, local travel and supplies, company credit card, other travel, purchases, labor, and other charges.

Fraudulent Trips

Shirley confessed that 38 of the 54 trips to El Paso, Texas, and St. George, Utah, were fraudulent. Some of the remaining 16 were questioned by management during the examination. She would submit the same voucher, sometimes on the same day, to a revolving set of managers in the same group. Many times she would attend meetings with management members at the same time she was supposedly traveling—and one of those managers would have approved the trip.

- *El Paso Trips.* Her El Paso trips were normally Tuesday through Thursday. Her approach was to stay home on Monday to pack and prepare the family for her absence. She would fly 40 minutes to El Paso around noon on Tuesday. She always upgraded her rental car to a luxury vehicle and her hotel to a suite. Tuesday night she would take someone from University of Texas at El Paso to a fancy restaurant. Rarely was the guest of any importance to recruiting efforts. Wednesday, she would drive to

Las Cruces, the home of New Mexico State University. She would stay at the Hilton, again upgrading her room. The receipts showed two adults in the hotel. She confessed that her son would be her guest for dinner and would spend the night in her hotel room; he was a student at NMSU. On Thursday, she would drive back to El Paso and fly home in the afternoon. She would spend Friday unpacking and tending to the family's needs.

*   *St. George Trips.* Shirley's trips to St. George, Utah, were similar to the El Paso trips regarding time frames. She would stay home on Monday preparing for the trip and stay home on Friday to take care of her family. Tuesday, she would fly to Las Vegas, because, according to her, it was a closer drive to St. George than from Salt Lake City. St. George is the home of Southern Utah University, where her daughter went to school. There was the usual rental car upgrade and the hotel upgrade to a suite or similar room. The receipts showed two adults in the room. When I asked who the other adult in the Las Vegas hotel was, I expected her to say it was her daughter. But her first words were "Don't tell my husband!"

She was actually having an affair with an employee of Southern Utah University. She confessed that often she did not go to St. George; rather, the two of them just enjoyed Las Vegas and its night life.

Local Travel and Supplies

Shirley lived approximately 10 miles north of the building in which she worked. We found a number of vouchers for local travel and supplies from the Office Depot within a mile of her house and on her route home. She would voucher mileage to and from the Office Depot when the receipt showed the purchases took place between 6:00 and 7:00 in the evening. During this time, she would be on her way home, and it was unnecessary to document mileage to be reimbursed due to the proximity of the store to her house. Also, the receipts showed items that were clearly available through the company's Just-in-Time benefit, allowing employees to order supplies that were delivered to the office. In fact, we found the same items that Shirley bought from Office Depot ordered through Just-in-Time on the same day listed on her receipt.

Company Credit Card

Shirley's company-issued credit card had a number of issues. Included on some of her travel vouchers were items that were clearly of a personal nature, such as makeup, underwear, hosiery, movies, and alcoholic drinks. All of these items are strictly prohibited for purchase on the company card. She would also charge her meals on the card and then inflate the meals on her travel vouchers to cover the cost of the personal items. She never admitted to this, insisting that she could not remember.

Other Travel

Shirley documented trips that were not considered necessary for her job. We reviewed all of her travel with Ted, Andrea, and Roger. There were two trips to conferences in Florida where other recruiters had been assigned. There were three trips to the parent company's recruiting office that were of no apparent value. She attended four expensive training classes at luxury locations that were deemed inappropriate. And one weekend trip to Phoenix occurred that she could not explain.

Purchases

We found a number of purchases for items that could not be located, mostly books and software. Shirley claimed that the books were recruiting texts that she gave to other recruiters. She could not remember to whom she gave any of the books, and none of the recruiters knew of them. She claimed the software did not work as she had hoped, and she deleted the programs on her machine and threw away the discs.

Labor

There was evidence that Shirley was not reporting her labor charges correctly. It appeared that she was trying to charge her time to the projects that she felt were most important to management. As her fraud became more complicated, her ability to charge her time faltered; she would charge a special project for the managers while being on travel with them. She confessed to finally losing complete control of her time, which she remedied by submitting random labor charges. And as stated, she stayed home before and after each trip and charged her labor as if she were at work. Our ability to re-create the proper charging of her time was severely hampered.

Other Charges

Shirley hosted three receptions that management rejected as appropriate after their second review. Also, two other lavish receptions were estimated as twice as expensive as necessary.

John and I ground out this estimated summary of the fraud:

Labor (loaded)		$26,000
Purchases Travel		5,500
	False vouchers	28,500
	False charges	17,500
	Local	1,000
Supplies		500
Other charges		5,000
Total estimate		$84,000

The report of our examination was passed through our legal department to the U.S. Attorney. During that process, our estimates were slightly reduced. Shirley A. Little never actually went to trial. We heard from a reliable source that a plea bargain resulted in five years of probation and some amount of restitution. Our attorneys would never confirm or deny this report due to the agreements embedded in the plea bargain.

Shirley's multifaceted fraud met the three corners of the fraud triangle: opportunity, rationalization, and pressure. There was plenty of opportunity to abuse the financial and travel administrative systems. She felt pressure to draw attention to herself by going above and beyond the call of duty, then to reward herself for her contribution with luxurious travel and extra money. The rationale was classic. In her words, "surely a little wouldn't hurt the company." She rationalized that she was only taking a few well-deserved dollars that she should have received in salary.

Lessons Learned

The personnel group learned an essential lesson: Management cannot shirk its responsibility. Rarely does anything replace physical observation, review, and examination by a human being. This is especially true when dealing with details. When the situation is exacerbated by the removal of internal controls, the barn door is swung open. Managers who are unable to perform their functions with due diligence either need to be retrained in their responsibilities or need to be asked to step down.

Senior management in personnel reluctantly learned that anyone within a group can go outside the lines, even if the person is highly rated and completely trusted. All employees must be subjected to the same set of controls, and management is responsible for ensuring it occurs. One result of the examination was an apology to Ted by management for blaming him for an overspent budget. Senior personnel accepted much of the blame for weakening the basic internal controls within the group.

John and I also learned about performing an examination. We must carefully review details and follow all the leads completely. First, we obtained a complete set of documentation, including personnel files and receipts. This significantly increased the possibility of a successful examination. Next, we reviewed all the data on each document, performing a simple "smell test" to sniff out aberrant documentation.

Finally, John and I learned that once people feel that they have beaten the system, their fraudulent activities will escalate. Shirley continued to commit fraud because she had not been caught in the act. Her rationalization was simple: "Surely a little wouldn't hurt."

Recommendations to Prevent
Future Occurrences

Based on our experience, the company has made many changes that I suggest as a program to reduce fraudulent activity.

Strengthen Requirements of Management and Employees

Human Resources has now changed their policy and strengthened the requirements of management in reviewing employee activities. Managers are asked to designate someone to take over when the first manager is out of the office.

Implement an Intense Process for Travel and Voucher Approval

All employees, especially recruiters, are now required to obtain at least an oral approval prior to travel, and that approval must be documented by the approving manager. Employees are required to have the receipts for all expense vouchers.

Surprise Reviews

The senior recruiter is required to review the recruiting budget with the manager each month. Periodically, the senior management conducts surprise reviews of the oversight activities.

In Case of Necessary Examination, Have Several Auditors Review Documentation

John and I instituted a process for all examinations to have at least two certified fraud examiners or auditors independently review all documentation. This provides us with a greater probability of recognizing all red flags.

In Closing

Every time we expand an examination, I am reminded of the perpetrator's rationalization in this story: "Surely a little wouldn't hurt." And every time management defends an employee in the face of strong evidence, I tell the story of "Shirley A. Little Wouldn't Hurt!"

A. T. "Chief" Schwyzer, CFE, MBA, is retired from Sandia National Laboratories, in Albuquerque, New Mexico, and is currently consulting in prevention, detection, and investigation of fraudulent activities. Mr. Schwyzer has both his MBA and BBA from the Anderson School of Business at the University of New Mexico and has over 35 years of experience in detecting, preventing, and investigating ethical violations.

CHAPTER 40

Just When You Thought It Was Safe

FRANK D. MORAN JR.

In high school, Ashley Becker was an attractive, popular girl with many friends. She certainly never had a problem finding dates, although she spent most of her time in the company of her on-and-off-again boyfriend, Ron Moore. The two met when his family moved to a home in Ashley's neighborhood during her sophomore year. Because they were the same age, they shared many classes. When high school ended, Ashley found herself spending time with Ron on a daily basis as most of their friends went off to college.

After graduation, Ashley worked a few low-paying, part-time, retail jobs while carrying a few credit hours at the local community college. Though it is not unusual for an 18-year-old to be unsure of her career path, Ashley felt particularly burdened by the fact that she had no direction. But that was all about to change.

Suddenly she found out that she was going to have Ron's baby. Faced with the daunting realization that she was going to be a mother, Ashley knew that she had to find a way to make a living—and fast. Ron and Ashley married just prior to the baby's birth, settling into the hectic world of young parents. Several months following the arrival of her first son, Ashley applied to Spring Hill Bank as a part-time teller. Ron had just taken a management trainee position with a local building supply company. Ashley knew that she was going to have to contribute to the financial security of her family, so she was relieved when she was hired at the bank.

Ashley found the job quite interesting and applied herself to all of the tasks required. The work environment was friendly and her position allowed her to interact with clients. Soon she was dealing with customers on a first-name basis, and her supervisor was receiving many accolades for her work and interpersonal skills. It wasn't long before Ashley was offered a full-time position.

Just as her job was progressing, so was her relationship with Ron and their new son. They found that being parents was an enjoyable and fulfilling experience, and they were finally starting to become somewhat financially independent.

Ashley's success at work continued. She learned her job well and was soon tasked with assisting new tellers to become proficient in their duties. Her outgoing personality and professional appearance caught the eye of management, and she was soon promoted to lead teller at her branch. This advancement brought more authority, responsibility, and income. Ashley Moore was on the road to success.

She and her husband were living comfortably as they raised their now four-year-old son. Ron's job also offered promotions and upward mobility. Ashley was being recognized in the company as someone to watch and learn from. Only one year after being crowned lead teller at the bank, Ashley was once again promoted. As a customer service representative (CSR), she would now have her own work area within the branch office and would be responsible for helping to grow deposits for the bank. Good news at work was coupled with good news at home; Ashley and Ron learned that they had a second child on the way. As a CSR, Ashley excelled in her position. Once again, her outgoing personality and professional demeanor were tools that helped her reach and even exceed her established goals. Life had blessed the couple with a silver lining.

CUTTING THE LOSSES

Spring Hill Bank of Mechanicsville, Maryland, was first chartered as a savings institution on March 30, 1868. Originally founded by a group of Quakers, the institution served the small agrarian community principally in savings and loans. After its first day of business, the bank held $383 on deposit. Within 10 years, its deposits grew to more than $100,000.

As the sleepy little town began to prosper, so did its bank. Reaching over 125 years of service, it experienced new growing pains. The realities of expansion and decentralization settled in. Staff growth, recruitment, employee turnover, fraud and robbery prevention, audits, regulation and oversight, and changing technology were all becoming daily management issues. In spite of these challenges, the bank continued to flourish through mergers and acquisitions.

Following my retirement after 28 years of service with the Maryland State Police, I was hired to replace the retiring director of corporate security at Spring Hill Bank. Upon my arrival, there were 32 branch offices in six Maryland counties. The bank had expanded its services to include commercial banking, retail banking and trust services, as well as owning a mortgage and insurance company. Total assets had grown to $2.7 billion. Clearly, the small-town community management concept had vanished. The current executives and directors at Spring Hill Bank wanted the organization to grow even more.

I found that the previous year's fraud losses were approaching $450,000. In my mind, this was a totally unacceptable figure. My predecessor, a quite capable person who had come to the bank after a successful career with the U.S. Secret Service, had fallen into the trap of paradigm paralysis. He became comfortable and complacent with managing his department based on a bank with only 10 branches. He had never moved forward and planned for the present-day challenges and changes to the company. I found, upon my arrival, a department and staff basically devoid of any current technology or fraud prevention skills and training. The department's database for case management was an archaic index card file. Employees were being hired without an FBI fingerprint check or other appropriate due diligence. It was no wonder that the bank had lost nearly a half million dollars to fraud the previous year.

Although I had faced many challenges throughout my law enforcement career, I knew that I had my work cut out for me. My mandate from the executives was clear: Reduce fraud, train staff, and bring the department back in line with current practices.

DISAPPEARING ACT

In October, with a little more than two years at Spring Hill Bank under my belt, I had begun to realize the benefits of the many goals I had set for overcoming the issues that plagued the Corporate Security Department in the past. Several key personnel changes had been made that allowed me to hire persons with the necessary skills to do the job properly.

I spent a lot of my time mending relationships with members from other departments. Many of the midlevel managers lacked confidence in the security operation in the face of rising losses. I knew that team building, gaining bank-wide support, and restoring faith in the security operation was the key to success. My boss, an executive vice president and general counsel for the bank, was always supportive and provided me with excellent guidance and advice as I maneuvered through the corporate mine field of egos and office politics. The chief operating officer and bank president seemed pleased with the positive changes that had taken place over the last 24 months, and, as long as I could convince them of the business need for a particular change, they were willing to support my request.

On October 27 I was in the process of reviewing the daily fraud prevention reports in my office when my telephone rang. The caller ID indicated that Larry Kay, the senior vice president of the Retail Administration Group, was on the other end of the line. Hardly a day went by that I did not speak or meet with Larry or other members of his staff. The Retail Administration Group ran the entire branch network for the bank. This was where I had focused the bulk of our fraud prevention, detection, and training resources—it continued to be where we suffered our heaviest losses.

After exchanging pleasantries, Larry told me that he had a problem at the bank's Dolefield branch. It seems that a client—a multilocation convenience store owner—was making a claim that $5,400 was missing from his Friday evening night drop deposit. To make matters worse, Larry informed me in a worried tone that it seemed that the branch manager at the Dolefield office had had a similar complaint from another business client two months ago. That client owned and operated a local fast food establishment. The investigation into that complaint, conducted by a member of my staff, had been closed for lack of evidence and a client who failed to cooperate.

After calming Larry down and asking some key questions to establish some basic facts, I hung up the phone and knew immediately that I had to get to the bottom of this issue quickly. Although $5,400 was missing and presumed stolen, a quick resolution would not only preserve our credibility but, more important, it would restore our client's faith in the bank.

Although the night drop in question was made on a Friday afternoon, the owner of the convenience store did not contact the Dolefield branch manager until the following

Monday. During this time period the store owner questioned his staff about the missing cash, thoroughly searched his store, and reviewed his security camera tapes in an effort to determine if his employees may have been involved in the theft. Finding no evidence to support this possibility, the business owner contacted his corporate loss prevention manager.

Following my telephone call with Larry Kay, I quickly accessed the department's case management system and searched for cases at the Dolefield office. In a matter of seconds, I was reviewing the file prepared by one of my investigators on the earlier allegation of the missing night drop deposit in August.

This investigator was someone that I had brought aboard at the bank during my first two years. He had a strong background in law enforcement and investigations, and I knew that his experience would be a plus for the department. Not only that, he had a great personality and an ability to get along with everyone. This personality trait also made him a great interviewer who could quickly put people at ease and, in the end, elicit a confession.

Upon reviewing the investigative notes from the August investigation at the Dolefield office, I was quick to see why the investigation was stymied and reached no conclusion: The fast food restaurant owner had not reported the loss for 30 days. The reason for the delay was that the deposit was not discovered missing by the company bookkeeper until the last days of July during their end-of-month finance summary. After speaking with the business owner, my investigator could never make contact with the store manager, as she had been transferred to another location. She was also the employee who allegedly made the deposit. Repeated telephone attempts to contact her went unanswered.

However, even though the client's employee was not cooperating, my investigator did go the Dolefield branch office and spoke with each employee who had been working the evening that the night deposit drop had allegedly been made. Based on the results of his interviews, he had some concerns about two of the branch employees. Unfortunately, without cooperation from the client or his employees, the case was eventually archived. Now, two months later, another allegation of the same nature and at the same branch office had surfaced.

WHERE CREDIT IS DUE

During the last couple of hours on Friday, after I had reviewed the notes from the previous case, I spent my time pulling the Dolefield branch employee personnel files. The staffing at the branch had remained unchanged in the last two months since the earlier investigation. There was the branch manager, Jennifer Heath; two customer service representatives, Sandy Woods and Ashley Moore; a financial consultant (FC), Tom Lilly; a teller supervisor, Beth Foreman; four daytime tellers; and two part-time drive-through tellers. The Dolefield branch, like the majority of our retail offices, had employees who worked closely together and seemed to enjoy each other. A friendly rivalry existed between bank branches as they compete to book deposits, loans, and other financial transactions. Being rated office of the month, branch of the quarter, or winning a branch-wide challenge to open the most deposit accounts in a year generates a spirit of competition that works to bring the employees together. After-hour dinners, office-wide pizza lunches, Christmas parties, and other light-hearted activities serve to develop a spirit of team building and friendship that often lasts for years.

The Dolefield branch was no exception. The majority of their staff had been together for quite a while. The manager, Jennifer, was an excellent coach who, through her leadership, had made it one of the best-performing offices in the bank. With the help of her CSRs, especially Ashley Moore, Dolefield had been transformed into a well-managed and creative office. The last thing Jennifer or her staff expected, the thing that was farthest from their minds, was about to be exposed.

My review of the branch employee personnel files that afternoon revealed nothing of significance outside of a few warnings for minor teller shortages and a reprimand to a part-time teller for being late in the past. I obtained current credit reports for the each of the staff members, as they are required to sign authorization for these checks as long as they are employed by the bank. An immediate red flag went up while reviewing these reports. It seemed that one of the branch employees' credit reports had changed dramatically during the past six months. She had an exorbitant number of revolving credit accounts, several of which were approaching the high end of her approved limit; two were delinquent. A recent new car loan appeared on the report with very high monthly payments, two of which were late. Other credit problems were detected that led me to believe that I already had one potential suspect: Ashley Moore.

On Monday, I bypassed going to my office and traveled directly to the Dolefield branch office. As my arrival was prior to the opening of the branch, I immediately met with the manager, Jennifer, and explained why I was there—she had been expecting me. With her assistance, I met in the conference room with all of the staff. I told them about the allegation. Most already had been made aware of the situation, as the branch manager had utilized them during her search for the missing funds. When told that I was going to interview each employee independently, Ashley Moore suddenly exclaimed, "I'm getting tired of being accused of stealing!" That was strike two.

Throughout the morning, I met with each staff member in private and through informal questioning learned as much as I could about their workmates, their personalities, their duties and responsibilities, and the inner workings of how the deposits were removed, recorded, and credited to client accounts. Although this activity is clearly spelled out in the bank's policies and procedures, it was important for me to hear of the process directly from those who performed it daily at the Dolefield office.

One of the most important aspects of handling cash at a financial institution is the concept of "dual control." Dual control ensures that no one person can enter certain areas of the bank without the assistance and presence of another employee who, in essence, acts as a witness. One such area that requires dual control is the branch night drop. Through my interviews, I heard firsthand that only four persons had access to that particular depository safe. Each of those individuals possessed only one-half of the safe combination. In order to open the safe, two employees with different parts of the combination would go into the night drop room. There the first employee would enter the first half of the combination and the second employee would enter the second half of the combination. Once the safe was opened, one employee would remove the contents. In the company of the second employee, the deposits would be taken behind the teller line and logged into the night drop log for processing. All of these duties were to be conducted under dual control.

THE CAMERA DOESN'T LIE

My investigation now took on a more focused approach. The night drop log for the date in question revealed that Ashley Moore, one of the CSRs at the branch, and Beth Foreman, the teller supervisor, had processed the night drop safe contents. During the initial interview, both employees denied any knowledge of or participation in this incident. Beth stated during her interview that she doubted that anyone at the branch was involved and felt that the client's own staff members were probably responsible for the theft. All four of the employees who possessed partial combinations to the night drop safe denied that they had anyone else's portion of the combination. If that statement was true, then this crime had to have been committed by two of our own workers.

Prior to my departure from the branch on Monday, I made each person who had a combination to the night drop safe fill out a statement analysis form. Statement analysis is a process of reviewing answers to specific questions. By reviewing and analyzing the use of personal pronouns and other subtle word usage within these responses, the reviewer is able to determine the veracity of the information provided. It is similar to a polygraph examination in written form. Through my training in this field, I wanted to see how these individuals answered the pertinent questions. I had no doubt that additional red flags would surface through this process.

Late in the afternoon on Monday, I began reviewing and scoring the four statements provided by the branch employees who possessed partial combinations to the night drop safe. Upon completion and based on the wording used in her answers, only one person gave me reason to be concerned: Ashley Moore. "Strike three!" I thought. I had only circumstantial evidence—her failing credit, her verbal statement, and now her written statement—but I knew I would need to obtain an admission when I confronted her during my next interview.

Banks use surveillance cameras to record the activities inside their institutions. Although there is no mandate to do so in the Bank Protection Act, their use is always helpful during robbery investigations, fraud investigations, and sometimes for internal investigations. Camera placement and field of view is most commonly focused on clients and nonclients alike. Therefore, teller cameras usually bypass the teller and record the customer. The same applies to the branch employees who open accounts and conduct other types of financial transactions. Our surveillance cameras are no different, with the exception that they are digital and color, and we retain the search and playback capabilities for six months. I hoped that I could retrieve an image of Ashley Moore with the night drop bag in question.

Since the missing deposit was made on a Friday afternoon, the probability was that the items in the safe were not removed or processed until Monday morning—the next business day. Branch employees will usually let night drop deposits sit over the weekend and then remove them from the safe on Monday for processing. In fact, that is what the Dolefield branch log indicated. However, a check of the alarm opening report indicated that Ashley disarmed it on Saturday morning, the day after the client made the deposit, at 8:13 a.m., 47 minutes prior to the opening time of 9:00 a.m.

A search of the Dolefield Branch digital cameras for the time period of 8:13 a.m. to 8:30 a.m. was conducted from various cameras within the branch. At 8:16 a.m., one of the cameras recorded Ashley walking past her desk and away from the night drop room with a night drop bag in her hand. There was no doubt now that Ashley, our six-year tenured employee with a bright future, not only had the full combination to the night drop safe, but she had also entered it and removed our client's missing deposit.

On Tuesday, I returned to the Dolefield office to reinterview her. Armed with this irrefutable evidence, it was only a matter of minutes before she made her confession. Later she also admitted to the earlier theft of the funds deposited in July by the fast food client. In total, Ashley Moore had stolen $7,900 over a two-month period.

THREE STRIKES AND YOU'RE OUT

During the final interview with Ashley, I concentrated on the details of her scheme. I needed to know the shortcomings in our security program that allowed this criminal activity to occur. Was she the sole person responsible? Had she confided in anyone else at the branch about her nefarious activity? Did her supervisor or even the branch manager do something by either commission or omission that allowed Ashley to perpetrate this crime? In my final interview with her, I needed to find the answers to all of these questions.

When she viewed the images from the branch security camera, Ashley knew her plot had been foiled.

"I'm so sorry," she uttered as she began to cry. "This is not like me. I really like working here."

The interview was not informal any longer, as I took control and made it clear that bank fraud was a serious felony.

"I can't go to jail. I have small children. Please don't send me to jail," she wailed.

Ashley Moore, the promising young businesswoman with a cheerful smile and bubbly personality, was overcome with grief, emotion, and—I think—a sense of relief.

In a written statement, she told all. Her debts were piling up from credit cards. Ron was unaware of this activity; she hid the bills from him. Even with her husband's paycheck, Ashley could not make ends meet. She developed her plot quite accidentally, thanks to the teller supervisor at the branch, Beth Foreman.

One evening while Beth and Ashley were opening the night drop vault, Beth verbalized the numbers to her half of the safe combination as she turned the dial. Ashley, hearing the

LESSONS LEARNED   **375**

other two numbers of the combination, could now have full access to the safe. At first, Ashley fought the urge to use her knowledge. She even considered telling the branch manager how she accidentally heard the numbers. But in the end, out of desperation, she decided to enter the night drop and take the cash.

In the end, in her mind, Ashley *had* to take the money. Paying down her credit cards was the only way to keep Ron from finding out about her spendthrift habits. As much as she liked her job at Spring Hill Bank, she loved her husband and her kids. She thought that her tenure with the bank and her excellent client relationship skills would deflect suspicion from her. Throughout our interview, Ashley Moore thought she was going to keep her job.

"I'll pay back the money. Send me to another branch; just let me keep my job," she begged. I believe she knew that that was not going to happen, but she had to try.

As it turns out, only part of the money she stole went to pay down her credit card. The rest bought her a personal shopping spree for clothes and shoes.

"I'm better than this; I'm ashamed of what I have done. My parents raised me to know better." Her remorse seemed sincere, but then again, she had been caught. What else could she say?

Ashley had acted alone on a plan born out of a coworker's lack of common sense. No one else at the branch knew what she was doing.

Ashley only got half of what she desired after our conversation ended. She was terminated immediately following our interview. She signed a restitution agreement that allowed the bank to offset her 401(k) fund for restitution. In return, she was not prosecuted. A suspicious activity report was filed with the Treasury Department, and she was eventually barred from working in the banking industry. However, her husband was not so forgiving. When he discovered the enormous debt created by his wife, coupled with her termination for theft, he left Ashley and took their children.

The teller supervisor, Beth, received a written reprimand and a transfer to another branch office at Spring Hill Bank. She never quite fit in at her new location and resigned within eight weeks of her transfer. When I questioned her about verbally articulating her half of the night drop safe combination, she told me, "That's the only way I can remember it, and besides, I trusted everyone here."

LESSONS LEARNED

Every investigation I have been involved with has led to lessons learned. Of course I always critique myself regarding how I conducted the inquiry, the steps I took, and the order I took them. Obviously, this goes directly to self-improvement for the next time. And there is always a next time.

The banking industry is one of the most heavily regulated businesses in the country. Individual banks must ensure that they comply with those regulations, or they will face a multitude of punitive actions up to and including the closing of the bank by federal regulators.

Bank security is much the same way. Each branch office must comply with literally hundreds of security policies and procedures on a daily basis. One of the most important policies is segregation of duties: dual control. Because these responsibilities rest on the shoulders of men and women who are hired principally to grow assets for the organization, they sometimes take a backseat to other revenue-producing activities. And because human nature is such that we all want to see the best in people, especially our coworkers, we sometimes bend or even overlook the rules in favor of promoting harmony and creating a positive work environment.

However, security professionals know that policies and procedures are in place to promote uniformity, responsibility, and accountability. I learned a long time ago that supervisors who overlook established policies and procedures in favor of creating a harmonious workplace suffer losses from fraud and theft more frequently. It is the principle role of security and fraud loss prevention professionals, as well as auditors, supervisors, and managers, to insure that the organization's rules are implemented and adhered to properly.

RECOMMENDATIONS TO PREVENT FUTURE OCCURRENCES

Branch Office Audits

The security department and the retail administration department now work closely together and conduct branch office audits. These audits review the practices of employees in an effort to determine whether they are following the bank's policies or not. We take the time to clearly explain the reasons for having the policies and the potential negative outcomes that could occur should they overlook them or elect not to comply.

Each branch is examined from top to bottom—everything from auditing teller cash drawers to examining their key control records. The point is not to catch someone who is not in compliance, but to explain why the policy was put into place, explain how to do it should they need assistance, and assist them in doing their job better. Following the audit, the branch is provided with a scorecard that lists their audit score. The branch manager, with assistance from his or her staff, must respond to the scorecard and articulate how the branch is going to improve and what steps will be taken to correct the listed deficiencies.

The goal is to show improvement in the audit scorecard and not have similar issues during the next security audit. The first audit develops a baseline for managers and supervisors. Deficient follow-ups have a direct impact on their evaluations. While some managers and supervisors were somewhat reluctant when the program began, our approach to the audits quickly put them at ease and allowed them to see that the program was all about personal development. Those who never gave this program the proper attention are either working in diminished roles at the bank or are working somewhere else.

Since the inception of the branch security audit program, the bank's incidences of internal issues have substantially diminished. Branch managers and key supervisors frequently call our office to ask questions and bring potentially suspicious activity to our attention. It is now everyone's intention not to repeat the mistakes of the past and to insure that all established security procedures are adhered to and documented.

Frank D. Moran Jr., CPP, is the senior vice president, director of corporate security, Risk Management Group, at a community bank in Maryland. He is a retired major from the Maryland State Police and a graduate of the FBI National Academy. Mr. Moran holds a bachelor's degree in sociology from the University of Maryland and a masters in criminology from the University of Baltimore.

41

How Many Ways Can I Defraud You?

DAVID CLEMENTS

Tony Hopkins came from a wealthy family. He had many advantages growing up: a large home, education from an exclusive Melbourne, Australia, private school, and well-connected friends. But he had a big problem: He wanted success and wealth without having to do any hard work. As a result, Tony dropped out of his university after two semesters and ended up in a low-level human resources (HR) job in a fruit canning company. By that stage in his life, he had destroyed his relationship with his parents. Time after time, Tony found himself in trouble for providing fake names and dates of births on loan applications. His dubious financial transactions required his parents to bail him out of trouble repeatedly. Many believed him to have all the qualities of a sociopath.

A human resources management position became available at the fruit company, for which Tony wanted to apply. The applicant was required to have a university degree and, because Tony hadn't completed college, he didn't qualify. Undaunted, he embarked on a scheme to create an accredited résumé. Tony found a student who had obtained a commerce degree and "borrowed" his academic record. He then stole university letterhead paper and managed to forge an acceptable document that stated that he held a college degree.

Unfortunately for him, one of his bosses had a feeling that Tony was a phony. This supervisor contacted a friend who happened to be a lecturer at the university in question, and his suspicions were quickly confirmed. Tony was soon fired and the police were informed. He was subsequently convicted of stealing university paper. The following year he declared bankruptcy.

Because he had worked for the fruit canning company for four years, Tony was concerned about how he would fill the employment gap in his résumé. He obviously needed to hide the fact that he had been fired and convicted of a criminal offense. This was easily dealt with by substituting the name of a bogus company during the four-year period of time in his application. He negotiated with Joe Foster, a friend of his who had also been the best man in his wedding, to be the director of the fake company and, therefore, a suitable reference. By this stage, Tony had a young family. It was imperative that he make a solid income. He had to gain employment in an organization that didn't know him, disregarded background checks, and needed an HR person. He finally found a local council located about an hour away from Melbourne that fit his criteria.

Dorset Local Council is located on the south coast of Victoria, Australia. The area is a favorite summer destination for Melbournians due to its proximity to the city, sandy beaches, camping and hotel facilities, and wineries. It originally consisted of two smaller local councils. Shortly after Tony was hired by one of them as an HR officer, the councils merged together and Tony ended up as general manager of resources. This position placed him in charge of a number of departments including HR, finance, payroll, maintenance, and fleet management. He had just been handed the keys to the cookie jar.

Tony had scored a great role; he was a senior council manager reporting directly to the chief executive officer (CEO). However, he now had another problem: he didn't have the skills to undertake such a complex role. One way to jump that particular hurdle was to return his bogus director's favor and hire his old friend, Joe Foster, as a contractor. Joe was a clever guy and between them, they managed to keep on top of the job. What Tony lacked in skills, he made up for in strategy. He knew that he needed to control those people working for him.

Tony took the stick-and-carrot approach. If employees stood up to him, he managed them right out of the organization. He was in charge of human resources. He had that kind of power. He gradually surrounded himself with his sycophants, treating them to meals and the occasional trip. With subordinates, he acted like a tyrant, berating them for disagreeing with him until they fell into submission. His role also included that of sexual harassment officer. It was ironic that when we finally analyzed his computer, we located a list of council staff he wanted to sleep with, together with ticks next to his conquests. Tony was indeed the textbook sociopath: superficially charming and glib, manipulative, callous, and lacking empathy.

He had few problems with his activities during the first 12 months employment at the council, but he had made a number of enemies within the staff ranks. Once a member of the council's finance section submitted a memo to the CEO alleging that he had received an anonymous phone call about $44,000 that Tony had falsely paid to Joe Foster's new business. The CEO called Tony into his office and showed him the memo.

"I've received this complaint about you. I thought I had better get your response," he began.

Tony read the memo. "That's an outrageous slur on my and Joe Foster's character. The allegation is totally false," he replied.

"Thought it would be something like that," said the CEO, who subsequently recorded his comments in an e-mail:

> I asked Tony if there was a fraud and he said no. I told him I was pleased to hear it; that kind of carelessness seemed inconsistent with what I had seen of his attention to matters of detail. I said that it was important that there could be no suspicion of fraud and that the audit trail had to be perfectly kosher.

The CEO had not bothered to undertake even the most basic investigation into the allegation. Tony subsequently typed up and sent two letters to the CEO, signing them as Joe, the "slandered vendor," in which he alleged that the finance staff member had created a fictitious anonymous call. Interestingly, the font and styles on Joe's letters were identical to Tony's letters. Furthermore, Joe's "signatures" were different on each letter. The fact that Tony had actually created them eventually surfaced. He was again trying to marginalize someone who opposed him.

In a further memo from Tony to the CEO, he wrote, "Thank you for your support with this matter. The suggestion of inappropriate action on my part, let alone 'fraudulent behavior' is upsetting and I found your response to be both professional and personal." He failed to include "and gullible." In any event, Tony was safe for another year. And what a year it was.

THE BEGINNING OF THE END

The time finally came when one or two people who worked with Tony couldn't hold back any longer. On the same day one fax was fired off to the Victoria Attorney General's Department, another fax found its way to the Victoria government department responsible for local councils. Further, rumors had spread through local councilors and even a federal member of Parliament about suspicious activity. Staff complaints had also reached the ear of another senior manager.

The accounting and auditing firm I worked for had undertaken some work for Dorset Council previously. At a crisis meeting with various state government agencies, it was decided that our firm should be appointed under the Local Government Act as inspector of municipal administration. One afternoon I was just about to leave my office in the forensic services group when one of the partners rang up.

"We need you guys on a job as soon as possible. Come and see me in five minutes." Three of us entered his office shortly after.

"Dorset Council has a potential fraud problem with one of their senior staff members," our partner said. "We are being appointed by the state government as inspectors."

"Is this senior staff person still on their premises?" one of my colleagues asked.

"They are suspending him with pay," our partner replied.

"What about his office? Have they changed the locks?" I queried.

"Why do you want to know that?"

"We don't want anyone touching his computer."

"They'll probably need a security guard until we get there as well," one of my colleagues added.

Our request was forwarded to the council's CEO, who agreed to get the office locks changed and organize a guard overnight. Although we had adopted our usual approach, what we didn't realize was that it probably wouldn't have made any difference with Tony.

His sociopathic behavior made him different from the majority of fraudsters I have dealt with in my career.

When I commenced the investigation, a staff member said, "You won't find anything on him; he's too smart." Boy, was that not the case. He hadn't hidden anything. Tony even had the original documents used to forge his academic record for which he had been fired from his HR job in the fruit canning company. Why would anyone keep such damning documents in an unlocked briefcase in his office so long after the event? The answer was now clear: Tony didn't care. Unlike the vast majority of the population, he had no sense of guilt. I doubt if he would even have failed a polygraph test. To him, fraud was a sport; how far could he go? What could he achieve?

Big Spender

We arrived at the council offices at 8:30 a.m. the following day.

A fraud crime scene is normally less distinctive than most. Fraud occurs over a period of months or years and in various locations. Our normal action is to treat the suspect's office or work area as the *initial* scene, focusing mostly on the computer. We obtained the services of one of our computer forensic experts to image both Tony's and his secretary's computers.

Two of us held discussions with the CEO while my other colleague set about reviewing every document in Tony's office. We obtained an overview of his role as an employee and the details of the anonymous allegations. It was during this meeting that the CEO mentioned the allegation from the previous year that he had failed to report. We added that to the list.

The first day was comprised of locating, documenting, and filing the various papers in Tony's office. We didn't know what their value would be, but at least we had a comprehensive description of the items to which we could refer later.

We then started the preliminary interviews of the staff. It became apparent that they fell into two categories: They either hated Tony or loved him; there was no middle ground. It also quickly became clear that we needed to investigate every activity in which Tony had been involved. Everywhere we looked we found evidence of suspicious behavior.

We reviewed his salary and performance bonuses, as he was in charge of payroll. The payroll clerk mentioned that, on occasion, Tony gave written instructions to amend various payments. These were usually signed only by Tony. When I looked at the amount of performance bonuses he received, I found that they were significantly greater than any of the other managers. The CEO confirmed that $12,000 of performance bonuses paid to Tony in one year were unauthorized. I then studied his salary payments. Again, he was receiving considerably more salary than equivalent managers. I located an authorization, which appeared to be signed by the CEO, to increase Tony's pay by $14,600 a year. The authorization also approved the payment to be backdated for a year, giving Tony a further $14,600 lump sum. He was now being paid more than the CEO! Of course, when I showed the document to the CEO, he stated that his signature was a forgery.

I interviewed Tony's former personal assistant about a credit card application made by him to be used for salary sacrifice purposes. "Salary sacrificing" requires some explanation. The Australian government has allowed certain government employees, including those working for councils, to sacrifice a certain percentage of their salary. This means that some personal expenditure (e.g., school fees or mortgage payments) is taken out of gross salaries prior to being taxed, therefore reducing the taxable income and thus the amount of tax paid. In this particular case, the council staff was permitted to sacrifice 10% of their total salary.

Tony had decided that he needed a credit card to use for his salary sacrifice expenditures. He was the only one to have such a card; we subsequently discovered that the CEO had decided that this practice was not permitted. Tony waited until the CEO was away from the office, then instructed his personal assistant to complete most of the credit card application form. Tony then located a letter containing the CEO's signature, cut it out, and pasted it on the application form in the authorization box. Next, he faxed the form to the bank. When his assistant queried this procedure, Tony responded, "Look, it's only to get the ball rolling. When the CEO gets back I'll ask him to sign another form." Tony received the credit card as a result of the false application. Needless to say, he never obtained a genuine signature from the CEO.

Evidently, Tony would go to nearly any length to defraud the council. One scam involved manipulating the procurement process. The council was looking to upgrade its payroll system, and he was interviewing various software providers. He decided he wanted to see a program "live" in a government location. He was offered a number of places in Victoria, but Tony wanted to go further—he could smell a nice trip coming up. After much discussion, it was decided that he and the council's payroll officer would travel to see the software program at the Cairns Port and Harbour Authority.

This meant that he would have to fly the length of the Australian east coast—no short journey. It was agreed that the software company would pay for the flights, and Tony would arrange for the council to pay for his and his manager's accommodations.

The hotel cost for the two-night trip was over $1,500, an outrageous amount. When I obtained a copy of the bill from the hotel, I found out why. Tony had booked a helicopter flight. We interviewed the payroll manager, who said, "Tony decided to visit the Great Barrier Reef while in Cairns. Because we were visiting the place where the payroll system was installed at 9 a.m., he didn't have time to catch the boats going out there. So he booked the chopper flight, went snorkeling, and then went back to Cairns on one of the boats." All this was paid for on the council's credit card. I found a brochure in Tony's office for the helicopter flight he took.

To end such a memorable trip, Tony treated his manager to a seafood dinner costing $300. When I reviewed his credit card payment authorization, I noticed that Tony had recorded that he had spent that money on "flowers for the office." The photocopy of the credit card statement he submitted simply showed "Tawny's." I recalled seeing that name on a bill in Tony's office. I went to our exhibits and located a credit card receipt for

"Tawny's Cairns—$300." I then recovered the original credit card statement and found that the entry had actually shown "Tawny's Restaurant—Cairns." Tony had deleted "Restaurant—Cairns" from the photocopy accompanying his payment authorization form to hide the fact that it was for a meal.

As previously mentioned, Tony had a number of illicit affairs with council staff. On one occasion he convinced his CEO that the Australian Institute of Human Resources had asked him to undertake a speaking tour in Tasmania. It didn't occur to the CEO that the council was actually paying for the trip instead of the institute. Obviously Tony just wanted a weeklong vacation with his current girlfriend. So the council paid for his car, accommodation, food, and drink for his holiday.

We established that Tony had recently obtained his master's of business technology from a state university. When we spoke to his personal assistant, she mentioned that he was taking the course by correspondence and was constantly being contacted for late assignments and failing subjects.

The rumor circulating the council was that Joe Foster, who was gone from work for about three months, had gone to the university to sit for a number of examinations in Tony's name. We were never able to establish the truth of the matter, but Joe was paid by the council during his absence and we could find no evidence of any work he had completed during that time.

Speaking of Joe, as Tony had originally employed him as a contractor, we followed up on the original allegation about him being paid $44,000 by the council. We undertook a number of business name searches on Joe and found that he had four separate business names and that he had used all of them to allegedly undertake work for Tony. In one year, Tony had authorized a total of $159,500 in payments to these four businesses. As far as we could ascertain, the council had received no benefit. Indeed, we were able to prove that another contractor had undertaken the same work as identified on one of Joe's invoices. We established that the other contractor, and not Joe, had actually performed the work.

After about a year, and without the CEO's authority, Tony hired Joe as a full-time council employee. He also paid him a salary for a higher position, irrespective of the fact that there was no higher position in his field of work, and gave him a council car although Joe's position did not warrant one.

After 10 months in this position, Joe ceased employment with the council. Tony authorized a severance package for him in the sum of $35,000. A day later, Tony rehired Joe on a part-time basis. It was at that time that Joe disappeared.

What happened to that $35,000 was an interesting investigative piece. When Tony set up his salary sacrifice account, he was supposed to ensure that all his expenses netted to zero at the end of each month. However, Tony actually built up a significant liability and at one stage owed $44,000 on it.

I noticed that a sum of $10,000 was deposited into his salary sacrifice account in one transaction. When I located the deposit slip, I found that Joe had put that money into Tony's account two days after Joe had received the $35,000; Tony had organized a round robin to reduce his account deficit.

Tony's wining and dining knew no bounds. To assist in hiding some of his excesses, he entered into a conspiracy with the owner of a local conference and restaurant facility. The agreement reached was that for those occasions when Tony wanted to hide his true purpose, the owner would create a bogus invoice showing that the premises had been used for "training" sessions. This had the added concern of defrauding the federal government. Dining expenses attract a fringe benefits tax, but training doesn't.

Using our inspector powers, we recovered all the genuine receipts from the facility and cross-referenced them to Tony's "training" invoices. We could not locate one genuine training document; they were all for meals and alcohol. It seemed that Tony and Joe would often go to the restaurant midmorning to enjoy a bottle of champagne and book it as "training room hire." On one occasion it appeared that he held a full-day training session. What actually occurred was that Tony took his staff out for a $1,500 lunch. I was reviewing the restaurant reservations book and found the date on which the training allegedly occurred. The lunch booking showed "Tony, Dorset Council; N.E.S."

I said to the owner, "What does N.E.S. mean?"

"No expense spared," she replied. "Tony wanted a lunch to remember. He didn't care what it cost."

The list of Tony's criminal activity began to mount. He and an ex-council employee bought a boat. Tony footed his half of the bill by paying the ex-staff member a $10,000 severance six months after she had left the organization, having already been given her entitlements. He booked Melbourne hotels during two Formula One Grand Prix events, for "training purposes." He obtained a council ride-on lawn mower, had his private-wheel drive vehicle serviced at the council workshop, and had an electric winch fitted to it, all at no cost to him.

Even after his suspension, Tony still had nearly everyone fooled. He remained on the council basketball team. "I'm getting reinstated soon," he would say. "Then I'm going to sue them for putting me through all this." Most people actually believed him.

A World of Denial

Our team conducted an investigation for three weeks to reach a stage where we had obtained enough evidence to interview Tony. As municipal inspectors, we had the power to put him under oath, which meant that if he told lies to us, he could be charged with perjury. However, by that time Tony was represented by a lawyer who was fighting to prevent him from being interviewed at all. As part of the delaying tactics, the lawyer queried the legislation governing our powers as municipal inspectors. The matter was heading to court for a judicial determination. The government, however, decided not to fight that particular battle, and it was determined that we wouldn't question Tony.

Even without any evidence that may have surfaced from the interview, we still had enough proof to pass the matter on to the police. At the same time, the evidence was used to enable the CEO to write a letter to both Tony and Joe requesting them to show cause for why they should not have their employment terminated.

This did, however, leave Tony with an opportunity to come up with some creative responses to the CEO's letter. A couple of classic "Tonyisms" related to his helicopter flight: "This was a business expense," he wrote. "I took it as an opportunity to better get to know my payroll manager. It also served to reward him because we had both been working very diligently during the trip."

The hard work had consisted of an hour's tour of the payroll function. The flight was the first thing Tony organized when he got to the hotel. If you've ever flown in a helicopter, you know that trying to think, let alone trying to "better acquaint" yourself with someone during the flight, is near impossible.

The "Tawny's" flower issue he dismissed, writing "The purchase was described as 'flowers' rather than 'restaurant' because, as you are aware, a number of staff at Council were being made redundant which had caused many Council staff to be extremely sensitive and critical in relation to the expenditure of Council funds on general business expenses." He didn't mention the additional $15,000 worth of meals he had also had at council's expense.

But he threatened to sue the CEO for having the audacity to allege that Tony created a false application for his salary sacrifice credit card. He wrote, "The allegation is untrue and should I become aware that your letter has been published to others I will take legal action for defamation." He then proceeded to blame his assistant for creating the document. Interestingly, when he finally did appear in court, Tony pleaded guilty to the offense of creating a false document.

As a final act of defiance, during his suspension, Tony submitted a work cover insurance claim for "stress and anxiety" caused by his job. If this claim had been accepted, all Tony's medical costs would have been covered by the council's insurance. Fortunately, it was rejected.

When Tony's employment was finally terminated, he commenced legal proceedings for unfair dismissal against the council. I was called to give evidence at the tribunal and waited around for two hours until we finally realized that Tony wasn't going to turn up. It was all part of his behavior. I found out later that Tony was actively looking for another job. He couldn't escape mentioning that he had been dismissed from the council but told his prospective employer that he was taking action against the council to prove his innocence. His ruse worked, and he was hired by the next gullible business. Within 18 months Tony was the subject of another police investigation.

Ultimately, both Tony and Joe were charged by the police with various criminal offenses. After obtaining legal advice as to the weight of evidence against them, they both pleaded guilty to all charges. Because of their guilty pleas and "remorse," they walked away with suspended prison sentences without serving any time. I could understand the result with respect to Joe, as he had been an accomplice. But Tony's sociopathic behavior enabled him to show total remorse without meaning a word of it.

In the end, the suspended sentence actually worked against him. He had embarked on another fraud campaign against his new employer almost as soon as he began work for that organization. When he was finally arrested and convicted for those offenses, the court also imposed the two-year suspended sentence given for the council frauds. In the end, Tony served four years in prison.

LESSONS LEARNED

From an investigative perspective, the major lesson that was reinforced to me was never to underestimate the amount and value of evidence that can be recovered from someone's workplace, especially from a computer. We never undertake an investigation now without imaging and analyzing computers or servers. Tony's office contained a wealth of information that provided vital corroboration.

It is also important to secure the location and correctly gather and document the evidence at the beginning of the investigation. Not only does this prevent loss, but it also ensures that the continuity of evidence chain is maintained. A few hours of collecting and documenting possible evidence at the beginning prevents major problems arising later in the prosecution.

We also need to be aware of the amount of emotional capital expended by innocent staff members caught up in these types of situations. Sometimes we tend to blow into an organization, fix the problem (in this case, undertake the investigation), and then leave. If Tony's employment had not been terminated, there were at least four staff members whose positions in the council would have been untenable because of the assistance they offered us.

It is also relevant to keep in mind that the vast majority of employees are honest people trying to do the right thing. Few of them have been involved in a fraud investigation, and some of them needed reassurance that they were not responsible for what occurred. With this particular case, the finance manager had many sleepless nights wondering if she could have done anything differently to prevent the frauds from occurring. In reality, given the type of person Tony was, there was only one way to prevent these frauds: not hiring him in the first place. On the other side of the coin, it is worth remembering that not everyone will be ecstatic at the sight of investigators. Some of the staff members aligned with Tony, particularly in the HR area, were at best uncooperative. And at worst, they actively hindered the investigation.

A lesson the CEO learned was to keep an open mind and not to dismiss allegations out of hand. Most of the losses the council suffered due to Tony occurred *after* the CEO's discussion with him. Following on from that point, the next lesson is that there is rarely any smoke without fire. People had been complaining about Tony for over 18 months but nothing was done until the anonymous faxes were sent to government departments.

This situation, to a certain extent, is linked to the so-called tone at the top. Tony was a senior manager reporting directly to the CEO, yet the culture that Tony developed was one of secrecy and favoritism. Moreover, the council learned the hard way not to put all of the eggs in one basket. Tony was in control of almost all of the money. He was in a prime position to commit fraud. His areas of management included finance (accounts payable), payroll, HR, fleet management, and maintenance.

RECOMMENDATIONS TO PREVENT FUTURE OCCURRENCES

We told the CEO that implementing a number of recommendations would help prevent future losses of this kind.

Background Checks

Tony's records were never checked before he was employed. If the council had done so, they would have realized that he had a history of dishonest behavior.

Hotlines

As Tony controlled the staff through fear, they quickly discovered that anyone who stood up to him was managed out of the organization. There was no process in place to allow allegations to be raised without the fear of losing their job or worse. Legislation now exists in Victoria which ensures that a person convicted of taking "detrimental action" against a public sector whistle-blower can be sentenced to a term of imprisonment.

Fraud Risk Assessment and Fraud Control Plan

The council had never assessed the fraud risk in its functions, nor had it created a fraud control plan. As such, there was no guidance on how allegations were dealt with. Furthermore, the council lacked protocols for undertaking investigations or notifying law enforcement agencies.

Fraud Awareness Training

Fraud awareness training was not provided for new employees, nor was ongoing fraud awareness training given to staff. Although a number of them knew that what Tony was doing seemed wrong, they were unable—and, in some cases, unwilling—to do anything about it. He used the classic "management override" to achieve his fraudulent ends.

Accept Only Original Receipts for Payment of Expenses

Do not pay expenses unless an original receipt is attached. A number of Tony's charges were not supported by adequate documentation. In addition, he altered the copy of his credit card statement to mask the true nature of his reimbursements.

Tone at the Top

Senior management must drive the tone of an organization. Tony was able to develop his culture because there was no strong leadership being shown from above. This lack of direction meant that the staff did not know what to do. As a result, Tony capitalized on that to the fullest extent.

David Clements, CFE, is a director in the Melbourne, Australia, Forensic Services Practice of PricewaterhouseCoopers. He has over 23 years of law enforcement experience with the Metropolitan Police in London, the Victoria Police, and the Australian Securities and Investment Commission. He is a graduate of Monash University and has worked for PricewaterhouseCoopers since 1997.

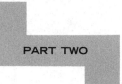

PART TWO

Corruption Schemes

CHAPTER 42

A Contract of Convenience

ROBERT B. WALSH JR.

Albert Thompson was one of Superior Insurance Company's success stories. He was hired right after college graduation and placed in the Basic TECH claims training program, a curriculum developed specifically to attract recent graduates to a career in insurance.

Superior doesn't accept just any applicant. The recruitment process requires applicants to have an excellent grade-point average and involves several rounds of interviews with a variety of company managers. Those accepted are the cream of the crop, and one of the program's challenges is to make the training investment pay off. Over time, certain alumnae are lured away by offers from competitors, keen to reap the benefits of the training without having to incur the expense themselves. Albert had talent, but after 10 years, he remained a faithful and valuable employee. Since his days as a trainee, he rose through the ranks and became a senior field claim representative.

Albert was a serious but generally affable fellow. Being five foot eight, a little round in the middle, and exhibiting a prematurely receding hairline, he didn't cast an extraordinary shadow—in any direction. However, in his mid-20s Albert married Ellen, an attractive young woman he met in college. Soon they had two beautiful girls and a well-maintained ranch-style home in middle-class suburbia, just a few miles away from Albert's boyhood home. His father was the founder and sole proprietor of a locally successful retail business, and Albert Sr. regularly reminded his son of the importance and benefits of exemplifying a lifestyle of achievement. So did Albert's wife. She constantly pressured him to buy her the nicest car or take the family on an extravagant vacation. Albert felt that he had "married up," and he was extremely motivated to assure that the means were available to provide for his young family in the manner to which they had become accustomed.

Albert's advancement over his 10-year career with Superior was noteworthy but certainly not meteoric. Some of his classmates from his trainee days were now supervisors, and he made it clear that he was eager to advance into management and, of course, the heftier paycheck that would accompany it. Albert was always quick to offer a rebuttal whenever he felt his work product was being unfairly evaluated. Lately he became particularly agitated and argumentative about criticism of his claim settlements during corporate file audits.

"You people from home office don't understand my territory," he protested. "The contractors in my part of the state service a wealthier clientele and they demand top dollar. I *have* to write my appraisals a little higher just to get someone to service our policy holders!"

Albert's arguments were met with some skepticism from Superior's corporate claims staff. But Albert had an advocate. His supervisor, Irma Westley, agreed with his assessment and consistently backed him up.

Irma liked Albert. She knew that he was bright and she felt that he could be relied on to make the extra effort. When the office's territory was hit with a hurricane, it was Albert who came in and helped her review other adjusters' closed catastrophe claims. Irma was so comfortable with Albert's abilities and his trustworthiness that she even authorized him to sign off on claims on her behalf.

SUPERIOR IN (ALMOST) EVERY WAY

Superior Insurance Company was established as a modest regional casualty insurance company in 1901 by brothers John and William Percy. By the mid-1980s, Superior had become a member of a group of regional property and casualty insurance carriers bound by their interest in surviving in a market dominated by large national carriers. The business plan is to offer independent agents and policy holders competitive rates while providing them excellent customer service. Before the merger, Superior faced challenges in completing this mission. Its procedures were somewhat disorganized and inefficient. Claims-handling procedures were archaic at best and undisciplined at worst. Claims-processing systems remained almost entirely manual. But the changes brought new blood into the organization, and new blood brought new ideas and efficiencies. Claims procedures were soon written or updated. Information systems were modernized, and programs were established to help claim staff negotiate and settle claims properly, efficiently, and fairly.

Training programs, such as Basic TECH, were part of this improvement. But other programs we developed provided policy holders with referrals to repairers and contractors who were reliable and trustworthy. Contractors were researched meticulously. Their work product was inspected and critiqued. Prior customers were solicited for assessments of the results. Contractors were required to endure an exhaustive financial review before they could be added to Superior's approved list of vendors. In an arena where Superior couldn't beat competitors consistently with pricing, customer service was going to be the key to success.

Superior's changes and improvements were not limited to the Claims Department. Before Superior expanded its operation, the Internal Audit Department consisted of one finance person. Not a lot of time and resources were available to dedicate to claim office audits or employee fraud investigations. Sure, employee frauds were identified and investigated occasionally. But the frauds were almost always reported by outside sources, such as policy holders or agents. Superior's only real proactive program in place was the claim confirmation letters sent to payees to verify that the payment issued was received and legitimate. But even this was a halfhearted effort.

After Superior's growth spurt, the internal audit department was expanded to a staff of four. Specific claim audits, fraud detection, and investigation responsibilities were defined for one of these new positions. After 10 years in claims, I leapt at the chance to broaden my experience and immediately submitted my résumé. Within a few months I was reporting to the new director of internal audits and developing a new claims audit program and fraud investigation procedures. I also tweaked the old confirmation letter program's random selection process so that it would concentrate on higher-risk transactions. We started getting periodic hits for potential fraudulent payments. Most were false alarms, but several turned out to be phony settlements issued by employees.

A CROOKED CONTRACTOR

If we had heeded conventional industry wisdom concerning the wasteful and unproductive nature of confirmation letter programs, we might have abandoned ours, as did many contemporary audit groups in the 1990s. However, Superior Insurance Company's periodic exposures of employee fraud and successful prosecution of these crimes motivated us to keep it going. Once again, a letter was received by the internal audit department by policy holders Arthur and Jennifer Accabo, stating that they never received a check we issued to them for $16,354. Our auditor, Dawn Mutuski, pulled the cancelled check over in the claims department. It was made payable to Mr. and Mrs. Accabo and J & B Contracting. Dawn observed that it did have endorsements for both policy holders and the contractor, so she sent the Accabos a copy of the check along with the typical "Does this jog your memory?" letter. Most days, that would be the end the story, but not this time.

A month later Dawn received a call from Mrs. Accabo. "My husband and I received your letter and the check copy, but we don't know anything about this payment," she said. "We had a claim for a leak in the roof of our store back in March, but the date of loss in your letter is June 20. We didn't have anything happen in June."

Mrs. Accabo was equally concerned that they had not signed the back of the check. The endorsements of Arthur and Jennifer were forgeries. It appeared that J & B Contracting had forged their endorsements on the check to deposit it without the couple's knowledge. Dawn knew this happened sometimes. A contractor would finish a job and forge the other payee's endorsements to avoid the hassle of getting the legitimate endorsements by mail or in person. It was still fraud, but most often policy holders would acknowledge that though they weren't too thrilled with the contractor's financial practices, the work was performed to their satisfaction and the payment could be honored; no harm, no foul.

Dawn called Albert Thompson at his office and asked him if he knew anything about the payment. She told Albert that Mr. and Mrs. Accabo were upset about the way the claim and repairs were handled.

"Oh, that case," he answered hurriedly. "Yeah, I had a problem with the original roofers on that claim. They actually caused more damage to the roof trying to repair it. I had to bring in someone else to clean up their mess, and I'm in the process of submitting a subrogation claim against his insurance carrier to get our money back. I'll contact the Accabos and clear everything up. Nothing for you to worry about."

The next day Dawn received a call from Jim Milligan, Mr. and Mrs. Accabo's insurance agent. Jim was obviously not in the mood for friendly, polite conversation.

"Dawn, something is not right with this claim," Jim said. "Arthur and Jennifer are here in my office. They got notice from your Underwriting Department today that Superior will not renew their policy because they had two large claims this year. You guys can't penalize them for this. First of all, they only had one claim for the roof, not two. Second, when Arthur reported this roof damage to me, he had a quote from Emerald Roofing, which said that they could make the repair for $900. But Albert Thompson insisted on hiring a company called Kraft Plus, and they charged almost $29,000. Then to add insult to injury, Kraft Plus screwed this up and Superior considered it another claim. What the hell is going on here?"

Dawn asked to speak with Mr. Accabo. When he took the phone, Dawn asked, "Mr. Accabo, can you tell me how Albert Thompson referred this contractor to you?"

"Sure," Mr. Accabo replied. "Albert told us that your company uses certain contractors to handle repair work and that he could get Kraft Plus out to our shop right away. I had no particular ties to Emerald, so as long as the roof was repaired, I didn't care who did it. The first repairs Kraft Plus made to the roof were so poor that we ended up with more leaks than we had in the first place. Albert then sent out another company named J & B Contracting to correct the problems. But you know what was weird? I'm pretty sure I recognized some of J & B's workers as the same guys that came here working for Kraft Plus who created the mess in the first place."

"This is obviously very suspicious," Dawn thought. She called me from her office and relayed the information. We shared a laugh at the thought of Kraft Plus employees showing up at Mr. Accabo's place working as J & B Contracting—maybe with phony mustaches and lame disguises, we quipped—but the jokes were overshadowed by the apparent revelation that one of our field adjusters, and one we had trained from the beginning of his insurance career, appeared to be somehow involved with a crooked contractor.

WEEDING OUT THE BAD GUYS

After we discussed the problems with the Accabo claims, Dawn reviewed all of the file notes. One of Albert's log entries jumped right off the screen. Just prior to closing the first claim, he had written: "Given the circumstances, no recovery potential exists for this loss." Yet Albert told her that he *was* going to pursue recovery on this very same file just two days before. Dawn called Peter Childs, Albert's manager.

"Peter, have you ever heard of contractors named Kraft Plus or J & B Contracting? We've been looking at a couple of claims involving these two companies, and we think that they could involve fraud." Dawn faxed him the information and evidence she had collected and asked him to give it a look.

Within an hour, Peter called. "I don't like what I see, Dawn. After what Albert told you on the phone, his notes in the file about recovery really disturb me. And that's not the only thing. There's not enough documentation in either of these files to support what Alfred paid. I'm going to look into this further and I'll get back to you." Another half hour went by, then another call from Peter. He sounded upset.

"Dawn, I asked my assistant managers about these two contractors. After I met with them, one sent an e-mail to the entire office telling them not to use Kraft Plus or J & B without his permission. Ten minutes later Albert walked into my office and stammered something about his job being too stressful—said he couldn't take it any more. He resigned on the spot and walked out the door!"

Our opportunity to interview Albert about these claims probably walked out with him.

Dawn and I ran some data reports on our claim system to identify all files handled by Albert and all cases where Kraft Plus or J & B Contracting were payees. Eighty-six claim payments were issued to one or the other and, with the exception of eight, all were made on files assigned to Albert. The other cases were handled by Dan Moore, and some of his documentation looked just as suspicious. Dawn and I decided to visit Dan unannounced and interview him. We arrived at his office early and settled into a small conference room. We asked Peter to bring Dan to us without explaining the nature of the meeting, and within a few minutes the two men returned. Dan's mop of unruly, brown-red hair bobbing as he walked made him look younger than his nearly 50 years. I introduced Dawn to Dan, and he and I greeted each other familiarly. We'd known each other for years. He looked concerned, but not particularly nervous.

"Bob, what's this all about?" he asked me in his unmistakable Scottish brogue.

"Dan, we've been auditing claims involving a couple of contractors named Kraft Plus and J & B Contracting, and we saw that you have used them on several occasions."

"Yeah, sure," Dan admitted. "I used them on a few cases. They're actually both run by a guy named Jack March. I got his name from Albert Thompson last year when we had all those hurricane claims. I was having trouble finding contractors that weren't all booked up and Albert offered up Kraft Plus. He told me they were professional and reliable so I used them on a few claims. Albert might have been happy with them, but I wasn't too impressed so I stopped using them straightaway."

We asked Dan about the cases that we felt had questionable transactions. "I opened those claims for Albert because he was on vacation," Dan said a little defensively. "When he got back he handled them because they were in his territory."

After a lull in the conversation, Dan suddenly looked like he had just been let in on a secret. He glanced over at me and said, "Albert's stealing from the company, isn't he?"

"What makes you say that, Dan?" I asked.

"Well, Albert and this Jack character seemed a bit cozy to me. I felt that there was something not quite right there, but there was never anything specific . . . until now, that is."

I said, "Look, Dan. We don't know what's going on at this point, and it would be unwise to jump to any conclusions or start any rumors. Let's keep this to ourselves, for now, okay?"

"You bet," Dan agreed. Dawn and I later confirmed that Dan had only used Kraft Plus for a short time and that Albert was responsible for the questionable payments on the claims initially assigned to him.

In all of the files we reviewed, the common denominator appeared to be that we were paying a lot more than the reasonable cost to repair the damages. I felt confident that we were looking at a kickback scheme, but my claims-handling background was in automobile physical damage and liability. After the first few file reviews, I realized that if we had any hope of a successful investigation, we had to recruit the assistance of a property claims expert to help us. I knew whom I should enlist.

I had worked closely with Chris Brown in several capacities over our nearly parallel 15-year careers at Superior, and we had an excellent working and personal relationship. I knew that his property estimating skills, his past experience with claims fraud, and his disposition with customers would be great assets to our team. I approached Superior's claim vice president and asked if he would lend Chris to our department. He readily agreed.

Chris jumped right in, reviewing Albert's claim files for questionable payments and suspicious supporting documents. I prepared a spreadsheet comparing original estimates, contractor estimates, and Albert's final settlement on all high-dollar claims. Dawn sent a confirmation letter on Albert's claims involving Kraft Plus, J & B, and a few other contractors that came to our attention. Based on the responses we received from those letters, Chris and I made our first appointments with 10 policy holders using the pretext that we were doing a quality control review. Just before Christmas, we hit the road.

Almost immediately, Chris had problems reconciling the amounts Albert paid to the work Kraft Plus and J & B performed. At our very first appointment, Chris pulled me aside. "Bob, my measurements are less than half what Albert documented, and he paid about three times what should have been paid on this claim. And look at the repairs!"

Chris pointed out the amateur roof replacement by Kraft Plus. Not only did we pay too much, but we were going to have to pay even more to replace the work the company had done. At some of the other inspections we arranged, I could immediately tell that some of the damages written and paid for by Albert did not exist. Chris confirmed that all of the claims were overwritten by using significantly larger measurements than what actually existed.

As Chris identified the problems with the measurements and the quality of the repairs, Dawn and I confided in the policy holders that we were actually investigating potential fraud and asked them to confirm their endorsements on checks and signatures on other file documents. I took signed statements from most of them confirming that their signatures had been forged. In one case we asked our policy holder, Diane Dabrowsky, to confirm her signature on a Direction to Pay, a document that allowed us to pay a contractor directly.

"That sure looks like my handwriting, but I don't remember signing anything like that." Chris studied the signature pensively, thumbed back through the file, and located the original assignment Mrs. Dabrowsky has signed.

"This might explain why," Chris said. He superimposed the signatures and they matched exactly. Clearly, Albert or Jack had cut out a photocopy of the signature, pasted it onto the Direction to Pay, photocopied it again, and used it to justify payments that were issued without Mrs. Dabrowsky's knowledge or consent.

Another policy holder we met was Carol Beaudin, a 92-year-old widow. She had wind damage to her home, and we had paid nearly $15,000 for its repair. As we inspected her house, Chris once again confirmed that the measurements were way off. I noted that the siding we paid to replace was never installed. The siding on the house was still damaged and was probably more than 40 years old. The chimney had obviously been damaged, and the broken pieces were just propped back up in place with no mortar. But Carol had nothing but praise for Jack March.

"He was such a polite man," she said. "He showed up here the day after I called my agent. He and the youngsters he had working for him cleaned the yard of every branch."

She had no clue that we had paid three times the cost of the damages, nor did she realize that some of the repairs Jack was paid for were never done. Her lawn was raked, her roof didn't leak, and a nice young man and his kids had helped make her life less lonely, if only for a day or two. We decided we couldn't pop Carol's balloon by discussing the fraud with her, but we did convince her to let us get someone over to complete the work that her newfound friend had neglected to repair—adding to the $278,000 in fraudulent payments we eventually identified through our fieldwork.

We decided it was time to try to interview Albert and Jack. I called Albert's home number, and he answered the phone.

"Albert, this is Bob Walsh at Superior Insurance," I said. "I've been reviewing some of your claims and I'd like to ask you about some of the transactions I've seen." There was a long pause, but Albert finally found his voice.

"I have an attorney. You'll have to talk to her," he said soberly. He gave me her name and phone number and hung up. Dawn was assigned the task of contacting Jack March.

Dawn called Chris and I and said, "I just spoke with Jack and he wants to meet you next Wednesday morning at 9:00 at Friendly's Restaurant at Exit 24."

Before the meeting, Chris and I discussed our strategy. We agreed that trying to confront Jack with all of the suspicious transactions we'd uncovered would risk a confusing, unproductive conversation. We decided to concentrate on four files. We arranged them so that our questions would first be interpreted by Jack as concerns about procedure and work product, and finish with cases that would leave him with no misunderstanding that our concerns were far more serious.

Chris and I arrived for our meeting with Jack just a little earlier than our 9:00 a.m. appointment. We had never met Jack, but a man fitting his description stood up from a booth and identified himself. He was tall, slender, had dark blond hair, a neatly trimmed beard, and what appeared to be a small diamond earring in his left earlobe. We introduced ourselves, handed him our business cards, sat in the booth facing him, and ordered coffee.

"Jack, do you know why we are meeting with you today?" I asked.

Jack replied, "Some of my customers have been contacting me to say that you're investigating me." From his expression, it was clear that Jack was not pleased to be hearing this from our policy holders.

Chris said, "That's right, Jack. We're investigating claims handled by Albert Thompson where you are the contractor. Are you willing to answer a few questions about the way some of these cases were handled?"

"Ah yeah, okay." Jack replied, hesitating a bit.

"How are things going on the Dabrowsky claim?" Chris asked.

When we interviewed Mrs. Dabrowsky, she showed us that there was work she was unhappy with and some that was never finished.

"When do you figure you can finish the work on her place?" Chris added.

Jack said, "I spoke to her yesterday and arranged to tear out her bedroom rug. The replacement rug is on order, and I'll have it installed as soon as it comes in. I'm going to get with her next week and schedule all the other work left at her place."

Chris continued, "You know, we were looking through Albert's file and some of his pictures didn't match any room in the house. Were you with Albert when he inspected the Dabrowsky house?"

"No, I wasn't. I never met with Albert on this claim," Jack replied.

Chris pressed on. "Do you remember a claim for Gerry and Brenna Lamson? Bob and I inspected their place and I have to tell you, they weren't happy people."

"What was their problem?" Jack asked a little wearily.

"Well," replied Chris, "to start with, the woodwork and wall-to-wall carpeting you installed were obviously nothing like the quality used in the rest of the house, and the painting was horrendous. To top it all off, they showed us $20,000 worth of Oriental rugs you apparently ruined when you tried to clean them with a wet vac."

Jack appeared a little nervous but sounded defensive. "My work didn't include cleaning rugs. My subcontractor did the painting, but they were happy with it when he left. And I took a sample of the damaged carpet right to my supplier and we matched it for quality," he insisted. "There was no satisfying them!"

"Okay. How about Regina Harmon? Do you remember her place?" asked Chris.

Jack got quiet. "Is that the place in Washington?" he asked.

"Yeah, that's the one," I said. "We just inspected her house a week ago and compared the estimate to the repairs you did. You know what? The only work we could find that you did was the replacement of a shed roof on the back porch. What happened to the rest of the damages? We paid you $5,700."

"I did every bit of the work written on that estimate," Jack swore.

"Oh, come on, the hallway you supposedly painted was wallpapered, and it obviously hadn't been touched since before either you or I were born," I said. He sat quietly.

Chris leaned toward Jack and almost whispered, "Do you remember Carol Beaudin?" Jack didn't say a word.

"You know the place, don't you? The little two-bedroom house that needed a new roof, electrical repairs, a rebuilt chimney, and new siding? What happened there? We paid you 15 grand for that claim and other than the roof repair, nothing else was done."

Jack said that he didn't know why this work was not completed, and he had no excuse for it being left unfinished.

After a while Jack said, "You know, I never had any intention of doing anything illegal. If you guys have some problems with the work I did, I'll make it right."

"Jack, this isn't our only concern," I replied. "We have affidavits from some of the mortgagees on these homes that their endorsements were forged on the checks we issued. Did you ever forge names of people or banks on the back of checks we issued?"

"Yeah, sometimes," Jack stated. "But everyone does that. That's not illegal, is it? When I was with Servicepro it was done all of the time."

"Jack, that's very illegal," I said. "In fact, we have affidavits from mortgagees that confirm these are forgeries."

Suddenly Jack slumped in his seat and looked down at the table. When he looked back up at us he said, "I have a family. They mean everything to me. Am I in trouble?"

"We're not police, Jack," Chris said. "We're just employees of an insurance company trying to investigate a former employee's claim handling." There was another long pause.

Finally I said, "The kind of activity we've seen in these claims is what we usually see in a kickback scheme."

Jack got agitated at this suggestion. "Do I need a lawyer?" he asked.

I followed Chris's lead. "We aren't police," I said. "We're here representing Superior Insurance Company's interests. We came here to ask you questions about these claims and your relationship with Albert, nothing more. You're free to help us with this case or not. You're the only person here who knows whether you need an attorney or not."

Our dialog with Jack was followed yet again by a long, uncomfortable silence. Chris got up to pay our coffee tab. I caught Jack's eye as Chris was returning to the table.

"You know, Jack, we've tried to contact Albert to ask him the same questions we've asked you. His response was to tell us he had an attorney. Your response to us was to talk to us, so I think I can speak for Chris when I say we know who the bad guy is here. I think you're trying to help, and I think you should tell us anything you feel might be helpful to our investigation because when it comes time for Thompson to talk to us, he's not going to think twice about leaving you out twisting in the wind."

Jack proceeded to tell us the whole story. Albert first asked him for a loan, and he paid the loan off by padding claims. Eventually Albert became more demanding. "He asked for $700 on this claim and $1,000 on the next, and soon we were inflating everything." Jack looked lost. "I don't know how it got so out of hand," he said, more to himself than to Chris and me. Jack looked up from the table. There were tears welling up in his eyes. His voice cracked as he said, "When you come to arrest me, please don't do it in front of my kids."

MARCHING FORTH

Once our investigation report was complete, we referred our case to the state insurance commissioner and the chief state's attorney's office for prosecution. We felt confident that our investigation, evidence, and the report we prepared were adequate to attract the interest of a prosecutor—and we were right. But it didn't happen without a little salesmanship.

During our first meeting, the investigator listened to us politely and then wondered allowed, "Explain to me again how this is a crime. I mean, insurance claims are overpaid every day, aren't they? Why isn't this just incompetence or a series of mistakes by your adjuster?"

We took the time to walk him through the transactions. We pointed out that Albert wasn't just paying more than the cost of needed repairwork. He was making up and paying for damages that never existed. And to top it all off, Jack was forging endorsements on numerous checks we had issued to prevent the intended recipients of claim payments from realizing how much we were paying on their claim. Eventually we had a convert, but for almost a year, we had to regularly rekindle the level of interest as the case was reassigned to several different investigators.

At the same time we were pursuing prosecution, we filed a civil suit against Albert and Jack to protect our rights of recovery. Our attorney filed a prejudgment remedy of attachment to identify all Albert's and Jack's known assets and prevent them from being liquidated or hidden from any judgment that we might ultimately receive from the trial. Additionally, the criminal action brought was based on only a fraction of the transactions involving the forgeries. We intended to recover as much of what was stolen as possible. The criminal charges being considered were based solely on the checks that had been forged.

In the process of filing the request for the prejudgment remedy, Chris and I were called as witnesses. I took the stand and recounted our discovery of the fraudulent activity amid numerous objections by Albert's and Jack's attorneys. When Chris took the witness stand, a lot of the questioning was redundant to what I had been asked, but he was also given expert witness status to speak about our claim-handling procedures. At one point, Jack's attorney addressed Chris.

"Mr. Brown, you've testified that Superior Insurance Company has a program that allows your claim employees to refer your policy holders directly to a contractor, is that correct?"

"Yes," Chris replied.

"And you've also testified that my client, Jack March, was never approved for this program and should not have been referred to your policy holders as a preferred contractor, correct?" the attorney asked.

"Correct," Chris responded.

Jack's attorney spun around and confronted Chris. It was a Perry Mason moment. "Then can you tell me why my client's name is stamped on the outside of this file jacket?

Does Superior Insurance Company make up a stamp for every nonpreferred contractor?" he demanded.

Chris was caught a little off guard. He knew we didn't stamp contractors' names on our file jackets and evidence to the contrary was not going to help our case. He looked concerned and asked if he could look at the file. Jack's attorney handed it over and Chris studied it for a minute. Then his furrowed brow relaxed.

"Sure, I can explain how your client's name got stamped on our file."

"Please do," the attorney replied almost smugly.

Chris said, "March . . . 22. It's the date the file was closed, counselor, not Jack March's last name." Jack's defense attorney was stunned.

The judge gave him a look that could only be described as a mixture of contempt and pity and said, "I've heard enough. I'll return from my chambers shortly with my decision."

Twenty minutes later the judge returned and announced, "I believe that plaintiffs have proven their case, and I'm granting the prejudgment remedy and interest for $300,000. And with a little encouragement, I could be convinced to authorize arrest warrants for these two defendants."

Eventually, Albert and Jack were convicted of felony theft, given five and four years probation, respectively, and ordered to pay restitution. We collected about half of the money we estimated was overpaid on Albert's claim files.

Lessons Learned

Chris, Dawn, and I spent nearly four years involved in this case. In that time, we learned some valuable lessons about how to organize and execute a successful investigation and prepare a report for prosecution.

I knew that it would be foolhardy to attempt to investigate this claim myself and rely on my limited property estimating skills. If you don't have the expertise to speak with authority to critical parts of your investigation, it is imperative that you enlist the help of an expert in the field capable of speaking and perhaps testifying to the subject. Chris Brown's expertise provided us with reliable and convincing proof of overpayments on each claim we reinspected. Without it, we had the unqualified opinion of an auditor—and not much of a case.

Also, it is appropriate to pursue a civil remedy to recover assets. With the investigation we did and the report we prepared we were able to convince a prosecutor to bring felony theft charges against Albert and Jack, but only for the transactions that involved endorsement forgeries. If we had relied on the criminal trial to provide us with the most equitable recovery, we would have received about $55,000 in restitution. By pursuing the matter in the civil courts concurrently, we succeeded in recovering nearly $140,000.

I found that law enforcement was eager to present our report to the prosecutor once they fully grasped the nature of the crime. The number of transactions and the general confusion about insurance claim settlements outside the industry were barriers to getting our case accepted and understood. Depending on the type of transaction, law enforcement might not fully understand the nature of the activity and why it is inappropriate. We concluded that it is beneficial to be patient and tenacious about pursuing prosecution.

The investigative report we presented to law enforcement was a comprehensive document. We included a summary page to allow law enforcement and the prosecutor the opportunity to see the highlights of our case up front. We also included exhibits of every questionable transaction we issued and the estimates and photographs supporting our argument that the settlements were being padded. As we walked through the report with the state's attorney's office, having examples of the fraudulent payment activity, the forged documents, and the numerous affidavits helped educate the investigator and make him an advocate for our case.

RECOMMENDATIONS TO PREVENT FUTURE OCCURRENCES

Segregate Vendor Setup from Claims Checks

Albert's success in this scheme was in part relative to his ability to add new vendors to the claim system's records. All staff authorized to add vendors to our system should be segregated from issuing claims checks. The task of adding vendors is now performed by a department outside the Claims Department.

Claim Check Processing

In order to control the flow of funds, we found that Albert frequently had checks returned to him rather than being mailed directly from the print room. Management should create and enforce strict controls over the distribution of claim checks. Now, if claim checks are returned to a file adjuster at Superior (which are rare occurrences these days), controls are in place that require management to confirm the need and sign off on the transaction.

Management Review

When we started reviewing Albert's claim files, we began to wonder why his supervisor, Irma, hadn't picked up on some of the blatant red flags. We later discovered that Albert had forged Irma's sign-off adequately to fool the file clerks that his cases had been properly reviewed. Irma's reliance on Albert to help her with management functions had helped educate him regarding what it takes to keep a file from reaching her desk. Using staff to perform certain management security functions should be forbidden.

Robert B. Walsh Jr., CFE, is a senior business analyst with Liberty Mutual in Keene, New Hampshire. He has been investigating internal and external insurance fraud for Liberty's Agency Markets Group for 25 years. Mr. Walsh attended Middlesex Community College and Salem State College in Massachusetts and has over 29 years of experience in the insurance industry.

CHAPTER 43

Corruption By Seduction

DOUGLAS M. WATSON

Many thought Carlton White was a bit player—after all, he was just an American expatriate working as an expediter for FARGO, Inc., an oil company that was embroiled in a messy internal fraud inquiry. But Carlton was one of the original Inner Circle members—a corrupt clique of fellow employees who greased palms, connived and cajoled executives, and schmoozed officials, coworkers, and even friends—all to facilitate whatever his boss, Sami A. Hamed, desired. His payoff? Promotions, great pay, and vacations on the company, which he'd been with for almost 14 years.

And then he got the phone call.

It was December 13—not a Friday, but it should have been. Carlton's nest egg cracked. The call came from a member of the company's fraud examination unit. The question the FEU wanted Carlton to answer seemed pretty simple: Could he justify a company-paid trip from the Middle East to the United States? Would he mind dropping by headquarters to chat? The FEU was so polite.

The problem was, the only business Carlton had on that trip was to marry his boss's girlfriend and bring her back to the Middle East so that she and the boss could continue their tawdry relationship.

Questions raced through Carlton's mind: "What do I do now? What else do they know? Why would the FEU want to talk to me about a trip that happened more than four years ago? What would Sami think?"

Sami was Carlton's boss's boss, according to the organization chart. But Carlton knew that the in-between guy was just for show. He answered only to Sami.

"Sami is powerful," thought Carlton, hoping he could pull the right strings to get him out of this one.

"But," he thought, "this is different." This time someone was asking questions that crept too close to the truth. And now here he was on the wrong end of a phone call with a fraud examiner, who was patiently waiting for him to respond.

Sami was the managing director for FARGO's Project Management Department. He had been a company man since his college days and now was on track for a vice presidency. For

22 years, Sami had given FARGO loyalty, efficiency, and creativity. But things changed as the years passed. He had hired Carlton to be his business manager, and looking back on it, that's when things began to happen. It began slowly at first. Carlton's job was "expediter extraordinaire." An expediter does those jobs that no one else can do. Carlton did not know much about business or project management, but he sure knew how to get his hands on things fast. If you needed anything—from a telephone pole, to a flush valve for a Kohler urinal—Carlton could get it quickly and at the best price.

Palestinian by birth, Sami held strong personal ties to the West, especially America. Sami was a young-looking 46 with a well-trimmed beard, dark wavy hair, and gentle eyes. When you met him, you couldn't help but like the guy. He was incredibly smart.

Sami was an exceptional engineer; soft-spoken with leadership qualities that made people want to work. The company had sent him to the United States for a master's degree in engineering, and as he rose through the ranks, he completed FARGO's senior executive seminars.

While in London attending college, he met and married his first wife, Penelope, whom he described as a bit of a prude, but quite pretty. Together, they had two daughters, Deena and Aysha.

During his 22 years with FARGO, Sami quickly took on a great deal of responsibility. It wasn't that long ago that he had been appointed to take charge of arguably one of the most important support operations in the company, the project management department. This department managed the most complex and, consequently, the most expensive projects. He ran it flawlessly, consistently meeting or exceeding performance milestones. He was a regular at the company awards ceremonies, either as a giver or a receiver, and was always praised by FARGO's senior executives and the many contractors who carried out all those construction and engineering tasks. His office "Wall of Honor" looked like a military officer's with all the plaques and recognition certificates hanging proudly.

Ashrafullah Chisti, or Ashraf, as he preferred to be called, was pissed. As Sami's department office manager, he had just received a phone call from the vice president's office informing him that Carlton White, his logistics guy, was being investigated by the FEU. Ashraf knew that Carlton always pushed the envelope, but never to the point that would rise to the level of interest of the FEU.

As he listened to the phone call, running through the back of his mind was the thought that no one in the company liked the Fraud Examination Unit, except the president, of course.

"Allahallah [*Oh God...*]," mumbled Ashraf, wondering out loud what was to come of this.

Ashraf's concern certainly wasn't for Carlton's well-being. He was worried because Carlton was Sami's confidant—Carlton knew all Sami's secrets. And Carlton looked out only for Carlton. So, Ashraf sat down and, before briefing Sami about the bad news, began to consider the options.

An Indian of marked intelligence, crafty, and with a special talent for identifying team players, Ashraf was described by friends and enemies alike as a survivor, a scoundrel, and a conniver. Imposing for a Kshatriya Indian, Ashraf stood just over six feet, with balding black hair and a pale, almost pasty, complexion. He had a roundish face, no mustache, but a well-trimmed beard that just managed to cover his chin. Ashraf saw everything through owl-like eyes lurking behind wire rims.

Nothing moved in the project management department without Ashraf's knowledge: time and attendance, vacation schedules, promotion recommendations, job position vacancies, business travel authorizations and vouchers, contract proposals and awards—all the administrative details passed through his hands. He was the brains behind the schemes, the glue that held the players together. He didn't know it now, but he would be the one who walked away untouched.

Ashraf walked into Sami's office and broke the news.

Pam got her phone call about an hour after Ashraf received his.

"PK, you got your divorce papers from Carlton?" Sami asked softly.

Pamela Kaye Hamed was Sami's new wife. Sami had divorced Penelope after a long separation, during which he met Pam.

Pam's former husband, Fred Coin, was a FARGO design engineer who worked in the province projects division. Sami met Pam at an office function.

Petite, with close-cropped blond hair, big blue eyes, and a figure that made the neighborhood teenage boys put down their bootlegged copy of *Playboy*, Pam was Sami's vision of perfection. It wasn't long before they struck up a relationship that quickly moved to more than just glancing flirtations.

Intriguingly and perhaps coincidentally, shortly thereafter Pam's husband found himself the victim of downsizing. The company calls it "surplusing," but it only happens to expatriates and is usually nonnegotiable. After about 10 years on the job, Pam's husband suddenly became expendable. Coincidences notwithstanding, Fred was given a "golden handshake" (a tidy severance award of several thousand dollars), and the family returned to the United States. Shortly thereafter, Pam and Fred divorced.

The divorce set in motion a series of events that cost FARGO hundreds of thousands of dollars, raised serious conflicts of interest, and involved bribes and kickbacks, all of which were supported by false statements, bid rigging, and leaking sensitive proprietary information.

FARGO, Inc., is a Middle Eastern oil company led by a president who oversees a team of vice presidents charged with managing exploration, production, refining, and distribution operations. The company is goal-oriented, with formal management policy statements established to guide and control employee actions. Part of its corporate culture is to embrace the customs of the host nation and ameliorate conflict with the flow of commerce and international law.

FARGO hires its workforce from many different nations, and at the time when the fraud schemes were hatched, the Project Management Department was staffed by American, British, Indian, Pakistani, Palestinian, Lebanese, Saudi, Australian, Philippine, and several other Arab nationalities, each of whom brought engineering, project management, computer and communication, contract management, cost accountant, and administrative skills to bear.

The Project Management Department, where the fraud spawned, is a subordinate arm of what amounts to a traditional business organizational structure. FARGO's business system is wrapped by a protective boundary made up of company regulations and administrative policies and procedures designed to bring together a multinational employee base. These formed all the necessary "antifraud" trimmings: an internal system of controls and procedures, a comprehensive conflict-of-interest and business ethics statement, and a training program that addressed the responsibilities of ethics in everyday business. Strangely, it was this carefully designed one-policy-for-all business ethics standard that served as entrée for corruption but, in the end, provided the foundation to right the wrongs of the Inner Circle.

WHO'S OVEREGGIN'?

Ken Riley was the epitome of investigators. A former chief of police with more than 30 years in law enforcement and investigative work, Ken took an early retirement from his city job to sign on as a consultant to FARGO's FEU.

I ran the FEU at the time. We were shorthanded and needed top-line investigators to teach our multinational staff of investigators how best to catch "bad guys." FARGO wanted a strong, viable business ethics program and an equally powerful special unit to investigate and prove allegations of corruption or fraud. The FEU's job was to root out the truth.

I have known Ken for more than 15 years. He is the best in his field. No one can elicit an admission like Ken. He lives by two investigative precepts: "Coincidences usually aren't" and "Con artists can be conned." A nondescript guy, he's of average height and build, with thinning reddish hair and blue, or maybe green, eyes—you can't really tell because they change with his mood. When they're blue, watch out because he's on the hunt. False statements, bid rigging, and leaking proprietary information are the fuel that run his engine.

Ken was assigned to Carlton White. He was on the phone waiting patiently for Carlton's answer. His eyes were turning blue.

Before Ken had called Carlton, before anyone had briefed senior management that one of their executives was suspect, before anyone in the FEU had even considered the ramifications associated with investigating a managing director, Ken interviewed Jason Q. Plank.

Formally known in the FEU as CS-1 to protect his identity, Jason didn't care about protection; he didn't care who knew that he was angry. He was being surplused and was convinced the reason was because he was "out of favor" with Sami Hamed and Ashraf Chisti, especially Ashraf, because he had challenged Sami's way of business.

"Sami is out of control," he had said. "He is exerting improper influence over the department by pressuring his division managers and bypassing them to pressure the project managers and project engineers into selecting and favoring certain contractors. He has also placed himself in a conflict-of-interest situation with at least three contractors and is presumed to be receiving money or gratuities in return. He has developed an illicit network of personnel throughout the department to keep him informed and to carry out his desires. He is actively engaged in bid slate manipulation and is leaking proprietary information to favored contractors in order to get them contracts."

And those were just the opening comments of the first of several taped secret sessions with Jason. There was no question about it. He held a wealth of information alleging fraud, corruption, and potentially serious malfeasance. Jason's credentials would hold up, too. He was a 20-year FARGO employee, a senior engineer with proven hands-on as well as supervisory successes. Gruff, direct, and a cigar-chomping Texan, he was eligible for early retirement but did not want to leave the company. On the surface, the FEU could find nothing—no business reason—for why Jason should have been surplused.

Meticulously detailed, Jason's debriefing sessions—over a period of three days— produced an extensive witness statement.

The only problem was that Ken's "insider" was now on the outside. Since he was on the surplus list, Jason couldn't get access to documents and other materials necessary to prove the allegations

The key to unlocking FARGO's Pandora's box was Carlton.

As Jason was chatting with Ken, he mentioned that everything seemed to happen after Sami and Pam got married, "Sami wanted to make everything special for Pam—a new villa, a special job, anything."

He explained that before Sami and Pam were married, "Carlton went back to the U.S., married Pam, brought her back as his dependent, just so she and Sami could shack up. And the company paid for everything."

Something clicked in Ken's mind. A while back he had been casually chatting with a woman who sometimes provided interesting tidbits about the employees. The FARGO community was pretty close-knit, and Mary seemed to know everything about everyone. British, single, gregarious, and a member of the local theater group, she was in touch with all the latest gossip.

Mary was talking about Pam, about how while she had been married to a guy in the Province Projects, she was shacking up with an executive.

"And, then," as Mary told it, "after her husband was surplused, she dumped him and married a Yank to get back to FARGO so she and her boyfriend could live together. Now, if that isn't overeggin' the pudding, I don't know what is."

It all made sense now. Pam's "overeggin'" hadn't added complexity. It actually provided a bit of clarity.

The records were all there—the marriage license, the U.S. visa applications, the household goods shipments, the business class airline tickets, the vouchers—all neatly filed away with Personnel and Finance. There was no doubt. Carlton and Pam had been married, and Pam was brought into the country as Carlton's wife and dependent.

Rummaging through the papers, Ken found the ace in the hole. A mail-order divorce. Carlton and Pam were divorced by mail—a Dominican Republic special: freedom for only $100.

Did You Get the Memo?

The interview room at the FEU was pretty stark. It had no windows, two relatively uncomfortable chairs, a small scarred and stained gray metal desk up against the far wall holding a single pad of paper and nothing else. It was also soundproofed. But behind the walls, everything was wired. We could listen while Ken and Carlton met face to face. It took two interview sessions. At the end of the second, Carlton made his offer.

"Will $25,000 cover it?" he asked, as he began to pen out a personal check to the fraud investigator. "I just want to put this behind me. Who should I make it out to? You or the company?"

Obviously, Ken didn't take the check, but he got the information he needed—Carlton's statement contained all the golden nuggets.

Before the interview, Ken kept saying "Find the slime and you'll find the crime." Well, we had the slime, but we hadn't found the catalyst—the gel to mold it together and reveal the fraud beneath the scum line.

In making his allegations, Jason provided clues as to how people had been strategically placed in the department. The interesting part was who those people were. Jason's statement had said, "Sami's system has been used in at least three cases. Contract Administration introduces new or unknown contractors on to a bid slate who either are not authorized to do the work being bid on or have not done this sort of work previously. Sami's design engineer will cost out all the details. Sami will leak company estimates to the preferred contractor, who then can easily underbid even the most experienced contractors. Once they start work, if there are problems with the service orders, they use their connection with Sami to obtain favorable business decisions or get change orders."

He didn't name names, but he was able to identify the choke points in the Project Management Department.

To guarantee control, Sami needed conspirators from each of four key divisions: Administration and Support Services, Engineering Services, Design and Architectural Services, and Contract Administration. Over time, Sami and Ashraf selectively introduced members of each of those into the conspiracy. There never was anything formal or special involved—no right of passage or Mafioso oath to enter the Inner Circle. It just evolved. Key people were given special favors by Sami or Ashraf, and then they were expected to fall in line.

In a nutshell, the Inner Circle was a hidden power structure. By co-opting at least one insider in each division, Sami and Ashraf had neatly established a clandestine link that provided advance notice of any potential problem.

As we looked closer into the circle, Ken and I discovered some interesting aspects. Ashraf had his finger on all Inner Circle members but one: Pam. And it is Pam's story that gelled the corruption.

Shortly after Carlton brought Pam back, Sami used his influence to place her as a contract coordinator in the Contract Administration Division. Normal human resources channels were bypassed even though conflict-of-interest and business ethics policies discouraged family members from working in the same department—Ashraf took care of that little detail.

FARGO hires employees from more than 20 different countries. And true to form, within the Project Management Department, as well as throughout the company, the different cultures mixed when business required, but socially, and by personal preference, employees tended to gather and trust according to national and cultural background.

Pam's hiring caused several responses. To the Arabs, Filipinos, and some others who were predominantly Muslim, the move was conflicting. In their eyes, a female held less status than a male, but Pam's position as a contract coordinator placed her in a position of some responsibility. She vetted contractor credentials for bid slate nominations, verified contractor charges, and certified contractor performance, each an important function of the system of managerial controls. Since by this time, she was the big boss's wife, they knew that even though they did not like what they saw, nothing could be done about it. To the Americans and Brits, the move was revealing. They saw it as something to use to weaken Sami's power.

What the Inner Circle did was infiltrate the day-to-day business and exploit areas of weakness where they could benefit. Pam was able to influence bid slate qualifications for "preferred contractors" and manipulate the selection scores, which were used to rank-select contractors. Her decisions went unquestioned because she was the boss's wife. With "preferred contactors" in place, everything else was simple.

With the Contract Administration Department under control, the other divisions easily followed suit—just as Jason said.

"It all goes back to Pam," Ken explained. "Sami started this all to protect his relationship with Pam. He wanted her, so he sent Carlton out to get her. Once she got here, he wanted to give her everything—and nothing was going to stand in his way. But for Sami to do what he wanted to do, he had to build the Inner Circle. He needed someone to keep control—manage things."

"Check out Jason's statement," I interrupted. "There's more going on here than a little adultery and travel fraud."

The impact occurred on two levels: personal and corporate. First, Sami was using his power and influence as a company executive to give his new wife luxury and status. But to do that, he compromised company ethical standards and his fiduciary responsibilities.

The company records confirmed what Carlton had told Ken. In order to get his mistress back, Sami had Ashraf authorize business assignments, travel orders, and other arrangements to facilitate Carlton's travel to the United States. The trip—purportedly to check on business in Houston—was a sham. Carlton never traveled to Houston and never did any business in the States. But he did travel to Las Vegas where, at 10:39 a.m. on March 24, he married Pam—U.S. court records confirmed that. FARGO's U.S. subsidiary then arranged and funded international travel for Pam, as Carlton's new wife, to return overseas.

When Pam and Carlton returned from the States, Pam immediately moved in with Sami, who at the time was occupying company executive housing.

Meanwhile, Carlton quietly submitted a travel voucher, claiming $5,240 in personal business expenses. The sum was minimal, but the impact was significant. The Project Management Department, and the Inner Circle in particular, accepted Sami's lead and decided that operating outside traditional company mores was justified *and* profitable.

Executive housing had become an enclave where expatriates were not truly welcome. Even though Sami fit in, his first wife and Pam never did. Sami wanted his own villa, one properly outfitted with all the amenities of Arab hospitality, but also equipped with the American opulence that Pam expected. The villa became Project Management's top priority.

That piece of information about the villa, coupled with the background in Jason's statement, prompted extensive contract reviews. An "archival" contract—which constitutes the official record—contains every document ever produced that has to do with a contractual agreement. Archival contracts even contain handwritten notes, each nicely dated and tabulated. They sit in filing cabinets patiently waiting for fraud investigators to discover their secrets.

We put together a team of four to review several contracts, all having to do with construction projects, all managed by Sami's crew. Here's a sample of what we found:

- Memo from a project manager to a vice president:

  > I would like to confirm our conversation that occurred approximately two months ago regarding my involvement with and assistance to our managing director, Sami A. Hamed, in building his own villa. Please be informed that the time I am spending in supervising this activity has no impact on my work as I am doing this either on my lunch hour or after working hours during my spare time. The only problem I could see is the utilization of one of my site supervisors. This site supervisor has been assigned to help supervise and coordinate construction activities for the last four months. I want to draw your attention to this fact and advise management about this situation. I will not be responsible for any consequences as a result of this action.

- Handwritten note by the vice president:

  > Discussed this with Sami. The matter is resolved.

Unfortunately, the VP's comments notwithstanding, little happened. But my team's contract reviews produced a revealing timeline. Construction projects matched villa progress from planning and design to the groundbreaking and construction. And costs were adroitly hidden between the lines of change orders, purchase orders, and time card reports.

For example, the team learned that Steve Phillips, Sami's man in Design Engineering and a trusted member of the Inner Circle, had earned a perk about three months before construction had begun on Sami's villa. Using a legitimate design project as justification, Phillips traveled to the United States to obtain 3D-CAD state-of-the-art design equipment, software, and training.

It did not take the FEU long to discover that even though a legitimate project was cited to justify the trip, under normal circumstances it would have been disapproved as an unnecessary expense, since the cited project did not justify that level of expertise. The real reason that Phillip's trip was approved was to design Sami's new villa; price was no object. Phillips, of course, got to add a newfound and coveted skill to his résumé as the company's 3D-CAD expert.

To build the villa, Project Management pulled out all the stops. Architectural and design services, surveyor services, and construction site supervision was completed under Sami's oversight. The jobs were assigned, performed, or certified by one of the Inner Circle but charged against legitimate projects. Except for some special-order items like Italian marble and teakwood trim, much of the villa's materials and building supplies were charged off to related projects by inflating quantities.

The site supervisor was identified and agreed to cooperate. During the ensuing series of interviews, he described how he rationalized his part:

> I worked as the villa site supervisor for about seven months and spent about four to eight hours daily on the site. I was taken off the job because rumor had it that someone had complained that we were being used on the villa but charging our time to other jobs. Sami visited the site frequently and he certainly knew who I was. He also knew that in order to get paid, I had logged my time on the other job: the security gate. Regardless, this all seemed fairly straightforward to me, and I don't think I've done anything wrong and I have never received anything from anyone for doing my job.

As the coup de grace, the FEU learned that Sami struck a deal with a local contractor who agreed to build the villa free of charge, but in return for assurances that future bids for FARGO jobs would be favorably considered.

After work had started on the villa, FARGO called for bids to participate in a major multimillion-dollar cross-complex project to lay fiber optic cable and complete associated communications and construction work. Sami's villa contractor submitted a bid to lay roadbed and complete construction on other tasks associated with the cabling setup and splicing. The contractor won the bid—uncontested.

TEARING DOWN THE VILLA

At its zenith, the Inner Circle comprised at least 14 key staff members, in addition to Pam and Sami. All operational functions of the Project Management Department were penetrated. Both field and headquarters operations were involved, but the four main headquarters divisions remained most important.

Ten local contractors were identified as being complicit. Each maintained a conspiratorial relationship with Sami and only Sami.

Over time, the Inner Circle members and the outliers—those who tangentially profited by taking advantage of Sami's compromise—had become proficient at manipulating purchase orders, contract work, and contractors. The principal beneficiaries were Sami and his wife. Others benefited from the benevolent acts Sami bestowed to them. Yet some became greedier, demanding undeserved promotions or special assignments. Some engaged in their own independent fraud with an expectation that, if discovered, they would be protected. As they continued their improper acts, they began to take uncharacteristically escalating risks, both individually and in concert with one another.

While the Inner Circle engaged in conspiratorial entropy, FARGO's management began to take notice. Routine work came under closer scrutiny, and checks and balances began to kick in. Division managers, all of whom always knew what was going on, saw a chink in Sami's armor. One came forward. So did more memos, like the one to the vice president.

Sami's response was strange. To Ken and me, as we reconstructed the events, it seemed like Sami took a bring-it-on attitude. It was almost as if he felt invulnerable.

Sami's department managed FARGO's multimillion-dollar project covering fiber optic installation. Instead of backing off, Sami ignored the signals and initiated an unparalleled case of contractor favoritism. In addition to guaranteeing a subcontract to his villa builder, he interceded in each phase of the project, the bid process, and the eventual contract awards by:

- Leaking key pricing information to favored contractors, thus subverting competition
- Altering engineering assessments that were critical of his preferred contractor to militate against technical disqualification
- Once a contract was awarded, allowing product substitution to favored contractors
- Allowing overcharges on service orders, but only to favored contractors
- Suppressing safety violations by his preferred contractors
- Interceding in favor of his preferred contractors during contract claims negotiations
- And, ultimately, endorsing payment for work not performed

Throughout the process, Sami required Inner Circle conspirators to support his acts. This overwhelmed their capabilities because of the number of outside agencies involved in the contractual process and an increased oversight by the company. Division managers were faced with externally originating complaints and were unable to defend the actions. The effect was that the Inner Circle was placed in a position of increased interaction with outsiders, causing greater scrutiny.

And then Sami surplused Jason.

Amar A. Ismael was the manager who came forward. He proved to be an interesting witness. Amar was an up-and-comer in Sami's department, but he knew he could only "up and come" so far. He saw an opportunity to advance his cause by helping to move Sami out—the domino theory in action.

He asked to talk privately with Ken.

Amar knew he should be a managing director, but also he knew his chances were slim. Opportunity knocked.

He spent several days with Ken. With meticulous patience, Ken recorded Amar's statements, independently validating point by point that which Jason had already provided. We were now ready to interview Sami.

I interviewed Sami three times and took two statements. He was very cooperative. First, he explained his affair with Pam, then he rationalized the eventual surplusing of her husband, and finally he justified the arrangements with Carlton. In his words:

> He did this for me as a personal favor. The real reason for the trip was to allow Carlton to go the U.S. to marry Pam. Pam and I had planned to be married after she obtained her divorce, but the paperwork was taking an extremely long time to process through the ministry. Carlton fixed it and we avoided all the governmental bureaucratic mess. It was the only way we could be together.

Then Sami let out another tidbit: Carlton played "Dad" for Sami's two daughters from his first marriage. While Sami was confirming our case against Carlton, he was also cementing our case against himself. He admitted sending Carlton to the United States to help enroll both daughters in school and help them obtain U.S. residency status. This admission confirmed and established the reliability of previously discovered computer files. It did not matter to Sami that Carlton's trips cost the company about $52,864. Of that, Carlton vouched for a total of $25,877. Sami was the string-puller who financed Carlton's work, using company money. Now we knew why Carlton offered to repay $25,000.

Everything about the villa was true. Sami's rationalization was simple: In his opinion his people were the best; he wanted his villa to be the best, so he used his people. He stated it as if it were just simple fact.

To the end, Sami maintained that he never abused his authority. Even when confronted with testimony and supporting evidence from seven employees that they had been fired or surplused for refusing to engage in Sami's frauds, he denied it.

When the Inner Circle collapsed, FARGO's management had to decide what to do. Middle Easterners are culturally very hospitable and nonconfrontational, even in their business dealings. Astute decision makers in the sense that they intuitively know the correct decision, most of FARGO's senior leadership would have preferred to have unpleasant decisions carried out by others to avoid causing a colleague to lose face. Unpleasant as it was, senior management recognized that action was necessary. This was, after all, the first case where a member of the executive staff had been caught in such blatant acts of deception.

The office suite for the vice president was appointed a bit differently from mine. When I passed by the security guard and through the secretary's office, I walked into a different world. The VP's gnarled walnut executive desk sat center rear in a room most would reserve for an office social function. The room was elaborately decorated; all the chairs had armrests. In the right corner, there were two Louis XV–style wing chairs covered in blue and gold vertical striped tufted cloth with that telltale bicolor shade of silk.

Hassan, the VP, was very pleasant. He wore the traditional Arab thobe—it was impeccable—white, crisply ironed, with small gold ball cufflinks. He was used to talking to politicians, princes, and presidents.

We drank tea. He listened intently.

The job of the FEU is to present facts, details, and offer countermeasures. The FEU is there to protect the company. What many people forget is that one of the most precious assets a company holds is reputation.

I carefully explained the fraud, all the accompanying parts, and each of the perpetrators. We discussed the Inner Circle relationships, the identity of CS-1 (Jason), the possible customs and immigration irregularities, and the direct chargeable losses to the company. We discussed the dynamics of cross-cultural interpretations of fraud and the value of awareness training for all employees, both management and worker. I made no action or disciplinary recommendations. Adjudication is not the FEU's job.

In the end, Sami was quietly offered the opportunity to retire, with compensation. He did so and shortly thereafter left for the United States. His punishment was more than it appears to western eyes. He lost respect, among both his peers and from his   extended family. Pam had already left the country and was somewhere in the States, waiting for Sami.

Carlton and three other expatriates were unceremoniously surplused. They did not get the coveted "golden handshake." Jason left the company, but not under a cloud. Special arrangements were made to provide him proper compensation—he received his golden handshake. Amar, the cooperative manager, was appointed to take Sami's position, which was a substantial promotion. However, many in the company were not pleased that Amar provided evidence against a member of senior management. He was shamed by his betrayal of his managing director and would see no further promotions.

Ashraf moved to a new position in the company and was eventually promoted.

LESSONS LEARNED

In order to educate the company, the FEU was invited to present a recurring session on business ethics at the Management Training Center to midlevel management—the leadership of the future. The FEU was also consulted as the company initiated an awareness program that emphasized the importance of mission, vision, and values.

Executive management had made an important business decision: Send a subtle but positive message to the company and business partners alike, a message that emphasized an ethical corporate culture and encouraged employees to embrace that in lieu of the strains placed by national or cultural markers.

An important lesson spawns from this case study: Culture matters. FARGO's management learned that the hard way. Employee attitudes, beliefs, and traditions are powerful motivators. They can be abused by fraudsters, but they also can be championed by management to build corporate pride. It depends on managerial ingenuity and adroit leadership. FARGO had all the ethical trimmings in place. It lost focus and allowed cultural pressures to override management objectives. Its corrective decision was bold, with a long-term outlook for success. Concepts of right and good carry considerable weight in the business world. Operating from a moral perspective actually encourages change and spawns trust.

For the investigator, this case underscored the need to pay attention to detail. Even small things like handwritten notes in archived files or seemingly unimportant computer file entries about family matters can provide the catalyst that makes the case.

RECOMMENDATIONS TO PREVENT FUTURE OCCURRENCES

Hotlines

Anonymous hotlines help identify fraud and corruption. Anonymity is important in every culture, but may be more so in multicultural environments. Middle Easterners in general tend to avoid public confrontation. A hotline offers another venue to report impropriety. A company-sanctioned anonymous means of reporting irregularity or malfeasance enhances the company's business ethics policy and at the same time provides a subtle deterrent effect. Hotlines are inexpensive and relatively easy to run.

Fraud Awareness

It is not unusual for companies and corporations to hold periodic business ethics training sessions for all employees. Most cover the basics like the costs of fraud, red flags that identify fraud and abuse, some common schemes, and the duties and responsibilities of each employee to protect against fraud. What frequently is missing is tying antifraud behavior to the company's value statements and identifying employees as stakeholders in preserving the reputation of the firm. Ingraining an antifraud attitude into a company's mission, vision, and values becomes an actionable principle of expected behavior and defines the organization's culture to its employees—new and tenured—and advertises it to customers and other outsiders.

Internal Controls

Nothing serves to prevent fraud and corruption better than effective internal controls. The key word is *effective*. FARGO had all the requisite corporate audit and accounting controls, but they were not employed effectively. FARGO responded by devising stricter independent oversight, much like an inspector general–type assessment of contracts and major purchases. The Auditing Department handles the responsibility for this initiative by providing no-notice random contract reviews as a supplement to the Sarbanes-Oxley–type mechanisms already in place.

Transparency

Mark "*Deep Throat*" Felt said it best. To find corruption, "Follow the money." Any company—or organization—that exploits methodological transparency as its business model has taken a first and most important step to countering corruption and fraud. Transparency is not a panacea, but offering a clear and objective road map that explains how business is conducted and how finances are managed builds ethical confidence.

Douglas M. Watson, Ph.D., CFE, has 35 years of investigative experience in the private and public sector, 25 of which were spent overseas. He works for the U.S. Department of Energy and is also an adjunct professor with George Mason University in Fairfax, Virginia. His area of expertise is cross-cultural dynamics of fraud, corruption, and trust betrayal.

CHAPTER 44

"Big Easy" Business

PATRICK W. MALIK AND JEFFREY R. SEBREE

Shortly after Herb Loft man sat down in his office chair, his wife called, again complaining about some of their daughter's wedding plans. This time it was about the deposit needed to book "BJ the DJ." Herb just couldn't get ahead. Only during the last two years of his marriage did he and his wife begin having problems. Perhaps their daughter's impending wedding was at the root of it. After all, it was crunch time for the plans, the commitments, and the costs.

When things were tight in the past, Herb had experienced strings of luck to tide him over. He began making frequent trips to the local casinos, or "the boats," as they were known locally. Herb recently found himself in the hole again, but it appeared that no matter what he tried, he just kept digging. It was not long before his latest attempts to bring home some extra cash turned into overdrafts and credit card debt. Ultimately, he filed for Chapter 13 bankruptcy.

Herb was a manager responsible for the administration of various items at South Bay Component Systems, Inc. Several years ago, when he awarded a deal to Heckler Contracting, a small company that maintained facilities for South Bay, he found a friend in Woody Heckler, the owner. Though they lived in different states, they became close and offered each other emotional support from time to time. During one of many telephone conversations, Herb confided in Woody: "I just can't keep living like this; my wife is about to leave me, I'm on the outs with my daughter, and I'm flat broke."

Woody consoled him. "You'll make it through this tough time. As a matter of fact, my contract is up for renewal. I'll be in town in the next few weeks to speak with your superiors about my contract renewal, so let's go hit the boats, have a few beers, and talk about it." When Woody made the trip and met with Herb, they talked about many avenues to get ahead: penny stocks, college football wagers, even the ponies. Herb talked more about his woes: how his daughter, who also worked at South Bay, was going to be married soon.

"Woody, I am so proud that my daughter has done well with the company and is getting married, but I have no idea how I'm going to pay for all this. I need to save face. With the threat of divorce and after filing for bankruptcy, I feel like I have really let my family down, especially my daughter. I need to come through for all of them."

"I think I know how we can ensure that your daughter will have a great wedding," said Woody. "Let's have another round."

Tip of the Iceberg

After dusting a few snowflakes out of my hair and making it to the coffeepot, I heard Raymond, my longtime cohort and coworker, approaching. We have worked together at South Bay for several years in construction and contract auditing. I've been here since the company's inception. Raymond was excited about a fax that he received from our hotline. It was a tip about a scheme that may have taken place recently.

As we examined the document and traced the telephone numbers, we determined that it had initially been sent to a machine in our Purchasing Department, which was located in an unsecured area. Subsequently, it had been faxed to our hotline by an unidentified individual from the same fax machine.

The fax was very precise when it came to the alleged fraud that had taken place. It was signed by George Harbour, who indicated that he was a former business partner of Woody Heckler. George and Woody were most recently involved in the profession of storm chasing—brokering roofing and tree removal services. The tip outlined a scheme whereby Woody, who owned a separate entity that subcontracts with South Bay, supposedly conspired with a company employee in our Purchasing Department to process fraudulent invoices exceeding $200,000. We thought this possible since we had discovered frauds in that area of the company before.

Suspicions Confirmed

Raymond initially focused on the assertion that fraudulent invoices had been paid. He first obtained a list of all contracts and related payments made to Woody Heckler. In recent years, South Bay had taken advantage of every opportunity to streamline accounts payable routines. Contractors could receive payments in three different ways: the contract management system, which electronically processes payments; procurement credit card transactions; and the traditional check requests. Due to its enhanced control features, the contract management system was the preferred method. It automatically compared line items on the invoice prior to payment. Procurement card transactions and check requests left the door open to potentially overlook the existence of a contract. In focusing on payments made to Woody, Raymond ran several queries against account payable data tables. In an effort to refine his search, he sorted the information in several ways: to identify payments that were not in accordance with agreements in effect at the time of payment; to evaluate accounting information to identify specific cost centers, cost codes, and whether the amounts were charged to a capitalized work order or to operating expense cost center; and to look for irregularities in invoice numbers, dates, amounts billed, and the usual payment procedure.

Suddenly I heard Raymond call out, "We've got a bingo!" Simply put, he identified two distinct abnormalities associated with six payments. Raymond noted that all of them had invoice numbers that were not comparable to others. They totaled $202,500. These findings prompted Raymond to locate the invoices and to examine the circumstances under which they were paid.

South Bay's electronic filing system is a great tool for auditors and investigators because all invoicing documentation is scanned after being paid. The images are readily available for review on demand, and hard copies can be retrieved from the offsite warehouse. Raymond continued his examination and confirmed his suspicions. The numbers were out of sequence, and more important, the format was different from other previously paid invoices. In addition, below Heckler Contracting in the header, the city name was misspelled. The final red flag was that the invoices were charged to a capitalized work order. This was strange as the description on the invoices appeared to be related to operating expense. Also, the documentation on the invoice showed it took place in Texas, but the capitalized work order claimed it was done in California. Work in that state would not have involved Heckler Contracting.

To confirm our suspicions, we took the next step in the investigation—contacting our source, George Harbour, to arrange to meet. Prior to calling, we performed a background check on him, but we could not find any public records linking him to Woody Heckler. We were not sure where George was located because the phone number on the border of the faxed tip had a Louisiana area code while the return number handwritten on the fax was a Texas area code. We determined that the phone number was a cellular.

We called the Texas number and found George in Louisiana, somewhere near Lake Pontchartrain. He sounded surprisingly calm, almost relieved that we had called. It did not take us long to get a read on why George was ratting out his business partner: revenge. Apparently, Woody had disappeared with some recent profits they had earned. Woody and George brokered jobs in a business called French Sky Roofing.

George lived in St. Tammany on the north side of the lake and recommended we meet him at a hotel. We moved quickly to ensure that he did not get cold feet. Initially, we were curious as to how George knew about Heckler Contracting and how he knew to send that fax to South Bay's Purchasing Department. He said he had found a letter from South Bay to Heckler Contracting in Woody's truck one day that contained the fax number. He had put the document in his pocket at the time, but could not explain why. After Woody ran off with some of George's part of the payment from the roofing business, he remembered Woody boasting about having a friend at South Bay and how they stole over $200,000 some time ago. He thought ratting him out might be a way to get some of his money back and seek revenge in the process.

While reviewing the information George provided, I asked him why he thought Woody may have a conspirator at South Bay. Without hesitation, he replied, "Woody made phone calls to someone at the company frequently. He was always telling this person what to do and not to worry about the consequences. I remember him saying something about how the money was going to a good cause. I think it was a wedding, but I can't remember exactly."

Incredibly, Woody's calls to South Bay were made on French Sky Roofing's cellular phone. George had access to the invoices and brought copies for the past six months. "Thanks, George," I said. "Investigations aren't supposed to be this easy, are they?"

As it turned out, George's information was right on the mark. We confirmed that the cell phone bills listed calls to a man named Herb Loftman. The case was coming together. At this point we decided to involve the regional postal inspector, Abigail Horn, since some of the evidence was processed through the mail. Abigail wanted to interview Herb as soon as possible. We informed Herb's superiors of our suspicions about his involvement in the fraud and advised that they should be prepared to relieve him of his duties. We summoned Herb to the office under the guise of other business that I had recently discussed with him. Abigail did not waste any time. She rolled up her sleeves and immediately told him that he was suspected of conspiring with Woody Heckler to have multiple fraudulent invoices paid. She told him that the penalties for his involvement could be quite stiff, but if he cooperated she would make sure prosecutors knew of his willingness to help with the case. Initially Herb denied the accusations. He was clearly weighing his options. For about an hour Abigail consoled him in a manner that sounded like she was his best friend. She impacted him with sound reasoning and conveyed an understanding of how good Herb will feel to get this off his conscience. After she went outside with him to get some fresh air, he confessed to his part in the fraud.

Justice Is Served

After Herb's confession, Abigail immediately proceeded to work with him, seeking cooperation in bringing Woody to justice. Prior audits of Heckler Contracting had given us a pretty fair idea of Woody's background and character, which meant that convincing him to confess would not be easy. But Abigail remained confident that she could not only find Woody but bring the investigation to a successful conclusion.

Based on what George had told us, all we knew was that he recently left Louisiana. Abigail attempted to locate and implicate him by having Herb contact him over a recorded line. Herb tried to casually lure Woody into incriminating himself to confirm his involvement. During one of the calls Herb said, "I've been researching those penny stocks we've talked about as I am trying to turn that money we stole into much more than it is now. What are your thoughts?"

Sounding confused, Woody replied, "Money we stole? I'm not sure what you're talking about, but if you're looking to invest, I hope you pick some winners."

Abigail encouraged Herb to carry on with the conversation.

"Woody, I'd like to try our cash machine again," Herb continued. "I need some extra cash and I know of some work orders to steal some from. What do you say? It will be easier than the last time we did it."

"Herb, I know you may be hard up right now. I'd love to help you out, but I can't afford to loan you any money." Even with our carefully devised angles, Woody chose his words carefully and was probably savvy enough to recognize what was going on.

Next, Abigail made the appropriate requests to identify real property and subpoenaed relevant banking records related to companies Woody either owned or acted in as a principle partner. This included checking, savings, and investments accounts. Ultimately, Abigail would take these to the United States Attorney. Bank records proved Woody deposited the check from South Bay in the amount of $202,500 and had subsequently written a check to Herb from that account in the amount of $20,000. We never expected that Woody would not have covered his tracks.

As criminal proceedings advanced, Woody took a different route from Herb by claiming innocence. In fact, Woody carried his innocence to the day of the trial when the prosecuting and defense attorneys exchanged offers one last time. Suddenly the defense counsel approached the bench and offered complete restitution, handing the judge a check in the amount of $202,500. This act indicated that Woody would plead guilty. Obviously the restitution, along with some sympathetic sob stories, was an attempt to affect the sentencing. Woody explained that he was genuinely sorry and told stories about how his family depended on him. The judge did not buy it. He reprimanded the defense counsel and Woody for taking things this far. The judge accepted the restitution and sentenced Woody to one year in federal prison without the possibility of parole.

Because Herb had cooperated and entered his guilty plea without going to trial, he received six months. Cooperation paid off. Subsequent to his sentencing and upon his release, his former coworkers maintained some degree of sympathy for the guy. Many people understood the circumstances he found himself in and have not condemned him personally. Herb has completed his sentence and has retired.

LESSONS LEARNED

Raymond and I believe that the ease with which the evidence was obtained and corroborated certainly contributed to the success of this case. We got everything out that we had hoped to: convictions, restitution, and jail time. We are convinced that a fraud of this amount would not have been pursued if it had taken months of dedicated effort. In the past, when we could not convince local authorities to pursue a case, we handled things internally. For example, we might fire the contractor or remove the company from future bidding lists. Conversely, we occasionally ended up working out a deal whereby we collected refunds for suspected overcharges.

We are of the opinion that fraud cases should be prosecuted when you are fairly certain of the outcome. Depending on the complexity, severity, and magnitude of the crime, some consideration should be given to turning the case over to state, rather than federal, authorities. In this particular case, we determined that the facts could not be manipulated in any manner that would lessen the charges. Regardless, before you hand over your case to law enforcement and to federal or state prosecutors, make sure you "put a bow" on it by presenting conclusive evidence that requires minimal legwork on their part. Prosecutors are usually more willing to take the case when they know there is a good chance of a guilty verdict.

Developing and maintaining a relationship with local law enforcement, postal inspectors, and prosecuting attorneys is very important in attaining cooperation from appropriate individuals. We make it a point to keep local officials somewhat involved with corporate functions and aware of particular issues we may be investigating. For example, when we have dignitaries such as members of our board of directors or other nationally recognized individuals visiting our headquarters, we always try to invite local law enforcement and other officials, providing them the opportunity to meet our senior management.

Regardless of how prepared you are, one thing that is always difficult to handle with sources is when they request a reward for supplying you with information. Our policy is to deny any rewards to avoid the perception of conflict of interest. George asked that we issue him a few hundred shares of company stock. Despite the solid evidence he provided, we could not honor his request.

The value of having a fraud hotline is immeasurable. Fraud is a problem that is faced by nearly all organizations. While employees are often the first to recognize a fraud, it is also important to publicize the existence of your hotline to customers and on your company's Web site. Law-abiding customers and citizens often respond in kind when made aware and given the opportunity to report suspicious activity. Tips are key in the fight against fraud. A fraud hotline provides consistent handling of tips because trained interviewers follow a designed protocol. In addition, many hotline providers also offer 24/7 communications and reporting services.

RECOMMENDATIONS TO PREVENT FUTURE OCCURRENCES

Update Technology

Technology allowed South Bay to eliminate manual or paper check requests. Electronic invoice processing systems actually provide improved controls related to the probability of identifying old-fashioned forgeries. We were recently involved in another case in which an employee who used to be a contractor for the company had forged manual check requests. Technological advances are making the outdated signature authorities obsolete. Evaluate your company's controls over the receipt of goods and invoice approval routines.

Review Work Orders

We have found that most funds that have been misappropriated have been charged to capital projects rather than departmental operating expense. The importance of reviewing capital work orders systematically cannot be underestimated.

Learn to Examine Data for Red Flags

Identifying unusual payments to regularly used contractors is another investigative technique. Red flags often are recognized after simply looking at the reasonableness, order, and sequencing of dates, invoice numbers, and amounts. Examine all available data by designing database queries to detect potential irregularities. Gain the skill to design and execute your own queries. You do not necessarily need to be a computer "guru." Many software packages make highly technical tasks simple.

Publicize the Results of the Investigation

As mentioned, you should publicize the results of the case. At South Bay, we have established a specific area in our online newsletter that is dedicated to reporting ethical concerns and the results of important fraud investigations. It is here that we continually remind employees to report any suspicious activity or concerns. The effectiveness of making fraud investigation public is based on deterrence. That is, if someone is aware that there is a significant possibility of being caught, this fear will deter the person from committing the crime.

Conflicts of interest often involve individuals with procurement responsibilities. Train your line personnel not to be intimidated or influenced by contractors. Give them the confidence to carry out their duties honestly and effectively.

Patrick W. Malik, CIA, CCSA, is the director of construction and contract audit with one of America's leading transportation companies. Mr. Malik is a graduate of the University of Texas at Arlington and has more than 20 years of corporate audit experience.

Jeffrey R. Sebree, CFE, CIA, is manager—CFO of joint ventures with one of America's leading transportation companies. Prior to his current position, he was an audit supervisor. Mr. Sebree received his BSBA, cum laude, and MBA degrees from Creighton University. He has over seven years of professional experience.

CHAPTER 45

Unlucky 13

GRAHAM J. THOMSON

Chris Mousley was a success story in anyone's language. At age 40, he lived in a luxurious house in a picturesque part of the English countryside. He'd spared no expense at his lavish wedding. Afterward, his young trophy wife gave birth to a healthy son. Chris was in the prime of his life: not bad for the son of a coal miner from the Welsh valleys.

Chris was raised in a small, dreary mining village in Wales by a hardworking family. His childhood memories were cluttered with sheep farms, foggy hills, and the musty smell of burned coal. Black Gold, they called it. "A fossil fuel consisting of carbonized vegetable matter deposited in the Carboniferous period," his dad would regurgitate at the dinner table. To most, coal is just a source of warmth on cold winter nights and the most common source of electricity in the world. But for Chris, it was different. He hated coal. It was a bitter reminder of his working-class upbringing and the source of his drive and ambition.

Almost all of Chris's family, friends, and neighbors had been miners. In Chris's father's era, most young boys could choose from dozens of coal mines within traveling distance of their homes. For many young men in the village, a life underground was not a choice—there were hardly any other employment opportunities. After a series of adverse events, there was only one deep mine left in all of South Wales.

With little local work available, poverty spread throughout in the village. As a youth, Chris had vowed that he would escape the misery. He would explore the world, work hard, and make sure that he would never have to endure the kind of paucity his parents and relatives endured.

To Chris, Black Gold was more like Black Death.

True to his word, he studied hard in school and was accepted by a decent college. After an undistinguished, but highly enjoyable, university career, Chris graduated and searched for a more prosperous life. Eventually he was hired as a junior manager by a retail store and worked his way up from the shop floor to the head office. With over 10 years at the company, he had reached senior management level and was a project manager in a new area of the Information Technology (IT) Department. A loyal and dedicated employee, he was respected by his peers and colleagues.

James Calder founded Jim's Store on his return from service with the British Royal Air Force during World War I. As a youth, he opened a small place in East London to sell goods. Bit by bit, the business expanded to other markets all over the city.

Jim's Store's growth since World War II involved a transformation of both its strategy and its image. The initial success was based on the pile-it-high, sell-it-cheap methodology. This plan made a poor impression with middle-class customers. By the late 1970s, the image was so negative that the company was advised to change the store name. Although this advice was not heeded, Jim's Store eventually became one of the largest retailers in the United Kingdom. A few decades later, it expanded internationally into Central Europe and even the Far East.

Originally specializing in food, Jim's Store now sells clothes, electronics, consumer financial services, DVDs, compact discs, music downloads, consumer telecoms, and Internet services.

13 REASONS

Roger Hawthorne-Wylde, a 27-year-old finance analyst, stared at the computer. He had been tasked with analyzing the accounts of the newly created online shopping division for Jim's Store. The department was packed full of IT project managers, contractors, software specialists, and hardware engineers. The budget was massive but not limitless.

During his analysis, Roger had come across some unusual payments. He'd printed off these peculiar invoices and thoroughly examined them. "»49,890 for 'professional recruitment services,' " he muttered to himself. It had been coded correctly and signed by a senior manager. The signature belonged to Chris Mousley, a project manager in the online shopping division who only a few months ago had been transferred to Thailand.

Despite the fact that the physical invoice looked no different from thousands he had seen before, there were some suspicious things about it. The description of the work was too vague, and for such a large value there was no breakdown. In addition, the amount was just under Chris's authorized sign-off level of »50,000. Roger vaguely remembered a seminar covering fraud indicators; he wished he'd paid more attention. He looked down at the invoice and read it once more, hoping that a reasonable explanation would suddenly jump out and hit him, but it didn't. "Why would a manager working in Thailand be paying a UK-based company? What does PJ Complete Recruitment do?"

Still hoping for that eureka moment, Roger logged on the web and typed "PJ Complete Recruitment" into a search engine. Results popped up instantly, and he clicked on the one that looked right. A sleek, well-designed, and professional site sprang to life. It was the company's homepage, containing an advertisement for its services. Roger cross-referenced all the contact details and numbers with the invoice; they matched up perfectly. Chris must have been using the company for recruitment—that made sense. There were certainly enough temps in the office. But there was no mention of them working in Asia. And something else still nagged at him. Chris had been told several times to pass on all UK work to a colleague back at headquarters. The first few invoices that Chris approved after starting the project were understandable; previous work he had ordered was complete, the bills were in, and only he could verify that they were correct. But now, after four months, there shouldn't be any work that his temporary replacement didn't know about.

Roger then accessed the UK Account Payables system on his computer and brought up all the invoices Chris Mousley had authorized. There were several million pounds worth to dozens of suppliers—thousands of payments in total. Roger downloaded the data into an Excel spreadsheet and sorted it in order of authorization date. He looked for the PJ Complete Recruitment payments; there were 13 of them, one per month. Using graphs, Roger could see that the quantity of payments to all the other suppliers declined slowly leading up to Chris's move to Thailand, and then stopped after about two months after his move. Chris's replacement was signing the work off now, so that made sense. But there was something odd. There were nine payments to PJ Complete Recruitment before his move date and four after, all for a similar amount—just under Chris's authorized limit. Each one had a vague description on the invoice, and all the numbers were in perfect sequence. Roger pulled up all the entries the company had for PJ Complete Recruitment. No one else except Chris Mousley had ever used them.

Roger reflected on the number 13 and thought, "Unlucky for some." He remembered where the saying came from: the tale of the Knights Templar. The order was taken down at the hands of Pope Clement V and King Philip of France on Friday the thirteenth in October of 1307, the original Friday the Thirteenth. The Templars were arrested on grounds of heresy. Roger shook himself out of his daydream; he'd made a decision. He picked up the phone, dialed the company switchboard, and said, "Put me through to the Fraud Department, please."

ALL SIGNS POINT TO CHRIS

The sun was warm on my skin as its rays shone through the Venetian blinds. I sat alone in my office, dutifully updating an investigation report for Evan Marshall, the director of security. I'd only been in the corporate investigations team for few months, and there was a steady flow of highly varied work: allegations of corruption, expenses fraud, abuse of   IT systems, breaches of security, and so on.

The phone rang. Annoyed at the distraction, I snatched it out of its cradle and mustered my most polite telephone voice. "Hello?"

"Hi, is this the Fraud Department?" asked the man at the end of line.

"This is Group Security. Yes, we investigate alleged frauds. Can I help you?" I replied.

"I'm Roger Hawthorne-Wylde from IT Finance. There is something suspicious about an invoice I have. Actually, 13 of them." Roger rapidly explained what he found.

"You've done the right thing by calling," I reassured him. "Have you discussed this with anyone?"

"Yes, I've talked to the manager who signed them off; he's not working in the UK at the moment. I phoned him last month to query one of the invoices, and he told me it was fine. I'm just not happy with the way he dismissed it. It's a lot of money, and he shouldn't be dealing with UK business anymore."

I told Roger that I would investigate this and arranged to meet with him at once.

Roger insisted that we hold the meeting away from the rest of the IT Department. He had never seen anything like this before and was clearly troubled. He showed me the 13 invoices.

"First, I'll look into all the available information covertly to build up background information before speaking to anyone. If there is nothing to this, then no one will have to know," I said. The facts were clear and simple: a registered supplier called PJ Complete Recruitment Limited; 13 suspicious invoices all paid by us and totaling almost »650,000; and, of course, the manager who approved them, Chris Mousley. "Just leave it with me, Roger," I said. "Your problem is now my problem, so relax and go home."

Back in my office, I sat behind my computer with the invoices laid out in front of me. I thought to myself, "First things first. What information does the company have on Chris Mousley?" This stage of an investigation is a link analysis, as it involves collating as much background data as possible from as many sources as are available and inputting everything into a software program specially designed to enable an investigator to create a pictorial representation of information and show any connections between things like people, addresses, phone numbers, and so on.

For starters, I logged on to the company human resources (HR) database and found the record for Chris Mousley. I copied all the available data: address, phone number, date of birth, next of kin, and so on, and input it into the program. Then I cut to the chase: an online directorship search—a credit agency's Web site linked straight into the UK companies' house data. I logged in and searched Chris Mousley. Five results popped up instantly. Since each record had a date of birth and zip code next to the name, I narrowed it down to the one that matched the details from HR. And there it was: a Chris Mousley with the same date of birth as our employee. I clicked on the entry and the full directorship details appeared on the screen. Bingo! He's a director of a company called PJ Complete Recruitment Ltd.

To dig further, I went to the online electoral rolls and clicked on the "search by name" feature. There were only a dozen entries for "Chris Mousley" in the United Kingdom, and because I had his wife's name from the HR data, it was easy to identify the relevant records. There were two addresses where both Chris and his wife, Penny Jane Mousley, were registered for voting. The UK Land Registry would have the ownership details of the properties, but I knew that would take some time to get and left that to our lawyers.

The picture was rapidly building up. Roger had said he'd found the Web site for the company, so I looked it up and found the URL. The PJ Complete Recruitment Web site was fairly flashy for the company's services. It would easily have fooled anyone into believing that the business was real. I navigated straight to the contact details and added them to the case notes. Interestingly, the phone number on the site was also the same as the HR number for Chris at his most recent address. A quick online "Whois" search confirmed that Chris had created the Web site. Again, all the information from the site went into the charting software.

Finally, I had completed the initial "link analysis" research. With a sigh of relief I sat back in my chair and looked up at the chart I'd created. There was no doubt that Chris Mousley was signing off invoices to a company he owned. It was highly likely that this was a fraud worth »648,890. I went to the director of security's office with the chart in hand and explained the news. Evan carefully scanned it.

"Well done. Let's brainstorm what we know and what we don't know. Then we will put together a list of the people we need to continue the investigation; we can't do it all on our own. And we should document our strategy. For starters, we want our money back, but we also want to prosecute—that's our policy," Evan said. Then he mapped out the plan. There were still a few details to check and a lot of work ahead, but the ball was rolling.

On the drive home I took a detour to pass by Chris's most recent address—the one on his HR file. As I rolled into the quiet cul-de-sac, I could just see the front of his house. It was an impressive property. Large black gates stopped me from snooping any further into the grounds. Although I would not have been surprised to find a board member living there, it was not the house of a typical senior manager—the company wasn't that prosperous. A few days later I would learn that the house had cost a cool »500,000. Satellite imagery showed that it even had an outdoor swimming pool—not particularly common in the UK. By this point I had no doubt that we had a major fraudster in our midst.

Over the following few days the remaining inquiries were made. Paperwork for setting up the supplier was found. The details on it had been faked, and we believed the handwriting to be Chris's. After speaking to a few senior people from the IT Department, it was clear that there was no evidence that PJ Complete Recruitment had ever done work for us. All the evidence was gathered and documented to support the legal and employment action that was now inevitable. One of our company lawyers was appointed to work with me, first to put together an affidavit and then to move forward with the legal proceedings.

"An affidavit? What's that?" I asked innocently.

"It's a formal, sworn statement, signed and witnessed by a notary public. I can do that for you. The name is Latin for 'he has declared upon oath,'" replied Carol Curry, our lawyer.

Also on the team was Robin Edwards, an external lawyer from a well-known London law firm, who specialized in civil recovery. Carol and Robin took the affidavit to a London court, where they stood before the presiding judge and requested he authorize an Anton Piller order, which provides for the right to search premises without prior warning and is used to prevent the destruction of incriminating evidence; it is basically a civil search warrant. The judge, impressed with the pile of documents, peered over his reading glasses and swiftly authorized this powerful but expensive legal tool.

Next, we got the team together to brief the Human Resources Department on the situation. It was essential that nobody do anything to compromise the investigation for a future court case. Once the news settled, they were instructed to draft a suspension letter and prepare for the inevitable. HR did have some good news for us: By sheer stroke of luck, Chris was back in the United Kingdom on leave for a couple of weeks. Not wanting to waste the opportunity, an action plan was expeditiously finalized with the legal team.

I followed the lawyers in my car to the Mousley mansion, as it was being referred to. The Anton Piller order only allowed our legal team and an independent observer—also a lawyer— to carry out the search. The letter of suspension from HR would be delivered as well. At the house, I kept my distance but maintained a good observation point, just in case things got nasty.

I watched as the pack of lawyers approached the front door and rang the doorbell. An attractive blond woman answered; she looked bewildered at the sight of so many Armani suits. She listened intently, then promptly retreated, closing the door on them. Seconds later, a casually dressed Chris appeared at the doorway with a nervous smile. For a few moments, words were spoken, heads nodded, and arms waved. Papers were eventually handed over, and Chris slowly digested it all. The deed was done, the investigation almost over.

A Just Reward

The lawyers carried out the order, which included freezing all of his bank accounts and assets, successfully and without hindrance from Chris or his family.

"Chris cooperated fully," Robin Edwards explained during a meeting. "He was visibly shocked and shaken, but quickly came to terms with the situation. I think he had been waiting for it to happen. He didn't deny that his conduct was fraud—he even said he'd pay the money back. Anyway, we found two laptops, one for work and one personal. We will send them for forensic analysis. We also found the bank statements for PJ Complete Recruitment." Robin paused with a grin. "There's something very interesting there. The first payment was for »250,000. It had been paid by a company called Axiom Computers Ltd. Anyone heard of it?"

"Yes, I have," I explained. I rifled through my case notes looking for some graphs. "It's a supplier that Chris used regularly. In fact, it's his most popular supplier, according to his sign-offs. It's a genuine company though; several other IT employees have also been using it. Chris, over the last five years, gave Axiom »3 million in business."

"Then it must be involved. Find out everything you can about them," Evan demanded. A new angle to the case had just opened.

Axiom Computers Ltd. was a small operation specializing in IT hardware repairs and software installations. It had also moved into recruitment, providing temporary IT specialists. The director of the company was a former British Navy sailor, Gary Kirkpatrick. When I met him, I guessed that he'd let himself go since his navy days; he was several pounds overweight, had greasy hair, and sweated profusely—perhaps that was nerves.

"Look, Chris asked for the money as a loan. He'd been a good friend to me; we've worked on big projects together, and I've known him for years. But the way he asked for the money that night—I just never expected him to pay it back," Gary explained during his interview. He had a lot at stake. Over 70% of his company's revenue came from us, but not for much longer. Gary continued, "After that conversation I kept him at an arm's length. I wanted nothing to do with him, other than normal business."

"Come on, Gary, a loan that you never expected to be paid back? Do you give money away on a regular basis? This was a bribe for more business, wasn't it?"

"No, it wasn't a bribe. I had no choice," Gary shouted; his face red.

"You always have a choice."

There was a long pause. "It was blackmail. He asked for the money. If we didn't pay he would have stopped giving us business." Gary sat back and relaxed a bit, the hard part over.

Despite serious doubts over some of the work Axiom Computers had done for us at the behest of Chris, Gary repeatedly denied that the money was a bribe. The end result was that Axiom Computers was dropped as a supplier. It later went bust.

Our quick-thinking lawyers realized that having accepted a bribe, Chris had breached his contract with the company and was liable for that money as well. He disagreed, but, yet again, the judge ruled in our favor. Carol explained that this was because a director owes a fiduciary duty to his employer: He must act in the best interests of the company and cannot profit at its expense. Chris was facing a double whammy of claims. In his daily liaisons with the lawyers, his assets were listed and valued. His company share options were frozen and added to the pot. Everything he owned was up for grabs. Chris's little gold mine had collapsed.

The nightmare of the situation was taking its toll on him and his family. The cracks in his marriage widened into a chasm. Digital forensic analysis on his laptops had revealed more than just false invoicing: There were dozens of e-mails to various young Thai women. He'd been keeping himself very busy. Although Chris had been summarily dismissed without a disciplinary proceeding, there was still a need to discuss a few matters with him, particularly the circumstances surrounding the bribe money. He was summoned to a "without prejudice" interview.

There Chris spoke quietly—he was barely audible—and faced the floor. His lawyer was also present and looked highly uncomfortable with the situation.

"He doesn't deny false invoicing," Chris's lawyer pointlessly interjected.

"Why did you do it?" I asked Chris.

"It was the pressure of work and being forced away from my family," Chris replied in a high-pitched squeak.

"What was the »250,000 from Axiom for? This was long before you went to Thailand."

"It was a business loan," Chris spouted. He did not elaborate.

The investigation and civil law process was completed in just a few weeks; the money would take over two years to trickle in. Chris lost everything: his home, wife, career, and even his freedom. Once the civil process had ended, I took the investigation package to the local fraud squad. There a detective took on the case. Chris was processed efficiently by the crown. He was duly charged with 13 counts of theft— the detective insisted that the issue of the bribe money be left out. During the trial Chris pleaded guilty. His reward was fours years at Her Majesty's pleasure.

LESSONS LEARNED

During his interview, Chris stated that "it was so easy" to commit the fraud. He was right. If Chris had stopped at a mere »400,000, then resigned from the company, he probably would have gotten away with it. This worried me, and I wondered how many other unscrupulous employees had done the very same thing.

There were many one-time supplier invoices (suppliers that do not regularly bill the company). At the time, a manager could sign off six invoices or more before the Accounts Payable Department would send an e-mail demanding that company be set up officially. Had there been a vetting process by the Corporate Purchasing Department, the fraud would have detected before any significant loss was incurred. At the time, the new supplier forms were filled out by the manager who was bringing the new company into the business: This represented a weakness in segregation of duties.

The key indicators of the fraud were in the data—both the employee and the supplier's phone number were the same. With a regular data mining process, the scheme could have been picked up quickly and the losses minimized.

I learned that the law is a very powerful tool, but it also proved to be prohibitively expensive. At the end of the case, our legal team stated that in the future, they would follow the same legal process only in very large frauds where the cost of using external lawyers outweighed the recovered funds.

Finally, the importance of keeping the investigation confidential and involving only those who need to know was paramount at all stages. Every decision and meeting was documented for complete transparency, should any decision have been challenged in court. Having an investigation strategy and constantly reviewing the case objectives was also essential.

RECOMMENDATIONS TO PREVENT FUTURE OCCURRENCES

The company made four policy changes.

1. Only two invoices can be paid to a company before it must be set up as an official supplier by the Corporate Purchasing Department. Corporate Purchasing also performs a basic inspection of all new suppliers, including director checks.

2. Data matching between the employee and supplier databases to identify fraud indicators is performed on an annual basis.

3. Comprehensive fraud awareness training workshops were implemented for senior management (who are statistically most likely to be the fraudsters), including management teams in countries where corruption is known to be endemic.

4. A whistle-blower line was also set up and has since been rolled out to almost all the operating countries. The phone number is also available to suppliers.

Graham J. Thomson is the corporate investigations deputy team leader for the United Kingdom's largest and most successful global retailer. Mr. Thomson is a graduate of the University of Glasgow and a former Military Intelligence operator of the British Army's Intelligence Corps. He has over 10 years of experience in managing intelligence and security matters.

CHAPTER 46

It's 11 p.m. Do You Know What Your IT Director Is Up To?

JOHN KULA

It's hard to say whether Lenny Wallace knew when he first walked through the door that he was going to steal from Toby Brands Retail (TBR). Events suggest that he did. Management at TBR believes that from the day he was hired as vice president of information technology, Lenny began defrauding them of $1,181,554 during his chaotic 13-month employment.

I spent about an hour interviewing Lenny during the last day he was allowed on TBR's premises. That was the extent of my direct contact with him. But more than two years later, after a very complex investigation, I knew a lot more. What I found painted a picture of a classic serial fraudster who operated brazenly, with impunity and without regard for those he hurt.

Divorced a few times, with a trophy wife and no children, Lenny had a penchant for embellishing the truth. Some said he was an accomplished liar, thief, and con man. One former coworker said, "Lenny didn't feel his day was complete if he couldn't lie to somebody about something." A consultant who was employed by Lenny characterized him as "a [expletive deleted] psychopathic liar and wacko."

You didn't have to dig very hard to find the red flags flying around Lenny. But TBR didn't look until it was too late. Its complacency was exacerbated by its vulnerability—a well-intentioned company that trusted certain employees far more than it should have. As a result, Lenny was able to commit a laundry list of unsophisticated fraud schemes.

Supposedly, a technical recruiting firm recommended Lenny to TBR. In actuality, Lenny knew Robert Taft, TBR's soon-to-be-retiring vice president of information technology (IT), through mutual business contacts. Taft hired Lenny to be his replacement. These mutual contacts turned out to be key conspirators in the frauds.

The recruiter alleged to have located Lenny through an Internet ad placed on behalf of TBR. He also claimed to have done a background check on Lenny, but we found out that it consisted solely of calling two of his references. Their comments about him were glowing. Taft said he made his hiring decision based on the strength of Lenny's résumé and those checks.

Unfortunately, the only thorough background on Lenny was done during our investigation. Had even minimal pre-employment screening procedures been completed a year earlier, at least some of these inconsistencies would have come to light and Lenny would never have been hired:

- He claimed to have undergraduate degrees in business administration and electrical engineering. When interviewed, he grudgingly admitted he had never attended college.

- Public records indicated at least 10 state and federal tax liens. At the time TBR hired him, his wages were being garnished by the state at the rate of $2,000 per month.

- Lenny filed for personal bankruptcy ($175,000 in debts) a few years before TBR hired him.

- He claimed past employment with IBM and NASA—he had never worked for either. In addition, he substantially exaggerated his titles with previous employers.

A month before TBR hired him, Lenny and his wife lived in a tiny, one-bedroom rented house in northern California. Within six months of joining TBR, they were living in a 4,000-square-foot home on the water with a 50-foot deep-water boat dock. In addition, Lenny acquired a brand-new Ford pickup truck, a mint condition 1980 Ferrari 308i, a new BMW M3 Roadster (a birthday gift for his wife), a Beechcraft five-seat airplane, a 21-foot speedboat, and a pair of Jet Skis.

How he paid for these items became the subject of our investigation. What our search ultimately revealed was shocking. Based on the West Coast, Toby Brands Retail is known worldwide for its popular, expensive, and trendy products favored by celebrities, business leaders, hip-hop stars, and regular folks.

Maybe it was the laid-back style of the company and its products, or maybe it was the distractions associated with a quickly growing business, but for some reason, TBR never focused much on internal controls, good governance, or setting an appropriate tone at the top. A number of midlevel managers repeatedly expressed concerns. But for the most part, they had trouble getting senior management's attention about their apprehensions.

Lenny Wallace reported to TBR's chief financial officer, a rising star in the company with a great background and a brilliant mind. The CFO gave him free rein on expenditures, most of which Lenny justified as the price for both developing an online catalog of products and for implementing a network in the company's new Hong Kong office.

THE BEST SYSTEM MONEY CAN BUY

Jackie Kim, a senior member of TBR's finance division, discreetly reported to the HR director that Lenny had a financial stake in one of the companies he used as a contractor in the IT Department. She never said how she came to know this fact. The CFO authorized an immediate review of Lenny's activities, and our investigation quietly began.

It took less than a day for TBR's loss prevention manager, Ed Griffin, to review Lenny's expense reports for any obvious anomalies. As it turned out, Lenny had submitted expenses for money never spent, for personal items unrelated to business expenditures, and for the same expenses on multiple reports—classic "double-dipping."

In the days that followed, I worked with Jim Roberts, TBR's director of loss prevention, on a comprehensive review of all IT vendors. While many were nationally known companies, a couple of local operations seemed to stand out. We dug further into these firms and found several troubling issues.

Invoices from one of the firms, Delta Partners, were for computer equipment and consulting services. But some were obviously exact duplicates with different invoice numbers. Others had prices that were much higher than TBR should have paid. In addition, Delta's fees seemed way out of line, with some consultants working 80 to 100 hours per week at excessive billing rates with no backup detail describing what they were working on. One common thread on these invoices was Lenny's personal, handwritten approval on each.

Around the same time, the CFO authorized a search of Lenny's office. We found a number of documents suggesting he may have extorted money or taken bribes from a vendor in Hong Kong, where he had gone five or six times to oversee the network installation at TBR's new office. On Lenny's desk was a photograph of a private airplane, the title of which we later learned had been transferred to him recently, under extremely unusual circumstances.

The preliminary investigation indicated approximately $50,000 in expense fraud, with the potential for several hundred thousand dollars in overbillings by one or two small local vendors.

One of the first interviews we conducted was with Dan Davis. During his first month at TBR, Lenny had hired Dan as an independent contractor to serve as a "technical project manager" in the IT Department. However, when we interviewed Dan, he said his last job was running a pool cleaning business. He had no college education and no experience related to computers or information technology, but he was learning "on the job and by reading manuals." Dan didn't have a good explanation for cleverly split billing records that, when analyzed closely, showed several instances of him working 40 hours at TBR in a one-day period at double his contract rate with TBR.

The interview came to an abrupt end when we asked Dan about corporate records showing he was the president of IT Engineering Associates (ITEA), a newly formed corporation. About two months after Lenny was hired, he engaged ITEA to provide consulting for TBR. In a very short time period, ITEA billed TBR almost $300,000, though no one in the IT Department had ever heard of the company and couldn't imagine what services they might have been providing. In addition, we discovered that one of TBR's checks to ITEA had been hand-endorsed by none other than Dan himself.

TBR's director of loss prevention said, "Dan, why don't you think about where all this is going? We will get to the bottom of things, and you can help yourself out immensely if you tell us what is going on. But the offer ends when we part today." Dan closed his eyes, put his head down and remained dead still for about a minute. Then he looked up and said, "I don't have anything more to say to you. I'll just take my chances." With that, he got up and left the building.

This marked the beginning of our field investigation, an odyssey that would take us around the country, to Hong Kong twice, and to countless meetings with attorneys, local police, county prosecutors, the Federal Bureau of Investigation, and TBR's insurance company.

TAKE MY CASE, PLEASE

At the start, we felt strongly about two things: Fraud losses from Lenny's double-dealing had the potential to be sizable, and this was not going to be easy. We were right on both counts.

On a Friday afternoon, very early in the investigation, TBR's CFO told us that management wanted Lenny questioned the first thing on Monday morning. Though we asked for more time to develop evidence, the message was clear: "Interview him now!"

During a detailed over-the-weekend inspection of Lenny's office, we recovered what later proved to be some incriminating data from his computer. We also visited his neighborhood and discovered his newly ostentatious lifestyle. But we had yet to find the smoking gun.

On Monday we interviewed him. We didn't want to show all our hand, so we picked our discussion points carefully. Lenny acknowledged a dozen separate instances totaling over $40,000 in which TBR reimbursed him twice for identical travel and other expenses, but he claimed the payments were "an inadvertent oversight" and blamed his administrative assistant for the mistakes.

Lenny also characterized $36,000 of duplicate invoices from Delta Partners as "a problem" and agreed that it was hard to imagine they were submitted in error. He said his approval was another oversight, but rationalized that he signed numerous invoices and could not be held accountable for the accuracy of each one.

After unsuccessfully trying to position himself as the victim, Lenny's attitude took a noticeable turn. With steely eyes and a defiant demeanor, he began answering questions with questions and claimed ignorance of even basic facts regarding the vendors he used in his department.

Lenny tried to turn the interview into a fishing expedition—he clearly wanted to know what else we knew. But it was apparent that he was not going to provide us with any more information. We ended the interview and escorted him to the CFO's office, where he was suspended pending the outcome of the investigation. Three months later he would be terminated for cause.

TBR blocked payment on ITEA's and Delta Partners' invoices. Not a peep was heard from ITEA, but within just a few days Allen Crain, the chief executive officer (CEO) of Delta, threatened to sue TBR over $85,000 in unpaid bills. Crain reluctantly agreed to meet with us and answer all of our questions. But he arrived with an attorney, and the meeting was brief. Crain fumed about the financial chaos his company would suffer if he was not paid quickly. His attorney threatened that, unless TBR immediately disbursed all Delta invoices, he would make sure the world knew TBR was "unfairly preying on one of the fastest-growing consulting firms in California."

During the discussion, Crain acknowledged the questionable invoices that clearly appeared to be double billings but blamed Delta's accounting system for the mistake. Oddly, he also turned over several additional invoices that TBR had paid, which we were unaware of, representing another $16,000 in duplicate billings that Lenny had approved. We later came to believe this disclosure by Crain and the demands by his attorney for immediate payments were intended to distract attention from other Delta billing improprieties we had not yet discovered.

TBR didn't take the bait and we continued our investigation, identifying what appeared to be fictitious invoices from fabricated companies, more apparent overbillings from real entities (mostly Delta Partners), and questionable deals from subcontractors to Delta on TBR projects. Within a month we also knew who owned the Ferrari (Allen Crain) and the ski boat (Dan Davis) just before Lenny did. We also traced the tail number of the airplane in the photo on Lenny's desk and discovered it was registered to ITEA at Dan's home address, which just happened to be Lenny's former address.

Lenny threatened to sue when he was terminated but ultimately said he'd settle for a generous separation package and a good reference. TBR said no. Any prospects for his cooperation ended there. Davis disappeared. Crain's demands for immediate payment waned when we discovered he had "sold" the Ferrari to Lenny for $35,000 but couldn't produce evidence that Lenny ever paid for it. Crain ultimately agreed to arbitration. But his attorney resigned after determining that his client had lied about the validity of the invoices. In the end, Crain didn't receive a dime.

We discovered documents that linked Robert Taft, who had hired Lenny, to two suspicious payments from ITEA totaling $47,000, just before he retired from TBR. I contacted Taft about it, but he had clearly gotten wind of how things were going with Lenny and Crain. The once-cordial, grandfatherly-type figure abruptly referred me to a criminal defense attorney, who advised that "Mr. Taft will have nothing to say without first receiving full immunity from prosecution." And this was before we even had our first discussion with a law enforcement agency!

In the meantime, we looked at Lenny's dealings in Hong Kong. We found the request for proposal Lenny had used to solicit bids for the Hong Kong network—we sent it to a few IT consultants, both in the United States and Hong Kong, to get their estimates for the work. Their bids were consistently tens of thousands of dollars less than the amount TBR actually had paid. In addition, each person we interviewed couldn't imagine why Lenny needed several Delta Partners consultants to make numerous trips to Hong Kong; they said the project wasn't that big or complicated.

In Hong Kong, we discovered that Lenny awarded the work to the smallest vendor that bid on the project. We found the original bid had been for less than $100,000, but it was later inflated, and TBR was actually invoiced for more than $140,000. The local vendor,

Mr. Tan, told us Lenny had insisted he raise his bid if he wanted the work—not unheard of when kickbacks are involved.

Lenny had TBR process Tan's invoices quite expeditiously, and he was paid in full well before his work was complete. He knew Lenny wanted money from him and understood why he was being paid so quickly. In fact, Mr. Tan stated that, just prior to one of Lenny's last trips to Hong Kong, Lenny told him he would be expecting "$40,000 in an envelope" the next time the two met. Tan believed Lenny needed the money to cover his extravagant living expenses in Hong Kong, which, Tan said, included helicopter tours of the area, lavish meals, gambling trips to Macau, and an escort service.

We presented these facts to the Independent Commission Against Corruption (ICAC) in Hong Kong. The ICAC raided Tan's offices, confirmed our findings, and obtained further incriminating evidence. Tan and his partner were arrested and quickly convicted of corruption. They would later flee to the United Kingdom and disappear. Lenny was convicted in absentia for his part in the scheme, and a warrant was issued for his arrest the next time he entered the country.

Back in the United States, our quest for prosecution was not so successful. We debated whom to present the case to first—the local police, county prosecutor, U.S. Attorney, FBI, postal inspectors, or the Internal Revenue Service because Lenny had received unreported income. TBR's counsel insisted that we start with the local police, who declined, citing lack of jurisdiction. Strike one. We spoke with the county prosecutor, who directed us to present our evidence to his chief investigator. The prosecutor's office declined to pursue the case. Strike two. We then presented the case to the FBI, but it was apparently not compelling enough. Strike three. The FBI's response was a real let-down, and TBR decided to put the investigation on hold indefinitely.

It's Not Over Till It's Over

Almost a year later (two years after the investigation began), I received a phone call from a woman named Darlene. She used to work for Allen Crain at Delta Partners, but the company owed her money and she was suing it. She said she had information I'd find interesting.

I met with her at her attorney's office. She was intimately familiar with Allen and Lenny's schemes and had documents to prove it. She received them when the county prosecutor's investigator contacted Allen for an interview. According to Darlene, Allen "was totally freaked out and convinced he was going to jail." He gave her all of Delta's business records pertaining to TBR to safeguard at her house. She took them, but shortly thereafter, her relationship with Allen soured. She went through the papers and they confirmed many of her suspicions about the extent of his unethical conduct.

Darlene provided the names of some former Delta employees and subcontractors. The first person I spoke with was Paul, a former partner at Delta. After a lengthy discussion, he signed a statement that included three key facts:

1. Shortly after starting at TBR, Lenny met with Paul, Crain, and Dan Davis at Delta's offices. Lenny announced he and Dan had formed a company called ITEA to provide services to TBR on a "revenue-sharing basis," and Delta was welcome to do the same. "Revenue sharing" was Lenny's euphemism for the payment of kickbacks. Delta became a vendor. One example of Lenny's revenue-sharing idea concerned the sale of a network monitoring station to TBR. For $700, Paul purchased a used station and sold it to TBR the following week as new equipment for $15,000. Lenny and Crain split the profit.

2. Several months after Delta became a TBR vendor, Crain instructed Paul to go to Delta's bank and pick up an envelope, which contained an $80,000 cashier's check payable to Lenny. Paul delivered it to Lenny at a small airport and watched as Lenny endorsed it over to the owner of the airplane that Lenny just "bought"—same Beechcraft airplane in the photo on Lenny's desk.

3. One invoice from Delta to TBR was for $6,600, for professional services and consulting by Paul on TBR's Hong Kong network. The problem, Paul said, was that he never did any consulting work for TBR on any project. The invoice was pure fiction.

Darlene also gave us the name of Eric, an independent IT contractor who told us he had known Crain for several years and, coincidentally, also knew Lenny. In fact, Eric reported that Lenny used to work for Crain. This was news to us, since neither man had mentioned it.

"I think Lenny is an idiot," Eric said, "and Crain knows it." That's why, Eric said, he was "beyond surprised" on the day that Crain called and told him Lenny wanted him to go to Hong Kong to "give [his] blessing to bring up the network." Eric thought the request was ridiculous, but decided to go if Lenny was dumb enough to pay him $10,000, plus expenses. Eric said, "I felt like I had won an all-expenses paid vacation to Hong Kong. They didn't need me, and they certainly didn't need Crain or most of the other consultants involved.

After returning to the United States, Eric billed Delta the $10,000 fee, but Crain paid Eric only $6,000, claiming that because of a misunderstanding, TBR refused to pay for any of the work Eric did. We showed Eric the only invoice TBR received from Delta pertaining to his work. The time period and description matched the dates of Eric's trip, but the invoice, for $25,503, had been paid in full by TBR. More "revenue sharing."

A LEOPARD DOESN'T CHANGE HIS SPOTS

All of us had been on a long roller-coaster ride, but we refused to let the case die. Once Darlene stepped forward, things got interesting again. Jim Roberts breathed new life into the case by authorizing us to track down and interview more of the people Darlene identified. Jim ran a Google search on Lenny's name just to see if anything new would come up—and indeed it did.

Jim found a fairly current quote from Lenny in an online business journal. Lenny was now vice president of IT for Virgo Technology in Fremont, California. The article described his use of a cutting-edge IT staffing model that relied heavily on a "partnership" with a Silicon Valley temp agency that specialized in providing highly skilled IT professionals. Lenny even mentioned the staffing company and its president by name. We didn't recognize the company, but the president was none other than Allen Crain.

In an effort to prevent another company from falling victim to Lenny and Crain's chicanery, Jim asked me to figure out a way to talk to senior management at Virgo without opening any of us up to potential claims for libel or slander. We called Virgo to see if Lenny still worked there and found that he had left its employ just a month or two earlier. Our first thought was that Virgo might have discovered some "issues" involving Lenny's relationship with Crain's new IT staffing company and let him go. And if that was true, we could possibly help them understand what happened to them and they could probably help us further cement our case against both Lenny and Crain.

I sent a brief letter to Virgo's CEO. To my surprise, the CEO himself called me the day the letter was delivered. We had a very short but cordial conversation, resulting in an invitation to meet with him.

Jim Roberts, TBR's attorney, and I met with Virgo's CEO, its director of internal audit, and its chief counsel. The discussion was a bit tentative at first, though it soon became evident that Lenny and Crain had struck again. Virgo uncovered their scheme early on when someone in the IT Department thought the details of one of Allen's temp agency invoices looked a bit odd and notified the Internal Audit Department. This led to the discovery of more odd-looking invoices, most of which involved both hours and billing rates that clearly deviated from the staffing contract. Internal audit's review of Lenny's expense reports also identified some double expenses, which, in a familiar refrain, they said he blamed on his administrative assistant.

Virgo's CEO said he knew Lenny was a thief when he heard the results of the internal audit review. He accepted Lenny's resignation and chose not to prosecute because the dollars were small. One of the CEO's final comments was that he wished Virgo had done a better background check. Curiously, Lenny's employment with TBR never appeared on the résumé he submitted to Virgo.

With this new evidence, we submitted our most comprehensive, best-documented, and compelling criminal referral to the FBI. Unfortunately, in many large jurisdictions, reasonably good corporate frauds are passed over in favor of very good, very large fraud cases. In the eyes of the FBI, our case required too much legwork and simply didn't make the cut. The game was over.

We had better luck with the insurance. We had prepared proofs of loss in support of a claim on TBR's commercial crime bond insurance coverage and submitted them to TBR's insurance company. After months of negotiation, TBR's commercial crime bond carrier paid the policy limits ($1 million) for the loss and an additional $200,000 for the cost of the investigation and associated attorneys' fees.

As for Lenny, I don't know whether he ever had a reason to go back to Hong Kong, nor do I know how long that warrant will remain. We've never heard anything from the ICAC indicating they had arrested him. In the end, Lenny dodged a bullet. As far as I know, he's still in the private sector and still poses a significant risk to the unsuspecting but well-intentioned people he may now be working for.

LESSONS LEARNED

The key points learned from this case are obvious, but worth restating:

- *Do background checks correctly.* Two "iffy" references by a recruiter do not comprise a good background check. A strong argument can be made that if TBR's Human Resources Department had paid an independent, professional pre-employment screening company to do a decent investigation on Lenny, it would never have hired him.

- *Pay close attention to IT expenditures—for both goods and services.* This is a significant challenge for many companies that don't have in-house resources that are both independent of the IT Department *and* have the technical standing to evaluate the propriety of expenditures and senior management conduct.

- *Be proactive about identifying fraud.* TBR had neither an Internal Audit Department nor an employee hotline. Yet studies have shown that most fraud schemes are detected as the result of tips, and most come from employees. This trend held true in TBR's case, as the investigation was kicked off by coworker Jackie Kim.

- *Companies may need to be patient when dealing with law enforcement agencies.* It's not unusual for cases to fall within multiple jurisdictions and have elements of both state and federal crimes. For many companies, getting to the point of seeking criminal prosecution can be a major hurdle because of concerns about adverse publicity and potential civil litigation, as well as costs associated with allocating resources and paying outside attorneys and investigators. Corporate frauds are often complex and frequently tax the resources and abilities of small to midsize police agencies. It can be very frustrating to present a good case to local police only to see it die because officers are uncertain how to investigate it or because the department does not have the necessary time or resources. Working with federal law enforcement agencies can be equally frustrating for different reasons, including the length of time it can take them to conduct investigations and their policies of not sharing many details with the victims. Many corporate fraud victims believe they must present their case to the FBI for federal prosecution, but other federal agencies should be considered, including the U.S. Postal Inspection Service if invoices, checks or other relevant documents were sent via U.S. mail, or to the Secret Service if the crime involves fraudulent access of a computer device, forgery, or false identification documents.

- *Companies should check their insurance policies.* Many companies are insured for large-dollar fraud losses resulting from employee dishonesty, but they forget to consider pursuing an insurance claim. Even though TBR didn't get the criminal prosecution it wanted, the company did recover almost $1.2 million from its insurer, which helped reduce the pain of some of the lessons it learned. In addition, organizations should verify whether the insurance policy reimburses at least a portion of the cost of the investigation. If TBR had not done this, $200,000 would have been left on the table.

RECOMMENDATIONS TO PREVENT FUTURE OCCURRENCES

Taking to heart the lessons learned would go a long way in helping prevent a similar fraud. The world is full of Lenny Wallaces and Allen Crains. Corporate fraud is big business. It is prevalent and expensive. One need only look at the growth of fraud examination, forensic accounting, and related fields for proof.

Large public companies have had little choice but to comply with Sarbanes-Oxley and other regulations in the post-Enron era. Antifraud programs, fraud mitigation strategies, fraud awareness training, hotlines, and other proactive steps are part of these regulations that actually work—but there is a cost associated with them, and therein lays a potential problem. I'm often surprised that companies won't spend money to detect fraud, even though proactively preventing it is almost always cheaper than responding to the problem. Midsize and small companies are at particular risk because robust internal audit and antifraud programs are more the exception than the rule.

Senior management that cares about fraud and unethical behavior and takes immediate steps to address both sends a powerful message to the workforce. If the workers are also educated and empowered through fraud-awareness training and ongoing positive reinforcement, and are given low-risk avenues to report fraud concerns, the chance of long-term ongoing fraud can be reduced and the likelihood of early detection may be greatly increased.

John Kula, CFE, MBA, is a director at Deloitte Financial Advisory Services LLP in Chicago. The practice provides forensic accounting, corporate investigation, expert witnesses, electronic discovery, and related services. Mr. Kula is a former financial crimes investigator with more than 25 years of experience in the field of corporate security and white-collar crime consulting.

CHAPTER 47

These Weights Didn't Measure Up!

JOSEPH R. DERVAES

Richard Langley was a party-hearty political activist in his community. As a rising political star, he worked on voter registration projects and was the campaign manager for an unsuccessful gambling initiative. He also made donations to many political campaigns in the state.

Chunky and boyish-looking, Richard was a self-promoter who loved to name-drop. Known as a high-roller, he threw large and lavish parties at his rented home on a lake near a major metropolitan city. Richard frequently entertained judges, mayors, ex-governors, lawyers, and councilpersons at his home. Valet service was provided for all who attended these gala events. Once inside, guests enjoyed the extensive display of autographed sports memorabilia that adorned the walls of his elegant home. But the primary purpose of these events was to provide a forum for the principal dignitaries to network with others participating in political activities.

Richard also hosted parties on his 80-foot leased yacht and in an executive box at the baseball stadium. He talked politics incessantly and liked to flash his wealth by bragging about the value of his watch and cars. However, at age 34 and unmarried, he didn't own any real estate and actually had no vehicles registered in his name.

When Richard needed money to fuel his extravagant lifestyle, he first formed a trucking business. Over time, he used his political contacts to secure a lucrative freight contract with the state's liquor control agency, referred to as simply the Agency. The Agency's decision to hire Richard as a contractor remains a mystery to this day. When examined later, his contract file was found to be unimpressive and practically empty. Of the two records in the file, one was a memorandum by a staff member indicating Richard had dropped the name of an agency executive when he first approached them for a job. The other was a letter of resignation. The Agency selected Richard as a contract vendor for one of its 14 liquor delivery routes.

He began delivering freight from the central warehouse to liquor stores along a 90-mile stretch of the interstate highway. In order to be paid for his services, he was required to submit invoices to the Agency. His company had never been in the freight business before, so even this relatively simple task was difficult for him. Richard didn't have a clue about how to complete the invoices in order to be paid promptly, as he lacked accounting skills.

To remedy this condition, he began to cultivate a relationship with Gerry Sparkle, an employee in the Accounts Payable (AP) Department at the Agency. She had been a fiscal technician at the company for five years. Gerry was a 42-year-old single mother with two teenage children. She had just ended a relationship with her domestic partner of four years. Due to her personal life and poor financial situation, she was vulnerable. Financial security was a major concern in her life, but the reality of being alone again scared her even more.

The AP Department was located at the Agency's headquarters in the state capital. One of Gerry's jobs was to process invoices for freight vendors that delivered liquor products in the statewide distribution system. It was a time-consuming job that involved processing about 1,400 invoices totaling $420,000 in payments every month. After Richard was hired as a contractor, she was required to process his invoices, as well. Invoices were first batched for review and approval. The data were then entered into the computer accounting system. Finally, invoices were processed for payment. While performing these duties, Gerry was required to verify information from vendor invoices to the Agency's computer database for all freight shipments from the central warehouse.

During the first year of his contract, when Richard encountered problems preparing accurate invoices, Gerry tried to help him. They spent a lot of time on the telephone discussing how to correct these documents. Gerry had no cause to believe that anything was really wrong with Richard's firm except poor business practices. She had come to believe that Richard was a good and honest man.

However, Richard's lack of business and accounting skills began to cause significant problems for them both. Richard was not being paid promptly because of the extra time required to correct his invoices. And Gerry did not have the time to devote all of her work to only one contractor.

Richard pleaded for help. Gerry decided that it would be easier to prepare his invoices herself rather than to fix them every time. They agreed to change procedures. Richard provided her with the freight transaction information. Gerry prepared his invoices, which allowed her to spend less time working on the accuracy of the transactions, and Richard began receiving his payments more promptly. Even with Gerry's help, things began to go awry. One of Richard's payments was lost in the mail. Another payment was mailed to the wrong company.

"What's wrong?" Richard asked.

"I don't know," Gerry replied, "but I'll fix the problem."

Rather than have the agency mail the delayed payments to Richard, Gerry made arrangements to pick them up at the headquarters. She called the check distributor.

"Will you return Richard's checks directly to me rather than mail them?" she asked.

"Sure I can. Think of all the stamps we'll save."

Gerry began meeting Richard in the parking lot to give him the checks. Richard now realized that he needed Gerry's assistance to do business with the Agency more than ever.

"Can I fax my transaction information to you to process information even faster?" Richard asked. Gerry agreed.

When Gerry was transferred to another department, she continued to help Richard prepare invoices. Once her review had been completed, she gave the invoices to the AP staff for further processing. Since she had already verified the information, the staff simply entered the information into the computer accounting system using their own passwords.

It wasn't long before Richard began to exploit his relationship with Gerry for his own personal and business advantage. Ultimately, he conducted a scheme to defraud the state of almost $840,000 over a three-year period.

BOOZE AND POLITICS: A DANGEROUS COMBINATION

The state legislature had established the liquor control agency in 1934. The Agency had a two-year operating budget of $157 million. It employed 950 full-time staff at the headquarters, a centralized warehouse, and 350 state-operated liquor stores throughout the state. The Agency is administered by three part-time commissioners appointed by the governor and confirmed by the state senate. Its mission is to serve the public by preventing the misuse of alcohol and tobacco through licensing, education, enforcement, and controlled distribution and merchandising systems. Principal activities include:

- Licensing and inspecting all activities pertaining to the manufacture, sale, and distribution of alcoholic beverages
- Enforcing liquor laws in cooperation with other governmental enforcement bodies
- Purchasing, warehousing, and selling liquor
- Collecting taxes on all liquor manufactured in or imported into the state
- Controlling and regulating alcoholic beverage advertising

Some liquor stores are operated by the Agency; others are operated by private businesses. The Agency contracts with freight vendors to haul products from its central warehouse to every store in the state. During a given fiscal year, the Agency pays around $45 million to these freight vendors.

One year after Richard was hired, a major computer change involving disbursements was made in the state's computer accounting system. This change caused a reduction in staff at the Agency's AP Department. The organization revised its disbursement policies and procedures to compensate for this cut in staff. It stopped verifying that all freight deliveries listed on vendor invoices actually represented valid freight shipments from the central warehouse.

The staff merely checked vendor invoices for mathematical accuracy and for agreement to the authorized rate structure specified in the contract negotiated with all freight vendors. While the Agency still maintained a computer database of freight shipments from its central warehouse, this important information was no longer used by the AP Department to verify the accuracy of freight vendor invoices. This change in operations turned out to be a fatal flaw.

The following June, when Gerry changed jobs and transferred to a different department, she had to train another employee to perform her duties in AP. Because there were many changes in personnel in that area, Gerry was repeatedly asked to train new staff and be of service by answering their questions about problem transactions. She even developed a training manual for the AP staff to help improve overall operations.

Over the years, Gerry developed good working relationships with all freight vendors—perhaps too good when it came to Richard's firm. While assisting the AP staff on a project two years later, Gerry noticed that one of Richard's invoices was a complete mess. In researching the problem, she noticed that the invoice significantly overstated the weights of some deliveries. Then, when looking at other invoices from his firm, she realized that all of his invoices significantly overstated delivery weights; some off by more than 20,000 pounds. Shocked, she contacted Richard the next day.

"Please meet me right away," she demanded.

"What's wrong?" Richard asked.

"Nothing specific. Let's just get together." Richard thought the reason for the meeting was personal. When Gerry met him in the parking lot at the Agency's headquarters, she hopped in the car and Richard drove a short distance to park so they could talk.

Gerry confronted him with her discovery. "You've been overbilling the Agency."

She hoped he would say that these transactions were only mistakes. But she was appalled when she found out what had really happened.

Though reluctant at first, Richard finally said, "I wondered how long it would take you to find that out. I've inflated weight information several times. I've even fabricated the information on entire shipments and falsified all of the invoices to obtain start-up funds for a new business venture. It's no big deal. Once the new business is operating, I'll have plenty of money to repay the Agency."

Essentially, Richard was using the state disbursement system to obtain a temporary loan.

"Don't worry about what you've found," he told her. "I'll eventually correct everything. Besides, does anyone else even suspect that anything is wrong?"

In disbelief, Gerry exclaimed, "No, nobody else knows! But Richard, this is theft!"

He didn't react much to this accusation. Instead, he simply responded, "I'll have enough money to hire a good defense lawyer if the scheme is somehow detected."

Gerry was now concerned about her participation in the fraud.

Richard made feeble attempts to comfort her. "Nothing will happen to you, Gerry. You don't know anything about the scheme, anyway. I'm the only person involved. If detected, I'll blame everything on the Agency's lack of shipment tracking."

Gerry knew that she couldn't condone stealing. "Richard, please stop doing this," she begged.

"I will, eventually," he promised. "If you get fired because of my actions, I'll pay for a defense attorney for you, give you a job at my firm, and provide for your needs during the ordeal." The meeting came to an abrupt end.

Gerry did nothing further to disclose Richard's scheme to the Agency's officials. Soon thereafter, the business relationship between Richard and Gerry turned personal. They began meeting for lunch to discuss her crumbling personal life. One day Richard handed Gerry an envelope full of cash.

"Please take this money," he said. "I want to help you through your hardships." Gerry didn't even open the envelope or count the money until later, when she discovered that it contained $6,000.

Gerry thought this was a nice gesture. A week later Richard gave her another envelope full of cash. Again she didn't open the envelope or count the money on the spot. Later she found that the envelope contained another $4,000. Over the next several weeks, Gerry tried to justify keeping the money for personal use. She even spent part of it to pay her living expenses.

Although she needed the money, she finally told Richard, "I just can't keep doing this."

After about six weeks, she returned $6,000 of the money to Richard and promised to pay back the remaining $4,000 soon thereafter. Gerry felt that keeping the money would make her an accomplice in the case. She didn't want to face the consequences of being prosecuted for her actions if she later decided to turn in Richard for this fraudulent billing scheme. She hoped the problem would go away and that Richard would start to submit accurate information for the invoices. Over the next several months, she stopped assisting the AP staff. She really didn't want to have to blow the whistle on Richard.

She even lied to him, saying "The auditors are in the office and are requiring us to properly verify the accuracy of all freight shipments."

"Thanks for the information," Richard barked. But that was his only reaction.

Gerry rationalized that her relationship with Richard was not a conflict of interest because processing his firm's invoices was not even her real job. Besides, their friendship was purely social. If the scheme was detected, she would only be guilty of being his friend. She continued to accompany Richard to parties and baseball games. She also spent endless hours on the telephone talking with him about his fun lifestyle and what she hoped would develop into a lasting relationship. Unfortunately, Richard had other plans.

Gerry then encountered a slew of medical and family problems. She was diagnosed with high blood pressure. A relative was killed in an automobile accident. Her stepfather died from a heart attack. She was barely able to do her job and cope with life at the same time.

Richard became depressed. Though he was taking home plenty of money, his emotional state made it increasingly difficult for him to keep up his lifestyle as a high-rolling political activist. "I think drugs and alcohol are contributing to my depression," Richard told Gerry. "Worst of all, my new business venture has failed."

Gerry was devastated. She decided to determine the extent of Richard's fraudulent billing scheme. Gerry knew he was supposed to make about $144,000 per year but soon found that he had been paid about $685,000 in 2001. Horrified, she knew now that she would have to become a whistle-blower and report Richard's activities to the Agency. She decided to meet with him one more time to resolve the matter. At the meeting, she was surprised to be met by Richard and his attorney.

"I'll hire an attorney for you, too, if the Agency finds out what we've been doing," he promised.

"No, thanks," Gerry responded. She was now more worried and depressed than ever before and soon began to fear for her life. She even prepared a will.

One day Richard called Gerry to ask her to help process a large invoice.

"Prepare the invoice yourself," Gerry snapped.

Richard realized that his scheme was about to unravel. Stunned by Gerry's sudden assertiveness, Richard knew his days were numbered. "I'm packing up my house and moving out of the state to get away from this mess!"

In the fall, Gerry decided to become a whistle-blower and to report Richard's scheme to the Agency. It took her over six months to notify the authorities about it. Obviously, it was a difficult choice for her to make, as she had become close to Richard.

ROLLING OVER

When February came, Gerry hired a lawyer. On the advice of her attorney, she disclosed the details of Richard's scheme to the state auditor's office. As the auditor for special investigations, I manage the statewide fraud program. Thus, Gerry's disclosure came to me for investigation. After making an initial assessment of the case, I immediately appointed my colleague, Franklin Smart, to review all payments the Agency made to Richard's firm during the five years that Richard had worked there.

As we began the investigation, I exclaimed, "From all indications, this will be one of the largest fraud cases ever investigated by the state auditor's office."

"I'm sure it will," Franklin agreed.

He spent six laborious months entering all of the information into a database. I then verified the accuracy of the information and conclusions prior to completing the audit. All of Gerry's allegations were confirmed. It was the largest fraud case we had ever investigated. Richard was later sentenced to nine months in jail.

This was a very complicated case involving a tremendous amount of coordination among six agencies.

1. *The Agency.* The executive director made all staff available for the audit and police investigation. In addition, the internal audit staff was responsible for assembling all freight vendor invoices from its disbursement files and all freight delivery documents from its central warehouse in Agency headquarters at the state capital. The organization provided office space for the auditors and police investigators working on the case. In addition, the internal audit staff analyzed a sample of the fraudulent transactions to demonstrate that Richard's firm was overpaid. The Agency used this information to suspend him from performing future work. This same information was also used to establish probable cause for the bank subpoenas that it needed for the police investigation.

2. *The state auditor's office.* This organization conducted the audit to determine the amount of loss in the case. The auditors used computer-assisted audit techniques to identify all payments the state made to Richard's firm. The auditors and police

investigators worked closely together on this case to ensure that the information the auditors developed would be exactly what the police investigators needed to build their case against Richard.

3. *The state patrol.* Once the audit was completed, the state patrol performed the police investigation. It reviewed the results of the audit, conducted all interviews, subpoenaed Richard's business and banking records, and then made recommendations for charges to the county prosecutor.

4. *The attorney general's office.* Legal representatives of both the Agency and the state auditor's office provided legal guidance and advice throughout the audit and police investigation.

5. *The state treasurer.* This organization had custody of the original checks associated with the case. Once the auditors prepared a list of all fraudulent disbursements, the treasurer removed all checks used in the scheme from its files, carefully placing all documents in plastic bags to preserve any fingerprint evidence. These documents were then used in the police investigation and were held in the office for any subsequent trial. All checks were made payable to and endorsed by Richard's firm.

6. *The county prosecutor.* This organization prosecuted the case. During the course of the investigation and audit, the prosecutor met with the auditors, the state patrol, and the defense attorney for the freight vendor. Ultimately the prosecutor was able to arrange for a plea bargain to resolve the case. The freight vendor agreed to make restitution for the amount of the loss and audit costs in this case. However, due to jurisdictional issues, the county prosecutor for the state capital region transferred the case to the county prosecutor for the region where Richard's firm was located. There was no trial.

The state auditor's office created a database of all transactions, including vendor invoices, agency disbursement documents, the checks, and documents for all freight shipments from the central warehouse. After analyzing the information in the database, the auditors were able to calculate the amount of the loss. Ironically, the auditors also determined that Richard had not submitted invoices to the Agency for some deliveries he had actually made. These transactions reduced the amount of the loss.

The audit revealed several weaknesses that allowed this scheme to occur undetected for over three years. First of all, the AP staff did not verify reported deliveries or the weights of deliveries from freight vendor invoices to its computer records of freight shipments from the central warehouse prior to making payments for services rendered. Second, the Agency's review of vendor invoices from Richard's firm was inadequate. Gerry, an employee assigned to a position outside the AP Department, received and approved Richard's invoices for payment. A subtle compromise of the AP system occurred when Richard's checks made a U-turn in the check distribution section and were returned to Gerry for hand-delivery to the freight vendor. Finally, Richard's firm was not required to submit original invoices to the Agency for payment. Instead, he submitted invoices by fax.

BAD PAPER

Richard's firm submitted false invoices to the Agency and received unauthorized payments for services he did not provide. He received $839,796.90 in unauthorized payments during the three-year period. The fraudulent transactions are summarized next:

Inflated weights on legitimate deliveries	$123,161.12
Deliveries that did not occur	600,527.84
Double billings	116,017.94
Total losses	$839,706.90
Unbilled legitimate deliveries	(67,843.31)
Net loss	$771,863.59

1. *Inflated weights on legitimate deliveries.* Payment for deliveries was determined by multiplying the weight of the freight load by the rate established in a contract between the Agency and all freight vendors. Richard made 1,103 freight deliveries during the audit period. He inflated 600 of these deliveries by over 5,000 pounds (i. c., 54.39% of all deliveries).

2. *Deliveries that did not occur.* Richard submitted 1,100 invoices reporting 1,370 deliveries that never occurred.

3. *Double billings.* Richard submitted 238 invoices requesting payment for 273 deliveries that had been previously billed to and paid by the Agency.

4. *Unbilled legitimate deliveries.* Richard did not bill the Agency for 382 legitimate deliveries valued at $67,843.31. The auditors gave him credit for this oversight, thus reducing the total loss.

Richard sent invoices to the Agency for transactions totaling $1,100,000 during his five years as an employee. Almost 76% of these invoices were bogus. When the state patrol visited Richard's home to arrest him, he had already fled the state to avoid prosecution. Since this was such an outrageous crime, the state formed a regional fugitive apprehension task force to track him down. Richard remained on the lam for six months. Acting on a tip, United States marshals traveled to another state and arrested him without incident at a friend's home. He was temporarily held in a county jail. After he waived extradition, he was escorted back to his home state and placed in jail to await the trial. "Richard doesn't have anything left but memories. He's penniless. The proceeds from the scheme have been squandered," the county prosecutor declared.

Richard even qualified for a public defense attorney due to his lack of assets. He eventually pleaded guilty and went before a superior court judge. His defense attorney tried to obtain a reduced sentence by citing the fact that Richard was a first-time offender who had drug and alcohol problems.

"He needs treatment," he said.

The judge denied first-time offender status based on the length of time the scheme had existed. Each and every false bill Richard submitted was considered to be a separate event. And practically all counts in the case involved first-degree theft, the most serious crime in the state.

"Drug and alcohol rehabilitation can be obtained while he is in jail," the judge assured Richard and his lawyer.

The judge then sentenced Richard to 57 months in the state penitentiary, the maximum sentence permitted for this crime by state law. The court also ordered restitution in the case for the amount of the loss plus audit costs. The likelihood that Richard will ever repay any money to the state is slim to nil.

Gerry also disclosed the details of Richard's scheme to the Agency. She was placed on administrative leave pending the outcome of the audit. After the state auditor's office issued its audit report, the Agency terminated Gerry for neglect of duty, gross misconduct, and willful violation of the organization's rules and procedures. This case was also referred to the Executive Ethics Board for violation of the ethics law applicable to all state employees.

Gerry was not prosecuted as an accomplice in this case. Instead, the prosecutor decided to use her testimony as a cooperating witness against Richard. She unknowingly assisted Richard in perpetrating this crime at first and then eventually blew the whistle on his fraudulent billing scheme. All of these things worked in her favor. Richard was the only individual who received the proceeds of the scheme. Gerry merely enjoyed some of the benefits from these funds while Richard lavishly spent the money on an extravagant life style. However, before agreeing to do this, the county prosecutor insisted that Gerry return the final $4,000 that she had not yet given back to Richard.

LESSONS LEARNED

At the completion of this case, the auditors learned a great deal about fraudulent billing schemes. In the future, managers will look for a "straight line" from the initiator requesting payment for the transaction, to accounts payable for review and production of the checks, and then to the individual making distribution of the checks. The risk of fraud increases when a check from any transaction makes a U-turn in the AP or Check Distribution department and is returned to the initiator. These transactions automatically become exceptions to the internal control structure and require intense scrutiny and monitoring by managers. Any compromise of the AP system will now be documented on a manual exception log to identify all transactions that have been processed outside normal parameters. These compromises include the use of any type of written communication, including Post-it Notes, or any verbal communications employees make with the accounts payable or check distribution staff. It also includes picking up checks after issuance when it is not the organization's normal procedure.

This particular weakness was the fatal flaw in the case. Managers periodically review the manual exception log. If any undesirable trends are identified, they will then review the validity of the supporting documents for each transaction as well as the bank endorsements on the checks.

Accounts payable duties will no longer be performed by anyone who works outside the AP Department. Also, fraud examiners will now examine vendor contracts in cases where the transaction analyses or analytical review procedures suggest high, increasing, or unusual volumes for specific vendors. For example, we may sort all expenditures by vendor, by accounting year, and then list them from highest to lowest dollar amount. Then we will compare the current accounting year to the prior accounting year for unusual or unexpected variances. If something appears out of the ordinary, we will find out why by obtaining an explanation from management officials, and then make our own professional judgment about the conditions found.

If vendors are selected through competitive bidding, fraud examiners will now review the contract selection files for completeness, determining if the selection process was documented properly and appears reasonable.

RECOMMENDATIONS TO PREVENT FUTURE OCCURRENCES

Recommendations to prevent future occurrences, based on the changes made in the Agency, follow.

Review Internal Controls and Procedures

Conduct a comprehensive review of all of the company's internal controls, accounting procedures, and management practices. Then implement revised procedures in areas where weaknesses are identified.

Review All Payments for Validity

While the case at the Agency represented a significant fraudulent billing scheme, it was an isolated case involving only one of its smallest freight carriers. It is vital to review all payments, regardless of the size of the transaction, for accuracy.

Surveillance

Implement procedures to closely monitor the work of key employees. The Agency recognized that an employee had compromised internal control procedures by allowing the freight carrier to use unauthorized procedures when submitting invoices for payment.

Training

Request a variety of fraud and ethics training classes from other state agencies. All staff members in the Agency's financial division receive fraud training from the state auditor's office, internal control training from the office of financial management, and state ethics law training from its attorney general's office representative.

Joseph R. Dervaes, CFE, ACFE Fellow, CIA, of Vaughn, Washington, is a retired Washington State Auditor's Office Special Investigations manager. He managed the state's fraud program for 20 years and participated in 730 employee embezzlement fraud investigations with losses of $13 million. He graduated from the University of Tampa and has over 42 years of audit experience.

CHAPTER 48

Swimming with the Sharks

PEDRO FABIANO

The second son of a wealthy, religious, and highly respected family in the Republic of Palms, Ivan Vichy had an unusual academic and work history. After obtaining his college degree in industrial engineering, he resolved to dedicate his life to religion. Ivan enrolled in a parochial school, but after a couple of years, he wanted a change. With the financial support of his family, he started his own business as a car dealer.

But dealing with used vehicles was not enough for him. Three years later Ivan established a consulting firm—CONSA—in partnership with his close friend, Serge Chupeta. Also the son of rich parents, Serge had traveled around the world as a result of his studies at the Navy University of Palms. After he earned his degree, he found himself back in his country and unemployed. Although the two men had no experience in corporate business, they had contacts with government leaders and potential international investors.

In the early 1990s, the government of the Republic of Palms announced the privatization of the gas generation, transportation, and distribution industry. Ivan and Serge agreed that CONSA should be a major player in this business, offering assistance to international investors. In addition, they would provide management services to these new companies. The two friends definitely had the entrepreneurial spirit. In fact, they had always dreamed of making it big on their own without the assistance of their wealthy parents.

Vito Rigatti was the founder and owner of Vafang Utilities, a major gas distribution company in southern Italy. He had established a profitable business in 1950 and ran his company with a small management team and two trainees—Frank and Nicky, his sons. The brothers did not like to work with their father because they considered him too tough. They preferred the *dolce vita*—enjoying life as sons of a rich man. However, Vito pressed them to continue working in the company, exclaiming "This is your future!"

Serge first met Nicky Rigatti on one of his trips to the French Riviera, where they had shared luxury parties and fabulous nightlife. They become close friends and planned to do business together in the future. Serge told Ivan about Nicky and the Rigatti family company. Ivan thought that Vafang Utilities had an excellent chance of winning the privatization of the gas distribution segment in his country. "Call Nicky Rigatti now!" he instructed Serge. This phone call would be the beginning of a close business relationship between Ivan Vichy and the Rigatti family.

After several meetings and negotiations in both Italy and Palms, Ivan reached an agreement with the Rigattis. Vafang Utilities would be the lead partner in a consortium for the privatization, and Ivan and Serge would advise the Rigattis in the preparation and presentation of the bid. They would also start contacting new partners. If the consortium won the bid, Ivan and Serge would became partners and members of the board of directors of the new company. This was potentially a very big deal.

Government regulations required the formation of a consortium with at least three partners, one of whom should have significant experience in the gas industry. Ivan had closed the deal with Vafang but needed two more partners to comply with the regulatory requirements.

The privatization law allowed investors to pay a significant part of the contract price in government bonds, which would be accounted at face value. This was a very advantageous deal for bond holders, as the market value of the Palms government bonds was nine cents for each dollar. International Financial Enterprises (IFE) was a U.S. financial institution listed in the New York Stock Exchange, with subsidiaries in Latin America, Europe, and Asia. The Equity Investments Division of IFE was looking for investment opportunities in Latin America. Moreover, IFE held a significant position in Palms government bonds at the time of the privatization. Ivan Vichy successfully contacted IFE and Lamas Preta, a local construction company, and both entities accepted to join Vafang in the consortium.

That December, the consortium, led by Vafang Utilities, won the bid for the privatization of the natural gas distribution business across the country. It was established as a new corporation under laws of the Republic of Palms and adopted the name of SAGCO (South America Gas Company).

Vafang Utilities owned 51% of SAGCO and would designate the chairman and the vice chairman of the board. The minority owners were: the government of Palms, 9%; Lamas Preta, 25%; and IFE, 15%. The new company would be governed by the steering committee of the board. Nicky was appointed chairman, and Ivan Vichy was designated vice chairman and chief executive officer (CEO). Serge was designated the third director representing Vafang. Alex Zabusky and Hannibal Perez were appointed directors, representing IFE and Lamas Preta, respectively. In addition, although not established in the company bylaws, Nicky had to report on a daily basis to his father, Vito, who would be making the significant decisions from Italy. The shareholders agreement stated that Vafang Utilities had the right to appoint the whole management team. The U.S. shareholder IFE was entitled to designate the general auditor, who would report to the board's steering committee.

I was the internal audit vice president for IFE at the time of the privatization. I had more than 10 years of experience in auditing U.S. financial institutions and had recently obtained the certified fraud examiner's (CFE) designation.

One day, about a year and a half after the formation of the consortium, Alex Zabusky, Equity Investments vice president for IFE, called me and said that he had "something very interesting to offer for my professional development." In fact, time would show me that it was not only interesting, but risky and challenging as well. Alex offered me the position of general auditor representing IFE in the new SAGCO. I accepted the position.

A Few Adjustments Will Take Care of That

It was a rainy and cold morning when I met Ivan Vichy for the first time. I was told that the interview with him was only a formality because my new position had been already approved by IFE, which had the right to appoint the general auditor. Although the meeting was scheduled for 10 a.m., I had to wait for more than an hour because Ivan had to attend an "unplanned meeting," according to his secretary. The interview lasted less than 30 minutes, including several interruptions. However, the message that I received during the meeting with respect to Ivan's expected audit approach was very clear.

After a brief introduction regarding my banking background, Ivan highlighted that SAGCO was not a U.S. financial institution and that I had to recognize this difference. Although this seemed an obvious assertion, I continued to listen attentively to his statements. He further explained that the two pillars of internal control were budgeting and internal auditing. He added: "I see auditors as good management advisors and not as *witch hunters.*" In fact, he was suggesting that I implement a "lapdog" audit approach. Although I felt this would conflict with my "bloodhound" style, I remained polite and simply replied, "Mr. Vichy, rest assured that I will implement an internal audit program that will perfectly fit the specific needs of the company."

Ivan's influence and control over decisions grew dramatically during the first years. Serge followed him unconditionally. Nicky initially consulted with his dad in Italy before approving Ivan's ideas, but after a few months he got tired of that and allowed Ivan to deal directly with his father. This situation gave Ivan almost absolute control of the company. He only had to maintain a good image with the partners. Moreover, the most important concern of the investors—the bottom line—was assured by the excellent profits of the first year. The company paid huge dividends, which kept everyone happy.

External auditors were not a problem for Ivan. He was able to convince them of almost anything. Several significant deficiencies were disclosed during the first financial statement audit. The partners of the firm were concerned because bank reconcilements were not performed as of the closing date, although management had promised to complete this task several times.

Gianni Nessuno, the chief financial officer (CFO), had a meeting with Ivan and stated that the auditors had been pressing him with this "minor administrative issue" of bank accounts reconciliation. Ivan told Gianni not to worry—he would handle it. And handle it he did. Ivan told the audit partner to just take the bank account balances and use those numbers in the financial statements. Any difference with the accounting records would be adjusted promptly with Ivan's personal oversight and approval. This would eliminate the need for a time-consuming reconciliation. Ivan stressed that, during this first year, personnel had been assigned mainly to the start-up of the new company and the continuity of operations. Ivan added that the business needed the cooperation of the auditors and would probably require some consulting services in the short term. The external auditors must have considered this a convincing argument because they accepted the non-reconciliation practice and issued an unqualified clean opinion.

PERHAPS I DIDN'T MAKE MYSELF CLEAR

I became aware of this story directly from Ivan in one of our weekly meetings. I was amazed by the deal with the external auditors, but did my best to avoid showing my feelings. Regrettably, it was at that point that I was submitting my first risk assessment report to Ivan. The lack of basic controls over cash management was the most significant issue in my report, which described, among others, the associated risks of misdirected collections, undue payments, and cash larceny.

"How dare you to write this?" Ivan asked after reading the report. He added in a hostile tone, "Why should *we* from inside the company criticize this, considering that a prestigious audit firm approved this practice and signed off the financial statements?" Moreover, he emphasized that he personally approved *all* the invoices before payment, signed *all* the checks, and had no doubts about Gianni. He was very upset, and my first reaction was to clarify that the report was not rendering any opinion about the CFO's honesty. Instead, it was only about risks and controls. I said matter-of-factly, "This is not a technical accounting issue, we just need to know where has the money gone and why."

A sudden call from the company president ended the meeting, but before I left, Ivan suggested I "review" the wording of the report. When I returned to my office, I started to think that there was something fishy going on with the CEO and decided to distribute the report to the executive committee without any changes.

One week after this meeting, my first presentation to the executive committee took place. All the "big bosses" who had received the report were in attendance: Nicky Rigatti (chairman), Alex Zabusky (IFE representative), Hannibal Perez (Lamas Preta), Serge Chupeta (Vafang), and obviously, Ivan Vichy (CEO). Alex asked me to comment on the report, and I briefed them about the issues and recommendations from the business perspective, avoiding accounting jargon. I also emphasized the importance of controlling collections and payments, mainly due to the cash-intensive business of SAGCO, which had daily average collections of about $700,000. Nicky attempted to ask me about the expression "undue payments," but he was suddenly interrupted by Ivan, who said that this issue had already been discussed with him and that we would better use our time to review the recommendations. Ivan finally told the directors, "I appreciate the audit recommendations, and I promise that our management team will effectively implement, *under my supervision*, all the suggested control measures."

It was a commitment he would fail to keep. Several key questions remained unanswered: How would management implement controls if the CEO signed all the invoices and all the checks? Would management dare to control the CEO? Why was Ivan working 15 hours a day? Why was he reluctant to delegate signing authority?

Two years had passed since my initial presentation to the executive committee. During this period I had recruited four auditors, implemented an audit policy, developed plans and programs, and issued several reports that included follow-up. The reports covered the main business processes, and the resulting control deficiencies were numerous:

- The marketing manager, Carlo Infraganti, had discretionary authority to negotiate contracts with corporate clients, which included price, discounts, and terms of payment provisions. Supporting documentation was not available, and not all the sales were formalized by written contracts. Corporate clients represented 40% of SAGCO's annual sales. Carlo challenged the report by saying that Ivan trusted him and that all negotiations were conducted in the best interests of the company.

- Payments were processed without backup documentation. The only strict requirement to process an invoice was the existence of Ivan's signature. In his response to this issue, Gianni Nessuno, the CFO, said that he was not there to control his boss. We found several cases of consulting fees for which the purpose and scope of the services were not clearly stated.

- Competitive bidding had not been implemented for significant purchases negotiated in the head office. However, three bids were required for minor purchases processed in the branches, which represented less than 10% of the total annual expenditures.

- The recommendation to develop a written code of ethics was not clearly understood. Nicky thought that it was unnecessary to write a policy stating how people should behave. However, and because of my insistence, he asked me to write a draft for the executive committee, but it was never discussed by the directors.

The latest follow-up report revealed that most of the recommendations had not been employed. Management continued to report that the implementation of basic controls were "in progress." Ivan kept promising that he would fix the issues, and the executive committee accepted his excuses again and again.

In addition to the traditional internal audit work, we had been gathering specific information regarding fraud indicators. The bulk of this information resulted from tips received from insiders who had developed a strong professional relationship with the auditors. We also maintained a so-called diamonds file that included documentation of strange or unusual transactions collected during the audits. I kept Alex apprised of my concerns, but he was still reluctant to believe that something was wrong with Ivan.

Unlike Ivan, Nicky had an excellent sense of humor and was friendly with all of the employees, especially the women. He also visited the offices of senior management to tell funny stories that were mixed with obscure corporate messages. In one my visits with him, after 20 minutes of his nonsensical jabber, I expressed my concerns about the company controls. He responded that the situation could be illustrated by using the metaphor of the sharks. As a degreed biologist, he had learned that sharks would never attack their victims without a "proper cause." In other words, no harm should be expected from sharks if we do not bother them. "All right, Nicky. I understand your metaphor" was my controlled response. His message was not very subtle—the sharks (CEO and management) were going to kill me if I continued to bother them with my audit reports.

This was enough for me! I immediately called Alex, the IFE representative, for an urgent meeting. Although he had received all these reports, he had not reacted according to my expectations.

The meeting started with my recommendation to perform a special investigation based on the persistence and the significance of the control deficiencies. But Alex kept saying that he did not want to upset Ivan because he was a hard worker and the company was exceeding the budgeted profits for the third consecutive year. They were all happy and things were going well, so why worry about controls?

"Just keep doing your good job with the audit reports, and don't mix your work with the investigation stuff," he replied. At this point I realized that I was not using the proper words to communicate the seriousness of the situation. Because there were some red flags that I had not mentioned in the audit reports, I decided to convince him by using the "dirty" word: "Alex, please consider that there are *fraud* indicators that we have been gathering, and again, we need to test them."

It still appeared that he was not fully convinced, and I realized that I had to shoot with my last bullet: "Ivan Vichy and the Rigattis might be siphoning funds from SAGCO for their private businesses and besides the criminal law considerations, they might be violating the shareholders' agreement with IFE. I feel I must investigate and formally report this to you as the IFE representative."

Alex was terrified by this statement. In an attempt to calm him down, I briefly explained the difference between control deficiencies and fraud indicators. In addition, I stressed that although IFE had a minority interest in SAGCO, it had appointed me as audit director, and therefore, IFE might have some degree of liability under the internal control provisions of the Foreign Corrupt Practices Act (FCPA). In my view, this potential liability deserved a detailed investigation and the opinion of IFE legal counsel in New York. Alex was also frightened by the possibility of a legal opinion. Finally, we agreed that I would prepare a confidential "red-flag report" for his review.

As soon as I returned to the office, I met with my two senior auditors in order to prepare for the investigation. The term "red-flag report" that I had employed with Alex was obviously a euphemism, used to speed up the investigation that we had already planned. One of the auditors had been tipped off that a "big boss" would be withdrawing a significant amount of cash from SAGCO Treasury Department for personal purposes.

I called Alex immediately, but he had traveled to New York to attend a meeting with his supervisor. I sent a fax to his hotel room explaining what we had found and asked him to call me at any time. The next day at 11 p.m., Alex called my home. He said that he had read my fax and had discussed the issues with his supervisor.

"Go ahead with your investigation plans quickly. I will be back next week with our legal counsel. You do have our support. Keep me posted and good luck!" Alex said.

Although initially I felt excited by this support, I was later disappointed regarding the actual cause of Alex's change of heart. IFE had a very profitable opportunity to sell its shares in SAGCO, but as stated in the shareholders' agreement, IFE needed a *no objection* from the majority owner (Vafang) for any divestment during the first five years after the establishment of the new company. For reasons that I will never know, the Rigattis did not want to allow a new U.S. partner to enter SAGCO. As a result of this conflict, Alex had decided to use the investigation to put pressure on Vafang in order to obtain the *no objection* for the sale.

To begin, I thought I'd start with the basics. I assigned the whole audit team to perform a surprise cash count the following morning at 8:00 a.m. At 1:00 p.m. the next day, I had no news about it. In the past, the auditors had completed this procedure in less than two hours. I was anxious and went to the treasury office to find out what had happened. Gianni, the CFO, saw me and said, "Your auditors say that there is a $500,000 discrepancy (shortage), but I have just found the supporting documentation, and therefore, there's nothing to worry about." The so-called supporting documentation was a computer-printed internal form used for petty cash withdrawals that was signed by Nicky, the president, with the inscription "cash advance." The amount was $500,000, and the date was four weeks ago. This transaction had not been recorded in the accounting system. However, Gianni was happy, because in his view, everything had been properly clarified. When asked why the transaction was not recorded, he explained that since the president usually reimbursed the "borrowed" money during the same month, the general ledger cash account remained unbalanced for a few weeks at the most; therefore, "it was unnecessary to record these transactions."

Moreover, Gianni said that no additional documentation was necessary because this form had the "blessing" of the president, as shown by his written approval. He added: "Well, you know what this means. . . ."

What Gianni did not know—or perhaps what he had intentionally forgotten—was that besides the accounting and potential criminal problems, this was a clear violation of the shareholders' agreement. In fact, the agreement required that any related party transaction in excess of $100,000 should be disclosed and approved by the executive committee.

In addition to the "presidential cash advance" issue, we had obtained information from public records regarding ownership and financial position of suspicious customers and vendors. We were able to link this information with the documents maintained in our "diamonds" file. The results follow.

THE DIAMOND FILE

Consa Consulting

Evidence obtained from public records confirmed that Consa—a consulting firm that supposedly provided services to SAGCO—was owned by Ivan Vichy (51%) and Serge

(49%). This situation had not been disclosed to the partners. During the last year, SAGCO had paid Consa $350,000 for services that were never rendered. Invoices were processed and paid with the written authorization of Ivan Vichy. Management was not able to provide any business rationale for these payments. "I don't know. I just follow Ivan's instructions" was the CFO's response when asked about the disbursements.

Lavergogna, Inc.

Our review of the financial statements revealed that 98% of their reported sales for the previous year were SAGCO purchases. This vendor supposedly specialized in construction works, but had no history of operations in Palms, although it had been incorporated more than two years ago. In addition, we discovered that Lavergogna was a wholly owned subsidiary of Menefreg Associates Ltd., a company incorporated in the Cayman Islands. Unfortunately, we were unable to find the names of the beneficial owners of Menefreg Associates.

However, we did find that SAGCO had awarded Lavergogna a large number of contracts (totaling more than $16 million) without competitive bidding and with prices significantly higher than other qualified competitors. Additionally, we discovered that this vendor received payments for construction work that had never been performed, amounting more than $6 million, all approved by Ivan.

Buonapietra Energy Co.

SAGCO entered into a gas sale contract with an entity called Buonapietra Energy, which was a Vafang subsidiary. This 10-year deal, worth $100 million, included a discount of 26% over market price. Moreover, our review of public records showed that Ivan was president of Buonapietra Energy. We also found that the original payment terms had been changed from 7 to 70 days. This gracious amendment was signed by Nicky, as president of SAGCO, and Ivan, as president of Buonapietra Energy. Once again, the shareholders' agreement had been violated because none of these decisions had been approved by the executive committee and no written justification was available.

AN OFFER THEY COULDN'T REFUSE

Our investigation report was presented in a meeting with IFE representatives, our New York legal counsel, and our local attorneys. The meeting lasted more than four hours, and each issue was thoroughly discussed. The lawyers concluded that there was more than sufficient evidence to seek a criminal referral against Ivan and Nicky for fraud and to begin a civil suit against them and Vafang Utilities for breach of the shareholders' agreement and conflicts of interest.

Alex and his boss from IFE headquarters told the lawyers that before any legal action was taken, they would like to offer an "opportunity" to the Rigattis first. This so-called opportunity was a promise that IFE would not pursue any claims against Vafang and the other parties if they would agree to these conditions:

- Ivan Vichy and Nick Rigatti would immediately resign their board and management positions without any special compensation.

- Vafang Utilities would pay IFE for all damages caused by the irregularities disclosed in the investigation report.

- Vafang Utilities would allow IFE to sell all its shares in SAGCO without objection.

- The new partner would have, for five years, the exclusive right to designate and remove senior management in SAGCO.

- IFE would not perform any additional investigation with respect to the transactions identified in the report that were more than three years old.

A month later, three months after the issuance of the investigation report, Vafang Utilities signed a new shareholders' agreement in which the Rigattis accepted all the conditions "offered" by IFE.

Ivan Vichy resigned his position in SAGCO without any compensation, but he later sued Vafang Utilities and obtained a $10 million compensation award. In the seven years following the scandal, he disappeared from the Palms business community. But then he suddenly reappeared in an interview with a local business newspaper. The title of the article was "Successful Businessman Wins Government Contract."

Nicky returned to Italy and continued his life as a biologist, perhaps with some additional knowledge about the behavior of sharks after his experience in Palms. I heard that his father, Vito, had reprimanded him severely for his performance in SAGCO.

I was congratulated by IFE headquarters for my performance in this case, and they offered me an executive position in a new media and entertainment company in which IFE would be a minority owner. The offer was so attractive that I found no reason to refuse to it.

LESSONS LEARNED

The five years I served as internal audit director in SAGCO were extremely important in my professional and personal development. I was exposed to high-stakes frauds perpetrated by the president, the CEO, and senior management. The schemes included undisclosed related-parties transactions, self-dealing, conflicts of interest, misappropriation of cash, fraudulent disbursements, and intentional breaches of contract.

In most cases involving frauds perpetrated by CEOs, they had used their position of power to override internal controls. However, in this case, the CEO and the president had no need to bypass internal controls since they were almost nonexistent in SAGCO. The external auditors were not a problem because they had been awarded a significant consulting contract and were happily ignorant. Moreover, the board did not fulfill its oversight responsibilities. With the exception of internal audit, management considered that the signature of one the "big bosses" was more than enough to process any transaction, regardless of its legitimacy. This corporate context, joined with the general perception of impunity, allowed Ivan, Nicky, and their management gang to perpetrate their frauds.

In this case we obtained full support only because IFE had a business reason to back our efforts. The investigation was used to press the Rigattis to allow IFE to sever its relationship with SAGCO. Ivan was considered a "star CEO," and the company was highly profitable. Everyone enjoyed remaining blissfully unaware of wrongdoing as long as business was good. I doubt, however, that the shareholders and the public would be so tolerant. The "limited fraud tolerance policy" of this case reminds me a statement generally attributed to gangster Charles "Lucky" Luciano: "There's no such thing as good money or bad money. There's just money."

RECOMMENDATIONS TO PREVENT FUTURE OCCURRENCES

Institute a Code of Ethics

My proposal to implement a code of ethics in SAGCO was never discussed by the board. Nicky took care of sending my draft to the freezer. Fortunately, IFE lawyers had included some basic antifraud provisions in the shareholders' agreement. These provisions would have allowed IFE to file a civil fraud claim against the majority owners in response to the findings of our investigation. It would be a good practice for all companies to include antifraud provisions in their partnership and joint venture agreements. As shown in this case, the inclusion of control provisions in the shareholders' agreement was the only resource available to protect the interests of the minority owners.

Establish a Hotline

Cultural issues are always an obstacle for fraud prevention and detection in foreign subsidiaries. A good example is the implementation of a hotline. People in many parts of the world are uncomfortable with reporting a problem, especially in places where there has been a history of repression or abuse. SAGCO did not have a hotline, but we did gain the trust of the employees and established excellent informal communications channels with honest staff members in key areas of the organization (accounts payables, collections, branches, etc). These allowed us to obtain relevant information for our case.

However, some of the improper actions being taken at SAGCO might have been found earlier if a reporting system was in place so that employees and vendors could report fraud anonymously. Again, depending on the culture, it may take some extra communication and training to teach employees that it is their duty to report misconduct or suspicious activities and to ensure them that they are safe in doing so.

Educate Directors and Management as to the Importance of Fraud Prevention

Some businesspeople do not care about internal control deficiencies until it is too late. Others expect that an internal audit will provide legal evidence for a fraud case. After this experience, I realized that businesspeople need to be trained about the different fraud responsibilities of management, board members, external auditors, internal auditors, fraud examiners, and lawyers. A better understanding of the CFE profession by those in senior positions will help to obtain their support in our fraud prevention and detection efforts.

Pedro Fabiano, CFE, is president and cofounder of the Argentine chapter of the Association of Certified Fraud Examiners (ACFE), the only chapter in Latin America. He has more than 15 years of international experience in overseeing internal audit, fraud examination, anti–money laundering, and operational risk. Mr. Fabiano is a regent emeritus and fellow of the ACFE.

CHAPTER 49

A New York State of Fraud

MARTIN T. BIEGELMAN

In the movie *Wall Street*, actor Michael Douglas portrays the character of Gordon Gekko, whose stock phrase is "Greed is good." Greed on Wall Street epitomized the 1980s with numerous insider trading cases and other financial scandals. But a few blocks away from Wall Street is John Street, the not-so-well-known insurance center of New York City. John Street had a dark and dirty secret. On John Street, greed and corruption had been good in every decade since the 1950s.

What I am about to tell you would make great fiction because it's hard to believe. But this is a true story about a way of life in New York City where corruption, kickbacks, fraud, and deceit were everyday occurrences—a life that the perpetrators thought would never end. And it wouldn't have ended if it weren't for persistence, strong detective work, and some very good luck.

For many years, a conspiracy existed in practically every segment of the New York insurance industry to fraudulently inflate and stage property claims and collect the proceeds. The corruption was so pervasive that almost everyone involved in the claims process was in on the scheme, from the insured property owner to the broker. Huge under-the-table payoffs and a strict code of silence kept this conspiracy going for 40 years.

Public adjusters are licensed professionals who adjust property claims on behalf of insured property owners. They typically work with the insurance company adjusters and other experts to determine a settlement amount to be paid to the insured. It is not uncommon for public adjusters and insurance company adjusters to disagree on the amount of damage on a claim. New York State law limits public adjusters to a maximum 12.5% commission on a claim. The usual compensation is 5 to 10%. Typically, the settlement check is sent to a public adjuster, who subtracts a fee and remits the balance to the insured property owners.

This particular scheme involved kickbacks paid by public adjusters to insurance company adjusters and other experts in order to convince them to comply with the conspiracy. Money for the payoffs came from the hugely inflated insurance settlements paid to the insured, who gave the public adjusters as much as one-half of the payments. The public adjusters then split the cash with the other participants in the scheme.

Years ago, the property claims community in New York was relatively small, so it became commonplace for the same public adjusters, company adjusters, accountants, and other experts to show up on many claims. Thus, the marriages of corrupt adjusters expanded, and this fraudulent conspiracy flourished for decades.

Almost every major insurance company in the United States was a victim of this fraud and corruption scheme. They had no idea that their employees had been corrupted and were taking kickbacks, often in the millions of dollars, to approve fraudulent insurance claims. Many of their corrupt adjusters were openly living like millionaires on salaries of $50,000, but no one ever caught on.

Thousands of phony claims were staged and inflated for as low as $8,000 all the way up to a staggering $19 million. Fraudulent claims included water damage, vandalism, burglary, fire, and arson. The fraudsters were imaginative in their work. Our investigation found machines constructed to blow powdered charcoal into buildings, simulating smoke damage. Pipes were installed for the sole purpose of breaking them to create water damage claims. Tea was sprayed on walls to look like water stain damage.

The subjects we identified were respected members of their communities. They were managers of their children's Little League teams; they belonged to the PTA; they were active members of their local churches and synagogues—they appeared to be upstanding citizens. But secretly, they were criminals, joined at the hip—or the wallet.

A Den of Thieves

As a United States Postal Inspector in New York City, I had just finished an investigation of a fast food restaurant called Mighty Burger. The owner was found guilty of mail fraud. Lou O'Malley, an insurance fraud investigator with the Insurance Fraud Prevention Bureau, had helped out on the investigation and was a tremendous asset. Lou had been a New York Police Department detective before becoming an insurance investigator. Short and stout with a reputation for being a detective's detective, he was a class act. Now in his late 60s, Lou still couldn't get police work out of his blood. He was a man on a mission.

Lou told me that a loosely knit conspiracy dating back 40 years existed in New York between all participants in the property claims settlement process. He learned about this from informants over the years who spoke in hushed tones. While Lou never received any substantial evidence, he believed in his heart that the informants were speaking the truth.

"I know truth when I hear it," Lou promised, "and I would bet the farm on it."

According to Lou, the fraud was so pervasive that everyone in the claims process was involved, and the scheme netted millions and millions of dollars. He said there had never been a successful large-scale investigation of the insurance industry because no one had been able to crack the criminal chain. Lou decided that I was the one to take on this monumental task. I asked what evidence he had collected to begin an investigation.

Lou looked me in the eye and said, "Well, boyo, that's the problem. I don't have any tangible evidence, but I have all the faith in the world that you will find what we need to make the case."

I like challenges, but this one had "impossible" written all over it. I didn't know where to start. Just when I was losing hope, lighting struck in the form of coincidence and luck. An investigator with the Champion Insurance Group told me of several anonymous telephone calls it had recently received.

Champion was one of the victim insurance companies in the Mighty Burger case that Lou and I had just wrapped up. The Champion adjuster who handled the restaurant's claims was Karl Miller. We had considered using Miller as a witness at the Mighty Burger trial, but decided against it. We had suspicions about him that we just couldn't put our finger on. One anonymous caller to Champion said that Miller was involved in fraudulent claims and received large amounts of payoffs. Another described a person who, while lounging at an exclusive country club, bragged about his fraudulent claims and all the money he made through his corrupt public adjuster, Herman Birnbaum. I decided we had enough information to commence the investigation.

MISSION: POSSIBLE

A task force began to investigate this systematic and entrenched fraud and corruption scheme. The Postal Inspection Service joined forces with the Federal Bureau of Investigation, the Internal Revenue Service–Criminal Investigation Division, and the United States Attorney's Office for the Eastern District of New York. Although nearing retirement, Lou O'Malley agreed to join us to watch his dream investigation come to fruition. We initially pulled hundreds of claim files where Miller was the Champion adjuster and Birnbaum was the public adjuster. Later we pulled files on other Champion adjusters.

It took many months for the task force to review these thousands of files thoroughly for red flags. There were files without backup documentation, files with no photos or photos that failed to show the claimed damage, mistakes as to the date of occurrence, field drafts routinely issued that did not require higher-level approval, files for claims paid within days of the occurrence, photos of damage already claimed in prior losses, multiple losses with the same insured property owners, and other files missing from storage. They were all red flags signaling insurance fraud, and we targeted them for further investigation.

We found numerous suspect claim files where Miller, Birnbaum, and additional Champion adjusters were involved. We learned the names of others who were involved in these suspicious insurance claims, and our list of suspects quickly grew. Following the concept of the "Six Degrees of Separation," we connected company adjusters with public adjusters.

We then contacted other insurance companies where these subject public adjusters had been involved in claims and requested those files. Soon there were thousands of additional files to review. The process took months to complete. We now had both homeowner and commercial claims that appeared to be fraudulent. Many of them were settled for millions of dollars. We knew that where there was fraud, there was corruption and kickbacks.

The task force began to interview homeowners about their suspicious claims. Homeowners were fairly easy to "roll over." They typically had filed few fraudulent claims and were quick to reveal the names of the public adjusters who involved them in the scheme. As the investigation progressed, other false claims and additional information were brought to our attention by other insurance companies, attorneys, investigators, informants, and cooperators.

The task force placed surveillance cameras in the homes and offices of cooperators to catch discussions of fraud and cash payments. We caught on video one public adjuster named Lester Ingram instructing an informant, undercover as an insured property owner, how to stage a burglary claim rather than arson.

"Are you a moron?" Ingram asked him incredulously. "You never want to claim fire because that brings in the cops *and* fire marshals. Do a staged burglary instead. No one asks questions and everyone gets rich."

Ingram and others like him were quietly arrested and quickly agreed to cooperate with the government in its ever-expanding investigation.

Ingram had a predisposition for fraud. In his prior job as the owner of a pest control business, he surreptitiously sprinkled dead termites in the homes of those he was inspecting.

"Oh my goodness," he would exclaim, "you have a serious termite infestation that I'll have to treat quickly."

The task force executed its first search warrant two years after Lou asked me to carry out the investigation. That search involved all the elements of imagination and tenacity we needed in order to crack these cases.

Jimmy Collier and his wife lived in an apartment in Queens, New York, a borough of New York City. Collier was a personable man in his early 30s. He was recently married and this was their first apartment. Collier filed an insurance claim with Champion Insurance alleging severe water damage in their apartment. He stated that the contents of his apartment, including his furniture, were completely damaged when the kitchen sink overflowed while the water was left running unattended. Somehow, a dish towel mysteriously fell into the sink by itself, clogged the drain, and caused the apartment flood. Within days, Collier's claim for thousands of dollars in damage was paid.

The task force couldn't substantiate whether the damage was legitimate from the few photographs—mostly of furniture—found in the claim file. Collier lived on the sixth floor, and although the water was allegedly left running for many hours, causing significant damage throughout the couple's apartment, none of the neighbors living below or on either side reported any damage.

Collier wanted the insurance company to believe that although water filled his apartment to the ceiling, destroying all furniture, clothes, and other contents, no water escaped next door or to any apartment below. Collier wanted us to believe that he lived in Toontown, not Queens. In Toontown, the imaginary city from the movie *Who Framed Roger Rabbit?* the laws of physics don't apply. But even more interesting was the fact that Karl Miller was the Champion insurance adjuster on the claim. As it turned out, Collier was a salvage expert who worked closely with Miller on many insurance claims.

When we went to the apartment to interview Collier, he and his wife had moved from the apartment to a house on Long Island. We were able to interview the current occupant of the apartment, who claimed to have no knowledge of the alleged flood. She let us pull up the carpet to reveal unfinished wood floors that displayed no water damage. We spoke to neighbors who lived below the Colliers at the time; none had any water damage in their apartments or knew of the alleged flood. We also spoke to the building superintendent. "There was no flood, no water damage, nothing. I would know; I was the super. They're *gonifs* [a slang Yiddish term for "thieves"]," he proclaimed.

The task force took a different approach to prove this particular fraud. We obtained a search warrant for the Colliers' new home to seize the furniture he had alleged was damaged. We made a unique argument to the federal judge in support of the search warrant. If Collier had incurred the amount of damage to his furniture as claimed, the furniture would have either been thrown out or refinished. If we found the furniture as depicted in the claim photographs in its original state, we could prove fraud and the corruption. "Now I've seen everything," commented the judge as she signed the search warrant.

You can imagine Jimmy Collier's surprise when we showed up at his residence almost five years after the original claim. After seeing the moving truck there to take his furniture away pursuant to the search warrant, Collier remarked, "This can't be happening. You're taking my furniture?"

At the Collier residence, we found several pieces of furniture from the claim. They were seized as evidence and sent to the Postal Inspection Service Crime Laboratory for analysis. The results didn't particularly surprise the task force. There was no evidence of either water damage or refinishing on any of the furniture. Collier was subsequently indicted, arrested, and convicted. He quickly became a cooperating defendant against Miller, along with numerous other suspects.

After reviewing thousands of claims files, the task force members could tell, just by reading, if a claim was staged and who did it. Certain public adjusters staged damages in particular ways; these were the signatures of those who worked the fraud. Some liked to break water pipes; some watered-down premises with hoses; some used smoke machines; and other brought in defective merchandise from other locations to create more damage. Others were fearful of actually staging a claim, so they just grossly inflated legitimate occurrences instead.

The investigation continued. The task force executed search warrants at the offices of five public adjusters, many of them on John Street, and unsealed the indictments of 24 additional people, including public adjusters, company adjusters, salvage experts, and others. The case went public. Almost immediately, numerous defendants and targets not yet charged came forward to work out plea agreements with the government. Included in the indictments were masterminds Herman Birnbaum and Karl Miller.

Shortly after Birnbaum's indictment and with the mounting number of cooperating defendants willing to testify against him, he decided to plead guilty and cooperate with the government's investigation.

"I'm not a young man anymore and I know when the game is over," said Birnbaum, a 74-year-old public adjuster for 40 years. When he sat down with the government, he had quite a story to tell.

Birnbaum described how he and other criminal-minded public adjusters realized 40 years ago that they could make a fortune in the growing property claims business through payoffs to insurance company adjusters. Most company adjusters were making very low wages in those days. It wasn't hard to persuade them to commit fraud with cash under the table. Birnbaum described the importance of getting all the participants in the claims settlement process "on board and with the program." Once they got on the money train, they couldn't get off. Even Birnbaum was shocked that the corruption and fraud lasted for so many years before its discovery. "All good things must come to an end, but I didn't think it would last this long or end this way," he lamented.

Birnbaum provided the names of hundreds of homeowner and commercial insureds, company adjusters, and other experts he conspired with over his long career in fraud. He also described the stacks of cash he handed out to his co-conspirators over the years. Interestingly enough, the person he paid the most in kickbacks was Karl Miller.

"It was hundreds of thousands, maybe millions of dollars over the years," Birnbaum said of the payoffs to Miller. "And that was just from me. Miller was dealing with many other public adjusters," he added.

The task force performed a net worth analysis on Miller, and Birnbaum was right. For an insurance company adjuster who never earned more than $50,000 a year, Miller was worth millions. He had huge positions in stocks and bonds, real estate holdings in several states, and, as we would later learn, millions in cash hidden away. Miller's corrupt career was over and he saw the light. He, too, decided to plead guilty and cooperate with the government.

The hard work that went into this investigation was paying off big time. The elusive dream of a veteran detective became reality with our investigation. Lou O'Malley was now able to retire knowing that his work was done.

SMOKE AND MIRRORS

The task force's first trial involved a fraudulent claim from three years prior. The claim involved Buyer's Choice Furniture, a discount furniture store located in a mall on Long Island, New York. An arsonist set fire to a store in the mall and was never caught. Buyer's Choice Furniture suffered some minor damage but submitted a grossly inflated claim to Worldwide Insurance Group.

Herman Birnbaum was the public adjuster for Buyer's Choice; Joe Rodriguez was the adjuster for Worldwide; and Kevin Bailey was the salvage expert who would determine the amount of smoke damage to the contents. Birnbaum, Rodriguez, and Bailey conspired with the insured, Buyer's Choice, to inflate the claim from less than $10,000 to over $100,000. As Birnbaum told Buyer's Choice, "I got these guys [the adjusters] in my pocket, and it's stuffed with cash."

In this case, Herman Birnbaum agreed to cooperate. Kevin Bailey was indicted and went to trial, where we used accomplice testimony and documents to prove fraud and corruption. Birnbaum and Rodriguez testified as to their involvement with Bailey in this fraudulent claim and admitted to promising cash payments in return for aiding the fraud.

An accountant who was not involved in the fraud testified that he couldn't verify the inventory used or the damage estimate that Bailey came up with. An attorney representing Worldwide testified that Bailey could provide no records showing how he verified the actual inventory and the amount of damage. This attorney also testified that Bailey refused to sign an affidavit as to the inventory and damage estimate he prepared and submitted to the insurance company. Finally, a store manager who had no part in the fraud testified as to how much inventory was in the store and how much damage really occurred.

At the conclusion of the trial, the jury found Bailey guilty on all the counts of mail fraud. While neither the claim nor the promised kickbacks were ever paid, the government was able to convict Bailey and send him to prison. After the trial, numerous other defendants awaiting trial decided to plead guilty. They correctly reasoned that if the government could prove a fraud when neither the phony claim nor the cash was ever paid, what chance would they have?

Next, the task force executed search warrants at the offices of seven additional public adjusters. "They're back" were the words that echoed on John Street and throughout the industry. The government unsealed indictments of 39 more individuals, including insured property owners, public adjusters, company adjusters, salvage experts, accountants, and brokers. In short order, most of these defendants pled guilty.

The second trial involved a series of insurance claims filed by Oceanview Manufacturing, an auto parts manufacturer located in Maspeth, New York. Champion was the insurance company for Oceanview. The defendant on trial was Ralph Murphy, whose real name was Ralph Miller. Murphy was a machinery expert hired by insurance companies to determine and appraise the amount of damage from a claim.

Murphy was also the brother of Champion adjuster Karl Miller. Murphy would receive loss assignments from his brother. To avoid arousing suspicion and the possibility of conflict-of-interest charges, he used the alias of Murphy. No one knew that they were brothers, and they wanted to keep it that way.

The public adjuster for Oceanview was our old friend Herman Birnbaum. Miller and Murphy had an agreement with Birnbaum that they would receive large kickbacks for inflating claims with him. Nasir Abdul was also a Champion adjuster and was involved in some of the Oceanview claims. He, too, had a standard agreement with Birnbaum to receive payoffs. An accountant who was retained by the insurance company was in on the scheme. Ralph Latoire, the owner of Oceanview, also conspired with Birnbaum and the others to fraudulently inflate these claims and then stuff their pockets with cash.

Murphy was charged with 10 counts of mail fraud involving a fire and water damage claim that occurred at Oceanview, for which Champion paid $678,000, and a water damage claim for which Champion paid $320,000. Murphy received kickbacks for claiming that undamaged machinery in the plant was damaged beyond repair. Birnbaum, Latoire, Abdul, and the accountant all testified as to their involvement in the fraud.

A volunteer fireman who responded to the scene testified how he saw little damage—under $10,000 worth. The Oceanview bookkeeper testified that she was aware of the kickbacks and even went to the bank to withdraw the cash for the payments.

"At the time, I felt like I was in a movie, stuffing cash in a briefcase, but now it's more of a nightmare," she told the jury.

Several employees of Oceanview who had no part in the fraud testified that the machines that Murphy claimed were ruined were not damaged and were still in working order. One of these machines had been sold, but was located by the investigators and photographed almost five years after the original claim. Murphy claimed this piece of machinery was damaged beyond repair. The photographic and witness testimony showed it was still in working condition, proving the crimes incontrovertibly. In addition, prior to his indictment, when Murphy was interviewed by the investigators, he made some admissions but lied about other aspects of his involvement. The government introduced these statements at trial.

Murphy testified in his own defense, and the government was able to prove that he perjured himself while on the witness stand. At the conclusion of the trial, Murphy was found guilty on all counts. He was sentenced to three years in prison and court-ordered restitution to Champion.

The enormity and long time frame of the conspiracy benefited the fraud examiners. While it might be possible for a defendant to fight criminal charges on one or two acts of corruption, it was impossible when one committed dozens if not hundreds of such crimes. With each new plea, the steamroller picked up speed with more and more defendants lining up to plead guilty.

Ultimately, the New York Insurance Fraud Task Force investigation resulted in charges and convictions against 256 defendants for insurance-related fraud, conspiracy, and tax evasion. Twenty-six search warrants were executed during the investigation. Almost every major insurance company in the United States was a victim. The total fraud loss was well over half a billion dollars.

Amazingly, only two individuals went to trial and were convicted. The sentences handed out to the defendants ranged from probation to 15 years in prison for a series of arsons for profit. Sentences usually included fines and court-ordered restitution. The largest fine was $1 million. The largest court ordered restitution was $293,301,435. Many of those charged were hit with civil Racketeering Influenced and Corrupt Organizations Act (RICO) lawsuits filed by the victim insurance companies.

LESSONS LEARNED

This investigation was a learning experience for the investigators. Prior to this, we never had a case with so many defendants and so many documents. The numerous search warrants and grand jury subpoenas yielded hundreds of thousands of documents that all had to be reviewed. In order to store, inventory, and review the documents, a warehouse-size building was needed. The amount of time and dedication required by the investigative team and me to examine the evidence was extraordinary.

We learned never to give up. Our motto was "Keep your eye on the prize." Large and complex cases take time. The team realized that cases such as this could take years to complete, and everyone was committed for the long haul. Organization was critical. We didn't allow ourselves to be overwhelmed by the volume of paper.

A systematic review allowed us to remove the wheat from the chaff, resulting in key and "smoking gun" documents. Computers greatly increased our productivity. Embracing and effectively using technology can significantly improve investigative results.

We also realized that in order to investigate fraud in the insurance business successfully, we needed to know the industry. That included education in how the business works, how insurance claims are filed and paid, the roles of the various participants in the claims process, and the terminology and lingo. The time and effort paid off. Whatever industry or business a fraud examiner investigates, it is absolutely critical to know how it operates.

We needed to use every available tool in the fraud examiner's toolkit. That included undercover operations, physical and electronic surveillance, search warrants, subpoenas, "flipping" defendants into cooperators, publicizing indictments and arrests, as well as adding tax evasion charges for the unreported cash payoffs. We even used a RICO indictment against one of the public adjusting firms.

Something else was reinforced for us: Know your case inside and out. We found it extremely beneficial to review constantly our notes and reports as well as our key evidence. With hundreds of defendants, witnesses, associated notes, and the large volume of evidence, there was always something discovered or remembered when we went back again. We also found that by having a small number of investigators who stayed together for most of the investigation, we retained our historical knowledge of the case.

Prepare, prepare, and prepare some more for possible testimony, whether at trial or any other related proceeding. You never know what question you will be asked. Your knowledge of the case could make or break the outcome.

RECOMMENDATIONS TO PREVENT FUTURE OCCURRENCES

Our case was successful because we identified numerous red flags of fraud and corruption, and were unrelenting in the investigation.

Understand Fraud Risk

We found that management at the victim companies had no idea that this corruption and fraud was going on. An executive at one of the companies told us at the beginning of the investigation that he would stake his reputation on the honesty of his adjusters. Furthermore, he stated that he believed that fraud has a minimal impact on his business. He was wrong on both accounts. At his company alone, we convicted four of his adjusters and the losses were in multimillions of dollars.

Those involved in the insurance industry must be aware that insurance fraud is a constant threat that results in billions of dollars in losses every year. Management of every organization needs to perform an ongoing fraud risk assessment and take appropriate action to mitigate those identified risks.

Rotate Employees

This conspiracy was successful for so long because the same company adjusters were allowed to work the same territories and with the same public adjusters and other external personnel year after year. Had adjusters been rotated, the "fraud marriages" may have been broken up. Rotation of employees in key roles is an internal control that should be always considered.

Respond to Rumors

Throughout the investigation, we learned that there were numerous rumors of unexplained wealth and extravagant lifestyles on the part of the company adjusters. It many cases, it was evident that the subjects were living beyond their means, but no one in authority did anything about it. One company executive told us that a particular adjuster was always providing investment information to other employees on what stocks and bonds to buy. The warning bells never sounded.

In another example, an adjuster was living in a million-dollar home on a salary of $40,000. Yet no one ever acted on this information. The corruption in this case was so vast that the illicit cash flowed like water. Rumors and other questionable activity must be appropriately and professionally investigated.

Review Claim Files

One of the constants that we found was a lack of a thorough review of the claim files by insurance company claim representatives. Those claims representatives must be trained thoroughly in detecting fraud through identification of red flags.

Ethics and Fraud Awareness Training

The victim insurance companies generally did not provide either ethics or fraud awareness training to their employees. This was a critical lapse that may have contributed to the culture of fraud. Ethical conduct and fraud prevention training is needed on at least an annual basis for all employees. In addition, it is highly recommended that all employees be told whenever any employees or others doing business with the company are arrested or discharged for fraudulent activity. This demonstrates to employees, customers, and investors that the organization takes a strong stand against fraud and abuse.

Hotlines

The anonymous calls that fueled this case did not come through a formal hotline. Instead, they were received ad hoc by employees. In fact, most of the victim companies did not have hotlines in place. All companies should institute hotlines to allow for anonymous and confidential reporting of allegations of fraud and violations of policy. The hotlines must be widely communicated internally and externally. Most important, all allegations received must be thoroughly vetted and investigated.

Certified Fraud Examiners

Today, with the certified fraud examiner certification as the gold standard for fraud detection and prevention, organizations are better served and protected by having CFEs on their investigative staffs. Every investigative unit must have CFEs to detect, investigate, and prevent fraud. Fraud examination expertise is absolutely critical in fostering a climate of honesty and integrity in every organization.

Martin T. Biegelman, CFE, is the director of financial integrity at Microsoft Corporation, Redmond, Washington. He has more than 30 years' experience in fraud detection, investigation, and prevention. Mr. Biegelman is the coauthor of *Executive Roadmap to Fraud Prevention and Internal Control: Creating a Culture of Compliance,* **published by John Wiley & Sons.**

CHAPTER 50

Information Superhighway

BARRY DAVIDOW

Phil Green served eight years on the New South Wales police force in Australia. He measured in at slightly over six feet, but his perfect, sharp posture made him appear taller. People guessed that he was in the military or law enforcement when they met him—he had the look of a respectable authority figure.

When Phil decided to quit the force, he was a highly regarded detective; he had made a name for himself as a hardworking and effective member of a specialist team. His superior officers tried to talk him out of leaving, convinced that he was destined to move quickly up the ranks. That's what he told me, at least.

He was in his early 30s when he left the force. He loved the police service but felt that he needed a less risky and more lucrative job for his family's sake.

So Phil opened an office as a private investigator. He relied on his vast network of personal contacts in the law enforcement and criminal world to obtain information about suspicious people and their activities. Phil could find people who ran away from their debts, families, and lovers. He received a steady stream of clients and felt secure within a year of starting his new business.

"I was doing okay but I wanted some real money," he said. "A client told me that if I wanted to get rich I should follow the cash, like Slick Willie, to the banks." He soon learned that banks and insurance companies were owed substantial amounts of money from clients absconding. The financial institutions were willing to pay high fees to get their money back.

Phil discovered that using the electoral roll for tracking people was not very helpful. Even though they were required by law to give the electoral office their real addresses, people who didn't want to be found didn't always do so. Phil learned that the most reliable database of addresses was in the New South Wales Roads and Traffic Authority (RTA). The RTA's major functions are to test and administer driving licenses, register and inspect vehicles, and improve road safety. In order to avoid losing their driving licenses, people made sure to inform the RTA about their changes of address. The difficulty was that the RTA didn't allow disclosure of information from their licensing and registration database to outside parties.

The financial institutions had a dilemma. The employees at the RTA didn't want to disclose personal information from the database, and the banks didn't want to bribe them because they considered bribery unethical. That is why they wanted Phil to get the information for them.

Phil was proud of the way that he could turn honest RTA employees into corrupt officials.

"I would find the most helpful, courteous, and sincere person at the motor registry," he said, adding that most of the workers who fit this description were male and more gullible than females. "I would then put a folder on the counter and tell him that I was so worried about the case I was working on that I couldn't sleep. Opening the folder, I would show documents and say something like 'This case here is about how a crook has built up a debt with Bill and Greta Johnston. They are the nicest people you could hope to meet—the real salt of the earth. They are in their 80s and run a small corner shop. A guy, Fred Bloggs, has been buying from them on credit and now owes them over $20,000. I checked on him and he has a criminal record longer than you could imagine—a real crooked fraudster. He's stolen from charities, orphans, and many people like Bill and Greta. He preys on good people. Anyway, Bill and Greta had to mortgage their home to finance their business, and now they're going to lose everything if I can't track down this Fred Bloggs. They'll lose their business and their home. They'll be out on the street. I can see that you're a good person. I've seen how you go out of your way to help people at the registry. Please help me to save Bill and Greta. I can't let them lose everything. Please, look up Bloggs's address. Nobody will ever know, and you'll help save this wonderful couple and make sure that this crook gets his just deserts.' Invariably the clerk would give me the address. I'd drop off a fancy box of chocolates and tell him that it was from Bill and Greta and although they did not know the name of the person who had helped them, they were extremely grateful. The person would feel good about what they had done and I would leave it at that for a couple of months. Then I would return with another 'case,' and I'd get them to help me again. After the second time I would not wait too long before the third. After that I would give them a short list of names. Before too long they would be giving me the addresses for a whole list of people in return for money.

"Of course," he added, "there had never been a Bill and Greta and the whole story was nonsense, but it got the clerks in and they earned a good income. Nobody got hurt, until this whole ICAC thing, but that's not my fault."

I met Phil at an audit conference a few years after the Independent Commission Against Corruption (ICAC) inquiry. I had presented a paper on it and other cases concerning unauthorized information disclosure and theft. During one of the breaks Phil introduced himself to me.

"I was one of the many key players who got away," he said, explaining his story and details of his involvement in the trade.

I have been a fraud investigator for over 20 years and have always found it fascinating to hear the accounts of people entangled in these activities. Phil was obviously very proud that he had been so successful in corrupting government employees and obtaining the information required for his clients. If he had any regrets, it was just that the game was over.

As a result of the ICAC inquiry, which seeks to reduce corruption against the government, many of the clerks lost their jobs, were publicly disgraced, or had their career prospects severely affected.

A large number of private investigators, inquiry agents, and debt collectors convinced government employees to release confidential information in contravention of their duties, often in breach of the law. People involved in the trade included those from the Department of Social Security, the Department of Immigration, the Australian Taxation Office, the Australian Customs Service, Medicare, Telecom, Australia Post, the RTA, police services, electricity suppliers, financial institutions, solicitors, and others.

The purchasers of information were not only those chasing "legitimate debts." Known criminals were also buying confidential police information. Money did not change hands for all of the data released or traded. For example, a chief superintendent in the police force stated that he dispensed information to a good friend "under the old chum's act," even though he knew that it was improper for him to do so.

Some government officials spent so much of their time improperly accessing data for sale that their work suffered. The ICAC commissioner noted a particular police officer. "When time permitted, he was the officer in charge of detectives at a large Sydney suburban police station," the commissioner said.

Some officials couldn't keep up with the demand from their "connections." They subcontracted or franchised this fraudulent business to other corrupt government officials. One investigator told me that in several government units, there were pyramids of people selling confidential information. "In some departments it was bigger than Amway," he said.

Many people who were supposed to be part of the solution became part of the problem. For example, the RTA established a team to set up a computer security program to better protect their records. Unfortunately, some of the people working on this team took the opportunity to download confidential records and sell them.

It's not known how many people participated because most were never detected. The ICAC report noted that more than 250 people have been identified as participating in the trade. A private investigator who had been actively involved told me that only a small minority of the people had been caught. "I would not know how many people there were, but I know that most of the private investigators and their connections got away clean. If 5 to 10% were caught, that would be a lot," he said.

There were probably thousands of people involved in some way. Some estimate that the most widespread corruption in Australian history occurred as a result of the improper trade of information.

DRIVER'S EDUCATION

The New South Wales RTA was established on January 16, 1989, from the amalgamation of three public sector agencies: the Department of Main Roads; the Department of Motor

Transport; and the Traffic Authority. As mentioned earlier, the RTA is responsible for testing and licensing drivers, registering and inspecting vehicles, and improving road safety. Managing the licensing of drivers and the registration of vehicles has resulted in two major corruption inquiries before the ICAC.

The first inquiry dealt with corrupt payments made by driving instructors to driver examiners of the RTA and its predecessor, the Department of Motor Transport. The ICAC noted that even though only a small number of perpetrators were involved, the payments made by those individuals were habitual. The investigation concluded that corruption was endemic at a number of motor registries in the Sydney metropolitan area over a 10-year period. There were times when all the driver examiners at a particular registry took money. Sometimes the cash was pooled between them on a daily or weekly basis.

Sixty-one people were involved in making bribes that were estimated to cost millions of dollars. ICAC acknowledged that they were unlikely to have identified all corrupt individuals, and the figures are likely significantly greater.

Jeffrey Williams was appointed to the position of corporate anti-corruption coordinator, reporting directly to the chief executive. The ICAC report noted that Mr. Williams "is a person from whom a good deal can be expected."

Many of the initiatives he introduced became standard practice in Australia and strongly influenced guidelines issued by regulatory authorities. His task was a major challenge due to many factors. According to ICAC, in the Department of Motor Transport, "the corrupt were encouraged." Corruption was widespread in certain areas, there was resistance to reporting corruption, and significant corruption was being ignored in other public sector agencies.

One of the most successful initiatives was an ethics campaign. The RTA ethics campaign slogan was: "Support Your Values." The Australian culture is traditionally one of rugged individualism combined with strong relationships. This results in fierce loyalty to friends and colleagues, along with skepticism of those managing others' conduct. Jeffrey reasoned that co-opting people into the campaign so that they could insist on an honest work environment would overcome this cultural resistance.

The campaign promoted colorful posters that encouraged people to "speak up" about unethical conduct. Humorous pictures, case studies, and light articles in internal publications, ethics workshops, and briefings, in addition to management awareness initiatives, all combined to enhance the ethical culture in the RTA substantially. It also encouraged people to report corruption.

Before the campaign, people were extremely reluctant to report corruption. After it, the number of reports and successful investigations increased dramatically. Other initiatives included the introduction of rigorous investigation standards, assessments of fraud risks, improving systems of internal control, close cooperation with internal audit so that they could better detect fraud and corruption, enhancing human resource and other policies to reflect high ethical standards, and so on. The initiatives resulted in major advances in the organization's efforts to tackle corruption.

LAW AND ORDER

The New South Wales police service came into possession of some documents from a private inquiry agent who unwittingly suggested that he had access to confidential information from police and RTA records. The commissioner of police passed the documents to ICAC.

When investigators interviewed the inquiry agent, he claimed that he was a lawyer with a bachelor of law degree from the University of Sydney. The investigators later found that he was neither a lawyer nor had he obtained a degree. With this in mind, the investigators were skeptical of the man's denial that he had access to confidential police and RTA records. The ICAC decided that there were sufficient concerns based on the actual evidence and complaints to launch an investigation. The RTA followed suit.

Searches were conducted of the records of private investigators who were suspected of being involved in the illicit trade of confidential government information. Parts of the investigation were relatively simple, as not all people involved in the information trade took steps to hide their involvement from showing in their financial and other records.

For example, an invoice was found in a private investigator's records that contained a charge for "corrupting several members of the Police Force and obtaining printouts relating to this man's criminal form, then drinking with them for long periods."

Another investigator showed his payments to RTA officials in his financial records listed neatly under the heading "bribes."

One private investigator printed a brochure for his clients showing the services he offered and the charges. The brochure showed the sources of information, including the Department of Motor Transport, Medicare, social security, immigration, criminal history, telephone, and post office. Since this information was not officially available, it was clear that the sources were not legitimate.

A number of private investigators kept records of the information they purchased. One particular investigator kept computer records that contained confidential government information concerning about 10,000 individuals.

Many other private investigators made sure that they did not keep any incriminating records. Some of them destroyed incriminating evidence when word of the ICAC investigation spread.

"I took all of my paper records to the garbage dump," one private investigator told me. "I know many of my colleagues shredded theirs or burnt them. I had too many records to shred. If I'd spent that long hunched over the shredder I'd have ended up looking like Quasimodo, and if I'd burnt them all the fire would have been so big it would have gotten out of control."

Private investigators were questioned about their involvement, and particularly about the people who were supplying them with the confidential information. Invariably, the answers were evasive. "My connection has been giving me information for over 10 years" was a typical response. This one came from a private investigator who had been a top detective in the police force for many years. He had years of training and experience in observing details and remembering names, places, and other relevant information. Yet, he continued, "I can't remember his name. I only ever knew him as John. I'm not sure where he worked or how he got the information. I met him in a pub. He is average looking. I can't really describe him more accurately than that."

Another private investigator claimed never to have seen a police officer who was selling him confidential information. "I received a telephone call," he explained, "from someone who said 'I think you may need some foreign orders done.' I knew that that was obviously police slang for obtaining confidential information I had requested. I agreed, and the man mentioned being paranoid about security. He explained that the security had to be 'watertight' and asked if I had a letter box and spare keys. I told him that I did." According to the private investigator, he used the post office box to make the payments and had "no personal dealings, no face-to-face dealings with the individual or individuals involved."

The identity of the person whom the private investigator was trying to protect ultimately came out, as many of the printouts had the unique registered number and access code of a certain police officer.

After a while, the private investigators' responses became fairly predictable:

Mr. Dark claimed that he received a phone call from "a gentleman who rang me up at work and said, 'I can provide DMT information. Are you interested?'"

"Now let me guess, he made some arrangement through a box or post office box or telephone, only gave you a Christian name or no name, and you've done business with him and you've paid him, and you can't tell us what he looks like or what his name is. How close am I?"

"I've never met him," he said.

"How close am I, Mr. Dark?"

"You were very close, and I'm sure you've heard it all before," he admitted.

The attempts of some private investigators to protect their government connections bordered on farcical. For example, the records of one private investigator indicated that he had paid "Jenson" for confidential information.

"Do you know someone by the name of Jenson?"

"Yes," he said.

"Who's that?"

"It's an alias," he said.

"For whom?"

"Me," he said.

Even though large quantities of documents and electronic evidence discovered, they were carefully examined to produce the maximum benefit. Handwriting was carefully examined, documents forensically assessed, and fingerprints lifted from papers and other articles.

Phil Green told me that many of the private investigators spoke to each other about the ICAC investigation. The general view was that they should deny their involvement as long as they could. "Our slogan was 'Lie till you die.' Many of us kept to that."

The government officials who were suspected of selling confidential information were also the focus of attention. Some of the corrupt public officials did not trust the private investigators who were bribing them, so they kept records of each item of confidential information that they accessed for sale.

"If they are crooked enough to bribe me, they are crooked enough to cheat me," said one official. The officials would use their own records to check that they were being paid the correct amount at the end of the week, fortnight, or month. Some of these officials kept these records in their diaries or even in their desk calendars, which sat in plain view to anyone walking past their desks. However, many were cautious and didn't keep any electronic or documentary evidence of their actions. Others destroyed evidence before investigators had an opportunity to collect it.

OFFICIAL DENIAL

Some of the government officials at first tried to deny that they had been involved in selling confidential information. Many changed their story after extended questioning and after documentary and other evidence was produced to show their involvement.

One constable repeatedly denied selling information. When evidence was produced, he still denied it. Finally he stated, "I misled you . . . I was confused." He then admitted that he had been paid for each piece of information that he provided but was later put on a monthly retainer. When he was questioned again roughly eight weeks later, he changed his story, even though he had given the previous information under oath.

"Have you supplied information from police records?"

"I could have," he replied.

"Why do you say you could have?"

"Well, I could have and I couldn't have. I don't remember," he said vaguely.

Some government officials at first denied supplying printouts of confidential information and photocopies of confidential documents. In many cases their denials evaporated when photocopies and printouts were shown to have their fingerprints and the occasional note handwritten by them.

Some government employees who had limited legitimate access to confidential information obtained the passwords and access codes of others who did have legitimate access.

There were government employees who wanted information from other government departments and misused their position to mislead staff in those departments that the information was required for legitimate official purposes. The employees then sold that information to private investigators.

A number of government employees were supplying information to more than one private investigator. When questioned, one police sergeant admitted to supplying information to seven private investigators.

The investigators gathered evidence about the involvement of banks and insurance companies in the illicit trade of confidential government information. Of course, typically the banks and insurance companies were reluctant to help. In many cases they attempted to place obstacles in the way of investigators and tried time and time again to mislead investigators. For example, one bank, when compelled to produce documents, handed over documents in which references to illegal checks had been whited out.

Here is an except from a typical interview.

"Were you aware that Smith Investigations Ltd. was used by the bank during that period?" Mr. Black was asked.

"That is correct," he said.

"What was it used for?"

"To obtain information," Mr. Black said.

"From where?"

"I really don't know sir," he responded.

Mr. Black later admitted that the bank used codes to indicate the source of information that it was using. For example, social security was code one, the RTA was code two, and so on.

"And why do you think it was deemed appropriate to hide where the information was coming from?"

"Because I believe it was probably incorrect, sir," he said.

"Improper?"

"Yes, sir," he admitted.

"Illegal?"

"Yes, sir."

When one of the banks was asked to respond officially to allegations that its staff had knowingly bought confidential government information, the bank replied that its staff never asked where the information came from.

Evidence had already been obtained to show that the bank's response was misleading. The bank then tried to distance itself from its misleading response by claiming that the author of the response was not authorized to put his signature to the letter and forward it as the bank's reply; in doing so he had acted without authority, "but in the belief that he did have authority." ICAC concluded that the corporate secretary's reply in the name of the bank is, indeed, the reply of the bank.

Some financial institutions went to significant lengths to hide the fact that it was obtaining confidential government information improperly. In some cases employees were told to put the information onto the computer records as if it had been contained in the original loan applications and other legitimate documents from the individuals concerned.

One file contained the following note to a new employee: "Remember, don't put info on screen about doing lic[ense] checks. It's illegal."

Employees admitted the true nature of confidential information once there was evidence that certain information should not be recorded in the computer records.

"Was there a policy against recording the type of inquiry that produced the information?" one employee was asked.

"Yes," she responded.

"And why was that?"

"Well, information that was obtained through license checks along with registration checks was obviously illegal information," she said confidently.

"And is that why it wasn't submitted into the computer?"

"I'd say so."

Senior management in many of the banks and insurance companies sought to distance themselves from the practice of obtaining confidential government information improperly. Some had even gone so far as to establish written policies forbidding the practice.

One such policy was produced to indicate that if anyone from the financial institution had been engaged in the illicit trade of government information, then that individual would be a "rogue employee" acting in contravention of instructions:

> The Corporation, in general, and Consumer Financial Services, in particular, will not condone any practice which we believe to be unethical or know to be illegal. Consequently, it is Consumer Financial Services Policy that we will not be a party, either directly or indirectly, to the procuring, or use, of any information which is not legally available.

This was supported by a memorandum that stated:

> At times it will be tempting for staff to seek and use such information which may be available, either directly or indirectly, from a number of sources including a number of government bodies . . . The Crimes Act of 1914 contains severe penalties which may be imposed upon informants, recipients and users of information which is not normally legally available. Please ensure all staff members are fully conversant with our policy in this matter and strictly adhere.

Despite these policies, in this particular financial institution, there was sufficient evidence to allow ICAC to conclude that the purchase of confidential government information "occurred with approval at the managerial level, managers indulging in the practice themselves."

It emerged that not only were some of the banks indirect purchasers of confidential government information, but some were also supplying confidential information about their own customers as part of the "information club."

CRIME AND PUNISHMENT

One of the outcomes of the investigation was the careful examination of the adequacy of legislation dealing with information protection in the commonwealth and state agencies found to have been used as sources of traded confidential government information. Privacy laws were eventually passed to help prevent the trade. The Crimes Act and other legislation was toughened to overcome loopholes and to introduce new offenses relating to unauthorized computer access and other methods of improperly obtaining information.

A number of employees in both New South Wales and the commonwealth public services resigned or took early retirement rather than face disciplinary action. Disciplinary action was taken against a number of people who were found to have engaged in corrupt conduct. The results of the disciplinary actions ranged from official warnings to dismissal.

Many private investigators who had earned a good living participating in the information trade found themselves blacklisted by financial institutions and insurance companies, many of which had been their customers in the trade.

Phil Green was one of these. He was bitter about what he described as "a betrayal by the financial institutions." "They were very keen players in the game," he explained, "yet after the inquiry they acted as though the only villains were the private investigators." He closed his private investigations business soon after the inquiry and accepted a position as a senior investigator for a large organization. He was one of the many participants in the information trade who escaped detection and prosecution.

Most of the financial institutions and insurance companies revised their practices to ensure that information would no longer be obtained in an illegal or improper manner.

Many debt recovery managers and other managers who were named in the ICAC report as having been purchasers of confidential government information were moved sideways in their companies or had their careers adversely affected.

There were a range of prosecutions of those considered to be corrupt and those who had lied under oath to ICAC.

Investigations in Commonwealth agencies were taken as a result of evidence uncovered by this investigation, which in turn led to suspensions and dismissals of staff, disciplinary actions, and improvements to the systems of control to protect confidential information.

LESSONS LEARNED

One of the most important lessons is that confidential information is a very valuable and sought-after commodity. We have undertaken a number of information protection assessments for government organizations in Australia and found that most organizations have a number of very valuable databases. Some public sector agencies have individual items of confidential information that are worth in the millions of dollars.

An important lesson was the ease with which endemic corruption had been accepted within a part of the community. I discussed this with a number of people who were involved in the illicit trade of confidential information. Many pointed out that people involved could rationalize their actions as being ethical because they were helping to ensure that debt-skippers, crooks, and other nefarious or irresponsible individuals were forced to meet their legal obligations to repay the debts that they had incurred. It was generally argued that no innocent people were hurt and society as a whole benefited.

The lesson for those fighting fraud and corruption is that it is difficult to combat "noble cause corruption" because people easily justify the fraud to themselves. It's therefore important to highlight the real damage to society and the harm to individuals caused by any form of corruption and the selective undermining of organizational norms. We have taken this approach in a number of situations and have been successful in preventing endemic fraud and corruption.

The investigation highlighted the importance of logging and reviewing read-only accesses to information on computer systems. The police information technology systems allowed investigators to identify who accessed certain information. These data proved extremely valuable to investigators. At the time, the RTA database of licensing and registration information did not allow the identification, which significantly hampered investigators.

The RTA database subsequently was enhanced to enable all computer accesses to be logged. This allowed auditing of accesses to see if they were legitimate and the identification of suspects who had access to information. Since that time, RTA investigators have completed many successful investigations based on the data obtained from the logs.

A number of approaches were taken in auditing the logged data. One approach was to select a list of high-profile individuals. If anyone accessed information about them, the accesses were reviewed and investigated if they did not appear to be legitimate. In one case, all people who had accessed the details of a model who appeared in a photograph on the front page of Sydney's newspaper were interviewed. Over 30 people had accessed the information, none for legitimate purposes. Another approach was to use statistical and analytic means to analyze access by individuals.

The number of improper accesses reduced dramatically when word spread of the analysis and investigation of accesses.

Confusion can cause corruption. Some government officials had never been told what information was confidential and what information could be given out freely or to specific categories of people. They therefore made their own decisions each time information was requested. It became very apparent that their decisions were based as much on who was asking for the information as on the category of information. Thus, some people were favored with information that others would be refused; it depended on whether you were liked or viewed negatively.

It appears that both confusion and the perception of corruption are factors in the decision that corruption is the best way to join the "information club."

It's important, therefore, to set the rules about what information may be freely disclosed, what information may be given out in specified circumstances, and what information is to be regarded as confidential. Once the rules have been set, it's important to ensure that they are clearly communicated and enforced.

The investigation showed the importance of getting the most value out of each piece of evidence. For example, many documents were used as valuable sources of information. Investigators used these documents for tests and comparisons. Forensically testing the handwriting on certain documents, comparing the handwriting to other documents, obtaining fingerprints from documents, using access evidence from documents for comparisons and for the basis of analytic reviews produced more valuable evidence.

The investigation showed that one should not overestimate the abilities of perpetrators in fraud and corruption. At the beginning of the investigation, some investigators and advisors said that it would be a waste of time to inspect the financial records of those paying bribes because they would not keep records of the bribes they paid. Yet a number of financial records either specifically listed bribes or disguised bribes in ways that were very obvious and easily spotted. An important lesson is to look for evidence in all places. Don't ignore some because they seem too obvious.

The investigation showed the importance of collecting evidence before it could be destroyed. Missing documents or electronic records should be investigated. It is possible that certain people had been involved in destroying and hiding evidence. Proving their involvement is often useful, and sometimes essential, in getting them to give more complete accounts of their involvement in the corruption being investigated.

It is important to record responses accurately and formally. Conversations and responses that appeared relatively unimportant at the time became very significant later in the light of new evidence. Sometimes in later questioning people contradict what they had said earlier or denied having said it. Being able to produce reliable records is very useful for investigators.

Getting people to commit to their accounts of events proved to be useful in the investigation, especially where people were under oath. Asking them for additional details, for clear clarification, and for confirmation made it more difficult for them to hide their involvement or for them to claim that what they said was being misunderstood, taken out of context or used unfairly.

RECOMMENDATIONS TO PREVENT FUTURE OCCURRENCES

Increase IT Security

It is important to increase information technology (IT) security, especially with regard to passwords. It was common for nicknames, favorite football teams, and acronyms to be used as passwords. Often it was easy to guess a computer user's password in order to access confidential information improperly. For example, it took investigators only one attempt to guess the password of the assistant commissioner of police.

It appears that some police officers had swapped passwords so that they would have "plausible deniability." Their computers could be improperly accessed with their own personal passwords while they were away on leave.

This fact highlighted the importance of performing analytic reviews of logged accesses to identify suspicious usage of the IT system. Thus, access should be carefully examined if it was made before or after office hours, when a person was on leave, excessively during the lunch break, at intervals that are too distant to be work-related, or too close together to have been made by only one person, or forming an unusual pattern. Statistical analysis is also useful for examining computer accesses.

Create Formal Procedures

Formalize and document procedures for legitimate transfers of confidential information between government departments. Official arrangements for the transfer of information between designated officers often had become informal and involved additional officials. It had reached the point that social functions had been organized for establishing contacts for exchanging information. After some time, invitations to join the "information club" had been extended to people who did not even work for the government, especially employees of banks and other financial institutions.

Documented procedures should cover which government departments can obtain confidential information, the categories of information covered, the form of the requests for the information, to whom it may be disclosed, and other prerequisites to be met before the information can be released. There should be formal recording of all disclosures of confidential information to other government departments.

Undertake Information Protection Assessments

Information protection assessments should be undertaken. Ideally these assessments or audits should be completed periodically. The frequency should be determined by the risks of unauthorized disclosure or theft of the information and its value. We have undertaken a number of these assessments for different organizations and found that invariably confidential information, including valuable information, is not protected nearly as well as senior management assumes it is. Serious internal control weaknesses are common.

The ICAC made an important recommendation that has, unfortunately, not been implemented. The recommendation stated: "In all departments it should be made a disciplinary offense for an officer to allow his or her access code to become known to another, or for an officer to gain access to computer-held information by the use of any code other than his or her own. For disciplinary purposes, the use of an officer's code should be treated as prima facie evidence that the relevant access was had by that officer." We have found that sharing of passwords and using one's password to allow access for another person are still occurring in many government organizations.

Barry Davidow, CFE, B.Com, B. Acc, M. Tax Law, MIIA, CA, is a director of Fraud Prevention Services Pty Ltd., a company specializing in all aspects of fraud control. He has over 20 years of experience in preventing, detecting, and investigating fraud and corruption in a wide range of industries and the public sector.

PART THREE

Financial Statement
Fraud Schemes

CHAPTER 51

Banking on Fraud

JASON LEE

Fraudulent merger and acquisition deals cost U.S. investment banks and their investors billions each year. And these are just the bogus deals that we know about; imagine how many scams go unnoticed. Investment banking on Wall Street is a high-stakes game, not merely because of the big bucks involved, but because of the plethora of potentially unwitting victims.

A decade ago, I took a job as the chief merger fraud investigator for one of the largest New York investment banks on Wall Street, Phelps Winston & Co. Prestigious, with over 40,000 employees worldwide, it deals primarily in the health care and biotechnology sectors. I had 10 members on my team and nearly 275 cases to go through each year. Many times senior investigators Dennis Rowiski, Sarah Cooper, and Mark Rosenthal were burning the midnight oil and sacrificing bedtime stories with their kids to slave over boxes of records, trying to find that one smoking gun. Dennis was a former cop in the New York Police Department's fraud and money-laundering team who left the police force after a botched raid on a drug-running operation he was investigating. Sarah was single and a workaholic; she was about six years out of business school, having worked for regulators like the National Association of Securities Dealers and the New York Stock Exchange. Mark was a retired Special Agent for the U.S. Secret Service. Together, they had an eye for financial chicanery like no others.

About six days before Christmas, Stan Murphy, Phelps Winston's associate director for the Pharmaceuticals Investment Banking Team, came to my office with a worried look on his face. He told me that he was working on a deal with Pharmamedix, PLC, a Chinese pharmaceutical company that was looking to sell itself to his client, an American company, to expand its sales market to the west. Stan's client, an obscure but stable public company called Medisure, LLC, was looking to globalize its operations too. Led by chief executive officer (CEO) Ned Corillo, Medisure employed about 1,100 PhDs who researched drug development, delivery, and sales to physician practices. Ned had called Stan about a week earlier and said that one of his Food and Drug Administration (FDA) contacts informed him that several of the highly touted drugs Pharmamedix was marketing hadn't even gotten past clinical trials. This puzzled Ned, so he asked Stan to do more in-depth due diligence on the development.

IT JUST DOESN'T ADD UP

Stan tried to set up interviews with some of the Pharmamedix research chemists who developed the drugs, only to reach disconnected phone numbers or people who said that they had never heard of the company before. A math wizard, Stan also ran the numbers for the proposed purchase through a proprietary financial model he created. The valuation he ended up with was millions of dollars off of the financial model that Investatrust Worldwide Capital Group, the bank advising Pharmamedix, had provided him with. By Investatrust's account, Pharmamedix was worth over $89 million more than what Stan calculated it to be. Owen Campbell, the lead banker on the deal, assured him that he had personally certified that the balance sheet was correct and that there was nothing to worry about. To make sure, Stan crunched the numbers six more times, each time with the same result, which was different from Owen's valuation. With the deal valued at about $432 million according to Investatrust's model, Stan believed that he may have stumbled on to something.

I called in Mark and Sarah to look at the financial model and other documents Stan had brought. Mark immediately took out a calculator and asked Stan what seemed like a hundred questions about Pharmamedix's books. Sarah jumped on her laptop and started doing Internet searches and database runs to find if Pharmamedix had any previous skeletons in its closet. I told everyone that they were moving too fast.

"First, we should take a look at the financial model and see what accounting line items make up this huge gap before we jump to conclusions. Sarah, can you use your spreadsheet macro to do a scan for anomalies? And Mark, can you talk to some of your old law enforcement buddies and see if Pharmamedix has been on anybody's radar?" We needed to see what we had in front of us first before we could launch a full investigation.

A HARD PILL TO SWALLOW

Pharmamedix was a state-sponsored pharmaceutical manufacturer in Shanghai, China, founded by Yin Li Sook and his wife, Mei Won Ho. The company was known for its unique business model, as it was run more like a venture capital fund than a pharmaceutical company. It would essentially raise money for a new drug it wanted to bring to market. Pharmamedix promised its investors that it would spend only a small amount of its capital on developing the drugs and utilize the rest as corporate equity. Backers were told that as long as Pharmamedix reported profits, the company would retain 10% of those profits internally and share the remainder equally over the total pool of investors. As good faith, Yin agreed that if a new drug experiment did not pan out, he would return the capital used to research it—a "no-loss proposition." Yin and his wife had created the business based on their dreams of creating new drugs that would save people's lives.

But as Yin aggressively tried to diversify into dozens of new medications, some of the projects failed miserably. Investors backing the unsuccessful drugs soon came knocking at his door asking for their promised capital back. To hedge lawsuits, he reimbursed them with "borrowed" profits from lucrative drug venture funds. But when it came time to pay investors, he had to borrow yet again from other areas in his company in order to continue the charade. Like an obsessed gambler, Yin tried in vain to raise even more money for medications—these being the most risky and ambitious yet. His hope was to hit the lottery with a groundbreaking drug that would give him enough profit to cover all his debts, both profit share payments and capital reimbursements, to investors in the failed venture funds. Disastrously, this last series were the biggest bust to date, partly because Yin ran out of money to hire competent talent to create these pie-in-the-sky superdrugs. He was now bankrupt and unable to attract new investors. His poor reputation spread. He traveled to other countries in Asia, soliciting money to raise new venture funds there. But this time, instead of trying to legitimately use it for drug development, Yin just collected the capital and fabricated stories to investors when they asked for updates—and it worked.

Yin was able to steal so much investor money that he returned to China and paid back all his debtors, seemingly redeeming himself as a trustworthy businessman. That's when he got the idea: To prevent future debt, he realized that pretending to have a successful drug development business was more profitable than having a real one—which had too many dramatic headaches and stresses. For three years, he repeatedly lied to investors, stating that drugs created by Pharmamedix were successes and profits were busting through the roof. In essence, these were shell companies. We would later find up to 16 venture funds having no corporate filings with any state entity, Chinese or American. Yin would make small good-faith share payouts to investors who wanted to see returns, but he said that the rest of the money was being reinvested to solicit the best doctors and buy the best equipment to work on the projects.

Finally, he had created so many fake drug venture funds that his house of cards was sure to collapse. Yin's only hope of keeping the sham a secret was to sell the company to the highest bidder and pray that when the fraud came out, it would be on the new company's watch. Unbeknownst to him, Chinese investigators were closing in and found enough evidence to arrest his wife and put her on trial. Yin then abandoned his family, jumped on a plane for the United States, and set up shop in one of Connecticut's highest-rent districts. Under the guise of not knowing much English, he hired a shrewd agent/lawyer, Louis Wilson, who was also a certified public accountant with the top-ranked accounting firm of MK Charles and Associates. Nicknamed "Groovy Louie" by his closest friends, he was known as a ruthless businessman who pushed the ethical envelope.

Louie exploited the MK Charles name, saying that the prestigious public accounting firm was representing an exciting new Chinese venture pioneering leading-edge drugs but seeking to sell itself to an American suitor in order to expand operations. Ned Corillo, searching for a way to rise above Medisure's competitors and truly diversify the company, answered the call.

Groovy Louie quickly phoned investment banker buddies at Investatrust Worldwide to begin the process and to put together a sales strategy. He even suggested that Investatrust draft an acquirer's engagement letter and fax it to Ned for signature as soon as possible. Essentially, Louis hoped that Medisure would use Investatrust as its advisor instead of finding its own investment banker. But Ned was a conservative businessman. He had a long-standing relationship with Stan Murphy and had previously used Phelps Winston, and decided that this deal should be no different.

Owen Campbell, the lead banker at Investatrust, was the complete opposite of Stan. Owen was into fast cars and women. He spent money like there was no tomorrow. Not including his debts from business school, Owen was nearly $340,000 in the hole. His Atlantic City gambling habits didn't help him either. With the prospects of closing this huge $432 million deal for Investatrust, Owen's boss promised, "You close this baby and you'll get the biggest office on this side of Manhattan; I'll double your salary and give you that expense account you've always been asking for—I mean it—the whole nine yards." Owen was so excited that he couldn't think about anything else. He even set up a meeting with Yin and Groovy Louie the day after Thanksgiving, when even Wall Street looks like a ghost town.

Louie opened the meeting. "Mr. Yin has a fabulous company in Pharmamedix, but there's something you should know, Owen. To better market ourselves to the bidders, we had to come up with some—how should we say—creative accounting. We rounded up the profits for the company this past year and kinda downplayed the expenses. Made a couple of other tweaks, too. Mr. Yin suggested that we report a couple of the venture funds as active even though some of them closed; this will make Pharmamedix's portfolio look a little bigger."

"What are you telling me?!" Owen retorted. "Are you saying that this only looks good on paper? It's too late. We have to close this deal. If we don't, I'll be bankrupt and fired. Look, just tell me what I can do to help you guys sell this thing to Medisure, and I'll do it."

In fact, not only did Owen do anything and everything to sell this deal, he decided to delve in a little fraud himself. He devised a plan to have Yin send a press release to the media announcing that he had been suffering from a rare form of cancer for the past two years and used one of the Pharmamedix drugs to effect a miraculous cure. The press release would be put out three days before the merger, a clear effort to make the stock price surge and, in turn, worth millions more. Owen also helped Groovy Louie think of catchy names and fabricate business descriptions for shell companies for the prospectus he wrote. He knew that he had to do something about the financial model in order to justify the deal's high price tag. Exaggerating a common merger asset called "goodwill" and making up categories like "short-term rotating capital assets sold within the fiscal quarter" and "professional expenses for executive management and venture operations," he was able to disguise money Yin made from illegal side businesses that couldn't be explained by legitimate Pharmamedix drug sales.

THE WAKE-UP CALL

After the meeting where I told Dennis, Sarah, and Mark to do a little more research, they hunkered down for an all-nighter. About 2 a.m., my phone rang. "Honey, its Dennis; something about crooks trying to ruin the bank," my wife said, trying to wake me. In a groggy voice, I said, "Hi, Dennis, what'd ya find?"

"Sixteen, maybe even 20 of the venture funds are all fakes—shell companies. I checked drug registration databases, tried to verify the medical licensing for the research chemists, and even tried to locate the phase testing reports for each stage of the drug's development. There was nothing, Jason," Dennis blurted.

I couldn't believe my ears. Of all the years I had been a banker and an investigator, I hadn't heard of anything so egregious. There was the occasional CEO trying to skim from the books, or some accountant attempting to take one too many write-offs on the income statement, but for a company to fabricate more than 16 subsidiaries . . . never.

Overnight, Sarah had combed through internal Phelps Winston bank records and found that Yin had opened up several accounts with our sister retail banking division. Tellers had filed several suspicious activity reports (SARs), as well as a number of currency transaction reports (CTRs) with the Financial Crimes Enforcement Network after Yin was observed making deposits of more than $10,000 in cash—occasionally multiple times on the same day. Sarah couldn't believe that the investment banking division hadn't heard about any of this before, especially since they were filed from our very own bank, albeit another division. Mark found out through some of his law enforcement contacts that Yin's wife was arrested a year earlier in China and convicted on securities fraud and money-laundering charges.

The Internal Revenue Service also had open investigations regarding unregistered tax shelters created by Louie for a series of unknown foreign-based drug development clients doing business in the United States. However, the agency was having a difficult time finding evidence linking these small subsidiaries to an unidentified parent company that owned them. Mark had put two and two together and theorized that Yin and Louie had a relationship even before Yin fled China for the United States. Louie must have planted the seed in Yin's mind that it would be less suspicious and more profitable for him to sell the firm in the States, as opposed to Asia or Europe. And as an added bonus, Groovy Louie would set up illegal tax shelters—another selling point for Yin—shielding any profit from the sale of the various venture funds from U.S. taxation. If the theory held true, it meant that the fraudulent merger was an organized, premeditated conspiracy by multiple parties. Mark's instincts were right on the mark; in trying to strike a deal with prosecutors, Louie later confessed that he indeed advised Yin to do these very things.

Mark decided to also contact fraud departments at other international banks. He found that overseas accounts had been opened in either Yin's or Pharmamedix's name. Yin was opening and closing them each month, rotating through different banks around the world, to ensure that the money collected by new investors for the fake venture funds was not being detected. Yin was also selling unmarked medications on the black market for extra cash on the side. Mark had a private detective intercept some of Pharmamedix's paper trash. Recipes and formulas for medications being created by other developers were found. Yin was essentially trying to copy these in a back-alley lab and sell them on the black market as generic brand products. The adventure at the landfill also yielded discarded letters from angry investors who wanted to sue and get their money back, as well as a number of invoices for various purchases of chemicals and drug manufacturing equipment.

In the ensuing days, Sarah labored over reconstructing Pharmamedix's income statement and cash flow. Suspiciously, the company made two bulk drug sales to two clinics, with different medications sold to each client that were recorded with exactly the same amount of units and the exact same dollar value of accounts receivable. Sarah would later find at least three other similar patterns of anomalies among the company's capital expenses, overhead, and cash flow. Clearly, Yin and Louie's lack of creativity led Sarah to unravel this sloppy financial statement fraud. Groovy Louie had hoped that the addition of pages of footnotes, annotations, caveats, and amortization tables would make the financial statements so frustrating to interpret that the reader would just give up. He clearly underestimated Sarah Cooper.

She also tried to milk whatever she could out of the discarded expense receipts taken from Yin's trash. There were certainly not enough to reconstruct Pharmamedix's entire accounting ledger, but Sarah thought that perhaps they could point to some kind of financial irregularity and offer at least one piece of the puzzle. Yin tried to double-count several of the expenses as both capital expenditures and as overhead costs in order to decrease his reported taxable profit.

Dennis was getting tired of trying to spearhead this investigation from an office. He was the kind of guy who wanted to get his leads right from the source. He decided to talk with some of Pharmamedix's competitors, and his first encounter was telling.

"I shoulda sued the pants off that guy, Yin, when I had the chance. I knew he was a no-good dirty rat. One day a whole shipment of my newest over-the-counter flu medications went missing from one of my trucks. Two days later I heard from one of my clients that this punk was selling samples of a flu drug he called RiddaFlu," shouted Tony Frachetta in a thick New York accent.

After finishing with the interviews, Dennis visited a long list of disgruntled customers. His travels brought him to a small town in Ohio. Alice Munder, who suffered from migraine headaches, told Dennis that she took Pharmamedix's extra-strength migraine aspirin for over a year and the headaches actually worsened. In a deposition taken shortly after his arrest, Yin admitted that he had counterfeited competitor's drugs and also sold placebos as if they were legitimate medication.

Would You Like That Meal to Go?

Stan had halted all work on the deal until hearing from me on our Pharmamedix investigation. Five weeks had passed since he first came to my office with that worried look on his face. Groovy Louie was becoming impatient, calling Stan at least twice a day for Phelps Winston's approval of the deal. I told Stan to set up a lunch meeting, requesting that all the major players show up: Ned Corillo, Yin Li Sook, Owen Campbell, Louie Wilson, me, and Stan himself. He made reservations at Le Bernadin, an upscale Manhattan restaurant. He had chosen it so as to not make Yin or Louis suspicious that the deal was not going forward. One by one, each gentleman arrived, all dressed in their best suits with money-hungry looks in their eyes. Groovy Louie was the last to show. With both arms extended in the air, he bellowed, "Hello, my friends. Are we ready to make the pharmaceuticals industry proud today?"

Then Louie turned to me and said, "I don't believe we've met. Do you work for Stan? One of his junior bankers?" I responded, "No, we haven't met before, Mr. Wilson, but I feel I know you quite well." He had a puzzled look on his face. Stan turned and in a nervous voice addressed the ice-cold lawyer. "Louie, Jason is a fraud investigator with Phelps Winston. That's why we wanted to have you meet us for lunch today. Medisure will not be pursuing a merger deal with Pharmamedix. We found some irregularities that really concern us. I think Jason can explain this better than I can." Shrewdly, Yin continued to pretend little comprehension of English and mumbled a few words in Chinese, seemingly to ask what was going on. Groovy Louie began to get defensive and pled ignorance.

"Mr. Wilson, I can't go into the specifics of our case here because we're in a public place. But I can tell you that we found evidence of fabricated financial statements and trade secret theft by your client. I also believe that you, Mr. Wilson, and you, Mr. Campbell, are fully knowledgeable about Mr. Yin's illegal practices; we have no other choice but to cease pursuing a merger and we will refer this case to the New York State Attorney's Office." Without waiting for any translation, Yin stormed out of the restaurant. Groovy Louie, in an angry but controlled voice, said, "I'm going to sue you guys for defamation. You have insulted a man who has spent his life making drugs to keep people alive. You should be ashamed."

"No, Mr. Wilson, I am not," I said. "I'm confident that we have made the pharmaceuticals industry very proud today by exposing these practices."

Yin Li Sook was arrested and extradited to China to face charges there. Owen Campbell lost his Series 7 license, was banned from the investment banking industry for life, and served six months of probation for his role as an accessory after the fact. Groovy Louie cracked under the pressure and decided to turn state's evidence, but charges were dropped against him and he continues to practice law today for investment banking clients after resigning from MK Charles. However, he was sanctioned for ethics violations and had his CPA license revoked. Ned Corillo engaged Stan Murphy to represent him in an acquisition bid of another drug development start-up, this time with a Canadian firm, which led to the delivery of three revolutionary allergy drugs. I left Phelps Winston about three years after the case closed to become a law enforcement officer. Dennis retired to spend more time with his grandkids in California. Mark was promoted as chief investigator for the bank, and Sarah continues to spend many late nights with her calculator and financial statements trying to save the next client from ruin.

Lessons Learned

Of the lessons that the Pharmamedix case taught me, I learned that there is no replacement for quantitative analysis through financial modelling to make assessments when there is a high volume of accounting data present. Stan's valuation model gave us a starting point and indicated several suspicious portions of the books. I also realized the value of pounding the pavement. Financial records can reveal only so much. Interviewing customers and competitors helps answer questions through firsthand observations.

I learned that investigating one corporate fraud can bring to light other crimes. What we first thought was a case of financial statement fabrication turned into a circus of trade theft, medication counterfeiting, and money laundering. Pharmamedix also highlighted that foreign investment banking deals are more apt to be riddled with fraud than their domestic counterparts.

Owen Campbell opened my eyes to those who abusively exploit their status as fiduciary protectors of investor interests. Greed drives them to close big deals, even if it means helping clients commit white-collar crimes, covering it up, or standing by idly while fraud unfolds.

Conspiracy and collusion in merger fraud can create obstacles for investigators as suspects attempt to erase their tracks. Therefore, everyone involved must be vigilant to spot fraud when the first red flags appear. CEO Ned Corillo conducted due diligence on his own and found early signs that something was wrong. His initiative may have saved his company. Luckily, he had a conscientious banker in Stan Murphy—a man who truly cared about his clients. Stan could have chosen to ignore the news by Ned's FDA contacts; instead, he looked into these suspicions even if that meant losing one of the biggest deals in his career.

It takes creativity to beat the bad guys. Mark leaned heavily on his experience as a former Special Agent to set up the dumpster dive with the private eye. It was also crucial that he checked Yin's legal record in China. Mark was willing to get lost on the back roads of Ohio to hear stories by devastated patients that Pharmamedix's products were bogus.

RECOMMENDATIONS TO PREVENT FUTURE OCCURRENCES

When I left Phelps Winston, I offered several recommendations. Investigators working in the banking or securities industry should carefully consider upgrading their safeguards to ensure successful policing of fraud penetration.

Transparency in information is paramount. Sarah uncovered a major vulnerability at Phelps Winston when she unearthed several SAR and CTR filings from the retail banking branch that were not shared with the investment banking division.

The next recommendation is controversial. Fraud teams should have the right and responsibility to vet all deals being conducted by the bank, which should be a natural part of the due diligence process.

There should be stiff penalties for investment bankers who assist clients in a fraud, help to hide it, or obstruct justice. With bankers being self-interested, negative reinforcement will certainly cut down on the crime rate. Investment banks cannot leave punishment to regulators and law enforcement. Financial institutions should communicate. There needs to be a searchable database that networks banks. Banks also should hire software developers to create proprietary algorithms aimed at vetting fraud indicators faster than human investigators can.

For international banks, it is important to station fraud investigators overseas. Foreign investments often involve different accounting standards, currency conversion issues, and compliance with home country laws that may directly contradict U.S. business laws. Investigators permanently stationed overseas should become experts in these issues with respect to the country they report on.

Most important, investment banks must maintain long-term relationships with federal, state, and local law enforcement agencies. These contacts will be invaluable when doing background checks on criminal involvement. Likewise, law enforcement can use ground-level intelligence on suspicious behavior.

Merger fraud may be the most underreported of all corporate frauds. Banks try to downplay deals that have collapsed from illegal activity for fear they too will be implicated or punished for their involvement. And bankers are often blinded by million-dollar commissions to allow ethics to rise above fame and fortune. It is up to investigators to remain vigilant. Corruption in the investment banking industry can never be eliminated, but attacking the problem head-on will mitigate it.

Jason Lee is an expert in investment banking fraud. He is an office chief for financial intelligence with a federal law enforcement agency in Washington, D.C. A chartered financial analyst, Mr. Lee has been published in over two dozen tier-one publications, including the Wall Street Journal Online, American Banker, Risk Management, Financial Executive, **and** KM World.

CHAPTER **52**

Just a Matter of Time

MARGARET SMITH

Ted Nickerson was a rough-and-tumble character, perhaps more comfortable in a barroom brawl than a boardroom meeting. Starting out as an 18-year-old high school graduate, he worked his way up from the assembly floor of Dally Industries, a manufacturer of clocks. Ted's job was to ensure that the company's name and the product registration number were affixed to the bottom of each assembled timepiece. He took great pride in his role at Dally but yearned for the day when he could assume a management position.

Ted realized that if he wanted to be successful, he would need a college education, so he enrolled in a local university. After Ted received his bachelor's degree in accounting, he informed Dally administration and asked to be considered for the management training program. Shortly thereafter, a position opened in the Purchasing Department for an accounts payable clerk. Ted jumped at the opportunity, and his ascension began.

Rising through the ranks, he took on roles with increasing responsibility. Ted worked in nearly all areas of the Accounting Department, including payroll, receivables, cash management, and financial reporting. He also had a leadership role in the development and implementation of the new computer systems for inventory management and accounting.

By the time Ted was promoted to chief executive officer (CEO), his tenure with the company exceeded 25 years. He knew virtually every detail about Dally Industries. But his meteoric rise left him with few allies. When Ted walked into a room, conversation ceased. Employees scattered to avoid confrontations with him, mainly because he believed in management by intimidation. He frequently made unreasonable demands and set unattainable goals.

Ted's entire existence and self-worth hinged on the successes and failures at Dally. He never married and routinely worked 15-hour days. The employees joked that he secretly lived at the corporate office. No matter how early they arrived or how late they left, Ted Nickerson was there. In the few hours he was not at work, he managed to cultivate expensive hobbies and tastes. It was also important to him to demonstrate his success with flashy vehicles, homes, and artwork. He lived in the most exclusive neighborhood in Philadelphia and drove a candy-apple-red Ferrari. In fact, Ted frequently sped off to Atlantic City to gamble with customers. He was known as a high roller.

Dally began in 1922 in a Philadelphia basement workshop of a Dutch immigrant, Art Dally. Art worked full time during the day as a butcher but came home each night to tinker with his collection of clocks. Word spread regarding Art's fascination with clocks and his skill in their repair. Eventually he had so many people requesting his services that he decided to quit his job and open Dally Clock Works. Art struggled through the Depression and World War II. But in the 1950s, he and his son, Bart, decided to expand the company. They became Dally Industries. To keep up with the ever-increasing demand, they built a state-of-the-art facility to assemble and package their timepieces. After Art retired, Bart, an energetic 28-year-old, took over the helm. Bart was less of a craftsman than his father, but had a keen sense for business. He decided to bolster the company's employee time clock business. This strategy paid off with the burgeoning industrial economy and increased focus on mechanization. Sales at Dally Industries grew to record levels. After being in the business for years, Bart took note of an ambitious employee named Ted Nickerson who had distinguished himself in the factory and was working toward becoming a manager. Bart developed a mentoring relationship with Ted, knowing that someday, he would be the leader of Dally Industries.

Dally experienced many highly profitable years, and Bart became very wealthy and decided to retire. Ted received a 20% interest in Dally when the company went public and became the new CEO. Bart appointed several of his close friends and business associates to the board of directors, regardless of their business acumen and leadership skills. A seat on the board, as Bart saw it, was his method of repayment for their support and loyalty throughout the years.

By the time Ted took over, technology had gradually outpaced the products Dally offered. For a while, the company did not realize this because the demand for replacement parts and clocks was still heavy. Ted felt it was important to portray a prosperous image, exemplified by the newest addition: a swanky corporate office adjacent to the factory. Before long, the company experienced a decline in both sales and margins.

Rumor Has It

When Dally hired a new chief financial officer (CFO), Chandler Sawyer, his first directive was to handle the financial statement audit for the current year. Chandler believed this task would be a piece of cake given his 20 years of experience with an international accounting and auditing firm. There he was the engagement partner on two prominent accounts in the timepiece industry. Over the course of Chandler's first few weeks at Dally, he met with supervisors in all areas of the company to obtain an understanding of the operations. During this time, he began the formal process of documenting the system of internal control. He created flowcharts of the key processes, such as accounts receivable/cash receipts, accounts payable/cash disbursements, inventory management and control, and purchasing and payroll. Chandler was astounded by the lack of documentation and cross-functional knowledge of the employees. He was even more alarmed when rumors of financial shenanigans surfaced in nearly all of his interviews with the managers. But everyone feared the wrath of Nickerson.

Chandler took the rumors very seriously. Utilizing the scant details, he began an investigation unbeknownst to Ted. He discovered many irregularities that required further analysis. To complicate matters, the year-end audit was scheduled to begin the very next Monday. Chandler did not want the auditors to be aware of the potential restatement of previously issued financials unless he established concrete evidence of fraudulent activity. He and the corporate legal counsel, Ross Guiler, scheduled a special telephone conference meeting of the board of directors to inform them of the allegations. It was clear to Chandler and Ross that the board was out of touch with Dally—they appeared to be merely puppets for Ted Nickerson. Ted tried to downplay the comments from the various managers and said that he did not think an internal investigation was merited. Chandler and Ross convinced the majority of the board members to authorize the retention of forensic accountants.

INVENTORY OVERHAUL

Chandler called the accountants recommended by Ross, the firm where I was employed: Collin, Cramer, Newman & Associates. Chandler provided George Collin, my boss, with a detailed description of what he had discovered. George told Chandler he would put an investigative team together and scheduled a meeting at Dally for the next morning. It consisted of four professionals: two junior staff accountants, who would be relied on for data entry and obtaining source documents; an accountant to supervise the staff and investigate the more complex questionable financial transactions; and me, the senior manager, to participate in the employee interviews with Ross and to assist George with the preparation of a written report documenting the findings and recommendations.

Chandler and Ross met with George and me the next morning. Chandler explained the four areas requiring investigation:

1. Manipulation of physical inventory quantities and unit costs

2. Exaggerated revenue recognition

3. Questionable fixed asset capitalization

4. Cash disbursements

I also began scheduling the questioning of current and former officers, which were to be conducted offsite to ensure privacy. Two of the former (CFO) had moved out of state, so arrangements were made for Ross and me to travel and meet with them. Collin utilized transcript-style notes that I prepared, documenting each interview, to establish the time periods and areas for the personnel who might have knowledge about the transactions in question. The consensus from all the former employees was consistent with that of the current staff: Everyone was afraid of Ted Nickerson. They stated that he ruled by intimidation and micromanaged every aspect of the business, including significant customers, the banking relationship, the audit, and the annual physical inventory. He frequently undermined the authority of senior management. As a result, there was constant turnover in key positions.

An investigation of the inventory commenced shortly after the interviews. Allegedly, the quantities on numerous tags had been altered after the stock was counted, apparently to reflect higher quantities than those originally counted. We located the tags for the years in question and put them in number order. Our plan was to compare them to those saved and stored by the inventory manager in a locked cabinet in the warehouse. A three-part form existed: one stayed on the inventory, one was pulled after the count and sent to accounting, and the third was saved in a locked cabinet in the inventory manager's warehouse office. But Ted Nickerson was unaware of the third copy.

The process of organizing and comparing the tags was tedious and time consuming. After several hours, we identified many where the quantity listed on the copy from the inventory manager's office did not agree with that on the tag attached to the inventory. In fact, the manipulation was quite obvious. For example, where it originally had indicated a quantity of 20, the tag had been changed to read 220. The handwriting and the color of the ink were clearly different; there was no attempt to hide it. Once we completed matching the tags to the form from the locked cabinet, we compared the tags with discrepancies to the final inventory report. We found, without exception, that the higher quantity had been recorded on the final inventory report. Next, we prepared a schedule of the differences, both quantity and extended cost, to determine the amount of the misstatement by year for the manipulated tags.

We had been told that the values had also been fudged by increasing unit costs. In his interview, a former CFO recalled a time when the physical inventory had been entered for one year, and he did a screen print to get the total value just before the end of the workday. It was $780,000. The former CFO had seen Ted Nickerson lurking around, and he was grumbling loudly that the inventory value had better be closer to $1,000,000 than $750,000 or the year-end numbers were not going to be good. One of the clerks performing the data entry was a longtime company employee and was very close to Ted. The next morning the former CFO checked and the value had jumped to $1,025,000. The former CFO confronted Ted and was told to mind his own business.

We obtained vendor price lists and began comparing them to the final inventory report. There were numerous instances of dramatically higher prices over a three-year period. For example, a unit cost of $125 became $1,250. We documented all of the exceptions and quantified them. Meanwhile, Collin and I investigated certain transactions identified by the former sales manager that were handled directly by Ted, who had forbade anyone else to have contact with this client because it was "*his* account." We found that the sales to this particular customer, who was also an inventory supplier to Dally, were always made near quarter-end and were for significant amounts but were never actually paid. More digging revealed that the inventory purchased by Dally was the same inventory it was selling to the supplier, but the supplier was buying it back for the inflated sales price. We had Chandler, the current CFO, run reports from the previous four years for this customer so he could analyze all of the transactions to determine their propriety.

Further, financial statements reflected significant increases in fixed assets during a two-year period, but the details were scant. In fact, Collin and I found that the additions were payments to a company owned by Ted Nickerson. Allegedly, these expenses were for the retooling of certain machines on the assembly floor, but according to the foreman, this work had not been performed in at least three years.

The final area we tackled was the review of cash disbursements. We asked Chandler to have his IT staff member export the check and wire transfer registers into Excel. After this was completed, we sorted and subtotaled the data by payee. Next we arranged information by total amount disbursed, highest to the lowest. Finally the team reviewed the paid bill files for the significant payments to ascertain if there was documentation supporting their business purposes.

CHECK THE STOCK

When Collin, Cramer, Newman & Associates completed their investigation, we delivered a comprehensive written report to Ross and the board of directors. A week later, Collin and I were scheduled to make an oral presentation summarizing the findings. We focused on three areas:

1. Dally had misrepresented its financial condition for at least four years. In some cases, it was facilitated by the falsification of certain of the company's books and records, particularly with respect to the inventory.

2. By all indications, there were inappropriate management overrides by the president and CEO, Ted Nickerson. The roadblocks established there, combined with Nickerson's mantra of "stay in your own lane," resulted in a litany of misstatements and mis-representations.

3. The broad categories of improprieties included:
    *   Inventory misstatements
    *   Erroneous revenue recognition
    *   Questionable fixed asset capitalization policies
    *   Disbursements and compensation issues

The board of directors was stunned and angered by the report. They fired questions at Collin and me. Over the years, the board had relied heavily on Ted's word and promises. They felt betrayed by his dishonesty.

A strategy had to be developed to minimize the long-term impact to the company and its shareholders. Dally was public, and the Securities and Exchange Commission (SEC) needed to be notified of the financial misstatements. The board, Chandler, and Dally administration also had to discuss the situation with their current auditors and their lenders, Penn Dutch Bank.

When Ross contacted the SEC and presented them with a copy of the investigative report, they requested that the company prepare the appropriate filings to rectify the situation. Ted Nickerson would be dealt with separately.

Chandler and Ross met with the partner from the auditing firm, an old friend of Ted's, to inform her about the forensic investigation and the results. Chandler also wanted to discuss why the auditors had not identified the irregularities during the course of their audits of the financial statements. He had not been able to locate a single letter from them recommending improvements in the system of internal controls. The partner was shocked by the news. The auditors determined it was necessary to conduct their own investigation.

Chandler and Ross also arranged a meeting with Dally's loan officer from Penn Dutch Bank. Also an old friend of Ted's, he appeared extremely agitated after hearing the news regarding the financial misstatements. The officer informed them that Penn Dutch Bank, in addition to providing the company with a line of credit secured by inventory, had loaned a considerable sum to Ted individually, and that the loan was secured by Dally stock. Chandler and Ross were not aware that of this. Now it all began to make sense to Chandler; Ted had committed the fraud to maintain the company's value at a price level to keep his loan from being undercollateralized. If the stock stayed above a certain price, Ted could continue to borrow funds to finance his extravagant lifestyle. Penn Dutch put Dally on a temporary credit hold and informed Chandler and Ross. The bank recognized that anything involving Dally would also adversely affect the loan to Ted, so it wanted to move forward cautiously. Penn Dutch also decided to send a team of auditors over to Dally to perform its own investigation.

Finally, Ted had to be confronted. The board of directors convened a special meeting with Chandler, Ross, and Ted. He was very quiet when the board chairman reviewed the findings of the forensic investigation and then began to cry hysterically, confessing and confirming that the misstatements were all his doings. In addition, Ted admitted that the manipulations had started five years ago. Because the company was underperforming, he had to be more aggressive to maintain positive financial results. He complained that when he stepped in to run the company, their state-of-the-art manufacturing facility was antiquated and needed a significant overhaul. He also believed Dally's products were on the verge of being obsolete. Sales had been decreasing for years. Newer and better products from competitors required Dally to reduce prices significantly, which greatly diminished profit margins. Ted also masked the overhead costs. His salary had been increased to $500,000 per year, and the newly constructed corporate office building was a huge financial burden. Ted admitted that he did not want to change his lifestyle or run the risk of tarnishing the company's image, but he just didn't think he had an alternative. He acknowledged that he was manipulating the financial information so that the stock price would not fall in order to keep his entire empire from collapse.

Ross and the board of directors informed the SEC of the financial misstatements and provided them with a copy of the investigative report prepared by Collin, Cramer, and Newman & Associates. The board also provided the SEC with an action plan, which included the removal of Ted Nickerson as CEO and the election of new board members with the requisite business skills to oversee Dally adequately. Because the company had been so forthright and diligent in its investigation, it was spared punishment. The SEC did not pursue Ted Nickerson due to his age and his fragile physical state. Surprisingly, the stock price of the company remained steady before and after the disclosure of the fraud.

LESSONS LEARNED

Forensic accountants learned that a variety of people rely on their work product and that it needs to be accurate with comprehensive documentation. The interview process is critical. In this instance it provided a road map of the areas that required investigation. Providing the findings in a clear and concise manner reduces confusion.

Chandler reflected back on when he was hired and how at the time he thought it strange that the company had an exceptionally high rate of management turnover. He realized that he should not have ignored the warning signs. A company managed by intimidation may have a problem. Employees should not be governed by fear. Issues they raise should be investigated. The CFO must make every effort to ensure that the system of internal controls is functioning.

The board of directors learned that members are not paid to be asleep at the wheel. Their collective role is a critical component of the company, and they need to remain objective, skeptical, and diligent. Individual shareholders who are not involved in the operation of the business are relying on the board to oversee the business and look out for their investments.

Penn Dutch Bank learned that when loaning funds to both the company and an officer or shareholder, their exposure to risk would be greatly reduced if they required the person to provide collateral not related to the company. Further, had the bank monitored Dally's financial results more closely, its internal analysts may have identified inconsistent financial relationships and market trends. If the bank had toured the manufacturing facility, it would have found the equipment to be outdated. It would have also observed the dust on the shelves in the finished goods inventory warehouse and the obvious obsolescence of many items that were collateral on the loan.

RECOMMENDATIONS TO PREVENT FUTURE OCCURRENCES

In order to improve Dally's overall financial reporting process and to avoid a repetition of the circumstances discussed, these practices should be implemented and maintained:

- A management tone that encourages fraud deterrence and accurate financial reporting
- Creation of an Internal Auditing Department and internal audit functions
- Reconstitute the board of directors

- Creation of an audit committee that:
  - Consists of informed, vigilant and effective overseers of financial reporting and internal controls
  - Has adequate resources and authority to discharge its responsibilities
  - Reviews management's evaluation of factors related to the independence of the company's auditing firm
  - Replaces the external auditors every three to five years
  - Oversees the quarterly financial reporting process
- Management should seek second opinions on significant accounting issues
- Formalize accounting policies and procedures
  - Document retention
  - Fixed asset capitalization
  - Computer backups
  - Inventory reserve estimates
  - Overhead rate determination
  - Purchase and sales cut-off
  - Monthly financial reporting package
  - Dual signatures on all disbursements in excess of a designated amount
  - Consider the use of an independent third party to assist with the counting and data entry of a physical inventory
  - Develop inventory cycle count procedures
- Appoint a compensation committee that must approve all management salary increases
- Formalize the employee complaint process and job training
- Establish and enforce mandatory vacations

While these practices will not eliminate fraud, they would certainly reduce the risk. In the case of Dally Industries, the illegal conduct likely would never have occurred if some or all of these policies and procedures had been implemented.

Margaret Smith, CFE, CPA/ABV, CIRA, CVA, is a principal with GlassRatner Advisory & Capital Group, a firm specializing in forensic and litigation accounting, and bankruptcy and restructuring advisory services. Ms. Smith has a bachelor's degree from Hillsdale College, with majors in accounting and Spanish.

Bury Me Not in Guyandotte

JOHN W. BURDISS

It's unclear why he chose Guyandotte, West Virginia. Perhaps it was because the town was notorious for lifestyles that were outside legal boundaries and accepted social mores. Indeed, lawlessness had long been fashionable in Guyandotte, an important fact in the tragedy that would unfold at a bank where Kenny Cox and his cohorts actively committed fraud for nearly two decades.

J. Kenneth "Kenny" Cox was a native of McKeesport, Pennsylvania, a small city near Pittsburgh. The record of his college studies is uncertain, but he did attend prep school at Parcourt Military Academy in Virginia. A banking colleague who knew Kenny well said, "He spiced conversations with exaggerations about his past. Cox claimed to have a master's degree from Stanford but no records could support it."

Kenny had begun his career in the credit department of a Pittsburgh bank in 1949. After two and a half decades of unremarkable jobs, he left the States in 1975 to work in Micronesia in a United Nations pilot project. Although he intended to stay much longer, Kenny lasted only two years An audit report about his tenure there criticized him for "excessive travel and poor collections and for issuing too few development loans."

In 1977 Kenny became the president of the Sanctuary Bank in Guyandotte, West Virginia, an institution that had $17 million in assets. The town, in a remote coal field location in the southern part of the state, had a population of only 600 people.

A longtime member of Sanctuary's board said of Cox, "His bank was small, in a depressed area and not worthy of a whole lot of attention. But he had a lot of drive to overcome that image. He was energetic, gregarious, and unconventional—and his braggadocio was never stymied."

Kenny made substantial campaign contributions that garnered political contacts. He plastered his office walls with photos of himself with presidents, and he was not shy about calling upon the White House and West Virginia's senators when bank examiners from the Office of the Comptroller of the Currency (OCC) pressed him.

Two Pittsburgh-area women, Sallie Bing and Susan "Susie" Schoolcraft, came to West Virginia with Cox. They had worked together in an apartment project in Pittsburgh where Sallie was the comptroller and Susie the bookkeeper. Although they had no banking experience and no college education, these two women were Kenny's trusted lieutenants for over 20 years at Sanctuary.

There was one other man in the Sanctuary family; he was Jerry Goodman, the executive vice president of the bank's mortgage subsidiary. Jerry had been a licensed certified public accountant (CPA). However, his license was revoked for improper conduct involving tax returns. Cox hired only women to work in the bank, calling them "Cox's foxes." Kenny never married.

Kenny was widely known to view representatives of the OCC with utter contempt, which led to very acrimonious dealings between Sanctuary Bank and the agency. VP Jerry said, "The mere mention of regulators outraged him. He would swear quite a bit." Once Kenny boldly told the *State Journal*, a West Virginia business weekly, "I don't care for examiners at all; I think we ought to do away with them."

After years of fighting with the OCC and running Sanctuary with an iron fist, Kenny died suddenly. The team picked and trained by him, including Sallie, Susie, and Jerry, along with many others among Cox's foxes, proved to be key figures in the huge fraud that was unearthed after Kenny's passing. Here is another success story that was too good to be true.

WHAT GOES UP MUST COME DOWN

Sanctuary attracted depositors' funds by paying above-market interest rates on certificates of deposit (CDs) to get the money to support its phenomenal growth. At one point, Sanctuary showed total assets of only $90 million, but less than seven years later, when the bank was finally closed down, total assets were reported at over $1 billion. Kenny had relied on the incredible growth of the bank's resources from the CDs to fund high-risk securitizations, a process whereby Sanctuary would aggregate loans, work with brokers who bundled and sold them as securities. Kenny's appetite for risk, coupled with his egotistical desire to report extraordinary levels of profits and asset growth (both highly exaggerated and false), reached new heights.

Sanctuary ostensibly had the unparalleled business acumen to cover the expense burden by managing extremely high risks in its loan portfolios. Securitizations were purportedly geared to create profits for the bank during the holding period and again when the bundles were sold.

This new buy-high-and-sell-higher scheme began to move at warp speed as Sanctuary and its mortgage subsidiary became a national player. Sanctuary was now actively making high-risk debt consolidation loans and at the same time purchasing large volumes of such loans from originators all over the United States.

Sanctuary reported staggering levels of growth and earnings. The bank's return on assets for a three-year period ranged from 2.61% to a whopping 8.45% in an industry where anything over 2% is viewed as exceptional. This astounding performance by Sanctuary consistently ranked the little bank from Guyandotte, West Virginia, in the ninety-ninth percentile compared to its peers.

Just two and a half years before Sanctuary imploded under the weight of a $500 million loan fraud, Kenny had told the *American Banker*, "We're going to keep it up. I don't see us making any less money in the foreseeable future, and I know we're going to do better this year."

Despite their apparent successes, Sanctuary's staff was always extremely combative when dealing with the National Bank Examiners. When the bank's management was incapable of subduing the OCC with their constant complaints, Sanctuary brought in some muscle. This little bank in Guyandotte, West Virginia, had two high-priced and well-known law firms on retainer—one from Washington, D.C., and another from Denver, Colorado.

Records showed that Sanctuary had been repeatedly cited for having poor systems of internal control. There were numerous instances of out-of-balance asset reconciliations involving millions of dollars. The bank was paying extremely high interest rates to obtain more deposits to fund more risky loans. Yet there seemed to be no drumbeat by regulators or outside auditors to question how, with this staff and these notable deficiencies, Sanctuary could maintain success at levels that were effectively stratospheric.

Finally the OCC clamped down on Sanctuary and insisted it ditch its local accounting firm and hire a national one to perform the annual audit. It was hoped the new auditors would look with fresh eyes and perhaps discover just what the secret to Sanctuary's success really was.

Unfortunately, the new auditors were no better at detecting the fraud. The new CPAs completed their audit for the year and released their report with a clean opinion. They had failed in their routine confirmation of the loans reportedly owned by Sanctuary and held by servicers in Detroit and San Diego. Of the $553 million in loans Sanctuary fraudulently represented as its assets, only $38 million were actually still owned by the bank. That $515 million discrepancy was ultimately discovered by a combined task force of examiners from the OCC and the Federal Deposit Insurance Corporation (FDIC).

The OCC had begun its examination just three months before the bank was closed. The relations between the examiners and the staff at Sanctuary hit all-time lows. Alleged threats of violence by Guyandotte citizens who had gotten wind of the "government" crackdown compelled the examiners to request on-site protection from the U.S. marshals—an unheard-of circumstance.

Examiners do not generally confirm assets; they rely on the auditors who have done so in their audit of the bank's financial statements. Unfortunately at Sanctuary, the auditors' confirmation was badly flawed. Failing to recognize the $515 million shortfall was an inexplicable and serious mistake. They apparently did not make the critical distinction between loans actually "owned" by Sanctuary and held by servicers and loans "formerly owned" by Sanctuary that had been sold as part of previous securitizations. The examiners were now pressing the officers at Sanctuary to provide some corroboration of just how the unbelievable performance had been achieved. In other words, the OCC and the FDIC wanted the truth. Clearly, the top officers were aware that the discovery of the fraud was imminent.

The Rush to Cover Up

Bank officers and employees had become very adept at conjuring up records. Testimony at the subsequent obstruction trial where Susie and Jerry were charged elicited some telling information. During the investigation, Susie had called a bank teller and asked him to create a false document that was needed as historical proof. The bank teller did so without hesitating. The purported account record was made on the spot, but the teller and some associates made an effort to "age" the document so it appeared to be decades old. They dropped it on the floor, stepped on it, spilled some coffee on it, and burned it with a cigarette. Their skills had been well honed with years of practice in deception, but soon, with the OCC and FDIC closing in, they would be called on to destroy records. Creating false documents was one thing; getting rid of them in volume and in a hurry was another.

Susie Schoolcraft and her husband owned Schoolcraft Ranch, a remote mountaintop property that had very limited access and seemed a great place to work on the plans of destruction. Staff members took files to the ranch and attempted to burn them. But they quickly discovered that in bulk, paper does not ignite well, and the fire needed constant tending to assure reasonable success. Those at the bank who had become skilled in creating false records found that microfilm could be destroyed in the microwave in the employees' kitchen, but that process was also too slow.

Meanwhile, back at the ranch, a new, larger scheme was hatched. They'd bury the records. And not just in any hole, but a trench 10 feet wide, 10 feet deep, and 100 feet long; big enough for a tri-axle dump truck to back in and dump the documents.

Some years prior, the bank had purchased the old Guyandotte High School, where it stored hundreds, perhaps thousands of boxes of bank records. Amazingly, while the examination was under way, Jerry, with the aid of five men—not regular bank workers, although some were husbands and relatives of the foxes—and other active female bank employees tossed those boxes in broad daylight from the third floor to a truck waiting below.

They drove to the ranch and dumped the loads in the huge hole, returning several times until the job was complete. Then they covered the trench. The audacity of this event corroborates the desperation and the breadth of involvement by employees, spouses, and others in this incredible fraud.

It's All Over

The OCC and FDIC examiners confirmed the shocking discrepancy one week before the bank was declared insolvent and closed. It turned out that the only significant funds that had been coming into the coffers of Sanctuary were not loan payments—since most of the loans did not exist—but the new money coming from investors for the purchase of CDs to keep this major pyramid scheme going.

The Federal Bureau of Investigation (FBI) got involved in the weeks following the bank's failure and closing. Aerial photos of the mountaintop Schoolcraft Ranch were made, and by using infrared technology, the recently disturbed earth was detected. Because there had been some rumors of the record destruction, the FBI had already searched the ranch. Some records were seized, including some computer disks that Susie had hidden in a picnic cooler.

Now the examiners insisted that they would, in fact, confirm the millions of dollars serviced by the third parties. In short order, they were told that Sanctuary did not have $553 million in loans. Rather, the bank in Guyandotte owned only about $38 million held by these two servicers—one in San Diego and one in Detroit. The examiners dispatched personnel in California and Michigan to determine whether there was a mistake in communication. There wasn't.

Immediately, plans were made to close the bank. The FDIC brought in its liquidation team; the OCC had on-site examiners and the West Virginia State Police were called in to provide security and protection for these unwelcome government workers. The bad news spread quickly in Guyandotte. A crowd surrounded the institution wanting to withdraw their funds, but it was too late; the scene was bedlam. Over the next few days, the predictable frenzy brought in not just local media, but news teams from every major U.S. television network, many prominent national newspapers and magazines, and reporters for at least two Japanese newspapers. This last economic boost to the town of Guyandotte from the scores of media and government employees was neither long-lived nor happy.

Digging Even Deeper

I began my career in banking in 1972 and was commissioned a National Bank Examiner three years later. In those days, we regularly did a 100% confirmation of cash, deposits held in other banks and the investment portfolio. Loan servicing was done almost exclusively in-house. In this case, I was engaged by the attorneys who were hired by Susie Schoolcraft. They were attempting to mount a defense regarding the initial charge of obstruction of a bank examination related to the destroyed and buried records.

As part of the examination, we reviewed the programs of internal and external audit to gain assurance that adequate measures had been taken to confirm the existence of the bank's loans. Thus, all liquid assets held by the bank or by others were verified and confirmed directly by the examiners. Over time, the OCC determined that this was an audit function and the examiners should be more concerned with asset quality, management systems, and the like. Since the external auditors were required to assert there were no material misstatements in the financial statements of the banks, it was believed that there was no need for bank examiners to act redundantly by confirming that significant assets actually existed. Unfortunately, this change in policy meant that if assets were not properly confirmed and verified, the examiners would be evaluating the quality of assets that might not exist.

In the Guyandotte fiasco, the actual failure by the auditors enabled Sanctuary's top officers to commit an incredible $500+ million fraud. On the surface, Guyandotte's reliance on third parties to service large numbers of the bank's loans was neither improper nor suspicious.

Ironically, in the old days when banks generally held and serviced their own loans, the onus was on the auditors to do a statistically sound sampling of them. Here, since third parties purportedly held the loans, that process should have been elementary. As with the standard confirmation and verification of investment securities, which are virtually all held and serviced by third parties, direct contact with these servicers should have been done. Obviously in the Guyandotte situation, that was not true.

While I was working with attorneys who were defending Susie Schoolcraft on charges of obstruction of a bank examination, she made an incredible statement to me. In her words, when the auditors needed to confirm and verify the loans allegedly held by third parties for the bank, she or Jerry would just make the "link" and they (the purported servicers) would just "modem them to us at the bank."

Despite Susie's inarticulate description, it was clear there was no valid, independent affirmation of the existence of loans allegedly being held and serviced for Guyandotte. Hence, like the "wire" scam in the memorable movie *The Sting,* where bets were being placed on races that had already occurred, the auditors were allowing Guyandotte's officers to rig the "wire" (here a phone line and modem) so that the "results" were totally predictable and, of course, controlled by the fraudsters. There is no evidence the third-party servicers did anything improper or in any way assisted Sanctuary Bank. Rather, the auditors simply did not confirm that the loans held by these third parties were really owned by Guyandotte.

Sanctuary was functioning as a pyramid scheme. Discovery of a major fraud rarely comes from a lightning bolt; most scams like this don't occur without warning. There are usually many indicators that, if heeded, could have either prevented or at least minimized the impact. The fraud at Sanctuary that would ultimately cost the FDIC's insurance fund nearly $1 billion was certainly no exception. A recap of some of the red flags that were missed, ignored, or purposely tolerated provides some insight about the lost opportunities to uncover the Ponzi scheme.

- While it is unlikely that anyone but top management really knew exactly what was going on, abundant evidence suggests that virtually any staff member at Sanctuary who was asked to do so was willing to alter records and to obstruct examiners and auditors. This endemic culture of lawlessness made it difficult for anyone to get to the bottom of anything.

- The fact that Sanctuary's staff was so highly paid should have raised questions. The tellers, bookkeepers, and proof operators routinely made in excess of $50,000 a year when most area banks weren't paying half that much. With the local job market perpetually in the doldrums, it's little wonder that so many employees were willing to commit criminal acts.

- How did supposedly objective observers come to believe these people were capable of such unbelievable financial achievements? The key players at Sanctuary had very limited work experience outside this little community bank that suddenly grew into a billion-dollar institution.

- The demeanor of the staff was unsophisticated, yet as compared to all other banks, this institution's published financial information would strongly support an argument that its employees were financial geniuses. If these guys and gals were so smart, why wasn't everybody trying to replicate their formula?

- Wasn't it suspicious that defrocked CPA Jerry Goodman was a key player in the reported fantastic growth and success?

- This little bank run by a motley crew was supposedly able to play at the high-risk end of the loan spectrum, outperforming every peer or standard while doing so.

The Losers

The main figures in this tragedy of fraud and bank failure all got substantial prison sentences. Susie was sentenced to 13 years for obstruction and 27 years for bank fraud. Jerry received 4 years for obstruction and 13 years for bank fraud. Sallie, who was also the mayor of Guyandotte, got 16 years.

The list of those who lost money in the Guyandotte fiasco is long. The latest tally shows the FDIC lost $870 million in its liquidation of the assets and payment of insured claims. Approximately 500 depositors had balances in excess of the $100,000 FDIC limits on accounts; they lost approximately $15 million.

The bank's directors were sued by a host of parties and settled for an undisclosed sum. Similarly, the bank's former auditors, longtime and local—not the ones who conducted the last audit—also settled for unknown amounts.

The OCC assessed a $300,000 fine against the auditors who did the final audit and sought to limit their ability to conduct future bank audits. The firm is still in litigation with numerous parties.

The "market capitalization" of Guyandotte shortly before it failed was $132 million—and not surprisingly, it fell to zero. Of course, this value was predicated on a house of cards and the huge ongoing fraud. The stockholders of the bank lost their investments.

The town of Guyandotte had received about $400,000 per year in taxes from the bank, amounting to two-thirds of the city's budget. When the bank went under, there were immediate layoffs and major cutbacks in services. In addition to at least one business owned by the Schoolcrafts (the local hardware store), other small companies failed due to their dependence on the financial institution.

Lessons Learned

We already know this axiom: If it sounds too good to be true, it probably is. Sanctuary Bank was offering dubiously high interest rates on certificates of deposit. It was suspiciously successful. There was not nearly enough skepticism in this case. That the scam went on for so long was in large part because no one seemed to sweat the details. Objectivity was lost, not only in the confirmation and verification process, but in the overall evaluation of the performance of this bank and its staff. In addition, the outside auditors and the examiners failed to look closely at the actual documents that allegedly supported the spectacular performance of Guyandotte.

Businesses can grow and even succeed at unexpected levels. However, any time a company is able to shift gears constantly, yet always outperform the market, it bears close scrutiny. There should have been some very quantifiable and fundamental reasons to explain this unbelievable success.

Outside directors should pay close attention. It is okay to assume, without specific knowledge to the contrary, that you have trustworthy management, but everything must be verified.

Here is a critical revelation: Missing or bogus or fake loans do not make regular loan payments. Files, documents, and reports can be faked, but cash cannot. If there were legitimately $553 million in loans, versus the actual $38 million that existed, a lot of payments would have been coming in. The bank should have been receiving several million dollars in cash each month in interest payments alone.

At the trial of Susie Schoolcraft and Jerry Goodman, midlevel bank officers testified that in the weeks and months before the discovery of the fraud, Sanctuary was almost always desperate for cash. The bank had to keep a certain amount of funds to operate, both in coin and currency and in cash in other banks to clear checks. The deposits held by Sanctuary were at high interest rates that had to be paid to the owners of the CDs. Further exacerbating the shortage was the bank's enormous payroll; the little bank was literally hemorrhaging cash.

The simple truth is that fraudulent loans don't make payments. The fraudsters could rig all the data and they could make up the needed document trail, but once the source of cash ended, so did the scam.

RECOMMENDATIONS TO PREVENT FUTURE OCCURRENCES

Follow the cash. If there must be a recurring theme about attempting to uncover fraud, this is it. Always remember that dollars matter. Also:

- Don't be afraid to ask dumb questions. And don't forget to ask the obvious.
- Have competent and objective people look at all key areas.
  - Ask the main what-if questions.
  - Auditors and/or examiners must investigate "facts" from a standpoint of objectivity and independence.
  - Use more critical analyses in situations of high growth and high profits. More objective measures must be in place to assure that risks are reasonably estimated and provided for with adequate reserves and sustainable capital and earnings.

- Make sure that performance matches, or is at least in sync with, processes and people executing them. In the Sanctuary Bank case, everything about the record keeping suggested sloppiness if not outright fraud. There were out-of-balance issues of millions of dollars. There were lots of violations of laws and regulations.

- Make certain confirmation and verification procedures used by internal and external auditors of all major assets meet industry standards.
  - Consider "testing" the auditors' work in a manner that will provide examiners with the assurance that such work was in fact performed adequately when above-average risk is involved.
  - Establish procedures for confirmation and verification of all major assets. In the Sanctuary case, the analysis was a worthless exercise since the actual assets did not exist.

- When noncompliance occurs, take timely, measured, and stringent actions that will mitigate or cure the problems.

- As another source of protection to the banking system, verify that professional liability insurance coverage for outside auditors and bank directors is sufficient to cover the risks identified.

John W. Burdiss, Esq., CFE, is a consultant/expert witness and solo practitioner in Cape Charles, Virginia. He has been engaged in over 150 fraud and banking cases since 1990. Also licensed in West Virginia, he began as a bank examiner in 1972, then graduated in 2005 from Regent University School of Law.

CHAPTER 54

The Woolly Mammoth Eats Its Prey

PAUL POCALYKO AND CHARLES N. PERSING

Mammoth Services, a division of Sparktech Technologies, was driven to succeed in the fast-paced technology world. Backed by research and development, Mammoth touted itself using its strengths in mobility, optical, software, data, and voice networking to create new revenue-generating opportunities for its customers, while enabling them to quickly deploy and better manage their networks. Mammoth's customer base included communications providers, governments, and enterprises worldwide.

At its launch, Mammoth Services was a major player in networking, web-based enterprise solutions that link public and private networks, communications software, professional network design, semiconductors, and optoelectronics. In four years, the company completed 38 acquisitions totaling more than $46 billion, including a $24 billion purchase of Rolfor Communications, which made Mammoth a leading supplier of data networking equipment for service providers.

To Mammoth's shareholders, creditors, and the public, all things appeared normal after its spin-off from Sparktech. The business was progressing and acquisitions were integrated. Mammoth had even weathered the start of the downturn in the telecommunications industry. What was not widely known was the magnitude of internal pressure for continued revenues in the face of the declining marketplace.

Preyton Communications, based in Boston, Massachusetts, was a publicly traded telecommunications company, offering a wide range of high-speed voice, data, and Internet services to small and medium-size businesses and the government. Preyton developed a unique "last-mile solution" for reaching its customers through the use of wireless technology, which was acclaimed within the industry and the investment community as a breakthrough for a competitive local exchange carrier (CLEC) to compete with incumbent local exchange carriers (ILECs). Preyton's business model was based on its desire to be recognized as the vendor of choice within the CLEC industry, offer cost-competitive services, and provide scarce and difficult-to-obtain broadband for end users who would no longer need to depend on the ILECs' expensive solutions.

Typically, Preyton would purchase telecommunications equipment from any number of suppliers as it began construction of its national network. One of its main suppliers was Mammoth. Since Mammoth began, the two companies had had a business relationship.

One year that vendor alliance grew when the companies entered into a supply agreement for the development, design, building, and implementation of a nationwide communications network. Preyton agreed to purchase products and services from Mammoth, which in turn arranged to provide the smaller company with the financing to purchase those products and services. The chairman and chief executive officer (CEO) of Preyton believed the relationship to be the defining moment of the business.

"Mammoth's major commitment of expertise and financing, combined with the overwhelming speed to market and cost advantages of Preyton's business model, clearly propels us to the top of the competitive local exchange carrier industry," he proclaimed. "With Mammoth behind us, we are positioned to be the first carrier to create a nearly ubiquitous end-to-end broadband network in the top 100 world markets."

WHEN MAMMOTH IS NOT ENOUGH

From Preyton's standpoint, the strategic partnership was a huge milestone. Mammoth had committed to design, supply, and build the company's network. The lopsided importance of the strategic partnership to was evident throughout the negotiations process. Preyton even created a code name for the project: the "Woolly Mammoth."

Mammoth expected to generate $2 billion of revenue with Preyton while at the same time provide a solid foundation to dominate the supplier market. Unfortunately, at the outset of the strategic partnership, Mammoth was unable to provide the required level of services requested by Preyton to construct its network. As a short-term solution, Mammoth agreed to execute a subcontract with Preyton's subsidiary until Mammoth could provide the services. As Preyton's expansion plans grew, its network build-out staff expanded rapidly. But Mammoth continued to be unable to perform.

Operationally, Preyton was almost entirely dependent on financing. Any disruption in its borrowing would put the network build-out in a precarious position. For two years, Mammoth allowed Preyton to borrow under its credit facilities. It used part of its loans to pay Mammoth for the services performed by the subsidiary. The large business had entered the relationship with the intent of selling its equipment to Preyton. By allowing the company to use it merely as a lender, Mammoth created a situation that was not generating the revenues and profits it expected. Further, the company had a debt on its books that was impaired.

It was understood that the construction of Preyton's network would require a significant amount of money, funding that would occur long before it expected to achieve profitability. In almost two years, Mammoth provided approximately $1.2 billion in financing. Although the agreement did not require repayment for another two years, Mammoth pressured Preyton for an early reimbursement. The smaller company obtained new financing to settle its debt. That same month Mammoth entered into a second credit agreement with Preyton for an additional $2 billion; the agreement contained a provision for refinancing when the debt passed $500 million. This gave Mammoth the ability to sell its debt or, in the absence of a sale, to reprice the interest and increase it. The borrowings under the second credit agreement reached approximately $930 million. Immediately thereafter Mammoth again put pressure on Preyton to reduce its borrowings or provide an early repayment plan.

The two companies crafted a series of transactions wherein Preyton was required to purchase an ever-increasing volume of Mammoth's telecommunications equipment. These purchases were aligned with the end of each calendar quarter, the Mammoth financial reporting period.

In November, two years after the business relationship commenced, Preyton obtained approximately $1 billion, which consisted of vendor financing, debt, and equity that included $270 million from a software company, a computer corporation, and a private equity fund. Additionally, an equipment supplier provided $200 million in senior debt through an amendment to Preyton's credit agreement with its outside banks. The new loan package closed in December, upon which Preyton paid Mammoth the net proceeds from the equipment supplier.

BAD PRESS

Shortly after Mammoth hired a new executive vice president and chief financial officer (CFO), an anonymous letter arrived that alleged, among other issues, improprieties in Mammoth's recognition of revenue. The company decided to conduct an investigation through its outside counsel and external auditors. No written report was produced. Since the investigation was conducted through outside counsel, they claimed attorney-client privilege in the numerous legal actions that followed.

The newly appointed chairman and CEO of Mammoth issued a November press release that stated:

> We have identified a revenue recognition issue impacting approximately $125 million in the fourth fiscal quarter, which ended Sept. 30th. The company estimates that the reduction in revenue could have an approximately two cent impact on earnings per share. The company previously reported $9.4 billion in revenues and eighteen cents per share on continuing operations for the quarter. We wanted to make this public as soon as it was discovered. I have asked our outside auditor and our outside counsel to assist us in doing a complete review of this and any related issues. We have also informed the Securities and Exchange Commission of our efforts.

As a follow-up press release in December, Mammoth stated:

> The company has completed the revenue review it announced last month. As a result, its fourth fiscal quarter revenue will be $8.7 billion and pro forma earnings will be 10 cents per share on continuing operations. This is lower than the previously announced $9.4 billion in revenues and pro forma earnings of 18 cents per share on continuing operations for the quarter ended Sept. 30th. For the fiscal year, the adjusted results will be $33.6 billion in revenue and pro forma earnings per share of ninety cents on continuing operations.

In the December press release, the company also announced that it was taking certain actions. For example, Mammoth found that in one case there had been misleading documentation and incomplete communications between a sales team and the financial organization with respect to offering a customer credits in connection with a software license. It was done with disregard for the clear revenue recognition procedures that Mammoth has in place. Appropriate disciplinary action, including the dismissal of an employee, was taken. As a result, we will reduce our fourth fiscal quarter revenues by $125 million.

In the course of the review, Mammoth identified two other cases in which the sales teams had verbally offered credits to be used at a later date, but that may have been related to transactions in the fourth quarter. We have decided to reflect those credits, reducing fourth fiscal quarter revenues by an additional $74 million.

In one case, we found that revenue had been recognized from the sale of a system that had been incompletely shipped. Accordingly, Mammoth reduced its fourth fiscal quarter revenues by an additional $28 million.

During the course of the review, we decided to take back $452 million in equipment that had previously been sold to certain systems integrators and distributors, but not utilized or passed on to customers due to changes in business strategies and the weakening of the emerging service provider market. In the interest of preserving customer and distributor relationships, and because there was some evidence that there may have been verbal agreements that led them to expect Mammoth to do so, we have decided to retrieve the equipment and resell it in the future. As a result, revenues for the fourth quarter will be reduced by an additional $452 million. Revenue from the resale of this equipment will be recorded as it occurs.

After the investigation was completed, it was clear that the numbers in the initial press release were substantially understated. The effect was 300% higher on earnings per share and was not only limited to Preyton; it was widespread and systematic.

The SEC charged Mammoth and 10 individuals with securities fraud. After a Mammoth representative was quoted in a national magazine as having said that the discrepancy was simply the result of miscommunications, the SEC required the company to pay a $25 million penalty for its lack of cooperation and to publicly acknowledge its fraudulent accounting.

Mammoth and three of the former employees agreed to settle with the SEC in a $1.1 billion accounting fraud case without admitting or denying the allegations.

UNDER PRESSURE

During the 27 months prior to Preyton's bankruptcy, the company's officers and staff assigned to the Mammoth account had experienced increasing pressure to recognize revenue through purchases of unneeded equipment and services in the name of the "strategic partnership." As noted in the bankruptcy judge's decision, Preyton did not need and would not have otherwise made a significant majority of the purchases. Essentially, these were front-loaded sales of equipment and services at a faster pace than Preyton ordinarily would have bought them. Under oath, the parties testified in depositions that Preyton staff was pressured into signing documentation that they knew was false. Ultimately this documentation was provided to Mammoth's auditors as part of justification for recognizing the transactions.

The documents indicated that Mammoth would, on a quarter-after-quarter basis, threaten to retroactively breach its agreement to finance the costs of the network-build in exchange for larger fraudulent purchase concessions by Preyton. Between October and Preyton's December repayment, Preyton's loan balance passed the refinancing notice threshold. This occurred at the same time a new treasurer had arrived at Mammoth.

Additionally, Mammoth held continual negotiations with Preyton to modify its loan agreements. The on-and-off negotiations appeared to be a tactic by the new CFO and the team at Mammoth to buy time and get out from under the Preyton debt. It was evident that Preyton was in a very precarious financial condition; this was confirmed by a due diligence effort undertaken by Mammoth. Shortly after a partial $188 million repayment in December, Mammoth issued its refinancing notice to Preyton. It became clear that Mammoth needed to end its relationship with Preyton because Preyton was unable to provide Mammoth with the revenue and profit anticipated now that the end-of-quarter deals were no longer acceptable. In a memo sent in January of the next year, Preyton executives analyzed the costs of the end of quarter they had provided Mammoth, identifying some $167 million of unneeded equipment purchases, as well as advance payments for services that were never obtained. These factors were directly responsible for Preyton exceeding the $500 million refinancing threshold. Sometime late in the first quarter of that year, Mammoth declared that Preyton was in breach of the purchase agreement and refused to fund any additional borrowing requests.

Without the continued financing, Preyton had no choice but to file bankruptcy. In April the company filed a voluntary petition for relief under Chapter 11 of the Bankruptcy Code, which would allow it to remain in business. In addition, Preyton filed a lawsuit against Mammoth. Ultimately, Preyton's Chapter 11 proceeding was converted to a Chapter 7 liquidation.

DEFINING MOMENTS

The bankruptcy trustee alleged that Preyton made a preferential payment in the amount of $194 million to Mammoth in December of the previous year. Because this was made more than 90 days before Preyton's filing for bankruptcy protection, the trustee believed that Mammoth was an insider on that date. Our firm was engaged to analyze the transactions between Preyton and Mammoth to determine if they were conducted at arm's length and whether Mammoth exerted undue influence and control over Preyton, facts that counsel to the bankruptcy trustee considered relevant to determining whether Mammoth was an insider.

An "arm's-length transaction" is one resulting from business dealings between independent parties presumed to have equal bargaining power. "Undue influence" is generally defined as the improper use of power or trust in a way that deprives a person of free will and substitutes another party's objective.

We performed our work by evaluating the detailed financial records and the written agreements executed between the parties. Our efforts focused on three questions: (1) Did the transactions make business sense for Preyton? (2) Did Preyton achieve a rational business objective from entering into the transactions? (3) Did the transactions favor Mammoth and harm Preyton?

We then evaluated the correspondence between the parties and their deposition testimonies. In essence, we wanted to determine whether contemporaneous written materials by individuals with direct knowledge regarding these transactions would support or refute our financial analysis.

BAD COMPANY

While some of these transactions were fashioned in a manner to appear to be performed at arm's length, most, if not all, revealed a pattern of concealment, manipulation, and deception that adversely impacted Preyton. We concluded:

- The parties' engaged in a series of end-of-quarter deals, in which Preyton purchased an ever-increasing volume of products and services in order for Mammoth to achieve its revenue goals. There was a significant increase in the transaction volume, almost 10 times those that occurred in the months when the quarter ended when compared to the non–end-of-quarter months. These transactions had no financial benefit for Preyton.

- Preyton's employees signed and executed numerous "bill and hold" letters at Mammoth's request that were designed to show imminent deployment for goods and services. These deals were completed without regard for Preyton's needs. In fact, significant amounts of equipment remained in the warehouses of both companies when Preyton filed for bankruptcy protection.

- Deployment schedules were consistently not met. Mammoth used these transactions to recognize revenue in a fraudulent manner.

- Mammoth prebilled Preyton on invoices that bundled equipment, engineering, and network services into one line item, thus enabling the recording of revenue prior to services performed (if ever) and, in most cases, before the network equipment was physically in Preyton's possession.

- There existed an agreement in which Mammoth purported to sell a total of $135 million of software to Preyton when it intended to deliver only $20 million of potential value.

- Mammoth used period-straddling billings and offsetting credits that accelerated revenue into its current year-end and maximized Preyton's purchases without violating lenders' covenants.

- The amount of vague invoicing was significant. We identified over $135 million of Preyton equipment purchases where Mammoth failed to detail the products with the numbers, descriptions, and quantities. This was approximately 27% of all Mammoth equipment purchased by Preyton over a two-year period.

Our examination of the correspondence between the parties buttressed our conclusion that the transactions just described were improper. When Preyton attempted to curtail or even diminish its participation, Mammoth exerted extraordinary pressure on Preyton to continue. And when Mammoth's new CFO banned the use of quarter-ended bill-and-hold transactions, the sales team creatively crafted software to generate approximately $115 million of fraudulent revenues without scrutiny of end-of-quarter deals.

Ultimately, the trial court ruled in favor of Preyton. Mammoth has appealed the ruling and the battle continues. At no point has Mammoth denied that fraud occurred.

LESSONS LEARNED

The significant level of revenue misstatement that occurred was attributable to a group of individuals who had the ability to circumvent accounting controls and policies. It is clear that the most stringent controls can be overridden if collusion exists. The atmosphere within Mammoth set the tone for this massive overstatement of revenue and income.

While certain internal controls were circumvented, others should have been in place to highlight:

- The significant increase in sales resulting from the end-of-quarter deals
- The buildup of sold product stored by Mammoth in its warehouses, supposedly for Preyton
- The issuance of credits and other offsets to sales
- The significant increase in Preyton's vendor loan balances
- The unusual nature of the transactions between Mammoth and Preyton

The bankruptcy trial judge offered a unique perspective. In the decision he stated:

> At its essence, this case is simply a tale of two companies—one large, one small—which entered into what each expected to be a mutually beneficial relationship to build a wireless communications network and deliver services to customers via that network. It became apparent as the evidence unfolded that what began as a strategic partnership to benefit both parties quickly degenerated into a relationship in which the much larger company bullied and threatened the smaller into taking actions that were designed to benefit the larger at the expense of the smaller. Along the way some executives of each company demonstrated their incompetence and arrogance, and in some instances, now find themselves targets of criminal investigations.

An important lesson to remember is that fraudulent documentation may be difficult to discover and hard to understand, but when it is evaluated in a systematic manner, the scheme can be uncovered. Such investigations are time consuming and require the utmost level of concentration and collaboration between team members.

RECOMMENDATIONS TO PREVENT FUTURE OCCURRENCES

Set the Tone at the Top and Develop Company Ethics

Ethical conduct must be set from the top down. Oversight and enforcement of a written code of ethics must be performed by company personnel who maintain operational independence not tied to financial performance. This group should report directly to the audit committee of the outside board of directors. Controls that prohibit and monitor apparent conflicts of interest in sales relationships with customers and suppliers must be put in place.

Encourage Anonymous Tips

In many instances of fraud, an anonymous tip has led to the initial discovery. While many times allegations are without merit, the fact remains that the method of detection in this case was from an employee and in an anonymous form. Tips are known to be the single largest source available for the detection of fraud; as such, they must be encouraged and embraced by management in order for corporate cultures to evolve properly. Over time, this deterrent effect can lead to prevention.

Paul Pocalyko, CFE, CPA, is a principal in the Forensic and Litigation Services Practice of Parente Randolph. He has provided a variety of financial, consulting, and accounting services to attorneys, insurance companies, governmental agencies, and corporations since 1982. Mr. Pocalyko has a bachelor of science degree and a master's degree in corporate finance from Lehigh University.

Charles N. Persing, CFE, CPA, CVA, CIRA, is the senior manager of Parente Randolph's Forensic and Litigation Services Group, in Philadelphia, Pennsylvania. His firm provides fraud examination, consulting, and expert witness services. Mr. Persing is a Drexel University graduate and has over 20 years of private industry experience, including financial, corporate development, and five years of experience in valuation, bankruptcy, and litigation services.

CHAPTER 55

Double Damage

MATTHIAS K. KOPETZKY

All his life, Herbert Kearns had been a salesman. At the tender age of five, he sold juice and snail shells to neighbors, proving his talent for deal-making early on. At every step along the job ladder, he excelled. However, he liked to live above his means, and this habit led to growing need for money and seemingly permanent debt.

His future partner, Simon Leary, was a quite different character. More introverted and a bit shy, he met Herbert when they both worked at CCC Computer Corp. in Vienna, Austria. Simon managed the assembling and tech support departments, and Herbert was a star marketer. Unlike Herbert, Simon was a family guy interested in good pay to support a comfortable—but not extravagant—lifestyle. He did not like to work overtime, and you would rarely find his car in the parking lot after five o'clock.

But Simon was very good at team building, and he managed a well-motivated department of almost 50 people. His style was calm but strict, and his staff valued his broad knowledge of computers and his ability to solve a myriad of problems. Even when the team was under stress to produce a big order, Simon acted without a hasty word and kept everyone on track.

With this attitude, he had become the invaluable backup for the stormy salesmen like Herbert, who often promised more than the company could deliver. Herbert was willing to do almost anything to land new customers. He realized very early the importance of a character like Simon in the management team of an aggressively growing computer hardware reseller.

After several years with CCC, Herbert, frustrated about a neglected salary increase, decided to start his own venture. He believed he had found his ideal partner in Simon, the team builder and back-office organizer. They started by working out of a small shop with only four employees near downtown Vienna. Herbert's business plan for the new company, Gamma Computer, Inc., was to lure away customers of CCC, and win new large accounts.

During his tenure at the old company, Herbert had learned how to deal with governmental agencies and organizations. Their needs and requirements are often quite different from those of private sector companies. Winning a contract with one of these entities often meant that you would need to move huge quantities of computer hardware in one deal—and quantity is always an issue in the computer-assembly business. The more units you can assemble and the more parts you are able to order, the better the profit margin.

Herbert knew that his timing was right. Virtual no-names like Gamma were now being allowed to bid on large government contracts. The tightening budgets in the public sector for governments to look beyond big companies like IBM and Siemens to see if they could procure what they needed at a lower cost from newcomers.

From the very beginning Gamma showed an ambitious and steep path of growth, which made it an attractive customer to the Second Savings Bank, one of the biggest financial institutions in the country. Second Savings backed Gamma by prefinancing its growing accounts receivable. It was a moderate risk. More than 95% of Gamma Computer's business was with national and local government entities, and its customer list included the departments of defense, agriculture, science, and education, and even the office of the prime minister. For Second Savings, this meant almost 100% secure accounts receivable, which the bank took in as collateral for the growing working capital needs of the company. The public sector was not famous for paying either fast or on time, but one could expect that every outstanding payment would come in sooner or later. And so it was at Gamma Computer, which showed a very low rate of write-offs within its accounts receivable during these years.

The rise of Gamma happened during one of the longest and most sustained bull market phases the stock markets ever saw. The 1990s were a gold rush time for investors all over the world, and stock indices seemed to grow without limits. It was the dawning of the Internet, and nearly every business involved with computers and software was making money. It was also the time when terms like "growth" or "cash-burn rate" seemed to turn market valuations upside-down. To be able to fulfill expectations in growth, more companies started to play the mergers and acquisition game. Gamma Computer, with sales upward of $100 million, soon came into focus as a takeover target. For Herbert Kearns, this was ultimate dream—to sell his company during a merger deal and start a new life as a wealthy man who could afford to stop working at the age of 45.

It didn't take long before firms were approaching him. Herbert had several meetings with a large investment group in Amsterdam. Gamma had just hit record high sales, and within a few short months, 100% of its stock was purchased by the Netherlands Holding Company, itself a rising star in booming Amsterdam.

To keep the party rolling, the former owners, Herbert and Simon, had to stay on for another three years. The price of the shares they sold to the Netherlands Holding Company was tied to certain success criteria, such as sales and recoverability of accounts receivable. Therefore, Herbert and Simon were able to cash in only one-third of the total price for Gamma Computer and had to "earn" the rest through another three successful years of business.

That's Odd

A few weeks after the sale, Simon turned in his resignation, citing "family reasons." This was quite astonishing—he left behind two-thirds of the sales price of the company, since he failed to remain the three years as required. At Second Savings Bank, the outstanding credit line of Gamma Computer had surpassed its limits, which brought up some "difficulties" for the company's account representative. Gamma should have been moved to the Large Commercial Accounts Section, a special department within the bank in which all big accounts are pooled. But this move would have been a significant change for Gamma and its longtime account representative, Jim Muller. Transferring the business would mean that Jim would have to pass it on to someone else. Both Gamma and Jim decided that this was not a desired outcome so—in violation of bank rules—Gamma remained within the regional branch office.

Only weeks after the sale of the shares to the Netherlands Holding Company, Jim received a strange call. A manager of the leasing branch of a well-known bank competitor informed him that it was buying all the receivables of Gamma Computer and that it would pay the outstanding credit to Gamma since Second Savings would no longer be holding the receivables as collateral. But the leasing bank also asked for a guarantee that it could sell back the receivables to Gamma at any time and that Second Savings would finance the sale. Since the overall risk picture for the bank didn't change, Jim was agreeable, but thought the transaction very odd. When Jim asked Herbert about the reason for this somewhat strange arrangement, he was told that the holding company asked for the move. Herbert added that he did not understand it either, but since Netherlands Holding Company was the new boss, he did not ask questions.

The sale of the receivables was finished by March 15, only two weeks before Gamma's end of the fiscal year on March 31. Eight weeks later, Gamma Computer bought back the entire group of receivables, which were again pledged to Second Savings, and the bank guarantee was rescinded. So within three months, the situation looked the same as before: Second Savings Bank had outstanding credit backed with receivables of Gamma Computer. The reason for this convoluted transaction would be become clear later.

Here Today, Gone Tomorrow

In October of that same year, Gamma Computer, Inc. declared bankruptcy because it could not pay its invoices on time, which in Austria is a cause for bankruptcy. One of the main reasons for the sale to the holding company was Netherlands Holding Company's insatiable need for additional revenues to show on its consolidated balance sheets. Herbert argued convincingly that Gamma's steep growth would continue if only it had more financing. But the increased sales didn't materialize, and the company was deeply in debt.

The sudden death of Gamma Computer was a shock for Second Savings Bank. It was totally unaware of the deep financial troubles of its customer—or so the bank said. But the bank was in a relatively comfortable position because it owned all the receivables as a backing for the credit line. And those receivables seemed to be almost as safe as real money because they were owed by slow but steady-paying government agencies and departments. Second Savings thought that it would be only a matter of time before the outstanding credit would be reimbursed. It was wrong.

Soon Second Savings became worried and decided to contact each debtor and ask for direct confirmation of the outstanding balances. The responses were devastating. The bank learned that in every instance, either the receivable never existed or the amount had been paid months—or even years—ago. This was astonishing because the policy at Second Savings stated that only receivables less than 180 days old could be accepted for collateral. At this point, Second Savings decided to hand over the case to the public prosecutor's office, which engaged our forensic accounting firm to check the allegations against Gamma and its management team—primarily Herbert Kearns.

Federal police seized a large amount of company records and documents, a load of almost 5,000 three-ring binders, computers, hard disks, and other data. The main focus was the allegation of the Second Savings Bank regarding the receivables, roughly $15 million, which it had reason to believe were fraudulent. So my team and I started with the receivables first and analyzed how they had been created within Gamma's accounting system. Strangely, we found duplicate databases with very different data in each. Herbert cooperatively explained to us that the company had two accounting systems for two lines of business it engaged in: assembling services and direct sales. This fact, although strange, would not have been a problem if the two systems showed the correct combined amounts. But we found the same receivables in both. We also found many more databases, which looked like backup or trial copies. Herbert explained this was due to some technical issues they had with the integration of the accounting system of Gamma into the systems of the Netherlands Holding Company.

Next, we found accounts receivable lists with the same date, but different totals—very different. Herbert told the investigators that they had real problems trying to show the sale of the receivables to the leasing company within the accounting system. He claimed that this was also why alternate versions of the accounting data could be found on Gamma's computers. Even harder, he said, was getting the receivables back into the system when the leasing company sold them back to Gamma a few months later.

We took the information and imported it into our data analysis software. The same receivables could be found in different "versions" with different dates of origin and different dollar amounts. It seemed that at least some of the receivables had been made to look "younger" by changing their dates. Obviously, the 180-day bank rule could be met more easily if Gamma could simply make the receivables seem current. These listings were sent to the bank every month to prove that the outstanding credit was backed with enough new receivables.

This was hard evidence that Gamma may have defrauded the bank by giving it falsified data. When confronted, Herbert insisted that the changes were made with the full knowledge of the bank because it knew that sometimes the government took longer than

180 days to pay. He also said that the bank told them it was all right to change the dates so that the list would comply with the rule.

We decided that the only way we could be certain of the validity of the receivables list was to check every single one with the original customer. We started with the highest single amounts and descended. A lot of explanations were in order—for most government agencies and departments, it was strange to be asked if a certain receivable was valid and still open. Some respondents failed to cooperate, and pressure from the office of the prosecutor was necessary to convince them to hand over information. This reluctance seemed odd to us, but Gamma had built very close relationships with these entities, so there was a lot of sympathy for the company and its staff. Additionally, we found signs of possible corruption. Gamma Computer had won the vast majority of biddings in the last few years. However, the prosecutor wanted us to concentrate on the alleged bank fraud, afraid that the matter could become unmanageable if it grew into a full-fledged corruption case.

NOT THE RESULT THEY EXPECTED

Our investigators were able to check 75% of the total receivables listed, or about $11 million out of the $15 million total. We only found two single receivables totaling $2,000 that appeared *not* to have been falsified. This raised a question: How was it possible to defraud Second Savings in such a brute and total manner? The bank got new lists of accounts receivable every month, and we couldn't understand why no one ever suspected anything. The prosecutor charged Herbert Kearns and his management team with defrauding Second Savings by presenting falsified evidence to prove valid receivables. This caused the bank to give Gamma increasing credit and leave the borrowing limits open.

But where normal fraud stories usually end, this one took another bitter turn for the defrauded Second Savings Bank. I had been appointed as an expert witness by the chief judge and had to present my findings to the four-person tribunal during court proceedings. (Note: In Austria, unlike many jurisdictions, where experts are chosen by the parties involved, expert witnesses are appointed. Also, in Austria experts are allowed to question witnesses.)

The trial started with the testimony of the defendants—primarily Herbert, as the main figure. His argument was that Gamma Computer could not possibly have defrauded the bank because Second Savings had been aware of the situation for a long time.

"We had financial problems and the bank knew of them. But I think they had problems internally showing the risk of the outstanding loan amount, so they constantly asked us to deliver lists of open receivables to formally cover the credit volume," Herbert told the court. "We had moved all of them to another group which cashed in the receivables, and that unit was planning to pay back Gamma, but this required some time. The whole group stood on shaky ground."

Second Savings Bank, represented by one of the country's leading law firms, denied these accusations, but Herbert added another "piece of evidence."

"The bank knew that we had to juggle the receivables in and out of our accounting systems. The real cash flows had been way too low not to raise eyebrows. In fact, Second Savings actively helped us cover the whole mess with that factoring deal. If these receivables would have been on our books at fiscal year-end, it never would have passed even the simplest audit. But because we managed to sell the receivables to the leasing company just before fiscal year-end, they weren't even on the books, so the auditors couldn't check them."

Deception is one of the indispensable ingredients of fraud. The longer the court proceedings went on, the more doubts surfaced about the real role of the bank. The court ordered Second Savings to produce Jim Muller as a witness, as well as other employees.

The people from the Credit Department explained how they regularly audited the debtor at least once a year, which was required under the internal rules of Second Savings. But the questioning brought up a picture of incompetence and bad communications within the bank. I asked if they had all the published financial statements from Gamma Computer. As it turned out, they only had an incomplete set. The bank also used interim statements as final ones. The audited final statements were never checked.

The Credit Department could show some activity, but the Securities Department could not prove any auditing. I asked one witness to explain the day-to-day auditing of the receivable lists.

Witness: Earlier, we received the list from Gamma Computer on paper. I checked the total on the last page and sent the figure to credit monitoring.

Question: What does that mean ... you checked the total on the last page?

Witness: I looked to see if there was a total at all.

Question: But that is not an audit procedure.

Witness: But I needed the figure to pass it along to credit monitoring.

Question: How did you know that the total was calculated correctly?

Witness: I did not know. But I was sure, because it was a computer printout.

Question: Did you check if there were only receivables younger than 180 days on the list?

Witness: Yes, by spot tests.

Question: And what else did you do?

Witness: I put the lists into a three-ring binder.

Question: And?

Witness: And what? That was it.

Question: How did you get list by mail electronically?

Witness: I don't know who had the idea, but we wanted to get rid of the annoying paperwork. So we urged Gamma to send us the lists electronically.

Question: So then it was easier to conduct audit procedures more effectively?

Witness: What kind of audit procedures are you talking about? I stored them electronically from then on.

Question: So do you have the old lists still on your hard disks? Could we see them?

Witness: No, every time we got a new one, we deleted the old one so we always only had the most recent one on file.

Jim Muller, Gamma's account representative at the bank, admitted that he had daily telephone conversations with Herbert about the true company situation and which payments would be allowed by the bank.

Later, the court asked to see the reports of internal audit at the bank and ordered the bank's lawyer to bring them to trial next morning. Instead of the papers, the bank brought its chief internal auditor to explain why there were no reports.

This last witness was the trigger of a very unusual and surprising court ruling. It was becoming clear that there were false statements and damage to the bank. But in the end, the court was convinced that the bank was not deceived; it knew the true situation at least during the last years and did not take any steps to protect itself.

The court found the defendants not guilty of fraud.

Because of the now-visible deficits within the bank, the bankruptcy trustee sued Second Savings, claiming that the bank's negligence made it possible for Gamma to survive longer than it would have if Second Savings had been properly guarding outstanding credit with diligence. That case was settled out of court.

LESSONS LEARNED

Obviously, Second Savings Bank had extremely weak controls. Assuming it did not conspire with Herbert, it was harmed by the failure to check Gamma's collateral. The bank had accounts receivable from federal and state agencies and other entities from the public sector. This, in turn, caused it to be negligent in its controls because it assumed the debt would be paid.

The next lesson is an old one. If a transaction is too complex to be understood, something is probably wrong. This was the case with the sale of all of Gamma's receivables to the bank competitor only weeks before fiscal year-end. Additionally, the factoring bank informed Second Savings that it planned to "sell back" the whole bunch in two to three months. At this point, the bank should have smelled a rat. It was not a cheap deal, and the factoring bank made a lot of money out of this fairly risk-free short-term position.

Second Savings should have asked Gamma and its parent company in Amsterdam why this was necessary. If a deal does not make sense, a red flag should go up. In this case, it seemed that Gamma wanted to get those receivables off the books before year-end, hoping that the auditors would not bother to test accounts that did not appear on the financial statements. Even the simplest audit procedures would have brought to light that all the accounts were falsified.

Another red flag in this case was the fact that one of the two founders of the company, Simon Leary, quit his job only weeks after the sale of his shares to the Amsterdam investor. This was astonishing because two-thirds of the sales price was contingent on his staying with the management team for the next three years. By leaving his post, he left behind two-thirds of the "value" of his shares. He cited "family reasons" as the cause, but an investigation would have revealed that he had just started a new and similar venture, and once again, his partner was Herbert Kearns.

RECOMMENDATIONS TO PREVENT FUTURE OCCURRENCES

Establish Effective Auditing Procedures

One of the weakest departments in Second Savings Bank was the Collateral Auditing Department. Effective auditing starts with healthy skepticism. Auditors should not accept the truth of every piece of information they are given. They should look for irregularities.

Using the Collateral Auditing Department as an example, the bank should require its staff to perform these simple procedures and checks with regard to the accounts receivable lists:

- Check for changes in the layout (especially in comparison to recent lists).
- Verify that the list is complete and that there are no missing or omitted pages.
- Recalculate the totals and subtotals.
- Search for duplicates or omissions.
- Conduct a line-by-line comparison between current and previous lists looking for:
  - Same line item, different date;
  - Same amount, same date, different text; and
  - Same amount, same text, different customer.
- Conduct random confirmations of items with the client's customer.
- Cross-check with other accounting statements and information provided.
- Trace from invoices to line items.

Test and Review the Functionality of Controls

Controls need to be tested to ensure they work as planned. In the Second Savings case, a lot of lists and reports were just filed without attention. If reports are not being used, then they should be stopped and management should find out why. As with Second Savings, a company could face liability if it receives information but take no steps to review it.

Look for Anomalies or Deviances from Normal Procedure

Rules are necessary for effective and efficient collaboration among businesses and individuals. But they are also a constant target of open or hidden criticism from those who feel too restricted.

Although many people are tempted to break or bend the rules, deviation can mean danger and risk for the entity and its employees. Salespeople and account representatives often are tempted to ignore regulations to keep their customers happy. In this case, Second Savings wanted Gamma as its customer, but the bank kept the company at its own expense. Gamma's account was supposed to have been transferred to the large unit of the bank. Presumably, that division would have been better equipped to review and audit the receivables list.

This rule also serves another function. Most of the problems with bank customers on the company level surface when the representative is changed. Rules are effective only if they are followed. It is useless to institute a rule if nobody ensures that it is followed. Broken rules could be a red flag and should be investigated.

Matthias K. Kopetzky, PhD, CFE, CPA, CIA, is chief executive officer of Business Valuation GmbH, in Vienna, Austria. The firm provides advisory services as expert witnesses to courts in Austria, South Germany, and Liechtenstein. Mr. Kopetzky teaches at different universities and, with Joseph T. Wells, wrote the German version of the *Corporate Fraud Handbook*.

CHAPTER 56

How to Steal a Million Dollars Without Taking the Cash

RICHARD A. RILEY

U pon entering the accounting offices of Carlton Chemical, Inc., one is met with drab fluorescent lighting, a few small cubicles, and dim morale. What one would not find, however, is the presence of Mr. Seneca Staunton, former accounts receivable (AR) clerk. Seneca left the company after being accused of posting AR payments to customers' balances due instead of applying amounts paid to specific invoices.

He may have come from modest beginnings, but Seneca achieved relative success and the possibility of a career when he accepted a position as an accounts receivable clerk at Carlton Chemical. Although he had completed no formal college accounting courses, he had excelled at bookkeeping duties at a small local company prior to applying to Carlton. Proud of his accomplishments and looking forward to his new opportunity, Seneca embarked on his accounts receivable duties with commitment and enthusiasm. He was happily married for the second time, a "Brady Bunch" union that combined two families for a total of seven children. On evenings and weekends, the family worked at a small farm in a rural part of the county.

At Carlton Chemical, Seneca's responsibilities included accounts receivable collections, posting payments, resolution of customer service inquiries, maintenance of the accounts receivable subledger, and reporting to management about the status of collections. Alfred Rollins, the former AR clerk, had recently been promoted to assistant controller. It was his job to train Seneca in his duties and be available as a supervisor. This gave Seneca confidence and, knowing that the last person in his position earned a substantial promotion, was especially positive for him. The sky was the limit.

Patrick Dawley, one of the initial owners of Carlton Chemical, had started the company over 30 years ago. Originally the idea was to provide chemicals to local manufacturers and a few small-scale customers to be used as raw materials. The company followed a path of slight, steady growth, but after 17 years of business, interest in the endeavor had waned in most of the owners except Patrick. He continued to see opportunity, and as the only hands-on owner, he determined that it was time to take sole possession of the business.

Generally, the margins in the chemical business are small. However, what drives profits in this industry are margins by specific product type and efficient operations, such as accurate order taking, billing, and collections, and perceived customer service, including availability and reliability of chemical deliveries.

Patrick loved his company and was viewed as the problem solver. He seldom engaged the staff related to clerical issues, inventory procurement, customer delivery, or similar day-to-day activities. But when challenges arose, Patrick was at the center, trying to solve the controversy. He also oversaw policy decisions (including pricing, credit, commitment to customer satisfaction, etc.) and was involved whenever necessary. Under Patrick's leadership, the company grew to approximately $125 million in revenues with record-setting sales, just two years prior to the discovery of the fraud. Net income was relatively modest, ranging from $450,000 to $950,000 under optimal conditions.

FUDGING AND WHINING

As in many businesses, Carlton Chemical's annual financial statement audit puts a strain on the entire organization. And this strain seemed to fall disproportionately on Seneca. Not uncommonly, the auditors observed some consistent behavioral patterns with Seneca. He often whined about assisting the auditors and complained that he didn't have time to prepare their schedules and pull their backup data.

When the schedules and data finally were delivered to the audit senior, she became concerned about unusual reconciliation items between the AR detailed list of balances due and the general ledger, reconciling items without support. The audit senior shared her concerns with Carlton Chemical's controller, Max Fairchild, who spent a long, late evening examining AR records. The accounts receivable posting process had not been followed recently, and Seneca had fudged the AR reconciliation. Max concluded his evening by preparing a formal reprimand to present to Seneca for "not following policy and procedure," including improper posting of deposits and failure to clear invoices per the customer remittance.

Due to nervousness and the crisis du jour, Max did not confront Seneca until late afternoon the following day. Seneca admitted to the policy violation, seemed to deeply regret his shortcuts, and begged for a second chance. Then in concert with Max, the two developed a formal "plan of resolution," as is required on all personnel reprimand forms, which included:

- Immediate reconciliation of accounts receivable balances by customer
- Additional temporary help for Seneca
- Agreement that all future payments must be applied properly to invoices per customer remittance statements
- Agreement that an Accounting Department supervisor would audit the application of customer payments on a monthly basis

The following morning, Seneca's time card read that he clocked in at 7:02 a.m. and clocked out at 7:40 a.m. During that time, he had been observed cleaning out his desk and removing personal items. Later in the day, shocked at his absence, Max and Alfred launched a more detailed review of AR and started making collection inquiries. Initial calls to customer Accounts Payable Departments revealed that many invoices listed as 30 days or older had already been paid.

Where, then, had the money gone, and why were paid invoices still listed in the accounts receivable subledger?

HEADING THE WRONG WAY

The day the perpetrator disappeared was not a good day for Max. As he entered the company parking lot, he waved to Seneca, who was heading in the other direction. That was Max's first clue. Upon arrival in the accounting area, he asked the staff about Seneca, who had apparently spoken to no one. Evidence suggested, though, that he would not be back.

Max was incredibly loyal and smart. Overworked but dedicated, he knew his first responsibility was to speak to Patrick. While the conversation would be difficult, the boss was known to be even-keeled and benevolent. Only later would it be revealed that Max had discovered just the tip of the iceberg in his initial investigation.

Collection of accounts receivable is the lifeblood that supports Carlton Chemical, so Patrick immediately launched an investigation using a three-pronged approach:

1. He brought in Alexa Hoffwire, a management information systems specialist, initially to lead and coordinate all aspects of an internal investigation. Patrick needed to ensure that Max was not involved. To do this, he needed eyes outside of accounting. Alexa examined the AR balances and supporting documentation, electronically mining the subledger data to determine what had happened.

2. Patrick asked Max to develop an investigation plan related to the underlying paperwork. He also hired a local outside certified public accounting firm to examine the investigation plan to ensure that the process championed by both Alexa and Max would result in detailed AR balances that were collectible and supported by underlying documentation.

3. Patrick hired a private investigator, a former Internal Revenue Service criminal investigations agent, to contact, interview, and investigate Seneca.

It was no surprise when Alexa confirmed that Max did not appear to be involved. Alexa's initial investigation of a sample of customer accounts receivable balances suggested that most of the 500 AR amounts likely had problems.

Patrick and Max were flabbergasted. Invoices are posted to the AR system through sales orders and proof of delivery information, data generated and keyed outside of accounting;

thus, Seneca had no access to posting into the AR subledger. Further, Seneca had almost no access to cash; 95% of customer payments were made to the company's lockbox, and the remaining 5% were brought to the company by delivery personnel who picked up customer checks. These checks were processed, copied, and sent to the bank by Patrick's administrative assistant. Seneca did not interact with the administrative assistant or the drivers, nor did he have access to or complete monthly bank reconciliations that were prepared on a timely basis.

Due to the nature of the chemical raw materials industry, Carlton must balance inventories on a daily basis in order to satisfy Environmental Protection Agency requirements. Related to this process, the company monitors chemical shrinkage. No large discrepancies were ever observed. The results from daily reporting were confirmed during the annual financial statement audit where inventory was counted. No big inventory overages or underages were discovered during this process either.

Max's credit authority limit was $25,000, while his combined limit with the vice president (VP) of sales was up to $75,000. Beyond that amount, Patrick personally approved all credit. Accounts receivable balances, in total, fluctuated in the past few years but had not risen as disproportionately to sales as one might expect, given the circumstances.

Most important, every Monday morning, the company held a customer service meeting that included a review of all outstanding AR balances for each customer. When in the office, Patrick attended these meetings along with the VP of sales, Max, and Seneca. The company was religious about customer service and collections.

This still left everyone scratching their heads. Where had the money gone? And why were paid invoices still listed in the AR subledger? More fundamentally, in an internal control environment centered on quality customer service and AR collections, how could this have happened?

THE GOOD, THE BAD, THE UGLY

The results of the private investigator's (PI) work provided news, both good and bad. The PI aggressively interviewed Seneca at his modest home in the presence of his wife and completed a public records search. The PI indicated that Seneca did not appear to have stolen any money. He observed no lifestyle changes; Seneca did not appear to have any wads of cash; there was no evidence that the Stauntons were living beyond their means. Seneca stated that he was simply overwhelmed from the beginning and that he had made a lot of mistakes. He had planned to clean up the mess, but the problems just snowballed out of control. Even with this information, Alexa and Max determined that they would remain vigilant for missing cash.

The PI's findings were consistent with the interviews of personnel that I conducted as part of my work as a fraud examiner. No employees observed Seneca as having an extravagant lifestyle, living beyond his means, nor did anyone indicate that Seneca had any pressing financial difficulties.

Once the scope of the investigation broadened to the majority of Carlton Chemical's customers, Patrick hired additional temporary accountants from outside the company. The investigation process involved calling each customer and requesting that the customer send in a listing of all accounts payable activity related to Carlton Chemical for the last four years, starting the period just before Seneca was hired as the AR clerk. Optimally, customers were requested to provide these data in electronic text files. Armed with this data, Alexa wrote a series of data-processing programs to match data from the electronic customer files to Carlton's AR files.

Open items were numerous and of a wide variety. Most disturbingly, the analysis revealed large numbers of alleged customer payments that did not appear in the customer AR detail for that customer. Fortunately, the payments were traced to bank statements to ensure the money was deposited in company accounts. But what Alexa found was that the money had been posted to the AR details of other customers, a sort of shell game. Another common open item included unpaid invoices and unpaid partial invoices older than 15 days. These open items were manually investigated by Max and the temporary accountants. Once the clean balance of AR was obtained, all remaining invoices were written off. These write-offs were manually tracked by customer in an Excel spreadsheet.

Some of the anomalies included:

- There was no apparent follow-up with customers regarding unpaid invoices.

  Some customers place the burden on Carlton Chemical to provide accurate invoices and supporting documentation before making payment. In order to process a payment, most customers require a valid purchase order, proof of delivery, and an accurate invoice. The absence of any of these three documents can delay payment. Seneca was supposed to contact customers about unpaid invoices and, where necessary, fax them the appropriate documentation. This process was not followed.

- Deposits from one customer were posted to another.

  In an effort to hide the fact that older invoices were unpaid, Seneca took new payments and posted them to old invoices, regardless of the source of the check. This created massive problems for reconciling AR balances and required extensive cooperation from Carlton Chemical's clientele. In that regard, some customers failed to acknowledge requests for information. However, no missing cash was discovered for those who provided documentation for payments we had not initially credited.

- There were payments to "balances" instead of invoices and payments applied to the oldest open invoices instead of those listed on the check remittance.

  To hide this activity, approximately two and a half years before he quit the company, Seneca stopped mailing monthly statements to customers. This anomaly was not noticed by Accounting Department leadership but was noted by customers during the reconciliation process.

- In a few instances, credit memos were posted to write off unpaid invoices.

  Max and Patrick must approve all AR write-offs. In a few cases, Seneca posted write-offs to AR invoices, but not enough to draw attention to him or for large dollar amounts.

- There was no apparent follow-up when customers claimed inappropriate discounts.

  Due to already thin margins, Carlton Chemical generally did not offer discounts for timely payment, such as "2/10 net 30." However, in some cases deals were negotiated with special clients. Some of those customers took discounts no matter when payment was made and put the onus on Carlton Chemical to follow up for collection. Evidence from the AR system indicated that Seneca simply reduced the invoice amount for the discounts taken that were outside the system time limits.

As part of my investigation, I formally reviewed approximately 45 customer payment remittance statements where the average customer payment might contain as many as 40 or more invoices. My investigation revealed that virtually every remittance had some payments applied to the wrong invoices when compared to the AR detail. They also contained inappropriate discounts. In at least two cases, the entire payment was not posted to the customer under examination.

The results of the investigation suggest that Seneca did not follow up with customers regarding missing or unpaid invoices. Carlton Chemical clients require an invoice, reconciliation to their own purchase order, and a signed delivery ticket before they are willing to make payment. Customers often place the burden of proof on Carlton Chemical to have accurate bills and provide the necessary supporting documentation. Further, clients are notorious for taking unearned discounts. Providing them with supporting documentation and following up on inappropriate discounts is time consuming. Seneca had neglected both of these activities to the detriment of the company. When faced with proof of unpaid invoices, some customers paid amounts owed. Several became upset about these debts, which sometimes went back several years, but Carlton Chemical only lost a handful of small customers during the multimonth clean-up process.

Most disconcerting is the fact that Seneca was taking deposits from one customer and posting those payments to other customers. Generally, he used payments from large customers to mask unpaid invoices from smaller customers. This issue created problems of massive proportion during the reconciliation process.

Based on the investigation, Patrick, Max, and I concluded that no cash was missing. The most compelling pieces of evidence included:

- Seneca had no access to the general ledger system, bank statements, or bank reconciliations.

- Generally, Seneca had no access to cash. Company representatives concluded that collusion would have been necessary for him actually to steal cash, and no collusive relationships were observed.

- Because supervision appears to have been minimal, it may have been possible for Seneca to credit memo away AR balances, but the evidence did not support this contention.

- During the investigation, no customers indicated that payments had been made but the payment had not been posted in a bank account.

Seneca had begun to cook the books within months of taking on the accounts receivable duties. Like most frauds, once on the slippery slope, it snowballed.

While these findings were interesting, questions remained. How much money was lost and how had Seneca pulled it off?

WHO'S BEEN MINDING THE STORE?

There is no doubt that lack of supervision provided an environment that allowed Seneca to operate unimpeded. Nevertheless, every Monday morning, the accounts receivable subledger was reviewed in detail by the VP of sales, Max, and, most weeks, Patrick himself. In this control environment, how did AR balances not balloon and the AR aging not reveal unpaid old invoices?

The answer to that question is relatively simple. Seneca was a quiet and shy person. He was much more comfortable working with the company's books and records than spending time on the phone contacting customers. Thus, instead of tracking down unpaid invoices, he spent time using the accounts receivable system's debit and credit memos. Every Friday afternoon, in preparation for Monday's customer service meeting, Seneca would write off all of the old unpaid invoices. It was this cleaned-up version of the AR subledger that he presented to and reviewed with Carlton Chemical leadership.

Then, on Monday afternoon, Seneca spent his time reversing all of the credit memos with debit memos. A review of credit/debit memos report provided by Carlton Chemical revealed:

	Year 1	Year 2	Year 3	Year 4*
Total number of debit/credit memos	285	600	1,000	150
Debit memos dollars related to specific invoices	$4,000	$50,000	$65,000	$4,000
Credit memo write-off dollars related to specific invoices	$9,000	$90,000	$75,000	$35,000
Number of offsetting credit and debit memos (to same company for the same amount)	100	250	330	20

* 2 months only

This evidence was compelling. The fact that Seneca put dollars back in the accounts receivable system after the customer service meeting rather than posting credit memos and leaving them off the system, coupled with no proof of missing money, strongly suggested that he was not stealing money. The evidence indicated that the problem was isolated to manipulation of data, which resulted in the destruction of the integrity of the electronic records in the accounts receivable subledger.

The investigation revealed no confirmation of physical destruction of supporting documentation. Some missing documents were observed, but no pattern emerged, and the number of those missing appeared to be no more frequent than in a normal filing system.

The initial individual customer reconciliation process took almost months and revealed a staggering $2 million in unexpected, unpaid, older accounts receivable balances. Max devoted his life to resolving this problem for Patrick. It consumed his every waking hour, including evenings and weekends. It haunted his dreams at night.

One of the hallmarks of Carlton Chemical is its devotion to quality customer service. This commitment paid handsome dividends during this difficult time. First, most customers cooperated and provided the company with the electronic and hardcopy records required to reconstruct the accounts receivable books and records. This data filled a "war room" where the primary investigation was completed. Second, when faced with unpaid but legitimate invoices, many customers made payment for past due amounts.

However, after another two months of dedicated work, Max still had $1.4 million of unreconcilable and uncollected balances. Without being able to demonstrate proof of delivery, a bona fide invoice and purchase order, and, most important, proof of non-payment, it was impossible for Carlton Chemical to approach its customers. Essentially, the AR write-off Excel summary sheet included upward adjustments for some customers and downward adjustments for others with the net being $1.4 million in downward adjustments:

Large customer write-offs	$2,000,000
Small customers balance increases	(600,000)
Net accounts receivable write-offs	$1,400,000

The company reviewed 100% of discounts taken and estimated that $700,000 of the large customer write-offs were due to inappropriately taken discounts. But a long period of time had passed and the company was worried about losing customers, so it chose not to pursue collection of unpaid discounts. After six months of round-the-clock work, the company had achieved its goal of having detailed accounts receivable balances that were collectible and supported by underlying documentation. However, the remaining unsubstantiated and uncollectible amounts totaled $1.4 million in losses.

In an interview with Seneca, I presented him with this amount. He was adamant that this number was far too large to have been caused by his mischief. His motivation: "I was just trying to keep my job." Seneca Staunton started as a $28,000-per-year accounts receivable clerk and received annual merit increases of approximately 5%. In his final full year with Carlton Chemical, he made a little more than $31,000. His effort to keep his job had cost his company $1.4 million in uncollectible AR losses. The reconstruction process cost another $125,000.

HALF A LOAF

Despite this gloom, all was not lost. Carlton Chemical had an all-risk property insurance policy that included a rider for accounts receivable. Thus, Carlton Chemical approached its insurance provider with a claim for property losses. There were several challenges here. First, the policy required that the insurance company be notified immediately upon discovery of losses. Carlton Chemical launched its investigation knowing about the insurance coverage but without reading the details of the policy. Second, although the insurance policy was all-risk, the rider included several situations where losses to AR were not covered; these included errors arising from bookkeeping, accounting, billing, or data entry. While Seneca's actions were not erroneous, they were deliberate; this still provided a "sticky wicket" for Carlton. Further, the insurance rider did not cover losses arising from discrepancies between legitimate invoice amounts due and receivable balances. Because the Excel spreadsheet essentially reflected unsupported discrepancies, coverage was at risk. Again, how the discrepancies arose provided a legitimate explanation for the losses, but the write-off amount could not be backed up with hard data. Finally, the insurance rider did not cover AR balances written off during the normal course of business, amounts traditionally characterized as bad debt. Since Carlton could not identify the source of the specific write-offs by company, it was difficult to prove that the amounts had not arisen in the normal course of business. In fact, the evidence suggested that some of Seneca's write-offs arose from customers that had historically been difficult collection problems.

All of these items muddied the waters for Patrick and Max. Ultimately, Carlton Chemical and the insurance company negotiated a settlement that reimbursed Carlton for the reconstruction costs of $125,000 and covered approximately $400,000 of the accounts receivable losses, leaving the company with a $1 million loss, which was greater than a year's profit in even the best of times.

LESSONS LEARNED

The most important lesson learned was that "the devil is in the details." Patrick and Carlton Chemical prided itself on being customer-service driven and tough on receivables collection. Each week Carlton leadership examined Seneca's work, but that was not enough. Details like internal audit testing of internal controls, ensuring that monthly customer statements are printed and mailed, and periodic examination of postings to the accounts receivable subledger could have prevented this fraud easily.

This fraud also reinforces the notion that once fraudsters start down the path, it is a choice that is almost impossible to reverse. Seneca threw in the towel when the situation was so desperate that reversing the damage took six months and a dedicated staff. In addition, as losses mounted, Seneca had no idea of their magnitude. Like many persons in this situation, he thought he could repair the problems himself and chose not to share them with supervisors and company leadership.

America is the land of opportunity, but success is where opportunity intersects with ability. Seneca may have had the aptitude and desire to be successful, but he did not possess the skills necessary to meet the demands of his position. Given his prior history, he had the potential to be a contributing employee instead of a one-man wrecking crew. But that potential was lost when training and supervision was not sufficient to assist him in reaching his potential.

Carlton Chemical is a company that any owner would be proud to own. Not only did it have an impeccable reputation as a service provider, the owner and leader was considered an outstanding corporate and community citizen. In addition, much of the management team had worked at the company for a long time, and they were proud of their work. The Personnel Department had an open door support policy for employees. Yet at least one employee felt he could go it alone. After Seneca Staunton's departure, Max Fairchild supervised his employees with a watchful eye. Max has dedicated much of his life to Carlton Chemical, but he learned the hard way a Russian proverb championed by Ronald Reagan: "Trust but verify."

RECOMMENDATIONS TO PREVENT FUTURE OCCURRENCES

Monitor Insurance Policies

Companies should monitor their insurance policies constantly to ensure that coverage is adequate. Carlton Chemical felt perfectly safe, given its accounts receivable rider. However, the policy had caveats and limitations that resulted in far less coverage than management realized.

Internal Controls

Internal controls must be in place and adequate. Seneca was not trying to steal money, and, generally, he was not trying to beat the system. He was simply a clerical employee trying to keep his job. He found a relatively simple way to deliver for management and deal with the fact that he was overwhelmed by his responsibilities. With closer supervision, his fraud would not have been successful.

Internal Audit Testing

Details like internal audit testing, ensuring that monthly customer statements are printed and mailed, and periodic examination of postings to the accounts receivable subledger could easily have prevented this fraud, and are advised as a preventive measure.

Solid Relationships with Stakeholders

The importance of solid relationships with the stakeholders, including customers and vendors, cannot be overemphasized. The dedication that Carlton Chemical had demonstrated to its customers during the past decades paid off. Without the customers' cooperation, the accounts receivable reconstruction would have been almost impossible and collection of old, unpaid amounts unimaginable.

Richard (Dick) A. Riley, CFE, CPA, is a Louis F. Tanner Distinguished Professor of Public Accounting at West Virginia University. In addition, he provides fraud examination, forensic accounting, consulting, and expert witness services. Dr. Riley is a graduate of the Wheeling Jesuit University, West Virginia University, and the University of Tennessee, where he received his PhD.

Other Fraud Schemes

CHAPTER 57

This Land Is Your Land, This Land Is My Land

ANDREW PAPPAS

Some guys just have that look about them—the darting, sloe-eyed leer; the gray grin without warmth or joy; cheap, ill-fitting clothes made of substances found nowhere in nature—that shouts *watch your wallet* to even the most naive mark and, to a more savvy target, is roughly as subtle as, to paraphrase Mark Twain, a peg-legged man having a spasm on a tin roof.

If Dennis Dixon had exhibited any of these or other telltale signs, perhaps this story would have had a different, happier ending. But Dennis not only lacked the look of a guy that a blind man could pick out of a police lineup, he looked more like someone who would help the blind man cross the street.

By all accounts, Dennis was a solid, soft-spoken guy whose generosity—his lunch companions had long ago quit trying to pick up the check—demeanor, and purity of speech contributed to his being liked and trusted by most everyone who knew him. In his early 40s, Dennis had just enough gray at the temples to radiate wisdom and maturity, but not so much as to dissuade the elderly ladies at church from wishing that their daughters had married him instead of their ne'er-do-well sons-in-law. The Dixon family's arrival at church each week looked like a scene from a Rockwell painting: Dennis and his wife, Debbie, in their modest Sunday best, hand in hand with their twin, auburn-haired, freckle-faced daughters in matching dresses. After church, the Dixons' five-year-old minivan was usually one of the last vehicles to leave the parking lot.

Few of Dennis's casual acquaintances knew for sure what he did for a living. College buddies remembered him earning a degree in management. He had a background in computer sales, and, judging by the way he dressed and the vehicle he drove, people who thought about it at all figured that he was reasonably successful, but certainly not enough to attract much attention or envy.

People closer to Dennis knew that, toward the end of his computer sales career, he got his real estate license. Not content with simply helping people buy and sell residences, he became a broker and began doing investment deals, putting together limited partnerships with relatives and some of his more well-to-do friends.

What most people in Dennis's world didn't know was that, in contrast to his modest public persona, the Dixons enjoyed a lifestyle open to only the uppermost tier of the local community. Their girls attended an exclusive private school that had an annual tuition higher than most people in town paid on their mortgage. And while Dennis "made do" with his aging minivan, Debbie drove a current-model Mercedes that they purchased during a trip to Europe and shipped to the United States.

And then there was their house—make that *houses*. Nestled in its own compound, out of sight in a wooded area, the Dixons' 6,400-square-foot principal residence cost more than $2 million, and a short time after buying it they had sunk at least that much more into renovations. For Dennis's real estate investors and their friends, an evening in the Dixons' media room was something not to be missed.

On long weekends, the Dixons would pile into one of Dennis's investors' airplanes for the two-hour flight to their second home overlooking Lake Tahoe. The "tree house," as the girls called it, was a sprawling three-level, 4,000-square-foot home surrounded on three sides by 15 acres of dense Ponderosa pines with unobstructed views of the lake and the mountain range beyond it. The $4 million that Dennis had paid for the house had seemed high at the time, but he was satisfied that with the proper "leveraging," he had more than tripled his money.

During the last several years, Dennis had assembled a number of real estate investment groups, in the form of limited partnerships, in which he served as general partner. Generally, his strategy was to buy potentially valuable land, hold it for the long term, and then sell when the appreciation would yield the desired return. Along the way, he had made a lot of money for himself and his grateful investors, who were almost always eager to pony up when he invited them to participate in the next good deal.

Two elections earlier, county voters had approved funding to expand the area's freeway system. By the time transportation planners unveiled the new routes, Dennis had already anticipated which parcels would be the hot properties and had cultivated relationships with the owners. He and a friend, "Monk" Mason, set their sights on one parcel in particular, a rural property that was adjacent to an anticipated freeway exit ramp, and bought it for $1.7 million with a cash down payment and a promissory note secured by a deed of trust.

They created a limited partnership, "Exit 41 L.P.," in which they were co-general partners. The 50 partnership interests sold quickly, for the most part to friends and relatives of the two men. The proceeds from the sale of the interests were properly used to repay the cash down payment to Monk and Dennis and to pay them roughly $100,000 for putting the deal together. At that time, the general partners made a nominal one-time cash contribution.

Pursuant to the partnership agreement, the limited partners made annual capital contributions, and the general partners made none. In order to provide a cash reserve, the total payments exceeded the amount required to make the annual payment on the land and to cover other partnership expenses. Since the partnership's strategy was not to develop the property but, rather, to hold it until a developer was willing to pay their price, they rented the land to farmers. The total rent was about the same as the management fee that the partnership paid to Monk and Dennis in their capacity as co-general partners.

SUM PROBLEMS

I am a certified public accountant (CPA) licensed to practice in the State of Arizona. I founded Pappas & Company, Ltd. over 25 years ago. Prior to that, I was with two international public accounting firms. I have extensive experience in auditing, fraud accounting, and the evaluation of complex business transactions.

One of my longtime clients, a construction company owner named Harmon Hilton, came into my office to discuss his individual income tax planning. Among the topics on his agenda were the tax ramifications of the pending sale of real estate by a partnership in which he and his wife, Helen, were limited partners. I remember thinking that the partnership was cleverly named: Exit 41 L.P.

The documentation that Harmon gave me included an e-mail from one of the general partners, Dennis Dixon. It described the amount per limited partnership unit that each limited partner was to receive upon the sale of the land.

I reviewed Harmon's documentation, and it didn't take long for red flags to start popping up. Multiplying the per-unit amount times the number of units that he and Helen owned produced a figure that seemed significantly lower than I thought it should have been. When I reached Harmon by phone that day and told him what I had discovered, he seemed reluctant to believe that his distribution was shorted since Dennis was Helen's brother, but he gave me the go-ahead to investigate further.

I gathered more information, including financial statements, cash flow statements, and correspondence that Dennis had provided to the Hiltons. I also reviewed the partnership agreement for direction regarding distribution of the sales proceeds. My investigation encountered a minor roadblock when Dennis refused to give Harmon a copy of the purchase contract because the sale had not yet closed, but he did provide the sales price per acre and the number of acres being sold, which allowed me to compute the gross sales price.

I consulted with a number of commercial real estate professionals who were experienced in sales of raw land for development in the area where the subject property was located, and I was able to determine what a reasonable real estate commission would be for this transaction. I also spoke with title companies regarding a range of closing costs. Finally, I asked Harmon to obtain from Dennis the total capital contributions by all partners since the inception of the partnership. Using the information from my client and other sources, I calculated the amount per unit that each of the limited partners should receive.

My calculation produced a sum that was more than 50% greater than the amount that Dennis had communicated to the Hiltons. Applying my calculations to all of the limited partners, the shortfall in proposed distributions was in excess of $1.5 million. I was confident that my original suspicions regarding my client's proposed distribution were correct, but I needed to explore further to determine the reason for the vast difference.

A BUM DEAL

Working with my associate, Denise Fritz, our investigation began by gathering more documents to help us paint an accurate picture of the situation. In addition to helping the Hiltons request from the Internal Revenue Service "certified court" copies of Exit 41 L. P.'s partnership tax returns, we also reviewed and analyzed the partnership's cash flow statements and financial statements and read all correspondence that Helen and Harmon had received from Monk and Dennis.

The detailed review confirmed our initial conclusion, that the amount of the Hiltons' distribution was substantially understated. While the financial information was relatively easy to obtain, our attempt to broaden the scope of the investigation hit a snag when Harmon asked Dennis for a copy of the contract for the pending sale. Dennis again replied that he would be unable to provide a copy until the sale had closed. Not wanting to spark a confrontation at this early stage, we did not insist that Dennis comply with the request. Rather, we asked Harmon to e-mail him to get the basics of the transaction: gross sale price, real estate commissions to be paid, closing costs, proposed distributions to repay capital contributions, and proposed distributions of the remaining cash. In his e-mail reply, Dennis reported a gross sales price of $4.7 million—that was $300,000 less than our calculation of $5 million.

Further, Dennis's proposed payments to the general partners and the limited partners did not comply with the distribution provisions in the partnership agreement. Per those provisions, the capital contributions were to be paid from the net sales proceeds *prior to* the distribution of the remaining cash. The distribution was to be an 80/20 split: 80% to the limited partners and 20% to the general partners. Dennis had applied the 80/20 split to the net sales price (less reserves for final expenses) and showed no line item for repayment of capital contributions. As a consequence, Dennis's method of distributions awarded him and Monk an extra $500,000.

From the information provided, we were able to perform a calculation that allowed us to re-create his result. We then helped Harmon draft an e-mail to Dennis that outlined our understanding of the assumptions used by him in his calculations. In his reply, Dennis wrote, "You nailed it."

Harmon again requested a copy of the purchase agreement, and Dennis still denied it, reiterating that the sale had not yet closed. In light of this information and Dennis's steadfast unwillingness to provide a copy of the purchase agreement, we recommended that the Hiltons engage an attorney.

In a letter to Dennis, the Hiltons' attorney, Gordon Goode, requested several documents: a copy of the purchase agreement, a list of limited partners who had made capital contributions and the amount of each, total real estate commissions to be paid and to whom, and an explanation of how the repayment of capital contributions factored into the distributions to the partners. Gordon's letter stated that Dennis's calculation of the proposed distributions was incorrect and not in compliance with the partnership agreement. He also suggested that Dennis hire an attorney.

A Hook from Hooker

Gordon soon received a letter from Dennis's attorney, Herb Hooker, stating that the general partners had asked him to handle the distribution of cash from the sale. Herb's letter included a copy of the much-awaited purchase agreement. We reviewed it, as did Gordon. In addition to calling for a $4.7 million gross sales price (6% lower than the $5 million price that we calculated), the purchase agreement, in an early paragraph, called for sales commissions to be paid to the general partners—3% to Monk and 3% to Dennis—despite the fact that the Exit 41 L.P. agreement prohibited the general partners from receiving compensation except as expressly provided, and the agreement did not provide for the general partners to receive a commission on the sale of the property.

At the end of the agreement was additional language indicating that a 6% commission was to be paid to a commercial real estate broker. It clearly provided for aggregate commission expenses of 12%— a total that both violated the partnership agreement and grossly exceeded the commission rate for transactions of this type.

In that letter and in subsequent correspondence to Gordon, Herb stated that the 12% real estate commission was reasonable and would be split equally between the buyer and the seller. He also provided the number of paid units, a listing of limited partners, and the capital contributions of each. In addition, Herb indicated that the proposed distribution had been corrected and that the applications of the 80/20 split would occur after repayment of capital contributions. Finally, he stated that he would instruct the title company not to close the sale prior to the closing date stated in the contract. Harmon told us that his total capital contributions were substantially greater than the amount indicated on the schedule provided by Dennis's attorney. He also explained that prior to investing in Exit 41 L.P., he had invested in another partnership with Monk and Dennis, where they also owned a parcel of undeveloped land. During an economic downturn, many of the investors defaulted on their required capital contributions, the partnership was in default on its debt, and it was going to lose the property. Monk and Dennis approached Harmon and the remaining partners with an opportunity to salvage their investment in the soon-to-be-defunct partnership by investing in Exit 41 L.P.

Monk and Dennis confided to Harmon and the others that Exit 41 L.P. was in a situation similar to the other partnership, but that their investment would save Exit 41 L.P. from losing its land. In order to induce him and others to invest in the deal, Monk and Dennis signed written agreements in which they promised, upon sale of Exit 41 L.P.'s land, to repay to Harmon and the prior partnership's other investors the amounts that they had contributed to the previous (now defunct) partnership.

Based on Harmon's information, we determined that the difference in the amount of capital contributions per his own records and of that provided by Dennis's attorney was the capital he had contributed to the defunct partnership. We met with Gordon to discuss Harmon's revelation and my findings regarding the contributions. We shared with him our opinion that Monk and Dennis did not intend to repay the capital that had been contributed to the defunct partnership.

After Gordon received from Herb schedules outlining the distribution of cash from the partnership, he asked us to analyze them to determine if the proposed distributions seemed proper. During our analysis, we discovered that the amount listed as "gross sales price" was actually gross proceeds less the 6% commission to be paid to the real estate broker. We also found that there was no money in the checking account. The distribution schedules did not provide for repayment of the capital contributions to the defunct partnership made by Harmon and the other partners. And finally, a portion of the amount reserved for preparation of the partnership's final tax returns was included in the amount to be distributed to the general partners.

As we analyzed the partnership tax returns, we noted that one partner, Nick Null, had not made capital contributions for four of the five years of the partnership's existence and, according to his Schedule K-1, he was treated as an expelled partner. The partnership agreement states that expelled partners are not entitled to any distributions in excess of their contributed capital. We further analyzed the schedules to determine the amount of proposed distribution to Nick and noted that he was to receive a distribution as if he were a current partner.

Correspondence between Gordon and Herb ultimately led Dennis to volunteer to give up his 3% real estate commission ($141,000), which reduced the total commissions to be paid from 12% to 9%. Dennis acknowledged that the zero balance in the partnership checking account was due to his personally withdrawing the remaining funds (approximately $41,000). Instead of depositing the funds back into the account, Dennis agreed to have his distribution reduced by $41,000. Nick, the partner who had not made all of his capital contributions, contributed $125,000 to the partnership prior to the sale closing and the distribution of the funds. Dennis then reported that, per his arrangement with Nick, he would make the capital contributions for him because Nick had loaned $51,000 to the partnership when it was short of cash. Dennis admitted that he did not make the payments because he did not have the funds at the time and then "forgot" that he had not made them. However, our analysis of the partnership's financial statements and tax returns showed no records of such a loan.

The joint efforts of Harmon, Gordon, and our firm resulted in Dennis's preparation of multiple revisions to the distribution schedules. The result was an increase of $1.4 million in proposed distributions to the limited partners and a corresponding decrease in the amount to be distributed to Monk and Dennis. However, not all the revisions that we requested were made, and we were still concerned that there were other improprieties of which we were not yet aware.

Dennis's attorney, Herb, refused to revise the distribution schedules to provide for repayment of the prior capital contributions of approximately $1,100,000. The impact of that at an 80/20 split meant that Dennis and Monk would receive an additional $220,000.

Dennis reportedly had informed Herb that he had no knowledge of any agreements promising repayment of the transferred capital. Gordon gave Herb a copy of Harmon's agreement with Dennis. When Herb presented the agreement to Dennis, he claimed not to recall signing the document and said that it must have been forged. Gordon proposed that he let Herb view the original of Harmon's agreement. Herb did not accept the offer but told Gordon that Dennis had changed his story and now admitted that he and Monk had signed the agreement. Despite that fact, Herb contended that it was not binding on Exit 41 L.P. as it was not in compliance with the partnership agreement.

Harmon sued Monk, Dennis, and Exit 41 L.P. for repayment of his $600,000 in transferred capital. During the discovery process, records were subpoenaed from the parties involved in the sale of the land. Included in the documents was correspondence from Dennis to the buyer of the Exit 41 L.P. property, instructing the buyer to pay directly to Dennis $141,000, which was 3% of the 6% commission that the buyer was supposedly paying to the real estate broker. We also found correspondence between Dennis and the broker confirming that they were to split the commission.

Harmon was represented in the suit by Gordon, who also subpoenaed bank records for all partnership accounts, including a line of credit that Dennis had opened in the partnership's name and was using personally, as well as an investment account that Dennis had opened in the name of the partnership.

We analyzed all information provided and re-created the accounting records as thoroughly as the quality of the documents available allowed. We discovered that, throughout the partnership's existence, Dennis had made large transfers of cash—calculated to be in excess of $1 million—from the partnership to himself and to various entities of his own, with sporadic repayments.

Our analysis of the investment account revealed that Dennis had invested $8,000 of partnership funds in technology company stock during the high-tech boom. He quickly doubled his investment, transferred $8,000 back to the partnership's checking account, and continued investing the profits personally. He pocketed over $28,000 through his misuse of partnership funds and the partnership investment account. We noted that the gains were reported only on Dennis's Schedule K-1.

According to our calculations, Dennis had failed to repay the partnership almost $100,000, including interest. We also noted checks, totaling $137,000 and paid from the trusts of two of Nick's children, that were deposited into the partnership checking account. The checks were signed by Dennis as trustee of the trusts. The partnership had no relationship to these entities.

A Good Day at Court

When we met with Harmon and Gordon to share the results of our investigation, Harmon expressed, in no uncertain terms, his desire to take legal action against Monk and Dennis to recover his rightful share of the excess funds that they had received. He also wanted to sue Nick to force a repayment of the full distribution that he had obtained from Exit 41 L.P.

despite the facts that he had made only 20% of the capital contributions required of him and he had been treated for tax purposes as an expelled partner.

In laying out his client's legal options, Gordon advised Harmon that he could file a "derivative lawsuit" on behalf of Exit 41 L.P. Generally speaking, in a derivative lawsuit, a partner, member, or shareholder (depending on the type of entity) initiates a legal action on behalf of, and ostensibly for the benefit of, the entity (in this case, Exit 41 L.P.). In a derivative lawsuit pertaining to this case, the limited partner (Harmon) would allege that the partnership is unwilling to pursue itself. This very frequently involves a claim brought by the limited partner in the name of the partnership against the general partners (Monk and Dennis) for alleged breach of fiduciary duty.

Gordon advised Harmon that, in a derivative lawsuit aimed at Monk and Dennis, the remedies that he could seek on behalf of the partnership should include the return of:

- The $141,000 real estate commission that Dennis received directly from the buyer of the property

- The portion of the $1,400 reserved for preparation of the partnership's tax returns that were included in distributions paid to Monk and Dennis

- The $28,000 gain on the sale of stock that Dennis had purchased through the personal use of partnership funds

- The $100,000 that, during the life of the partnership, Dennis had taken from the partnership and failed to repay

Harmon's lawsuit against Dennis and Monk to recover his capital contributions continued separately from the derivative suit. This was a direct claim by Harmon, and he therefore was not required to pursue the claim in a derivative capacity.

As for Nick, Gordon advised Harmon that the partnership could expand the scope of its derivative lawsuit to go after Nick in an attempt to recover the excess $150,000 that the partnership had improperly paid to him as if he were a paid-in-full partner. Nick's position was that he was in fact a partner and was actually entitled to more than he had received.

As one might assume, Harmon quickly decided to move forward with the derivative lawsuit as Gordon had outlined for him.

Because of the likelihood that the legal interests of Dennis and Monk might be in conflict with each other, Herb informed the two men that he could not represent both of them in the lawsuit. Herb continued to represent Monk, while Dennis went with a new attorney, Ted Fink.

Monk, Herb, Dennis, Ted, Nick, and his attorney met in an attempt to reach a settlement on the issues that Harmon raised in his derivative claim. They hatched this following plan for painlessly settling the lawsuit: Dennis would pay $35,000 to the partnership, and Nick would receive $10,000 from the partnership and release the partnership from all future claims by him. The defendants submitted their proposed settlement agreement, with its net $25,000 restitution, to the limited partners for their approval.

Predictably, Harmon viewed the settlement offer—which would allow Dennis effectively to steal almost $300,000 and to repay a relatively paltry $35,000—as an insult, and he expected his fellow limited partners to be of the same opinion. To Harmon's dismay, however, a majority of the partners—more than 60% of them—voted in favor of the settlement. Most of the "yes" votes came from partners who were close friends or relatives of Monk, Dennis, or Nick. They appeared either to believe Dennis's position that these claims were unfounded or were just eager to receive the balance of their distributions.

Because the limited partners' vote was not sufficient to accept the settlement and negate Harmon's derivative claim, the defendants were required to submit the settlement in court. Despite the disparity between what the defendants owed the limited partners and what they were offering to pay, the trial judge approved the settlement proposal that the limited partners, by their majority vote, had accepted.

Harmon was outraged by the judge's decision to grant the settlement of the derivative claims, especially since there was overwhelming evidence supporting the claims against Dennis. Far from being deterred by the judge's decision, though, he became even more committed to his fight for his transferred capital from the prior, defunct partnership.

Regarding Harmon's lawsuit to recover his capital contributions, as is common in such cases, the judge ordered the parties to mediate their dispute. Mediation, which is a form of alternative dispute resolution, is an informal process in which a trained mediator tries to help the parties reach a negotiated resolution of their dispute. The mediator does not decide who is right or wrong and has no authority to impose a settlement on the parties. The attempted mediation failed after Dennis and Monk offered Harmon $75,000 and refused to go higher, despite the fact that Harmon's capital contribution totaled $600,000.

At trial, Gordon's examination of Dennis and Monk produced a litany of inconsistent, contradictory, and conflicting testimonies that exposed the general partners' dishonest practices and generated jury sympathy for Harmon's position. At one of the trial's most dramatic moments, jurors reacted audibly when Dennis, in the face of document after document contradicting his claim that they made the agreement only with Harmon, finally admitted that he promised repayment of the transferred capital to *all* of the investors from the prior defunct partnership who invested in Exit 41 L.P.—this after adamantly denying that he had an agreement with *any* partners other than Harmon.

Notwithstanding the financial and contractual complexities of the dispute and the evidence and testimony presented by the two sides, the jury deliberated for just one hour before arriving at a verdict. In the end, Dennis and Monk were ordered to repay to Harmon his $600,000 capital contribution and to pay him $90,000 in interest. Further, the court ordered the general partners to reimburse Harmon $150,000 for attorney fees that he incurred in his legal battle.

The general partners had attempted to misappropriate over $2.2 million with almost no one noticing. The efforts of Harmon, Gordon, and our firm resulted in recovering almost $1.8 million from the general partners for the limited partners, plus interest and attorney fees.

LESSONS LEARNED

More accurately, I *relearned* a few lessons in the saga of Harmon, Dennis, et al.

First, good guys don't always win. Harmon Hilton is as solid as they come, but he suffers from a trait that is common among honest men: They too often assume that the people with whom they are dealing are as honest as they are.

Second, when money is involved, no friendship (or, in this case, blood relationship) is sacred. Dennis and Monk were able to profit from their venture not because they valued their relationships with their investors, but because they correctly anticipated that their investors would be forgiving of the wrongs done to them.

Third, one should never assume that a transaction is legally binding until one has sought and received informed advice from a professional who has no stake in the deal. An opportunity that "can't wait" for the due diligence process is usually an opportunity to avoid.

Fourth, people are not always what they appear. The investors who thought they knew Dennis Dixon, from casual acquaintances to close friends, probably had little knowledge of the house of cards on which Dennis's business deals rested or of the manner in which he went about constructing it.

Finally, even if you catch the thief, you are not guaranteed to have your money returned. Therefore, it is better to have never been cheated than to catch the perpetrator.

RECOMMENDATIONS TO PREVENT FUTURE OCCURRENCES

Investors in limited partnerships and other business entities may be able to avoid the fate of the fainthearted limited partners in Exit 41 L.P. by exercising a higher degree of due diligence on the front end and ongoing scrutiny as the business progresses.

Trust, but Verify

Even when placing their money with close friends, acquaintances, or relatives, investors owe it to themselves to do their homework. Investors should look past the facade and the promise of greater wealth, asking for business and personal references on the general partners and checking them all. They should also carefully scrutinize the periodic financial information they receive and seek independent review and verification. In this case, Harmon should have asked me, as his CPA, to look at the periodic financial information he received.

Know Your Business Partner(s)

Investors should develop a real knowledge of the people with whom they're placing their money: their level of sophistication, their relationship to one another and with other investors, their financial strength, their risk tolerance, and so on.

Enforce Terms of Partnership Agreement

Investors should seek to enforce the terms of the partnership agreement. In this case, the agreement required annual audited financial statements, but the general partners produced only *compiled* financial statements. The partners should have demanded audited statements, not reviewed or compiled ones. In an audited financial statement report, the CPA expresses his or her opinion as to whether the financial statements, taken as a whole, are fairly presented. This opinion is given after extensive tests of the accounting records are made. The tests include confirmation with outside parties, analytical procedures, inquiry of client personnel, and a detailed study of the accounting records. In a reviewed financial statement report, the CPA expresses limited assurance that there are no material adjustments that should be made to the statements in order for them to be in conformity with accepted standards. In order for the CPA to express this limited assurance, he or she must be satisfied as to the reasonableness of the statements through inquiry and analytical procedures. In a compiled financial statement report, the CPA expresses no assurance on the correctness of the financial statements. The CPA only presents, in the form of financial statements, information that is the representation of the management of the business entity. To do this, he or she obtains the information from management and assembles it. Reviews and compilations are usually allowed only when the potential risk to outside parties is relatively low.

Use Legal Counsel

Investors should use their own legal counsel to review transactions and draft legal documents. They should not rely on the general partners—especially when the general partners may be the ultimate cause of any problems that arise.

Andrew Pappas, CPA, is the founder of Pappas & Company, and has over 30 years of experience as a CPA and business advisor in Arizona, with an emphasis on forensic accounting and litigation support. His firm offers business owners and litigators extensive experience in fraud accounting and the evaluation of complex business transactions.

CHAPTER 58

Paradise Lost

PIERRE E. LAUTISCHER

A true Caribbean paradise, the Cayman Islands boast palm trees, sand, surf, and no taxes! That's right—no income taxes, no corporate taxes, and no property taxes of any kind. As a business owner, you keep every dollar you earn, and there are no government financial reporting requirements. However, employers must comply with two mandatory benefit programs: pension plan participation and health care insurance. Both require payments to approved plans funded by deductions from the employees' salaries and contributions from the employer.

The National Pensions Law was created under the criminal statutes about 10 years ago. All funds are administered in the private sector by financial institutions. Every business must enroll in one of the six plans available. The money is deducted from employees' paychecks, matched by the employer, and must be paid by the fifteenth of the following month. The National Pensions Office is the government arm that oversees and ensures compliance by both the pension plan providers and the private employers.

Most employers abided, as this was the law—and there were steep penalties for failure to comply. But one businessman did not.

Bob Walker was smart. He was born in the United States and had moved to the Cayman Islands in his youth. He had been married a few times and had a son who lived with one of his ex-wives in Costa Rica. Bob had had numerous jobs, including a brief stint as a police officer. He liked to drink, party, and enjoyed the fast lane.

As the owner and operator of Caycar Printing Ltd., Bob had built it into a successful company and earned a respectable market share of the printing business in the country. He had some 15 employees, including salespersons, printers, office workers, and maintenance personnel. The operation was quite profitable—until about six years ago.

If one could pinpoint the start of Bob's problems, it would have to be when he purchased Sentinel Doors and Installations Ltd. The company sold and installed pedestrian, overhead, garage, heavy-duty commercial doors and an array of accessories. Bob knew nothing about the door business but felt he could quickly learn it as the owner. He considered himself very shrewd and once said, "You show me how to do doors and I will show you how to make money."

Bob was in his late 30s when he bought Sentinel Doors and was going through a serious midlife crisis. Most fraudsters live well above their means. Bob was no exception—he surrounded himself with new cars, boats, and planes and traveled extensively. He enjoyed the facade of being extremely wealthy. But at the moment, his two companies were experiencing cash flow problems; workers' earnings were progressively delayed and what had started as weekly pay went to biweekly, to monthly, and then to installments on the monthly paychecks. And despite the fact that he had been deducting pension contributions from the employees' salaries, he had not made payments to the pension plans for several years for either of his companies.

However, there was no reason for the cash flow problems. Business was extremely brisk, and there was more work than they could handle. And pricing for the jobs included a very large percentage allotted to profit. Apparently Bob had been pulling out a tremendous amount of money from both of his businesses to support his lavish lifestyle—an estimated $6,000 every two weeks from each of the companies. Between the two businesses, 50 employees had been financing the yacht, the airplanes, the new cars, and the high living. Representatives of the National Pensions Office had known of the situation for at least four years. The superintendent had had numerous meetings with Bob at which he'd agreed to begin making payments for current and past due contributions. But Bob did not make any payments until four years later. When one of his employees quizzed him about the National Pensions Office, he replied, "I'm not worried about them; they're a toothless tiger."

Getting Teeth

The pensions office realized it needed enforcement to get compliance, so it hired me as the first pensions inspector. My previous experience primarily included law enforcement and accounting. Just before being hired, I had become a certified fraud examiner, which was a major factor in me getting the position. My initial duty was to prepare a standard operational plan for the investigation and prosecution of noncompliant employers. Most of them were just tardy with their payments, but a small percentage were actively trying to avoid their responsibilities. Bob fell into this category. He and his companies would become one of the country's first successful prosecutions under the pension laws.

I became involved with the case when I received a phone call from the pension plan administrator for Sentinel Doors. He said Bob Walker had written a check drawn on Caycar Printing that was dishonored by the bank. The amount of $5,100 was to be the initial installment—though four years late—to pay off his debt, as agreed on between the superintendent of pensions and Walker.

I phoned Bob and set a date with him to see the superintendent. During the call, he was calm and polite and seemed genuinely interested in resolving the issues. On the day of the meeting, 15 minutes prior to the appointment, Bob phoned me to cancel. We scheduled another date, and I advised him it was in his best interest to bring money with him when we met. Should he not show up, I warned him, we would take legal action.

On the day of the second meeting, Bob phoned our office, declined to speak to either the superintendent or me, but instead left a message with the administrative assistant that he was leaving the country within the hour. He claimed that he was not trying to avoid the meeting but had a family emergency and would call us upon his return. That call never came, and the National Pensions Office began prosecution proceedings. We initially focused on Sentinel Doors, as the debt was older, bigger, and affected more employees.

My investigation included collecting documentary evidence, conducting witness interviews, calculating the debt owed, and liaising with the solicitor general. I had to determine the scope by identifying the charges and the availability of sufficient evidence. Over the years, the pensions office had compiled a copious case file on Bob Walker and his businesses, so I did not conduct an interview or attempt to get a statement from him. I reviewed his case to determine the significance of the items and to see what could be used as evidence. From the documents, I was able to piece together a chronology of events. The file also held a number of complaints that had been submitted to the National Pensions Office by ex-employees.

The first interview I conducted was with the pension plan administrator who had called about the dishonored check. He told me the last good payment received from Sentinel Doors was four years ago. Shortly after that last payment, the pensions office sent a letter informing Bob that his company was in arrears. The first payment plan was arranged at that time—but he waited four years before sending the $5,100 check that bounced.

I spoke with previous employees who had submitted complaints. All had similar stories: Deductions were taken from their pay for pension contributions, but neither the employer's share nor their contributions ever made it to the pension plan. I verified this with the pension plan providers, interviewing both the superintendent and the deputy superintendent of National Pensions Office.

STORMY WEATHER

Supported by the solicitor general, we charged 43 counts against Sentinel Doors. During the investigation information had surfaced that showed Bob's other company, Caycar Printing, was also seriously in arrears in making pensions payments, and it was charged with 39 counts. We also charged Bob personally with 82 counts. The prosecution of this case would set an important precedent, so the solicitor general herself would become the lead prosecutor in court.

Bob Walker pleaded guilty to the Sentinel Doors charges for the last four years he admitted to running the company and the two years that Caycar Printing was on the record. He maintained he was innocent of the first year of charges against Sentinel Doors and the remaining charges related to Caycar Printing because "the business ceased to operate after Hurricane Ivan."

Just two years earlier, in 2004, the Cayman Islands faced the worst storm in its history, Hurricane Ivan. This catastrophic class 5 hurricane caused dozens of deaths and a lot of property damage in the Caribbean, wiping out records of businesses and government. This created a recipe for noncompliance excuses that Bob Walker used to his advantage by saying he could not provide us with accounting records for the investigation. Thus, we had to calculate amounts owed using previously submitted information, employee pay detail stubs, and witness statements. (Coincidentally, later on, Bob did manage to find some documentation that he tried to use to reduce his obligations, which led us to believe that he did not lose the records in the hurricane.)

Bob tried any way he could to reduce his pension debt and to mitigate the charges against him personally. One of his defense tactics was to claim that he did not take over Sentinel Doors officially until four years ago and that someone else was responsible before that. He also blamed Hurricane Ivan for destroying Caycar Printing and said the business had closed its doors two years previously. Without any supporting documentation, Bob furnished us with new figures of the amounts owed that were substantially less than what he had previously submitted. It was apparent that he was trying anything to reduce the debt.

Bob agreed to a figure owed for Caycar Printing but then changed his mind a few days later. As a result, we failed to come to an understanding on either company. His defense lawyers worked the angle that the companies, not Bob, were liable. None of these ploys reduced any of the charges against him. As a last resort, Bob made the decision to go to trial and let the judge decide.

The Prosecutor's Case

It took the prosecutor 12 days to present her evidence. She introduced 60 exhibits and 25 witnesses. I had gathered, at her direction, statements from more than 50 employees from both companies and 10 additional witnesses including management, workers, accountants, customs and immigration officials, and even one of Bob's ex-wives. In interviews with ex-employees of Sentinel Doors, we discussed pension deductions and established that Bob—not some other person—had been the mind and management of the entity for five years, which was the period in which the pension fund had not been paid. The statements taken were backed up by pay stubs, letters, or other documentation that showed that:

- Five years earlier, Bob Walker was introduced to the employees as the new owner of Sentinel Doors.
- At that time, Bob started signing documents as president of the company.
- Bob became the only signatory on the bank account.
- Bob did the hiring and firing.
- According to the bookkeepers and accountants, Bob was receiving draws in excess of $6,000 every two weeks.
- The bookkeepers prepared monthly payables for the pension contributions payment, but Bob never issued a check.
- All eligible employees had pension contributions deducted from their pay.
- Bob had a collection of "toys," which included a half-million-dollar yacht, new cars, a brand-new Wave Runner, two airplanes, and plans to buy a jet.

- Statements showed no contributions were made to the pension plans.
- The pensions were not being paid, Bob knew of his responsibility, and he willfully neglected it.
- Health insurance premiums and vehicle insurance payments also were neglected.

My investigation further proved that Caycar Printing continued in business for at least two years after Hurricane Ivan, and Bob Walker operated as he had before, taking pension deductions from employees' pay, missing contributions to the pension fund, and taking hefty draws for himself.

This new information enabled a more accurate calculation of pension obligations and resulted in an increase of the amount Bob owed. At that time, I felt somewhat confident the figures accurately reflected Bob's debt, but I was wrong. Subsequent evidence tendered by Bob during the trial increased the obligations even more.

In the early stage of the trial, the magistrate ruled that the employer was responsible for contributing to the pension plan regardless of whether he took a deduction from an employee.

THE DEFENSE

Bob Walker spent two days, including cross-examination, on the witness stand. He explained what happened to Caycar Printing: Prior to 9/11 he was making $1.2 million profit per year. He blamed the terrorist attacks and new competition for reducing his margin to $600,000 a year. When Hurricane Ivan hit, it destroyed all his equipment, and because he was uninsured, he claimed to have closed it down. He said all the Caycar funds made before Ivan were injected into Sentinel Doors, as it was failing miserably.

He said he had bought non–business-related goods, made possible through loans and dividends. In fact, he testified that he purchased three planes over the years, including a jet. He maintained that he had never received any money from Sentinel Doors. He claimed that he had taken over as president of the company as a favor to a childhood friend and his father, Bert. Bob said he acted as an advisor, not really a manager, and that Bert actually ran the company. He could not call Bert to testify because the man had just died. As it happened, Bob Walker did not offer this information regarding his father's alleged control of the companies until after Bert was dead. Incidentally, during the years of negotiation with the National Pensions Office, Bob never had mentioned anything about the debt belonging to Bert. Cross-examination caused Bob quite a bit of stress, and it was apparent to me that he was not credible; I only hoped that it was apparent to the magistrate.

THE CROSS-EXAMINATION

The solicitor general was methodical, polite, and tenacious. She started her cross-examination by inviting Bob to explain what it meant to be the president of Caycar

Printing and what his duties were. She then switched to Sentinel Doors and drew comparisons, as he had admitted that his title was president for both.

The solicitor general went over testimony and entered as evidence a number of documents that showed Bob had received money from Sentinel Doors, contrary to his testimony. Bob's answer to this was that all the bookkeepers were either wrong or incompetent; he said he was sure an error had been made. The final document in the series had been filled out and signed by Bob himself. It listed the pension contributions paid for each employee and was attached to the dishonored check. On it Bob posted a contribution of $833 for himself in his own name. When questioned, he was momentarily speechless and then squeaked out, "I don't know why I put that there."

During the cross, I recognized his deceitful tactics. Apparently, so did the solicitor general, as she challenged Bob's credibility. Bob tightened up, changed explanations, could not remember important details, seemed to be fabricating stories, and simply could not provide proper answers. The solicitor general charged he was lying to the court.

On the last day of the trial, documentary evidence was reviewed, proving that Bob was in control of Sentinel Doors, that he had employees in Caycar Printing after he claimed it was closed, and that the company was still collecting money on accounts after that date. During summation, the prosecution again addressed Bob's credibility. The defense still contended that the companies were liable and Bob was not.

Throughout the entire process, I made calculations regarding what was owed to the individual pension funds of each employee. Considerations included the amount of their earnings and what deductions should have been taken as well as the interest owed as dictated by law. The total obligation was $318,000.

A powerful piece of legislation provided us an ace in the hole—a means to recoup some monies for the pension debts. We were able to place a restriction on the sale of developed property Bob owned in the amount of $360,000. This money was placed in trust at an independent lawyer's office. Any cash left over after the distribution for pension obligations would go back to Bob.

The Verdict

Bob had already pleaded guilty to the charges against the companies early in the proceedings so on the day the magistrate announced the verdict, it concerned only the charges against Bob Walker. In the end, she found him personally liable for all the charges presented, which included failing to contribute to a pension plan as well as failing to provide information. The magistrate said there was no doubt that Bob was the mind and management of the companies.

She accepted the figures I had provided but wanted to do some fine-tuning. Finally, the magistrate closed by setting another date for sentencing and a final assessment of amounts owed.

At sentencing, she ordered Bob to pay the arrears and interest, less his personal contributions. In addition, he was fined $74,000 (in default, he faced 26.5 years in prison) and had to pay $25,000 in costs. I breathed a sigh of relief and knew I had won a victory for the employees affected and the rest of the Cayman Islands workforce.

LESSONS LEARNED

Hindsight provides the opportunity to improve. I would do a few things differently in future investigations. I would conduct an interview and take a statement from the accused. If I had done this with Bob, I might have been able to obtain accounting records in the case. I could have brought out Bob's excuses and reasons for noncompliance with the law. This would have enabled the prosecution to better anticipate defense strategies and prepare for them.

We should have seized all of the records. The National Pensions Law has a provision that allows, under an inspection order, seizure of payroll and accounting information from all types of premises, including private dwellings. The order is the same as a search warrant obtained under the penal code. This would have produced all types of additional evidence.

Finally, it is important first to charge offending entities with "failure to provide information" for many reasons. First, it is much easier to prove in court. Second, it shows that the National Pensions Office will enforce the law for noncompliance. And it allows the entity to get its house in order and become compliant in the interim.

RECOMMENDATIONS TO PREVENT FUTURE OCCURRENCES

Some actions just make the investigator's work easier and more productive.

Track Complaints

The development and implementation of procedures for complaints would provide a uniform and consistent practice. At any time in the process, one could refer to the status of a particular file and see what the next step should be.

Enlist the Services of a Forensic Accountant

A forensic accountant would be invaluable to the National Pensions Office. The offending entity would be billed for his or her time, which would offset the costs.

Restrict Use of Money Set Aside

The legislation regarding the sale of property needs to be changed so that we are able to restrict the use of the resulting funds set aside. These monies should be used specifically for disbursement of pension obligations. Upon satisfying these, the remainder would be distributed to the rightful owner.

Prompt Enforcement

The National Pensions Office should contact employers quickly after they become delinquent. If a payment agreement is reached, enforcement should begin immediately upon default. If the office had begun proceedings against Bob Walker sooner, the employees and the government would not have faced such a large shortfall.

Pierre E. Lautischer, CFE, CIG, CFI, secured the first conviction under the National Pensions Law as the pioneer pension inspector in the Cayman Islands. Capitalizing on 28 years of experience as an accountant, police officer, and inspector, he now operates his own investigation firm with locations in the Cayman Islands and Canada.

CHAPTER 59

Bodies for Rent

REBECCA S. BUSCH

Rent-a-patient fraud schemes usually involve an outpatient surgical center that supplies unnecessary medical services to low-income insured people who have employer-sponsored benefit programs. The workers of particular companies are recruited to become patients for cash rewards. The clinics reward themselves with the reimbursement checks from the insurance companies. The perpetrators in this particular fraud scheme fall victim to an addictive cycle of greed, deceit, and lies—all for monetary gain, despite the ramifications.

There are four groups of perpetrators in these schemes. The *clinic owners* are the ones who set up the clinics to offer the unnecessary services. The *providers* include the doctors and nurses who performed the procedures. The *recruiters* are individuals who seek out patients. The last group is the *patients*, who willingly donate their bodies to have unnecessary medical services performed. Unfortunately, these individuals frequently end up with scars and lifelong injuries due to their wrongful participation in this fraud scheme.

Danh and Ly Tran were a Vietnamese couple living in southern California. They had worked in a number of retail businesses before deciding to open a medical clinic specifically to engage in rent-a-patient fraud. New to the medical environment, they opened up a weekend outpatient medical office called the Palm Springs East Outpatient Surgical Center. They did not have any formal contracts with insurance company health benefit programs. Therefore, Mr. and Mrs. Tran's weekend clinic was viewed as an Out-of-Network provider. They used local newspapers to advertise for physicians and nurses to work there on the weekends. The doctors they hired often were already in high-paying positions in their weekday jobs. Many entered the clinic fully understanding the intent of the rent-a-patient fraud, while others were blind to the scheme. Regardless, all developed the ability to rationalize their participation.

Dr. Bao Chu is a typical example of a provider perpetrator. He worked for a major university medical center. Married with children, Dr. Chu had an active practice making a high six-figure income. He also worked in the Trans' clinic Saturdays and Sundays and averaged $30,000 each weekend performing unnecessary medical services for willing participants. The nurses who worked in the clinics and in the operating rooms typically made between $60 and $70 an hour. They also held full-time jobs in reputable hospitals during the week. At some point, the nurses may have understood that many of these surgical procedures were not necessary. Once again, the prospect of money overpowered their ability to behave ethically.

Mr. and Mrs. Tran employed other Vietnamese workers to hunt for patients. These recruiter perpetrators are commonly referred to as cappers or coyotes. Recruiters are typically of ethnic background, including Vietnamese, Hispanic, and Bosnian. In this case, it was Due Voung, an individual working for a large self-insured employer called Recycle Industries Company. His mission was to seek out other Vietnamese employees from his weekday workplace who had insurance benefits and encourage them to have unnecessary procedures at the outpatient surgical centers for cash. Due also recruited and advertised by word of mouth through several Vietnamese nail salons. Some employees even found advertisements posted in their workplace cafeterias. A recruiter averaged $2,000 per employee, or "patient," found. The clinic owners' potential revenue from an individual and his or her family members was typically up to $400,000.

Finally, the patient perpetrators are typically low-wage earners with language barrier issues. In this case, they were recruited by Due and others to have medical work performed on them and/or their family members, including spouses and children, for approximately $300 to $1,000 per procedure. The patients would receive cash from the clinics, which would then submit their medical insurance claims to the patients' insurance carriers. In most circumstances the insurance check was sent to the patient, who was instructed to bring it back to pay the doctors, nurses, and clinic owners. Many of the patients became recruiters themselves, which perpetuated the cycle.

Recycle Industries Company was a well-established U.S.-based corporation with annual sales exceeding $1 billion. The division involved with this investigation had a medical participant plan with over 5,000 employees.

Palm Springs East Outpatient Surgical Center was also doing well. The clinic had recruited up to 30 physicians and 10 to 20 support staff. Danh and Ly Tran became so successful at this game of deceit that they eventually operated four weekend outpatient surgical centers in the southern California area.

Due, who was employed at Recycle Industries Company, was a capper who recruited at least 50 claimants. The clinic owners paid him a significant amount of money to find insured employees. Due was just one of many recruiters the Trans were using in over 40 different states. Like Due, the recruiters targeted workers at businesses with health insurance coverage.

At times, the recruiters had to convince or pressure the patients into receiving these medically unnecessary procedures. The cappers/recruiters arranged the transportation, flying or driving the patients to California. It was the recruiter's job to schedule the procedures, instruct the patients what to say, and return the employees back home once everything was completed. If the employees did not tell the doctor the correct symptoms, they would be returned to the recruiter for additional "coaching" and be presented to the clinic a second time. Often the clinic billed these visits as emergency services, since these typically do not require precertification by the insurance company. All of these patients had one thing in common: They were healthy from the start.

The clinics kept themselves under the radar screen by performing very common procedures—typically colonoscopies, upper gastrointestinal procedures, sweaty palm removal surgery, hemorrhoid operations, and pain management. The capper often stayed with the patient during the doctor visit.

Many patients were unaware of the effects of these operations. A man who was interviewed on a national network program about his participation in such a procedure stated that after his sweaty palm removal surgery, "When the sun shines on me, it feels like my skin is on fire." The inability to sweat on one side of his body is a permanent condition. False claims and misrepresentation of services, such as billing for services never rendered or for performing cosmetic surgery disguised as a covered illness, have been around a long time. The rent-a-patient scheme is unique in that physicians are performing completely medically unnecessary services.

They began by performing minor cosmetic work, then for emergency services, and eventually evolved into performing surgical procedures at 5000% above gross price. The clinic owners maximized their reimbursement from a perpetrator patient by double-billing services. For example, they changed the dates of the medically unnecessary services that actually were rendered. The alteration would make it appear as if the procedure took place more than once. They often recruited as many as 200 employees from the same company. Performing the surgeries on Saturdays and Sundays was common to avoid detection by the employer.

OUT IN THE OPEN

Most frauds surface from a quiet inside tip. This particular fraud scheme materialized publicly. As stated earlier, these out-of-network checks often were mailed to the patients. As you can imagine, a $200,000 check in the mail would certainly generate temptation among minimum-wage workers. As a result, patients began to cash the insurance checks instead of turning them over to the clinics. The clinics began to sue the patients for the fraudulently obtained monies. A group of employees from Recycle Industries found legal representation. A local newspaper reporter got wind of the litigation, starting a series of publications, and the patients struck back by telling their horror stories from the clinic.

In an interview with the paper, Hien Trung, an employee at Recycle Industries Company, stated that he did not have any health problems before being recruited to undergo several surgeries. The 31-year-old New Jersey resident was paid to undergo a number of medical procedures, including a circumcision, removal of his sweat glands, a nose operation, a colonoscopy, and an endoscopy. Hien disclosed that he participated even though he knew that he did not need any of these surgeries. He felt pressured by Due, his coworker, who repeatedly urged him to travel to southern California for the unnecessary operations. He reported that he was told what to say to the doctors and, in turn, "They just did all these surgeries." However, Hien did admit to cashing insurance checks totaling $250,000. He further explained, "I let them do it. Afterward, I felt like I was their experiment. When they came to get the insurance check, I decided to just cash the check and keep the money."

When other patients like Hien were interviewed, they described how they received payments from Due of $400 for each procedure they participated in. Due denied knowledge of this or any other health care insurance scam. But advertisements for recruiting employees were found in the cafeteria listing Due's cell phone number. He denied this as well, claiming that his cell phone had been stolen.

Like Hien, other patients starting cashing their insurance checks too. The recruiters were supposed to collect the money from the employees when they received them. However, when the patients started cashing the checks themselves, problems surfaced for Mr. and Mrs. Tran.

Overall, this clinic took in excess of $2.6 million from Recycle Industries Company. It is estimated that more than $100 million was stolen from over 1,200 different employers. Their victims also included third parties, such as collection firms that buy receivables at a discounted rate.

The Trans operated with impunity for a long time by creating multiple companies, changing tax identification, and changing the billing location address while keeping the same physical location of the clinic. It is important to note that the Trans were among many clinic owner perpetrators who existed during the time. It is estimated that rent-a-patient frauds cost the market over $500 million.

DEEP IN THE DATA MINES

I was hired by Recycle Industries Company to assist in investigating the extent of the damage from the rent-a-patient fraud. An additional layer to this particular scheme existed. Since this was a self-funded insurance program, the employees were stealing money directly from the company. Because this scheme was, in essence, theft of corporate assets, the losses were potentially covered under Recycle Industries' fidelity or employee crime policy. These policies are designed to reimburse a company for losses due to the theft or dishonesty of its employees.

My role in this investigation involved confirming that the fraud took place, identifying the total loss, and providing expert opinions in filing the fidelity claim.

Confirmation of the fraud began by gathering the available documents. Since employees of Recycle Industries Company had been interviewed by the media, we searched and obtained all publications that involved discussion of them. In addition, several workers had been questioned as part of a national network television show. We obtained a copy of it. Significant publicity existed in this case, so proof was fairly established at the time of my participation.

The televised segment included some of these quotes:

> "They offered me money, and I thought—why not?"
> "I rented my body. I know it's really bad, but I'm human."
> "They give you $1,000. I thought, how bad can this be? It's only one hour."

The program continued with additional employee interviews.

> "Did you get your money?" asked the interviewer.
> "Yes, we received $2,000—me and my son."
> "Was it worth it?"
> "No," confirmed the employee, "we could have died right there."

Recruiters were also interviewed. Vietnamese nail salons were a common place to find potential patients. The program had an investigative reporter attempt to receive cosmetic health care services. One of the recruiters told the reporter, "You can get insurance to pay for your surgery. It's really cheating but we need to cheat' em good. You just lie—lying does not hurt." Once at the clinic, on-site cappers would coach the employees by telling them the appropriate symptoms to report to the doctor. One person was instructed not to state that she wanted cosmetic surgery. The recruiter explained, "We have to actually do the colonoscopy. We need to prove to the insurance company that you had the colonoscopy. Then they'll do the cosmetic surgery on your eyes."

Another employee took five trips to the clinics and was subjected to all of these procedures. The public exposure, as well as the employer documents, provided sufficient predication for continued discovery and filing of a fidelity claim. Additional employer documents included an interview matrix in order to evaluate and screen for employees who were involved with the fraud. They were fired from the organization.

I found many patterns, one of which demonstrated that the clinic owners understood the claims-processing aspect extremely well. I also found billing statements that arrived at the third-party administrator (TPA) with stamped notations such as "out-of-network claims; process." This was to further confuse a claim adjuster when reviewing the files. Companies with self-insured plans often outsource claims processing to an independent company called a third-party administrator. In conducting an investigation of a provider clinic, it is important to understand how information moves from one operational function to another.

The identified claims demonstrated consistent weaknesses and documentation issues, thus making it possible to separate legitimate from fraudulent claims. Similar understanding of the movement of health information is important with respect to the TPA functions.

The clinic owner perpetrators often stated that the high volume of patients required emergent care, which is why these clinics treated so many out-of-state employees. The term "emergent" implies unplanned, unexpected, and an acute situation. Data mining helped analyze this statement. We found that, on average, the pre-certification occurred up to four weeks in advance of the service. It is interesting to note how many of the pre-certification numbers were traced to nonfunctioning cell phones. However, the calls for collection of payments often went back to home addresses as well as clinic and billing office locations. This pattern is consistent with the cappers, confirming that the employee they were recruiting did, in fact, have valid insurance.

My discovery documents from the employer included a list of employees, their respective files, and interview notes. I also obtained an electronic file of the claims paid data and the employers' data dictionary directly from its third-party administrator. The most involved aspect of this investigation was the electronic data mining of the claims. It contained 1,123,891 records and the electronic file size was 1,194,176 kilobytes.

I pulled a general profile of the dated claims and noted increased expenditures by the employer during the relevant time periods. In addition, we profiled the identified employees. The file contained the typical diagnosis themes of excessive sweating, diarrhea, and abdominal pain—typical day-to-day symptoms. In terms of procedures, one of the common rent-a-patient procedures included thoracoscopy, removal of sweat gland procedure, colonoscopy, and endoscopy.

I isolated the claim activity by dependent and providers. The TPA involved in processing claims by this provider had a national presence. It contained the names of the providers for the in-state, home-based TPA center for the employer. The file was complicated because the providers' names from out-of-state locations were deleted from the host TPA processing center. As a result, I had to depend on other factors, such as address data, employee Social Security numbers, and other rent-a-patient profiler tools to pull together all the relevant information.

Once the data were gathered and sorted, a written report was submitted to the fidelity insurance carrier. The initial claim was for $2,049,310 stolen from the employer's benefit plan via the rent-a-patient fraud scheme. This figure was submitted after data analysis of 70 targeted employees, 25 of whom were identified to have been involved in the scheme.

The fidelity carrier responded with a few challenges. The first expert hired by the carrier was not able to extract data from the original claim file. Informal follow-up conversations with the data support personnel indicated that he was able to confirm the numbers. The fidelity report was processed internally. I never received a copy of it.

I then began to work with a second certified public accountant expert hired by the fidelity carrier. He said that the TPA-processed claim file did not qualify as evidence that actual cash was taken from the employer, and he wanted bank transactions to justify proof of loss. At that point, I had my staff repeat the analysis process with the bank statements. Upon completion of the review, we noticed additional data integrity issues. Many of the patients involved had ethnic names. At times, the names were incorrectly spelled or had other variations, such as the first and last name switched. In addition, I found missing letters in a name. This could include a claim for "John Smith" and others under "John Smih." Significant additional management, testing, and processing of the data was required. Similar issues were found in the TPA electronic claim file.

The outcome of this additional investigation resulted in a revised report, which increased the loss to $2.6 million. This was primarily from newly identified claimants with stolen Social Security numbers of legitimate employees that were incomplete in the original payer claim file.

The Outcome of the Investigation

After a two-year investigation by the county district attorney's office, with the assistance of the state's Department of Insurance and the Franchise Tax Board, charges were brought forward against the clinic owners, Mr. and Mrs. Tran. They were each charged with 46 counts of conspiracy, grand theft, insurance fraud, capping, and tax evasion. The couple was accused of recruiting thousands of healthy patients from all over the United States to have medically unnecessary surgeries at their weekend outpatient surgical center and stealing more than $100 million from insurance companies and employers. If convicted, they could face a maximum sentence of up to 38 years in a state prison.

My client, Recycle Industries, was lucky because it had fidelity insurance to cover its loss of over $2 million.

Lessons Learned

When I was conducting the investigation, I paid particular attention to flowcharting all players involved, such as "patient," "provider," "TPA," and any other vendors. Although cumbersome in the beginning, this was particularly helpful when reevaluating patterns.

Due to the many data integrity issues, obtaining employee information for corroboration was required from more than one source. Additionally, among the players, it is important to understand system limitations and determine alternative sources for missing data elements that were routinely dropped in the normal course of business. Repetition of tasks can be avoided by having a comprehensive listing of all documents. Finally, sufficient information systems and data analysis support is critical to any claims investigation. The greatest challenge was handling the information that could be received only in hardcopy format. Be prepared with resources to convert those items into electronic format and to analyze them properly.

RECOMMENDATIONS TO PREVENT FUTURE OCCURRENCES

Company Awareness

The rent-a-patient scheme represents a new level of employee corruption. Employers must realize that their corporate assets are at risk. This is an area that is rarely on the internal audit checklist. Health care benefit programs involve significant corporate expenditures. The rent-a-patient fraud scheme demonstrates vulnerabilities that employers can suffer without proper oversight of their health plans. Management should understand that proactive monitoring and training of employees is critical in putting a dent into this problem.

Obtain Fidelity Coverage

If an insurance plan is self-funded, theft may be covered by an employee crime policy, often referred to as a fidelity bond or fidelity insurance. Such policies are a good idea because they cover all types of employee theft and embezzlement. You should check to make sure that your company has such coverage under its insurance policies.

Employee Awareness Programs

Employers should institute fraud awareness within the health care benefit program. They should understand how these rent-a-patient schemes work and the medical dangers involved. Additionally, they should be informed that this practice is illegal.

Data Mining and Proactive Review

Employers should implement internal data mining processes of their claim activity and regular third-party audits of their benefit programs. In this case, such reviews may have picked up the anomalies of excessive claims on Saturdays and Sundays and for common rent-a-patient procedures, such as sweat gland removal.

Reviews should also be conducted to look for other common schemes, such as:

- Billing for services never received
- Double-billing services
- Inflated prices
- Unbundling charges
- Fake insurance cards
- Fake discount cards
- Identity theft

My key recommendation is for employers to beware. Fraudsters are after your money in more ways than one, and many companies are oblivious to the costliness and prevalence of rent-a-patient frauds.

Rebecca S. Busch, CFE, RN, MBA, CCM, FHFMA, is president of MBA Inc., in Westmont, Illinois. Her firm provides audit, fraud examination, exploratory data analysis, consulting, health care industry analysis, and expert witness services. Ms. Busch is a graduate of Rush University, DePaul University, and Lewis University and has more than 20 years of experience in the health care industry.

CHAPTER 60

The Million-Dollar Breach of Trust

HOLLY FROOK GRAHAM

Clara Hatfield was born and raised in Caldwell, a rural, dusty town on the midwestern side of Arizona. People in this community prided themselves on their quiet and neighborly way of life. No one was too busy to help out another and certainly not too busy to ignore newsworthy gossip. Clara grew up surrounded by family and friends of all ages. She quickly became known as the little mother because she had a tendency to take care of others. Although some might argue the perception was undeserved, this reputation of caretaker stayed with Clara even through adulthood. In fact, one former employer was quoted as saying that Clara "went around portraying herself as another Mother Teresa."

A short woman with a kind and expressive face, Clara was endearing to many people. She was well known in her country neighborhood as someone who could be counted on to help with any project, but she also had another side. Some of those close to her thought at times that she was mulish and hard to deal with, liked control a little too much, could be manipulative to get what she wanted, and was even somewhat cagey.

As she grew older, difficulties surfaced with her personal relationships, and she soon found herself to be a single mother of two children, a boy and a girl. She had additional burdens with ailing relatives who depended on her for care and assistance. When time allowed, Clara took on various jobs to feed her family, but it seemed they were always just barely making ends meet. She became transient, moving to several different towns in search of better-paying jobs. It was in one of these towns that she fell in love with the son of a Baptist minister. Together, they started a new life back in her hometown where her roots were and where she felt the strongest. Clara believed her luck had finally changed for the better. They found a modest trailer park where they could establish a home and settle in. Within weeks they both found stable and secure government jobs.

Clara started working as a secretary for the Los Ramos County Board of Supervisors. In this capacity, she met many people and learned a great deal about the inner workings of county business. It was in this position that she came to discover the occupation of her dreams. She could spend her days serving people who were most in need: the frail and elderly, those with diminished mental capacity, and vulnerable people who had nowhere else to turn. Clara thought that she may well become the county's public fiduciary. She would manage the physical and financial needs of these defenseless individuals, the wards of the county. Little did she know that this culmination of her professional and personal aspirations would tempt her beyond her capacity and she would lose herself to the insidious disease of greed, failing those who so desperately needed to be served.

Los Ramos County in Arizona covers about 5,000 square miles of stunning, unique, and rugged terrain. There is something for everyone: majestic mountains with pine trees, jagged and dangerous cliffs, weeping willows bordering the banks of cool running streams, and even desert landscape complete with cholla cactus. The county boasts of its colorful proliferations of wildflowers during the spring season; hence its Spanish name, Los Ramos, or "The Bouquets." More than half of the area belongs to the U.S. Forest Service and nearly 40% is owned by the Apache Indian Reservation.

The region has a turbulent and violent history that personifies the idea of the Wild West. The land was initially inhabited by Apache Indians who fiercely defended their territory from encroaching prospectors. Word had spread that the land was rich with minerals such as silver and copper, and miners were all eager to make their stake. The conflicting ambitions launched a chaotic and cruel beginning for the establishment of Los Ramos County. The vicious "Apache Wars" were followed by horrific murders, stagecoach robberies, brutal public hangings, and pervasive drunkenness. Although order eventually came to the beautiful Los Ramos County, a robust and pioneering spirit is still present.

The locals are an industrious and humble group. They still mine for copper, but farming and ranching have taken over as the main livelihoods. While most of the 60,000 citizens have at least graduated from high school, only a small percentage have gone on to complete college degrees. The typical household income of just over $20,000 is a fraction of the national average. Maintaining the bucolic lifestyle has inhibited growth and industrial development in the area. Some may prefer this countrified standard of living, but the declining economy has impelled many to leave the community for more prosperous regions. Consequently, family members may live apart from one another and often do not have the means to help support each other when health fails or other needs arise.

Like many in Arizona counties, Los Ramos officials saw the need to assist residents who required care but did not have familial support and were unable to help themselves due to poor health or mental capacity. In 1974 the Arizona legislature required each county board of supervisors to appoint an individual to the position of public fiduciary and serve these citizens. The county was to be responsible for funding the operating costs of the public fiduciary office. A series of state laws, rules, and procedures followed this mandate to ensure that public fiduciaries are properly trained to make medical, financial, and general welfare decisions benefiting the vulnerable citizens under their care. In order for a person to receive the services of a county's public fiduciary, the court must make a formal determination that because of mental or physical impairments, an individual is in need of guardianship and thereby appointed to the oversight of the public fiduciary. This appointment means that the person becomes a ward of the county, dependent on the public fiduciary for health and property management.

When Clara began serving as the Los Ramos County Public Fiduciary, she had a staff of five to assist her. Although the number of wards in her care varied over time, she had an average caseload of about 60 persons. Most of these people were indigent; however, some came with wealth. In those situations, Clara was responsible for prudently managing their income, in addition to handling their assets, such as money market, savings, and checking accounts; certificates of deposit; real estate; personal property like furnishings, precious gems, and jewelry; and even rare stamp collections. For the first time in her life, Clara was surrounded by a cornucopia of treasures.

ROBBING PETER TO PAY PAUL

It was the time of year just before autumn, when Clara thought the mornings had a fresh and familiar feel, reminiscent of a less complicated life when childhood school days were just beginning. For a short while, the air was muted and cool with a nearly sweet smell. But by noon this enchanted sensation was gone, replaced with the intense and bright sunshine typical of Arizona.

On her desk this September morning was yet another note detailing a message from Sarah Byler. It read: "Clara, Sarah called again at 3:30 and said that she hadn't heard from you. She said it was urgent that you call her in regard to Virginia May's estate." Virginia was Sarah's aunt. She had passed away several months earlier, and her final accounting had not been completed yet. As she had done for a handful of other wards, Clara had personally taken care of Virginia's estate. Other office staff had no access to any of the records for the wards that Clara managed. She hoarded the paperwork associated with their finances and restricted communications with them as an overprotective mother might do for a sick child.

Clara could not put this task off any longer. She gathered the other notes on her desk and went home to prepare the final accounting report for Virginia May. Staying away from the office would help her focus and keep her stress level down. Virginia was one of the few wards who had money so it would take Clara some time to prepare this final accounting. In the end, Virginia should have had nearly $300,000 left in her estate. Clara reported this on the final accounting that she submitted to the court. Although she had completed her paperwork duties as required, Clara's stress level had increased, and she was now feeling physically ill. It pained her to think of just how she could explain that Virginia's money was gone. Clara made a silent wish that the demands would all go away and people would forget about Virginia May. For the rest of the year, court and county staff hardly saw Clara as she tried to keep a low profile and make herself scarce.

However, Virginia's estate was not paid to her heirs, and niece Sarah was not satisfied. Numerous phone calls were made to Robert Black, the attorney representing the Los Ramos Public Fiduciary Office, but no one could get hold of Clara.

Finally, on a cold and wintry evening during the first week of January, Clara answered her home telephone and spoke to Mr. Black. She admitted that the money was gone. She said that she had made some serious mistakes and had used Virginia May's money for other wards' expenses. "I robbed from Peter to pay Paul." This was the rationale she reported to anyone who would listen.

Clara's declaration to Mr. Black that Virginia's money had been consumed was the catalyst for a flurry of communications with numerous county officials. Clara was placed on administrative leave. Jim Wilkins, the county manager, was concerned about how this recent chain of events would affect the financial audit his county was currently undergoing. He informed the lead auditor from the Arizona Auditor General's Office who passed the information on to us, a small group of forensic accountants who dealt with fraud in the public sector. The special investigative unit is a unique component of the Auditor General's Office that specifically handles allegations of corruption, misuse of public money, and theft. Thus, we began an arduous and time-consuming inquiry into the improper dealings that occurred under Clara Hatfield, Los Ramos County Public Fiduciary.

All Mixed Up

Our first step was to meet with county officials. We needed to hear their concerns, ascertain the organizational structure, find out what records were available, and arrange for access to county buildings and contact with employees. The two-hour drive from Phoenix to Caldwell provided time to forget about the hectic, congested thoroughfares of a major metropolis. We drove on one-lane roads that intermittently curved around undulating land speckled with cactus and sheer jagged cliffs overlooking rocky canyons that glowed with amethyst and golden hues in the morning sunlight. It was beautiful. Our thoughts, however, were focused on the task that lay ahead: not only did we need to find out what happened to the $300,000 belonging to Virginia May; we needed to see if any other money was missing.

Seated around an aged oval cherrywood table with the county attorney, county manager, finance director, health director, and public fiduciary program manager, we learned that Clara had resigned the Friday prior to our meeting. Her husband, concerned about how stress was affecting her health, had just taken her to the hospital. It would be difficult, at least for the time being, to arrange for any kind of meeting with Clara.

Directing our attention to the history and goings-on of the public fiduciary's office, we discovered that Clara had far-reaching and unchecked control of extensive amounts of money belonging to the wards. She was able to write checks at will without anyone ever verifying the propriety of her actions. However, this level of authority was also available to the five people working for Clara. Accordingly, we had many avenues to consider. The money could be missing because of inept management, or it could have been pilfered by any public fiduciary or county employee. Clara could be covering up for somebody or even colluding with another worker.

Our troubles were compounded when we learned that a year earlier, county officials neglected to look into improper dealings at the public fiduciary's office they were informed about that involved the "incorrect disbursement of client funds." Instead, they covered the shortfall with a loan of nearly $12,000 from the county's general fund monies. Further, officials admitted to knowing about false annual accountings that Clara had filed with the court, yet they failed to take any corrective or remedial actions. Another complexity involved the role of the private attorney contracted for handling duties associated with the public fiduciary's office. Robert Black was a personal friend of Clara's and had been for several years. There seemed to be many sticks in the fire, and we had a lot of digging to do.

It didn't take long before peculiarities began to surface. We visited the public fiduciary's office, which was actually an old rundown house on the outskirts of town. The dirt parking area, turned muddy by recent rains, led to a dusty and unkempt place of work. Papers were strewn carelessly on desks, shelves, and even the floor. The wards' personal property was treated no differently. Valuable items such as jewelry, property deeds, and stamp collections were not secured; in fact, the public fiduciary's office did not even maintain a safety deposit box. In an effort to bring some sort of normalcy and order to the chaos, county employees had begun searching for and organizing what they could find. Not unexpectedly, they located several boxes of original records in Clara's home.

Our interviews of public fiduciary personnel exposed Clara's harsh and rather callous side. She managed her staff with a domineering and oppressive style, very uncharacteristic of the compassionate and thoughtful person she attempted to portray publicly. Clara had a hold over her employees, creating a climate in which they feared asking questions lest they be fired. In this community, jobs were hard to come by. Staff understood that certain files—the wards with money—were handled solely by Clara. All of the mail for these wards was supposed to go directly to her, unopened. She also controlled all of the bank statements and cancelled checks. There were no written policies and procedures that staff could look to for guidance. Clara was often away from the office, claiming to be visiting with wards and tending to their needs, so it was difficult to ask her questions anyway.

Before the end of January, we had found enough evidence to have a preliminary interview with Clara. She was still under the care of a physician for stress but was able to travel to Phoenix and meet with us. Clara was a short lady in her mid-50s, carried about 50 pounds more than she should, and wore clothes that might be described as out of date, but on this occasion, she had noticeably prepared herself to impress us as a credible businesswoman. Her eyes were hidden behind glasses, yet they still revealed a hint of trepidation and worry that could not be superficially camouflaged with dress and presentation.

We had concerns about the financial management of many wards and allowed her to explain the circumstances. Clara was the master at speaking in circles. She answered no question directly and continued on ceaselessly with meaningless or irrelevant information. Her most often used justification for undocumented transfers of money was that she was "robbing Peter to pay Paul." She claimed that although it was the wrong thing to do, she had used money from wards that were wealthy to pay for expenses of wards that were indigent. We had reviewed enough of the available financial information to know there were significant transfers among the different wards' accounts; however, we did not have records to support how the money was actually spent. In particular, we wanted to know about Virginia May's estate. She should have had $300,000. After being redirected and asked to focus again, Clara responded, "I'm so mixed up on what we were doing. I was robbing Peter to pay Paul to try to take care of this, so I will be honest with you, I really don't know exactly because and I'm not saying this to be off the record or to be off the mark or something, but it's like sometimes everything is so confusing and you think you're trying to do it, and I would think I was doing right and then I would think no, that's not right."

And so it went for the explanations. Clara couldn't remember specific information, but claimed the problems all stemmed from trying to take care of the wards that did not have any money. She reiterated that her function as the public fiduciary was to assist and nurture the wards, those who were too ill or incapacitated to care for themselves. During the interview, she repeatedly tried to convey that she was a true caretaker; her only concern was for their physical well-being.

As we continued our search through records and compared the information with the listing of wards receiving services from the public fiduciary's office, it became apparent that the complete files for 10 wards were missing. Bank records indicated that all of these wards, at one time, had quite a lot of money. However, the bank records were incomplete. An account had been established for each of these 10 wards, with Clara as the authorized signatory. The statements showed the typical activity, with deposits, transfers, and withdrawals, but the cancelled checks normally included with the bank statement were not presented in their entirety. Additionally, the check stubs on which the preparer normally recorded the date, purpose, payee, and amount were also missing.

It was time to request documentation from the bank. Financial institutions, like any business, can't keep records indefinitely. As a result, our focus was limited to a five-year span. We had to find nearly 700 checks.

REALITY CHECK

As the missing checks came in from the bank, we found that each and every one of them was prepared and signed by Clara. They were payable to a variety of entities, including major credit card conglomerates, retail stores, utility businesses, and gasoline companies. For five years, Clara wrote 695 checks totaling $750,159 for which the purpose was unknown, undocumented, and clearly suspicious. Our work was not finished. We needed to know what and who was behind the assortment of credit card and other innumerable payments.

After reviewing copious documents and statements, we knew it was time to bring Clara back in for another interview. We wanted to hear her explanation for why wards' money was used to pay personal credit card bills, telephone utilities, home improvements, and insurance premiums. She had spent the majority of money on seven major credit card accounts for herself, her husband, her daughter, and her son-in-law. For this five-year period, with bills totaling $665,772, the credit cards held by Clara and her husband were used for Las Vegas and Arizona Indian Reservation casinos; trips to California, Alaska, Missouri, and Colorado; electronic equipment, repairs on their recreational vehicle and personal car; dining at restaurants and going to the movies, buying jewelry, and even a spa to relax in. The credit cards that Clara had given to her daughter and son-in-law were used for their groceries, gasoline, and medical-related purchases.

The residual amount of misspent money totaling $84,387 was for charges to family gasoline credit cards, retail store credit cards, cellular and long-distance telephone charges, home improvement supplies and materials, and personal cancer and hospitalization insurance policies for Clara and her husband.

Because the availability of documentation was limited, we were unable to identify specifically where at least an additional $217,729 was spent. We were able to determine that because of Clara's misspending of ward money over five years, she caused a loss on earning interest income totaling $101,717. Further, Clara failed to send $52,566 in fees to the county from wards' uncashed checks. We found some of these checks, dated nearly five years earlier, on her desk. Moreover, Clara paid her family members directly out of the public fiduciary checking account and hid the evidence. She wrote 111 checks to her husband, son, and son-in-law totaling $31,709 for unsubstantiated purposes. Despite her initial claim of robbing Peter to pay Paul, we found that Clara had actually used only $24,004 of the wealthy wards' money for needs of the indigent.

Clara agreed to come to the office for another interview. She had moved from her hometown of Caldwell and was now much closer to Phoenix. Our first order of business was to establish that the great majority of these transactions were personal. We showed Clara different spreadsheets, initially demonstrating the smaller thefts and gradually moving on to the larger amounts. Not unexpectedly, Clara's initial response was one of denial and defense. She lamented, "You know, I'm so tired and so weary of this whole thing! I came in here today telling myself that I don't care what you guys do. I gave my best to that office and tried my very, very hardest and the circumstances are very, very adverse and I can't even keep track of where I was or what I did—and that's not a copout."

When asked how long she had been writing public fiduciary checks to pay her credit card bills, Clara responded, "It wasn't—it wasn't in the beginning, it was when things became overwhelming and I didn't have the means to continue to take care of everything. I don't know. Time has no. . ." Her voice trailed off, leaving her sentence hanging in the air.

Like many fraudsters, Clara had great difficulty comprehending the vast amount she had stolen. She had nothing to show for it. All of the money was spent and had been simply frittered away. As the million-dollar figure was discussed, Clara offered, "I'm so sorry. The amount just did not seem like it was that much. . .and I can vow to you that I didn't realize it was that much. I—I'm not saying that I'm stupid and I'm not saying that I wasn't trying to do everything right in that office. I know sometimes it was just escaping to get away from there 'cause its mind game, mind game, mind game, mind game. . .I'm just—I don't—I feel like I was I was stupid but haywire. I can't explain. I know that's what you're saying and I'm not saying that's not what it is. I'm just. . .is just overwhelming to me." As the interview came to a close, Clara could no longer maintain her composure, and she began crying. Her concluding statement was uttered between tears. "This is extremely hard on me. . . I didn't mean to ever do anything. I just. . .I'm not a bad person."

After being indicted by the grand jury, Clara Hatfield pled guilty to fraud and theft, both felonies. She was sentenced to seven years in prison and ordered to pay restitution in the amount of $1,177,884.

LESSONS LEARNED

A frequent and dismaying lesson learned all too often by administrators is that they have placed an excessive amount of trust in one person. This blind faith is so pervasive that the manager of our special investigative unit at the Arizona Auditor General's Office has half-jokingly suggested that audits and reviews always include the question, "Who is your most trusted employee?" Management should think twice before being impressed by those who seem to work harder and longer, never take vacations, and have no difficulty doing the work of several people.

County management also learned that they should have more thoroughly investigated seemingly minor disturbances with the public fiduciary's office that came to light a year before. The public fiduciary had failed to pay fees to the county on behalf of the wards, although she had falsely reported to the courts otherwise. They accepted Clara's rationalization of not receiving money from federal and state agencies on a timely basis and not only loaned the public fiduciary $11,770 for "incorrect disbursement of client funds," but also failed to notify the court about the false annual accountings. If the county officials had responded diligently, Clara's thieving could have been cut short.

Just months before the initial theft discovery, Clara let her public fiduciary certification lapse and the county was required to temporarily hire a replacement, who identified 12 "issues of concern." The county failed to investigate those issues and terminated the replacement's contract early in order to bring Clara back.

The importance of having a productive and professional relationship with your auditors can be very beneficial. Proactive communications can support solid business practices and keep employees cognizant of diligent and detailed oversight. Company dealings should be lawful and reasonable, able to stand up to scrutiny. Administrators should be candid with auditors to help ensure the integrity of management and company operations. These departments should be allied with a strong policy against fraud.

Although there are no guarantees that internal controls can prevent fraud from occurring, sound business practices are very helpful at deterring individuals who may be tempted to steal. Public corruption is an affront to all taxpayers and must be rigorously prosecuted. Clara's stealing from vulnerable citizens who were entrusted to her care is intolerable and injurious in the worst way. She victimized defenseless and incapacitated people to serve her own avaricious desires. We will not soon forget the hollowness of her disingenuous words, "I just want to take care of them."

RECOMMENDATIONS TO PREVENT FUTURE OCCURRENCES

Segregation of Duties

In order to help deter and prevent frauds like this from occurring, management is best served by establishing an adequate segregation of duties among employees. Three main functions that must be kept separate: custody, authorization, and recording (CAR). For instance, three individual employees should handle the wards' disbursement activities: one who is responsible for maintaining *custody* of the bank accounts; another who has *authorization* to sign checks; and one who *records* transactions. An additional control is having an employee in a supervisory position perform reconciliations between the company books and the bank statements.

Effective Communication

Communications also need to be effective and efficient. Although county personnel became aware that Clara had filed false accountings, they failed to inform the court or the judge. If one hand knew what the other hand was doing, then corrective actions could have taken place at a much earlier time.

Organize Recorded Data

Client (ward) files should have consistent structure and organization. Having a regular categorizing system would assist in managerial oversight. It is extremely difficult and time-consuming to analyze files that are in disarray; conversely, it is much easier to hide improper financial activities in a hodgepodge of jumbled records.

Internal Auditors

An internal auditor can provide great assistance to management by performing periodic reviews. It is important that the internal auditor report to the highest level of management appropriate, such as the board of supervisors, in order to facilitate an unbiased and unconstrained audit that is free of political or work-related pressure.

Holly Frook Graham, CFE, CPA, is the former Special Investigative Unit manager of the Arizona Auditor General's Office, which investigates allegations of public corruption, assists in criminal and civil prosecutions, issues reports on investigations, and provides fraud detection and deterrence training. Ms. Graham is an Arizona State University graduate and has over 15 years of financial and forensic accounting experience.

CHAPTER 61

Troubled Water

DIMITER PETROV DINEV

Mich Jacobs was a civil engineer specializing in water and wastewater distribution and management systems. Born in London, he started his career of over 25 years when he moved from designing water systems for municipalities to actually running them. He served as the operations manager for water utilities in several cities in Central and Eastern Europe.

Mich knew he had a head for business. Many European municipalities were seeking to privatize their water systems, and Mich believed there was money to be made. He talked to some friends in the United Kingdom and convinced them that if they could provide the funds, he could use his extensive experience to secure lucrative contracts.

With cash from his U.K. backers, Mich formed two companies, InvestCap 1 and InvestCap 2. These entities would serve his plan to seek out water privatization contracts in Europe.

The city of Sofia in Bulgaria has a population of approximately 1.5 million. Much of its infrastructure was aging and needed improvement. Sofia's leaders had been reviewing their water supply and wastewater systems and desperately wanted to develop them through the introduction of modern management, operation, and maintenance practices. They also needed to implement a plan to repair and extend existing systems.

The city decided to award an exclusive concession contract for the operation of Sofia's water and wastewater system through an international tender. The mayor approached an international monetary fund, the MIBRD, to help the city form a private sector participation (PSP) arrangement and for support in carrying out a process of competitive bidding to select a concessionaire. The MIBRD provides assistance in developing countries to improve their services and infrastructures. Next, the MIBRD set up a team of transaction advisors to work with city leaders to select the best bidder.

International competitive bidding for a 25-year concession took place, and a winning bidder, Water Luxury AD, was selected. It was a Bulgarian company, owned indirectly by a joint venture between InvestCap 1 and InvestCap 2. As part of the contract, the city of Sofia was a 25% shareholder. Water Luxury approached the MIBRD and a loan agreement was signed for $35 million to finance an initial investment program. The chief executive officer was Mich Jacobs. This arrangement was supposed to be a classic concession, in which Water Luxury had the full responsibility for operation and maintenance, along with the financing and implementation of capital investments. At the time this arrangement was designed, there was no national regulatory agency in Bulgaria with responsibility for water and wastewater services. In fact, city officials were enjoying the recent decentralization of many powers and were reluctant to cede responsibility back to the government.

It was understood, nevertheless, that it would be important for the municipality to establish a dedicated unit for oversight and monitoring rather than rely on a city department to do the job. One reason was that it would allow the unit staff to be paid better salaries, thus encouraging the recruitment of experts with high competence.

The agreement therefore provided that a "concession screening unit" (the acronym in Bulgarian being "Aquamon"), acting as an agent of the municipality, would be established to monitor the concessionaire. I was one of the directors.

During the first two years of the contract, there were some problems, but Water Luxury did improve service, and Mich told anyone who would listen that the company had overcome these initial difficulties and that things were progressing smoothly. He loved to give speeches and interviews extolling how Water Luxury was working hard to present a transparent and open face to the community. Mich made sure that Water Luxury played a full role in many aspects of life in Sofia. Not only did the company provide high-quality water supply and wastewater treatment, but its staff actively participated in many committees and supported area events. He was particularly proud of the company's internship program, which on an annual basis allowed over 60 young people to sample work life in a utility environment. He often praised the youth of Bulgaria, proclaiming they were intelligent, thoughtful, and, above all, honest. He asserted that Bulgaria has a great and sustainable future if left in the hands of the next generation. As we discovered later, he meant those words. Mich replaced many of the skilled and experienced employees with young ones who had no experience at all in water management, but who would work for lower salaries.

He continually praised Bulgaria as a good investment opportunity with its stability and qualified human potential. "The country," he would explain, "is an extremely dynamic market that is going to become more and more attractive to foreign investors." He claimed to have assembled an excellent team comprised of the best specialists in the field of water and wastewater services in Bulgaria. Additionally, the MIBRD was a shareholder in the company. With its backing, he promised there was no way this investment could lose.

THE CITY THAT DROWNED WITH BILLS

The first sign something was wrong was the increasing number of overbilled customers. When angry clients came into the office, Mich often met with them personally. He always blamed the errors on the computer software and assured them that the problem was being fixed. His charm and sincerity smoothed their ruffled feathers, and as long as the bill was corrected, they were satisfied. Fortunately, around this time Aquamon, the concession monitoring and screening unit, was up and running, and we began our look at Water Luxury. It didn't take us long to discover that the city had not been provided with the required documentation and information. We immediately began an in-depth investigation of the company and its finances. It took many months of digging, but we eventually discovered some very disturbing facts.

Mich Jacobs was being paid a monthly wage of $45,300 ($544,000 per year), a record-high remuneration for Bulgaria. The company also paid rent ($3,000 a month) for a house for Mich's family, along with many of their household bills and the education of his children.

The eight other expatriates in top positions at Water Luxury also had their full expenses covered. The total amount of their annual wages was $3,530,000, with monthly remunerations between $16,500 and $23,460. The business paid for numerous items, including home rentals, heating, power, water, and even meals. As a local newspaper later described it, "Bills for Shopska salad [a popular Bulgarian meal] and Rakia [the country's most preferred grape brandy] are presented as investments and paid by the Sofians through their water bills."

We also discovered several contracts that were to be performed not by Water Luxury but by InvestCap 1. The use of Water Luxury as a middleman increased the cost of the contract by as much as 20%, and the expenses were passed on in the form of higher water bills to Sofians. Based on these findings, in my view, the municipality had every reason to try to improve or to terminate the contract with Water Luxury.

As we were conducting our investigation, the National Audit Office (NAO), the country's top financial control body, also became interested in the contract between the Sofia municipality and Water Luxury. The NAO auditors discovered that the municipality had never received any fees from the concession it awarded to Water Luxury.

In fact, the NAO said that because of a lack of reliable information, the auditors could not establish the amount spent by the Sofia municipality on consultancy fees and financial advisors to procure the original consultancy. The contract also provided that Water Luxury was to pay "a concession fee" to the city. Amazingly, it did not set forth the amount to be paid. The Sofia municipality further disobeyed the law by guaranteeing the $35 million loan from the MIBRD to Water Luxury. The audit also found violations in the way in which the price of services was determined. Based on our report and the NAO audit, government prosecutors became interested in Water Luxury. We provided them with copies of everything we had and promised to continue our investigation.

THE DIGITAL WHISTLE-BLOWER

One morning as I was just sitting down for my first cup of coffee, our office manager brought me an envelope that had been sent from Paris. To my surprise, I found copies of e-mail correspondence between the top management of Water Luxury and InvestCap 1 and InvestCap 2. The sender of this envelope was anonymous. After reading some of the e-mails, I was shocked. We had been concerned that Mich Jacobs and his cohorts from the investment companies had intentionally diverted funds. These e-mails provided exactly what we needed.

I nearly spilled my coffee as I began reading the first e-mail. It was sent by Mich to one of the principals in InvestCap 1:

> Patrick,
>
> I am aware that you received a copy of the draft letter handed to us by Mr. Mechev [the deputy mayor]. The last few days I have had a number of meetings with the Concession Screening Unit (CSU) and Christiane Mancheva [the advisor to the mayor and a member of the board of directors of Water Luxury] to ensure that there is absolute clarity that the payments made by Water Luxury to InvestCap 1 and InvestCap 2 are according to the Contract and if the Mayor does write a letter to Board that the numbers we give him are at least factually correct and at best any reference to the 16.2m and 5.82m [investment amounts not used to provide services] is removed.
>
> In speaking with Christiane this morning, she believes the only thing that could cause embarrassment is the fact that there is no "contract" between InvestCap 1 and InvestCap 2 and Water Luxury to cover the reimbursement of these costs. I am not aware of a contract but I believe it would be simple to put one in place with the appropriate date and perhaps we should take this action.
>
> The Aquamon continues to ask questions, but these will be on the quantum, and proof of benefits which while a nuisance, cannot constitute a threat to the Concession. For example they would like copies of all InvestCap 1/InvestCap 2 timesheets for development costs and also would like proof of the deliverables from this work. In my meeting with Christiane and Mechev my aim is to provide them with enough confidence in the legality that they will place pressure on Aquamon to reduce these ridiculous requests.
>
> Regarding the capital program, clearly we were slower off the mark than the municipality would like. This, coupled with the higher level of expenditures on transition than anticipated, has created a difficult comparison between material and non-material assets.
>
> In addition, we recharged a significant figure of operating expenses to capital expenditures which in the Municipality's eyes is not real work. Of course, this will be corrected over time. This subject needs two clear activities: firstly, demonstrable delivery. It is far too risky and could provide an opportunity for termination if the Municipality strongly contests the contents. Secondly, we need a "charm offensive," particularly on the capital program, explaining step-by-step the progress and benefits. With the arrival of Jens and now Jean Paul, I am sure we have the team in place.
>
> Regards,
> Mich

After investigating the facts presented in this e-mail, we were able to confirm these points:

- Water Luxury management had sent money received as a credit from MIRBD to its mother companies in the United Kingdom.

- There was no legal contract as a basis for this transfer.

- A fake contract would be prepared and simply put it in place with the appropriate date.

- The management of Water Luxury had some high-level accomplices—the deputy mayor and his advisor were members of the board of directors of Water Luxury.

- Pressure would be placed on the concession screening unit to stop its "textbook requests" for information.

- The company was engaging in accounting gymnastics by changing the allocation of operating expenses to capital expenditures in order to manipulate the amount spent on material assets.

After reading the first e-mail, I was eager to know what other information our anonymous benefactor provided. Another important e-mail, from Mich again, follows.

Patrick,

Further to our meeting today, I briefly note the following actions: (i) Gudsen [one of the principals of InvestCap 1 and 2] will produce a note which outlines a commercial structure to undertake capital works and which allows the withdrawal of fees for InvestCap 1 and InvestCap 2; (ii) Gudsen will review the transfers to maximize capital expenditures; (iii) Gudsen will arrange to adjust the "non revenue water" (NRW) graph to ensure that it meets the Level of Service Schedules given to the city as part of the capital program.

Mich

Based on this e-mail, we learned:

- Fees paid to the investment companies would be disguised as payments for capital works.

- The transfers were indeed used to maximize reported capital expenditures.

- The achievement of level of services would be falsely presented.

The third e-mail to one of Mich's executives regarding inflating prices follows.

Subject: Invoice for Models
David,

Please arrange for an invoice to be submitted to Water Luxury from InvestCap 1 "for the provision of hydraulic software and licenses." Total invoice of $113,000 should be dated 28 September.

The actual cost to InvestCap 1 of these licenses will be approximately $53,000 and the net difference of $60,000 is to be shared equally between InvestCap 1 and 2 in the same manner as the billing software.

I believe that the rates at which we are billing for this software and licenses is in line with the prevailing prices and we could be criticized if we try for more, but probably only by engineering companies who know the market, and only then if they had access to the numbers.

We could invoice more if we were comfortable, but I would suggest that we only do this in the event that we need to make up our 75% investment for the year.

Mich

Again, Mich had advised one of the executives to inflate the prices, and he set forth how "the investors" would share the margin and cover the clues. The fact that it was a repetitive action ("in the same manner as the billing software") shows his real intent to defraud the company.

Still reeling from these revelations, I read the next e-mail:

Subject: Modeling Project Structure
Gudens,

Please see attached note. This is a summary of what I believe to be successful discussions last week in regard to modeling in Sofia and I think it meets all our objectives in respect of project delivery. Gudens, please advise if you have any comments before I progress with the software purchase and the procurement of project managers from Ivan Stroj. The procurement will be backdated to be included in the first year.

Mich

Attachment:

Ivan Stroj Ltd. provides project managers through InvestCap 1 at close to market rates. These are then passed through to Water Luxury under the TSA (Technical Service Agreement) as InvestCap 1 staff. InvestCap will have a confidential contract with Ivan Stroj to cover this.

During an initial three-month evaluation and development period, a contract will be developed to provide all necessary modeling support that is not capable of being provided by Water Luxury staff. A public procurement process must be followed, subsequently for the tendering of this contract. But this must be presented in a way that allows the Fobos Joint Venture to win.

A success fee will be payable to Fobos (only Fobos—as lead of the JV) who will pass this through to InvestCap 1 and 2. It is proposed that the money should be equal to the penalties for three months delay in the delivery of the Strategic Models. This is approximately $600K to be paid over three stages of $200K each, at the end of months three, nine, and eighteen. This level of success fee is seen as realistic, given the high level of penalty that can be levied on Water Luxury.

It seemed that there was no end to the chicanery of Mich Jacobs and his friends— inflated bills, fake contracts and consulting services, phantom ventures, big margins, offshore affiliates, possibly even tax fraud and money laundering. Conducting some further searches, I found that Ivan Stroj was a company formed in the United

Kingdom. Its Web site noted that the business had recently secured a record number of framework contracts, creating a deluge of career opportunities. Dozens of posts were being advertised, ranging from divisional directors and principal engineers to technicians and graduates, during what was called its most exciting period of growth in the past 20 years. Obviously, the business it was receiving from Mich Jacobs was paying off—particularly for Mich and the other participants in the InvestCap companies. Although we still had many details to confirm, this information was extremely damning, and we thought it best to notify the mayor and the city leaders about our discoveries.

WATER UNDER THE BRIDGE

When we informed the mayor about all this evidence, he immediately called Mich Jacobs. Not surprisingly, Mich denied everything and insisted that none of it was true. He proposed that the anonymous sender was simply a disgruntled former employee who just fabricated these stories to seek revenge. Unfortunately for the citizens of Sofia, the story was true. But two events transpired that would prevent swift justice.

First, we were notified that our investigation would end. Aquamon's contract with the city for screening and monitoring was being cancelled. The main reason was that there was now a new state water regulator whose responsibilities would include the same oversight services. Second, a new mayor was elected who did not believe that the investigation of Water Luxury was a high priority—or a priority at all. He declined to meet with us and although he said he would correct the problems we identified in our report, he never took any action.

However, the municipal council reviewed the evidence and stated that it was ready to consider all options available to revise the concession contract for the operation of Sofia's water and wastewater services with Water Luxury. Bowing to pressure, the mayor presented a list of 15 conditions to the company that it would have to meet in order to preserve the concession. Also, in response to public interest, prosecution authorities said again they were investigating the alleged violations.

Some members of the Sofia city council asked for immediate termination of the contract with Water Luxury. However, other council members opposed such an extreme measure, mainly fearing the penalties for early termination.

Several of the council's advisors claimed that the termination of the contract could cost the city in excess of $30 million. Additionally, they said a ruling would be required from an international court of arbitration in order to end the ordeal, which could take years. The advisors believed that the water concession should continue, and, if possible, the city should share in the dividends of the corruption since it was a shareholder!

Prosecution is reportedly ongoing, but no charges have yet been filed. The city was able to renegotiate the terms of the contract with Water Luxury (under new management), and the citizens of Sofia continue to have water. Mich Jacobs was a master magician—he truly turned water into gold.

LESSONS LEARNED

My team and I learned some valuable lessons about the frustrations of dealing with local governments. The leaders and citizens of Sofia found out that when you turn control of a community service over to a private company, you cannot simply sign the contract and walk away.

The Municipality learned these hard lessons regarding these types of concession contracts:

- Partnerships between public entities and private companies can be a tool for corruption if not well planned and organized and if the risks of fraud are not assessed.

- Some companies seeking these concessions are looking for a high-fee, low-risk deal whereby the city or other groups guarantee or assume the risk for repayment of the loans needed to improve systems and services.

- Cities should be extremely wary of giving a private company a monopoly on essential services. There is always a risk that profit will prevail over the interests of the citizens.

RECOMMENDATIONS TO PREVENT FUTURE OCCURRENCES

City governments, no matter where they are located across the globe, have an enormous responsibility. They are charged with providing many of the basics that their constituents need to survive, such as electricity and water. However, many cities are faced with aging equipment, high operating costs, and limited funds. Privatization often looks like the perfect solution: The citizens receive improved service, and supposedly the city just has to sit back and receive money. Unfortunately, privatization does not mean that the government takes it easy. Any taxpayer-funded institution that is considering privatizing services should keep five points in mind:

1. *Hire reliable consultants to design the program and write the contracts.* In the case of Water Luxury, the agreement was missing basic terms, such as the amount of the initial fee to be paid the city. The deal should clearly set forth the responsibilities of the contractor and provide stiff penalties for violations.

2. *When selecting a contractor, conduct an extensive investigation of the company.* You should understand how the organization is structured, who the principals of the company are, and where their funds will be coming from. Background checks should be conducted on all the principals.

3. *Once the contractor is selected, examine the qualifications of the managers and other key employees.*

4. *Set up a system of independent and effective monitoring.* Every fraud perpetrator is looking for opportunities. Although an annual audit should be conducted, this is

not enough. Continuous monitoring should be undertaken so that there is ongoing oversight of what the contractor is doing.

5. *Establish a complaint hotline whereby customers and vendors can call to report problems with either services or billing.* The monitors should have access to these reports so that they can identify potential problems before they escalate.

Dimiter Petrov Dinev, PhD, CFE, is the chairman of the Association for Counteraction to Economic Fraud, Sofia, Bulgaria. His firm, Omonit, has provided consulting services for the municipality in Sofia. Dr. Dinev is a graduate of the Timirjazev Agriculture Academy in Moscow and has over 20 years of experience in teaching financial control and consultancy and six years in detecting and preventing white-collar crime.

CHAPTER 62

Con Artists Gone Wild

HEINZ ICKERT

At only 35 years old, Jeff Davidson, an entrepreneur from a small town just south of Chicago, made it big fast. Not only did he have his own certified public accountancy practice, but it was dwarfed by his other business interests, including real estate holdings, a major restaurant and bar in town, and, most important, his escrow company, Secure Escrow Services. Jeff owned one of the largest houses in the city and was in the process of building another that would surpass anything Aurora, Illinois, had ever seen. Without a doubt, his success and wealth made Jeff the most eligible bachelor in his part of the state.

Only four years earlier, he had been a small-town CPA struggling to keep his practice afloat. He was a defendant in a number of lawsuits, had to deal with state tax liens filed against him, and was going nowhere fast. Now he was gaining a reputation as the "go-to guy" in Chicago—and throughout the country, for that matter—if you needed a sharp financial player who could access a lot of capital quickly.

Having grown up in a prominent and well-respected family, Ryan Jenkins had lived his entire life in Springfield, Illinois. He earned an MBA from a prestigious university's business school, then married his high school sweetheart. They had two beautiful daughters. At 36 he was a successful businessman with extensive real estate holdings, but most of his success was from his insurance-related business, Omega Capital Ltd.

Donna Delgatti was a registered nurse before she left the medical field in search of a way to earn more money. In her early 40s, she accomplished her goal. Donna had worked for a company involved in the viatical industry for a while and then opened her own business,

Phoenix Capital Funding in Davenport, Iowa. With growth, this business would take care of her family for life.

Omega Capital Ltd. and Phoenix Capital Funding were both involved in the viatical insurance business. The two companies sought investors to buy the life insurance policies of the terminally ill. The investors were promised a return on their investment that far exceeded interest rates available from bonds or certificates of deposit. Omega and Phoenix would pool investor money and buy the policies of terminal individuals (otherwise known as viators). The viators would receive cash they could use immediately for medical treatments and to support them in their remaining time. A portion of the investor funds would be set aside in escrow to pay the premiums on the life insurance policies until the viators passed away.

Investors were assured their investment was safe and insured by the various state insurance departments. Based on a medical exam of the viators, underwritten by Omega or Phoenix, it was known that the insured were likely to die within a short period of time. Investors could expect a double-digit return on their investment in two to three years. The purported safety and superior return earned by viatical investments, compared to bonds or certificates of deposit, made this an ideal investment for the senior citizens Omega and Phoenix representatives targeted.

Omega and Phoenix had agents and representatives that scoured the country to find terminally ill individuals with life insurance policies that they would be willing to sell for fast cash. AIDS victims were the initial impetus to the creation of the viatical industry. Many AIDS victims were relatively young and were not, nor had they ever been, married. Thus, they seldom had dependents or heirs. Rarely was anyone financially dependent on the life insurance policies he had purchased. In the late 1990s, treating AIDS was expensive, and the prognosis certain. These unfortunate people were the ideal candidates to sell their insurance policies for fast cash to pay for treatments in order to alleviate their suffering and perhaps prolong their lives.

Omega and Phoenix used Secure Escrow Services to escrow investor funds until the investors could be matched to a life insurance policy of a terminal individual. Secure would prepare a closing statement indicating which investors owned a particular policy and the fees due on the transaction and set up the insurance premium escrow. Secure Escrow Services would pay the viator for his policy and make all commission payments to Omega or Phoenix, the agents who secured the viators, and agents who located the investors. Secure would check up on the viators regularly, file death claims when the time came, and finally send the investors their share of the death proceeds representing their original investment and profit. In return for its services, Secure received a small fee for each closing it processed, usually $300 to $400, but was entitled to keep all or half of the money earned by the funds Secure held in escrow for investors not yet matched to life insurance policies or held to make future premium payments.

Jeff, through his CPA firm, maintained all of the accounting records for the viatical business for Omega and Phoenix, related investments entities of both firms, and of Ryan, personally.

NOT SO SECURE, AFTER ALL

I received a call from an attorney I had recently met through a close friend of mine. Bill Gleason was the managing partner of a midsize law firm in Chicago. His specialty was bankruptcy. Bill informed me that he had just been appointed receiver by a federal judge in the matter of *Omega Capital/Phoenix Capital Funding v. Secure Escrow Services and Jeff Davidson, et al.*, a civil action filed in federal court. A receiver is assigned by the court in some cases to manage a business or property during litigation. The plaintiffs alleged that millions of dollars of their own and their investors' money were missing from Secure. They sought to have the defendants removed from control over their funds and their investors' funds. Bill was aware of my background in litigation matters, my firm's abilities as CPAs, and my additional designation and experience as a certified fraud examiner. He would need a knowledgeable accountant to assist him in accounting for the funds during his charge as receiver. More important, the plaintiffs were charging the defendants with misappropriation of funds on a massive scale. They further asserted that the accounting records maintained by Secure and Jeff's accounting firm were incomplete and fraudulent. Funds had been transferred between accounts and entities to such an extent that there was great doubt as to what had happened to the monies entrusted to Secure.

My initial responsibility was to gain control of the assets of Secure and assist Bill with his responsibilities. Bill and I met with the legal counsel of Phoenix, who provided us with the specific allegations of misconduct on the part of Secure and Jeff Davidson. We then met with Jeff and his legal representation. Naturally, they had quite a different perspective concerning the dispute, and insisted neither Jeff nor Secure had acted inappropriately and that all actions had been authorized by the plaintiffs. Approximately $10 million had been transferred to Omega to permit them to make insurance premium payments. Boxes of accounting records had been seized from Secure. But Jeff and his company still retained control over all other assets and a sizable portion of the accounting records for Secure and the viatical operations of Omega and Phoenix. Bill advised all parties that as the receiver, he was taking control over the assets held both by Omega and Secure and that I would assume responsibility to oversee the accounting function. Somewhat surprisingly, both the plaintiffs and the defendant rejected that idea. The plaintiffs preferred that the funds be seized from Secure and turned over to them. They would assume control over accounting and other duties that had previously been administered by Secure. However, the federal court reiterated its decision to appoint a receiver. Bill would be taking over control and I would assist him by performing the required accounting.

The accounting records seized by the plaintiffs had been returned to the custody of Secure's attorney. Bill quickly gained control of these documents. My first task was to examine them and provide Bill with an initial status report. I went to Secure's attorney's office and proceeded to review over 30 boxes of records during four very long days.

Upon completing my initial review, I met with Bill to tell him what I found.

"What's going on here?" he asked.

"It appears really simple," I replied, "Crook Number Two has stolen from Crook Number One, and Crook Number One is pissed."

I filled him in with all the details I had uncovered. Secure was supposed to have invested the funds received from Omega and Phoenix in safe government-insured investment vehicles. Virtually none of the funds held by Secure was invested in that way. An initial review of the accounting records and other documentation indicated that funds were being shuffled through accounts of various entities. Numerous investments had been made that can only be described as outside the normal course of business for an escrow agency. It was apparent that substantial losses had already been incurred and that the viability of other investments was doubtful.

In reviewing the boxes held by Secure's attorney, I found numerous uncashed checks from insurance companies, along with correspondence that insurance policies were being rescinded due to fraud.

A review of Omega and Phoenix's marketing literature, viatical closing statements, and correspondence between Jeff and Ryan led me to believe this case ran much deeper than anyone realized—and far beyond Jeff and Secure Escrow Services.

GETTING TO THE BOTTOM OF IT

From the beginning it was obvious I would have to move through the investigation quickly. Jeff maintained 22 bank accounts among Secure, Omega, and Phoenix, into and between which millions of dollars flowed and moved freely. The first step was to gain control over these accounts via the court order appointing the receiver, Bill, to do so.

I had also identified securities accounts held with two brokerage firms totaling over $7 million. A review of the account statements indicated the investments were largely in small over-the-counter companies—penny stocks. The accounts had been heavily margined, very actively traded, and were incurring substantial losses. I advised Bill to gain immediate control over these accounts as well. He advised the brokers involved of the receivership and instructed them to cease trading. The accounts were transferred to a different broker and liquidated, which stopped the losses and the significant margin interest expense that was being incurred.

The accusations between Plaintiffs Omega and Phoenix and Defendants Secure and Jeff Davidson were flying fast and furious while their attorneys were in court filing motions. I had to cut through the clutter and get to the heart of the matter quickly to protect the investors. It was important to gain control over all the accounting records held by Secure's attorney and those still in Jeff's possession. I made an appointment to meet with Jeff at his office.

I arrived at Jeff's office and was escorted to the conference room. I would have to wait a bit since Jeff was tied up on an important conference call. To be kept waiting was no surprise. Jeff held himself in high regard, and the wait was certainly designed to let me know the pecking order. The conference room doubled as his accounting business's library. As a CPA myself, I observed that most of the publications were out of date.

His accounting business was obviously not his first priority and had not been in some time.

Having downed the cup of coffee that was provided when I first arrived, I wandered down the hall to ask the receptionist where I might get a refill. I was directed to the employee lunchroom and passed Jeff's office along the way. He was indeed present and occupied on the telephone. In the lunchroom, I found the coffee and decided to remain there as I waited for Jeff in case I needed another refill. It was then that I met Bonnie and Paula.

Bonnie and Paula were two of the few remaining employees at Secure. Since the lawsuit and the temporary restraining order, most of the staff had been terminated. Bonnie was an accountant in the CPA practice who provided accounting work for Secure, Omega, and Phoenix, while Paula worked largely with maintaining records related to the life insurance policies that were sold to investors. When I told them who I was, they became curious and concerned for the company. They were aware that there was serious trouble. With minimal coaxing, they divulged that the raid to seize accounting records, while certainly disruptive and upsetting, was poorly executed. The most important accounting records had yet to be seized.

Bonnie, who had a job interview scheduled for the next day, then divulged her concerns regarding Secure and how it conducted business. She told me how death benefits had been received but not disbursed to the investors for months. The investors, upon learning of the death of the viator, would call to inquire as to when their funds would be disbursed. They were given all kinds of excuses regarding why payments were not made. Usually, some weeks or months later, when the proceeds of a different policy were received, these investors would be paid and the process of delay and lies would begin again.

Paula explained her job function in maintaining policy and investor records. She told me how, lately, insurance companies believed that life insurance policies had been fraudulently obtained and were rescinding the policies and returning all premium payments. Jeff had told her not to cash the rescission checks because Secure was going to fight the rescissions.

I was advised that Jeff had finished his conference call and could see me. If I had any lingering doubts regarding Jeff's personality and ego, they were quickly quelled upon entry into his office when I viewed the golden dollar-sign lamp over his desk and the dollar signs woven into the fabric of the office chairs. We spent just over an hour together, where I learned far less than I had in 15 minutes with Bonnie and Paula.

The following Monday I learned that Bonnie's job interview was successful and she had been offered a position at the new company. Paula had been terminated at Secure due to a lack of work.

About two weeks later, after much legal wrangling, I was able to relocate the accounting records held by Secure's attorney and those important documents that had been left behind the first time documents were seized. The records were now in an office rented by Bill, where his new employee, Paula, was setting up the office.

I provided several reports to the court regarding Secure and its operations. The plaintiffs were seeking control over all remaining funds and wished to take charge of their own policies for the purpose of protecting their investors. From a review of the accounting records for Secure and those maintained for Omega and Phoenix by Jeff, it was apparent that the records were not up to date and did not accurately reflect the financial condition and operations of the entities. It was apparent that there had been mass transfers of funds between accounts and entities that had no economic purpose other than to get cash where it was needed on a particular day. Money was flowing into Secure from Omega and Phoenix at the rate of hundreds of thousands of dollars per day, and it was flowing out almost as quickly.

In reviewing the life insurance policies that had been purchased by Omega and Phoenix, I found that Secure had been designated as the owner and beneficiary of the policies. I found multiple policies for the same individual. A few individuals had over 20 life insurance policies that they had sold to Omega or Phoenix. Poring through correspondence, I found a letter from Jeff to Ryan indicating that Omega's premium escrow fund was short $19 million. I then began reviewing the policy closing summaries. It was apparent the economics of viatical investing, as practiced by Omega, Phoenix, and Secure, were not sustainable. The financial details of one life insurance policy sold to three investors follow:

Face value	$50,000
Proceeds from investors	$17,043
Payment to viator	$5,500
Agent securing viator	$6,135
Broker for investors	$3,000
Profit (Omega)	$1,688
Closing fees (Secure)	$325
Premium escrow account	$395

The terminally ill viator sold his life insurance policy with a face value of $50,000 for $5,500. The agent who secured the viator actually received more from the transaction than the viator. The agent was often either Omega or Phoenix. The numerous dealings among Omega, Phoenix, Secure, Ryan, Jeff, and Donna provided overwhelming evidence that all were involved in what appeared to be a Ponzi scheme.

The claims of the insurance companies that the life insurance policies had been fraudulently obtained were in the documentation in Secure's files. The various insurance carriers were asserting that Secure, Omega, and Phoenix were utilizing a technique known as cleansheeting. Cleansheeting often involved independent insurance brokers soliciting gay men to purchase life insurance policies. Ideal candidates were in their 20s or 30s and unmarried. The participants typically had contracted AIDS, which was a fatal disease at the time. These men had short life expectancies. Individuals would apply for life insurance in amounts less than $100,000, which required no physical exam, and would not reveal their diagnosis on the application. Some brokers just had the participant sign blank applications for them to complete and submit at a later time. The terminally ill viator received several thousands of dollars for securing a life insurance policy on which he had made no payments. The viator had little concern about the deception as he did not expect to live long enough to deal with legal consequences. A review of the medical examinations performed on the viators established the fact that Omega and Phoenix were aware of the deception. Exams were often dated prior to the application for insurance.

The insurance industry had slowly become aware of the practice of cleansheeting. Conseco, Inc. had noticed that a number of policies were being transferred to a new owner within 60 days of purchase. Conseco had acquired numerous smaller insurance companies but continued to operate them under their original names. A data sort of policies issued by all subsidiary companies found multiple policies covering the same individual written by the same independent broker. Additional data mining revealed Secure to be the owner and beneficiary of hundreds of policies.

Omega had another problem in maintaining its viatical business. Money was flowing in from investors faster than it could be covered with cleansheet policies. A new twist was needed—and necessity is the mother of all invention. Ryan came up with the idea of "senior policies." A senior policy was a life insurance policy on a senior citizen in good health whose only immediate mortality issue was age, usually over 70 years old. The policy was obtained with the key deception being the intent of acquiring the policy. The insured did not indicate that the policy was being obtained for sale with assignment of the death benefit to a third party. One senior viator was a retired doctor living in Boca Raton. Fred had obtained policies on his life totaling $15 million that he sold to Omega. But he had not made the first premium payment. One of Fred's policies was syndicated in this way:

Face value	$6,000,000
Proceeds from investors	$2,751,667
Payment to viator (Fred)	$180,000
Insurance agent commission	$60,000
Investor agents	$790,528
Secure closing fee	$6,625
Insurance premium escrow	$4,231,499

All the payments to the viator, the agents, the broker, and Secure were made. But the premium escrow account was underfunded by $2,516,985. The premium on the policies was $58,770 per month. The escrow had sufficient funds deposited to pay premiums for 29 months if the funds remained untouched. The escrow fund was to have been funded for 72 months based on the closing documents on file. Through consultation with an insurance actuary who did not know Fred personally, I learned the insurance carrier was basing its premium on the expectancy that Fred would live for at least nine years. There would seem to be no reasonable expectation that the policy would be funded and remain in force until Fred died. Although he was supposed to live for approximately nine years, the Omega investors were unknowingly wagering their entire investment on his passing in 27 months or less.

Our examination identified senior policies with a total face value of nearly $90 million that had been sold to investors for just in excess of $35 million. We found further problems with the senior policies. Omega itself was an investor in a number of the policies; in those policies, it owned 25 to 40%. Although in line for what was touted to be a tax-free death benefit, we could find no evidence that Omega actually had invested a dime to any of the policies it purportedly owned.

JUSTICE IS SERVED

Bill sought permission to sue various parties and companies to recover funds they had received from Secure and/or Jeff. Included in his request was permission to sue plaintiffs Omega and Phoenix. This put Bill at odds with the plaintiffs, who did not approve of his appointment in the first place. A lot of wasted time and legal wrangling ensued, resulting in the dismissal of Bill and the appointment of a new receiver, for whom I continued to be an accountant. The court had ordered that Omega and Phoenix, which argued that they had the best interests of their clients at heart, be permitted to make insurance premium payments themselves as the payments were due. Omega was given funds sufficient to make required premium payments, but Phoenix received more than what would be required to meet its premium payments. Phoenix convinced the court that it should have funds returned in proportion to the total funds that should have remained in Secure's accounts. At that point, the court restricted Phoenix's use of the funds to premium payments. I was certain that Phoenix would not comply with this order.

I was instructed to complete an accounting of the funds received by Secure from Omega and Phoenix and to trace those funds to their ultimate disposition. As part of this, I was to report to the court exactly how funds given to Phoenix and Omega were disbursed. I believe it was my insistence on obtaining accounting records from Phoenix that led to my being replaced as the accountant for the receiver. But for the defendants and plaintiffs, it was too late. Prior to being dismissed, I had completed two extensive volumes detailing the transactions and asset diversions that had taken place. I was able successfully to trace funds through accounts and entities, and tied several disbursements and wire transfers to companies I identified as being owned and controlled by Ryan or Donna.

Bill and I had been instructed to cooperate with the Federal Bureau of Investigation, which had become involved in the case as a result of political pressure from Congress that emanated from the insurance industry. During the case, I met with agents from the FBI, Secret Service, Internal Revenue Service Criminal Investigation Division, and numerous state departments of insurance. During these meetings I provided the agents and investigators with the evidence and copies of the volumes of data that had been prepared for the court but were sealed.

Civil suits are still pending by investors who lost their money. The second receiver and later, his successor, have continued to be involved in suits with the banks, brokerage firms, companies, and individuals who received funds that came from Secure. The brokers and agents who secured viators and investors have also become involved in extensive civil litigation. Little money has found its way back to the victims.

Omega and Phoenix have been shut down. Donna served a 3-year sentence for insurance fraud and money laundering. Jeff is serving 12 years for numerous charges, including insurance fraud, wire fraud, and money laundering. Ryan is currently serving 20 years without parole in federal prison and was ordered to pay $92 million in restitution to investors. Jenkins's conviction on 157 counts was recently upheld, although the sentence has been remanded for reconsideration.

Lessons Learned

This case provided a number of lessons. For me, the case presented a tremendous challenge from a management standpoint. I also learned a lot about conducting an investigation along multiple lines simultaneously. Not only was I required to continue the operations of Secure in filing death benefit claims, collecting policy proceeds, making premium payments, and filing routine reports with the court, but I also had to conduct an investigation into possible criminal conduct on the part of the plaintiffs and the defendant. While doing that, I had to assist Bill in identifying assets of the receivership and securing those assets to prevent further erosion in value or loss.

The case presented numerous challenges since accounting records were poor. Many aspects had to be re-created, including listings as to who the investors were and what policies existed. Attention to detail proved valuable as money was transferred from entity to entity, account to account, and back again. Assigning staff to different parts of the investigation became essential due to the complexity of the case and the numerous transactions and entities involved. Coordination was essential in order to bring all the pieces together.

Tracking down and interviewing numerous individuals who were or had been involved in the case and Secure Escrow Services was critical to pulling the complete picture together. Interviews led to the identification of additional persons to contact, which often provided leads to previously unknown transactions or crucial case facts. The importance of interviewing and listening cannot be overstressed. I remembered what I had learned years before: Some of the seemingly least important people can become your most valued sources of information.

It was eye-opening for me to see how, when there are huge sums of money involved, people can become greedy quickly and have total disregard for their victims. I observed firsthand how, once blinded, these perpetrators can convince themselves they are innocent of wrongdoing.

The banks that maintained the accounts Secure Escrow Services and Jeff controlled now know how important it is to monitor account activity. Large transfers between Omega and Phoenix attracted no attention.

The investors and the agents who solicited the investments were reminded of the old adage: "If it sounds too good to be true, it probably is." Many investors poured huge sums of money into viatical investments, which supposedly would earn more than government bonds or bank certificates of deposit. The financial advisors who recommended the investment were found to have little background with viaticals, performed little due diligence on the investment or the companies offering it, and had become blinded by what appeared to be an easy 10% commission.

RECOMMENDATIONS TO PREVENT FUTURE OCCURRENCES

Background Checks

Background checks are not only relevant for employers; they can be valuable for investors or companies dealing with those they do not know. A corporate background check on Omega or Phoenix would have disclosed actions by a number of state departments of commerce related to the sale of unregistered securities. The limited operating histories of Omega, Phoenix, and Secure should have made investors wary. Jeff's troubled financial history was easily obtained through public records of lawsuits and tax lien filings.

Due Diligence

Investor agents, brokers, and other financial advisors need to understand the importance of performing independent due diligence on any investment offered through their agency. This includes checking with the Department of Commerce to ensure the investment is properly registered for sale, as well as understanding the risks involved in the investment. Many advisors paid little heed to investment diversification in advising their clients to invest disproportionately in viaticals.

Check for Credibility of Businesses

Viatical companies offer a sobering lesson to all organizations: Know whom you are doing business with. The credibility and veracity of your vendors is important. The viatical companies in this case made no effort to ensure the funds they entrusted to Secure were actually retained or invested in the manner agreed on. Secure was not required to provide an audit report, submit to an inspection, or provide any documentation. Taking those extra measures could have reduced the fraud infinitely.

Heinz Ickert, CFE, CPA, heads the litigation support and forensic accounting section of Rea & Associates, Inc. He provides fraud detection, investigation, and deterrence services in addition to litigation support and expert witness offerings. Mr. Ickert is a graduate of Ohio State University and has over 30 years of experience in forensic accounting and investigation.

Index

CPSIA information can be obtained
at www.ICGtesting.com
Printed in the USA
LVOW04*0959110318

568510LV00002B/1/P

9 780470 134689